Domicile as Residence?

A Guide to Part 2 Finance Act 2025

By Adrian Shipwright

assisted by Julian Hickey

First published December 2025

by

Spiramus Press Ltd

102 Blandford Street

London W1U 8AG

www.spiramus.com

ISBN

9781913507886 Paperback

9781913507893 Digital

British Library Cataloguing-in-Publication Data.

A catalogue record for this book is available from the British Library.

Preface

This work was originally written as a supplement to the earlier publication called *Taxation of Entertainers and Sportspersons*[1] following the enactment of changes announced by Rachel Reeves on Budget Day 2024.[2] These were essentially the replacement of a domicile-based system with a residence-based system and the abolition of the Remittance Basis which had been around in its current form since the beginning of the First World War.[3]

These changes were, in the main, enacted in Part 2 Finance Act 2025. People suggested that the work would be of use to a wider audience following the changes coming into force after 5 April 2025 – hence this publication.

The text is essentially that of the Supplement and so has many references to and examples based on the circumstances of entertainers and sportspersons. However, these are essentially of a general application. The discussion of Performance Income which applies particularly to Entertainers and Sportspersons has been left in as it can be a trap for the unwary. Such income does not benefit from the advantages of FIG relief.

The approach of the Main Volume and the Supplement remain as said in the Preface:

> "The Book is intended as a starting point when dealing with a particular case or matter. To that end, as explained below, I have tried to put together in one place what I think are the basic matters (including statute and Manual extracts etc.) that will aid the adviser in dealing with the particular case or matter. It is almost a Cases and Materials publication with added commentary in that respect. To make the abstract more concrete it has been sought to include many examples intended to help in understanding. The Reader may think that an example is an illustration of the obvious, but the examples and illustrations derive from explanations sought from me and where difficulties in understanding have been encountered in practice."

This is continued in this publication.

---

[1] Published by Spiramus Press Limited in hardcopy (four volumes) and electronically and as a Specialist Tax Text on Croner-I. First published November 2024 - see www.spiramus.com (ISBN 9781910151099 Paperback, 97819101511204 Digital)

[2] Wednesday, October 30, 2024

[3] See section 5 FA 1914:
https://www.legislation.gov.uk/ukpga/Geo5/4-5/10/pdfs/ukpga_19140010_en.pdf

The text of the legislation is included in the publication. Each provision is gone through using the headings Overview, Relevant Legislation, Detail and Commencement. This is followed by a section on some thoughts as to how the provisions can be used for the benefit of clients.

It is hoped that the Reader will find the publication practical and useful.

Any constructive criticism should be sent to the Publisher.

I am grateful to my colleague at Burnell chambers Julian Hickey for his assistance in the production of this work. As ever any mistakes my own unaided work and not those of Julian.

I also wish to thank Carl Upsall, the publisher and his colleagues for their patience, kindness and help in the production of this work.

Happy reading.

AJS

6 October 2025

1 The New Residence Based Regime after Finance Act 2025

Key Points

- The purpose of this Supplement is to consider the New Residence Based Regime replacing the Domicile Based Regimes in IT, CGT and IHT brought about by Part 2 FA 2025
- At a high level this is the abolition of the Domicile Basis for taxation but as ever with tax it is never quite so simple
- These are significant changes which can affect ESPS which will require review often of a detailed nature of existing arrangements e.g. Image Right Structures and whether the UK is the right base for the HINWI ESP in question.
- The Remittance Basis abolished from 6 April 2025 but care is needed with income and gains which arose or are treated as arising before that date or where there is a straddle of the start date.
- Four-year FIG Regime introduced essentially in place of the Remittance Basis
- Not apply to "Performance Income" of ESPs -- trap for unwary
- Residence based OWR (Overseas Workday Relief) introduced now with a four-year period
- IHT changes including 10-year tail charge on Long Term Residents ("LTR")
    - UK resident 10 or more out of the previous 20 tax years to determine long term residence.
    - Change announced in the Budget led to many UHNWIs leaving the UK
    - How get information for 20 years? Practical problem with real impact
- LTR used elsewhere instead of domicile
- TRF (Temporary Repatriation Facility) introduced a Lower rate for three years for income and gains
- "remitted" in some circumstances. Change to remittance rules for unremitted income arising before the change which some (including the CIOT) consider may give rise to double taxation
- Ending of relief for Excluded Property and Excluded Property Trusts based on Domicile
- Accordingly, Settlor Interested Trusts will not benefit from Domicile based reliefs such as that from IHT for Excluded Property Trusts and the Remittance Basis for IT and CGT
- Subject to the Four-Year FIG Relief
- CGT rebasing for Non-Doms to market value on 5 April 2017 see paragraph 1 Schedule 11

1.1 Summary

The UK has introduced a new residence-based tax regime starting from the 2025-26 tax year, replacing the previous domicile-based system for income tax (IT), capital gains tax (CGT), and inheritance tax (IHT). This significant policy shift affects many internationally mobile individuals, especially those long-resident in the UK, and requires careful review of existing tax and trust structures.

- **New regime replaces domicile basis:** The New Residence Based Regime abolishes the old domicile-based rules, introducing residence-based taxation for foreign income, gains, and inheritance tax from 6 April 2025.
- **Abolition of remittance basis:** The preferential remittance basis for non-domiciled individuals is abolished, meaning foreign income and gains (FIG) will be taxed on a residence basis without the previous remittance protections.
- **Four-Year FIG relief:** New arrivals to the UK who have not been resident in any of the previous ten years receive 100% relief on foreign income and gains for their first four years of UK residence. Others will be taxed on worldwide income.
- **Temporary Repatriation Facility (TRF):** A transitional relief allows individuals previously taxed on the remittance basis to remit pre-6 April 2025 foreign income and gains with reduced tax rates for three years following the abolition of the remittance basis.
- **CGT rebasing for remittance users:** Individuals who used the remittance basis can rebase foreign capital assets to their market value as of 5 April 2017 for CGT purposes, easing transition.
- **Inheritance Tax changes:** IHT shifts from domicile-based to residence-based, applying to worldwide assets for individuals resident in the UK for ten years prior to the chargeable event, with a 10-year tail extending IHT liability after leaving the UK.
- **End of Excluded Property Trusts:** The special IHT treatment for Excluded Property Trusts is removed, exposing assets held in such trusts to UK IHT, prompting review of existing trust arrangements.
- **Impact on structures and residency decisions:** The changes necessitate review and possible restructuring of common tax arrangements, including Image Right structures and trusts, and may influence where internationally mobile individuals choose to reside.

- **Legislative framework:** The Finance Act 2025, particularly Part 2, enacts these changes with Chapters covering foreign income and gains, ending special non-domicile treatment, trusts, and inheritance tax provisions.

1.2 General

This Supplement is concerned with the New Residence Based Regime ("**the New Regime**") introduced for 2025-26 and subsequent tax years to replace the Domicile based regimes for IT, CGT and IHT that applied for tax years up to 2024-25 which ended on 5 April 2025.

The purpose of the Supplement is to consider:

- the changes involved in this replacement; and
- especially the legislation implementing the change.

In particular, this Supplement looks at the specific changes made by Part 2 FA 2025 headed "Replacement of Special Rules Relating to Domicile".

These are significant changes which are likely to impact many people especially internationally mobile ESPs and in particular those who have chosen to base themselves in the UK and have done so for a number of years. The longer the period in the UK the more important that the position is reviewed in the light of the New Regime.[4] Some first thoughts on the changes and possibilities are set out at the end of this Supplement.

It is particularly important to check whether such persons based in the UK are US Citizens or Green Card Holders in practice they are potentially caught by the legislation and, if so, what the effect would be. Such individuals may have the benefit of FTC's as they will have US Tax liabilities on income and gains that continue which may reduce the impact of the IT and CGT changes. They may also be able to benefit from the UK US Double Taxation Convention on death duties and gift taxes.[5] These are discussed in more detail in the section at the end headed "Some Thoughts etc".

---

[4] as the number of years resident in the UK is an important determinant.

[5] See e.g. Statutory Instrument SI 1979 No. 1454

The Double Taxation Relief (Taxes on Estates of Deceased Persons and On Gifts) (United States of America) Order 1979

EXPLANATORY NOTE

The Double Taxation Convention with the United States of America which forms the Schedule to this Order applies to death duties and gift taxes. The taxes covered by the Convention are the United Kingdom capital transfer tax and the United States estate and gift taxes. The Convention will also apply to any tax of a substantially similar character which may be imposed by either country…

See also https://www.gov.uk/guidance/inheritance-tax-double-taxation-relief#countries-the-uk-

A limited number of other countries have such Death Duties Conventions with the UK.[6] This is discussed in more detail towards the end of this Supplement.

Various common structures will need review and possible modification in the light of the change. For example, Image Right structures that relied on the Remittance Basis, at least in part, for their efficacy will require careful consideration as well as the difficult question as to where ESPs should base themselves in the light of the various competing interests.[7] Is the UK still the right place?[8] Whether existing structures need unwinding and if so how and when and what replacement if any is needed also needs detailed consideration.[9] Trust structures will also need to be looked at. Non-Dom ESPs resident in the UK will need to consider whether they should become resident elsewhere in the light of the changes and particularly in light of the IHT position on death which can be 40% on worldwide assets. It will take time to modify the position for some purposes (e.g. the IHT 10-year tail). It may be worthwhile taking out term insurance to cover this. The insurability of the individual should be investigated and the cost considered with appropriate spread sheets.

Much of the necessary work considering such matters will be bespoke and require a deep understanding of what was done before and why and how flexible the arrangements are as well as profound knowledge and understanding of the New Regime. An early triggering of tax charges may not gratify the ESP. However, in some circumstances it may in fact give an overall saving which will require calculations to be done on agreed assumptions. The issue then will often be funding of the tax bill as the ESP in question may have limited liquidity and as the phrase goes be asset rich and cash poor.

has-double-taxation-conventions-with

[6] See again https://www.gov.uk/guidance/inheritance-tax-double-taxation-relief#countries-the-uk-has-double-taxation-conventions-with

[7] These depend on the particular personal circumstances of the ESP in question. Tax will often play a major part in this but the views of any partner and the needs of any children and of their education etc. will need careful consideration and balancing.

[8] I am aware of several ESPs who have concluded that the UK is no longer the right place for them. This has been for a number of reasons which are not always tax related. Some no longer feel welcome in the UK and many do not trust the UK government whatever its colour.

[9] This can be a complex matter which may well need specialist advice.

1.2.1 *Previous Domicile based approach*

The previous Domicile based approach (**"the Old Regime**") was discussed in detail in *Taxation of Entertainers and Sportspersons* to which the Reader is referred.[10] This domicile-based approach is sometimes referred to as "the Old Regime" here and is not discussed in detail in this Supplement. However, the Old Regime is likely to remain important in practice for a significant period in the future, so it is important to retain access to the relevant materials. Further, Domicile remains important where DDCs are in point as they still apply by reference to Domicile.

The new residence-based regime is sometimes referred to in this Supplement as the New Regime ("**the New Regime**").

1.2.2 *The New Regime*

The New Regime replaces "Domicile"[11] for UK tax purposes with a "New residence-based regime for foreign income and gains"[12] and a "New residence-based regime for inheritance tax".[13]

There had been much talk of a so called "Non-Dom Loophole"[14] which this is seemingly aimed at. This is a change of policy rather than closing a so-called "loophole". The Non-Dom treatment was what the statute actually said to apply. It was not trying to take advantage of an omission or poor wording of the statute. The "Non-Dom" regime was a deliberate policy of the legislation. Changing a policy is the right of Parliament but that is not closing a loophole. It is replacing a policy. This is a happier approach in my view rather than the false moral certainties that were common in earlier discussions of this area. "Clear"[15] data on which to base such policy changes is also a good basis for such a change. The lack of a full Impact Assessment for the IHT changes is to be regretted and particularly on this ground.

---

[10] See Chapter 3 and its Appendices

[11] For a discussion of Domicile see Chapter 3 in *Taxation of Entertainers and Sportspersons.*

[12] See Non-UK domiciled individuals- Policy Summary - GOV.UK (www.gov.uk) Updated 8 August 2024

[13] *Ibid*

[14] It was not a loophole as it was what the legislation provided specifically and clearly rather than an omission in the legislation or a contrived interpretation. "A loophole is an ambiguity or inadequacy in a law or a set of rules that allows one to circumvent the intent of the law or rule."https://www.quora.com/What-is-the-meaning-of-the-word-loophole Politicians are fond of using this inaccurate description presumably for political advantage.

[15] A word beloved of politicians in recent times which often does not bring clarity. Nor does "bearing very clear" necessarily make something right. Something may be clear and wrong e.g. two and two makes five.

The previous government had announced changes to the Non-Dom Regime at the Spring Budget 2024 essentially to IT and CGT but in general not to IHT and Trusts. The Autumn 2024 Budget following the election on 4 July 2024 added to the announced changes particularly removing the benefit of Excluded Property Trusts which led to the significant exodus of billionaires from the UK in my experience. These were often the very people who paid significant amounts of UK tax and funded much investment in the UK[16]. Their worldwide assets were to be liable to IHT for 10 years even if they left the UK.

The government elected in July 2024[17] published a document entitled "Changes to the taxation of non-UK domiciled individuals). This ls - Policy Summary - GOV.UK (www.gov.uk) on 29 July 2024[18] (**"the Policy Summary"** or **"the Policy Paper"**). This document set out the new government's intention to reform the taxation of non-domiciled individuals ("**non-doms**") etc. It said that the new government considered that that "approach [i.e. the previous government's] left several advantages for existing non-doms, which the government is committed to ending."

The Policy Paper confirmed, in particular, as previously announced:

- the abolition of the remittance basis;
- the change of Inheritance Tax from a domicile-based system to a residence-based system. This is broadly what the legislation enacted. The Policy Paper announced the IHT changes which led to the exodus of billionaires etc. mentioned above.

1.2.3 The Policy Summary - Some matters to note [19]

In particular, the Policy Paper (*inter alia*):

1.2.3.1 Confirmed the Abolition of the Remittance Basis

- The preferential tax treatment under the Old Regime based on domicile status for all new foreign income and gains (FIG) that arise from 6 April 2025 will be abolished. This is the abolition of the Remittance Basis.
- From 6 April 2025, the protection from tax on income and gains arising within settlor-interested trust structures will no longer be available for non-

[16] Much has been written on this topic, but The Oxford Economics documents are particularly useful in my view (peripheral involvement disclosed)

[17] Election on 4 July 2024

[18] Updated 8 August 2024 https://www.gov.uk/government/publications/2024-non-uk-domiciled-individuals-policy-summary/changes-to-the-taxation-of-non-uk-domiciled-individuals

[19] This is a broad overview and not exhaustive.

domiciled and deemed domiciled individuals who do not qualify for the 4-year FIG[20] regime mentioned below.

- "Limited Transitional Relief" mentioned next is provided for.

1.2.3.2 *"Limited Transitional Relief" - Temporary Repatriation Facility (TRF)*

- The policy paper said provision was intended for some "Limited Transitional Relief"
- A new Temporary Repatriation Facility ("**TRF**") will be available for individuals who have been taxed on the remittance basis. Individuals that have previously claimed the remittance basis will be able to remit FIG that arose prior to 6 April 2025 and pay a reduced tax rate on the remittance for a limited time period after the remittance basis has ended. The period for the relief is three years i.e. 2025-26, 2026-27 and 2027-28.

1.2.3.3 *Arrangements for affected non-UK domiciled individuals include:*

- *CGT payable if no 4-year relief*

UK resident individuals who are ineligible for the 4-year FIG regime[21] (or who choose not to make a claim for a tax year) will be subject to CGT on foreign gains in the normal way.

- *CGT Rebasing for former remittance basis users*

Transitionally, for CGT purposes, current and past remittance basis users will be able to rebase foreign capital assets they hold to the market value of the assets at the rebasing date when they dispose of them. The rebasing date is 5 April 2017.

- *Pre-6 April 2025 non-relieved FIG*

Any FIG that arose before 6 April 2025, while an individual was taxed under the remittance basis, will continue to be taxed if when remitted to the UK, as before the changes. This includes remittances of pre-6 April 2025 FIG after that date for those who are eligible for the new 4-year FIG regime.

1.2.3.4 *New Four-Year FIG Regime*

The Policy Paper confirmed the intention to introduce a Four-Year FIG Regime.

New residence-based regime for foreign income and gains (FIG).[22]

The Policy Paper says:

> "To replace the remittance basis of tax, the government will introduce ... [a] residence-based regime, providing 100% relief on FIG for new arrivals to the UK

[20] Foreign Income and Gains

[21] E.g. because have already been in the UK for more than four years

[22] "The government will implement the 4-year foreign income and gains regime announced by the previous government at the Spring Budget". Policy Summary

> in their first four years of tax residence, provided they have not been UK tax resident in any of the 10 consecutive years prior to their arrival."

The new regime will exempt foreign income and gains ("**FIG**") from UK IT and CGT for a specified period. The paper confirms that:

- The period in which relief is available is up to 4 years; and
- It will be available to anyone who has not been UK tax resident in any of the ten consecutive tax years prior to their arrival in the UK.

Those who do not qualify for the Four-Year FIG Regime will be fully taxable on their worldwide FIG in the usual way. This will include those previously protected by the Remittance basis as that is abolished and so such FIG is taxable in the usual way.

Protected trust status will be abolished from 6 April 2025. Accordingly, a UK resident non-UK domiciled settlor interested in the trust will not be protected from that date from income tax, and capital gains tax on income and gains arising in the trust structure. This is subject to the four-year FIG regime which may apply where the settlor has not been resident in the UK in the previous 10 years.

1.2.3.5 Limited Transitional Relief is introduced

There will be rebasing of foreign assets for CGT purposes for current and past remittance basis users. The rebasing date was not announced then. The legislation tells us that it is 5 April 2017 see Schedule 11.

Any FIG that arose before 6 April 2025, while an individual was taxed under the remittance basis, will continue to be taxed if and when that FIG is remitted to the UK, as is the case under the current rules. This includes remittances of pre-6 April 2025 FIG for those who are eligible for the new 4-year FIG regime. Remittance under the old rules will remain of relevance for some time so it is important to keep those rules in mind. Remittance is discussed in Chapter 3 and particularly Appendix 6 to that Chapter in *Taxation of Entertainers and Sportspersons* to which the Reader is referred.

There are some questions on the DTT articles which limit relief on income not remitted and its conflict with the FIG regime which strictly speaking is not 'remittance'.

1.2.3.6 OWR

A form of OWR will be preserved. This will be for four years rather than for three years as under the previous Domicile based regime. The new regime will be Residence Based.

1.2.3.7 Confirmed the introduction of a new residence-based regime for inheritance tax IHT.

- The domicile-based IHT system is replaced by a new residence-based system from 6 April 2025 with a 10 Year Tail.
- This will affect the scope of the charge on property for UK IHT for individuals and trusts. Essentially an individual's worldwide assets will be potentially liable to UK IHT. There will essentially be a 10 Year Tail when a person has continued to be treated as a UK resident.
- The basic test from 6 April 2025 whether non-UK assets are liable to IHT will be whether a person has been resident in the UK for 10 years[23] prior to the tax year in which the chargeable event (including death) occurs.
- There will be provision to keep a person within IHT potential liability for 10 years after leaving the UK. IHT charges arising on deaths occurring before 6 April 2025 will be unaffected by the change and will be charged according to the rules existing before the change. The new rules will apply to deaths after 5 April 2025.

1.2.3.8 End of "Excluded Property Trust" treatment

The Policy Paper also confirmed the end of "Excluded Property Trust" treatment. This has been a particular bone of contention for Non-Doms and led many, in my experience to leave the UK as a potential liability at 40% on their worldwide assets for 10 years after leaving the UK was "the last straw".[24]

The Paper said that the government also intended to end the use of "Excluded Property Trusts" for IHT and to alter the IHT charge on non-UK assets held by Excluded Property Trusts so that any long-term UK residents benefiting from the beneficial treatment of Excluded Property Trusts would no longer be protected from UK IHT. In other words, IHT charges would arise. Great care is therefore needed in respect of existing structures and arrangements. These should be carefully reviewed.

The use of Excluded Property Trusts to keep assets out of the scope of IHT has accordingly been stopped.

It was said that the government intends to change the way IHT is charged on non-UK assets which are held in such trusts, so that everyone who is in scope of UK IHT pays their taxes in the UK.

It was also said that "The government will not carry out a formal policy consultation on moving to a residence-based system for IHT. Instead, it will review

---

[23] There are complex rules concerning this.

[24] Some ESPS put this in somewhat more pithy language.

stakeholder feedback provided following the Spring Budget and officials will carry out further external engagement over the summer on IHT policy design." This was what happened which was a pity as the earlier proposals were not the same as the new government's proposals. The ten-year tail for IHT after leaving the UK for many was "the straw that broke the camel's back."[25] It was not part of the earlier proposals. The new government also sought to rely on some interesting publications suggesting only 77[26] non-doms would leave the UK in similar circumstances. These estimates proved inaccurate. The UK is set to lose the second highest number of millionaires in the relevant period, the highest being from the PRC.[27] It is helpful for there to be reliable data and full consultation and transparency if changes are to be accepted and effective.

The Finance Bill as introduced confirmed this and it is now part of the Finance Act 2025 which is the legislation under discussion here.

1.2.4 *Further Review*

It was also announced that the government intended to conduct a review of offshore anti-avoidance legislation, including the Transfer of Assets Abroad and Settlements legislation, to modernise the rules and ensure they are fit for purpose. The intention for this review was to be to remove ambiguity and uncertainty in the legislation, make the rules simpler to apply in practice and ensure these anti-avoidance provisions are effective. Further details on the review will be provided in due course. It was said that it is not anticipated that this review would result in any changes before the start of the 2026/27 tax year. However, some changes have been made by FA 2025 to these provisions see

---

[25] https://www.quora.com/What-is-the-origin-of-the-phrase-the-straw-that-broke-the-camels-back

[26] https://warwick.ac.uk/fac/soc/economics/research/centres/cage/publications/policybriefings/2022/reforming_the_non_dom_regime_revenue_estimates/ "... Our estimates suggest that abolition of the remittance basis would lead to 0.3% of RBUs (77 people) leaving as a result of the reform."
I am personally aware of more than 21 seriously rich Ultra HINWIs who have already left the UK at the time of writing. It is very easy for such persons with residential properties all over the World to do so. They only have to alter their travel plans so as to become non-UK resident and many such individuals are not employees and do not need to work to maintain their income. Many are of an age where children are of an age where schooling has been completed or they are already in International schools abroad. Altering travel plans does not generate publicity if not wanted. For many the IHT additional changes to the earlier proposals were the last straw. Seemingly it is the relatively small proportion of HINWIs who are super rich who pay most of the tax in question. It will be interesting to see how much the measure actually raises. It is understood that the OBR and the Treasury are not over optimistic it will raise that much.

[27] Peoples Republic of China. Some of the figures have been disputed but are borne out anecdotally. https://www.theguardian.com/commentisfree/article/2024/jun/21/britain-millionaires-leave-tax-havens-ukhttps://www.ftadviser.com/investments/2024/10/09/uk-millionaire-exodus-expected-by-2028/

Chapter [3] Part 2 FA 2025 discussed below. They apply form 6 April 2025 – See paragraph 70 of Schedule 12.

1.3 The Relevant Legislation

Key Points

- Part 2 FA 2025 implements the changes foreshadowed in the Policy Paper and confirmed by the 2924 Autumn Budget
- Four Chapter in Part 2
  - Chapter FIG and new residents
  - Chapter 2 ending of special treatment for Non-Doms
  - Chapter 3 Trusts
  - Chapter 4 IHT
- Note in particular
  - TRF
  - Four-year rule for FIG [and qualifying new residents] [Not cover Performance Income]
  - New four-year OWR
  - CGT rebasing
  - Ending of special treatment of Excluded Property Trusts
- Remittance basis gone from April 2025 but can apply to remittances of earlier income.

The relevant legislation providing for the changes is found in Part 2 FA 2025 headed "Replacement of Special Rules Relating to Domicile".

Part 2 is divided into four chapters. These are headed:

- Chapter 1 New rules for foreign income and gains of individuals becoming UK resident
- Chapter 2 Ending the special treatment of individuals not domiciled in the UK
- Chapter 3 Trusts etc.
- Chapter 4 Inheritance Tax

In more detail, the legislation providing for the changes in Part 2 is as follows:

1.3.1 *Chapter 1 New Rules for Foreign Income and Gains of Individuals becoming UK Resident*

- Section 37 Claim for relief on foreign income);
- Section 38 Claim for relief on foreign employment income;
- Section 39 Claim for relief on foreign gains).

1.3.2 *Chapter 2 Ending The Special Treatment of Individuals Not Domiciled in United Kingdom*

- Section 40 Remittance basis not available after tax year 2024-25;
- Section 41 Temporary repatriation facility;

- Section 42 Rebasing of assets).

1.3.3 *Chapter 3 Trusts Etc*

- Section 43 Trusts: connected amendments, transitional provision etc;

1.3.4 *Chapter 4 Inheritance Tax*

- Section 44 Excluded property: domicile test replaced with long-term residence test;
- Section 45 Corresponding change for settled property;
- Section 46 Consequential, connected and transitional provision.

2 Specifics: Replacement of Special Rules Relating to "Domicile"

2.1 Summary

2.1.1 Introduction

From 6 April 2025, the UK implemented a significant shift in its tax framework by replacing the domicile-based taxation system with a new residence-based tax regime. This overhaul, established primarily through the UK Finance Act 2025 (FA 2025), introduces comprehensive changes affecting individuals, trusts, foreign income and gains, inheritance tax, and reliefs for qualifying new residents. The legislation also abolishes the Remittance Basis and introduces transitional mechanisms like the Temporary Repatriation Facility (**TRF**) to ease the transition for affected taxpayers.

2.1.2 Residence-Based Tax Regime - Overview

The new regime, effective from 6 April 2025, replaces domicile as the basis for taxation with residence status, impacting income tax, capital gains tax, and inheritance tax (IHT). The Finance Act 2025 structures these reforms into four chapters addressing trusts, anti-avoidance rules, individual taxation of foreign income and gains, and inheritance tax implications.

2.1.3 Trusts and the 4-Year Foreign Income and Gains (FIG) Regime

Settlor-interested trusts, including Excluded Property Trusts, lose UK tax protection for income and gains unless the settlor qualifies for the FIG regime, which is available to individuals not UK resident in any of the 10 preceding tax years. The FIG regime grants exemption from UK tax on foreign income and gains for the first four years of UK residence, subject to a claim. However, it excludes "performance income," which notably affects entertainers and sportspeople (ESPs). Trusts created before 5 April 2025 generally lose protection unless within the FIG regime, and capital gains within trusts are taxable if settlors or beneficiaries are UK residents without FIG protection. Offshore anti-avoidance rules remain but are under review, and rebasing relief may apply in some cases.

2.1.4 Inheritance Tax and Anti-Avoidance Changes

The existing Transfer of Assets Abroad (ToAA) and settlements legislation continue but are scheduled for reform starting in 2026–27. Excluded Property

Trusts lose domicile-based IHT protection, replaced by a long-term residence test. Individuals UK-resident for 10 years become liable to IHT on worldwide assets, with a 10-year IHT tail applying after residence ceases. Clients are advised to review trusts and offshore arrangements, considering exit strategies or insurance to mitigate IHT risks.

2.1.5 *Transitional Considerations for Trusts and Income*

Income and gains arising before 6 April 2025 may still be remitted under the old rules, requiring trusts to track pre- and post-change income and gains to avoid double taxation. An urgent review of trust arrangements and strategic use of the FIG regime is recommended, alongside anticipation of forthcoming offshore anti-avoidance reforms.

2.1.6 *Foreign Income and Gains for New UK Residents*

2.1.6.1 *Qualifying New Residents and Relief Claims*

Qualifying new residents are individuals not UK resident in any of the 10 tax years before arrival and who are UK resident in the tax year. They can claim relief on foreign income and gains for up to four tax years from arrival, provided claims are made within 12 months after the tax return deadline. Members of Parliament are excluded. Relief deducts qualifying foreign income from net income but results in loss of the capital gains tax annual exempt amount for the claim year.

2.1.6.2 *Definition of Qualifying Foreign Income*

Qualifying foreign income includes profits from trades wholly outside the UK, overseas property business profits, foreign interest, dividends, royalties, and certain pensions. Disqualified income includes performance income, certain settlement income, transferred income streams, and some pension payments.

2.1.7 *Performance Income and Impact on Entertainers and Sportspersons (ESPs)*

Performance income, encompassing earnings from entertainment or sport performances, commercial appearances, and endorsements, is excluded from FIG relief. The legislation broadly defines performance to cover any physical activity made publicly available, regardless of payment or location, significantly affecting ESPs.

2.1.8 *Overseas Workday Relief (OWR)*

2.1.8.1 *Eligibility and Limits*

OWR provides relief on income from employment duties performed outside the UK and is available to qualifying new residents for their first four years of UK residence. Relief is capped at the lesser of £300,000 or 30% of total employment income and must be claimed via a foreign employment election within 12 months after the tax return deadline.

2.1.8.2 Types of Qualifying Income and Claim Effects

Qualifying employment income includes general earnings, third-party income, and securities income related to foreign employment duties. Claiming relief reduces net taxable employment income but results in loss of personal allowances and the capital gains tax annual exempt amount for the claim year. Adjusted net income calculations treat the relieved income as if relief had not been deducted to prevent double benefits.

2.1.9 *Abolition of the Remittance Basis and Legislative Amendments*

2.1.9.1 End of Remittance Basis

From 6 April 2025, the remittance basis—previously allowing non-domiciled individuals to be taxed only on UK income and gains and on overseas income if remitted—is abolished. Existing remittance provisions continue to apply for prior years, but from 2025-26 onwards, remittance basis claims are disallowed.

2.1.9.2 Legislative Changes Across Tax Acts

Amendments to ITTOIA 2005, ITEPA 2003, TCGA 1992, and FA 2022 remove domicile references and adjust provisions accordingly. The meaning of "remitted to the United Kingdom" is expanded to include indirect benefits enjoyed in the UK from property used abroad, broadening the scope of remittance. Relief is introduced for repeated remittances of the same income or gains upon becoming UK resident, under specified conditions.

2.1.9.3 PAYE and Transitional Provisions

Employer notification and HMRC direction mechanisms are introduced for PAYE treatment of qualifying new residents' income, allowing proportionate PAYE application on qualifying foreign employment income. Transitional provisions affect qualifying new resident status and relief limits for tax years 2025-2028.

2.1.10 *Temporary Repatriation Facility (TRF)*

2.1.10.1 Purpose and Operation

The TRF offers a transitional mechanism for individuals who previously used the remittance basis, allowing them to designate qualifying overseas capital and pay a reduced tax charge to remit such capital without triggering income or capital gains tax charges. The facility is available for three tax years: 2025-26, 2026-27, and 2027-28.

2.1.10.2 TRF Charge Rates and Qualifying Capital

Charges apply at 12% for 2025-26 and 2026-27, and 15% for 2027-28. Qualifying overseas capital includes foreign income or gains accrued before 6 April 2025 that have not been remitted or are remitted during the TRF period. Designations must be made in tax returns within 12 months of the filing deadline by individuals who were subject to the remittance basis before 2025-26 and are UK resident in the designation year.

2.1.10.3 Mixed Funds and TRF Capital Accounts

TRF capital is treated as a distinct category within mixed funds for remittance ordering and offshore transfers. Individuals may nominate TRF capital accounts to manage remittances and avoid inadvertent tax charges, with a 30-day grace period for rectifying breaches. An annualised basis applies to mixed funds containing TRF capital during the TRF period, simplifying remittance ordering.

2.1.10.4 Business Investment Relief (BIR) and TRF Capital

BIR qualifying investments cannot be made after 5 April 2028 and cannot be funded using TRF capital. Provisions clarify the treatment of TRF capital in BIR investments, including disposal order and mitigation to avoid double taxation.

2.1.11 Rebasing of Assets for Former Remittance Basis Users

Former remittance basis users may rebase personally held foreign assets to their market value as of 5 April 2017 for capital gains tax purposes, subject to conditions such as non-UK situs between 6 March 2024 and 5 April 2025 and remittance basis status between 2017-18 and 2024-25. Rebasing applies to disposals between spouses and shares reorganisations treated as the same asset. An irrevocable election can opt out of rebasing.

2.1.12 Settlements Legislation and Qualifying Overseas Capital

Income treated as arising under settlements or transfer of assets abroad legislation may qualify as overseas capital if matched with pre-2025 foreign income or gains and designated appropriately. These provisions aim to prevent tax avoidance by attributing income to settlors or close family members when diverted through trusts or settlements.

2.1.13 Removal of Domicile References in Education and Digital Tax Requirements

The legislation removes domicile references in education funding regulations and income tax digital reporting requirements, aligning with the residence-based tax system. This includes amendments to music, ballet, choir school grants, student support regulations, and removal of exemptions for foreign businesses of non-UK domiciled individuals.

This wide-ranging legislative reform marks a fundamental transition in UK taxation from domicile to residence basis, affecting trusts, foreign income and gains, inheritance tax, and reliefs for new residents. The abolition of the remittance basis and introduction of the TRF provide transitional mechanisms to mitigate tax impacts. Detailed rules on relief claims, anti-avoidance, and asset treatment ensure clarity and fairness under the new regime.

2.2 General

Some Key Points

- Major change to remove the Domicile basis and associated reliefs from IT, CGT and IHT particularly the Remittance Basis and replace with Residence Basis - see discussion above
- Purpose of this section of the Supplement is to outline the principal changes and help understanding of the legislation
- Changes made by Part 2 FA 2025 headed "Replacement of special rules relating to domicile" which is divided into four chapters headed:
    - Chapter 1 New rules for foreign income and gains of individuals becoming UK resident
    - Chapter 2 Ending the special treatment of individuals not domiciled in the UK
    - Chapter 3 Trusts
    - Chapter 4 Inheritance Tax
- The Appendix X contains a list of some definitions words and phrase used in this legislation and of some associated matters for the convenience of the Reader. They are important in understanding the legislation
- Start date 06 April 2025
- Chapter 1 is considered first below
- The other matters are considered later not necessarily in Chapter order

2.2.1 *General*

The legislation introducing these changes is found, in the main, in Part 2 FA 2025 which is headed "Replacement of special rules relating to domicile".

As noted above, the Part is divided into four Chapters.

The sections in each of these Chapters are considered in turn in the rest of this Supplement (not necessarily in the same order as the legislation).

The sections in each Chapter of Part 2 of the Act are listed above in the key points.

This section of the Supplement is focused on the **implications and planning opportunities** arising from the **UK's New Residence-Based Tax Regime**, following the **Finance Act 2025 (FA 2025)**. It builds on the general changes introduced in previous material and dives into **specific areas of impact**, including trusts, anti-avoidance legislation, capital gains tax (**CGT**), and inheritance tax (IHT).

Outline of key content:

2.2.2 *Trusts Under the New Regime*

- From **6 April 2025**, settlor-interested trusts (including Excluded Property Trusts) **lose protection** from UK tax for income and gains unless the **settlor qualifies for the new 4-Year Foreign Income and Gains (FIG) regime**.
- Trusts created **before 5 April 2025** do **not retain protection** unless within the FIG regime.
- The **scope of taxation on trust gains** now includes **UK resident settlors and beneficiaries** under various situations.

2.2.3 *4-Year FIG Regime Specifics*

- Available to individuals who haven't been **UK tax resident in the 10 years** prior to arrival.
- Provides exemption for **foreign income and gains** (FIG) during their **first four years** of UK tax residence.
- Does **not apply** to:
    - "Performance Income" (especially for entertainers/sportspeople).
        - Long-term residents or trust structures post-2025 unless qualifying.

2.2.4 *Trust Gains and Tax Exposure*

- **Capital gains arising in trusts** are **taxable** if:
    - A **UK resident settlor** is not protected by the FIG regime.
    - A **UK resident beneficiary** receives benefits from the trust.
- The **offshore anti-avoidance rules** are retained (e.g., **TCGA s86** for settlors, **s87** for beneficiaries), though under review.
- **Rebasing relief** may apply in some trust cases, but further detail is required (to be addressed in regulations or guidance).

Anti-Avoidance Rules and Reforms

- The **Transfer of Assets Abroad (ToAA)** and **Settlements Legislation** remain in place for now but are due for further review.
- Some changes are already made in FA 2025 (e.g., **Schedule 12**), but comprehensive reform is expected from **2026–27 onwards**.

- Until then, care must be taken in using **corporate or trust structures**, especially those involving **UK resident participators or settlors**.

2.2.5 *Inheritance Tax (IHT) and Excluded Property*

- Excluded Property Trusts lose their IHT protection based on **domicile status**.
- The new **"long-term residence test"** replaces the domicile test:
  - If UK-resident for **10 years**, a person is subject to **UK IHT on worldwide assets**.
  - An individual remains exposed to IHT for **10 years after ceasing UK residence** ("**IHT tail**").
- **Structures relying on** the **old Excluded Property Trust regime** must be **reevaluated**.

2.2.6 *Planning Considerations*

- Clients are advised to:
  - Review all **pre-existing trusts** and offshore arrangements.
  - **Consider exit strategies** from the UK if not yet caught by the IHT tail. This is to allow a fully formed decision to be made.
  - Explore **insurance** options to mitigate IHT exposure.
  - Understand how **existing and future income/gains** are treated under transitional provisions and remittance rules.
  - See also Some Thoughts at end of Supplement.

2.2.7 *Key Transitional Points*

- Income and gains **arising before 6 April 2025** may still be **remitted under old rules**.
- Trust income/gains before the change might remain subject to previous treatment **if not distributed or matched** until after April 2025. Potential double charge where payment to offshore non doms before April 2025 and later distribution.
- Trusts must track the **source and nature** of pre- and post-change income and gains for accurate tax compliance.

2.2.8 *Conclusion*

This Chapter provides an in-depth look at the **technical tax treatment** and **compliance traps** following the shift to a residence-based tax regime. It especially emphasizes:

- The need for **urgent trust reviews**.
- Strategic use of the **4-year FIG regime**.
- Anticipation of **future reforms** to offshore anti-avoidance rules.
- Caution regarding **IHT exposure** for long-term UK residents.

2.3 Chapter 1 of Part 2 of the Act: New rules for foreign income and gains of individuals becoming UK resident

Key Points Chapter 1 Part 2 FA 2025

- Chapter 1deals with FIG and with qualifying new residents
- Qualifying new residents are broadly new arrivals to the UK in the first four years of UK residence, provided they were not UK resident in any of the ten consecutive years prior to their arrival
- Relief from FIG may be available to such new residents for up to four tax years
- Chapter 1 also deals with OWR now residence based and for up to four years rather than domicile based for three years
- However, restrictions for Performance Income which will apply to many ESPs, so care needed

2.3.1 *General*

2.3.1.1 *Introductory*

Chapter 1 of Part 2 FA 2025 deals with the new rules for Foreign Income and Gains ("**FIG**") for "**qualifying new residents**", a defined term for these purposes discussed below. It also deals with Overseas Workday Relief ("**OWR**") discussed below.

2.3.1.2 *Qualifying new residents*

Qualifying new residents are broadly new arrivals to the UK in their first four years of UK tax residence, provided they have not been UK tax resident in ***any*** of the 10 consecutive years prior to their arrival (see the various examples considering this in the discussion below).

Relief on such foreign income and gains for such persons may be available for up to four tax years from arrival (including the year of arrival) as discussed below. The relief needs to be claimed.

However, this may not be of much use to ESPs where Performance Income is involved (see the discussion on Performance Income below). Performance Income does not benefit from the reliefs (see section 843J ITTOIA).[28]

---

[28] **845JPerformance income**

(1) Performance income is any income chargeable to income tax (however that charge arises) that results, directly or indirectly, from the performance of a relevant activity by a performer (whether performed in the United Kingdom or not).

(2) "Performer" means any individual who gives performances of entertainment or sport.

(3) For the purposes of this section "performances of entertainment or sport" includes any activity of a physical kind performed by an individual (alone or with others) which is or may be made available to the public or any section of the public, whether for payment or not.

(4) The following are "relevant activities"—

On 29 July 2024 the government published a policy paper outlining its plans to change the taxation of non-UK domiciled individuals[29] (referred to in this Supplement as "**the Policy Paper**" or "**the Policy Summary**"). "This included replacing the remittance basis of tax with a residence-based regime, providing100% relief on foreign income and gains for new arrivals to the UK in their first four years of UK tax residence, provided they have not been UK tax resident in any of the 10 consecutive years prior to their arrival." [30]

Example

Rick Pawtay is a Domchirian resident ESP who comes to the UK for the first time aged 25. He has not been UK resident for any of the previous 24 tax years, and so Rick has not been UK tax resident in any of the 10 consecutive years prior to his arrival.

Prima facie, Rick could be entitled to the Four-Year FIG Relief on foreign income and gains assuming the right claims etc. are made, and it is not "disqualified income" such as Performance Income mentioned next. Depending on employment status Rick might qualify for OWR if all the conditions are met. (See the discussion below)

2.3.1.3 *Special rule for ESP's – Performance Income*

In the context of ESP's, it is important to be aware of section 845J ITTOIA headed "**Performance Income**".

This covers income resulting directly or indirectly from performances of entertainment or sport whether performed in the UK or not by an individual. Such Performance Income is disqualified from the relief from tax for four years for FIG in this Chapter (see *section 845I Disqualified Income*). This includes Performance Income, but an example may give some context.

Section 845J is discussed below in greater detail below.

(a)the giving of a performance of entertainment or sport;

(b)the participation of the performer in any sound or video recording;

(c)any activity in connection with a commercial occasion or event (including the appearance of the performer in connection with the occasion or event).

(5) The reference to a commercial occasion or event includes any description of occasion or event—

(a)for which any person might receive or become entitled, as a result of anything done by the performer, to receive anything by way of cash or any other form of property; or

(b)which is designed to promote commercial sales or activity by advertising, the endorsement of goods or services, sponsorship, or other promotional means of any kind.]

[29] 2024: Non-UK domiciled individuals- Policy Summary - GOV.UK (www.gov.uk)

[30] See the Explanatory Notes to the Bill which became FA 2025 under the heading "Background Note".

Example

Sam Woth-Lees is a concert pianist who also works as a computer coder who would be a qualifying new resident.

He plays a concert at the Wigmore Hall, London for which he is paid. He also performs at the Konzerthaus in Berlin and the Musikverein in Vienna again for which he is paid. These all take place in the same tax year. He does his coding whilst travelling and when not performing, practising, or sleeping.

His income from the concerts in London, Berlin and Vienna would be directly from the performance of entertainment performed in the UK or abroad and so would be Performance Income under section 845J. Consequently, it would be Disqualified Income under section 845I (d) [31] and not eligible for FIG relief even if the other conditions are met.

Sam's income from his coding activities would not generally be directly or indirectly from the performance of entertainment or sport and so would not, without more, be disqualified income. [32]

The wording of income directly or indirectly from performances of entertainment or sport should be noted. This gives a wide ambit to the provision. It would seem likely that HMRC would consider that this can cover endorsement income and the like which has been the subject of debate in the past in the context of the 1987 Regulations see e.g. the *Agassi* case (see 8.3.5 ff and 8.4.3.2 in *Taxation of Entertainers and Sportspersons*) and Chapter 8. The interesting question is why the different wording? Why "results" rather than derived from?

2.3.1.4 OWR

This Chapter I Part 2 also sets out the new Overseas Workday Relief ("**OWR**") (see below).

2.3.2 *Consideration of the sections in Chapter 1 Part 2*

2.3.2.1 Sections in question

Chapter 1 of Part 2 consists of sections 37 – 39 FA 2025.

The text of these sections is set out below.

2.3.2.2 Hansard – Standing Committee Debates

James Murray MP, the Exchequer Secretary to the Treasury said this of sections 37-39 in the Finance Bill Standing Committee debates. (28 January 2025).

"Clauses [now sections] 37 to 39 make changes to ensure that from April 2025, individuals moving to the UK who have not been tax resident in the UK for the

---

[31] Section 845G Disqualified income
Income is disqualified income if— ...
(d) it is performance income (see section 845H), or ...

[32] If Sam was involved with Electronic music and used his computer skills to produce code etc. to perform such music that he had composed the position is more complicated. What constitutes a performance of that music. Is the coding directly or indirectly linked to the performance? What if he had a separate company through which he carried on his coding business?

10 previous years will not pay tax on their foreign income or gains for the first four years of UK residence.

For context, the Government are removing the outdated concept of domiciled status from the tax system and replacing it with a new, internationally competitive, residence-based regime from 6 April this year. Currently, where a non-UK-domiciled individual moves to the UK, they are able to access the remittance basis of taxation, under which foreign income and gains are not taxable unless they are brought into the UK. Similarly, when undertaking work abroad, newly UK resident, non-UK-domiciled individuals are able to access overseas workday relief, which means that overseas employment income is not taxable unless brought into the UK. The arrangements create a disincentive to invest in the UK and are being changed as a result of these measures.

The changes made by clauses [now sections] 37 and 39 will provide full tax relief on foreign income and gains for new arrivals to the UK for their first four years of tax residence, provided that they have not been UK tax resident for 10 years before their arrival. To align with the new regime, clause 38 and schedule 8 extend the period of overseas workday relief to four years, and decouple overseas workday relief from domiciled status to align it with the new foreign income and gains regime. Claims to the relief will be capped at the lower of £300,000 or 30% of an individual's total employment income. Furthermore, the removal of the remittance basis means that it will no longer be necessary to keep income offshore to benefit from relief...

[He also referred to some government amendments.] [33]

The Government are committed to ensuring that everyone who is long-term resident in the UK pays their taxes here. The new regime ensures that that will be the case, while also being more attractive than the current approach as individuals will be able to bring income and gains into the UK without attracting additional tax charges. That will encourage people to spend and invest those funds here in the UK."

2.3.3 *Section 37: Claim for relief on foreign income*

2.3.3.1 *Summary*

2.3.3.1.1 General

Section 37 introduces a new income tax relief for "qualifying new residents" [34] of the UK on foreign income and makes consequential amendments.

[33] Government amendment 20 amends clause 37 to add an additional category of income to the list of eligible incomes, which will ensure that all eligible income for relief is referenced correctly. Government amendments 44 to 53 have also been tabled to schedule 8 to ensure that the relief on travel costs for qualifying newly resident employees in the UK functions as the legislation intended. Furthermore, Government amendment 54 amends schedule 8 to clarify that it is a general direction made by HMRC, rather than a public notice. This is included for the purposes of completeness.

[34] Discussed below at 24-29

Foreign gains (i.e. capital gains) are dealt with separately by section 39 headed "Claim for relief on foreign gains" discussed below.

The replacement for Overseas Workday Relief ("**OWR**") is dealt with by section 38 also discussed below.

2.3.3.1.2 New Chapter 5 Part 8 ITTOIA - Relief for New Residents on Foreign Income

Section 37 adds a new Chapter 5 to Part 8 ITTOIA. This new Chapter consists of Sections 845A to 845J ITTOIA. The Chapter is headed "Relief for New Residents on Foreign Income."

Sections 845A makes provision in respect of a "claim" for relief for "qualifying new residents".

The phrase "Qualifying new residents" is a defined term for these purposes.

The definition of "Qualifying new residents" is found in section 845B ITTOIA discussed below.

Section 845C deals with the "Effect of claim, foreign employment election or foreign gain claim on losses". It is discussed below.

Section 845D deals with the "Effect of claim, foreign employment election or foreign gain claim: costs of dwelling-related loan." It is discussed below.

Section 845E provides that "Effect of claim, foreign employment election or foreign gain claim on personal allowance etc". It is discussed below.

Section 845F is headed "Effect of claim on relief for contributions to registered pension schemes." It is discussed below.

Section 845G is headed "Foreign income relief ignored for purposes of determining adjusted net income". This is discussed below.

Section 845H is headed "Qualifying foreign income" what income qualifies is listed in a Table in the section.

Section 845I deals "Disqualified Income".

Section 845J tells us what is "Performance Income" which is generally disqualified income see below.

2.3.3.2 The legislation

845A Claim for relief for qualifying new residents.

(1) An **individual may make a claim for relief for a tax year** under this section (a "**foreign income claim**") **if** the individual is a **qualifying new resident** for that year (see section 845B).

(2) Where an individual makes a foreign income claim for a tax year, the individual is entitled to **relief for the tax year** that is **equal to so much of the total income** of the individual for that year as—

(a)**reflects qualifying foreign income** (see section 845H), and

(b)is identified as such in the claim.

(3) The **relief is given by deducting the amount** of the relief **in calculating** the **individual's net income for the tax year** (see Step 2 of the calculation in section 23 of ITA 2007).

(4)A foreign income claim must be made in a return.

(5)A foreign income **claim in relation to a tax year must be made before** the end of the period of **12 months beginning with 31 January after the end of that tax year**.

(6)A **foreign income claim may not be made as a consequential claim** (within the meaning of section 43C(5) of TMA 1970) if the circumstances which give rise to the consequential claim result from a loss of tax brought **about carelessly or deliberately by the individual** or a person acting on the individual's behalf.

(7) See also—

(a)Chapter 5C of Part 2 of ITEPA 2003 which provides for a claim for relief that may be made in respect of foreign employment income where a foreign employment election is made, and

(b)Schedule D1 to TCGA 1992 which provides for a claim for relief that may be made in respect of foreign gains (a foreign gain claim).

(8) Sections 845C to 845E set out **some income tax consequences** of a foreign income **claim**, a foreign employment election or a foreign gain claim.

(9) See also section 1K of TCGA 1992, which provides for the **loss of an individual's annual exempt amount** for capital gains tax **where** a foreign income claim, a foreign employment election or a foreign gain **claim is made**.

(10) For the purposes of this section—

(a) "return" means a return under section 8 of TMA 1970 (personal return),

(b)references to a claim being included in a return include a claim being so included as a result of an amendment of the return, and

(c)subsections (5) to (7) of section 118 of TMA 1970 (loss of tax brought about carelessly or deliberately) apply for the purposes of this section as they apply for the purposes of that Act.

845B Qualifying new residents

(1) For the purposes of this Chapter, an individual is a **qualifying new resident for a tax year** if—

(a)the **individual** is **UK resident** for that tax year,

(b)the individual is **not disqualified** for that tax year, and

(c)for each of the **10 tax years before** that tax year, the individual was **not UK resident.**

(2) An individual is **also** a qualifying new resident for a tax year if—

(a)the **individual** is **UK resident for that tax year,**

(b)the individual is **not disqualified for that tax year**, and

(c)that **tax year is one** of the **next three tax years after a qualifying tax year** in relation to the individual.

(3)A tax year is a **qualifying tax year in relation to an individual if—**

(a)the individual was a qualifying new resident for that tax year as a result of subsection (1),

(b)the individual **would have been** a qualifying new resident for that tax year as a result of that subsection, **but was not only** as a result of the individual being **disqualified for that tax year, or**

(c)the tax year—

(i)is the tax year **2022-23, 2023-24 or 2024-25**, and

(ii)is a tax year to which paragraph (a) or (b) would have applied in **relation to the individual had this section had effect for that tax year.**

(4) An **individual is disqualified** for a tax year **if the** individual would, for the purposes of section 41 of the Constitutional Reform and Governance Act 2010, be regarded as—

(a)**a member of the House of Commons** for any part of that tax year, or

(b)**a member of the House of Lords** for any part of that tax year.

845C Effect of claim, foreign employment election or foreign gain claim on losses

(1) Subsection (2) applies where—

(a)an individual who carries on a relevant business wholly outside the United Kingdom makes a foreign income claim, a foreign employment election or a foreign gain claim for a tax year,

(b)the individual has a loss for that tax year from the relevant business, and

(c)the profits (if there were any) of the business would be qualifying foreign income for that year.

(2) No relief for that loss is available in the tax year for which the claim or election is made or in any other tax year.

(3) In this section "relevant business" means—

(a)a trade, profession or vocation, or

(b)a property business.

845D Effect of claim, foreign employment election or foreign gain claim: costs of dwelling-related loan

(1) This section applies where an individual—

(a)has a relievable amount for a tax year in respect of an overseas property business for the purposes of section 274A (reduction for individuals: entitlement), and (b)makes a foreign income claim, a foreign employment election or a foreign gain claim for the tax year.

(2) The individual is not entitled to relief under section 274A for that tax year in respect of that relievable amount.

(3) For the purposes of section 274A, the individual's brought-forward amount for the following tax year in respect of the overseas property business is nil.

845E Effect of claim, foreign employment election or foreign gain claim on personal allowance etc

Where an individual makes a foreign income claim, a foreign employment election or a foreign gain claim for a tax year, the individual is not entitled, for that year, to—

(a)any allowance under Chapter 2 of Part 3 of ITA 2007 (personal allowance and blind person's allowance),

(b)any tax reduction under Chapter 3 of that Part (tax reductions for married couples and civil partners),

(c)any tax reduction under Chapter 3A of that Part (transferable tax allowance for married couples and civil partners), or

(d)any relief under section 457 or 458 of ITA 2007 (payments for life insurance etc).

845F Effect of claim on relief for contributions to registered pension schemes.

(1) Subsection (2) applies where—

(a)an individual makes a foreign income claim for a tax year,

(b)the individual is entitled to relief under section 188 of FA 2004 (relief for contributions) for that tax year, and

(c)the maximum amount of relief to which the individual is entitled under that section for that tax year is greater than the basic amount within the meaning of section 190(4) of that Act.

(2) The maximum amount of relief to which the individual is entitled under section 188 of that Act for that tax year is to be reduced by the lesser of—

(a)the relevant amount, and

(b)the amount that would reduce the maximum amount of relief to the basic amount.

(3) The "relevant amount" is the amount of the relief to which the individual is entitled under section 845A (2) of this Act as a result of making the foreign income claim, so far as that amount reflects relevant qualifying foreign income.

(4) An amount of qualifying foreign income is "relevant qualifying foreign income" if the income is relevant UK earnings within the meaning of section 189(2) of FA 2004.

845GForeign income relief ignored for purposes of determining adjusted net income.

(1) Subsection (2) applies for the purpose of determining the adjusted net income under section 58 of ITA 2007 of an individual for a tax year for which the individual has made a foreign income claim.

(2) The adjusted net income is to.be determined as if the relief allowed by the claim had not been deducted in calculating the individual's net income for the tax year.

845H Qualifying foreign income

Income is qualifying foreign income if it—

(a) falls within a description set out in the following table, and

(b) is not disqualified income (see section 845I).

No.	*Description*
1	Profits of a trade carried on wholly outside the United Kingdom (see Chapter 2 of Part 2).
2	A UK resident partner's share of the profits of a trade carried on by the firm wholly outside the United Kingdom.
3	Profits of an overseas property business.
4	Adjustment income (within the meaning of Chapter 17 of Part 2) in respect of a trade carried on wholly outside the United Kingdom (see that Chapter).
5	Income chargeable under Chapter 2 of Part 4 (interest) that arises from a source outside the United Kingdom.
6	Income chargeable under Chapter 4 of Part 4 (dividends from non-UK resident companies).
7	Income chargeable under Chapter 7 of Part 4 (purchase life annuity payments) that arises from a source outside the United Kingdom.
8	Income chargeable under Chapter 8 of Part 4 (profits from deeply discounted securities) that arises from a source outside the United Kingdom.
9	Income chargeable under section 579 (royalties and other incored.me from intellectual property) that arises from a source outside the United Kingdom.
10	Income chargeable under Chapter 3 of Part 5 (films and sound recordings: non-trading businesses) that arises from a source outside the United Kingdom.
11	Income chargeable under Chapter 4 of Part 5 (certain telecommunication rights: non-trading income) that arises from a source outside the United Kingdom.
12	Income that arises from a source outside the United Kingdom and that is treated as arising to an individual under section 624 or 629 (income arising under settlement attributed to settlor).
13	So much of any amount of income treated as arising to an individual under section 633 (capital sums paid to settlor by trustees of settlement) for the tax year as falls within the foreign amount of income available up to the end of the tax year.

	The foreign amount of income available up to the end of a tax year is the amount that would be determined, in accordance with sections 635 to 637 (amount of available income), as the amount of income available up to the end of the tax year if all income arising under the settlement from a source in the United Kingdom were ignored.
14	Income treated as arising to an individual under section 643A (benefits paid out of protected income).
15	Income chargeable under section 649 (estate income) that arises from a source outside the United Kingdom.
16	Income chargeable under Chapter 7 of Part 5 (annual payments not otherwise charged) that arises from a source outside the United Kingdom.
17	Income chargeable under Chapter 8 of Part 5 (income not otherwise charged) that arises from a source outside the United Kingdom.
18	Accrued income profits (within the meaning of Part 12 of ITA 2007) made by an individual as a result of a transfer of securities if income from the securities would be qualifying foreign income.
19	Income treated as arising under regulation 17 of the Offshore Funds (Tax) Regulations 2009 (offshore income gains).
20	Income that is treated as arising to an individual under section 721, 728 or 732 of ITA 2007 (transfer of assets abroad: deemed income) and that is "foreign" for the purposes of (respectively) section 726, 730 or 735 of that Act.
21	Pension income that arises from a source outside the United Kingdom (see Part 9 of ITEPA 2003).
22	A benefit to which section 678 of ITEPA 2003 applies (foreign social security benefits).
23	The foreign proportion (see paragraph 46 of Schedule 2 to FA 2022) of income arising as a result of the payment of interest, or the making of a distribution or qualified distribution (within the meaning of paragraph 45(5) of that Schedule), by a QAHC (within the meaning of that Schedule).

845I Disqualified income

Income is disqualified income if—

(a)it is income of a settlement (within the meaning of Chapter 5 of Part 5) arising in the tax year 2024-25 or an earlier tax year that is treated as arising in tax year 2025-26 or a later year as a result of section 648(3) to (5),

(b)it is income arising from a security treated as situated in the United Kingdom as a result of section 138ZB of TCGA 1992 (share exchanges involving non-UK incorporated close companies),

(c)it is income chargeable to income tax as a result of section 809AZB of ITA 2007 (transferred income streams),

(d)it is **performance income** (see section 845J),

(e)it is income from a pension to which section 629 of ITEPA 2003 applies (pre-1973 pensions paid under the Overseas Pensions Act 1973), or

(f)it is a payment made to or in respect of—

(i)a relieved member of a relevant non-UK scheme (within the meaning of Schedule 34 to FA 2004), or

(ii)a transfer member of such a scheme,

to which the member payment provisions (within the meaning of that Schedule) apply.

845J Performance income

(1) **Performance income** is any **income chargeable to income tax** (however that charge arises) **that results, directly or indirectly, from the performance of a relevant activity** by a performer (whether performed in the United Kingdom or not).

(2) "**Performer**" means any individual who gives performances of entertainment or sport.

(3) For the purposes of this section "**performances of entertainment or sport**" includes **any activity of a physical kind performed by** an **individual (alone or with others)** which is or **may be made available to the public or any section of the public**, whether for payment or not.

(4) The following are "**relevant activities**"—

(a)the giving of a performance of entertainment or sport;

(b)the participation of the performer in any sound or video recording;

(c)any activity in connection with a commercial occasion or event (including the appearance of the performer in connection with the occasion or event).

(5) The reference to a **commercial occasion or event** includes any description of occasion or event—

(a)for which any person might receive or become entitled, as a result of anything done by the performer, to receive anything by way of cash or any other form of property; or

(b)which is designed to promote commercial sales or activity by advertising, the endorsement of goods or services, sponsorship, or other promotional means of any kind.

2.3.3.3 Details of Section 37

2.3.3.3.1 Insertion of Chapter 5 Part 8 ITTOIA – subsection 37 (1)

As noted above section 37 inserts Chapter 5 (relief for new residents on foreign income) into Part 8 ITTOIA. This new Chapter in ITTOIA consists of new sections 845Ato 845J the text of which is set out above.

The insertion into Part 8 is provided for by subsection (1) of section 37.

Sections 845A to 845J are discussed below. This text is set out above.

2.3.3.3.2 Section 37 (2) Amendment of section 24 ITA

Subsection 37 (2) deals with some of the mechanics of the charge and the effect on calculation. It reads as follows:

"(2) In ITA 2007—

(a) in section 24 (reliefs deductible at Step 2, in subsection (1)(a))—

(i) at the end insert—

"section 845A of ITTOIA 2005 (claim for relief for qualifying new residents), and", and

(ii) at the end of the entry for section 193(4) of FA 2004, omit the "and",

(b) in section 38 (personal allowance and blind person's allowance) for subsection (3) substitute—

"(3) See also

(a)section 809G, in relation to tax years before 2025-26 where a claim for the remittance basis to apply is made, and

(b) section 845E of ITTIOA 2005, in relation to tax years from 2025-26 where a foreign income claim, a foreign employment election or a foreign gain claim is made.

Those sections provide that where an individual makes such a claim or election for a tax year, the individual is not entitled to any allowance under this Chapter for that tax year.",

(c)in section 55A (transferable tax allowance for married couples and civil partners) for subsection (3) substitute—

"(3) See also—

(a)section 809G, in relation to tax years before 2025-26 where a claim for the remittance basis to apply is made, and

(b) section 845E of ITTIOA 2005, in relation to tax years from 2025-26 where a foreign income claim, a foreign employment election or a foreign gain claim is made.

Those sections provide that where an individual makes such a claim or election for a tax year, the individual is not entitled to any tax reduction under this Chapter for that tax year.",

(d)in section 460 (residence of claimants for relief under section 457 or 458) for subsection (4) substitute—

"(4) See also—

(a)section 809G, in relation to tax years before 2025-26 where a claim for the remittance basis to apply is made, and

(b)section 845E of ITTOIA 2005, in relation to tax years from 2025-26 where a foreign income claim, a foreign employment election or a foreign gain claim is made.

Those sections provide that where an individual makes such a claim or election for a tax year, the individual is not entitled to any relief under section 457 or 458 for that tax year.", (e)in section 809EZA (disguised investment management fees: charge to income tax)—

(i)in subsection (2A), for paragraphs (d) and (e) substitute—

"(d)the individual makes a foreign income claim for the relevant tax year.", and

(ii)in subsection (2C), for "before the end of the period of non-residence" substitute "in any period—

(a)ending immediately before a qualifying tax year in relation to the individual (within the meaning of section 845B (3) of ITTOIA (qualifying new residents)), and

(b)that consists only of tax years for which the individual is not UK resident.", and

(f)in section 989 (the definitions), at the appropriate places insert—

""foreign income claim" means a claim under section 845A of ITTOIA 2005";

""qualifying new resident" has the meaning it has in Chapter 5 of Part 8 of ITTOIA 2005 (see section 845B of that Act)."

Section 24 ITA before the amendments read as follows:

"24. **Reliefs deductible at Step 2 [Section 23 Calculation]**

(1) If the taxpayer is an individual, the provisions referred to at Step 2 of the calculation in section 23 are—

(a)the following—

- section 72 (early trade losses relief),
- Chapter 6 of Part 4 (share loss relief),
- Chapter 3 of Part 8 (gifts of shares, securities and real property to charities etc),
- sections 457 and 458 of this Act or section 266(7) of ICTA (payments to trade unions or police organisations),
- section 193(4) of FA 2004 (pension schemes: relief under net pay arrangement: excess relief), and
- section 194(1) of FA 2004 (pension schemes: relief on making of claim), and

(b)the following—

- section 64 (trade loss relief against general income),
- section 83 (carry-forward trade loss relief),
- section 89 (terminal trade loss relief),
- section 96 (post-cessation trade relief),
- section 118 (carry-forward property loss relief),
- section 120 (property loss relief against general income),
- section 125 (post-cessation property relief),
- section 128 (employment loss relief against general income),

- section 152 (loss relief against miscellaneous income),
- Chapter 1 of Part 8 (interest payments),
- Chapter 1A of Part 8 (irrecoverable peer-to-peer loans),
- Chapter 4 of Part 8 (annual payments ...),
- section 574 (manufactured dividends on UK shares: payments by non-companies),
- section 579 (manufactured interest on UK securities: payments not otherwise deductible),
- Part 2 of CAA 2001 (plant and machinery allowances), in a case where the allowance is to be given effect under section 258 of that Act (special leasing of plant and machinery),
- ...
- Part 8 of CAA 2001 (patent allowances), in a case where the allowance is to be given effect under section 479 of that Act (persons having qualifying non-trade expenditure),
- section 555 of ITEPA 2003 (deduction for liabilities related to former employment),
- section 446 of ITTOIA 2005 (strips of government securities: relief for losses),
- section 454(4) of ITTOIA 2005 (listed securities held since 26 March 2003: relief for losses: persons other than trustees), and
- section 600 of ITTOIA 2005 (relief for patent expenses).

(2) In any other case, the provisions referred to at Step 2 of the calculation in section 23 are—

(a)the provisions listed in subsection (1)(b), and

(b) regulation 18 of the Unauthorised Unit Trusts (Tax) Regulations 2013.

2.3.3.4 Section 23 referred to in section 24

Section 23 ITA is referred to in section 24. Section 23 is headed "The calculation of income tax liability". It is set out here for the convenience of the Reader and reads as follows:

"To find the liability of a person ("the taxpayer") to income tax for a tax year, take the following steps.

Step 1

Identify the amounts of income on which the taxpayer is charged to income tax for the tax year.

The sum of those amounts is "total income".

Each of those amounts is a "component" of total income.

Step 2

Deduct from the components the amount of any relief under a provision listed in relation to the taxpayer in section 24 to which the taxpayer is entitled for the tax year.

See sections 24A and 25 for further provision about the deduction of those reliefs.

See also section 24B which provides that a taxpayer's net income is taken to be £0 in certain cases.

The sum of the amounts of the components left after this step is "net income".

Section 24 after amendment

After the amendments section 24 reads as follows:

24 Reliefs deductible at Step 2

(1) If the taxpayer is an individual, the provisions referred to at Step 2 of the calculation in section 23 are—

(a)the following—

section 72 (early trade losses relief),
Chapter 6 of Part 4 (share loss relief),
Chapter 3 of Part 8 (gifts of shares, securities and real property to charities etc),
sections 457 and 458 of this Act or section 266(7) of ICTA (payments to trade unions or police organisations),
section 41P of ITEPA 2003 (deduction for amount that reflects qualifying foreign employment income),]
section 193(4) of FA 2004 (pension schemes: relief under net pay arrangement: excess relief), ...
section 194(1) of FA 2004 (pension schemes: relief on making of claim), and
section 845A of ITTOIA 2005 (claim for relief for qualifying new residents), and]

(b)the following—

section 64 (trade loss relief against general income),
section 83 (carry-forward trade loss relief),
section 89 (terminal trade loss relief),
section 96 (post-cessation trade relief),
section 118 (carry-forward property loss relief),
section 120 (property loss relief against general income),
section 125 (post-cessation property relief),
section 128 (employment loss relief against general income),
section 152 (loss relief against miscellaneous income),
Chapter 1 of Part 8 (interest payments),

Chapter 1A of Part 8 (irrecoverable peer-to-peer loans),
Chapter 4 of Part 8 (annual payments ...),
section 574 (manufactured dividends on UK shares: payments by non-companies),
section 579 (manufactured interest on UK securities: payments not otherwise deductible),
Part 2 of CAA 2001 (plant and machinery allowances), in a case where the allowance is to be given effect under section 258 of that Act (special leasing of plant and machinery),
Part 8 of CAA 2001 (patent allowances), in a case where the allowance is to be given effect under section 479 of that Act (persons having qualifying non-trade expenditure),
section 555 of ITEPA 2003 (deduction for liabilities related to former employment),
section 446 of ITTOIA 2005 (strips of government securities: relief for losses),
section 454(4) of ITTOIA 2005 (listed securities held since 26 March 2003: relief for losses: persons other than trustees), and
section 600 of ITTOIA 2005 (relief for patent expenses).

(2) In any other case, the provisions referred to at Step 2 of the calculation in section 23 are—

(a)the provisions listed in subsection (1)(b), and

(b) regulation 18 of the Unauthorised Unit Trusts (Tax) Regulations 2013

Consequential amendment to para 46 Schedule 2 – FA 2022 - QAHC (Section 37(3))

2.3.3.4.1 Section 37 (3) QAHC – Consequentials

This subsection makes consequential amendments to the QAHC legislation.

QAHCs are "qualifying asset holding companies." These were introduced in 2022 to attract managed investments to the UK. They can give tax benefits if they meet certain conditions See IFM 40000.

Section 37(3) amends paragraph 46 of Schedule 2 to Finance Act 2022 (qualifying asset holding companies)[35] as a consequence of new subsection 845H (discussed below).

---

[35] Payments of distributions etc to individual to whom the remittance basis applies:

46(1) This paragraph applies in relation to income or a chargeable gain arising to an individual in a tax year if—

(a)section 809B, 809D or 809E of ITA 2007 applies to the individual for that tax year,

(b)the income or gain arises as a result of—

(i)the payment of interest by a QAHC,

(ii)the making of a distribution or a qualified distribution by a QAHC, or

(iii)the disposal by the individual of shares in a QAHC,

(c)in the case of a payment of interest or the making of a distribution or qualified distribution, the

Section 845H is headed "Qualifying foreign income" and discussed below.

Commencement (Section 37(4))

2.3.3.4.2 Section 37(4) Commencement of section 37 (6 April 2025)

Section 37(4) provides for commencement of the amendments made by section 37. This is essentially 6 April 2025.

The subsection reads:

> "(4) The amendments made by this section [37] have effect for the tax year 2025-26 and subsequent tax years."

Accordingly, the section and the amendments made by it apply for the tax year beginning 6 April 2025 and for following tax years.

---

individual provided investment management services in connection with investment arrangements to which the QAHC is party, and

(d)in the case of a disposal of shares, the shares were acquired by the individual during the course of the individual providing investment management services in relation to such arrangements.

(2) The foreign proportion of the amount of any such income is to be treated, for the purposes of income tax, as relevant foreign income.

(3) The foreign proportion of the amount of any such gain is to be treated, for the purposes of capital gains tax, as a gain accruing on the disposal of foreign assets.

(4)For the purposes of this paragraph, the "foreign proportion" of an amount of income or of a gain is equal to the proportion of the profits of the QAHC in the relevant period that was derived from foreign sources, apportioned on a just and reasonable basis in accordance with sub-paragraph (6).

(5) The "relevant period" means—

(a)where the QAHC has been a QAHC for at least three accounting periods, the three most recent complete accounting periods of the QAHC, or

(b)otherwise, the period beginning with beginning of the day on which the QAHC became a QAHC and ending with—

(i)where the income or chargeable gain arose to the individual on that day, the end of that day, or

(ii)otherwise, the end of the day before the income or chargeable gain arose to the individual.

(6) For the purposes of determining the proportion of profits of a QAHC that were derived from foreign sources in the relevant period—

(a)include any profits that would have arisen had the QAHC disposed of all of its assets for a consideration equal to the market value of the assets immediately before the end of the period, and

(b)whether profits are derived from foreign sources is to be determined by reference to the ultimate underlying income or assets to which the profits relate (so, for example, the extent to which profits arising from an interest in another company are derived from foreign sources depends on the extent to which the profits of that company are derived from income arising outside the United Kingdom or the disposal of assets outside the United Kingdom).

(7) In this paragraph—

"foreign asset" has the meaning it has in Schedule 1 to TCGA 1992 (see paragraph 5 of that Schedule);

"profits", in relation to a company, means income and chargeable gains;

"qualified distribution" has the meaning given by paragraph 45(5).

2.4 Details of New Chapter 5 Part 8 ITTOIA

2.4.1 *Introduction*

As noted above section 37(1) inserts Chapter 5 into Part 8 of ITTOIA. This Chapter consists of consists of sections 845Ato 845J ITTOIA.

Each of these sections will be considered in turn in the following paragraphs. The text of these provisions is set out above. Some of that text is repeated in the following paragraphs where it is thought it might assist the Reader.

2.4.2 *Section 845A*

2.4.2.1 *Overview*

Section 845A provides that "**an individual**" who is a "**qualifying new resident**" (defined in section 845B) may make a claim (a "**foreign income claim**") for relief from tax on "**qualifying foreign income**" (defined in section 845F discussed below).

A claim for the relief must be made and made in a tax return no later than 12 months after the 31 January following the end of the tax year for the relief to be available. [36] This is discussed below.

Section 845A also "signposts" the income tax consequences of:

- a foreign income claim;
- a foreign employment election; or
- a foreign gain claim; and

  provides that making such a claim for a tax year result in the Capital Gains Tax annual exempt amount not being available for that year.

The meaning of "a foreign income claim, a foreign employment election or a foreign gain claim" is discussed below.

Example

Liam Cofering is an ESP who performs globally for which he is paid. In the particular circumstances, Liam is a qualifying new UK resident [37]. He makes a foreign income claim in respect of qualifying foreign income. This means he will have lost annual his annual exempt amount. He sells some shares soon after arriving in the UK and becoming UK resident.

The claim cannot apply to his Performance Income (see sections 845 I and J discussed below) as it is Disqualified Income for these purposes.

If Liam had other income which was not related directly or indirectly to the performance, then potentially that income might be eligible for the relief. Liam

---

[36] See subsections (2) and (5)

[37] As this is Liam's first tax year in the UK and he has never been in the UK before

will not be entitled to the CGT annul exempt amount on the wording of the section as he has made a claim.

2.4.2.2 *The Legislation*

Section 845A is headed "Claim for relief for qualifying new residents". It reads as follows.

"(1) An individual may make a claim for relief for a tax year under this section (a "**foreign income claim**") if the individual is a qualifying new resident for that year (see section 845B [discussed below]).

(2) **Where** an individual **makes a foreign income claim** for a tax year, the **individual is entitled to relief** for the tax year that is equal to **so much** of the **total income** of the individual for that year as—

(a) **reflects qualifying foreign income** (see section 845F), **and**

(b) is **identified as such in the claim**.

(3) The **relief** is given **by deducting the amount** of the relief **in calculating the individual's net income** for the tax year (see Step 2 of the calculation in section 23 of ITA 2007).

(4) A foreign income **claim must be made in a return**.

(5) A foreign income claim in relation to a tax year must be made **before the end of the period of 12 months beginning with 31 January after the end of that tax year.**

(6) A foreign income claim may **not be made as a consequential claim** (within the meaning of section 43C(5) of TMA 1970) if the circumstances which give rise to the consequential claim result from a loss of tax brought about carelessly or deliberately by the individual or a person acting on the individual's behalf.

(7) See also—

(a) Chapter 5C of Part 2 of ITEPA 2003 which provides for a claim for relief that may be made in respect of foreign employment income where a foreign employment election is made, and

(b) Schedule D1 to TCGA 1992 which provides for a claim for relief that may be made in respect of foreign gains (**a foreign gain claim**).

(8) Sections 845C and 845D set out some income tax consequences of a foreign income claim, a foreign employment election or a foreign gain claim.

(9) See also section 1K of TCGA 1992, which provides for the loss of an individual's annual exempt amount for capital gains tax where a foreign income claim, a foreign employment election or a foreign gain claim is made.

(10) For the purposes of this section—

(a) "return" means a return under section 8 of TMA 1970 (**personal return**),

(b) references to a claim being included in a return include a claim being so **included** as a result of an **amendment of the return**, and

(c) subsections (5) to (7) of section 118 of TMA 1970 (loss of tax brought about carelessly or deliberately) apply for the purposes of this section as they apply for the purposes of that Act."

2.4.2.3 Detail

2.4.2.3.1 Some questions arising

A number of questions arise in respect of section 845A including the following:

- What is a foreign income claim?
- When is a claim made in a return?
- What is the allowed time within which to make a claim?
- What is a consequential claim?
- Who is a qualifying new resident?

These questions will now be considered in turn.

2.4.2.3.2 What is a "Foreign income claim"

Section 845A allows an individual who is a "qualifying new resident" for the year in respect of which the claim is made to make a claim under section 845A.Such a claim is called in the legislation a "foreign income claim". [38] This is discussed below.

2.4.2.3.3 Foreign Income claim must be made in a return

General

By subsection 845A (4) a foreign income claim must be made in a return.

This raises the questions as to:

- What is a return for these purposes?
- When is a claim included in a return?

Return

By section 845A (10) for these purposes a "return" means a return under section 8 of TMA 1970 (personal return). [39]

---

[38] See section 845(1)

[39] Section https://www.legislation.gov.uk/ukpga/1970/9/section/88 TMA is headed "Personal return". It provides:

"(1) For the purpose of establishing the amounts in which a person is chargeable to income tax and capital gains tax for a year of assessment, and the amount payable by him by way of income tax for that year, he may be required by a notice given to him by an officer of the Board—

(a)to make and deliver to the officer ..., a return containing such information as may reasonably be required in pursuance of the notice, and

(b)to deliver with the return such accounts, statements and documents, relating to information contained in the return, as may reasonably be so required.

(1A) . . . . .

(1AA) For the purposes of subsection (1) above—

(a)the amounts in which a person is chargeable to income tax and capital gains tax are net amounts, that is to say, amounts which take into account any relief or allowance a claim for which is included in the return; and

(b)the amount payable by a person by way of income tax is the difference between the amount in which he is chargeable to income tax and the aggregate amount of any income tax

2.4.2.4 *Amendment*

In most cases it will be obvious from the face of the return what is included in it. This may not be so obvious if the return is amended.

The issue of amendment is dealt with by section 845A (10) (b) which provides that references to a claim being included in a return includes a claim being so included as a result of an amendment of the return.

Example

Artur Dendemen is a qualifying new resident who submits a return which includes a foreign income claim. The return is subsequently amended. This could be by the taxpayer e.g. to correct an error or by HMRC on review.

---

deducted at source ...

(1B)In the case of a person who carries on a trade, profession, or business in partnership with one or more other persons, a return under this section shall include each amount which, in any relevant statement, is stated to be equal to his share of any income, loss, tax, credit or charge for the period in respect of which the statement is made.

(1C) In subsection (1B) above "relevant statement" means a statement which, as respects the partnership, falls to be made under section 12AB of this Act for a period which includes, or includes any part of, the year of assessment ....

(1D) A return under this section for a year of assessment (Year 1) must be delivered—

(a)in the case of a non-electronic return, on or before 31st October in Year 2, and

(b)in the case of an electronic return, on or before 31st January in Year 2.

(1E) But subsection (1D) is subject to the following two exceptions.

(1F) Exception 1 is that if a notice in respect of Year 1 is given after 31st July in Year 2 (but on or before 31st October), a return must be delivered—

(a)during the period of 3 months beginning with the date of the notice (for a non-electronic return), or

(b)on or before 31st January (for an electronic return).

(1G) Exception 2 is that if a notice in respect of Year 1 is given after 31st October in Year 2, a return (whether electronic or not) must be delivered during the period of 3 months beginning with the date of the notice.

(1H) The Commissioners—

(a)shall prescribe what constitutes an electronic return, and

(b)may make different provision for different cases or circumstances.

(2) Every return under this section shall include a declaration by the person making the return to the effect than the return is to the best of his knowledge correct and complete.

(3)A notice under this section may require different information, accounts and statements for different periods or in relation to different descriptions of source of income.

(4) Notices under this section may require different information, accounts and statements in relation to different descriptions of person.

(4A) Subsection (4B) applies if a notice under this section is given to a person within section 8ZA of this Act (certain persons employed etc by person not resident in United Kingdom who perform their duties for UK clients).

(4B) The notice may require a return of the person's income to include particulars of any general earnings (see section 7(3) of ITEPA 2003) paid to the person.

(5) In this section and sections 8A, 9 and 12AA of this Act, any reference to income tax deducted at source is a reference to income tax deducted or treated as deducted from any income or treated as paid on any income."

By Artur

If Artur amended his tax return to include a foreign income claim which was done in time but was not originally in the claim submitted without section 845A (10) (b) it would not be clear that the claim was made in the return. The claim would be treated as made in the return by virtue of subsection (10).

There may be arguments that if the amendment is made after the time for a claim that the time of original submissions should be taken. However, I am not optimistic that they would succeed. I think the purpose of the legislation is to deal with the effect of amendment not to change the period on which a claim needs to be made.

By HMRC

If HMRC amend a return after its submission, then it would not be clear without this subsection whether the claim was made in the return. This subsection makes it clear that it would be treated as made in the claim for this purpose.

Subsections 845A (10)(c) deals with causing loss of tax carelessly or deliberately in this context. The subsection provides:

> "subsections (5) to (7) [40] of section 118 of TMA 1970 (loss of tax brought about carelessly or deliberately) apply for the purposes of this section as they apply for the purposes of that Act."
>
> This is relevant *inter alia* to "consequential claims" discussed below.

2.4.2.5 Time to make claim

The section itself covers the time within which a claim must be made in subsection (5). This reads:

> "A foreign income claim in relation to a tax year must be made before the end of the period of 12 months beginning with 31 January after the end of that tax year."

---

[40] These read as follows:

"(5) For the purposes of this Act a loss of tax or a situation is brought about carelessly by a person if the person fails to take reasonable care to avoid bringing about that loss or situation.

(6) Where—

(a)information is provided to Her Majesty's Revenue and Customs,

(b)the person who provided the information, or the person on whose behalf the information was provided, discovers some time later that the information was inaccurate, and

(c)that person fails to take reasonable steps to inform Her Majesty's Revenue and Customs,

any loss of tax or situation brought about by the inaccuracy shall be treated for the purposes of this Act as having been brought about carelessly by that person.

(7) In this Act references to a loss of tax or a situation brought about deliberately by a person include a loss of tax or a situation that arises as a result of a deliberate inaccuracy in a document given to Her Majesty's Revenue and Customs by or on behalf of that person."

Example

Liam Metic makes a foreign income claim in respect of tax year WWAA in the return for that tax year (i.e. WWAA). That tax year ends on 5 April AA. The 31 January following is 31 January YY which is the date by which the return for tax year WWAA has to be filed electronically. The following 31 January is 31 January ZZ i.e. end of period of 12 months following. The following table may help to explain the steps to work this out.

Matter	Legislation	Date etc.	Comment
Tax year in question	"claim in relation to a tax year" in sub-section	Tax year WWAA	It is assumed that the self-assess-ment return is made in time
End of tax Year WWAA	Tax year begins 6 April one calendar year and ends 5 April the following year see section 4(3) ITA	5 April AA	This is the date that tax year WWAA ends
Following 31January	period of 12 months beginning with 31 January after the end of that tax year.	31 January YY	This is the follow-ing 31 January
12 months later	period of 12 months beginning with 31 January after the end of that tax year.	31 January ZZ	This is the date 12 months later

2.4.2.6 *Not if Consequential Claim?*

2.4.2.6.1 General

A foreign income claim may not be made as a "consequential claim" [41] where the consequential claim results from a loss of tax brought about carelessly or deliberately by the individual or a person acting on the individual's behalf. [42] We are told in the legislation that for these purposes a consequential claim here is one that falls within section 43A(5) [43] TMA.

---

[41] See section 845A (6) "A foreign income claim may not be made as a consequential claim (within the meaning of section 43C (5) of TMA 1970) if the circumstances which give rise to the consequential claim result from a loss of tax brought about carelessly or deliberately by the individual or a person acting on the individual's behalf."

[42] See Section 845 (10) (c) discussed above

[43] "(5) In subsection (4) above "consequential claim" means any claim, supplementary claim, election, application or notice that may be made or given under section 36(3), 43(2), 43A or 43D(6)(as it applies by virtue of subsection (1) or (2) above or otherwise).

Subsection (4)Where it is necessary to make any adjustment by way of an assessment on any person—

(a)in order to give effect to a consequential claim, or

(b)as a result of allowing a consequential claim,

the assessment is not out of time if it is made within one year of the final determination of the claim.

2.4.3 *Section 43A*

Section 43A (1) TMA reads as follows.

"43A Further assessments: claims etc.

(1) This section applies where—

(a)... by virtue of section 29 of this Act an assessment to income tax or capital gains tax is made on any person for a year of assessment, and

(b)the assessment is not made for the purpose of making good to the Crown any loss of tax brought about carelessly or deliberately by that person or by someone acting on behalf of that person.

(2) Without prejudice to section 43(2) above but subject to section 43B below, where this section applies—

(a)any relevant claim, election, application or notice which could have been made or given within the time allowed by the Taxes Acts may be made or given at any time within one year from the end of the year of assessment] in which the assessment is made, and

(b)any relevant claim, election, application or notice previously made or given may at any such time be revoked or varied—

(i)in the same manner as it was made or given, and

(ii)by or with the consent of the same person or persons who made, gave or consented to it (or, in the case of any such person who has died, by or with the consent of his personal representatives),

except where by virtue of any enactment it is irrevocable.

(2A) In subsection (2) above, "claim, election, application or notice" does not include [an election under—

(a)... any of sections 47 to 49 of ITA 2007 (tax reductions for married couples and civil partners: elections to transfer relief),

(aa)section 55C of ITA 2007 (election to transfer allowance to spouse or civil partner),

(b..

(c)section 35(5) of the Taxation of Chargeable Gains Act 1992 (election for assets to be re-based to 1982).

[(2B) For the purposes of this section and section 43B below, a claim under Schedule 1AB is relevant in relation to an assessment for a year of assessment if it relates to that year of assessment.

For this purpose a claim is not taken to be finally determined until it, or the amount to which it relates, can no longer be varied, on appeal or otherwise."

(3) For the purposes of this section and section 43B below, any other claim, election, application or notice is relevant in relation to an assessment for a year of assessment if—

(a)it relates to that year of assessment] or is made or given by reference to an event occurring in that year of assessment, and

(b)it or, as the case may be, its revocation or variation has or could have the effect of reducing any of the liabilities mentioned in subsection (4) below.

(4) The liabilities referred to in subsection (3) above are—

(a)the increased liability to tax resulting from the assessment,

(b)any other liability to tax of the person concerned for—

(i)the year of assessment to which the assessment relates, or

(ii)any year of assessment which follows that ear of assessment and ends not later than one year after the end of the year of assessment in which the assessment was made.

(5)Where a claim, election, application or notice is made given, revoked or varied by virtue of subsection (2) above, all such adjustments shall be made, whether by way of discharge or repayment of tax or the making of assessments or otherwise, as are required to take account of the effect of the taking of that action on any person's liability to tax for any year of assessment.

(6) The provisions of this Act relating to appeals against decisions on claims shall apply with any necessary modifications to a decision on the revocation or variation of a claim by virtue of subsection (2) above.

2.4.3.1 *Consequential Claim?*

A "consequential claim" is a claim to which certain subsections of sections 36, 43A, 43D and sections 43 (1) and (2) TMA apply. These allow claims to be made in some circumstances after an assessment has been made. This can include a discovery assessment. However, if the assessment, in broad terms, is made because of a loss of tax carelessly or deliberately an effective claim cannot be made for the purposes under consideration.

Example

Fred Tarus consciously omits certain income from his tax return so as to pay less tax.

HMRC find out and make a discover assessment in time which is correctly made. The amount omitted includes income which could qualify for relief as a qualifying new resident but also other income that would not so qualify. If this was not done deliberately but only carelessly then of Fred might be able to make the appropriate claim as a qualifying new resident for relief under section 43 (1) and (2) as a matter of general tax law. It might be that it is accepted that Fred was new to the UK and did not understand the system and got it wrong as he could not afford appropriate advice. This could affect the amount of tax due and any tax geared penalty. However, Fred appears to have done this deliberately here. Even if Fred was only careless there could be no effective claim for these purposes because of the wording of section 845A (6).

Fred planned this as "a tax fiddle" and was sure that he would never be found out this would be deliberate conduct. We are told he did so consciously to save tax so there could be no successful claim made. This could be important as to the amount of tax due as well as penalties. It could also have implications for criminal liability.

2.4.3.2 *"Qualifying new resident"*

This is discussed in the following section.

2.4.4 *Section 845B "Qualifying new resident"*

2.4.4.1 *Overview*

This is an essential requirement for a foreign income claim. Section 845A (1) provides that such a claim may be made "if the individual is a qualifying new resident" for the tax year in question.

Broadly, a qualifying new resident in relation to a tax year is an individual who:

- is not "disqualified"
- is resident in the UK for the year in question
- but was not UK resident for **each** of the ten preceding tax years before that tax year.

This phrase is a defined term for the purposes of Chapter 5 of Part 8 ITTOIA.

Section 845B sets out the conditions an individual must meet in order to qualify for relief.

It also sets out conditions that disqualify an individual from qualifying for relief.

2.4.4.2 *Detail "qualifying new resident"*

As noted above the definition of the phrase "qualifying new resident" is found in section 845B. It applies for the purposes of the Chapter i.e. Chapter 5 Part 8 of ITTOIA 2005.

2.4.4.3 *Relevant Legislation*

The relevant legislation is found in section 845B headed "Qualifying new residents". This is repeated here for the convenience of the Reader.

It reads as follows.

"(1) For the purposes of this Chapter, an **individual** is a **qualifying new resident for a tax year if—**

(a) the **individual** is **UK resident for that tax year,**

(b) the individual is **not disqualified** for that tax year, and

(c) **for each of the 10 tax years before** that tax year, the **individual** was **not UK resident**.

(2) An individual is also a qualifying new resident for a tax year if—

(a) the **individual** is **UK resident** for that tax year,

(b) the individual is **not disqualified** for that tax year, and

(c) that **tax year is one of the next three tax years after a qualifying tax year** in relation to the individual.

(3) A tax year is a **qualifying tax year** in relation to an individual if—

(a) the **individual was a qualifying new resident** for that tax year as a **result of subsection (1),**

(b) the individual would have been a qualifying new resident for that tax year as a result of that subsection, but was not only as a result of the individual being disqualified for that tax year, or

(c) the **tax year**—

(i) is the tax year **2022-23, 2023-24 or 2024-25**, and

(ii) is a tax year to which paragraph (a) or (b) **would have applied** in relation to the individual **had this section had effect for that tax year**.

(4) An **individual is disqualified** for a tax year if the individual would, for the purposes of section 41 of the Constitutional Reform and Governance Act 2010, be regarded as—

(a) a member of the House of Commons for any part of that tax year, or

(b) a member of the House of Lords for any part of that tax year.

2.4.4.4 *Details of section 845B and conditions*

2.4.4.4.1 General

New section 845B sets out:

- the conditions an individual must meet in order to qualify for relief as a qualifying new resident; and
- the conditions that disqualify an individual from qualifying for relief as a qualifying new resident.

Subsection (1) of section 845B deals effectively with the first year of residence as a qualifying new resident. Subsection (2) deals with the following three years i.e. the three years after the first year of residence.

2.4.4.4.2 Subsection (1) – first year of residence

To qualify for the relief for a tax year under subsection (1):

- the claimant must be an **individual**;[44]
- that individual must be **UK resident for that tax year,**
- the individual must **not be disqualified for that tax year**, and

[44] The meaning of individual is discussed at a number of points in this Supplement.

- for **each of the 10 tax years before that tax year**, the individual must **not have been UK resident**. Essentially looking at 11 years because requirement is non-resident for the ten years before the year in question.

This essentially applies to the first year of UK residence. See the Example below. Later years are dealt with by subsection (2) considered next.

2.4.4.4.3 Subsection (2) – following three years of residence

To qualify for the relief for a tax year under subsection (2):

- the claimant must be an **individual**;
- the individual must be UK **resident for that tax year**,
- the individual must n**ot be disqualified for that tax year**, and
- that t**ax year is one of the next three tax years after a qualifying tax year** in relation to the individual.

This essentially applies to the three years following the first year of UK residence which was a qualifying tax year. This allows the relief for four years in all. See the Example below.

The difference between the two subsections is that:

- subsection (1) essentially relates to the first year of UK residence;
- whereas subsection (2) relates to the three years following the first i.e. years 2,3 and 4.

Example

Year 11

This is the year in question i.e. the potentially qualifying year.

Ray Tendilsique arrives in the UK in year 11.[45]

This is Ray's first year of UK residence which HMRC accept.

Ray was not resident in the UK during any of the years 1 to 10 (inclusive).

Accordingly, Ray meets the conditions in subsection (1) for year 11 as

- Ray was not UK resident for any of the preceding 10 tax years
- He was UK resident and not disqualified for year 11.

Next three years – Years 12, 13 and 14.

For years 12, 13 and 14 i.e. the next three years following year 11 which is a "qualifying year" Ray meets the conditions in subsection (2) for each of years 12, 13 and 14.

Ray is a UK resident for each of those years.

Ray is not disqualified for those years and remains UK resident.

[45] Which is after 5 April 2025

They are the three years following a "qualifying year" i.e. year 11.

Year 11 falls within subsection (1) and so is a qualifying year by virtue of section 845(3)(a) as it falls within Section 845 (1).

Accordingly, Ray meets the conditions in Section 845 (2) (b) as he is resident for the tax year in question and not disqualified for each of these years. Consequently, he meets the requirements of Section 845 (B) (3).

2.4.4.4.4 Table

The following table may assist the Reader when considering this Example.

Year	Residence status	Comment
14	UK resident one of three years following a qualifying year	UK resident and falls within Section 845 (b) (2)
13	UK resident one of three years following a qualifying year	UK resident and falls within Section 845 (b) (2)
12	UK resident one of three years following a qualifying year	UK resident and falls within Section 845 (b) (2)
11	UK resident – year of arrival a qualifying year	UK resident and falls within Section 845 (b) (1)
10	Not UK resident	*Outside UK tax charge*
9	Not UK resident	*Outside UK tax charge*
8	Not UK resident	*Outside UK tax charge*
7	Not UK resident	*Outside UK tax charge*
6	Not UK resident	*Outside UK tax charge*
5	Not UK resident	*Outside UK tax charge*
4	Not UK resident	*Outside UK tax charge*
3	Not UK resident	*Outside UK tax charge*
2	Not UK resident	*Outside UK tax charge*
1	Not UK resident	*Outside UK tax charge*

Note it is assumed Ray is not disqualified for any of these years.

2.4.4.5 Some Questions arising from section 845B

Section 845B raises a number of questions including the following:

(1.) Who is an individual for these purposes?

(2.) Who is a claimant?

(3.) How is the individual's tax residence to be determined for these purposes?

(4.) When is an individual disqualified?

(5.) What is a qualifying tax year in relation to the individual?

(6.) What is meant by "for each of the 10 tax years before that tax year, the individual was not UK resident"?

(7.) When is a tax year "one of the next three tax years after a qualifying tax year in relation to the individual?"

(8.) What is a qualifying?

2.4.4.5.1 Who is an individual for these purposes?

"Individual" is not a defined term for the purposes of the legislation.

Accordingly, the word bears its ordinary meaning. Broadly, this is a human being who is not a legal or juridical person such as a company or corporation.

The capacity is which the person acts can also sometimes be relevant.

IRC V Longford [1928] AC 252 Lady Longford was a trustee of a settlement for the benefit of Frank Pakenham aka Lord Porn [46] [1928] UKHL J0322-2. She was held not liable for super tax because (*inter alia*) she was not an individual in her capacity as a guardian or trustee.

2.4.4.5.2 Who is a claimant?

Broadly, a claimant is an individual claiming the relief in question here. It is not a defined term in the legislation. It is used here for the sake of convenience and should be so interpreted purposively in the context in which it is used.

2.4.4.5.3 How is the individual's tax residence to be determined for these purposes?

Essentially, the SRT is to be used to determine the individual's tax residence for UK tax purposes here. The question is whether the individual was UK tax resident for the year under consideration which may be a year other than the year of claim e.g. one of the three years following a "qualifying year".

The SRT is discussed in the main text of Chapter 3 of the *Taxation of Entertainers and Sportspersons* at 3.3 and Appendices 1, 2, 3 and 4.

2.4.4.5.4 When is an individual disqualified?

2.4.4.5.4.1 Introductory

Essentially, a person is disqualified if they are a sitting member of the House of Commons or the House of Lords. Entertainers and Sportspersons are and have been members of the Lords and Commons. [47] However, not many would be "qualifying new residents" if they were a sitting member of either House. They would be disqualified for the year in question if they were.

Whether an individual is disqualified for a tax year is dealt with in the legislation.

---

[46] Frank Pakenham, 7th Earl of Longford see https://en.wikipedia.org/wiki/Frank_Pakenham,_7th_Earl_of_Longford

[47] e.g. Glenda Jackson who was an MP and an actress and Seb Coe who was both an athlete and an MP. He was a member of the House of Lords from 16 May 2000 to 31 January 2022 according to the UK parliament website.

2.4.4.5.4.2 Legislation - Disqualification

Section 845B (4) provides:

> "An individual is disqualified for a tax year if the individual would, for the purposes of section 41 of the Constitutional Reform and Governance Act 2010, be regarded as—
> (a) a member of the House of Commons for any part of that tax year, or
> (b) a member of the House of Lords for any part of that tax year."

What is a "qualifying tax year" in relation to the individual?

Qualifying tax year

"Qualifying tax year" is a defined term for these purposes. The definition is found in section 845(B)(3). It reads:

> "(3) A tax year is a **qualifying tax year** in relation to an **individual if**—
> (a) the individual was a **qualifying new resident for** that tax year as a result of subsection (1) [i.e. year of arrival],
> (b) the individual would have been a qualifying new resident for that tax year as a result of that subsection, but was not only as a result of the individual being disqualified for that tax year, or
> (c) the **tax year**—
> (i) is the tax year **2022-23, 2023-24 or 2024-25**, and
> (ii) is a **tax year to which paragraph (a) or (b) would have applied** in relation to the individual had this section had effect for that tax year."

See the Examples above involving Ray.

Ray is a qualifying new resident in year 11 as a result of section 845B (1) (year of arrival).

Accordingly, year 11 is "a qualifying tax year" in relation to Ray as a result of section 845B (3).

This affects the following three years by virtue of section 845B (2) where the tax year "is one of the next three tax years after a qualifying tax year in relation to an individual.

Example above **at 47**

In relation to Ray

- year 11 is the qualifying tax year
- Years 12,13 and 14 are the next three tax years after the qualifying tax year i.e. Year 11.

2.4.4.5.4.3 What is meant by "for each of the 10 tax years before that tax year, the individual was not UK resident"?

The phrase "that tax year" means the tax year under consideration (Year 11 in the Ray example). This refers back to the phrase "an individual is a qualifying new resident *for a tax year*" earlier in subsection (1) of section 845B.

The phrase "the 10 tax years before that tax year" means the 10 years before the tax year in question. Accordingly, there is a period of eleven years that needs consideration consisting of the current year and the ten tax years before it.

Example (see also Ray Example above)

Liam Cant is a recent arrival in the UK. Liam is UK resident in the year in question. Liam is not a member of the House of Commons or the House of Lords at any time in the period under consideration and so is not a disqualified person see X above.

There are two scenarios as to his earlier residence status as set out in the following table.

Tax Year	Scenario A Residence status	Scenario B Residence status	Comment
Year in question, year of Arrival year 0.	UK	UK	Year of arrival in UK for period in question
1	Not in UK	Not in UK	Year(s) preceding Year of arrival
2	Not in UK	Not in UK	Outside UK tax charge
4	Not in UK	Not in UK	Outside UK tax charge
5	Not in UK	Not in UK	Outside UK tax charge
6	Not in UK	Not in UK	Outside UK tax charge
7	Not in UK	Not in UK	Outside UK tax charge
8	Not in UK	Not in UK	Outside UK tax charge
9	Not in UK	UK	Outside UK tax charge
10	Not in UK	Not in UK	Outside UK tax charge
11	UK	Not in UK	Outside UK tax charge
12	Not in UK	UK	Outside UK tax charge

Scenario A

Although Liam has been Resident in the UK before the year in question this was 11 years before the year of arrival i.e. year 0. Accordingly, in Scenario A Liam meets the requirements that "for each of the 10 years before that year [i.e. the year in question Year 0] the individual [i.e. Liam] was not UK Resident" in any of them.

Scenario B

The position here is that Liam was UK resident in Year 9. Accordingly, Liam does not meet the requirement that "for each of the ten years before that year" i.e. the year in question Year 0 as Liam was UK resident in Year 9. Accordingly, Liam would not be a qualifying new resident.

i. *When is a tax year "one of the next three tax years after a qualifying tax year in relation to the individual?"*

a. Qualifying tax year

The first question to consider is what is a qualifying year for these purposes.

"**Qualifying tax year**" is a term used in the section in relation to an individual which is given a specific meaning. It is used as a mechanism to allow the relief for four years i.e. the first year of residence and the next three tax years.

By section 845B (3)

"A **tax year** is a **qualifying tax year in relation to** an **individual** if—

(a) the individual was a **qualifying new resident for that tax year** as a **result of subsection (1)**,

(b) the individual would have been a qualifying new resident for that tax year as a result of that subsection, but was not only as a result of the individual being disqualified for that tax year or

(c) the tax year—

(i) is the tax year 2022-23, 2023-24 or 2024-25, and

(ii) is a tax year to which paragraph (a) or (b) would have applied in relation to the individual had this section had effect for that tax year."

b. Tax year

We also need to remind ourselves is that a tax year is the period from 6 April one calendar year to 5 April the next calendar year. [48]

It may help to understand the position if some examples are considered.

Examples

(i) General

Desi Tern arrives in the UK in year 1.[49] He is an Asturian national who has lived in Asturia all his life till then. He is 25 years old and has never been resident in the UK before. He is first resident in the UK for year 1. Accordingly, Year 1 is a qualifying year. Desi is not disqualified for any of the years under discussion here.

(ii) Qualifying new resident for that tax year as a result of subsection (1)

Section 845B (3)(a) includes the phrase "the individual was a qualifying new resident for that tax year as a result of subsection (1) …"

Subsection (1) of section 845B reads:

"(1) For the purposes of this Chapter, an individual is a qualifying new resident for a tax year if—

(a) the individual is UK resident for that tax year,

(b) the individual is not disqualified for that tax year, and

[48] See section 4(3) ITA

[49] This is after 2024-25

(c) for each of the 10 tax years before that tax year, the individual was not UK resident."

In the General Example Desi is (a) resident in the UK for the year in question (b) not disqualified for that year; and (c) was not resident in the UK for any of the ten years before the year in question.

> *"... one of the next three tax years after a qualifying tax year in relation to the individual..."*

It is provided by section 845B (2) that

"An individual is also a qualifying new resident for a tax year if—

(a) the individual is UK resident for that tax year,

(b) the individual is not disqualified for that tax year, and

(c) that tax year is one of the next three tax years after a qualifying tax year in relation to the individual."

(iii) What is the qualifying tax year in relation to an individual?

Desi is a qualifying new resident for his first year of UK residence and is not disqualified for any subsequent year. He is UK resident for the following three tax years. Accordingly, Desi is also a qualifying new resident for each of the three years after his first year of UK residence i.e. the year of qualification.

This has been discussed above.

Section 843B (1) would have applied i.e. the individual was UK resident for that year and was not disqualified for that year and was not UK resident in any of the preceding ten tax years.

A tax year is a qualifying tax year if:

(1) The year in question is 2022-23, 2023-24, or 2024-25 as

(2) The year in question would have been a qualifying tax year if the year was the year of arrival the individual would have been qualifying new resident as it was the year of arrival.

This is probably best illustrated by an Example.

Section 845B (3) deals with this "A tax year is a qualifying tax year in relation to an individual if—

Example

Desi Tern is a resident of the UK in the year in question and not disqualified for the tax year. Desi was UK resident in the preceding tax year (years) and resident in the tax year in question and the next two tax years (years 2 and 3). The meaning of an individual has been discussed above as has Qualifying new resident. Section 843 (3) (b) deals with the situation where an individual has been a qualifying new resident but for being disqualified for that year. It does not matter for late years.

2.4.4.5.4.4 Arrival in UK before 6 April 2025 and Qualifying Tax Year

Section 843 B (3) (c) deals, (*inter alia*) with the situation where the individual has come to the UK before 6 April 2025 when the new regime first applied. It also deals with disqualification for the individual's year of arrival. It would have helped in my view if these matters had been separated. Section 845(3)(3) reads as follows,

> "A tax year is a qualifying tax year in relation to an individual if
>
> (a) the individual was a qualifying new resident for that tax year as a result of subsection (1),
>
> (b) the individual would have been a qualifying new resident for that tax year as a result of that subsection, but was not only as a result of the individual being disqualified for that tax year, or
>
> (c) the tax year—
>
> (i) is the tax year 2022-23, 2023-24 or 2024-25, and
>
> (ii) is a tax year to which paragraph (a) or (b) would have applied in relation to the individual had this section had effect for that tax year."

The first thing to remind ourselves is that a tax year is the period from 6 April one calendar year to 5 April the next calendar year. [50]

This raises the question how does paragraph (a) work if the individual arrived pre 6 April 2025 given that section 37(4) tells us that the amendments made by section 37 apply for the tax year 2025-26 and subsequent years.

On that basis an arrival before 6 April 2025 could not, without more, give rise to a qualifying new resident.

In my view, paragraph 843B (a) has to be read in the context of paragraph (c)(i) which extends the meaning of qualifying tax year and is to be read independently of (a) despite the reference to it i.e. paragraph (a). Accordingly, was the individual a new resident for the year of arrival.

Paragraph (c) refers to the three tax years before 2025-26 the first year which was the first year the new regime applied.

An example may help to understand what seems to be intended.

> **Example**
>
> David Nuili arrived in the UK for the first time in 2023-24 never having been to the UK before. He was UK resident for that year and was not disqualified. This is before 2025-26. However, paragraph (a) would have applied if the new rules had been in force. Accordingly, paragraph (c)(ii) is met.

---

[50] See section 4(3) ITA

2.4.5 *Section 845C Effect of claims on loss relief*

2.4.5.1 *Overview*

Loss relief may be restricted, where certain claims have been made.

Section 845C sets out that the effect of making certain claims on loss relief.

The effect of Section 845C where it applies is that in some circumstances where claims are made this may result in loss relief being lost.

2.4.5.2 *What claims covered?*

The claims in question are:

- a foreign income claim; [51]
- a foreign gain claim; or [52]
- a foreign employment election. [53]

These are defined terms for these purposes. They are discussed below.

These sometimes referred to in this section of the Supplement together as the Claims ("**the Claims**").

2.4.5.3 *Loss Relief*

If, in respect of a tax year an individual makes:

- a foreign income claim (under section 845A ITTOIA),
- a foreign gain claim (under Schedule D1 TCGA) or
- a foreign employment election (under section 41 ITEPA),

no loss relief will be available for any foreign losses for that year arising from a relevant business in that tax year or any other tax year.

Loss relief where the section applies arising in the year of the claim will not be available for the year of the claim, or any other tax year.

> **Example**
>
> Liam Caing carries on business as a trader in Astoria.
>
> He makes a loss in the current year from that business which HMRC treat as "relevant" business. See below.

The effect of section 845C is that no relief for that loss is available in the year of claim or in any other tax year. The loss relief is not available in future or past years nor in the year in question. This restriction can also apply to Rental Businesses which are not trades.

---

[51] Under section 845A to ITTOIA

[52] Under Schedule D1

[53] Under section 41M ITEPA

2.4.5.4 *Relevant Legislation*

Section 845C is headed "Effect of claim, foreign employment election or foreign gain claim on losses". It provides:

"(1) Subsection (2) applies where—

(a) an **individual** who carries on a **relevant business wholly outside the United Kingdom** makes a foreign income **claim**, a foreign employment election or a foreign gain claim for a tax year,

(b) the individual has a **loss for that tax year from the relevant business,** and

(c) the profits (if there were any) of the business would be qualifying foreign income for that year.

(2) No relief for that loss is available in the tax year for which the claim or election is made or in any other tax year.

(3) In this section "relevant business" means—

(a) a trade, profession or vocation, or

(b) a property business."

2.4.5.5 *Some Questions*

This raises a number of questions including the following:

(1.) Who is an individual for these purposes?

(2.) In respect of what claims does the section apply?

(3.) What is a "relevant business" for these purposes?

(4.) When is it carried on wholly outside the United Kingdom?

(5.) When does an individual have a loss for the tax year from the relevant business?

(6.) When would the profits from the relevant business (if any) be qualifying foreign in for the year in question.

(7.) For what periods does the restriction apply?

These questions will now be considered in turn.

2.4.5.5.1 Who is an "individual" for these purposes?

"Individual" is not a defined term for the purposes of the legislation. Accordingly, the word bears its ordinary meaning. Essentially, that meaning is an individual human being as opposed to a company or trustee. It does not cover juridical persons or entities with a separate legal personality.

A trustee is not treated in practice as an individual in their capacity as a trustee even if the person who is the trustee is in fact an individual human. *Lady Longford et al v IRC* 1928 AC [1928] UKHL J0322-2

This is discussed above (see 23.3.4.6.1).

2.4.5.5.2 In respect of what claims does the section apply?

The section applies for a tax year to a loss for that tax year from the relevant business for that tax year.

> **Example**
>
> See above (part of which duties are abroad).
>
> Ant Fever is employed as a consultant in the UK. Ant Fever is a qualifying new resident of Dystopian heritage. He carries a rental business in Dystopia. In the year in question, he makes a loss in the land business on UK computation principles.
>
> That loss would be caught by the restriction.

2.4.5.5.3 What is a "relevant business" for these purposes?

This phrase is a defined term for the section.

Section 845 C provides in subsection (3):

> "In this section "**relevant business**" means—
>
> (a) a **trade**, profession or vocation, or
>
> (b) a **property business**."
>
> The HMRC Manuals give some guidance as to HMRC's views on "a trade, profession or vocation" and "a property business".

Some extracts follow from the Manuals.

2.4.5.6 Trade, profession or vocation

The HMRC Manuals provide a useful practical starting point here:

> **BIM14010 - Trading income: trades, professions and vocations**
>
> The word 'trade' is not comprehensively or generally defined in tax law although some activities, such as a venture in the nature of trade, are specifically included. 'Trade' therefore takes its ordinary meaning, which normally involves commercial operations by a trader who provides goods or services to his or her customers in exchange for a reward. Whether a trade exists in any given circumstances is a question to be decided on the facts of the case. The Courts do not claim to have defined 'trade' exhaustively, but over the years characteristics indicative of trading have been identified. These are considered in detail at BIM20050 onwards.
>
> Neither 'profession' nor 'vocation' has any statutory definition and they, too, take their ordinary meanings.
>
> A 'profession' historically meant the three learned professions of the Church, Medicine and the Law but today the term goes much wider and normally involves some substantial exercise of intellectual skill.
>
> 'Vocation' has a wide meaning related to the way a person passes his or her life and indicates a calling, although not necessarily one related to religion or high-minded service to others. A bookmaker and a jockey have been held to engage

in vocations and authors, dramatists and professional singers have all been dealt with by the Courts on the basis that they carried on vocations.

The difference in practice causes few problems and it is rarely necessary to debate the point when a taxpayer is clearly carrying on one or the other. If the question is at issue then it has to be decided on the facts of the case (as with the meaning of 'trade', see BIM20070).

There are specific statutory provisions which apply only to a 'trade' or only to a 'profession or vocation' so that the distinction is of some practical significance. Those provisions include the valuation of work in progress at discontinuance (see BIM33540), expenses of research and development (see S87 Income Tax (Trading and Other Income) Act 2005) and expenses for patents, designs and trademarks (see BIM45950 onwards).

There is no practical distinction between a profession and a vocation.

2.4.5.7 *"property business."*

PIM1020 - Introduction: what is a UK property business?

UK property business – legislation

'UK property business' includes all activity for generating income from land in the UK. See section 264 of the Income Tax (Trading and Other Income) Act 2005 (for taxpayers in charge to income tax (IT)) and section 205 of the Corporation Tax Act 2009 (for taxpayers in charge to corporation tax (CT)).

A UK taxpayer may also have an overseas property business – see PIM1025.

Property business: what is it?

Profits from UK land or property are treated, for tax purposes, as arising from a business.

Since the 2017-18 tax year the cash basis (see PIM1090 onwards) is the default way of reporting the profits or losses of a property business for IT customers. However, profits or losses of a tax year must be calculated in accordance with GAAP if certain criteria are met - most notably if the landlord is a company or other CT customer (see PIM1100 onwards). Before this change however, the vast majority of landlords had to use GAAP.

The broad scheme is that property business profits are computed using the same principles as for calculating the profits of a trade, but the taxpayer is not actually treated as if they are trading – unless they meet the normal trading tests (see BIM60000). Thus, for example, CGT reliefs for traders are not normally available.

More information about rents and other receipts is given at PIM1050 onwards.

More information about the expenditure that can be deducted from receipts to arrive at taxable property business profit is given at PIM1900 onwards.

Who carries on a property business?

Any person or body of persons carries on a UK property business if:

- they own or have an interest in land or property in the UK; and
- they enter into transactions that produce rents or other receipts liable to IT or CT from that land or property.

The list of those who carry on a property business includes individuals, partners, trustees, personal representatives, trustees in bankruptcy and companies, including non-residents with UK property income. For more about trusts see PIM1045.

A person will carry on a property business even if they engage an agent to handle it for them. The person carries on the business through the agent.

All property business activities treated as one

In most cases all the various types of income from land and property in the UK are treated as parts of the same, single property business. It does not matter how many properties the taxpayer has, or how many different types of income from land and property. This is clear from section 264(a) (UK property businesses) and section 265(a) (overseas property businesses).

This means that normally all the property business receipts, and expenditure can be amalgamated and, hence, that the expenses on one property can be deducted from the receipts of another.

However, if a landlord has income from property in the UK and income from property outside the UK, the landlord is treated as having two businesses: a UK property business and an overseas property business – legislation does not amalgamate them.

...

There are also special rules for:

- jointly owned property and partnerships - PIM1030,
- trusts and trustees - PIM1045,
- properties which are not let on commercial terms - PIM2130,
- agricultural land - PIM4224,
- receipts from letting a room or rooms in the taxpayer's own home under the rent-a-room scheme - PIM4000 onwards,
- furnished holiday lettings - PIM4100 onwards; and
- activities carried on in different capacities - see the paragraph below.

Activities carried on in different capacities

In law, an individual can act in different legal capacities. Property business activities are treated as parts of a single business where the activities are carried on by the same person acting in the same legal capacity.

Where different legal capacities are involved different property businesses will generally result.

It may be that an individual has property income in a number of different capacities. The individual could, for example:

- hold property in their own right,
- be a member of a partnership, and have a part share in property which the partnership lets,
- be a trustee of a trust receiving rental income.

These would all have to be treated as belonging to different property businesses.

Trustees, executors and partners are common examples of cases where a person acts in a different legal capacity. Executors, for instance, act on behalf of the estate of the deceased and not for themselves. Any property business conducted in a different capacity must be kept separate from any personal property business. A loss on one cannot be set against a profit on another. For more about life interest trusts see PIM1045.

Who is charged to income tax

Normally it is the person who carries on the property business who is charged to tax. But the law says the IT charge falls on the 'person receiving or entitled to the profits', ITTOIA05/S271. In most cases the person entitled to the rental income will also receive it. But different people could be involved where, for example, the landlord engages an agent to handle the property business. The landlord will then carry on the property business through the agent. It will still usually be the landlord who is chargeable to tax. But where the landlord normally lives abroad, we may collect tax from the agent.

Where the taxpayer normally lives abroad and engages the services of an agent in the UK, see PIM4800.

On Overseas Property Business see PM 1020. Such a business is a separate business from a UK property business. On what is an Overseas Property Business see in particular PM 1025ff.

Where is there a loss from the relevant business for that year?

Thus, will essentially be a question of fact and accounting. When will profits, if there were any, of the relevant business be "qualifying foreign income" for that year? Again, this will essentially be a matter of fact and of accounting.

For what periods does the restriction apply?

Essentially, the restriction applies to all periods. Subsection (2) of section 845C reads " (2) No relief for that loss is available in the tax year for which the claim or election is made or in any other tax year."

Essentially, the restriction applies to all periods.

2.4.6 *Section 845D- Effect of claims on personal allowances etc.*

2.4.6.1 *Overview*

Where certain claims are made this can affect the availability of certain allowances and reliefs. This includes personal allowances, and the restriction applies as it does for losses.

Section 845D sets out the **effect of making**:

- a claim for **foreign income relief**;
- a claim for **foreign gain relief**; and
- making an election for **foreign employment relief**;

on personal allowances and other allowances.

Such a claim or election for relief means the individuals who make such claims for a year are not entitled to:

- the personal allowance;
- the blind person's allowance;
- the marriage allowance;
- the married couples' allowance; or
- relief for payments for life insurance.

for that year i.e. the year of claim.

In summary, making such a claim results in the loss of the individual's personal and the other allowances etc. listed above for the year of claim.

Example

Alan Walonce, who is a qualifying new resident, makes a claim for foreign income relief.

Th effect of Alan making such a claim is for that year he is ***not*** entitled for that year to:

- the personal allowance;
- the blind person's allowance;
- the marriage allowance;
- the married couples' allowance; or
- relief for payments for life insurance.

The relevant calculations should be made to determine whether it is advantageous to make the claim. If there is significant overseas income it is likely to be advantageous to make the claim. If the overseas income is small or insignificant it is unlikely to advantageous. However, it all depends on the particular circumstances and the relevant calculations should be done for each year to determine where the balance of advantage lies.

2.4.6.2 Relevant Legislation – Effect of claim

Section 845D is headed "Effect of claim, foreign employment election or foreign gain claim on personal allowance etc". It provides:

"Where an individual makes a foreign income claim, a foreign employment election or a foreign gain claim for a tax year, the individual is not entitled, for that year, to—

(a) any allowance under Chapter 2 of Part 3 of ITA 2007 (personal allowance and blind person's allowance),

(b) any tax reduction under Chapter 3 of that Part (tax reductions for married couples and civil partners),
(c) any tax reduction under Chapter 3A of that Part (transferable tax allowance for married couples and civil partners), or
(d) any relief under section 457 or 458 of ITA 2007 (payments for life insurance etc)."

2.4.6.3 *Some Questions*

This raises a number of questions including the following:

- Who is an individual for these purposes?
- What reliefs does the restriction apply to?
- In respect of what period does the restriction apply?

Who is an individual for these purposes

"Individual" is not defined in the legislation for these purposes.

Accordingly, it bears its ordinary meaning. Broadly, it means a human being in their natural capacity not as acting as a trustee see *IRC v Lady Langford* (1928).

This is discussed above see 23.3.4.6.1.

2.4.6.4 *What reliefs does the restriction apply to?*

The reliefs to which this restriction applies are set out in the section.

By way of reminder, they are:

(a) any allowance under Chapter 2 of Part 3 ITA (personal allowance and blind person's allowance),
(b) any tax reduction under Chapter 3 of Part 3 ITA (tax reductions for married couples and civil partners),
(c) any tax reduction under Chapter 3A of Part 3 (transferable tax allowance for married couples and civil partners), or
(d) any relief under section 457 or 458 ITA (payments for life insurance etc)."

It should be noted that these restrictions apply to a tax year where:

- a foreign income claim;
- a foreign employment election; or
- a foreign gain claim;

is made for that year.

Example

Liam Cenicom arrived in the UK in year 0 and becomes UK resident for that year. He has not been UK resident before and meets the criteria to be qualifying new UK resident for that year.

Liam makes a foreign income election.

> Accordingly, Liam will not be entitled to a personal allowance for that tax i.e. the year of claim.

In respect of what period does the restriction apply?

The restriction applies for the year in which the claim is made.

This follows from the wording of section 845C. So far as relevant this reads "Where an individual makes a [relevant] claim ... for **a tax year**, the individual is not entitled, **for that year**, to" the relief listed above.

If no claim is made the relief may be available if the other relevant conditions are met.

It may be worthwhile for the relevant calculations to be done to see where the balance of advantage lies.

If no claim is made the following year etc. Then the notification does not apply for that year as no claim is made in respect of that year. The restriction is for the year in respect of which a claim is made.

2.4.7 *Section 845E No deduction for relieved foreign income in determining "adjusted net income"*

2.4.7.1 *Overview - "Adjust net income"*

"Adjust net income" is relevant for certain matters such as income related reduction in personal allowances and High-Income Child Benefit Charges. A relief as a result of a relevant claim is ignored for the calculations of income for these purposes.

Section 845E provides that, for the purposes of determining an individual's adjusted net income, any foreign income relieved from tax will be included as part of the calculation for that tax year and will not be deducted. Presumably, this is intended to stop there being a double benefit.

2.4.7.2 *Relevant Legislation*

Section 845E is headed "Foreign income relief ignored for purposes of determining adjusted net income". It provides:

> "(1) Subsection (2) applies for the purpose of determining the adjusted net income under section 58 of ITA 2007 of an individual for a tax year for which the individual has made a foreign income claim.
> (2) The adjusted net income is to be determined as if the relief allowed by the claim had not been deducted in calculating the individual's net income for the tax year."

Section 58 ITA is referred to in Section 845E.

Section 58 ITA is headed "Meaning of "adjusted net income"". It reads as follows:

"(1) For the purposes of Chapters 2 and 3, an individual's adjusted net income for a tax year is calculated as follows.

Step 1

Take the amount of the individual's net income for the tax year.

Step 2

If in the tax year the individual makes, or is treated under section 426 as making, a gift that is a qualifying donation for the purposes of Chapter 2 of Part 8 (gift aid) deduct the grossed-up amount of the gift.

Step 3

If the individual is given relief in accordance with section 192 of FA 2004 (relief at source) in respect of any contribution paid in the tax year under a pension scheme, deduct the gross amount of the contribution.

Step 4

Add back any relief under section 457 or 458 (payments to trade unions or police organisations) that was deducted in calculating the individual's net income for the tax year.

The result is the individual's adjusted net income for the tax year.

(2) The grossed-up amount of a gift is the amount of the gift grossed up by reference to the basic rate for the tax year ....

(3) The gross amount of a contribution is the amount of the contribution before deduction of tax under section 192(1) of FA 2004.

(4) Subsection (6) of section 809ZM (removal of income tax relief in respect of tainted donations etc) excludes certain donations from being deducted at step 2 in subsection (1).

2.4.7.2.1 What is adjusted net income? [54]

Adjusted net income is total taxable income before any Personal Allowances and less certain tax reliefs.

2.4.7.2.2 When your tax liability can be affected by adjusted net income

Your adjusted net income will affect your tax if [certain matters apply]. [This includes where] you are liable to the:

- income-related reduction to the Personal Allowance — where you have an adjusted net income over £100,000 (regardless of your date of birth)
- High Income Child Benefit Charge — where you have an adjusted net income above £60,000".

These matters now include the claims listed above because of this section. This can affect the amount of liability to tax.

[54] See Guidance Personal Allowances: adjusted net income on Gov.uk

Example

Alan Cowel is a qualifying new resident who makes a foreign income claim. He has a taxable income of £110,000 of which £20,000 is Qualifying Foreign Income (discussed in the next section). If Alan makes the claim (discussed in the next section) the £ 20,000 FIG will not be charged saving him some tax on current figures, but he will loss certain allowances and loss relief. If no claim is made on £110,000 will be liable to IT. His personal allowance will be reduced by the excess over £100,000. This is less than the full personal allowance however £20,000 will be outside the UK's IT so the claim is likely still advantageous. However, the detailed calculations should be done to see where the balance of advantage lies.

2.4.8 *Section 845H - "Qualifying foreign income"*

2.4.8.1 *Overview -"Qualifying foreign income"*

"Qualifying foreign income" is what attracts the relief under discussion. Accordingly, it is important to know what such income is.

Section 845F sets out the foreign income that is eligible for relief. This is listed in the table in the section the text of which is set out next.

2.4.8.2 *Relevant Legislation*

Section 845 H is headed "Qualifying foreign income". It provides:

845HQualifying foreign income

Income is qualifying foreign income if it—

(a)falls within a description set out in the following table, and

(b)is not disqualified income (see section 845I).

No.	Description
1	Profits of a trade carried on wholly outside the United Kingdom (see Chapter 2 of Part 2).
2	A UK resident partner's share of the profits of a trade carried on by the firm wholly outside the United Kingdom.
3	Profits of an overseas property business.
4	Adjustment income (within the meaning of Chapter 17 of Part 2) in respect of a trade carried on wholly outside the United Kingdom (see that Chapter).
5	Income chargeable under Chapter 2 of Part 4 (interest) that arises from a source outside the United Kingdom.
6	Income chargeable under Chapter 4 of Part 4 (dividends from non-UK resident companies).
7	Income chargeable under Chapter 7 of Part 4 (purchase life annuity payments) that arises from a source outside the United Kingdom.
8	Income chargeable under Chapter 8 of Part 4 (profits from deeply discounted securities) that arises from a source outside the United Kingdom.
9	Income chargeable under section 579 (royalties and other incored.me from intellectual property) that arises from a source outside the United Kingdom.

10	Income chargeable under Chapter 3 of Part 5 (films and sound recordings: non-trading businesses) that arises from a source outside the United Kingdom.
11	Income chargeable under Chapter 4 of Part 5 (certain telecommunication rights: non-trading income) that arises from a source outside the United Kingdom.
12	Income that arises from a source outside the United Kingdom and that is treated as arising to an individual under section 624 or 629 (income arising under settlement attributed to settlor).
13	So much of any amount of income treated as arising to an individual under section 633 (capital sums paid to settlor by trustees of settlement) for the tax year as falls within the foreign amount of income available up to the end of the tax year. The foreign amount of income available up to the end of a tax year is the amount that would be determined, in accordance with sections 635 to 637 (amount of available income), as the amount of income available up to the end of the tax year if all income arising under the settlement from a source in the United Kingdom were ignored. The foreign amount of income available up to the end of a tax year is the amount that would be determined, in accordance with sections 635 to 637 (amount of available income), as the amount of income available up to the end of the tax year if all income arising under the settlement from a source in the United Kingdom were ignored.
14	Income treated as arising to an individual under section 643A (benefits paid out of protected income).
15	Income chargeable under section 649 (estate income) that arises from a source outside the United Kingdom.
16	Income chargeable under Chapter 7 of Part 5 (annual payments not otherwise charged) that arises from a source outside the United Kingdom.
17	Income chargeable under Chapter 8 of Part 5 (income not otherwise charged) that arises from a source outside the United Kingdom.
18	Accrued income profits (within the meaning of Part 12 of ITA 2007) made by an individual as a result of a transfer of securities if income from the securities would be qualifying foreign income.
19	Income treated as arising under regulation 17 of the Offshore Funds (Tax) Regulations 2009 (offshore income gains).
20	Income that is treated as arising to an individual under section 721, 728 or 732 of ITA 2007 (transfer of assets abroad: deemed income) and that is "foreign" for the purposes of (respectively) section 726, 730 or 735 of that Act.
21	Pension income that arises from a source outside the United Kingdom (see Part 9 of ITEPA 2003).
22	A benefit to which section 678 of ITEPA 2003 applies (foreign social security benefits).
23	The foreign proportion (see paragraph 46 of Schedule 2 to FA 2022) of income arising as a result of the payment of interest, or the making of a distribution or qualified distribution (within the meaning of paragraph 45(5) of that Schedule), by a QAHC (within the meaning of that Schedule).]

2.4.8.3 Detail

Section 845H sets out the foreign income that is eligible for relief. The legislation refers to this as "Qualifying foreign income".

"Qualifying foreign income" is the income for which relief under section 845A headed "Claim for relief for qualifying new residents" can be given.
The relevant part of section 845 A reads:

> "(1) An individual may make a claim for relief for a tax year under this section (a "**foreign income claim**") if the individual is a qualifying new resident for that year (see section 845B).
>
> (2) Where an **individual makes a foreign income claim for a tax year**, the **individual is entitled to relief for the tax year** that **is equal to so much of the total income of the individual for that year as—**
>
> (a) **reflects qualifying foreign income** (see section 845F), **and**
>
> (b) is **identified as such in the claim**...." [Emphasis supplied]

The Table in section 845F sets this out. For the text of Table see above.

"Disqualified income" i.e. income that does not qualify for the relief in question is dealt with by section 845I discussed below.

2.4.9 *Section 845I - Disqualified income*

2.4.9.1 Overview

Not all foreign income attracts the relief under section 845A. Some such income is specifically disqualified.

Section 845I sets out the foreign income that is disqualified from receiving relief from tax under the provisions under consideration i.e. section 845A in particular see extract above for the income disqualified from relief.

2.4.9.2 Relevant Legislation

Section 845I is headed "Disqualified income". It provides:

> "**Income is disqualified income** if—
>
> (a) it is **income of a settlement (within** the meaning of Chapter 5 of Part 5 [**the Settlement Provisions] arising in the tax year 2024-25 or an earlier tax year** that is **treated as arising in tax year 2025-26 or a later year as a result of section 648(3) to (5),**
>
> (b) it is income arising from a security treated as situated in the United Kingdom as a result of section 138ZB of TCGA 1992 (share exchanges involving non-UK incorporated close companies),
>
> (c) it is income chargeable to income tax as a result of section 809AZB of ITA 2007 (transferred income streams),
>
> (d) it is **performance income** (see section 845J), or
>
> (e) it is income from a pension to which section 629 of ITEPA 2003 applies (pre-1973 pensions paid under the Overseas Pensions Act 1973), or
>
> (f) it is a payment made to or in respect of—
>
> > (i) a relieved member of a relevant non-UK scheme (within the meaning of Schedule 34 to FA 2004), or
> >
> > (ii) a transfer member of such a scheme, to which the member payment provisions (within the meaning of that Schedule) apply."

2.4.9.3 Detail

Section 845I sets out the foreign income that is disqualified from relief in this context.

In essence, the following is the foreign income that is relevant there which disqualified from relief, namely:

(a) income of a settlement within the Settlement Provisions arising in 2024-25 or an earlier tax year that is treated as arising in tax year 2025-26 or a later year as a result of section 648(3) to (5),

(b) is income arising from a security treated as situated in the United Kingdom as a result of section 138ZB of TCGA 1992 (share exchanges involving non-UK incorporated close companies),

(c) Transferred Income Streams within section 809AZB ITA (see Chapter 6)

(d) **Performance Income** within section 845J – which is particularly relevant to ESPs and is discussed below.

(e) certain pension payments.

The income in question should always be carefully considered to see if it is disqualified from relief. The most important category here is "Performance Income" the meaning of which is considered in the next section.

2.4.10 *Section 845J - Meaning of performance income which can be disqualified income for ESPs*

2.4.10.1 Overview

One of the items of disqualified income i.e. income which is not "qualifying foreign income" eligible for relief under section 845 A is "Performance Income".

Section 845J defines what is meant by "Performance Income" which is disqualified from receiving relief from tax by section 845G (d) (set out above).

This is of particular significance for ESPs as such income most likely will not qualify for relief under section 845A. This depends on whether it is "income that results, directly or indirectly, from the performance of a relevant activity by a performer".

For a high-level example see the example above at page [11] [Sam Woth-Less].

The meaning of the phrase "Performance Income" is discussed further in the following paragraphs.

2.4.10.2 Relevant Legislation - "Performance Income"

The relevant legislation is found in section 845J.

Section 845J is headed "Performance income". It reads as follows:

"(1) **Performance income** is **any income chargeable to income tax** [55] (however that charge arises) **that *results*, directly or indirectly, from** the **performance of a relevant activity by a performer** (whether **performed in the United Kingdom or not**).

(2) "**Performer**" means any individual who gives performances of entertainment or sport.

(3) For the purposes of this section "**performances of entertainment or sport**" includes any **activity of a physical kind performed by an individual** (alone or with others) which is or may be made **available to the public** or any section of the public, whether for payment or not.

(4) The following are "**relevant activities**"—

(a) the giving of a performance of entertainment or sport;

(b) the participation of the performer in any sound or video recording;

(c) any activity in connection with a commercial occasion or event (including the appearance of the performer in connection with the occasion or event).

(5) The reference to a **commercial occasion or event** includes any description of occasion or event—

(a) for which any person might receive or become entitled, as a result of anything done by the performer, to receive anything by way of cash or any other form of property; or

(b) which is designed to promote commercial sales or activity by advertising, the endorsement of goods or services, sponsorship, or other promotional means of any kind."

(2) In ITA 2007—

(a) in section 24 (reliefs deductible at Step 2, in subsection (1)(a))— 25

(i) at the end insert—

"section 845A of ITTOIA 2005 (claim for relief for qualifying new residents), and", and

(ii) at the end of the entry for section 193(4) of FA 2004, omit the "and",

(b) in section 38 (personal allowance and blind person's allowance) for subsection (3) substitute—

"(3) See also—

(a) section 809G, in relation to tax years before 2025-26 where a claim for the remittance basis to apply is made, and

(b) section 845D of ITTIOA 2005, in relation to tax years from 2025-26 where a foreign income claim, a foreign employment election or a foreign gain claim is made.

[55] Presumably UK IT

Those sections provide that where an individual makes such a claim or election for a tax year, the individual is not entitled to any allowance under this Chapter for that tax year.",

(c) in section 55A (transferable tax allowance for married couples and civil partners) for subsection (3) substitute—

"(3) See also—

(a) section 809G, in relation to tax years before 2025-26 where a claim for the remittance basis to apply is made, and

(b) section 845D of ITTIOA 2005, in relation to tax years from 2025-26 where a foreign income claim, a foreign employment election or a foreign gain claim is made.

(c) Those sections provide that where an individual makes such a claim or election for a tax year, the individual is not entitled to any tax reduction under this Chapter for that tax year.",

(d) in section 460 (residence of claimants for relief under section 457 or 458) for subsection (4) substitute—

"(4) See also—

(a) section 809G, in relation to tax years before 2025-26 where a claim for the remittance basis to apply is made, and

(b) section 845D of ITTOIA 2005, in relation to tax years from 2025-26 where a foreign income claim, a foreign employment election or a foreign gain claim is made.

Those sections provide that where an individual makes such a claim or election for a tax year, the individual is not entitled to any relief under section 457 or 458 [56] for that tax year.",

(e) in section 809EZA (disguised investment management fees: charge to income tax)—

(i) in subsection (2A), for paragraphs (d) and (e) substitute—

"(d) the individual makes a foreign income claim for the relevant tax year.", and

(ii) in subsection (2C), for "before the end of the period of non-residence" substitute "in any period—

(a) ending immediately before a qualifying tax year in relation to the individual (within the meaning of section 845B (3) of ITTOIA (qualifying new residents)), and

(b) that consists only of tax years for which the individual is not UK resident.", and

[56] Section 457 applies to "profits … taken to arise on a disposal of a deeply discounted security by trustees" which are treated as income arising under the settlement and so potentially chargeable on the settlor. By section 458 (1) Tax is not charged under this Chapter if the disposal is made by the trustees of a settlement and they are non-UK resident. The section This section ensures that non-UK resident trustees are not generally charged to tax on profits and gains from deeply discounted securities.

(f) in section 989 (the definitions), at the appropriate places insert—
""**foreign income claim**" means a claim under section 845A of ITTOIA 2005";
""**qualifying new resident**" has the meaning it has in Chapter 5 of Part 8 of ITTOIA 2005 (see section 845B of that Act)."

(3) In paragraph 46 of Schedule 2 to FA 2022 (qualifying asset holding companies)—

(a) in the heading for "applies" substitute "applied or who makes a foreign income claim",

(b) in sub-paragraph (1)— 5

(i) in the words before paragraph (a), for "This paragraph applies" substitute "Sub-paragraphs (2) and (3) apply", and

(ii) in paragraph (a), for "applies" substitute "applied", and

(c) after sub-paragraph (6) insert—

"(6A) Sub-paragraphs (4) to (6) also apply for the purposes of item 22 in the table in section 845F of ITTOIA 2005 (qualifying foreign income for the purposes of foreign income claim)."

(4) The amendments made by this section have effect for the tax year 2025-26 and subsequent tax years."

2.4.10.3 Detail

Subsection (1) of section 845J sets out the main description of "Performance Income".

It reads as follows:

"(1) **Performance income** is **any income chargeable to income tax** (however that charge arises) **that results, directly or indirectly, from the performance of a relevant activity by a performer (whethe**r performed **in the United Kingdom or not**)."

The rest of the section elaborates on this overall description.

2.4.10.4 Some Questions

Subsection (1) raises a number of questions including the following.

- What is income chargeable to income tax (however that charge arises)?
- What is income that results, directly or indirectly, from the performance of a relevant activity by a performer?
- What is a performance?
- What is a relevant activity?
- Who is a performer?
- What is the significance of "whether performed in the United Kingdom or not?"

There is a certain familiarity to some of these questions as they are very similar to those connected with the 1987 Regulations discussed in Chapter 8 of the *Taxation of Entertainers and Sportspersons*.

Each of the questions listed above will now be discussed in turn.

2.4.10.4.1 What is income chargeable to income tax (however that charge arises)?

"Income" is not a defined term generally for UK tax purposes. A useful starting point, in my view as a rule of thumb is how the receipt would to be treated for accounts purposes. The reality though is whether the receipt in question is included in the legislative list of what is chargeable to Income Tax.

The legislation specifically refers to income tax and so would not include CT on general principles of construction. However, the word "indirectly" should be borne in mind when considering whether a payment to a company involved in the arrangements, say at the request or direction of the ESP, would be "income that results indirectly from the performance of a relevant activity by a performer".

A further difficult question is "Does this cover endorsement income?"

It would also seem to exclude capital gains tax. IT generally takes precedence over CGT.[57]

The Reader is referred to Chapters 2,4 ,6 etc. of *Taxation of Entertainers and Sportspersons passim*.

2.4.10.4.2 What is income that results, directly or indirectly, from the performance of a relevant activity by a performer?

The answer to the question what does the income "result" from is not always an easy answer to find. The legislation does not give guidance on the necessary causality or whether correlation alone may be sufficient. The word "results" suggest more than correlation is needed to my mind, it suggests a degree of causation in my view.

The word not being defined in the statute therefore bears its ordinary meaning. The SOD tells that *inter alia* ["results"] means "1. Arise as a consequence, effect or conclusion from some action, process etc. to end or conclude in a specified manner actual or follow as logical consequence ....; have outcome or end in a specified manner esp. *in* failure or success (*resulted badly, in a large profit...*"

Example

Fermo Prance, a professional ESP, contracts to perform "his thing" on stage at a variety show for a specified fee which is duly paid after the show that would

---

[57] Section 37 TCGA is headed 2Consideration chargeable to tax on income." It provides *inter alia* "(1)There shall be excluded from the consideration for a disposal of assets taken into account in the computation of the gain any money or money's worth charged to income tax as income of, or taken into account as a receipt in computing income or profits or gains or losses of, the person making the disposal for the purposes of the Income Tax Acts..."

seem to be covered. It would seem to be a result of the performance that the fee is received.

However, it is not just income that directly results from the performance that is caught. Income that results indirectly from the performance is also caught. How much wider does this make the ambit of the meaning. How wide does the addition of the word "indirectly" make the ambit of "results from the performance"?

Does this cover income from merchandising? If so, just merchandising at the "gig"? What about online merchandising? What about enhanced merchandising after an ESP's death. [58]

What about the question of endorsement income? That income may in part result indirectly from a number of performances that give the reputation or personal brand. How does that fit with "results"? is an apportionment needed? If so on what basis?

The wording here differs from that in the 1987 Regulations. For those regulations to apply there needs to be a "prescribed connection."

Regulation 3(2) provides "Subject to paragraph (3) [59] a payment or a transfer made for, in respect of, or which ***in any way derives either directly or indirectly from, the performance of a relevant activity, has a connection of a prescribed kind*** with the relevant activity."

Regulation 3 uses the word "derives" whereas section 845H uses the word "results". In my view, "derives" [60] has a wider scope and ambit than "results". The SOD definition (set out above) talks of something arising as an actual or logical consequence, almost in the sense of cause and effect. The extension by the word "indirectly" means that the meaning can be wider. The question the is how much wider.

Would offshore endorsement income be caught by "results" in the way the House of Lords tells us it is by "derived" (see the discussion of the *Agassi* Case in Chapter 8 of the *Taxation of Entertainers and Sportspersons*).

Has different language been used deliberately? If so, why? [61]

---

[58] Assuming it is not a "performance" because there is video of it.

[59] Descriptions of payments to which paragraph (2) shall not apply

[60] Derives comes from the Latin and is treated as broadly equivalent to flows from. That is not the same causality in my view as results from.

[61] I have not found anything to answer this question but the search continues.

The wording ""whether performed in the United Kingdom or not" might suggest that something wider was intended. However, it may be that it is used to cover the position of performance in a studio outside the UK, but where the outcome is consumed in the UK. It could also include playing in a FIFA World Cup Final abroad which is televised in the UK. We are then back to whether it "indirectly" results from that game.

I can see this giving rise to interesting discussions with HMRC.

2.4.10.4.3 What is a performance?

> Section 845J(3) provides "For the purposes of this section "**performances of entertainment or sport**" includes any **activity of a physical kind performed by an individual** (alone or with others) which is or may be made **available to the public** or any section of the public, whether for payment or not."

Would an open training session to which the public are admitted for free be covered? It seems to meet the words.

2.4.10.4.4 What is a relevant activity?

The legislation gives some idea as to what this covers in section 845J(4) ff. This reads as follows.

> "The following are "**relevant activities**"—
>
> (a) the giving of **a performance of entertainment or sport**;
>
> (b) the **participation of the performer in any sound or video recording**;
>
> (c) any ***activity in connection with a commercial occasion or event*** (including the appearance of the performer in connection with the occasion or event).
>
> (5) The reference to a ***commercial occasion or event includes*** any description of occasion or event—
>
> (a) for which any person ***might receive or become entitled, as a result of anything done by the performer, to receive anything by way of cash or any other form of propert***y; or
>
> (b) which is ***designed to promote commercial sales or activity*** by advertising, the endorsement of goods or services, sponsorship, or ***other promotional means of any kind***."

This is similar to but not the same as the matters in Regulation 6 of 1987 Regulations. (See Chapter 8 of *Taxation of Entertainers and Sportspersons*).

2.4.10.4.5 Who is a performer?

The meaning of "Performer" is given in the section.

Section 845J(2) provides that "Performer" means any individual who gives performances of entertainment or sport. This is not of the clearest of definitions in my view.

2.4.10.4.6 What is meant by "performances of entertainment or sport"?

The definition of performer raises this question.

Section 845J provides some guidance itself as to what this covers:

> "(3) For the purposes of this section "performances of entertainment or sport" includes any activity of a physical kind performed by an individual (alone or with others) which is or may be made available to the public or any section of the public, whether for payment or not."

This is quite general in its drafting. It has similarities to the 1987 Regulations discussed in Chapter 8 of *Taxation of Entertainers and Sportspersons.*

Subsection (3) gives an "inclusive" definition of Performance of entertainment or sport. It would seem from the context that this is not meant to be an exhaustive definition in the sense of only this core meaning being covered. I think it would be inadvisable to take the view that it is an exhaustive definition.

Subsection (3) raises a number of questions including the following.

(1.) What is an "Activity of a physical kind"?
(2.) When is it "performed by an individual"?
(3.) What is meant by "alone or with others"?
(4.) When is it "available to the public"?
(5.) What is meant by "is or may be made available"?
(6.) What is meant by "whether for payment or not"? Payment by whom?

This will be considered in turn next.

i. *What is an "Activity of a physical kind"?*

   This requires activity rather than passivity. It seems to require that the individual does something.

   Issues have arisen in the past in related areas to whether chess or bridge would qualify. It is likely in practice to be a matter of fact and degree. This gives a fair degree of discretion to HMRC and the Tribunals and Courts. Would it cover a "living statute" i.e. someone who stands still so as to look like a statute?

ii. *When is the matter "performed by an individual"?*

   The paradigms would be:

   - an actor with others on the stage playing their parts in a Shakespeare play;[62]
   - a violinist performing the Bach A minor concerto[63] at a concert;

[62] E.g. As You Like It "All the world's a stage, and all the men and women merely players", Act II, Scene VII, Jaques's speech on the "seven ages of man,"
[63] In front of a paying audience **playing** BWV 1041

- a professional golfer at a PGA tournament in front of a paying public.

The penumbra of meaning gets more complicated.

What if an individual produces something to be "performed" electronically? Is it performed by the individual. This might be the coding or algorithm for computer generated music. If the individual actually switches on the computer from which the work is heard would that be a performance by the individual? It involves some physical activity. Does it matter if the individual wrote and / or owns the copyright of the piece?

What if the electronics decide on the order in which sounds are played randomly? Does it matter if the human "wrote" the sounds and/or the programme or just switched the machine on? Does whose machine it is that is involved? Does it matter if someone else switches the machine on?

iii. *What is meant by "alone or with others"?*

This covers performances of a solo nature. It also covers performances as part of a group, ensemble. Troupe or band, combo etc.

Does "with" cover "against"?

Group or troupe can give a wide meaning.

When is it with others rather than against?

iv. *When is the matter "available to the public"?*

"Available to the public" suggests that people can go and watch. This would clearly cover going physically to a football match. It would seem likely to cover a televised football match. What about a match behind closed doors that is not televised or recorded?

"Public or any section of it" implies something more generally accessible. A private affair which is invitation only would seem not covered. However, this is likely to be a matter of fact and degree.

What about a football match behind closed doors with no spectators?

What if televised?

v. *What is meant by "is or may be made available"?*

"May be made available" is phrase of wide potential. In Theory anything may be made available. Accordingly, there would seem a need for a limit of some sort. I would expect this to be dealt with as a matter of fact and degree. This gives a practical outcome but does not help certainty.

vi. *What is meant by "whether for payment or not"? Payment by whom?*

Again, this is something of potentially wide impact. Would playing in a charity match or testimonial match be covered? Seemingly, Yes as the spectators would pay and so "… may be made available to the public or …, whether for payment or not." Interesting question is what about a free concert in Hyde Park where the performers are paid? Again, this is likely to be a matter of fact and degree.

2.4.10.4.7 What is the significance of "whether performed in the United Kingdom or not?"

The exclusion applies wherever the performance takes place.

"Commercial Occasion or Event".

2.4.10.4.8 Why does this matter to ESPs?

This matters to ESPS because "Performance Income" is "Disqualified Income". Consequently, such income such income cannot benefit from the relief for qualifying new residents.

Example

Ron Fige is a qualifying new resident. He is a professional actor who is paid for his appearances on stage. These would not attract relief. Ron also acts as a director for stage and film productions. The activity as a director would not be blocked as it is not a performance. Interesting questions can arise if Ron plays the leading role in the production and is also the director. Separate contracts can help minimise difficulties if the payments are commercially justifiable.

2.5 Section 38 – The New Overseas Workday Relief

2.5.1 Introduction

Overseas Workday Relief ("**OWR**") provides a form of relief for earnings from work done abroad as an employee in certain circumstances. It will now be available to qualifying new residents for up to four years for the earned income that reflects the work done abroad as an employee.

OWR was available before the 2025 changes on a domicile basis for certain employment income. This is discussed at 3.4.3.3.13.1ff in the *Taxation of Entertainers and Sportspersons*.

As was announced in the Policy Paper this relief is continued on a residence basis in the New Regime. It was formerly domiciled based which it would have been inconsistent to continue on that basis given the move away from a domicile-based system.

OWR is now available for four years rather than three-year periods as under the Old Regime. However, it no longer seems as easy as before because of the residence requirements. It applies to "qualifying foreign employment income" (see section 41Q ITEPA headed "Amount of relief available," in particular).

Broadly, this relief applies to income from an employment the duties of which are performed wholly or partly outside the UK during the qualifying year (see section 41T) for the amount which reflects the overseas performance. This appears to be less prescriptive than under the Old Regime when who the employer was could matter (see the *Taxation of Entertainers and Sportspersons* passim) and the income needed to be kept offshore so there was no remittance.

The new OWR is available to qualifying new residents for the first four years of UK residence.

This new OWR is introduced by section 38 FA 2025 which is considered next.

2.5.2 *Section 38 and Schedule 8: Claim for relief on foreign employment income*

2.5.2.1 *Overview*

Section 38 introduces the new rules governing Overseas Workday Relief ("**OWR**") for new residents after the abolition of non-UK domiciled status and the remittance basis for tax purposes.

Accordingly, OWR will continue to provide Income Tax relief on qualifying employment income which relates to *employment duties performed outside the UK.*

Individuals will now be able to benefit from Overseas Workday Relief for their first four years of residence instead of three years in the earlier version and their foreign employment income can now be brought to the UK without charge as the Old Remittance Basis OWR has been replaced with the new residence-based regime described in the following paragraphs.

There is one difference though as, the new relief will now be subject to financial limitations. The maximum relief per year is now £300,000. It can also be a subject to a lower cap as discussed below.

Section 38 inserts "Chapter 5C Relief for New Residents on Foreign Employment Income Foreign employment election" into Part 2 of ITEPA 2003 (employment income: charge to tax).

Chapter 5C consists of sections 41M to 41Z. The text of these is provisions set out below.

The rules introduced by section 38 started on 6 April 2025.

The newly inserted Chapter 5C applies to give relief for new residents on "foreign employment income". What "foreign employment income" etc means is discussed below under the heading "Key Definitions Section 41N".

This is the new version of OWR on a residence rather than the domicile basis.

"Foreign employment election" The "foreign employment election" is an election made under section 41(3) ITEPA which is discussed below.

A qualifying new resident (within the meaning of section 845B see 41M (2)) may make a foreign employment election in respect of the qualifying year. This must be done in a return and within a specified. See section 41M (7) and (8).

It should be noted that section 41N sets out the key definitions for OWR. The text of this section is set out below at page 82.

2.5.2.2 The Legislation

Section 38 is headed "Claim for relief on foreign employment income". It reads as follows:

"(1) In Part 2 of ITEPA 2003 (employment income: charge to tax), after Chapter 5B insert—

"Chapter 5C Relief for New Residents on Foreign Employment Income Foreign employment election"

Section 41M – Foreign employment election for qualifying new residents

(1). This Chapter applies if an **individual** is a **qualifying new resident** for a tax year (the "**qualifying year**").

(2) An individual is a qualifying new resident for a tax year for the purposes of this Chapter if the individual is a qualifying new resident for the tax year for the purposes of Chapter 5 of Part 8 of ITTOIA 2005 (see section 845B of that Act) [discussed above].

(3) The individual may make an election for the qualifying year under this section ("**a foreign employment election**").

(4) Section 41P makes provision about a claim for relief—

(a) which an individual can make for the qualifying year or any subsequent tax year, where the individual has made a foreign employment election, and

[(b)] which entitles the individual to relief in that year calculated by reference to employment income that is in respect of the qualifying year.

(5) Sections 41Q (amount of relief available) and 41R (limit on relief) set out how to determine the amount of relief to which the individual is entitled.

(6) See also—

(a) sections 845C and 845D of ITTOIA 2005, which set out some income tax consequences of a foreign employment election, and

(b) section 1K of TCGA 1992, which provides for the loss of the individual's annual exempt amount for capital gains tax where a foreign employment election is made.

(7) A foreign employment election must be made in a return.

(8) A foreign employment election for the qualifying year must be made before the end of the period of 12 months beginning with 31 January after the end of the qualifying year.

(9) A foreign employment election may not be made as a consequential claim (within the meaning of section 43C(5) of TMA 1970) if the circumstances which give rise to the consequential claim result from a loss of tax brought about carelessly or deliberately by the individual or a person acting on the individual's behalf.

(10) For the purposes of this Chapter—

(a) "**return**" means a return under section 8 of TMA 1970 (personal return),

(b) references to a claim or election being included in a return include a claim or election being so included as a result of an **amendment** of the return, and

(c) subsections (5) to (7) of section 118 of TMA 1970 (loss of tax brought about carelessly or deliberately) apply as they apply for the purposes of that Act.

41N Key definitions

(1) This section sets out some definitions that apply for the purposes of this Chapter.

(2) "**Qualifying employment income**" means—

(a)qualifying general earnings,

(b)qualifying third party income, and

(c)qualifying securities income.

(3) "**Qualifying foreign employment income**" means—

(a)qualifying foreign general earnings,

(b)qualifying foreign third-party income, and

(c)qualifying foreign securities income.

(4) Section 41T defines what it means—

(a)for general earnings to be "**qualifying general earnings**", and

(b)for qualifying general earnings to be "**qualifying foreign general earnings**".

(5) Section 41U defines what it means—

(a)for third party income to be "**qualifying third party income**", and

(b)for qualifying third party income to be "**qualifying foreign third-party income**".

(6) Section 41V defines what it means—

(a)for securities income to be "**qualifying securities income**", and

(b)for qualifying securities income to be "**qualifying foreign securities income**".

2.5.2.3 An Individual

- Who is a" qualifying new resident" (as to which see section 38(2) discussed below)
- For the "qualifying year"
- Makes a "foreign employment election" in respect of the qualifying year and the relevant income.

It allows relief in respect of the income attributable to the work overseas when a claim has been made in a return.

2.5.2.3.1 Some questions arising

This raises a number of questions including the following:

- Who is an individual for these purposes?
- Who is the qualifying new resident?
- What is the qualifying year?
- What is a foreign employment election?
- What are the consequences of a foreign employment election sections 845 C and D
- What income is covered?
- Other questions also arise such as:
- What is the amount of the relief?
- What limits are there on the relief?
- What are the income tax ions consequences?

These questions will be considered after some of the relevant legislation has been set out. Before that it is helpful to consider some of the Key Definitions here. This is done next.

2.5.3 *Key definitions*

2.5.3.1 *Section 41M – foreign employment election for qualifying new residents*

2.5.3.1.1 Overview

Section 41M is headed "Foreign employment election for qualifying new residents". It provides that an individual who is a qualifying new resident (defined at new section 845B ITTOIA 2005) for a tax year (defined as a qualifying year) may make an election for that qualifying year (defined as a foreign employment election).

Section 41M signposts that a foreign employment election will allow an individual to make a claim for relief for the qualifying year or any subsequent tax year, which entitles the individual to relief in that year on employment income which relates to the qualifying year. Section 41M signposts the income tax consequences of a foreign employment election, and signposts that making an election for a tax year results in the CGT annual exempt amount not being available for that year.

Section 41M provides that a foreign employment election must be made in a tax return no later than 12months after the 31 January following the end of the tax year. Section 41M provides that a foreign employment election may not be made as a consequential claim if the consequential claim results from a loss of tax brought about carelessly or deliberately.

2.5.3.2 Section 41N key definitions

2.5.3.2.1 Overview

Section 41N is headed "key definitions". It provides key definitions *(inter alia)* for qualifying employment income qualifying foreign employment income consists of definitions for sections 41T, 41U, and 41V for the purposes of Chapter 5C.

These are essentially found in section 41N. See Table below.

2.5.3.2.2 Legislation

Section 41N reads as follows:

"(1) This section sets out some definitions that apply for the purposes of this Chapter.

(2) "**Qualifying employment income**" means—

(a) qualifying general earnings,

(b) qualifying third party income, and

(c) qualifying securities income.

(3) "**Qualifying foreign employment income**" means—

(a) qualifying foreign general earnings,

(b) qualifying foreign third-party income, and

(c) qualifying foreign securities income.

(4) Section 41T defines what it means—

(a) for general earnings to be "**qualifying general earnings**", and

(b)for qualifying general earnings to be "**qualifying foreign general earnings**".

(5) Section 41U defines what it means—

(a) for third party income to be "**qualifying third party income**", and

(b)for qualifying third party income to be "**qualifying foreign third party income**".

(6) Section 41V defines what it means—

(a) for securities income to be "**qualifying securities income**", and

(b) for qualifying securities income to be "**qualifying foreign securities income**"."

2.5.3.3 *Table of some definitions etc for OWR*

Word or phrase	Meaning and/ or statutory reference	Comment
"consequential claim"	*Consequential Claim?* A "consequential claim" is a claim to which certain subsections of sections 36, 43A, 43D and sections 43 (1) and (2) TMA apply	See 23.4.3.4 *Consequential Claim?*
"foreign employment election"	means an election under section 41M of ITEPA 2003	See section 989 ITA
"general earnings"	See Section 7(3) ITEPA 2003	See EIM00511 -Employment income: general earnings https://www.gov.uk/hmrc-internal-manuals/employment-income-manual/eim00511
"loss of tax brought about carelessly or deliberately"	Section 845A(10) (c) Section 118 TMA	See section 41P
"net taxable employment income"	Section 41P (8) For the purposes of this Chapter "net taxable employment income", in relation to a tax year, means the employment income on which the individual is charged to tax for the tax year (see section 9(1)).	
"no later than 12months after the 31 January following the end of the tax year"	Section 41M	See section 41M
"Qualifying employment income"	41N(2) (2) "**Qualifying employment income**" means— (a) qualifying general earnings, (b) qualifying third party income, and (c) qualifying securities income.	
"Qualifying foreign employment income"	41N (3) "**Qualifying foreign employment income**" means— (a)qualifying foreign general earnings, (b)qualifying foreign third-party income, and (c)qualifying foreign securities income.	

“**qualifying foreign general earnings**”	41T“(1) General earnings are “qualifying general earnings” if they are— (a) “for” the qualifying year determined in accordance with sections16 and 17, (b) if the qualifying year is a split year as respects the individual, attributable to the UK part of the year, and (c) from an employment the duties of which are performed wholly or partly outside the UK during the qualifying year.	
“**qualifying foreign securities income**”	Section 41N tells us (6) Section 41V defines what it means— (a)for securities income to be “**qualifying securities income**”, and (b)for qualifying securities income to be “**qualifying foreign securities income**”.	
“**qualifying foreign third-party income**”	41U (2) Third party income is “**qualifying third party income**”— (a) if it is in respect of an employment the duties of which are performed wholly or partly outside the UK during the qualifying year, and (b)to the extent that the **value** of the relevant step that counts as employment income (see section 554Z3) is— (i) **“for” the qualifying year** determined in accordance with **section 554Z4(2),** and (ii) if the qualifying year is a split year as respects the individual, attributable to the UK part of the year.	
“**qualifying general earnings**”	section 41T	
“qualifying new resident”	defined at new section 845B ITTOIA 2005	

"**qualifying securities income**"	Section 41N tells us 6) Section 41V defines what it means— (a)for securities income to be "**qualifying securities income**", and...	
"qualifying year"	See **section** 554Z4(2)	
"tax return"	Section 845 (10) For the purposes of this section— (a) "**return**" means a return under section 8 of TMA 1970 (personal return), (b)references to a claim being included in a return include a claim being so included as a result of an amendment of the return	
"tax year"	Section 4 ITA	Period from 6 April one year to 5 April the following year
"third party income"	Section 41U "(1) For the purposes of this Chapter, "**third party income**" is an amount that counts under Chapter 2 of Part 7A (treatment of relevant step for income tax purposes) as employment income in respect of an employment.	

2.5.3.4 *Section 41P– "Claim for relief for qualifying new residents"*

2.5.3.4.1 Overview

Section 41P is headed "Claim for relief for qualifying new residents". It provides that where an **individual** has **made a foreign employment election**, they **may make a claim for relief for the qualifying year, or any subsequent tax year** (defined as a **foreign employment relief claim**) on **so much of the net taxable employment income for that year as is qualifying foreign employment income** (determined under section 41Q).

The relief claimed may not exceed the limit determined under section 41R (discussed below).

Relief claimed is given by deducting this amount at step 2 of the calculation of their income tax liability for the tax year under section 23 of ITA 2007.

Section 41P provides that a foreign employment relief **claim must be made in a tax return no later than 12 months after the 31 January following the end of the tax year**.

Section 41P provides that **a foreign employment relief claim may not be made as a consequential claim if** the consequential claim results **from a loss of tax brought about carelessly or deliberately.**

Section 41P defines "**net taxable employment income**" for the purposes of Chapter 5C.

The relief (i.e. OWR) needs to be claimed.

2.5.3.4.2 Legislation

Section 41P is headed "**Claim for relief for qualifying new residents**"

It reads as follows:

> "(1) Where an individual has made a foreign employment election, the individual may make a claim for relief for the qualifying year or any subsequent tax year ("**a foreign employment relief claim**").
>
> (2) Where an individual makes a foreign employment relief claim for a tax year, the individual is entitled to relief that is equal to so much of the net taxable employment income for that year as—
>
> (a) reflects **qualifying foreign employment income** (see section41Q), and
>
> (b) is identified as such in the claim.
>
> (3) But subsection (2) only applies to the extent the total amount of the relief given does **not exceed the limit (see section 41R)**.
>
> (4) The relief is given by deducting the amount of the relief in calculating the individual's net income for the tax year for which the claim is made (see Step 2 of the calculation in section 23 of ITA 2007).
>
> (5) A foreign employment relief claim must be made in a return.
>
> (6) A foreign employment relief claim for a tax year must be made before the end of the period of 12 months beginning with 31 January after the end of that tax year.
>
> (7) A foreign employment relief claim may not be made as a consequential claim (within the meaning of section 43C(5) of TMA 1970) if the circumstances which give rise to the consequential claim result from a loss of tax brought about carelessly or deliberately by the individual or a person acting on the individual's behalf.
>
> (8) For the purposes of this Chapter "net taxable employment income", in relation to a tax year, means the employment income on which the individual is charged to tax for the tax year (see section 9(1)).

Section 9 is headed "Amount of employment income charged to tax". It reads as follows.

> "(1) The **amount of employment income which is charged to tax under this Part** for a particular tax year is as follows.

(2) In the case of **general earnings**, the amount charged is the **net taxable earnings from an employment in the year**.

(3) That amount is calculated under section 11 by reference to any taxable earnings from the employment in the year (see section 10(2)).

(4) In the case of specific employment income, **the amount charged is the net taxable specific income from an employment for the year**.

(5) That amount is calculated under section 12 by reference to any taxable specific income from the employment for the year (see section 10(3)).

(6) Accordingly, no amount of employment income is charged to tax under this Part for a particular tax year unless—

(a)in the case of general earnings, they are taxable earnings from an employment in that year, or

(b)in the case of specific employment income, it is taxable specific income from an employment for that year."

Sections 11 and 12 ITEPA

These read as follows.

Section 11 is headed "Calculation of "net taxable earnings"" It reads as follows.

"(1) For the purposes of this Part the "net taxable earnings" from an employment in a tax year are given by the formula—

TE - DE

where—

TE means the total amount of any taxable earnings from the employment in the tax year, and

DE means the total amount of any deductions allowed from those earnings under provisions listed in section 327(3) to (5) (deductions from earnings: general).

(2) If the amount calculated under subsection (1) is negative, the net taxable earnings from the employment in the year are to be taken to be nil instead.

(3) Relief may be available under section 128 of ITA 2007 (set-off against general income)—

(a)where TE is negative, or

(b)in certain exceptional cases where the amount calculated under subsection (1) is negative.

(4) If a person has more than one employment in a tax year, the calculation under subsection (1) must be carried out in relation to each of the employments.

Section 12 is headed "Calculation of "Calculation of "net taxable specific income"". It reads as follows.

"(1) For the purposes of this Part the "net taxable specific income" from an employment for a tax year is given by the formula—

TSI-DSI

where—

TSI means the amount of any taxable specific income from the employment for the tax year, and

DSI means the total amount of any deductions allowed from that income under provisions of the Tax Acts not included in the lists in section 327 (3) and (4) (deductions from earnings: general).

(2) If the amount calculated under subsection (1) is negative, the net taxable specific income from the employment for the year is to be taken to be nil instead.

(3)If a person has more than one kind of specific employment income from an employment for a tax year, the calculation under subsection (1) must be carried out in relation to each of those kinds of specific employment income; and in such a case the "net taxable specific income" from the employment for that year is the total of all the amounts so calculated."

2.5.3.4.3 Details

Section 41P provides that where an individual has made a foreign employment election, they may make a claim for relief for the qualifying year, or any subsequent tax year foreign employment relief claim) on so much of the net taxable employment income for that year as is qualifying foreign employment income (determined under section 41Q). The relief claimed may not exceed the limit determined under section 41R. Relief claimed is given by deducting this amount at step 2 of the calculation of their income tax liability for the tax year under section 23 of ITA 2007.

Section 41P provides that a foreign employment relief claim must be made in a tax return no later than 12 months after the 31 January following the end of the tax year. Section 41P provides that a foreign employment relief claim may not be made as a consequential claim if the consequential claim results from a loss of tax brought about carelessly or deliberately.

Section 41P defines "net taxable employment income" for the purposes of Chapter 5C.

2.5.3.4.4 *Effective Date*

06 April 2025

2.5.3.5 Section 41Q "Amount of Relief Available"

2.5.3.5.1 Overview

Section 41Q is headed "Amount of relief available". It sets out how the amount of qualifying foreign employment income in respect of which a foreign employment relief claim for a tax year can be made is to be determined. This includes the extent to which any deductions in that tax year affect the relief available.

As mentioned before there is a cap on the relief available in Section 41R. This section helps to work out the amount of relief. Section 41Q tells what amount "reflects qualifying general earnings".

2.5.3.5.2 Legislation

Section 41Q is headed "Amount of relief available". It provides:

"(1) For the purposes of section 41P (2), the **amount of net taxable employment income for a tax** year that **"reflects" qualifying foreign employment income is** the **total** of—

(a) the total of the amount of the **net taxable earnings from each employment in the tax year** that **reflects qualifying foreign general earnings** (see subsections (2) to (5)), **and**

(b) the **total** of the amount of the **net taxable specific income from each employment** for the tax year that reflects qualifying foreign third-party income or **qualifying foreign securities income** (see subsection (6)).

(2) The amount of the net taxable earnings from an employment in a tax year that "**reflects**" qualifying foreign general earnings is—

(a) the amount of the taxable earnings from the employment in the tax year that are qualifying foreign general earnings, minus

(b) the amount of the qualifying deductions.

(3) If the amount calculated under subsection (2) is nil or a negative amount, then none of the net taxable earnings from the employment in the tax year reflect qualifying foreign general earnings.

(4) If the foreign employment relief claim is for the qualifying year, the amount of the **qualifying deductions** is the proportion of the total deductions that is the same as the proportion of the claim year taxable earnings that are qualifying foreign general earnings.

(5) If the foreign employment relief claim is for a subsequent tax year, the amount of the qualifying deductions is the amount resulting from the following steps—

Step 1 Deduct the claim year taxable earnings from the total deductions.

If the result is nil or a negative amount, there are no qualifying deductions.

Step 2 Deduct any other taxable earnings that are not qualifying foreign general earnings.

If the result is nil or a negative amount, there are no qualifying deductions.

(6) The **proportion** of the net taxable specific income from an employment for a tax year that "**reflects**" qualifying foreign third-party income or qualifying foreign securities income is the same as the proportion of the taxable specific income for the employment in that year that is qualifying foreign third-party income or qualifying foreign securities income.

(7) In this section—

> "claim year taxable earnings" means the taxable earnings from the employment in the tax year that are "for" the year for which the claim is made determined in accordance with section 16and 17;
> "total deductions" means the total amount of any deductions allowed from the taxable earnings from the employment in the tax year under provisions listed in section 327(3) to (5) (see section 11(1))."

2.5.3.5.3 Details

This section 41(Q) as the heading suggests deals with the amount of relief available. Section 41P tells us that the individual who has made a foreign employment claim that individual is entitled to relief for so much "net taxable employment income" for the year in question as:

(a) "reflects" the "qualifying foreign income", and

(b) is identified in the claim.

2.5.3.5.4 Some questions arising

This raises a number of questions including the following:

- What is the net taxable employment income?
- What is qualifying foreign employment income?
- What is meant by "reflects"?
- What is meant by identified in the claim?

These questions will be considered in turn next.

2.5.3.5.4.1 What is net taxable income?

This is defined in section 41P.

Subsection (8) reads as follows:

> "(8) For the purposes of this Chapter "net taxable employment income", in relation to a tax year, means the employment income on which the individual is charged to tax for the tax year (see section 9(1))." [64]

---

[64] Section 9 is headed "Amount of employment income charged to tax". It reads as follows.

"(1) The amount of employment income which is charged to tax under this Part for a particular tax year is as follows.

(2) In the case of general earnings, the amount charged is the net taxable earnings from an employment in the year.

(3) That amount is calculated under section 11 by reference to any taxable earnings from the employment in the year (see section 10(2)).

(4) In the case of specific employment income, the amount charged is the net taxable specific income from an employment for the year.

(5) That amount is calculated under section 12 by reference to any taxable specific income from the employment for the year (see section 10(3)).

(6) Accordingly, no amount of employment income is charged to tax under this Part for a particular tax year unless—

(a)in the case of general earnings, they are taxable earnings from an employment in that year, or

(b)in the case of specific employment income, it is taxable specific income from an employment for that year."

This is essentially the employment income on which the individual is taxed for the year in question within the meaning of section 9 (set out above). This is enlarged upon by sections 11 and 12 set out above.

2.5.3.5.4.2 What is qualifying foreign employment income?

This is defined by section 41 N (3). It reads as follows.

> "(3) "Qualifying foreign employment income" means—
>
> (a)qualifying foreign general earnings,
>
> (b)qualifying foreign third-party income, and
>
> (c)qualifying foreign securities income."

Section 41Q (discussed below) sets out how the amount of qualifying foreign employment income in respect of which a foreign employment relief claim for a tax year can be made is to be determined. This includes the extent to which any deductions in that tax year affect the relief available.

2.5.3.5.4.3 What is meant by reflects?

i. *General*

This is dealt with by section 41Q (2). This reads as follows.

> "(2) The amount of the net taxable earnings from an employment in a tax year that "reflects" qualifying foreign general earnings is—
>
> (a)the amount of the taxable earnings from the employment in the tax year that are qualifying foreign general earnings, minus.
>
> (b)the amount of the qualifying deductions.
>
> This requires a deduction calculation. There is to be deducted from the amount of the taxable earnings from the employment in the year in question that are "qualifying foreign general earnings".

ii. *"qualifying foreign general earnings"*

This is discussed above.

iii. *the amount of "qualifying deductions".*

Qualifying deductions are dealt with by subsection (4). This reads as follows.

> (4) If the foreign employment relief claim is for the qualifying year, the amount of the qualifying deductions is the proportion of the total deductions that is the same as the proportion of the claim year taxable earnings that are qualifying foreign general earnings.

iv. *Identified in the claim?*

The meaning of claim is discussed above. This can include an adjusted claim. It does not include a consequential claim where there has been careless or deliberate conduct causing loss of Revenue (as to which see the TMA *passim*).

2.5.3.5.5 ***Effective Date***

06 April 2025.

2.5.3.6 Section 41R – Limit on relief

2.5.3.6.1 Overview

The Revised OWR has a limit on the amount of OWR available.

Section 41R determines the limit on the amount of relief the individual is entitled to under section 41P.

There is an overall maximum relief of £300,000 but it may be lower at 30% of the relevant qualifying employment income if it is less than £300,000 (see section 41R (2) and (3) set out below).

2.5.3.6.2 Legislation

Section 41R is headed "Limit on relief". It reads as follows.

"This section sets out how to determine the limit on the amount of relief the individual is entitled to when making a foreign employment relief claim for a year for the purposes of section 41P (3).

(2) The limit is the lesser of—

(a) **30%** of the relevant qualifying employment income, and

(b) **£300,000.**

(3) For the purposes of this section "**relevant qualifying employment income**" means—

(a) **so much** of the **net taxable employment income** for the tax year for which the claim is made as **reflects qualifying employment income**, and

(b) if the foreign employment relief claim is for a tax year that is subsequent to the qualifying year, so much of any net taxable employment income for any earlier tax year (but not any tax year before the qualifying year) as would reflect qualifying employment income if that earlier year was the year for which the claim was made.

(4) If the foreign employment relief claim is for a tax year that is subsequent to the qualifying year, the limit is reduced by the total of any amounts reflecting qualifying foreign employment income that have previously been relieved under section 41P.

(5) To determine the amounts mentioned in subsection (3)(a) and (b), apply section 41Q, but as if—

(a) the references in that section to qualifying foreign employment income were to qualifying employment income, the references in that section to qualifying foreign general earnings were to qualifying general earnings, and the references in that section to qualifying foreign third-party income and qualifying foreign securities income were references to qualifying third party income and qualifying securities income.

For section 41 Q see above.

2.5.3.6.3 Details

There is a limit on the amount of the relief under a foreign employment relief claim. This is dealt with by section 41R. Foreign employment relief ignored for purposes of determining adjusted net income. By section 41R (2) this is the lesser of:

- 30% of the relevant qualifying employment income; and
- £300,000

This means the relief is not available on amounts exceeding £300,000 for the year. The relief may be less as there is also the lower limit of 30% of the relevant qualifying employment income. This raises the question: what is relevant qualifying employment income?

What is relevant qualifying employment income?

This is defined in section 41R (3). It reads as follows:

> "(3) For the purposes of this section "**relevant qualifying employment income**" means—(a) so much of the net taxable employment income for the tax year for which the claim is made as reflects qualifying employment income, and if the foreign employment relief claim is for a tax year that is subsequent to the qualifying year, so much of any net taxable employment income for any earlier tax year (but not any tax year before the qualifying year) as would reflect qualifying employment income if that earlier year was the year for which the claim was made."

2.5.3.6.4 Effective Date

06 April 2025

2.5.3.7 Section 41S Amount ignored in determining adjusted net income.

2.5.3.7.1 Overview

Section 41S is headed "Foreign employment relief ignored for purposes of determining adjusted net income". It provides that, for the purposes of determining an individual's "adjusted net income", any qualifying foreign employment income relieved from tax will be included as part of the calculation for that tax year and will not be deducted.

2.5.3.7.2 Legislation

i. Section 41S

Section 41S is headed "Foreign employment relief ignored for purposes of determining adjusted net income". It reads as follows.

"(1) Subsection (2) applies for the purpose of determining the adjusted net income under section 58 of ITA 2007 of an individual for a tax year for which the individual is entitled to relief under section 41P.

(2) The adjusted net income is to be determined as if the relief had not been deducted in calculating the individual's net income for the tax year."

ii. *Section 58 ITA*

Section 58 ITA is headed 58 "Meaning of "adjusted net income"". It reads as follows.

"(1) For the purposes of Chapters 2 and 3, an individual's adjusted net income for a tax year is calculated as follows.

Step 1

Take the amount of the individual's net income for the tax year.

Step 2

If in the tax year the individual makes, or is treated under section 426 as making, a gift that is a qualifying donation for the purposes of Chapter 2 of Part 8 (gift aid) deduct the grossed-up amount of the gift.

Step 3

If the individual is given relief in accordance with section 192 of FA 2004 (relief at source) in respect of any contribution paid in the tax year under a pension scheme, deduct the gross amount of the contribution.

Step 4

Add back any relief under section 457 or 458 (payments to trade unions or police organisations) that was deducted in calculating the individual's net income for the tax year.

The result is the individual's adjusted net income for the tax year.

(2) The grossed-up amount of a gift is the amount of the gift grossed up by reference to the basic rate for the tax year ....

(3) The gross amount of a contribution is the amount of the contribution before deduction of tax under section 192(1) of FA 2004.

(4) Subsection (6) of section 809ZM (removal of income tax relief in respect of tainted donations etc) excludes certain donations from being deducted at step 2 in subsection (1)."

2.5.3.7.3 Details

These provisions set out how the calculations are to be done.

2.5.3.7.4 Effective Date

06 April 2025.

2.5.3.8 Section 41 T Meaning of Qualifying foreign employment income

2.5.3.8.1 Overview

Section 41T is headed "Qualifying general earnings and qualifying general income". It defines 'qualifying general earnings' and 'qualifying foreign general earnings'.

Section 41T sets out the definition of **"Qualifying foreign employment income."** This an important definition for OWR purposes as it is by reference to this that is relief. The definition relies on the definition of "qualifying general earnings"

2.5.3.8.2 Legislation

i. Section 41T

Section 41T is headed "Qualifying foreign general earnings". It reads as follows:

"(1) General earnings are "qualifying general earnings" if they are—
(a) "for" the qualifying year determined in accordance with sections16 and 17,
(b) if the qualifying year is a split year as respects the individual, attributable to the UK part of the year, and
(c) from an employment the duties of which are performed wholly or partly outside the UK during the qualifying year.
(2) Any attribution required for the purposes of subsection (1)(b) is to be done on a just and reasonable basis.
(3) Qualifying general earnings are "qualifying foreign general earnings" if they are neither—
(a) in respect of duties performed in the United Kingdom, nor
(b) from overseas Crown employment subject to United Kingdom tax (see section 41W).
(4) For the purposes of subsection (3), the extent to which qualifying general earnings are in respect of duties performed in the United Kingdom is to be determined on a just and reasonable basis."

ii, Section 16 ITEPA

Section 16 is headed "Meaning of earnings "for" a tax year.
It reads as follows.

"(1) This section applies for determining whether general earnings are general earnings "for" a particular tax year for the purposes of this Chapter.
(2) General earnings that are earned in, or otherwise in respect of, a particular period are to be regarded as general earnings for that period.
(3) If that period consists of the whole or part of a single tax year, the earnings are to be regarded as general earnings "for" that tax year.

(4) If that period consists of the whole or parts of two or more tax years, the part of the earnings that is to be regarded as general earnings "for" each of those tax years is to be determined on a just and reasonable apportionment.

(5) This section does not apply to any amount which is required by a provision of Part 3 to be treated as earnings for a particular tax year."

iii. Section 17

Section 17 is headed "Treatment of earnings for year in which employment not held".

It reads as follows.

"(1) This section applies for the purposes of this Chapter in a case where general earnings from an employment would otherwise fall to be regarded as general earnings for a tax year in which the employee does not hold the employment.

(2) If that year falls before the first tax year in which the employment is held, the earnings are to be treated as general earnings for that first tax year.

(3) If that year falls after the last tax year in which the employment was held, the earnings are to be treated as general earnings for that last tax year.

(4) This section does not apply in connection with determining the year for which amounts are to be treated as earnings under Chapters 2 to Part 3 (the benefits code)."

2.5.3.8.3 Detail

This deals with "Qualifying foreign general earnings", an important concept in the calculation of OWR.

2.5.3.8.4 Effective Date

6 April 2025

2.5.3.9 Section 41V Qualifying foreign third-party income

Qualifying foreign third-party income.

2.5.3.9.1 Overview

Section 41V is headed "Qualifying third-party foreign income". It defines 'qualifying third party income' and 'qualifying foreign third-party income'.

Third party income is 'qualifying third party income if it is (a) in respect of an employment the duties of which are wholly or partly outside the UK during the qualifying year, and (b) to the extent that the value of the relevant step that counts as employment income (in section 554Z3 ITEPA 2003) is (i) 'for the qualifying year determined in accordance with section 554Z4(2) ITEPA 2003 and, (ii) if the qualifying year is a split year as respects the individual, attributable to the UK part of the year. Qualifying third party income is 'qualifying foreign third-party income' to the extent that it is not in respect of duties performed in the UK. The extent to which qualifying third party income is not in respect of duties performed in the UK is to be determined on a just and reasonable basis.

2.5.3.9.2 Legislation

Section 41V is headed "Qualifying foreign third-party income". It reads as follows.

> "(1) For the purposes of this Chapter, "**third party income**" is an amount that counts under Chapter 2 of Part 7A (treatment of relevant step for income tax purposes) as employment income in respect of an employment.
>
> (2) Third party income is "**qualifying third party income**"—
>
> (a) if it is in respect of an employment the duties of which are performed wholly or partly outside the UK during the qualifying year, and
>
> (b)to the extent that the **value** of the relevant step that counts as employment income (see section 554Z3) is—
>
> (i) **"for" the qualifying year** determined in accordance with **section 554Z4(2),** and
>
> (ii) if the qualifying year is a split year as respects the individual, attributable to the UK part of the year.
>
> (3) Any attribution required for the purposes of subsection (2)(b)(ii) is to be done on a just and reasonable basis.
>
> (4) Qualifying third party income is "**qualifying foreign third-party income**" to the extent that it is not in respect of duties performed in the United Kingdom.
>
> (5) The **extent** to which qualifying third party income is not in respect of duties performed in the United Kingdom is to be **determined on a just and reasonable basis.**"

2.5.3.9.3 Detail

Section 41V is headed "Qualifying Foreign Securities Income". It defines 'qualifying securities income' and 'qualifying foreign securities income'.

a. Securities income (SI) is qualifying foreign securities income (FSI)
   - (a) if the duties of the relevant employment are performed wholly or partly outside the UK during the qualifying year, and
   - (b) to the extent that it
     - (i) accrues during the qualifying year, or
     - (ii) accrues during the UK part of the qualifying year if it is a split year for the individual.

b. When SI accrues is determined by treating an equal amount of the SI as accruing on each day of the relevant period determined in accordance with section 41G, unless the result is not just and reasonable, in which case the qualifying SI is then such amount as is just and reasonable.

c. Qualifying SI is wholly qualifying FSI if the duties of the relevant employment are performed wholly outside the UK. If some, but not all, of the duties are performed outside the UK (a) the qualifying SI is apportioned (on a just and reasonable basis) between duties performed in and outside of the UK, and (b) the income apportioned in respect of duties performed outside the UK is qualifying FSI. But qualifying SI from overseas Crown employment subject to UK tax is not qualifying FSI.

2.6 Schedule 8 Relief on foreign employment income: consequential and transitional provision

2.6.1 *Overview*

The changes made by section 38 require consequential amendments to be made and for there to be transitional provision. This is dealt with in the main by Schedule 8.

Section 38 (2) introduces Schedule 8. The subsection provides

"In Schedule 8—
(a) Part 1 makes general consequential amendments;
(b) Part 2 makes consequential amendments relating to the operation of PAYE;
(c) Part 3 contains transitional provision.
(3) The amendments made by this section and the provision made by Schedule 8 have effect for the tax year 2025-2026 and subsequent tax years.".

The changes made by the section and Schedule 8 apply from 6 April 2025 (see section 38 (3)).

2.6.2 *Legislation*

The Schedule is quite long. Accordingly, the particular legislation is set out by reference to paragraphs in what follows.

2.6.3 *Details*

The details of Schedule 8 are given under the heading "Details" for each paragraph in what follows.

2.6.4 *Effective Date*

06April 2025 see section 38 (3)

2.6.5 *Details of the Schedule*

2.6.5.1 *Part 1: General consequential amendments*

Paragraph 1 – General Consequential amendment to ITEPA

Paragraph 1 makes general consequential amendments overview to ITEPA 2003. This removes reference to "domicile" in ITEPA and where appropriate making reference to "qualifying new resident" etc.

2.6.5.1.1 Legislation

Paragraph 1 provides as follows.

"1(1) ITEPA 2003 is amended as follows.

(2) In section 28 (meaning of "general earnings from overseas Crown employment subject to UK tax"), in subsection (2)(b), after "or of" insert "Wales, Scotland or".

(3) In section 225 (payments for restrictive undertakings), for subsection (6) substitute—

"(6) This section only applies where—

(a)if there are general earnings from the employment that are earned in, or otherwise in respect of, the tax year mentioned in subsection (3), subsection (7) applies to any of those general earnings, or

(b)it is reasonable to assume that, if there were such general earnings, subsection (7) would apply to any of those general earnings.

(7) This subsection applies to general earnings if either—

(a)section 15 applies to the general earnings and the general earnings are not—

(i)qualifying foreign general earnings within the meaning of section 41T (qualifying foreign general earnings), or

(ii)general earnings to which section 22 or section 26 would apply if the individual made a claim under section 809B of ITA 2007 (claim for the remittance basis) for the tax year mentioned in section 22(1) or 26(1) (being a tax year before tax year 2025-26), or

(b)section 27 applies to the general earnings."

(4) In section 290E (calculation of earnings rate for a tax year), in subsection (4), for "non-domiciled", in each place it occurs, substitute "non-resident or qualifying new resident".

(5) In section 333 (scope of this chapter: expenses paid by the employee), in subsection (3)(b), for "non-domiciled" substitute "qualifying new resident".

(6) In section 341 (travel at start or finish of overseas employment), in subsection (4), for the words from "domiciled" to the end substitute "not a qualifying new resident for the purposes of Chapter 5C of Part 2 of this Act or Chapter 5 of Part 8 of ITTOIA 2005 (see section 845B of that Act)."

(7) In section 342 (travel between employments where duties performed abroad), in subsection (7), for the words from "domiciled" to the end substitute "not a

qualifying new resident for the purposes of Chapter 5C of Part 2 of this Act or Chapter 5 of Part 8 of ITTOIA 2005 (see section 845B of that Act)."

(8) In section 355 (deductions for corresponding payments by non-domiciled employees)—

(a)in the heading, for "non-domiciled" substitute "qualifying new resident";

(b)in subsection (2), for the words from "not domiciled" to the end substitute "a qualifying new resident for the purposes of Chapter 5C of Part 2 of this Act or Chapter 5 of Part 8 of ITTOIA 2005 (see section 845B of that Act)."

(9) In section 360 (disallowance of certain accommodation expenses of MPs), in subsection (1), for "non-domiciled" substitute "non-resident or qualifying new resident".

(10) In section 370 (travel costs and expenses where duties performed abroad), in subsection (6), for paragraph (b) substitute—

"(b)either—

(i)if the tax year is tax year 2024-2025 or an earlier tax year, would be taxable earnings under section 15 even if the employee made a claim under section 809B of ITA 2007 (claim for remittance basis) for that year, or

(ii)if the tax year is tax year 2025-2026 or a later tax year and the employee is a qualifying new resident for the purposes of Chapter 5C of Part 2 for that tax year, are not qualifying foreign general earnings within the meaning of section 41T (qualifying foreign general earnings)."

(11) In the italic heading before section 373 for "non-domiciled" substitute "non-resident or qualifying new resident".

(12) In section 373 (employee's travel costs and expenses where duties performed in UK)—

(a)in the heading, for "Non-domiciled" substitute "Non-resident or qualifying new resident";

(b)in subsection (1) for "not domiciled in the United Kingdom" substitute "non-UK resident or a qualifying new resident for the purposes of Chapter 5C of Part 2 of this Act or Chapter 5 of Part 8 of ITTOIA 2005 (see section 845B of that Act)";

(c)in subsection (4)(a)—

(i)for "the country" substitute "a country";

(ii)after "normally lives" insert "at the time the journey is made";

(d)in subsection (4)(b), for "that", in both places it occurs, substitute "such a";

(e)omit subsection (7).

(13) In section 374 (spouse's, civil partner's or child's travel costs and expenses where duties performed in UK)—

(a)in the heading, for "Non-domiciled" substitute "Non-resident or qualifying new resident";

(b)in subsection (1) for "not domiciled in the United Kingdom" substitute "non-UK resident or a qualifying new resident for the purposes of Chapter 5C of Part 2 of this Act or Chapter 5 of Part 8 of ITTOIA 2005 (see section 845B of that Act)";

(c)in subsection (3)(a)—

(i)for "the country" substitute "a country";

(ii)after "normally lives" insert "at the time the journey is made";

(d)in subsection (5)(c)—

(i)for "the country" substitute "a country";

(ii)after "normally lives" insert "at the time the journey is made"

(e)omit subsection (10).

(14) In section 376 (foreign accommodation and subsistence costs and expenses (overseas employments))—

(a)in subsection (1)(c), for "domiciled in the United Kingdom" substitute "not a qualifying new resident for the purposes of Chapter 5C of Part 2 of this Act or Chapter 5 of Part 8 of ITTOIA 2005 (see section 845B of that Act)";

(b)omit subsection (6).

(15) In section 395C (meaning of "foreign service" in section 395B), for subsection (4) substitute—

"(4) In subsection (2) "relevant earnings" means—

(a)for service in or after the tax year 2025-26, earnings—

(i)to which section 15 applies, and

(ii)if the employee is a qualifying new resident for the purposes of Chapter 5C of Part 2 for that tax year, which are not qualifying foreign general earnings within the meaning of section 41T (qualifying foreign general earnings), and

(b)for service before tax year 2025-26, earnings to which section 15 applies and to which that section would apply even if the employee made a claim under section 809B of ITA 2007 (claim for remittance basis) for that year."

(16) In section 413 (exception in certain cases of foreign service), for subsection (3ZA) substitute—

"(3ZA) In subsection (2A) (a) "relevant earnings" means—

(a)for service in or after the tax year 2025-26, earnings—

(i)to which section 15 applies, and

(ii)if the employee is a qualifying new resident for the purposes of Chapter 5C of Part 2 for that tax year, which are not qualifying foreign general earnings within the meaning of section 41T (qualifying foreign general earnings), and

(b)for service before tax year 2025-26, earnings to which section 15 applies and to which that section would apply even if the employee made a claim under section 809B of ITA 2007 (claim for remittance basis) for that year."

2.6.5.1.2 Details

(a.) Sub-paragraph 1(1) provides that the Schedule amends ITEPA 2003.

(b.) Sub-paragraph 1(2) amends section 28 to insert the words "Wales, Scotland or" after "or of" in subsection (2)(b).

(c.) Sub-paragraph 1(3) amends section 225 by removing references to a claim to the remittance basis at subsection 225(6) and inserting a requirement that the general earnings are not qualifying foreign general earnings if the individual's earnings meet the requirements as set out in 41TChapter 5C of Part 2 , or general earnings to which section 22 or 26 apply through a claim made under section 809B ITA 2007, or section 27 applies to the general earnings

(d.) Sub-paragraph 1(4) amends section 290E by substituting the words "qualifying new resident" for the words "non-domiciled" in each instance it occurs in that section.

(e.) Sub-paragraph 1(5) amends section 333 by substituting the words "qualifying new resident" for the words "non-domiciled" in subsection (3)(b).

(f.) Sub-paragraph 1(6) amends section 341 by substituting the words "is not a qualifying new resident for the purposes of Chapter 5C of Part 2" for the words "is domiciled in the United Kingdom" in subsection (4).

(g.) Sub-paragraph 1(7) amends section 342 by substituting the words "is not a qualifying new resident for the purposes of Chapter 5C of Part 2" for the words "is domiciled in the United Kingdom" in subsection (7).

(h.) Sub-paragraph 1(8) amends section 355 by substituting the words "qualifying new resident" for the words "non-domiciled" in the heading and by substituting the words "a qualifying new resident for the purposes of Chapter 5C of Part 2" for the words "not domiciled in the United Kingdom and section 835BA of ITA 2007 (deemed domicile) applies for the purposes of this subsection" in subsection (2).

(i.) Sub-paragraph 1(9) amends section 360 by substituting the words "qualifying new resident" for the words "non-domiciled".

(j.) Sub-paragraph 1(10) amends section 370 by substituting paragraph (b) in subsection (6) for a new paragraph (b).

(k.) Sub-paragraph 1(11) amends the italic heading before section 373.

(l.) Sub-paragraph 1(12) amends section 373 headed "Non-resident or qualifying new resident employee's travel costs and expenses where duties performed in UK" by substituting the words "Qualifying new resident" for the words "Non-domiciled" in the heading, by substituting the words "a qualifying new resident for the purposes of Chapter 5C of Part 2" for the words "not domiciled in the United Kingdom" in subsection (1) and by omitting subsection (7).

(m.)Sub-paragraph 1(13) amends section 374 by substituting the words "Qualifying new resident" for the words "Non-domiciled" in the heading, by substituting the words "a qualifying new resident for the purposes of Chapter 5C of Part 2" for the words "not domiciled in the United Kingdom" in subsection (1) and by omitting subsection (10).

(n.) Sub-paragraph 1(14) omits section 375 headed "Meaning of "qualifying arrival date"".

(o.) Sub-paragraph 1 (15) amends section 376 by substituting the words "is not a qualifying new resident for the purposes of Chapter 5C of Part 2" for the words "is domiciled in the United Kingdom" in subsection (1)(c) and by omitting subsection (6).

(p.) Sub-paragraph 1(16) amends section 395C by substituting subsection (4) on the meaning of relevant earnings for service before 2025-26 and for service from 2025-26.

(q.) Sub-paragraph 1(17) amends section 413 by substituting subsection 3ZA on the meaning of relevant earnings for service before 2025-26 and for service from 2025-26.

2.6.5.1.3 Effective Date

6 April 2025 see section 38(3).

2.6.5.2 Paragraph 2 – General Consequential Amendments to ITA

2.6.5.2.1 Overview

Paragraph 2 makes general consequential amendments to ITA 2007.

2.6.5.2.2 Legislation

Paragraph 2 is headed "General Consequential Amendments to ITA" and reads as follows.

"2(1) ITA 2007 is amended as follows.

(2) In section 24 (reliefs deductible at Step 2), in subsection (1)(a), after the entry for section 266(7) of ICTA insert— "section 41P of ITEPA 2003 (deduction for amount that reflects qualifying foreign employment income),".

(3) In section 989 (the definitions), at the appropriate place insert—

""foreign employment election" means an election under section 41M of ITEPA 2003,".

2.6.5.2.3 Details

i General

Sub-paragraph 2(1) provides that the Schedule amends ITA 2007.

ii Section 24 ITEPA

Sub-paragraph 2(2) amends section 24 by inserting the words

"section 41P of ITEPA 2003 (deduction for qualifying foreign employment income)," in subsection (1)(a) after the entry for section 266(7) of ICTA

Section 41P is headed "Claim for relief for qualifying new residents" and is discussed above.

iii. Section 989

Sub-paragraph 2(3) amends section 989 headed "Definitions" by inserting the following ""foreign employment election" means an election under section 41M of ITEPA 2003,".

2.6.5.2.4 Effective Date

6 April 2025 see section 38(3).

2.6.5.3 Part 2: Consequential amendments relating to PAYE

2.6.5.4 Paragraph 3 in Section of Sections 690C and 690D

2.6.5.4.1 Overview

i. General

Paragraph 3 inserts two new sections. These are section 690C and new section 690D.

ii. New Section 690C

New section 690C sets out the circumstances where an employer of an employee who is likely to be a qualifying new resident, can give notice to apply PAYE on a proportion of the qualifying earnings.

Subsections (1) sets out that this section may apply to qualifying new residents with subsection (2) and (4) providing effect for a notice by an employer upon acknowledgement to treat qualifying payments made to the employee as not subject to PAYE.

Subsection (3) provides the definitions of "qualifying payment and "foreign proportion".

Subsections (5) and (6) provide circumstances where the notice will either not have effect, or cease to have effect Subsection (9) sets out the treatment of specific income at section 695A, section 696 for the purpose of this section and new section 690D.

iii. New Section 690D

New section 690D allows an officer of HMRC to issue a direction where a notice is received under new section 690C for qualifying new residents. Under subsection (2) an officer may give a direction to determine the proportion of a qualifying payment by an employer that is not a payment of PAYE income, and it is applied to any qualifying payment at subsection (4). Subsection (3) specifies what information is to be included within a direction. The circumstances under which a direction ceases to have effect is detailed at subsection (5).

2.6.5.4.2 Legislation

Paragraph 3 reads as follows.

"3 In Part 8 of Schedule 3 to the Social Security (Contributions) Regulations 2001 (S.I. 2001/1004), in paragraph 5 (travel costs and expenses where duties performed in the United Kingdom) —

(a) in the heading, for "non-domiciled" substitute "non-resident or qualifying new resident";

(b) in paragraph (a), for "non-domiciled" substitute "non-resident or qualifying new resident"."

2.6.5.4.3 Details

Paragraph 3 inserts new section 690C and new section 690D. New section 690C sets out the circumstances where an employer of an employee who is likely to be a qualifying new resident, can give notice to apply PAYE on a proportion of the qualifying earnings. Subsections (1) sets out that this section may apply to qualifying new residents with subsection (2) and (4) providing effect for a notice by an employer upon acknowledgement to treat qualifying payments made to the employee as not subject to PAYE. Subsection (3) provides the definitions of "qualifying payment and "foreign proportion". Subsections (5) and (6) provide circumstances where the notice will either not have effect or cease to have effect. Subsection (9) sets out the treatment of specific income at section 695A, section 696 for the purpose of this section and new section 690D. New section 690D allows an officer of HMRC to issue a direction where a notice is received under new section 690C for qualifying new residents. Under subsection (2) an officer may give a direction to determine the proportion of a qualifying payment by an employer that is not a payment of PAYE income, and it is applied to any qualifying payment at subsection (4). Subsection (3) specifies what information is to be included within a direction. The circumstances under which a direction ceases to have effect is detailed at subsection (5).

2.6.5.4.4 Effective Date

6 April 2025 see section 38 (3).

2.6.5.5 Part 3: Transitional provision

2.6.5.6 Paragraph 4

2.6.5.6.1 Overview

Paragraph 4 provides transitional provisions which apply to individuals who met the requirement of section 26A ITEPA 2003 for the tax year 2022-2023 and to whom section 809B ,809D or 809E of ITA 2007 applies in that year, or for tax year 2023-2024 or 2024-2025.

2.6.5.6.2 Legislation

The legislation Part 2 is headed "Consequential amendments relating to PAYE" and reads as follows.

"After section 690C of ITEPA 2003 (employees who were internationally mobile etc. before 2025-2026) (as inserted by section 21 of this Act) insert—

"**690D Employer notification for qualifying new residents**

(1) This section applies in relation to an employee if—

(a)the employee is or is likely to be a qualifying new resident for a tax year ("the qualifying year"), and

(b)the employee works or is likely to work outside the UK during the qualifying year.

(2) The appropriate person may give a notice to an officer of Revenue and Customs at any time during the qualifying year—

(a)that the employer is proposing to treat the foreign proportion of any qualifying payment made by the employer to the employee as not being PAYE income of the employee for the purposes of PAYE regulations, and

(b)specifying that proportion.

(3) For the purposes of this section and section 690E—

(a)a "qualifying payment" means a payment of, or on account of, an amount of employment income of the employee that is likely to be qualifying employment income;

(b)the "foreign proportion" of a qualifying payment is the proportion of the employment income that, on the basis of the best estimate that can reasonably be made, is likely to be qualifying foreign employment income.

(4) If a notice given under this section has effect, the proportion of any qualifying payment made by the employer to the employee in any tax year which is to be treated for the purposes of PAYE regulations as not being a payment of PAYE income is the proportion specified in the notice.

(5) notice given under this section—

(a)does not have effect if a direction has previously been given to the appropriate person under section 690E (direction by HMRC in relation to qualifying new residents) in relation to the employee and the qualifying year;

(b)otherwise, has effect when it is acknowledged by an officer of Revenue and Customs.

(6)A notice given under this section ceases to have effect if—

(a)a direction under section 690E is given to the appropriate person in relation to the employee and the qualifying year,

(b)a subsequent notice is given by the appropriate person under this section and is acknowledged by an officer of Revenue and Customs, or

(c)a subsequent notice—

(i)is given by the appropriate person under section 690A (employer notification for internationally mobile employee) on the basis that the employee is or is likely to be non-UK resident in the qualifying year, and

(ii)is acknowledged by an officer of Revenue and Customs.

(7)A notice given under this section must be in such manner and form, and contain such information, as may be specified in a general direction made by the Commissioners for His Majesty's Revenue and Customs.

(8) Subsection (4) is without prejudice to—

(a)any assessment in respect of the income of the employee in question, and

(b)any right to repayment of income tax and any relevant debts overpaid and any obligation to pay income tax underpaid and any relevant debts that remain wholly or partly unpaid.

(9) For the purposes of this section and section 690E—

(a)where an amount of employment income is treated as PAYE income paid by the employer for the purposes of PAYE regulations by virtue of section 687A or 695A (employment income under Part 7A) or section 696 (readily convertible assets), the employer is to be treated as making payment of that amount of employment income, and

(b) "qualifying new resident", "qualifying employment income" and "qualifying foreign employment income" have the same meaning as in Chapter 5C of Part 2 (relief for new residents on foreign employment income).

690E Direction by HMRC in relation to qualifying new residents

(1) This section applies where—

(a)a notice given during the qualifying year under section 690D has effect, and (b)it appears to an officer of Revenue and Customs that the proportion of any qualifying payment made by the employer to the employee that is treated as not being a payment of PAYE income for the purposes of PAYE regulations should not be the proportion specified in the notice.

(2) An officer of Revenue and Customs may give a direction—

(a)for determining a proportion of any qualifying payment made by the employer to the employee which is to be treated for the purposes of PAYE regulations as not being a payment of PAYE income, or

(b)that any such payment is to be treated entirely as PAYE income for the purposes of PAYE regulations.

(3)A direction under subsection (2)—

(a)must specify the employee and the qualifying year,

(b)must be given by notice to the appropriate person, and

(c)may be varied by notice to the appropriate person from a day specified in the notice (which may not be earlier than 30 days from the date on which the notice is given).

(4) If—

(a)a direction under subsection (2) has effect, and

(b)any qualifying payment is made by the employer to the employee in any tax year,

the direction applies to the payment.

(5)A direction under subsection (2) has effect when it is given.

(6)A direction under subsection (2) ceases to have effect if a notice has subsequently been—

(a)given by the appropriate person under section 690A (employer notification for internationally mobile employee) on the basis that the employee is or is likely to be non-UK resident for the qualifying year, and

(b)acknowledged by an officer of Revenue and Customs.

(7) Subsection (4) is without prejudice to—

(a)any assessment in respect of the income of the employee in question, and

(b)any right to repayment of income tax and any relevant debts overpaid and any obligation to pay income tax underpaid and any relevant debts that remain wholly or partly unpaid."

Section 26A ITEPA reads as follows.

"26ASection 26: requirement for 3-year period of non-residence

(1) An employee meets the requirement of this section for a tax year if the employee was—

(a)non-UK resident for the previous 3 tax years, or

(b)UK resident for the previous tax year but non-UK resident for the 3 tax years before that, or (c)UK resident for the previous 2 tax years but non-UK resident for the 3 tax years before that, or

(d)non-UK resident for the previous tax year, UK resident for the tax year before that and non-UK resident for the 3 tax years before that.

(2) The residence status of the employee before the 3 years of non-UK residence is not relevant for these purposes."

2.6.5.6.3 Details

Paragraph 4 provides transitional provisions which apply to individuals who met the requirement of section 26A ITEPA 2003 for the tax year 2022-2023 and to whom section 809B, 809D or 809E of ITA 2007 applies in that year, or for tax year 2023-2024 or 2024-2025. If these provisions apply, an individual who would otherwise be a qualifying new resident for the tax year 2025-2026 for the purposes of Chapter 5C of Part 2 of ITEPA 2003, is treated as not being a qualifying new resident for that year for the purposes of that Chapter.

2.6.5.6.4 Effective Date

6 April 2025 (see section 38(3)).

2.6.5.7 Paragraph 5 – Transitional Provisions Section 26A

2.6.5.7.1 Overview

Paragraph 5 provides transitional provisions which apply to individuals who meet the requirement of section 26A ITEPA 2003 for the year 2025-2026 or 2026-2027, and who met the requirement of section 26A ITEPA 2003 for the year 2023-2024 or 2024-2025 and to whom section 809B, 809D or 809E of ITA 2007 applies in that year. If an individual to whom this paragraph applies would not otherwise be a qualifying new resident for the tax year 2025-2026 or 2026-2027 in which they meet the requirement of section 26A ITEPA 2003, Chapter 5C of Part 2 of ITEPA2003 has effect as if the individual were a qualifying new resident for that year. Accordingly, OWR could be available to such a person.

2.6.5.7.2 Legislation

Paragraph 5 reads as follows.

Individuals no longer meeting section 26A requirement not qualifying new residents

5(1)If an individual falling within sub-paragraph (2) would otherwise be a qualifying new resident for tax year 2025-26 for the purposes of Chapter 5C of Part 2 of ITEPA 2003 (relief for new residents on foreign employment income), the individual is to be treated as not being a qualifying new resident for that year for the purposes of that Chapter.

(2) An individual falls within this sub-paragraph if—

(a)the individual met the section 26A requirement for tax year 2022-23, and
(b)section 809B, 809D or 809E of ITA 2007 (remittance basis) applied to the individual for that year or for tax year 2023-24 or 2024-25.

26ASection 26: requirement for 3-year period of non-residence

(1) An employee meets the requirement of this section for a tax year if the employee was—
(a)non-UK resident for the previous 3 tax years, or
(b)UK resident for the previous tax year but non-UK resident for the 3 tax years before that, or
(c)UK resident for the previous 2 tax years but non-UK resident for the 3 tax years before that, or
(d)non-UK resident for the previous tax year, UK resident for the tax year before that and non-UK resident for the 3 tax years before that.

(2) The residence status of the employee before the 3 years of non-UK residence is not relevant for these purposes."

2.6.5.7.3 Details

Paragraph 5 provides transitional provisions which apply to individuals who meet the requirement of section 26A ITEPA 2003 for the year 2025-2026 or 2026-2027, and who met the requirement of section 26A ITEPA 2003 for the year 2023-2024 or 2024-2025 and to whom section 809B, 809D or 809E of ITA 2007 applies in that year. If an individual to whom this paragraph applies would not otherwise be a qualifying new resident for the tax year 2025-2026 or 2026-2027 in which they meet the requirement of section 26A ITEPA 2003, Chapter 5C of Part 2 of ITEPA 2003 has effect as if the individual were a qualifying new resident for that year.

2.6.5.7.4 Effective Date

6 April 2025 see section 38(3)

2.6.5.8 Paragraph 6 Transitional Provisions disapplying the Limit in Section 41R in some cases

2.6.5.8.1 Overview

Paragraph 6 provides transitional provisions which disapply the limit on relief under section 41R in certain circumstances. These provisions apply to individuals to whom the provisions in paragraph 5 apply. These provisions also apply to an individual who met the requirement of section 26A ITEPA 2003 for the year 2023-2024 or 2024-2025 and to whom section 809B, 809D or809E of ITA 2007 applies in that year, who is a qualifying new resident for the purposes of Chapter 5C of Part 2 of ITEPA 2003 in 2025-2026, 2026-2027 or 2027-2028, and who meets the requirement of section 26A ITEPA 2003 for the tax year 2025-2026.

2.6.5.8.2 Legislation

i. Paragraph 6

Paragraph 6 is headed "Certain individuals meeting section 26A requirement treated as qualifying new residents". It reads as follows.

> "6(1) If an individual falling within sub-paragraph (2)—
> (a)meets the section 26A requirement for tax year 2025-26 or 2026-27, and
> (b)is not a qualifying new resident for that year for the purposes of Chapter 5C of Part 2 of ITEPA 2003,
> the individual is to be treated as a qualifying new resident for that tax year for the purposes of that Chapter.
> (2) An individual falls within this sub-paragraph if—
> (a)the individual met the section 26A requirement for tax year 2023-24 or tax year 2024-25, and
> (b)section 809B, 809D or 809E of ITA 2007 (remittance basis) applied to the individual for that tax year."

ii. Section 26A

Paragraph 6 refers to section 26A which is set out here for the convenience of the Reader.

Section 26A is headed "Section 26: requirement for 3-year period of non-residence." It reads as follows.

> "(1) An employee meets the requirement of this section for a tax year if the employee was—
> (a)non-UK resident for the previous 3 tax years, or
> (b)UK resident for the previous tax year but non-UK resident for the 3 tax years before that, or
> (c)UK resident for the previous 2 tax years but non-UK resident for the 3 tax years before that, or
> (d)non-UK resident for the previous tax year, UK resident for the tax year before that and non-UK resident for the 3 tax years before that.
> (2) The residence status of the employee before the 3 years of non-UK residence is not relevant for these purposes."

2.6.5.8.3 Details

Paragraph 6 provides transitional provisions which disapply the limit on relief under section 41R in certain circumstances. These provisions apply to individuals to whom the provisions in paragraph 5 apply. These provisions also apply to an individual who met the requirement of section 26A ITEPA 2003 for the year 2023-2024 or 2024-2025 and to whom section 809B, 809D or 809E of ITA 2007 applies in that year, who is a qualifying new resident for the purposes of Chapter 5C of Part 2 of ITEPA 2003 in 2025-2026, 2026-2027 or 2027-2028, and who meets the requirement of section 26A ITEPA 2003 for the tax year 2025-2026.

2.6.5.8.4 Effective Date

6 April 2025 see section 38(3).

2.6.5.9 Paragraph 7 Definition "foreign employment claim", "qualifying year" and "section26A requirement"

2.6.5.9.1 Overview

This paragraph provides some transitional relief.

2.6.5.9.2 Legislation

Paragraph 7 reads as follows.

"Limit on relief not to apply to certain foreign employment relief claims

7(1) Section 41R of ITEPA 2003 (limit on relief) does not apply to a foreign employment relief claim made by an individual for a tax year if the claim falls within sub-paragraph (2) or (3).

(2)A foreign employment relief claim made by an individual for a tax year falls within this sub-paragraph if—

(a)the qualifying year is tax year 2025-26 or 2026-27, and

(b)paragraph 6(1) [65] applies to the individual for that tax year.

(3)A foreign employment relief claim made by an individual for a tax year falls within this sub-paragraph if—

(a)the qualifying year is tax year 2025-26, 2026-27 or 2027-28,

(b)paragraph 6(1) does not apply to the individual for that tax year,

(c)the individual falls within paragraph 6(2), and

(d)the individual meets the section 26A requirement for tax year 2025-26."

2.6.5.9.3 Details

The limit on relief in section 41R does not apply to a foreign employment relief claim made by an individual for a tax year if the claim

A.

(i) is for a qualifying year that is tax year 2025-26 or 2026-27, and

(ii) paragraph 6(1) applies to the individual for that tax year; or

[65] This reads "6(1) If an individual falling within sub-paragraph (2)—

(a)meets the section 26A requirement for tax year 2025-26 or 2026-27, and

(b)is not a qualifying new resident for that year for the purposes of Chapter 5C of Part 2 of ITEPA 2003, the individual is to be treated as a qualifying new resident for that tax year for the purposes of that Chapter."

B.

(i) is one where the qualifying year is tax year 2025-26, 2026-27 or 2027-28,
(ii) paragraph 6(1) [66] does not apply to the individual for that tax year,
(iii) the individual falls within paragraph 6(2),[67] and
(iv) the individual meets the section 26A requirement (see above) for tax year 2025-26.

2.6.5.9.4 Effective Date

06 April 2025 (see section 38(3)).

2.6.5.10 Paragraph 8 Meaning of "foreign employment relief claim" and "qualifying year" and "the section 26A requirement"

2.6.5.10.1 Overview

Paragraph 8 provides definitions of:

"foreign employment claim",

"qualifying year", and

"section26A requirement"

for the purposes of Part 3 of Schedule 1.

2.6.5.10.2 Legislation

Paragraph 8 reads as follows.

> "8 For the purposes of this Part of this Schedule—
>
> "**foreign employment relief claim**" and "**qualifying year**" have the same meanings as in Chapter 5C of Part 2 of ITEPA 2003 (relief for new residents on foreign employment income);
>
> "**the section 26A requirement**" means the requirement of section 26A of ITEPA 2003 (requirement for 3-year period of non-residence)."

Foreign employment relief claim and qualifying year in the context of Chapter 5C of Part 2 of ITEPA are discussed above.

ii. Section 26A

Paragraph 8 refers to 26A. It is set out here for the convenience of the Reader.

Section 26A is headed "Section 26: requirement for 3-year period of non-residence." It reads as follows:

---

[66] Set out in the preceding footnote.

[67] This reads "(2) An individual falls within this sub-paragraph if—
(a)the individual met the section 26A requirement for tax year 2023-24 or tax year 2024-25, and
(b)section 809B, 809D or 809E of ITA 2007 (remittance basis) applied to the individual for that tax year."

"(1) An employee meets the requirement of this section for a tax year if the employee was—
(a)non-UK resident for the previous 3 tax years, or
(b)UK resident for the previous tax year but non-UK resident for the 3 tax years before that, or
(c)UK resident for the previous 2 tax years but non-UK resident for the 3 tax years before that, or
(d)non-UK resident for the previous tax year, UK resident for the tax year before that and non-UK resident for the 3 tax years before that.
(2) The residence status of the employee before the 3 years of non-UK residence is not relevant for these purposes."

2.6.5.10.3 Details

This paragraph provides the meaning of Part [3] of Schedule 8 of

a. "foreign employment relief claim"; and

b. "qualifying year".

These are discussed above.

2.6.5.10.4 Effective Date

6 April 2025 see section 38](3).

2.7 Abolition of the remittance basis

2.7.1 Section 40 and Schedule 9: Remittance basis not available after tax year 2024-25

2.7.1.1 Abolition of the remittance basis after tax year 2024 - 25

2.7.1.1.1 Overview

The government Policy Paper published on 29 July 2024 outlined the government's plans to change the taxation of non-UK domiciled individuals included bringing the remittance basis of taxation to an end and removing references to domicile in the legislation to reflect the change.

This is in line with the announced policy that starting on 6 April 2025 the domicile of an individual will generally no longer be relevant for UK direct taxes after 5 April 2025.

Broadly, the remittance basis provided that any income or gains that arose overseas were only taxable in the United Kingdom to the extent that they were remitted to (brought into, used in, or enjoyed in) the United Kingdom where the taxpayer was not domiciled or treated as domiciled in the UK. This is discussed at length in the *Taxation of Entertainers and Sportspersons* see particularly Chapter 3.

As announced in the 30 October 2024 Budget the Remittance Basis was abolished for the tax year starting on 6 April 2025 and for subsequent tax years.

The Explanatory Notes to the Bill told us that what is now Section 40 and Schedule 9 abolish the special income tax and capital gains tax regime (the Remittance Basis) for persons who were resident but who were not domiciled in the United Kingdom for tax years 2025-26 and subsequent years.

They also say that Section 40 "signposts" that the remittance basis will not be available for tax year 2025-26, or for subsequent tax years. However, the remittance basis will continue to have effect on income and gains that have been remitted in previous tax years to 2025-26 or dealt with in a way that affected this. It also signposts further amendments to legislation consequential to those changes.

2.7.1.1.2 The Legislation

Section 40 is headed "Remittance basis not available after tax year 2024-25".

It reads as follows.

"(1) **Amendments** made by paragraph 1 of Schedule 9 have the **effect** that **the remittance basis is not available for tax year 2025-26, or for subsequent tax years.**

(2) But **provisions relating to the remittance** of income and gains will **continue** to have effect in relation to income and gains subject to the remittance basis **in previous tax years.**

(3) Other provision is made by that Schedule [i.e. Schedule 9] (including provision amending the Income Tax Acts and TCGA 1992)—

(a) in consequence of ending the availability of the remittance basis,

(b) clarifying the circumstances in which amounts are remitted (see paragraph 5), and

(c) in connection with otherwise ending the relevance of domicile to income tax and capital gains tax.

(4) Subject to subsection (5), the provision made by that Schedule has effect for the tax year 2025-26 and subsequent tax years.

(5) Paragraph 6 of Schedule 9 (relief for amounts remitted again on becoming UK resident) is to be treated as having always had effect.

(6) The amendments made by paragraphs 9 and 10 of Schedule 9 (residence of personal representatives) have effect where the deceased person died on or after 6 April 2025."

2.7.1.1.3 Details of Section 40

As noted above section 40 "signposts" that the Remittance Basis will not be available for tax year 2025-26, or for subsequent tax years. However, the Remittance Basis will continue to have effect on income and gains that have been remitted in previous tax years to 2025-26 or arose before then and are remitted.

It also signposts further amendments to legislation consequential to those changes as noted above.

Domicile is also relevant for certain DDCs as discussed in more detail towards the end of the Supplement.

Issues can also arise where matters straddle 6 April 2025.

2.7.2 *Details of Schedule 9*

2.7.2.1 General

Schedule 9 is divided into three parts:

- Part 1 Remittance Basis;
- Part 2 Removal of Domicile (Primary legislation);
- Part 3 Removal of Domicile (Secondary legislation).

These are each considered in turn next.

2.7.2.2 Schedule 9 Part 1: Remittance Basis

Paragraph 1 General

2.7.2.2.1 Overview

Paragraph 1 Schedule 9 amends Chapter A1 of Part 14 of ITA (which deals with the Remittance Basis), so that the remittance basis is only available in the tax year 2024-25 or an earlier tax year.

Accordingly, the remittance basis is not available after 5 April 2025.

2.7.2.2.2 Legislation

Paragraph 1 reads as follows.

> *"No remittance basis for tax years after 2024-25*
>
> 1(1) Chapter A1 of Part 14 of ITA 2007 (remittance basis) is amended as follows.
>
> (2) In section 809B (claim for remittance basis to apply), in subsection (1)—
>
> (a)in the words before paragraph (a) omit "the individual";
>
> (b)before that paragraph insert—
>
> "(za) **the tax year is the tax year 2024-25 or an earlier tax year,**";
>
> (c)in each of paragraphs (a), (b) and (c), at the beginning insert "the individual".
>
> (3) In section 809C (claim for remittance basis by long-term UK resident), in subsection (1)—

(a)in the words before paragraph (a) omit "the individual";

(b)before that paragraph insert—

"(za)the tax year is the tax year 2024-25 or an earlier tax year,";

(c)in each of paragraphs (a) and (b), at the beginning insert "the individual".

(4) In section 809D (application of remittance basis where income and gains under £2000) in subsection (1), before paragraph (a) insert—

"(za)the tax year is the tax year 2024-25 or an earlier tax year,".

(5) In section 809E (application of remittance basis without claim: other cases) in subsection (1), before paragraph (a) insert—

"(za)the tax year is the tax year 2024-25 or an earlier tax year,".

(6) In consequence of the amendments made by sub-paragraphs (2) to (5), in section 809A—

(a)for "are" substitute "were";

(b)after "Kingdom" insert "in tax years before tax year 2025-26".

2.7.2.2.3 Detail

Paragraph 1 amends Chapter A1 of Part 14 of the Income Tax Act (ITA) 2007 (remittance basis), so that the remittance basis is only available in the tax year 2024-25 or an earlier tax year.

2.7.2.2.4 Effective Date

06 April 2025 see section 40(4).

2.7.2.3 Paragraph 2 Consequential Amendments TCGA

2.7.2.3.1 Overview

Paragraph 2 makes amendments to the TCGA consequent upon the ending of the remittance basis.

2.7.2.3.2 Legislation

Paragraph 2 reads as follows.

"Amendments of TCGA 1992 connected with end of remittance basis.

2(1) TCGA 1992 is amended as follows.

(2) In section 1A (territorial scope), in subsection (2)(a), for "applies" substitute "applied".

(3) In section 1K (annual exempt amount), omit subsection (3).

(4) In the italic heading before section 3D, for "Non-UK domiciled individuals" substitute "Individuals who were non-UK domiciled".

(5) In section 3D—

(a)for the heading, substitute "Individuals who were non-UK domiciled";

(b)in subsection (1)—

(i)for "a tax year" substitute "tax year 2024-25 or an earlier tax year";

(ii)for "is", in each place it occurs, substitute "was".

(6) Section 16ZA (losses: non-UK domiciled individuals) is omitted.
(7) In Schedule 1 (UK resident individuals not domiciled in UK)—
(a)in the heading, for "not domiciled in the UK" substitute "to whom the remittance basis applied";
(b)in paragraph 1(1) for "applies" substitute "applied";
(c)omit paragraphs 2, 3 and 4."

2.7.2.3.3 Detail

Paragraph 2 amends the Taxation of Chargeable Gains Act 1992 (TCGA) as a consequence of the ending of the remittance basis.

The past tense is substituted in some instances to help to make matters less unclear.

2.7.2.3.4 Effective Date

06 April 2025 see section 40(4).

2.7.2.4 Paragraph 3 amendments to ITEPA 2003

2.7.2.4.1 Overview

Paragraph 3 makes consequential amendments to ITEPA 2003 following the ending of remittance basis.

2.7.2.4.2 Legislation

Paragraph 3 reads as follows.

"***Amendments of ITEPA 2003 connected with end of remittance basis.***
3 (1) ITEPA 2003 (employment income: charge to tax) is amended as follows.
(2) In section 6 (nature of charge to tax on employment income), in subsection (3)—
(a)in paragraph (a), omit "and domicile";
(b)in paragraph (aa), for "applies" substitute "applied".
(3) In section 20 (taxable earnings under this Chapter), for subsection (1) substitute—
"(1) This Chapter contains provision for determining how much of the following are taxable earnings from an employment in a tax year—
(a)general earnings that are for a tax year for which section 809B, 809D or 809E of ITA 2007 (remittance basis) applied to the employee (being a tax year before tax year 2025-26), and
(b)general earnings that are for a tax year for which the employee is non-UK resident."
(4) In section 22 (chargeable overseas earnings for year when remittance basis applies and employee outside section 26)—
(a)in the heading and in subsection (1)(a), for "applies" substitute "applied";

(b)in subsection (1)(b), for "does not" substitute "did not".

(5) In section 23 (calculation of "chargeable overseas earnings"), in subsection (2)—

(a)in paragraph (a), for "applies" substitute "applied";

(b)in paragraph (aa) for "does not" substitute "did not";

(c)in paragraph (b) for "is" substitute "was";

(d)in paragraph (c) for "are" substitute "were".

(6) In the italic heading before section 25, for "meet" substitute "met".

(7) In section 26 (foreign earnings for year when remittance basis applies and employee meets section 26A requirement)—

(a)in the heading, for "applies and employee meets" substitute "applied and employee met";

(b)in subsection (1), in the opening words—

(i)for "applies", in the second place it appears, substitute "applied";

(ii)for "meets" substitute "met".

(8) In section 41F (taxable specific income: internationally mobile employee etc), in (a), for "applies" substitute "applied".

(9) In section 41H (section 41F: chargeable and unchargeable foreign securities income)—

(a)in subsection (4)—

(i)in paragraph (a), for "applies" substitute "applied";

(ii)in paragraph (b) for "does not" substitute "did not";

(iii)in paragraph (c) for "is" substitute "was";

(iv)in paragraph (d) for "are" substitute "were";

(b)in subsection (7)—

(i)in paragraph (a), for "applies" substitute "applied";

(ii)in paragraph (b) for "meets" substitute "met";

(iii)in paragraph (c) for "are" substitute "were".

(10) In section 271 (limited exemption of removal benefits and expenses: general)—

(a)in subsections (2)(a) and (2)(b), for "applies" substitute "applied";

(b)in subsection (2), for "meets" substitute "met".

(11) In section 554Z9 (remittance basis: A does not meet section 26A requirement)—

(a)in the heading, for "does not" substitute "did not";

(b)in subsection (1)—

(i)in paragraph (b) for "applies" substitute "applied";

(ii)in paragraph (c) for "does not" substitute "did not";

(iii)in paragraph (d) for "is" substitute "was";

(iv)in paragraph (e), for "are" substitute "were".

(12) In section 554Z10 (remittance basis: A meets section 26A requirement)—

(a)in the heading, for "meets" substitute "met";
(b)in subsection (1)(b), for "applies" substitute "applied";
(c)in subsection (1)(c), for "meets" substitute "met".

(13) In section 576A (temporary non-residents), in subsection (5), for "applies" substitute "applied".

(14) In section 698 (PAYE: special charges on employment-related securities), in subsection (8), for "remittance basis" substitute "internationally mobile employees".

(15) In section 700 (PAYE: gains from securities options), in subsection (7), for "remittance basis" substitute "internationally mobile employees".

(16) In section 700A (employment-related securities etc: remittance basis), in the heading, for "remittance basis" substitute "internationally mobile employees".

2.7.2.4.3 Detail

This paragraph amends ITEPA including section 6 headed "nature of charge to tax on employment income". It also makes a number of consequential changes following the move away from domicile for UK tax purposes.

2.7.2.4.4 Effective Date

06 April 2025 see section 40(4).

2.7.2.5 Paragraph 4 section 832 ITTOIA only before 2025-26

2.7.2.5.1 Overview

Paragraph 4 amends section 832 ITTOIA (Relevant foreign income charged on remittance basis) to clarify that the remittance basis only applies before tax year 2025-26 and not for that year or subsequent years.

2.7.2.5.2 Legislation

Paragraph 4 reads as follows.

"*Amendment of ITTOIA 2005 connected with end of remittance basis.*

4 In section 832 of ITTOIA 2005 (relevant foreign income charge on remittance basis), in subsection (1)—

(a)for "applies", in the second place it appears, substitute" applied";
(b)after "that year" insert "(being a tax year before tax year 2025-26)"."

Section 832(1) ITTOIA after amendment reads as follows.

"(1) This section applied to an individual's relevant foreign income for a tax year ("the relevant foreign income") if section 809B, 809D or 809E of ITA 2007 (remittance basis) applies to the individual for that year (being a tax year before tax year 2025-26)."

2.7.2.5.3 Detail

Paragraph 4 amends section 832 of the Income Tax (Trading and Other Income) Act (ITTOIA) 2005 (Relevant foreign income charged on remittance basis) to clarify the remittance basis only applies before tax year 2025-26. It does so by using the past tense and make it clear it only applies to tax years before 2025-26.

2.7.2.5.4 Effective Date

06 April 2025 see section 40(4).

2.7.2.6 Paragraph 5 Amendment of ITA 2007

2.7.2.6.1 Overview

Paragraph 5 amends ITA 2007 as set out below. This is essentially consequential on the ending of the remittance basis and the associated use of "domicile" in UK tax legislation.

However, it is not a provision without controversy. The Remittance Basis is closed down from 5 April 2025. However, there is no general "grandfathering" of the charge on remittance. Some relief was introduced at Report Stage but has specific requirements for its application (see paragraph 6).

Paragraph 5 widens the meaning of "remitted to the UK".[68] There was no consultation on the changes. The scope of remittance is extended by the changes. These can lead to "double remittances" (see paragraph 5(11)). If the first remittance did not give rise to a UK tax charge than a second remittance after 5 April 2025 may. In the past it had been understood that in effect there was only one bite of the cherry for HMRC. This is no longer the case in simple terms because of the charge to tax requirement.

The Reader is referred to the exchange of correspondence between the CIOT and HMRC published on the CIOT website and its briefings[69].

2.7.2.6.2 Legislation

Paragraph 5 reads as follows.

> *"When amounts will be remitted.*
>
> 5(1) ITA 2007 is amended as follows.

---

[68] HMRC described it as "clarification". This is not accepted as accurate by many e.g. the CIOT.

[69] E.g. https://assets-eu-01.kc-usercontent.com/220a4c02-94bf-019b-9bac-51cdc7bf0d99/558b4385-216d-49d6-953d-0a51d22c1ea1/CIOT%20FB24-25%20report%20stage%20briefing%20Part%202%20Non-doms%20FINAL.pdf

(2) Section 809L (meaning of "remitted to the United Kingdom" [70]) is amended in accordance with sub-paragraphs to (3) to (8).

(3) In subsection (2)—

(a)omit the "or" at the end of paragraph (a);

(b)at the end of paragraph (b) insert ", or

(c)money or other property is used outside the United Kingdom (directly or indirectly) for the benefit in the United Kingdom of a relevant person."

(4) In subsection (4)—

(a)in paragraph (a), for "is enjoyed by a relevant person" substitute "either—

(i)the property is enjoyed by a relevant person, or

(ii)as a result, a benefit is enjoyed by a relevant person.";

(b)after paragraph (b) (but before the "or" at the end) insert—

"(ba) is used outside the United Kingdom (directly or indirectly) and as a result a benefit is enjoyed in the United Kingdom by a relevant person,".

(5) In subsection (5)—

(a)in paragraph (a), for "is enjoyed by a relevant person" substitute "either—

(i)the property is enjoyed by a relevant person, or

(ii)as a result, a benefit is enjoyed by a relevant person.";

(b)after paragraph (b) (but before the "or" at the end) insert—

"(ba) is used outside the United Kingdom (directly or indirectly) and as a result a benefit is enjoyed in the United Kingdom by a relevant person,".

(6) In subsection (6)—

(a)for "or (b)", in each place it occurs, substitute ", (b) or (ba)";

(b)after "property", in the second place it occurs, insert ", benefit".

(7) At the end of subsection (9) insert "and cases where the property is used to secure the debt."

(8) After subsection (9) insert—

"(9A) For the purposes of this Chapter, any reference to property being brought to the United Kingdom includes—

(a)sending, or otherwise effecting a transfer of, the property to the United Kingdom, and

(b)in the case of intangible property, taking any steps, or permitting steps to be taken, that would result in property situated outside the United Kingdom becoming situated in the United Kingdom.

(9B) Sections 275 to 275C of TCGA 1992 (location of assets) apply for the purposes of subsection (9A) (b) as they apply for the purposes of TCGA 1992.

---

[70] See https://www.gov.uk/hmrc-internal-manuals/employment-income-manual/eim40302

(9C)But subsection (9B) does not apply where the intangible property is a debt other than a judgment debt."

(9) In section 809N (section 809L: gift recipients, qualifying property and enjoyment)—

(a)in subsection (7)(c), after "(b)" insert ", (ba)";

(b)in subsection (9)—

(i)in the opening words, after "property" insert ", a benefit";

(ii)in paragraph (a), at the beginning insert "in the case of enjoyment of property or a service,";

(iii)after paragraph (a) insert—

"(aa)in the case of enjoyment of a benefit—

(i)if the qualifying property being dealt with as mentioned in section 809L(4)(a) or (ba) results in a benefit being enjoyed by relevant persons and persons who are not relevant persons, and

(ii)the enjoyment by all relevant persons is no more than negligible,";

(iv)in paragraph (c), after "property" insert ", benefit".

(10) In section 809O (section 809L: dealings where there is a connected operation)—

(a)in each of subsections (2), (3), (4) and (5) after "(b)" insert ", (ba)";

(b)in subsection (6)—

(i)in the opening words, after "property" insert ", a benefit";

(ii)in paragraph (a), at the beginning insert "in the case of enjoyment of property or a service,";

(iii)after paragraph (a) insert—

"(aa)in the case of enjoyment of a benefit—

(i)if the property being dealt with as mentioned in section 809L(5)(a) or (ba) results in a benefit being enjoyed by relevant persons and persons who are not relevant persons, and

(ii)the enjoyment by all relevant persons is no more than negligible,";

(iv)in paragraph (c), after "property" insert ", benefit".

(11) In section 809P (section 809L: amount remitted)—

(a)in subsections (6) and (8), for "or (b)" substitute ", (b) or (ba)";

(b)in subsection (12), after "***previously remitted***", in each place it occurs, insert "**that has been charged to income tax or capital gains tax**"."

2.7.2.6.3 Detail

Paragraph 5 amends ITA 2007 essentially as follows.

a) Sub-paragraphs 5(2) to (8) amend section 809L (meaning of "remitted to the United Kingdom").

b) Sub-paragraph 5(3) inserts subsection 809L(2)(c) to capture the use of property in a wide range of situations, which results in a relevant person receiving a benefit in the United Kingdom. This includes, but is not limited to, property used outside of the United Kingdom to settle an obligation within the United Kingdom, as this would be a benefit for the relevant person.

c) Sub-paragraph 5(4)(a) amends subsection 809L(4)(a) so that qualifying property of a gift recipient is now caught where it results in property being enjoyed by a relevant person, or a benefit is enjoyed by a relevant person. The property would still need to be brought to, received or used in the United Kingdom for this to apply.
d) Sub-paragraph 5(4)(b) introduces subsection 809L (4) (ba) to address situations where qualifying property of a gift recipient is used outside the United Kingdom, and as a result a relevant person enjoys a benefit in the United Kingdom. The use of the qualifying property can be a direct use or an indirect use.
e) Sub-paragraph 5(5)(a) amends subsection 809L(5)(a) so that property of a non-relevant person (apart from qualifying property of a gift recipient) is now caught where it results in property being enjoyed by a relevant person, or a benefit is enjoyed by a relevant person, in circumstances where there is a connected operation. The property would still need to be brought to, received or used in the United Kingdom for this to apply.
f) Sub-paragraph 5(5)(b) introduces subsection 809L(5)(ba) to address situations where property of a non-relevant person (apart from qualifying property of a gift recipient) is used outside the United Kingdom, and as a result a benefit is enjoyed in the United Kingdom by a relevant person. The use of the property can be a direct use, or more indirect uses are also caught in circumstances where there is a connected operation.
g) Sub-paragraph 5(6) amends subsection 809L (6) to ensure the timing of the remittance is consistent with regards to the addition of S809L (4) (ba) and S809L (5) (ba).
h) Sub-paragraph 5(7) amends subsection 809L (9) to include "and cases where the property is used to secure the debt." to clarify that loans which are secured with Foreign Income and Gains (FIG) are considered to be a use of that FIG.
i) Sub-paragraph 5(8) introduces subsection 809L(9A) to clarify that property brought to the United Kingdom also includes situations where the property is sent or transferred. It further clarifies that intangible property is brought to the United Kingdom when steps are taken, or permitted to be taken, which result in the property being regarded as having a United Kingdom Situs under TCGA 1992. All references to property throughout Chapter A1 of Part 14 of the Income Tax Act (ITA) 2007 (remittance basis)

includes intangible property. There are various ways intangible property can be remitted, however, in order to be brought to the UK steps must have been taken, or permitted, in order for there to have been a change in situs.

j) Sun-paragraph 5(9) amends subsection 809N (section 809L: gift recipients, qualifying property and enjoyment).
k) Sub-paragraph 5(9)(a) amends subsection 809N(7)(c) to reflect the addition of S809L (4) (ba).
l) Sub-paragraph 5(9)(b)(i) amends subsection 809N (9) to clarify that a benefit will also be taken into account when evaluating whether any of the conditions for disregarding enjoyment apply.
m) Sub-paragraph 5(9)(b)(ii) amends subsection 809N(9)(a) to include the benefit, ensuring the benefit can be considered as disregarded if the enjoyment by all relevant persons is no more than negligible.
n) Sub-paragraph 5(9)(b)(iii) introduces subsection 809N (9) (aa) to clarify when a benefit may result in enjoyment by a relevant person which is to be disregarded.
o) Sub-paragraph 5(9)(iv) amends subsection 809N(9)(c) to include the benefit, ensuring the benefit can be considered as disregarded if it was made available for the general public to enjoy in the same manner as the relevant person experiences enjoyment.
p) Sub-paragraph 5(10) amends subsection 809O (section 809L: dealings where there is a connected operation), at subsections (2), (3), (4) and (5) to reflect the addition of S809L (5) (ba).
q) Sub-paragraph 5(10)(b)(i) amends subsection 809O (6) to clarify that a benefit will also be taken into account when evaluating whether any of the conditions for disregarding enjoyment apply.
r) Sub-paragraph 5(10)(b)(ii) amends subsection 809O(6)(a) to include the benefit, ensuring the benefit can be considered as disregarded if the enjoyment by all relevant persons is no more than negligible.
s) Sub-paragraph 5(10)(b)(iii) introduces subsection 809O (9) (aa) to clarify when a benefit may result in enjoyment by a relevant person which is to be disregarded.
t) Sub-paragraph 5(10)(b)(iv) amends subsection 809O(6)(c) to include the benefit, ensuring the benefit can be considered as disregarded if it was made available for the general public to enjoy in the same manner as the relevant person experiences enjoyment.
u) Sub-paragraph 5(11)(a) amends section 809P (section 809L: amount remitted), at subsection (6) to reflect the addition of S809L (4) (ba); and at subsection (8) to reflect the addition of S809L (5) (ba).

v) Sub-paragraph 5(11)(b) amends subsection 809P (12) to reflect that **previous remittances need to have been charged to tax in order for this subsection to apply.**

w) Sub-paragraph 5(12)If the amount remitted (taken together with any amount previously remitted that has been charged to income tax or capital gains tax) would otherwise exceed the amount of the income or chargeable gains, the amount remitted is limited to the amount which (when taken together with any amount previously remitted that has been charged to income tax or capital gains tax) is equal to the amount of the income or chargeable gains.

Section 809P (12) now reads as follows.

> "(12)If the amount remitted (taken together with any amount previously remitted that has been charged to income tax or capital gains tax) would otherwise exceed the amount of the income or chargeable gains, the amount remitted is limited to the amount which (when taken together with any amount previously remitted that has been charged to income tax or capital gains tax) is equal to the amount of the income or chargeable gains."

This, as the CIOT pointed out in its Budget responses etc.,[71] can lead to Double Taxation e.g. where there was an appointment to a non-resident who keeps what is appointed for themselves offshore and does not pass it on to a close family member. This would not reduce the amount available for charge on a subsequent appointment as there has been no UK charge to IT or CGT and the "pool" [72] is accordingly not reduced. [73]

Section 809L ITA before amendment read:

> **809LMeaning of "remitted to the United Kingdom".**
>
> (1) An individual's income is, or chargeable gains are, "remitted to the United Kingdom" if—
>
> (a)conditions A and B are met,
>
> (b)condition C is met, or
>
> (c)condition D is met.

---

[71] https://www.tax.org.uk/finance-bill-2024-25 and https://assets-eu-01.kc-usercontent.com/220a4c02-94bf-019b-9bac-51cdc7bf0d99/558b4385-216d-49d6-953d-0a51d22c1ea1/CIOT%20FB24-25%20report%20stage%20briefing%20Part%202%20Non-doms%20FINAL.pdf

[72] In the sense of the amount that can be taxed. It only escapes if there is the right kind of UK tax paid. Payment to someone outside the UK tax net where tax is paid seems outside the net. This is a policy change for no obvious reason.

[73]https://assets-eu-01.kc-usercontent.com/220a4c02-94bf-019b-9bac-51cdc7bf0d99/558b4385-216d-49d6-953d-0a51d22c1ea1/CIOT%20FB24-25%20report%20stage%20briefing%20Part%202%20Non-doms%20FINAL.pdf cf 3.5 ff It is hard to see any policy justification for the change. I am not aware of any being forthcoming.

(2) Condition A is that—

(a)money or other property is brought to, or received or used in, the United Kingdom by or for the benefit of a relevant person, or

(b)a service is provided in the United Kingdom to or for the benefit of a relevant person.

(3) Condition B is that—

(a)the property, service or consideration for the service is (wholly or in part) the income or chargeable gains,

(b)the property, service or consideration—

(i)derives (wholly or in part, and directly or indirectly) from the income or chargeable gains, and

(ii)in the case of property or consideration, is property of or consideration given by a relevant person,

(c)the income or chargeable gains are used outside the United Kingdom (directly or indirectly) in respect of a relevant debt, or

(d)anything deriving (wholly or in part, and directly or indirectly) from the income or chargeable gains is used as mentioned in paragraph (c).

(4) Condition C is that qualifying property of a gift recipient—

(a)is brought to, or received or used in, the United Kingdom, and is enjoyed by a relevant person,

(b)is consideration for a service that is enjoyed in the United Kingdom by a relevant person, or

(c)is used outside the United Kingdom (directly or indirectly) in respect of a relevant debt.

(5) Condition D is that property of a person other than a relevant person (apart from qualifying property of a gift recipient)—

(a)is brought to, or received or used in, the United Kingdom, and is enjoyed by a relevant person,

(b)is consideration for a service that is enjoyed in the United Kingdom by a relevant person, or

(c)is used outside the United Kingdom (directly or indirectly) in respect of a relevant debt,

in circumstances where there is a connected operation.

(6)In a case where subsection (4)(a) or (b) or (5)(a) or (b) applies to the importation or use of property, the income or chargeable gains are taken to be remitted at the time the property or service is first enjoyed by a relevant person by virtue of that importation or use.

(7) In this section "relevant debt" means a debt that relates (wholly or in part, and directly or indirectly) to—

(a)property falling within subsection (2)(a),

(b)a service falling within subsection (2)(b),

(c)qualifying property dealt with as mentioned in subsection (4)(a),
(d)a service falling within subsection (4)(b),
(e)qualifying property dealt with as mentioned in subsection (5)(a), or
(f)a service falling within subsection (5)(b).

(8) . . . .

(9) The cases in which property (including income or chargeable gains) is used in respect of a debt include cases where the property is used to pay interest on the debt.

(10) This section is subject to sections 809V to 809Z6 (property treated as not remitted to the United Kingdom)."

2.7.2.6.4 Effective Date

06April 2025 see section 40(4).

2.7.2.7 Paragraph 6

2.7.2.7.1 Overview

Paragraph 6 deals with "Relief for amounts remitted again on becoming UK resident". This came in at Report Stage following representations from the CIOT et al.

2.7.2.7.2 Legislation

Paragraph 6 reads as follows.

"*Relief for amounts remitted again on becoming UK resident*

6(1) This paragraph applies where—

(a)income or chargeable gains of an individual have been remitted to the United Kingdom during a period that exceeds 5 years—

(i)that ends before 6 April 2024, and

(ii)in which there was no period for which the individual was UK resident, and

(b)after the end of that period, but before 6 April 2025—

(i)the same, or part of the same, income or chargeable gains ("the repeated remitted amount") were again remitted to the United Kingdom, and

(ii)a relevant charge has arisen in relation to that remittance.

(2)A "relevant charge" in relation to a remittance means—

(a)income tax becoming chargeable on that remittance, or

(b)a gain accruing under paragraph 1(2) of Schedule 1 to TCGA 1992 on that remittance.

(3) Any relevant charge that has arisen on the first occasion on which the repeated remitted amount is remitted in circumstances falling within sub-paragraph (1)(b) is to be treated as never having arisen.

(4)But a remittance that is not charged to income tax or capital gains tax as a result of sub-paragraph (3) is to be treated as if it were charged to income tax or capital gains tax (as the case may be) for the purposes of section 809P(12) of ITA 2007.

(5) This paragraph is to be treated as never having applied where—

(a)for either, or each, of the tax years 2024-25 and 2025-26, the individual is not UK resident, or

(b)either, or each, of those tax years is a split year as respects the individual.

(6) References in this paragraph to amounts being remitted to the United Kingdom are to be construed in accordance with Chapter A1 of Part 14 of ITA 2007 (see, in particular, sections 809L to 809O of that Act)."

2.7.2.7.3 Detail

Paragraph 6 applies where:

(1) income or chargeable gains of an individual have been remitted to the United Kingdom
  (a) during a period that
    (i) exceeds 5 years—
    (ii) ends before 6 April 2024, and
    (iii) in which there was no period for which the individual was UK resident,

(2) after the end of that period, but before 6 April 2025—
  (a) the same, or part of the same, income or chargeable gains ("the repeated remitted amount") were again remitted to the United Kingdom, and
  (b) a relevant charge has arisen in relation to that remittance.

A relevant charge is one falling within paragraph 6(2)). This tells us "A "relevant charge" in relation to a remittance means—

(a)income tax becoming chargeable on that remittance, or

(b)a gain accruing under paragraph 1(2) of Schedule 1 to TCGA 1992 on that remittance. [74]

References in paragraph 6 "to amounts being remitted to the United Kingdom are to be construed in accordance with Chapter A1 of Part 14 of ITA 2007 (see, in particular, sections 809L to 809O of that Act)." [75]

[74] See paragraph 6(2)

[75] See subsection (6)

(3) Any relevant charge that has arisen on the first occasion on which the repeated remitted amount is remitted in circumstances falling within sub-paragraph (1)(b) is to be treated as never having arisen.

(4)But a remittance that is not charged to income tax or capital gains tax as a result of sub-paragraph (3) is to be treated as if it were charged to income tax or capital gains tax (as the case may be) for the purposes of section 809P(12) of ITA 2007.

By paragraph 6(5)

"This paragraph [i.e. 6] is to be treated as never having applied where—

(a) for either, or each, of the tax years 2024-25 and 2025-26, the individual is not UK resident, or

(b) either, or each, of those tax years is a split year as respects the individual."

The effect of paragraph 6(5) is that if the conditions are met paragraph 6 is treated as never having applied.

Example

Mitt Crene had been UK resident between 1999-2000 and 2002-2003. He was not resident before those years nor after. Accordingly, Mitt was not UK resident for either of 2024-25 or 2025-26 and so does not fall within paragraph 6.

If Mitt's residence position were different then paragraph 6 could apply. If Mitt's residence position were as follows namely that Mitt was resident in2024-25 or 2025-26 paragraph 6(5) would not apply and so 6 could apply.

2.7.2.7.4 Effective Date

06 April 2025 see section 40(4).

2.7.3 *Part 2 Removal of domicile (primary legislation)*

2.7.3.1 *Paragraph 7 Removal of exemption for persons not domiciled in United Kingdom*

2.7.3.1.1 Overview

Paragraph 7 repeals the legislation giving exemption for persons not domiciled in United Kingdom. Chapter 1A of Part 14 of ITA 2007 is the legislation repealed by the paragraph.

2.7.3.1.2 Legislation

Paragraph 7 reads as follows.

"Removal of exemption for persons not domiciled in United Kingdom

7(1) Chapter 1A of Part 14 of ITA 2007 (exemption for persons not domiciled in United Kingdom) is repealed."

2.7.3.1.3 Detail

Paragraph 7 repeals Chapter 1A of Part 14 of ITA 2007 (exemption for persons not domiciled in United Kingdom) as this will no longer apply after tax year 2024-25.

This is the main engine of change to give effect to the move away from a Domicile based system.

2.7.3.1.4 Effective Date

06 April 2025 (see section 40(4).)

2.7.3.2 *Paragraph 8 Transferable tax allowance for married couples etc*

2.7.3.2.1 Overview

Paragraph 8 substitutes "not a qualifying new resident" for "domiciled in the United Kingdom" in the conditions to election to reduce a spouse's personal allowance for the benefit of the other spouse.

2.7.3.2.2 Legislation

Paragraph 8 reads as follows.

> *"Transferable tax allowance for married couples etc*
>
> 8 In section 55C of ITA 2007 (election to reduce personal allowance), in subsection (3)(b), for "domiciled in the United Kingdom" substitute "not a qualifying new resident"."

As discussed, section 55 ITA as amended reads as follows.

"55C Election to reduce personal allowance

(1) An individual may make an election for the purposes of section 55B if—

(a)the individual is married to, or in a civil partnership with, the same person ("**the gaining party**")] —

(i) for the whole or part of the tax year concerned, and

(ii) when the election is made [F3or, where the election is made after the death of one or each of them, when they were last both living],

(b)the individual is entitled to a personal allowance under section 35 ... for that tax year,

(c) assuming the individual's personal allowance was reduced as set out in section 55B(6), the individual would not for that year be liable to tax at a rate other than the basic rate, the default basic rate, the savings basic rate, the dividend nil rate, the Scottish basic rate, a Scottish rate below the Scottish basic rate, the Scottish intermediate rate, the Welsh basic rate, the dividend ordinary rate, the savings nil rate or the starting rate for savings,

(ca)where on that assumption the individual would for the tax year be liable to tax at the dividend nil rate, the individual on that assumption would for that year neither be liable to tax at the dividend upper rate, nor be liable to tax at the dividend additional rate, if section 13A (dividend nil rate) were omitted, and

(d)where the individual meets the requirements of section 56 (residence) for the tax year by reason of meeting the condition in subsection (3) of that section, the individual meets the condition in subsection (2) of this section.

(2) The condition is that the individual's hypothetical net income for the tax year concerned is less than the amount of the personal allowance to which the individual is entitled for that tax year under section 35 ....

(3) For the purposes of subsection (2), an individual's "hypothetical net income" is the amount that would be that individual's net income calculated at Step 2 of section 23 if that individual's income tax liability were calculated on the basis that the individual—

(a)was UK resident for the tax year concerned (and the year was not a split year),

(b)was not a qualifying new resident] for that tax year,

(c)in that tax year, did not fall to be regarded as resident in a country outside the United Kingdom for the purposes of double taxation arrangements having effect at the time, and

(d)for that tax year, had made a claim for any available relief under section 6 of TIOPA 2010 (as required by subsection (6) of that section).

(4) An individual's hypothetical net income for a tax year is, to the extent that it is not sterling, to be calculated by reference to the average exchange rate for the year ending on 31 March in the tax year concerned.

(5) The personal representatives of an individual may make any election for the purposes of section 55B that the individual (if living) might make in relation to—

(a)the tax year in which the individual dies, or

(b)an earlier tax year.

2.7.3.2.3 Detail

This moves the "Transferable tax allowance for married couples" away from domicile and restricts it whilst a qualifying new resident.

Example

Mark and Fru are both UK resident and have been resident in the UK for more than five years and in circumstances such that they could not be qualifying new residents for the current year (which is post 2025-2026). Fru was born in Cieland and has a domicile of origin there which HMRC accept.

In the past the election could not have been made but seemingly now could.

2.7.3.2.4 Effective Date

06 April 2025

2.7.3.3 *Paragraph 9 Residence of personal representatives: domicile of deceased no longer relevant section 834 ITA amended.*

2.7.3.3.1 Overview

Paragraph 9 amends section 834 ITA (residence of personal representatives) so the domicile of the deceased is no longer relevant and is replaced by "long-term UK resident within the meaning of IHTA 1984". This fits in with the change from a domicile-based system to a long-term residence-based regime.

Example

Johan was born in Dewsen and has a domicile of origin there. He had been living in the UK for a time but had not become a long-term UK resident and had left the UK two years before his death. Before the change Johan's PRs would have been treated as UK resident in their capacity as such if Johan was UK resident at his death. However, he was not and so his PRs are non-UK resident. after the change as Johan was not a long-term UK resident when he died and was the PRs in their capacity as such as non-UK resident (see section 834 (3) and (4).

2.7.3.3.2 Legislation

Paragraph 9 reads as follows.

"Residence of personal representatives: domicile of deceased no longer relevant

9(1) Section 834 of ITA 2007 (residence of personal representatives) is amended as follows.

(2) In subsection (3), for "domiciled in the United Kingdom" substitute "a long-term UK resident within the meaning of IHTA 1984".

(3) Omit subsection (5).

2.7.3.3.3 Detail

Paragraph 9 amends section 834 ITA (residence of personal representatives) so the domicile of the deceased is no longer relevant and is replaced by "long-term UK resident within the meaning of IHTA 1984".

2.7.3.3.4 Effective Date

06 April 2025

2.7.3.4 *Paragraph 10 Amendment of section 62 TCGA (residence of personal representatives)*

2.7.3.4.1 Overview

Paragraph 10 amends Section 62 of TCGA 1992 (residence of personal representatives) removing reference to domicile.

2.7.3.4.2 Legislation

Paragraph 10 reads as follows.

"10 In section 62 of TCGA 1992 in subsection (3), for the words from "having" to the end substitute "UK resident if the deceased was UK resident or a long-term UK resident within the meaning of IHTA 1984 at the date of death.""

2.7.3.4.3 Detail

Paragraph 10 amends subsection 62(3) of TCGA 1992 (residence of personal representatives) removing the concept of domicile with the effect that the personal representatives are treated as UK resident if the deceased was a UK resident or a long-term UK Resident.

2.7.3.4.4 Effective Date

06 April 2025 (see section 40(4)).

2.7.3.5 Paragraph 11 Amendment of section 476 ITA Condition C for Trustees residence for IT

2.7.3.5.1 Overview

This relates to the residence of trustees and stops the domicile of the Settlor being relevant after 5 April 2025. This is in line with the move away from domicile for tax purposes. Broadly the residence of the Settlor at the time of creation, death etc. is what is to matter.

2.7.3.5.2 Legislation

Paragraph 11 reads as follows.

"*Residence of trustees: domicile of settlor no longer relevant*

11(1) Section 476 of ITA 2007 (residence of trustees: how to work out if settlor meets condition C) is amended as follows.

(2) In subsections (2)(b) and (3)(b), omit "or domiciled in the United Kingdom".

(3) After subsection (3) insert—

"(3ZA) In relation to a settlement—

(a)that arose before 6 April 2025 on S's death, or

(b)that S made (or is treated for the purposes of the Income Tax Acts as having made) before 6 April 2025,

subsections (2)(b) and (3)(b) have effect as if after "UK resident" there were inserted "or domiciled in the United Kingdom"."

(4) In subsection (3A), for "subsections (2)(b) and (3)(b)" substitute "subsection (3ZA)".

(5) In subsection (4)(c), for "subsection (2) or (3) or this subsection" substitute "this section"."

Before amendment section 476 headed "How to work out whether settlor meets condition C" read as follows.

"(1) This section applies for the purpose of working out whether a settlor ("S") in relation to a settlement meets condition C at a time.

(2) If—

(a)the settlement arose on S's death (whether by S's will, on S's intestacy or in any other way), and

(b)immediately before S's death, S was UK resident ***... or domiciled in the United Kingdom***, [words in bold removed]

then S meets condition C from the time of S's death until S ceases to be a settlor in relation to the settlement.

(3) If—

(a)the settlement is not within subsection (2)(a), and

(b)at a time when S made the settlement (or is treated for the purposes of the Income Tax Acts as making the settlement), S was UK resident ... ***or domiciled in the United Kingdom***, [words in bold removed]

then S meets condition C from that time until S ceases to be a settlor in relation to the settlement.

(3A) Section 835BA (deemed domicile) applies for the purposes of subsections (2)(b) and (3)(b).]

(4) Further, if—

(a)there is a transfer of property in relation to which section 471 applies,

(b)S is a settlor in relation to settlement 2 as a result of that section, and

(c)immediately before the disposal by the trustees of settlement 1, S meets condition C as a settlor in relation to settlement 1 as a result of subsection (2) or (3) or this subsection,

then S meets condition C as a settlor in relation to settlement 2 from the time S becomes such a settlor until S ceases to be such a settlor.

(5) "Settlement 1" and "settlement 2" are to be read in accordance with section 470(1)."

This relates to section 475 ITA headed "Residence of trustees".

Subsection (5) provides "Condition B is met at a time if at that time—

(a)at least one person who is a trustee of the settlement is UK resident and at least one such person is non-UK resident, and

(b)***a settlor in relation to the settlement meets condition C*** (see section 476)."

2.7.3.5.3 Detail

Paragraph 11 amends subsections 476(2)(b) and (3)(b) of ITA 2007 (residence of trustees: how to work out if settlor meets condition C) to remove domicile. Subsection (3ZA) is introduced to remove the condition on the settlor not being domiciled in the UK at the relevant applicable time such that only the residence of the settlor is considered rather than both their residence and residency test (as it applies to the settlor).

2.7.3.5.4 Effective Date

06 April 2025

2.7.3.6 Paragraph 12 Amendment of section 69 of TCGA 1992 (trustees of settlements) CGT

2.7.3.6.1 Overview

Paragraph 12 amends section 69 of TCGA 1992 (trustees of settlements) to remove references to domicile in respect of post 5 April 2025 settlement. Domicile continues to be relevant before that date. See new section 69(2CA).

2.7.3.6.2 Legislation

Paragraph 12 reads as follows.

"12(1) Section 69 of TCGA 1992 (trustees of settlements) is amended as follows.

(2) In subsection (2B) (c), omit "or domiciled".

(3) After subsection (2C) insert—

"(2CA) In relation to a settlement—

(a)that arose before 6 April 2025 on the settlor's death, or

(b)that the settlor made (or was treated for the purposes of this Act as making) before 6 April 2025,

subsection (2B) (c) has effect as if after "resident" there were inserted "or domiciled"."

(4) In subsection (2F), for "(2B) (c)" substitute "(2CA)".

2.7.3.6.3 Detail

Paragraph 12 amends section 69 of TCGA 1992 (trustees of settlements) at subsection (2B) (c) to remove the reference to domicile. Subsection (2CA) is introduced to remove the condition on the settlor not being domiciled in the UK at the relevant applicable time such that only the residence of the settlor is considered rather than both their residence and domicile.

For existing trusts, the trustees will continue to use the pre-April 2025 residency test (as it applies to the settlor). A consequential amendment is made to s69(2F) to provide for the correct cross reference.

2.7.3.6.4 Effective Date

06 April 2025 see section 40(4).

2.7.3.7 Paragraph 13 Amendment of regulation 42(2) (application of Part 5) of the Money Laundering, Terrorist Financing and Transfer of Funds (Information on the Payer) Regulations 2017

2.7.3.7.1 Overview

Paragraph 13 amends Regulation 42(2) (application of Part 5) of the Money Laundering, Terrorist Financing and Transfer of Funds (Information on the Payer) Regulations 2017 (S.I. 2017/692), to remove the reference to domicile. It also inserts a new paragraph (2A) into the Regulation to deal with pre-6 April 2025 settlement to continue the relevance of domicile.

2.7.3.7.2 Legislation

Paragraph 13 reads as follows.

> "13(1) In the Money Laundering, Terrorist Financing and Transfer of Funds (Information on the Payer) Regulations 2017 (S.I. 2017/692), regulation 42 (application of Part 5) is amended as follows.
> (2) In paragraph (2)(d)(ii), omit "and domiciled".
> (3) After paragraph (2) insert—
> "(2A) In relation to a trust that was set up before 6 April 2025, paragraph (2)(d)(ii) has effect as if after "resident" there were inserted "and domiciled"."

2.7.3.7.3 Detail

Paragraph 13 amends regulation 42(2)(d)(ii) (application of Part 5) of the Money Laundering, Terrorist Financing and Transfer of Funds (Information on the Payer) Regulations 2017 (S.I. 2017/692), to remove the reference to domicile. Paragraph (2A) is also inserted into regulation 42 to remove the condition on the settlor not being domiciled in the UK at the relevant applicable time such that only the residence of the settlor is considered rather than both their residence and domicile. For existing trusts, the trustees will continue to use the pre-April 2025 residency test (as it applies to the settlor).

2.7.3.7.4 Effective Date

06 April 2025 see section 40(4).

2.8 Application of Income Tax Acts in relation to deemed employment

2.8.1 *Paragraph 14 Income Tax Acts and deemed employment.*

2.8.1.1 Overview

This is essentially a consequential tidying change following the move away from domicile for UK tax.

2.8.1.1.1 Legislation

i. General

Paragraph 14 reads as follows.

"14 In sections 56, 61G and 61R of ITEPA 2003 (chargeability to tax in respect of deemed employment payment), omit subsections (4) and (5)."

ii. Section 56(4) and (5)

Section 56 (4) and (5) before omission read as follows.

"(4) The worker is not chargeable to tax in respect of the deemed employment payment if, or to the extent that, by reason of any combination of the factors mentioned in subsection (5), the worker would not be chargeable to tax if—

(a)the client employed the worker,

(b)the worker performed the services in the course of that employment, and

(c)the deemed employment payment was a payment by the client of earnings from that employment.

(5) The factors are—

(a)the worker being resident or domiciled outside the United Kingdom or meeting the requirement of section 26A,]

(b)the client being resident ... outside the United Kingdom, and

(c)the services in question being provided outside the United Kingdom."

Section 61G and 61R had broadly similar provisions.

2.8.1.1.2 Detail

This is essentially a consequential tidying change following the move away from domicile for UK tax. purposes.

2.8.1.1.3 Effective Date

06 April 2025 see section 40(4).

*2.8.2 **Pension schemes***

2.8.2.1 Paragraph 15 Pension Schemes

2.8.2.1.1 Overview

This is a consequential tidying change following the move away from domicile for UK tax purposes.

2.8.2.1.2 Legislation

Paragraph 15 reads as follows.

"(1) Part 4 of FA 2004 (pensions schemes etc.) is amended as follows.

(2) In Chapter 3 (payments by registered pension schemes), in section 185G, in subsection (3)(a) omit "and domiciled".

(3) In the following provisions of Chapter 5 (registered pension schemes: tax charges) and Chapter 6 (schemes that are not registered pension schemes) omit "or domiciled"—

(a)section 205(3);
(b)section 206(3);
(c)section 207(3);
(d)section 208(4);
(e)section 209(5);
(f)section 237A (2);
(g)section 237B (8);
(h)section 239(4);
(i)section 242(3);
(j)section 244J (6).

2.8.2.1.3 Detail

This is a consequential tidying change following the move away from domicile for UK tax purposes.

2.8.2.1.4 Effective Date

06 April 2025 see section 40(4).

2.8.2.2 Paragraph 16 Pension schemes – amendment F (No. 2) A 2005

2.8.2.2.1 Overview

This is a consequential tidying change following the move away from domicile for UK tax purposes.

2.8.2.2.2 Legislation

i. General

Paragraph 16 reads as follows.

"16 In section 7 of F(No.2) A 2005 (social security pension lump sum), in subsection (3) omit "or domiciled".

ii. Section 7 F(No.2) A 2005

Before the amendment section 7 headed "Charge to income tax on lump sum" read as follows.

"(1)A charge to income tax arises where a person becomes entitled to a social security pension lump sum.

(2) For the purposes of the Tax Acts (including subsection (5)) a social security pension lump sum—

(a)is to be treated as income, but
(b)is not to be taken into account in determining the total income of any person.

(3) The person liable to a charge under this section is the person ("P") entitled to the lump sum, whether or not P is resident ... ~~or domiciled~~ [words omitted] in the United Kingdom.

(4) The charge is imposed on P for the applicable year of assessment (see subsection (6)).

(5)A charge under this section for a person who is neither a Scottish taxpayer nor a Welsh taxpayer in the applicable year of assessment is a charge in respect of the amount of the lump sum at the following rate—

(a)if P's Step 3 income for the applicable year of assessment is nil, 0%;

(b). . . .

(c)if P's Step 3 income for that year of assessment is greater than nil but does not exceed the basic rate limit for that year, the basic rate ... for that year;

(d)if P's Step 3 income for that year of assessment exceeds the basic rate limit for that year but does not exceed the higher rate limit for that year, the higher rate ... for that year.

(e)if P's Step 3 income for that year of assessment exceeds the higher rate limit for that year, the additional rate ... for that year.

(5A) Where P is a Scottish taxpayer in the applicable year of assessment, a charge under this section is a charge in respect of the amount of the lump sum at the following rate—

(a)if P's Step 3 income for the applicable year of assessment is nil, 0%;

(b). . . .

(c)if P's Step 3 income for that year of assessment is greater than nil], the highest Scottish rate for that tax year that would be applicable to an amount of income that is equal to P's Step 3 income(2) for that year if such amount were wholly chargeable to income tax at Scottish rates.

(5B) Where P is a Welsh taxpayer in the applicable year of assessment, a charge under this section is a charge in respect of the amount of the lump sum at the following rate—

(a)if P's step 3 income for the applicable year of assessment is nil, 0%;

(b)if P's step 3 income for that year of assessment is greater than nil but does not exceed the basic rate limit for that year, the Welsh basic rate for that year;

(c)if P's step 3 income for that year of assessment is greater than the basic rate limit but does not exceed the higher rate limit for that year, the Welsh higher rate for that year;

(d)if P's step 3 income for that year of assessment is greater than the higher rate limit for that year, the Welsh additional rate for that year.

(6) Section 8 makes provision as to the meaning of "the applicable year of assessment" for the purposes of this section.

(7) Section 9 contains further definitions and makes provision as to commencement.

(8) Section 10 contains consequential amendments.

> (9) For the purposes of this section P's "Step 3 income" means P's net income less allowances deducted at Step 3 of the calculation in section 23 of ITA 2007 (calculation of income tax liability).

2.8.2.2.3 Detail

This is a consequential tidying change following the move away from domicile for UK tax purposes.

2.8.2.2.4 Effective Date

06 April 2025 (see section 40(4)).

2.8.2.3 Paragraph 17 Domicile of overseas electors IHT

2.8.2.3.1 Overview

There was at one time controversy as to the effect on domicile of registering etc. as an overseas elector. This led to legislation for IHT found in section 200 FA 1996.This legislation is now repealed as it is now effectively redundant post 5 April 2025 and the move away from domicile for IHT.

2.8.2.3.2 Legislation

Paragraph 17 reads as follows.

> "17 In FA 1996 omit section 200 (domicile for tax purposes of overseas electors).
> Section 200 FA 1996 was headed "Domicile for tax purposes of overseas electors."

Before its omission it read as follows.

> "(1) In determining—
> (a)for the purposes of inheritance tax... or capital gains tax where a person is domiciled at any time on or after 6th April 1996, or
> (b)for the purposes of section 267(1)(a) of the Inheritance Tax Act 1984 (deemed UK domicile for three years after ceasing to be so domiciled) where a person was domiciled at any time on or after 6th April 1993,
> there shall be disregarded any relevant action taken by that person (whether before, on or after that date) in connection with electoral rights.
> (2) Relevant action is taken by a person in connection with electoral rights where—
> (a)he does anything with a view to, or in connection with, being registered as an overseas elector; or
> (b)when registered as an overseas elector, he votes in any election at which he is entitled to vote by virtue of being so registered.
> (3) For the purposes of this section, a person is registered as an overseas elector if he is—
> (a)registered in any register of parliamentary electors in pursuance of such a declaration as is mentioned in section 1(2)(a) of the Representation of

the People Act 1985 (extension of parliamentary franchise to certain non-resident British citizens); or

(b)registered under section 3 of that Act of 1985 (certain non-resident peers entitled to vote at European Parliamentary elections).

(4) Nothing in subsection (1) above prevents regard being had, in determining the domicile of a person at any time, to any relevant action taken by him in connection with electoral rights if—

(a)his domicile at that time falls to be determined for the purpose of ascertaining his or either other person's liability to any of the taxes mentioned in subsection (1)(a) above; and

(b)the person whose liability is being ascertained wishes regard to be had to that action;

and a person's domicile determined in accordance with any such wishes shall be taken to have been so determined for the purpose only of ascertaining the liability in question."

2.8.2.3.3 Detail

There was at one time controversy as to the effect of on domicile of registering etc. as an overseas elector. This led to legislation for IHT found in section 200 FA 1996.This is now repealed.

There was at one time controversy as to the effect of on domicile of registering etc. as an overseas elector. This led to legislation for IHT found in section 200 FA 1996.This is now repealed.

2.8.2.3.4 Effective Date

06 April 2025 see section 40(4).

2.8.2.4 Paragraph 18 Domicile of overseas electors

2.8.2.4.1 Overview

There was at one time controversy as to the effect of on domicile of registering etc. as an overseas elector. This led to legislation for IT now found in section 835 B ITA for IT purposes. This is now repealed.

2.8.2.4.2 Legislation

Paragraph reads as follows.

"18 In ITA 2007 omit section 835B (domicile for income tax purposes of overseas electors).

Before its omission section 835B reads as follows.

"835B Domicile for income tax purposes of overseas electors

(1) In determining for income tax purposes where a person is domiciled, disregard any relevant electoral action taken by the person (whether taken before on or after the day on which TIOPA 2010 is passed).

(2) For the purposes of this section, relevant electoral action is taken by a person if—

(a)the person does anything with a view to, or in connection with, being registered as an overseas elector, or

(b)the person, when registered as an overseas elector, votes in any election at which the person is entitled to vote as a result of being registered as an overseas elector.

(3) For the purposes of this section, a person is registered as an overseas elector if the person is—

(a)registered in any register of parliamentary electors in pursuance of such a declaration as is mentioned in section 1(2)(a) of the Representation of the People Act 1985 (extension of parliamentary franchise to certain non-resident British citizens), ...

(b)................................

(4) Subsection (1) does not prevent regard being had, in determining a person's domicile at any time, to any relevant electoral action taken by the person if—

(a)the person's domicile at that time is being determined for the purpose of ascertaining that or any other person's liability to income tax, and

(b)the person whose liability is being ascertained wishes regard to be had to that action.

(5) If a person's domicile is determined in accordance with any such wishes, that domicile is to be regarded as having been determined for the purpose only of ascertaining the liability concerned."

2.8.2.4.3 Detail

As noted above there was at one time controversy as to the effect of on domicile of registering etc. as an overseas elector. This led to legislation for IT now found in section 835 B ITA for IT purposes. This is now repealed.

2.8.2.4.4 Effective Date

06 April 2025 see section 40(4).

2.8.2.5 Paragraph 19 Situs of debt

2.8.2.5.1 Overview

This deals with the situs of certain bank debts

2.8.2.5.2 Legislation

Paragraph 19 reads as follows.

"19(1) Section 275 of TCGA 1992 (location of assets) is amended as follows.
(2) In subsection (1), omit paragraph (l).
(3) Omit subsection (3A)."

Section 275 (1) before its omission read as follows.

"(1) For the purposes of this Act—

(a) the situation of rights or interests (otherwise than by way of security) in or over immovable property is that of the immovable property,

(b) subject to the following provisions of this subsection, the situation of rights or interests (otherwise than by way of security) in or over tangible movable property is that of the tangible movable property,

(c) subject to the following provisions of this subsection, ***a debt***, secured or unsecured, is situated in the United Kingdom if and only if the ***creditor is resident in the United Kingdom***,

(d) shares or debentures issued by any municipal or governmental authority, or by any body created by such an authority, are situated in the country of that authority,

(da) subject to paragraph (d) above, shares in or debentures of a company incorporated in any part of the United Kingdom are situated in the United Kingdom,

(e) subject to paragraphs (d) and (da) above, registered shares or debentures are situated where they are registered and, if registered in more than one register, where the principal register is situated,

(f) a ship or aircraft is situated in the United Kingdom if and only if the owner is then resident in the United Kingdom, and an interest or right in or over a ship or aircraft is situated in the United Kingdom if and only if the person entitled to the interest or right is resident in the United Kingdom,

(g) the situation of good-will as a trade, business or professional asset is at the place where the trade, business or profession is carried on,

(h) patents, trademarks, registered designs and corresponding rights are situated where they are registered, and if registered in more than one register, where each register is situated, and licences or other rights in respect of any such rights are situated in the United Kingdom if they or any right derived from them are exercisable in the United Kingdom,

(j) copyright, design right, franchises and corresponding rights, and licences or other rights in respect of any such rights, are situated in the United Kingdom if they or any right derived from them are exercisable in the United Kingdom,

(k) a judgment debt is situated where the judgment is recorded,

(l) a debt which—

(i)is owed by a bank, and

(ii)is not in sterling, and

(iii)is represented by a sum standing to the credit of an account in the bank of an individual who is not domiciled in the United Kingdom, is situated in the United Kingdom if and only if that individual is resident in the United Kingdom and the branch or other place of business of the bank at which the account is maintained is itself situated in the United Kingdom."

Subsection (3A) of section 275 before its omission read as follows.

"(3A) Section 835BA of ITA 2007 (deemed domicile) applies for the purposes of subsection (1)(l)(iii)." [see above]

2.8.2.5.3 Detail

Section 275 of TCGA 1992 (location of assets) is amended notably as far as the situs of a debt is concerned. These are debts owed by a bank in a currency other than sterling which is represented by a credit in the bank account of a non-UK domiciled individual. These are only relevant if the individual was UK resident and the account was maintained at a branch in the UK. This provision is repealed. This is catching up with the number of bank branch closures it seems.

2.8.2.5.4 Effective Date

06 April 2025 (see section 40(4))

2.8.2.6 Paragraph 20 Trust reporting requirements Schedule 5A TCGA

2.8.2.6.1 Overview

Paragraph 20 amends Schedule 5A to TCGA 1992 (settlements with foreign element: information) so that references to domicile are removed and to ensure that the individual is both resident and does not qualify for the new CGT relief for new residents on foreign gains.

2.8.2.6.2 Legislation

Paragraph reads as follows.

"20(1) Schedule 5A to TCGA 1992 (settlements with foreign element: information) is amended in accordance with sub-paragraphs (2) and (3).

(2) In paragraph 3—

(a)in sub-paragraph (3) omit "is domiciled in the United Kingdom and";

(b)at the end of sub-paragraph (3) insert "and is not a qualifying new resident within the meaning of Schedule D1";

(c)omit sub-paragraph (3A).

(3) In paragraph 4—

(a)for sub-paragraph (2)(b) substitute—

"(b)where that time was before 6 April 2025, did not fulfil the condition mentioned in sub-paragraph (3) below at that time or at any time before 6 April 2025,

(ba)where that time was on or after 6 April 2025, does not fulfil the condition mentioned in sub-paragraph (3A) below at that time,";

(b)in sub-paragraph (2)(c)—

(i)for "that condition" substitute "the condition mentioned in sub-paragraph (3A) below";

(ii)for "the commencement day" substitute "6 April 2025";

(c)in the closing words of sub-paragraph (2), for "the relevant day" substitute "31 January after the end of the tax year in which the relevant day falls";

(d)after sub-paragraph (3) insert—

"(3A) The condition is that the person concerned is resident in the United Kingdom and is not a qualifying new resident within the meaning of Schedule D1."

(4) Sub-paragraph (5) applies where a settlor fulfils the condition in paragraph 4(3A) of Schedule 5A to TCGA 1992 (settlements with foreign element: information) on 6 April 2025.

(5) For the purposes of paragraph 4(2)(c) of that Schedule, the settlor is to be treated as first fulfilling that condition on 6 April 2025."

2.8.2.6.3 Detail

Paragraph 21 amends Schedule 5A to TCGA 1992 (settlements with foreign element: information) so that references to domicile are removed and to ensure that the individual is both resident and does not qualify for the new CGT relief for new residents on foreign gains. This is essentially a consequential tidying up change.

2.8.2.6.4 Effective Date

06 April 2025 (see 40(4))

2.8.2.7 Paragraph 21

2.8.2.7.1 Overview

Paragraph 21 amends Finance Act 2005. References to domicile are removed at section 28(4) and Schedule 1 where the assumption that the vulnerable person is domiciled in the UK is removed.

2.8.2.7.2 Legislation

Paragraph 21 reads as follows.

"*Trusts with vulnerable beneficiary*

21 (1) FA 2005 is amended as follows.

(2) In section 28 (vulnerable person's liability: VQTI), in subsection (4)—

(a)at the end of paragraph (a) insert "and";

(b)omit paragraph (c) and the "and" before it.

(3) In Schedule 1 (non-UK resident vulnerable person), in paragraph 7(1)(a) omit "and domiciled".

2.8.2.7.3 Detail

Paragraph 21 amends Finance Act 2005. References to domicile are removed at section 28(4) and Schedule 1 where the assumption that the vulnerable person is domiciled in the UK is removed.

This is essentially consequential on the removal of domicile basis from UK tax.

2.8.2.7.4 Effective Date

06 April 2025 (see section 40(4))

2.8.2.8 Paragraph 22 amendment of section 459 of ITTOIA 2005 (application of transfer of assets abroad legislation to disposals of deeply discounted securities),

2.8.2.8.1 Overview

Paragraph 22 section 459 of ITTOIA 2005 (application of transfer of assets abroad legislation to disposals of deeply discounted securities).

2.8.2.8.2 Legislation

Paragraph 22 reads as follows.

> *"Disposals of deeply discounted securities*
> 22 In section 459 of ITTOIA 2005 (application of transfer of assets abroad legislation to disposals of deeply discounted securities), in subsection (1) omit "or domiciled".

2.8.2.8.3 Detail

Paragraph 22 is essentially a tidying up change following the move away from domicile for UK tax purposes.

2.8.2.8.4 Effective Date

06 April 2025 (see section 40(4))

2.8.2.9 Paragraph 23 (Digital Requirements) Regulations 2021

2.8.2.9.1 Overview

Paragraph 23 removes the exemption at regulation 26 (exemption for foreign businesses of non - UK domiciled individuals) in the Income Tax (Digital Requirements) Regulations 2021 (S.I. 2021/1076).

This is essentially a consequential change following the move away from domicile for UK tax.

2.8.2.9.2 Legislation

Paragraph 23 reads as follows.

> *"The accrued income scheme*

23(1) ITA 2007 is amended as follows.

(2) In section 667 (trustees' accrued income profits treated as settlement income), in subsection (2)—

(a)in paragraph (a) omit "or domiciled outside the United Kingdom";

(b)in paragraph (b) omit "or domiciled in the United Kingdom".

(3) In section 680 (interest on securities involving accrued income losses: foreign trustees), in subsection (1)—

(a)in paragraph (a) omit "or domiciled outside the United Kingdom";

(b)in paragraph (d) omit ", or domiciled in the United Kingdom,".

2.8.2.9.3 Detail

This is essentially a consequential change following the move away from domicile for UK tax.

2.8.2.9.4 Effective Date

06 April 2025 (see section 40(4)

2.8.2.10 Paragraph 24 FOTRA (Free of Tax to Residents Abroad) Securities

2.8.2.10.1 Overview

This is essentially a consequential change following the move away from domicile for UK tax.

2.8.2.10.2 Legislation

Paragraph 24 reads as follows.

"FOTRA securities

24(1) In section 22 of F(No.2) A 1931 (Treasury power to issue securities with a FOTRA condition), in subsection (1)(b) for "neither domiciled nor" substitute "not".

(2) In section 154 of FA 1996 (FOTRA securities), omit subsection (1).

(3) Any security issued with a FOTRA domicile condition is treated in relation to times on or after 6 April 2025 as if—

(a)it was a security issued with the post-1996 Act FOTRA conditions (and with no other FOTRA condition), and

(b)the post-1996 Act FOTRA conditions had been authorised in relation to the issue of that security by virtue of section 22 of F(No.2) A 1931.

(4) In sub-paragraph (3)—

"a FOTRA condition" means a condition about exemption from taxation authorised by section 22 of F(No.2) A 1931;

"a FOTRA domicile condition", in relation to a security, means a FOTRA condition requiring the security to be in the beneficial ownership of persons who are not domiciled in the United Kingdom for an exemption from taxation to apply;

"the post-1996 Act FOTRA conditions" means the FOTRA conditions with which 7.25% Treasury Stock 2007 was first issued.

2.8.2.10.3 Detail

This is essentially a consequential change following the move away from domicile for UK tax.

2.8.2.10.4 Effective Date

06April 2025 (see section 40(4))

2.8.2.11 Paragraph 25 Reliefs in respect of income from investments etc. of certain pension schemes

2.8.2.11.1 Overview

This is essentially a consequential change reflecting the move away from a domicile-based system for UK tax.

2.8.2.11.2 Legislation

Paragraph 25 reads as follows.

"25 In section 614 of the Income and Corporation Taxes Act 1988 (exemptions and reliefs in respect of income from investments etc. of certain pension schemes), in subsections (4) and (5), omit "not domiciled and".

Section 614 ICTA read as follows before the amendment.

"614Exemptions and reliefs in respect of income from investments etc. of certain pension schemes.

(1) . . . . .

(2) Any interest or dividends received by the person in whom is vested any of the Family Pension Funds mentioned in section 273 of the Government of India Act 1935, and having effect as a scheme made under section 2 of the Overseas Pensions Act 1973, on sums forming part of that fund shall be exempt from income tax.

(2A) The reference in subsection (2) above to interest on sums forming part of a fund include references to any amount which is treated as income by virtue of Chapter 8 of Part 4 of ITTOIA 2005 (profits from deeply discounted securities) and derives from any investment forming part of that fund.

(3) Income derived from investments or deposits of any fund referred to in section 648, 649, 650 or 651 of ITEPA 2003] shall not be charged to income tax, and any income tax deducted from any such income shall be repaid by the Board to the persons entitled to receive the income.

(4) In respect of income derived from investments or deposits of the Overseas Service Pensions Fund established pursuant to section 7(1) of the Overseas Aid Act 1966, the Board shall give by way of repayment such relief from income tax as is necessary to secure that the income is exempt to the like

extent (if any) as if it were income of a person ***not domiciled and not resident*** in the United Kingdom.

(5) In respect of dividends and other income derived from investments, deposits or other property of a superannuation fund to which section 615(3) applies the Board shall give by way of repayment such relief from income tax as is necessary to secure that the income is exempt to the like extent (if any) as if it were income of a person ***not domiciled and not resident*** in the United Kingdom.

(6) A claim under this section shall be made to the Board."

[Words omitted in bold italic]

2.8.2.11.3 Detail

This is a somewhat specialist area but is a reflection of the move away from domicile for UK tax purposes.

2.8.2.11.4 Effective Date

06April 2025 (see section 40(4))

2.8.3 Part 3 Removal of domicile (secondary legislation) Education funding

2.8.3.1 Paragraph 26 Removal of domicile (secondary legislation) Education funding

2.8.3.1.1 Overview

Paragraph 26 amends various regulations related to education funding to remove the concept of domicile. This is essentially a consequential change reflecting the move away from a domicile-based system.

2.8.3.1.2 Legislation

26(1)In the Appendix to Schedule 1 to the Education (Grants) (Music, Ballet and Choir Schools) (England) Regulations 2001 (S.I. 2001/2743 [76]) (aided pupil

[76] Explanatory Note *(This note is not part of the Regulations)*

These Regulations consolidate, with amendments, the Education (Grants) (Music, Ballet and Choir Schools) Regulations 1995 which, with Regulations amending them, are revoked by regulation 15(1). They come into force on 1st September 2001 and apply in relation to a school year beginning on or after that date (regulation 1).

The Regulations provide for the payment of grant to the schools of music and ballet referred to in regulation 3(1) to reimburse them for their expenditure in operating the aided pupil scheme described in Schedule 1. That scheme allows schools to remit tuition and other fees, and to pay uniform and travel grant in respect of aided pupils.

The Secretary of State is also empowered to pay grant to—

(a)the Royal Ballet School in respect of their expenditure incurred in connection with the provision of education at the school, the staging of auditions and associated activities to attract new pupils to the school, and the maintenance of the school's premises at White Lodge, Richmond Park (regulations 9 and 10), and

(b)the Choir Schools' Association Bursary Trust in respect of education provided to choristers aged between 8 and 13 attending a choir school supported by the Trust which is a finally registered independent school (regulations 11 to 14).

scheme: computation of income), in paragraph 2, in sub-paragraph (a) omit ", ordinarily resident or domiciled".

(2) In Part 2 of Schedule 2 to the Education (Student Support) (European University Institute) Regulations 2010 (S.I. 2010/447 [77]) (calculation of contribution), in paragraph 4(5)(a), omit "or domiciled" in the first place it appears.

The amount of grant payable to the Royal Ballet School and the Trust is to be determined after consultation with them. Payment of grant may only be made in the case of a choir school in respect of pupils who satisfy the residence requirements specified in Schedule 1, paragraph 2.

Apart from minor drafting amendments, the main changes from the previous Regulations are set out below:

1. In Part III the purposes in respect of which grant is payable to the Royal Ballet School have been extended so as to include the staging of auditions and associated activities to attract new pupils to the school and the maintenance of the school's premises at White Lodge, Richmond Park, as well as the provision of education at the school (this is no longer limited to the Upper School).

2. In Schedule 1 (which establishes the aided pupil scheme, sets out conditions of eligibility for aided places, provides for remission of fees and payment of grant and makes administrative provisions):

(a)the condition relating to residence (paragraph 2), which also applies in relation to grants to choir schools, has been revised to add a category of a child aged 16 years or over who has been ordinarily resident throughout the period of three years preceding the first day of the first academic year of the course in the European Economic Area. Where a child qualifies for an aided place by reason of this provision, there will only be an entitlement to remission of tuition fees and not costs of board and lodging;

(b)in paragraph 5 (conditions as to liability for payment of fees) we have added a provision that a school shall not select for an aided place a child the whole of whose fees for the school year in which he would take up his aided place if selected are required to be paid pursuant to a qualifying agreement (a legally enforceable agreement under which a person, being either a body corporate or an individual who is not a parent of the aided pupil, is required to pay school fees for the aided pupil);

(c)in paragraph 8, the reduction to be made in relevant income in respect of dependent relatives pursuant to sub-paragraphs (3) and (5) has been increased to £1,430 (from £1,400 in the previous Regulations);

(d)in paragraphs 14 and 15, the means test for the remission of fees has been amended: the level of income at or below which fees are to be wholly remitted is set at £9,798 instead of £9,832 (in respect of boarding pupils) and £12,148 instead of £11,804 (in respect of day pupils). In addition, the structure of the parental contribution scales has been changed, and tables have been added;

(e)in paragraphs 18 and 19, the means test for uniform and travel grants are relaxed and the amount of grant payable increased; and

(f)in paragraph 25(1) archaeology has been added to the list of subjects and the list of examinations has been expanded to include the Advanced Subsidiary and the Advanced Vocational Certificate of Education.

3. In Schedule 2 a new provision has been added (paragraph 5) which provides for the transfer of aided places from one school of music or ballet to another.

[77] Explanatory Note *(This note is not part of the Order)*

These Regulations provide support for eligible students taking designated higher education courses at the European University Institute in respect of an academic year beginning on or after 1st September 2010. These Regulations apply in relation to England only.

Grants for living and other costs, a disabled students' allowance and a grant for dependants are available for up to twenty eligible students at the European University Institute.

The Regulations set out the eligibility criteria for the grants, the application procedure and the method for calculating the amount of grant payable. The Regulations also set out the arrangements for payment of the grants and recovery of any overpayments.

These Regulations revoke the Education (Student Support) (European Institutions) (No. 2) Regulations 2006 and amending regulations in relation to England. The extent of the revocation is set out in regulations 4 to 6 and under Schedule 3.

(3) The Education (Student Support) Regulations 2011 (S.I. 2011/1986 [78]) are amended in accordance with sub-paragraphs (4) and (5).

(4) In Schedule 4 (financial assessment)—

(a)in paragraph 5(7)(a)—

(i)omit "or domiciled" in the first place it appears;

(ii)omit "so";

(b)in paragraph 7(7)(a)—

(i)omit "or domiciled" in the first place it appears;

(ii)omit "so".

(5) In Schedule 6 (assessment of eligible part-time student's household income)—

(a)in paragraph 5(6)(a)—

(i)omit "or domiciled" in the first place it appears;

(ii)omit "so";

(b)in paragraph 7(7)(a)—

(i)omit "or domiciled" in the first place it appears; The

(ii)omit "so";

2.8.3.1.3 Detail

This is essentially a consequential change reflecting the move away from a domicile-based system.

The paragraph amends the Education (Grants) (Music, Ballet and Choir Schools) (England) Regulations 2001 (S.I. 2001/2743), removing references to "ordinarily resident or domiciled" from the Appendix to Schedule 1(aided pupil scheme: computation of income).

Paragraph 22(2) amends the Education (Student Support) (European University Institute) Regulations 2010 (S.I. 2010/.447), removing the reference to domicile from Part 2 (calculation of contribution) of Schedule 2 (student's contribution) to the Education (Student Support) (European University Institute) Regulations 2010 (calculation of contribution).

Paragraphs 22(3) to 22(5) amend the Education (Student Support) Regulations 2011 (S.I. 2011/1986) to remove references to domicile in paragraph 5 (calculation of parent's residual income) and paragraph 7 (calculation of parent's partner's residual income) of Schedule 4 (financial assessment) and paragraph 5

An impact assessment has not been produced for this instrument as it has no impact on the costs of business, charities or voluntary bodies. The impact on the public sector is minimal.

[78] Long regulations see https://www.legislation.gov.uk/uksi/2011/1986

(calculation of parent's residual income) and paragraph 7 (calculation of parent's partner's residual income) of Schedule 6 (assessment of eligible part-time student's household income).

2.8.3.1.4 Effective Date

06 April 2025 (see section 40(4))

2.8.3.2 Paragraph 27 Making Tax Digital

2.8.3.2.1 Overview

Again, this is a consequential change reflecting the move away from a domicile-based system.

2.8.3.2.2 Legislation

Paragraph 27 reads as follows.

> *"Making Tax Digital*
>
> 27 In the Income Tax (Digital Requirements) Regulations 2021 (S.I. 2021/1076) omit regulation 26."

Regulation 26 read as follows before its omission.

> *"Exemption for foreign businesses of non-UK domiciled individuals.*
>
> 26.— (1) The digital requirements do not apply to a person in respect of that person's foreign businesses for a tax year in which the person is not domiciled in the United Kingdom.
>
> (2) For the purposes of paragraph (1), a person's foreign businesses are—
>
> (a)that person's overseas property business within the meaning of section 265 of ITTOIA 2005; and
>
> (b)any trade, profession or vocation carried on by that person outside the United Kingdom.
>
> (3) Where a person carries on a trade, profession or vocation partly in the United Kingdom and partly outside the United Kingdom, the part carried on outside the United Kingdom is a foreign business for the purposes of paragraph (1), but the part that is carried on in the United Kingdom is not.
>
> (4) Section 835BA (deemed domicile) (1) of ITA 2007(2) applies for the purposes of this regulation."

2.8.3.2.3 Detail

This is essentially a consequential tidying up matter reflecting the move away from a domicile-based system.

2.8.3.2.4 Effective Date

06 April 2025 (see section 40(4))

2.8.4 *Section 41 and Schedule 10: Temporary repatriation facility ("TRF")*

2.8.4.1 *Overview – Introduction of the TRF*

Section 41 and Schedule 10 provide for a 'Temporary Repatriation Facility' ("**TRF**") under which former remittance basis users may designate and pay a charge on qualifying foreign capital in order to secure that the remittance of amounts of that capital does not result in a charge to income tax or capital gains tax.

The Policy Paper published by the new government on 29 July included making available a new 'Temporary Repatriation Facility' for individuals who have been taxed on the remittance basis such that they will be able to remit FIG that arose prior to 6 April 2025 and pay a reduced tax rate on the remittance for a limited time period after the remittance basis has ended.

The limited time is 4 years.

The Explanatory Notes say:

> "This [section] and Schedule provide for a 'Temporary Repatriation Facility' (TRF) under which former remittance basis users may designate and pay a charge on qualifying foreign capital in order to secure that the remittance of amounts of that capital does not result in a charge to income tax or capital gains tax."

2.8.4.1.1 The Legislation

Section 41 is headed "Temporary repatriation facility". It provides:

"Schedule 10 makes provision for a "temporary repatriation facility" for individuals who have been subject to the remittance basis".

2.8.4.1.2 Detail

This provides for the TRF as signposted in the Policy Paper as described above.

2.8.4.1.3 Effective Date

06 April 2025

2.8.5 *Details of Schedule 10*

Schedule 10 is divided into 3 parts. These are:

- Part 1: Temporary repatriation facility charge (paragraphs 1 to 7)
- Part 2: Exemptions etc for designated qualifying overseas capital (paragraphs 8 to 10)
- Part 3: Effect of designation on when amounts remitted etc paragraphs 11 to 17)

Each of these Parts will be considered in more details next.

Part 1: Temporary repatriation facility charge ("TRF charge")

2.8.5.1 Paragraph 1 Introduction of TRF charge

2.8.5.1.1 Overview

Paragraph 1 introduces the TRF charge. The TRF charge is a charge on an amount of designated qualifying overseas capital. This charge is at a reduced rate.

Sub-paragraphs 1(3) to (8) provide that an individual, who is UK resident, will be charged to tax on designations of qualifying overseas capital for the tax years 2025-26, 2026-27 and 2027-28. The rate of the TRF charge on designated qualifying overseas capital will be:

- 12% for the tax years 2025-26 and 2026-27, and
- 15% for 2027-28.

The paragraph also introduces the concept of "qualifying overseas capital". This is discussed below (see paragraph 2 headed "definition of qualifying overseas capital ").

2.8.5.1.2 Legislation

Paragraph 1 reads as follows.

> "*Introduction and charge*
>
> 1(1) This Part of this Schedule sets out a charge on amounts of qualifying overseas capital of individuals previously subject to the remittance basis.
>
> (2) The charge is to be known as the temporary repatriation facility charge, and is referred to in this Schedule as the "**TRF charge**".
>
> (3) Paragraphs 2 to 6 set out when amounts are, or are to be treated, as qualifying overseas capital.
>
> (4) Amounts of qualifying overseas capital of an individual are **subject to the TRF charge only if the individual designates them** in accordance with this Part of this Schedule.
>
> (5) An **individual may only designate qualifying overseas capital if** the individual was **subject to the remittance basis for at least one tax year** (being a tax year **before the tax year 2025-26**).
>
> (6) An **individual designates** qualifying overseas capital **by making an election** (a "**designation election**") **in a return** for the tax year 2025-26, 2026-27 or 2027-28 (see paragraph 8 for further provision about designation elections).
>
> (7) A **designation election may only be made in a return if, for the tax year to which the return relates, the individual is UK resident** for the purposes of income tax and capital gains tax (see Schedule 45 to FA 2013).

(8) The amount of the TRF charge on qualifying overseas capital designated by an individual is—

(a)in the case of amounts of qualifying overseas capital designated in a return for the tax year 2025-26 or 2026-27, the amount equal to 12% of the amount of that capital, and

(b)in the case of amounts of qualifying overseas capital designated in a return for the tax year 2027-28, the amount equal to 15% of the amount of that capital.

(9) **Part 2 of this Schedule sets out exemptions and reliefs from income tax and capital gains tax** that apply **where amounts of qualifying overseas capital are designated.**

(10) **Part 3 of this Schedule amends or modifies rules about the remittance of amounts where an individual has designated qualifying overseas capital**.

(11) For the purposes of this Part of this Schedule—

(a)an **individual is subject to the remittance basis for a tax year**—

(i)in relation to the tax years **2008-09 to 2024-25,** if any of **sections 809B, 809D or 809E of ITA 2007 apply to the individual for that year**, or

(ii)in relation to **any tax year before 2008-2009, if any income or gains of the individual for that year were subject to the remittance basis** (including any income or gains that would have been regarded as arising in the tax year but were not as a result of the application of the remittance basis), and

(b)"**return**" means a return under **section 8 of TMA 1970** (personal return for income tax and capital gains tax), and

(c)references to an **election being included in a return include** an election being so included as a result of an **amendment** of the return.

2.8.5.1.3 Detail

This is essentially introductory to TRF. Paragraph 1 introduces the TRF charge. The TRF charge is a charge on an amount of designated qualifying overseas capital.

Sub-paragraphs 1(3) to (8) provide that an individual, who is UK resident, will be charged to tax on designated qualifying overseas capital for the tax years 2025-26, 2026-27 and 2027-28.

The rate of the TRF charge on designated qualifying overseas capital will be

- 12% for the tax years 2025-26 and 2026-27, and
- 15% for 2027-28

HMRC say the following about this paragraph in their Manuals.

> "**Overview**
> Paragraph 1 Schedule 10 Finance Act 2025

The temporary repatriation facility (TRF) is only available to individuals who:

- are UK resident in the tax year of designation
- have previously been subject to the remittance basis for at least one tax year
- have 'qualifying overseas capital' (see RDRM72100 onwards) available to designate

UK residence is determined by the statutory residence test (SRT) – see RFIG20000 onwards. If an individual is non-UK resident under the SRT for a tax year they are not eligible to make a designation election in that tax year.

Subject to the remittance basis

For tax years 2008-09 onwards, an individual having been 'subject to the remittance basis' for a tax year means that section 809B, 809D or 809E ITA 2007 applied to the individual for that year. This means that an individual is eligible to use the TRF even if they did not make a claim for the remittance basis but instead it applied, for example, by their having less than £2,000 of unremitted foreign income and gains for a year. See RDRM32020 for claims under section 809B and RDRM32105 for exceptions to the claim under sections 809D and 809E.

For tax years before 2008-09, an individual having been 'subject to the remittance basis' for a tax year means that in the tax year they had income or gains to which the remittance basis applied, whether it was applied automatically (to gains and employment income) or was claimed (for relevant foreign income) – see RDRM36005. It is not sufficient for an individual to have been not ordinarily resident or non-domiciled for that year; the remittance basis must have applied to income or gains arising in that year, or that would have arisen in that year but for the remittance basis applying.

Designation on behalf of a third party

Designations under the TRF are restricted to individuals that would otherwise have been taxable on the remittance of the income or gain. It is not possible for an individual or entity to make a designation of qualifying overseas capital that relates to an amount that they themselves would not otherwise be taxable on were the funds to be remitted. However, this does not prevent a person, such as an advisor, assisting an individual in the managing of their tax affairs by completing a return or making a payment.

Example 1

Amber and Romolo are both UK residents and former remittance basis users. They have been married to each other for 20 years.

On 6 April 2025 Amber transfers £150,000 of her foreign employment income from 2023-24 from her overseas bank account to Romolo's overseas bank account, which he opened on 6 April 2025 and contains no other funds.

On 30 June 2025 Romolo spends £30,000 in the UK on hiring a venue in London, catering and entertainment for a wedding anniversary celebration, transferring the funds to the vendors from his overseas bank account containing

Amber's foreign employment income. This is a remittance of £30,000 which Amber would be taxable on, as it has been brought to the UK by a relevant person to her (see RDRM33030 for a definition of 'relevant person').

Even though Romolo is himself a UK resident and former remittance basis user and was the person who brought the funds to the UK, he cannot designate the £30,000 in his Self Assessment tax return for 2025-26. It is Amber who must either designate the £30,000 in her 2025-26 tax return and pay the TRF charge or pay tax on the remittance at the usual rate.

Example 2

Jared is 17 years old and has been UK resident and subject to the remittance basis since his arrival in the UK on 6 April 2020.

His father Riccardo has also been UK resident and subject to the remittance basis since 6 April 2020. In 2023-24 Riccardo sold overseas shares for £100,000 making a gain of £50,000. He used the funds to purchase a sports car which he keeps in Monte Carlo.

On 6 April 2025 Riccardo gives the car to Jared, because Riccardo has secured a 3-year contract working in Canada and will not have much use for it in that time. This is on the understanding that Jared will be responsible for paying all taxes on the car.

On 7 April 2025 Jared drives the car to the UK and keeps it at the family home in London. When the car reaches the UK, this will be a remittance of the £50,000 gain (providing one or more of the exempt property rules do not apply - see RDRM34070), because it has been brought to the UK by a relevant person to Riccardo. Even though Jared has been gifted the car and is the one who brought it to the UK, the remittance still relates to a gain on which Riccardo is taxable.

Although Jared is UK resident in 2025-26 and a former remittance basis user, he is not eligible to use the TRF to designate the £50,000. It is Riccardo who will need to decide if he would like to make an election to designate this gain in his 2025-26 tax return.

Riccardo may find that due to his work and time spent in Canada he is non-UK resident for 2025-26, and for the remainder of the TRF period, so is not eligible to designate the gain at all. However, even though Riccardo may want it to be designated, for example, because the temporary non-residence rules may apply to him on his return (see RDRM32530), neither Jared nor anyone else is eligible to designate the £50,000 on his behalf."

2.8.5.1.4 Effective Date

06 April 2025

2.8.5.2 Paragraph 2 definition of qualifying overseas capital

2.8.5.2.1 Overview

Paragraph 2 defines qualifying overseas capital.

2.8.5.2.2 Legislation

Paragraph 2 is headed "Qualifying overseas capital: main cases". It reads as follows.

"2(1) An amount of capital is "qualifying overseas capital" of an individual if it falls within sub-paragraph (2), (5) or (8).

(2)An amount of capital falls within this sub-paragraph if—

(a)it is an amount that arose in the tax year 2024-25 or an earlier tax year as income or as a gain,

(b)the amount has not been remitted to the United Kingdom, and

(c)the amount, if remitted to the United Kingdom, would have the effect mentioned in sub-paragraph (3)(a) or (b).

(3)That effect is that—

(a)the individual becomes chargeable to income tax by reference to the amount remitted in accordance with section 22, 26, 41F, 554Z9 or 554Z10 of ITEPA 2003 or section 832 of ITTOIA 2005 (income charged on remittance basis), or

(b)a gain is treated as accruing to the individual by reference to the amount remitted in accordance with paragraph 1(2) of Schedule 1 to TCGA 1992 (gains charged on remittance basis).

(4)In determining whether an amount of capital falls within sub-paragraph (2) for the purposes of making a designation election for a tax year, the condition in sub-paragraph (2)(b) is to be regarded as met if it was met at the end of that tax year.

(5)An amount of capital falls within this sub-paragraph if—

(a)it is an amount that arose in the tax year 2024-25 or an earlier tax year as income or as a gain,

(b)the amount is remitted to the United Kingdom in the tax year 2025-26, 2026-27 or 2027-28, and

(c)that remittance has the effect mentioned in sub-paragraph (3)(a) or (b).

(6)An amount that is qualifying overseas capital falling within sub-paragraph (5) (and that has not previously been designated as result of the amount falling within sub-paragraph (2)) may only be designated in a designation election for the tax year in which it was remitted.

(7)For the purposes of sub-paragraphs (2)(c) and (5)(c), a remittance is to be treated as having the effect mentioned in sub-paragraph (3)(a) or (b) if it would have that effect ignoring—

(a)Part 2 of this Schedule (exemptions etc for designated qualifying overseas capital),

(b)section 809VA of ITA 2007 (business investment relief), and

(c)section 809X of that Act (exempt property).

(8)An amount of capital falls within this sub-paragraph if—

(a)it does not fall within sub-paragraph (2) or (5),

(b)it was held by the individual immediately before 6 April 2025,

(c)it was situated outside the United Kingdom—

(i)immediately before it was most recently acquired by the individual before that date, and

(ii)throughout the period beginning with the time referred to in sub-paragraph (i) and ending with that date.

(9)References in Parts 1 and 2 of this Schedule to amounts being remitted to the United Kingdom are to be construed in accordance with Chapter A1 of Part 14 of ITA 2007 (see, in particular, sections 809L to 809O of that Act)."

2.8.5.2.3 Detail

i. General

Paragraph 2 defines "qualifying overseas capital".

Paragraph 2(1) provides that "An amount of capital is "qualifying overseas capital" of an individual if it falls within sub-paragraph (2), (5) or (8)."

This requires us to consider sub-paragraphs (2), (5)and (8).

This will be done next having noted that "an amount of capital" is not defined for these purposes. My starting point would be to look to its accounting treatment. This not determinative but it helps in my view.

ii. Sub-paragraph (2)

Sub-paragraph (2) reads as follows.

"(2) An amount of capital falls within this sub-paragraph if—

(a)it is an amount that arose in the tax year 2024-25 or an earlier tax year as income or as a gain,

(b)the amount has not been remitted to the United Kingdom, and

(c)the amount, if remitted to the United Kingdom, would have the effect mentioned in sub-paragraph (3)(a) or (b)."

Sub-paragraph (3) provides as follows.

"(3)That effect is that—

(a)the individual becomes chargeable to income tax by reference to the amount remitted in accordance with section 22, 26, 41F, 554Z9 or 554Z10 of ITEPA 2003 or section 832 of ITTOIA 2005 (income charged on remittance basis), or

(b)a gain is treated as accruing to the individual by reference to the amount remitted in accordance with paragraph 1(2) of Schedule 1 to TCGA 1992 (gains charged on remittance basis)."

iii. Sub-paragraph (5)

Sub-paragraph (5) reads as follows.

"(5)An amount of capital falls within this sub-paragraph if—

(a)it is an amount that arose in the tax year 2024-25 or an earlier tax year as income or as a gain,

(b)the amount is remitted to the United Kingdom in the tax year 2025-26, 2026-27 or 2027-28, and

(c)that remittance has the effect mentioned in sub-paragraph (3)(a) or (b)."

Sub-paragraph (3)(a) or (b) is set out above under the heading ii[ ].

iv. Sub-paragraph (8)

Sub-paragraph (8) reads as follows.

"(8)An amount of capital falls within this sub-paragraph if—

(a)it does not fall within sub-paragraph (2) or (5),

(b)it was held by the individual immediately before 6 April 2025,

(c)it was situated outside the United Kingdom—

(i)immediately before it was most recently acquired by the individual before that date, and

(ii)throughout the period beginning with the time referred to in sub-paragraph (i) and ending with that date."

Sub-paragraphs (2) and (5) are considered in the preceding paragraphs.

HMRC say the following on this in their Manuals.

"**RDRM72200 - Temporary repatriation facility: Qualifying overseas capital: Pre-6 April 2025 foreign income and gains**

Paragraph 2(2) and (5) Schedule 10 Finance Act 2025

An amount of income or gains which arose in a year in which the individual was subject to the remittance basis will be qualifying overseas capital for the purposes of the temporary repatriation facility (TRF) if it has never been remitted or it is remitted during the TRF period, and if remitted the individual would be chargeable to Income Tax on income, or a gain is treated as accruing, under one of the following provisions:

- section 832 ITTOIA 2005 - income charged on the remittance basis
- paragraph 1(2) schedule 1 TCGA 1992 - gains charged on the remittance basis
- sections 22 and 26 ITEPA 2003 - chargeable overseas earnings
- section 41F ITEPA 2003 - foreign securities income
- sections 554Z9 and 554Z10 ITEPA 2003 - foreign employment income provided through third parties

This includes amounts that otherwise would be taxable under those provisions but for being treated as not remitted as a result of being exempt property (see RDRM74400) or as a result of a claim for business investment relief (see RDRM74710).

An individual may also have amounts overseas where they are uncertain as to the source of the funds. These amounts can also meet the definition of qualifying overseas capital – see RDRM72300. Amounts that are qualifying overseas capital under the definition at paragraph 2(2) must not have been remitted before or during the tax year of designation.

Amounts that are qualifying overseas capital under the definition at paragraph 2(5) are amounts that have been remitted in the year of designation, so there is no requirement under subparagraph (5) for amounts to have never been remitted previously.

If an individual wants to designate an amount that they remit to the UK during the TRF period (that has not already been designated in an earlier year), it must be designated in their Self Assessment tax return for the same tax year as the remittance, if the individual wishes to benefit from the low TRF rate. An individual could not, for example, remit an amount in 2025-26 then designate it in their 2026-27 tax return. See RDRM73100 onwards for the designation process and time limits.

Whether amounts are qualifying overseas capital under paragraph 2(2) or (5), once the designation election has been made and the TRF charge has been paid, no further tax charges will arise on the remittance of any of these amounts in the year of designation or a future tax year.

Unremittable income and gains, on which the charge to tax has been deferred due to an individual making a claim under section 842 ITTOIA 2005 or section 279 TCGA 1992, are not qualifying overseas capital.

Example 1

Augusta is UK resident and a former remittance basis user. On 6 April 2025 she has an overseas bank account containing £300,000 of foreign gains from the sale of 2 overseas properties in 2022-23, when she was subject to the remittance basis.

Augusta has never previously remitted any of these gains and doesn't make any remittances from her account in 2025-26. Anticipating remittances in future, Augusta wants to designate the gains in her 2025-26 tax return.

The foreign gains meet the definition of qualifying overseas capital under paragraph 2(2) because they arose before 6 April 2025, they have not been remitted by the end of the 2025-26 tax year nor previously, and if Augusta remitted them, they would be treated as accruing in the tax year of remittance under paragraph 1(2) schedule 1 TCGA 1992.

Therefore, Augusta can designate the gains in her 2025-26 tax return and when she remits them, whether this is during or after the TRF period, there will be no further tax charge on remittance.

Example 2

Darius is UK resident and a former remittance basis user. He has foreign dividend income of £40,000 which arose in 2024-25 when he was subject to the remittance basis. Darius used these funds to purchase a painting in France which has remained in his apartment in Paris.

If Darius were to bring the painting to the UK this would result in the remittance of the £40,000 of foreign income from which the painting derives. Darius has the option to designate up to £40,000 in any one of the 2025-26, 2026-27, or 2027-28 tax years.

Darius has not yet designated any of the £40,000. On 31 March 2027 Darius brings the painting to the UK to hang in his London home. The foreign income meets the definition of qualifying overseas capital under paragraph 2(5) because it arose before 6 April 2025, has been remitted during the TRF period and is chargeable to Income Tax on remittance under section 832 ITTOIA 2005.

However, because it was remitted in 2026-27, Darius must designate the £40,000 in his 2026-27 tax return if he wants to take advantage of the low tax rate; he cannot wait until 2027-28. If Darius does not designate some or all of the £40,000, the undesignated amount will be taxable as an ordinary remittance at the usual tax rate in 2026-27. "

2.8.5.2.4 Effective Date

06 April 2025

2.8.5.3 Paragraph 3 "Capital payments made by settlement: section 87 and 89 TCGA 1992 cases".

2.8.5.3.1 Overview

Paragraphs 3 and 4 apply when a non-UK resident settlement makes a capital payment in any tax year 2025-26 to 2027-28 to an individual beneficiary who is not a settlor of the settlement. So much of the payment that could be matched, in accordance with section 87A of the Taxation of Chargeable Gains Act (TCGA) 1992, to gains that accrued to the trustees prior to 2025-26 (on an assumption that there are no gains after 2024-25 that could be matched to the payment) is an amount of qualifying overseas capital of the individual.

2.8.5.3.2 Legislation

Paragraph 3 is headed "Capital payments made by settlement: section 87 and 89 TCGA 1992 cases". It reads as follows.

"3(1)This paragraph **applies for the tax year 2025-26, 2026-27 or 2027-28 in relation to an individual if—**

(a)**chargeable gains are treated as accruing to the individual in that tax year** as a result of **section 87(2) or 89(2)** of TCGA 1992 **in relation to a capital payment from the trustees of a settlement for which the individual is a beneficiary**, and

(b)the settlement has a **section 1(3) amount that is greater than nil for one or more tax years before 2025-26**.

(2) **So much of the payment as is matched with section 1(3) amounts for tax years before 2025-26 is qualifying overseas capital.**

(3)For the **purposes of matching** those amounts, **apply section 87A** of TCGA 1992 **as if—**

(a)the **section 1(3) amount for each tax year after the tax year 2024-25 were nil**, and

(b)the reference in Step 2 in subsection (2) of section 87A of that Act to the total amount of capital payments received by the beneficiaries were to the **total amount of capital payments—**

(i)**received by the individual and other beneficiaries that are qualifying individuals for the relevant tax year**, and

(ii)to which **section 87(2) or 89(2)** of that Act **applies**.

(4)For the purposes of this paragraph**, ignore any reduction of a section 1(3) amount for the tax year 2024-25 or an earlier tax year resulting from the application of section 87 or 89(2**) of TCGA 1992 in the **tax year 2025-26 or any subsequent tax year**.

(5)Sub-paragraph (6) applies where—

(a)an amount of a **capital payment has been matched with a section 1(3) amount under sub-paragraph (2)**, and

(b)that **amount is designated as designated qualifying overseas capital**.

(6)The section 1(3) amount is to be taken to have been reduced (but not below nil) by so much of it as matches with the capital payment for the purposes of any subsequent application of this paragraph.

(7)This paragraph is not to be taken as affecting the application of section 87A of TCGA 1992 for any purpose other than for the purposes of this paragraph and paragraphs 4 and 5 (and no section 1(3) amounts or capital payments are to be taken to have been reduced as a result of the application of this paragraph for any other purpose).

(8)For the purposes of this paragraph—

(a)"**section 1(3) amount**" has the meaning it has in section 87 of TCGA 1992, and

(b)section 97 of TCGA 1992 (supplementary provisions) applies as it applies for the purposes of sections 86A to 96 of that Act.

(9)For the purposes of this paragraph, and paragraphs 4 and 5, an individual is a **qualifying individual in a tax year if** the individual—

(a)is **UK resident** for the purposes of income tax and capital gains tax **for that tax year**, and

(b)was **subject to the remittance basis for at least one tax year** (being a tax year **before the tax year 2025-26**)."

2.8.5.4 Paragraph 4"Capital payments made by settlement: offshore income gains cases."

2.8.5.4.1 Overview

This paragraph deals with capital payments made by settlement: offshore income gains cases.

2.8.5.4.2 Legislation

Paragraph 4 is headed "Capital payments made by settlement: offshore income gains cases". It reads as follows.

"4(1)This paragraph **applies for the tax year 2025-26, 2026-27 or 2027-28 in relation to an individual if—**

(a)**chargeable gains are treated as accruing to the individual** in that tax year as a **result of section 87(2) of TCGA 1992**, as it applies in relation to OIG amounts as a **result of regulation 20 of the OFT Regulations, in relation to a capital payment from the trustees of a settlement for which the individual is a beneficiary**, and

(b)**the settlement has an OIG amount that is greater than nil for one or more tax years before 2025-26.**

(2)**So much of the payment as is matched with OIG** amounts for tax years before 2025-26 **is qualifying overseas capital.**

(3)For the purposes of matching those amounts, **apply section 87A** of TCGA 1992 **as if—**

(a)**the OIG amount for each tax year after the tax year 2024-25 were nil,** and

(b)the reference in Step 2 in subsection (2) of 87A of that Act to the total amount of capital payments received by the beneficiaries were to the **total amount of capital payments—**

(i)**received by the individual and other beneficiaries that are qualifying individuals for the relevant tax year**, and

(ii)to which section 87(2) of that Act applies in relation to OIG amounts (as a result of regulation 20 of the OFT regulations).

(4)For the purposes of this paragraph, ignore any reduction of an OIG amount for the tax year 2024-25 or an earlier tax year resulting from the application of section 87 or 89(2) of TCGA 1992 in the tax year 2025-26 or any subsequent tax year.

(5)Sub-paragraph (6) applies where—

(a)an amount of a capital payment has been matched with an OIG amount under sub-paragraph (2), and

(b)that amount is designated as designated qualifying overseas capital.

(6)The OIG amount is to be taken to have been reduced (but not below nil) by so much of it as matches with the capital payment for the purposes of any subsequent application of this paragraph.

(7)This paragraph is not to be taken as affecting the application of section 87A of TCGA 1992 for any purpose other than for the purposes of this paragraph and paragraphs 3 and 5 (and no OIG amount or capital payments are to be taken to have been reduced as a result of the application of this paragraph for any other purpose).

(8)For the purposes of this paragraph—

(a)the "**OFT Regulations**" means the Offshore Funds (Tax) Regulations 2009, (b)"**OIG amount**" is to be construed in accordance with the OFT Regulations, and

(c) section 97 of TCGA 1992 (supplementary provisions) applies as it applies for the purposes of sections 86A to 96 of that Act".

2.8.5.4.3 Detail

Paragraphs 3 and 4 apply when a non-UK resident settlement makes a capital payment in any tax year 2025-26 to 2027-28 to an individual beneficiary who is not a settlor of the settlement. So much of the payment that could be matched, in accordance with section 87A of the Taxation of Chargeable Gains Act (TCGA) 1992, to gains that accrued to the trustees prior to 2025-26 (on an assumption that there are no gains after 2024-25 that could be matched to the payment) is an amount of qualifying overseas capital of the individual.

2.8.5.4.4 Effective Date

06 April 2025

2.8.5.5 Paragraph 5 "Capital payments made by settlement: Schedule 4C cases

2.8.5.5.1 Overview

Paragraph 5 provides that income treated as the income of an individual because of certain capital payments made during the 2025-26, 2026-27 or 2027-28 tax years is to be treated as qualifying overseas capital, provided that the individual has been subject to the remittance basis for at least one tax year before the 2025-26 tax year.

2.8.5.5.2 Legislation

Paragraph 5 reads as follows.

"Capital payments made by settlement: Schedule 4C cases

5(1)This paragraph applies for the tax year 2025-26, 2026-27 or 2027-28 in relation to an individual if—

(a)chargeable gains are treated as accruing to the individual in that tax year as a result of paragraph 8(1) of Schedule 4C to TCGA 1992 in relation to a capital payment from the trustees of a relevant settlement for which the individual is a beneficiary, and

(b)the section 1(3) amount in the Schedule 4C pool is greater than nil for one or more tax years before 2025-26.

(2)So much of the payment as is matched with section 1(3) amounts in the Schedule 4C pool for tax years before 2025-26 is qualifying overseas capital.

(3)For the purposes of matching those amounts, apply section 87A of TCGA 1992 as if—

(a)the section 1(3) amount in the Schedule 4C pool for each tax year after the tax year 2024-25 were nil, and (b)the reference in Step 2 in subsection (2) of section 87A of that Act to the total amount of capital payments received by the beneficiaries were to the total amount of capital payments—

(i)received by the individual and other beneficiaries that are qualifying individuals for the relevant tax year, and

(ii)to which paragraph 8(1) of Schedule 4C to that Act applies in relation to section 1(3) amounts in the Schedule 4C pool.

(4)For the purposes of this paragraph, ignore any reduction of a section 1(3) amount in the Schedule 4C pool for the tax year 2024-25 or an earlier tax year resulting from the application of paragraph 8(1) of Schedule 4C to TCGA 1992 in the tax year 2025-26 or any subsequent tax year.

(5)Sub-paragraph (6) applies where—

(a)an amount of a capital payment has been matched with a section 1(3) amount in the Schedule 4C pool under sub-paragraph (2), and

(b)that amount is designated as designated qualifying overseas capital.

(6)The section 1(3) amount in the Schedule 4C pool is to be taken to have been reduced (but not below nil) by so much of it as matches with the capital payment for the purposes of any subsequent application of this paragraph.

(7)This paragraph is not to be taken as affecting the application of section 87A of TCGA 1992 for any purpose other than for the purposes of this paragraph and paragraphs 3 and 4 (and no section 1(3) amount in the Schedule 4C pool or capital payments are to be taken to have been reduced as a result of the application of this paragraph for any other purpose).

(8)For the purposes of this paragraph—

(a)"section 1(3) amount in the Schedule 4C pool" and "relevant settlement" are to be construed in accordance with Schedule 4C to TCGA 1992, and

(b)section 97 of TCGA 1992 (supplementary provisions) applies as it applies for the purposes of sections 86A to 96 of that Act.

2.8.5.5.3 Detail

Paragraph 5 provides that income treated as the income of an individual because of certain capital payments made during the 2025-26, 2026-27 or 2027-28 tax years is to be treated as qualifying overseas capital, provided that the individual has been subject to the remittance basis for at least one tax year before the 2025-26 tax year.

HMRC say the following on this in their Manuals.

"RDRM72400 - Temporary repatriation facility: Qualifying overseas capital: Capital payments made by non-resident settlements

Paragraphs 3, 4 and 5 Schedule 10 Finance Act 2025

Section 87, 89(2) and Schedule 4C TCGA 1992 treat UK beneficiaries of non-UK settlements, or a trust that has migrated to the UK, as accruing chargeable gains to the extent that they receive a capital payment that is matched to the trustees' gains (see CG38570+ and CG39100+). Regulation 20 of the Offshore Funds

(Tax) Regulations 2009 (SI 2009/3001) performs a similar function in respect of offshore income gains.

Where chargeable gains are treated as accruing to an individual in tax years 2025-26 to 2027-28 because of a capital payment, the 'qualifying overseas capital' an individual may designate for TRF purposes is, broadly, so much of the payment that, in relation to them, is matched to trustees' gains relating to tax years before 2025-26. (Where a chargeable gain is treated as accruing to the individual in tax years before 2025-26 because of a capital payment from a non-resident settlement, and the remittance basis applied for the year in which the gain was treated as accruing, then any unremitted amount of the capital payment will be qualifying overseas capital – see RDRM72550.

To calculate the amount that is 'qualifying overseas capital' for TRF purposes for an individual, the normal capital gains matching rules are applied (see CG38700P onwards) to the 'section 1(3) amounts', 'OIG amount' or 'Schedule 4C pool' (as the case may be) that remain after any matching in 2024-25 but with the following modifications:

it is to be assumed that the 'section 1(3) amount', 'OIG amount' or 'Schedule 4C pool' (as the case may be) for each tax year after the tax year 2024-25 is nil

any capital payments made to other beneficiaries in a relevant tax year are to be ignored (and the total amount of capital payments made by the settlement is to be reduced accordingly) to the extent they are made to beneficiaries who are ineligible for the TRF because they are either not UK resident in that year or were not subject to the remittance basis for at least one tax year before 2025-26

Any matching that occurs for the purposes of calculating the amount that can be designated for TRF does not affect any matching for other purposes. In effect, this means that a parallel matching exercise is carried out for TRF purposes only.

See RDRM72450 for guidance on capital payments made by non-resident settlements where a 'supplementary charge' applies.

Example

At the end of 2024-25 a non-resident settlement has unmatched 'section 1(3) amounts' as follows:
2019-20 = £30,000
2020-21 = £50,000

A further £60,000 of gains accrue in 2025-26.

Capital payments of £60,000 in 2025-26 and £70,000 in 2026-27 are made to beneficiaries as follows:

To Alan (who qualifies for and makes a TRF designation): £20,000 in 2025-26; £20,000 in 2026-27.

To Bridie (who qualifies for but chooses not to make a TRF designation in 2025-26 as she has personal capital losses, but she does make a designation in 2026-27): £20,000 in 2025-26; £30,000 in 2026-27.

To Craig (who does not qualify for TRF): £20,000 in 2025-26; £20,000 in 2026-27.

In 2025-26:

For TRF purposes only Alan and Bridie are considered; and the 'section 1(3) amount' for 2025-26 is assumed to be nil (instead of £60,000).

Total payments to relevant beneficiaries = £40,000, split on a 50%:50% basis. This is all matched to 2020-21 and is therefore qualifying overseas capital. Both Alan and Bridie can designate up to £20,000 each. Alan designates their full £20,000.

For future TRF purposes the 'section 1(3) amounts' are reduced irrespective of whether a person makes a TRF designation and become:
2019-20 = £30,000
2020-21 = £50,000 - £40,000 = £10,000
2025-26 = £60,000

For non-TRF purposes, Alan, Bridie and Craig each receive a £20,000 capital payment matched against 2025/26 gains, which is chargeable to CGT in the normal way.

As Alan designates £20,000 for TRF purposes, he is given a CGT exemption for the same amount, reducing his amount chargeable to CGT to nil.

For future non-TRF purposes the 'section 1(3) amounts', after all the capital payments have been matched, become:
2019-20 = £30,000
2020-21 = £50,000
2025-26 = £60,000 - £60,000 = nil

In 2026-27:

For TRF purposes only Alan and Bridie are considered; and the 'section 1(3) amount' for 2025-26 is again assumed to be nil (instead of £60,000). There is no 'section 1(3) amount' for 2026-27.

Total payments to relevant beneficiaries = £50,000, split on a 40%:60% basis. £10,000 is first matched to 2020-21 'section 1(3) amounts' and then £30,000 to 2019-20 amounts. These are therefore amounts of qualifying overseas capital. The remaining £10,000 cannot be matched to pre-2025-26 'section 1(3) amounts' and is not qualifying overseas capital.

Of the £40,000 qualifying overseas capital, Alan can designate up to £16,000 and Bridie up to £24,000. They both make their full designations.

For future TRF purposes the 'section 1(3) amounts' become:
2019-20 = £30,000 - £30,000 = nil
2020-21 = £10,000 - £10,000 = nil

2025-26 = £60,000

For non-TRF purposes, £50,000 of the capital payments are first matched against the available 2020-21 gains as follows:

For Alan: (£20,000/£70,000) x £50,000 = £14,286

For Bridie: (£30,000/£70,000) x £50,000 = £21,428

For Craig: (£20,000/£70,000) x £50,000 = £14,286

and the remaining £20,000 of capital payments are then matched against the available 2019-20 gains as follows:
For Alan: (£20,000/£70,000) x £20,000 = £5,714
For Bridie: (£30,000/£70,000) x £20,000 = £8,571
For Craig: (£20,000/£70,000) x £20,000 = £5,714

For Alan, as he designates £16,000 for TRF purposes, a CGT exemption is given for the same amount against the total £20,000 matched payment otherwise chargeable to CGT (see 73600). The remaining £4,000 is charged to CGT in the normal way.

For Bridie as she designates £24,000 for TRF purposes, a similar CGT exemption is given for the same amount against the total £30,000 matched payment otherwise chargeable to CGT. The remaining £6,000 is charge to CGT in the normal way.

For future non-TRF purposes, the 'section 1(3) amounts' after the capital payments have been matched become:
2023-24 = £30,000 - £20,000 = £10,000
2024-25 = £50,000 - £50,000 = nil
2025-26 = nil

2.8.5.5.4 Effective Date

06 April 2025

2.8.5.6 Paragraph 6 Amounts of income treated as qualifying overseas capital

2.8.5.6.1 Overview

Paragraph 6 deals with what amounts

2.8.5.6.2 Legislation

Paragraph 6 reads as follows.

"Amounts of income treated as qualifying overseas capital
6(1) This paragraph applies—
(a)where an individual is treated as having an amount of income as a result of section 643A of ITTOIA 2005 (benefits paid out of protected foreign-source income or transitional trust income) for any of the tax years 2025-26, 2026-27 or 2027-28,
(b)where an individual would have been treated as having an amount of income as a result of any other provision of Chapter 5 of Part 5 of ITTOIA

2005 (settlements: amounts treated as income of settlor or family) in the tax year 2024-25 or an earlier tax year but was not only as a result of the application of section 648(3) of that Act (relevant foreign income treated as arising under settlement only if and when remitted), or

(c)where—

(i)an individual is treated as having an amount of income for any of the tax years 2025-26, 2026-27 or 2027-28 as a result of section 732 of ITA 2007 (individuals receiving a benefit as a result of relevant transactions),

(ii)under section 735A of that Act (if it applied also for this purpose) that amount would be matched with relevant income that arose in the tax year 2024-25 or an earlier tax year, and

(iii)that amount would have been treated as relevant foreign income of the individual if it had been treated as accruing in the tax year 2024-25 and the individual had been subject to the remittance basis for that tax year.

(2) An amount of income falling within paragraph (a), (b) or (c) of sub-paragraph (1) is to be treated as an amount of qualifying overseas capital of the individual.

(3) An amount of income treated as qualifying overseas capital falling within sub-paragraph (1)(a) or (c) may only be designated in a return for the tax year in which the income was treated as arising to the individual.

(4) For the purposes of this paragraph "relevant foreign income" has the meaning it has in the Income Tax Acts."

2.8.5.6.3 Detail

HMRC say the following on this in their Manuals.

"**RDRM72100 - Temporary repatriation facility: Qualifying overseas capital: Overview**

Individuals do not have to remit their pre-6 April 2025 income and gains during the temporary repatriation facility (TRF) period in order to benefit from the low tax rate, although they can if they choose to. Instead, individuals designate amounts on which they pay the TRF charge, which can then be remitted in the future without incurring any further tax charges.

In order to be designated, amounts must meet the definition of 'qualifying overseas capital'.

There are, broadly, six types of qualifying overseas capital:

First are amounts that arose in the tax year 2024-25 or an earlier tax year as personal foreign income or gains when the individual was subject to the remittance basis – see <u>RDRM72200</u> for the relevant criteria. This includes amounts that have either not been remitted to the UK or are remitted during the TRF period.

Secondly, former remittance basis users may have amounts overseas that they are uncertain as to the source. These amounts can also be qualifying overseas capital – see RDRM72300.

Third are capital payments received in tax years 2025-26 to 2027-28 matched to section 1(3) TCGA 1992 amounts that arose within an offshore structure (or migrated settlement) prior to 6 April 2025 see RDRM72400 for the relevant criteria.

Fourth are amounts treated as being the individual's income under the settlements legislation because of benefits received from a non-resident trust in any of the tax years 2025-26 to 2027-28 that is matched with pre-6 April 2025 protected foreign source income or transitional trust income of a non-resident trust– see RDRM72500 for the relevant criteria.

Fifth are amounts that would have been treated as being the individual's income in tax years before 2025-26 because of them being the settlor of a settlement but were not because it was treated as arising only when remitted – see RDRM72500 for the relevant criteria.

Sixth are amounts treated as being the individual's income in any of the tax years 2025-26 to 2027-28 because of receiving a benefit from a non-resident trust that is assessable under the transfer of asset abroad legislation where the benefit is matched with relevant foreign income arising before 6 April 2025 – see RDRM72550.

For details of how to designate qualifying overseas capital see RDRM73000 onwards."

They also say as follows.

"**RDRM72500 - Temporary repatriation facility: Qualifying overseas capital: Settlement income treated as qualifying overseas capital**

The settlements legislation

The settlements legislation is a wide-ranging anti-avoidance provision aimed at preventing an individual obtaining a tax advantage by making arrangements to divert their income to another person whilst retaining an interest in the property or income. The legislation works to deem the income to belong to the settlor, and they will be liable for the income tax as it arises in the same way that they would be had they actually received the income.

From 2018-19 benefits and onward gift charges were introduced into the settlements legislation. If the settlor or a close member of their family receives a benefit, either directly or routed through another individual, that can be matched with 'Available Protected Income' (API) then an income tax charge will arise on the settlor or the close family member, depending on the circumstances.

Detailed guidance can be found in the Trust, Settlements and Estates Manual at TSEM4000 onwards.

Qualifying overseas capital

Paragraph 6(1)(a) and (b) Schedule 10 Finance Act 2025

In relation to the settlements legislation, income can be treated as qualifying overseas capital for the purposes of the temporary repatriation facility (TRF) in two circumstances.

Firstly, where an individual is treated as having an amount of income under section 643A ITTOIA 2005 (benefits paid out of protected foreign-source income or transitional trust income). Section 643A applies a tax charge on individuals in relation to benefits paid to the settlor or a close member of the settlor's family and onward gifts. Any amount treated as qualifying overseas capital can only be designated for the year in which it is treated as arising to the individual.

Secondly, where an individual would have been treated as having an amount of income under any of the other provision of Chapter 5 part 5 of ITTOIA 2005 in the tax year 2024-25 or earlier (amounts treated as income of settlor or family), but was not charged to tax on that income because of section 648(3) ITTOIA 2005 (relevant foreign income treated as arising under settlement only if and when remitted).

Example 1

Mark is a former remittance basis user and created the MR Family Trust whilst he was resident and domiciled in France in 2001 for the benefit of himself and his family. He moved to the UK in 2002 and became deemed domiciled under condition B from 2017-18. The trust generates income of £150,000 per year outside of the UK. From 2008-09 to 2016-17 the income is Transitional Trust Income (TTI) and from 2017-18 to 2024-25 the income is Protected Foreign Source Income (PFSI) and forms a pool of 'Available Protected Income' within the settlement.

2008-09 to 2016-17 (TTI total): £1,350,000
2017-18 to 2024-25 (PFSI total): £1,200,000
Total API: £2,550,000

In tax year 2025-26 the trustees purchase an £800,000 property for Mark and transfer ownership to him. This is treated as an amount of income chargeable on him under section 643A because it forms his 'untaxed benefits total' and there is sufficient API to match it against.

Mark is able to designate the £800,000 benefit that he received in his 2025-26 tax return and benefit from the low TRF rate. He must designate it in his 2025-26 tax return; he cannot designate it in a later year of the TRF period, because it is treated as arising to Mark in 2025-26. In 2027-28 Mark asks for £600,000 to undertake some renovations of the property. The trustees agree to pay this benefit to him. It is treated as an amount of income chargeable on him under section 643A, because it forms his 'untaxed benefits total' and there is sufficient API to match it against.

Mark is able to designate the £600,000 benefit that he received in his 2027-28 tax return and benefit from the low TRF rate. He must designate it in his 2027-28 tax return; he cannot designate it in an earlier year in anticipation of receiving the benefit, because it is treated as arising to Mark in 2027-28.A further distribution is made to Mark in 2030-31 of £500,000. This is treated as an amount of income chargeable on him under section 643A because it forms his 'untaxed benefits total' and there is sufficient API to match it against. The TRF period has ended by this date and Mark is therefore unable to designate any amount to qualify for the reduced TRF rates. Mark will pay tax on this amount at the usual rates.

Example 2

Pamela created a Jersey trust known as the PD Family Trust in 1999 whilst resident and domiciled in Austria for the benefit of her, her family and a number of charities that she wanted to support. The trust held investments in Austrian companies which generated income of £50,000 per year from 2000. Pamela moved to the UK in 2000 and was subject to the remittance basis for all tax years she was UK resident.

Pamela would have paid tax on the income arising to the trustees under section 624 ITTOIA 2005 because she was the settlor of the 'settlement' and retained an interest because she was able to benefit from the trust. However, because she was a remittance basis user any relevant foreign income arising under the settlement is not deemed to arise until the year it is remitted to the UK by virtue of section 648(3).

In 2007 the trust re-organised and moved all investments to UK companies. Pamela pays UK income tax on all of the income arising to the trustees under section 624 on the arising basis on that now UK source income.

In 2025-26 the trustees make a distribution of £200,000 to Pamela from the relevant foreign income that arose prior to the re-organisation of assets in 2007. Pamela is able to designate this amount and pay tax at the low TRF rate because she would have been taxable on this amount in the years that it was paid to the trustees, had it not been for section 648(3)."

2.8.5.6.4 Effective Date

06 April 2025

2.8.5.7 Paragraph 7

2.8.5.7.1 Overview

Paragraph 7 provides that the designation of qualifying overseas capital will be chargeable to TRF in the tax year that the return in which the designation is made relates to.

The paragraph also provides that, although the TRF is a charge on an amount of capital, the income tax framework will be used to administer the TRF charge.

2.8.5.7.2 Legislation

Paragraph 7 reads as follows.

> **"Deemed income under section 732 of ITA 2007 where pre-2025 gains available for matching**
>
> 7(1)Sub-paragraph (2) applies where—
>
> (a)an individual is treated as having an amount of income for any of the tax years 2025-26, 2026-27 or 2027-28 as a result of section 732 of ITA 2007 (individuals receiving a benefit as a result of relevant transactions),
>
> (b)the amount of income does not fall within paragraph 6(1)(c), and
>
> (c)the benefit by reference to which that income is treated as arising would, if it were not chargeable to income tax, be an amount of qualifying overseas capital of the individual by virtue of paragraph 3 or 5 (capital payments).
>
> (2)The amount is to be treated as an amount of qualifying overseas capital of the individual.
>
> (3)The amount may only be designated in a return for the tax year in which the income was treated as arising to the individual.

2.8.5.7.3 Detail

HMRC say the following in their Manuals about this paragraph.

> **"RDRM72600 - Temporary repatriation facility: Qualifying overseas capital: Treatment of post-2024-25 income where pre-6 April 2025 gains available for matching**
>
> Paragraph 7 Schedule 10 Finance Act 2025
>
> When matching capital distributions or other benefits it is usual for such amounts to be matched with all the relevant income of the overseas entity before such benefits are matched with capital gains. For details of how capital payments can be subject to Capital Gains Tax see CG38570C.
>
> For temporary repatriation facility (TRF) purposes, this rule is ignored where:
>
> - an individual is treated as having an amount of income for any of the tax years 2025-26, 2026-27 or 2027-28 as a result of section 732 ITA 2007 (individuals receiving a benefit as a result of relevant transactions)
> - the income does not fall within paragraph 6(1)(c) (benefits matched with pre-6 April 2025 relevant foreign income)
> - the benefit by reference to which that income is treated as arising would, if it were not chargeable to income tax, be an amount of qualifying overseas capital of the individual by virtue of paragraph 3 or 5 (capital payments)
>
> In such cases the amount is treated as an amount of qualifying overseas capital and can be designated by the beneficiary.
>
> If the deemed income is qualifying overseas capital because of paragraph 7, the transfer of assets abroad (ToAA) provisions have effect as though the benefit by reference to which the deemed income was treated as arising had never been

provided. So, in applying section 733(1) ITA 2007 to any individual for subsequent years:

- the benefit will not be taken into account at step 1
- no deduction in respect of the deemed income will be made at Step 2 or Step 5
- the total untaxed benefits will not be reduced in respect of that benefit by virtue of section 734 (previous capital gains charge)"

For further details of the step calculation see INTM601740.

Example

Jemima is the beneficiary of a non-resident trust which was established by a non-UK resident in Jersey, the J Trust. Jemima has been resident in the UK since 2015-16 and for all years until 2024-25 has been a remittance basis user.

The J Trust has made a number of offshore investments which have resulted in the following income and gains arising:

Year	Foreign income (£)	Foreign gains (£)
2017-18	10,000	0
2020-21	10,000	0
2022-23	10,000	20,000
2023-24	10,000	30,000
2024-25	10,000	0
2025-26	50,000	0

In 2025-26 the trustees make a capital distribution to Jemima of £90,000. Jemima decides that she wants to designate as much of the capital distribution as she can under the TRF.

Note: this example is to demonstrate the impact on the relevant foreign income of the trust. For a more detailed calculation of the trust gains under the TRF see RDRM72400.

Under the normal matching rules at section 735A ITA 2007 the capital distribution will be matched as follows:

Year	Foreign income (£)
2017-18	10,000
2020-21	10,000
2022-23	10,000
2023-24	10,000
2024-25	10,000
2025-26	40,000

Leaving unmatched income of £10,000.

However, as part of the capital distribution matched under section 735A ITA 2007 is matched with £40,000 of income that arose after 2024-25 it does not come within paragraph 6(1)(c) and therefore cannot under this paragraph be qualifying overseas capital within the TRF. However, paragraph 7(1)(c) will apply and for the purposes of the TRF Jemima is able see if there are any pre-6 April 2025 gains that would be available for matching. As there are pre-6 April 2025 gains totalling £50,000 there are sufficient gains available and so Jemima can treat the £40,000 as qualifying overseas capital by virtue of the gains.

Jemima is therefore able to designate the full £90,000 under the TRF.

When applying the matching rules at section 733(1) ITA 2007 in subsequent years the amount of benefit taken into account will be £50,000 (this is because the benefit treated as matched with gains is ignored for the purpose of the TRF) and the amount of deemed income at step 2 and step 5 will be £50,000 (because the deemed income treated as matched with gains is not deducted for the purpose of the TRF).

2.8.5.7.4 Effective Date

06 April 2025

2.8.6 Part 2: Exemptions etc for designated qualifying overseas capital

2.8.6.1 Paragraph 8 Designated qualifying overseas capital not liable to IT on remittance

2.8.6.1.1 Overview

Paragraph 8 provides that designated qualifying overseas capital will not be taxed to income tax on remittance to the UK.

2.8.6.1.2 Legislation

Paragraph 8 is headed "Designation of qualifying overseas capital". It reads as follows.

"8(1)A designation **election for a tax year** must be made before the end of the **period of 12 months beginning with 31 January after the end of that tax year**.

(2) The **designation must**—

(a)**set out the total amount designated**, and

(b)**identify which** (if any) of the **amounts** designated have been remitted in the tax year to which the return relates.

(3) Where an amount of relevant foreign tax has been paid, or is payable, in respect of an amount of qualifying overseas capital, only so much of the amount as remains after deducting the amount of relevant foreign tax paid, or payable, may be designated.

(4) For the purposes of this paragraph, **relevant foreign tax** means a tax imposed by the law of a territory outside the United Kingdom **that corresponds to—**

(a)income tax, or

(b)capital gains tax.

(5) An **individual may designate an amount where it has not yet been determined**[79]**—**

(a)**whether** the amount **is qualifying overseas capital**, or

(b)**whether**, or to what extent, **relevant foreign tax is, or was, payable in respect of the amount.**

(6) An **amount designated—**

(a)that is **determined to not be qualifying overseas capital**, or

(b)that **should not have been designated as a result of sub-paragraph (3)** [deduction of foreign tax]**,** is to be nevertheless treated as designated qualifying overs**eas** capital, other than for the purpose of Part 2 of this Schedule (exemptions etc).

(7) **Where an amount is designated**, it is **treated as designated qualifying overseas capital from the beginning of the tax year** to which the return in which it is designated relates.

(8) **An individual who makes a designation election must keep a record of each amount designated**."

2.8.6.1.3 Detail

This paragraph as noted above deals with the designation of qualifying overseas capital. This is defined in paragraph 6 discussed above. TRF treatment needs in effect to be claimed in a relevant return within the appropriate period.

It deals with a number of matters including the following.

(i.) Time Limit

This is dealt with by subparagraph 8(1).

This reads as follows.

> "A designation election for a tax year must be made before the end of the period of 12 months beginning with 31 January after the end of that tax year."
>
> **Example**
>
> Sade Tingdion has qualifying overseas capital in respect of year AB for which she wants TRF treatment.

[79] See https://www.gov.uk/hmrc-internal-manuals/residence-domicile-and-remittance-basis/rdrm72300

She therefore needs to make a designation election which may only be made in a return. [80]A designation election may only be made in a return if, for the tax year to which the return relates. [81]

Sade needs to make a return for tax year AB in time. She needs to designate the relevant qualifying overseas capital in respect of year AB for which she wants TRF treatment in that return. [82]

The designation needs to be made before the end of the period of 12 months beginning with 31 January after the end of that tax year.

The tax year here is AB which ends on 5 April B.

The following 31 January will be year C. It is 31 January year C. 12 months after 31 January year C is 31 January year D.

Sade therefore needs to make the designation before 31 January year D.

(ii.) *Minimum content*

By subsection (2):

"The **designation must**—

(a)**set out the total amount designated**, and

(b)**identify which** (if any) of the **amounts** designated have been remitted in the tax year to which the return relates."

It should also be noted that by sub paragraph (4):

"For the purposes of this paragraph, **relevant foreign tax** means a tax imposed by the law of a territory outside the United Kingdom **that corresponds to—**

(a)income tax, or

(b)capital gains tax."

This is relevant to subparagraph 3 and I would include such figures in the return where possible.

---

[80] Paragraph 1 (7) "A **designation election may only be made in a return if, for the tax year to which the return relates, the individual is UK resident** for the purposes of income tax and capital gains tax (see Schedule 45 to FA 2013)".

By paragraph 1 (11) (b) "(b) "**return**" means a return under **section 8 of TMA 1970** (personal return for income tax and capital gains tax) ..."

[81] Paragraph (7)A **designation election may only be made in a return if, for the tax year to which the return relates, the individual is UK resident** for the purposes of income tax and capital gains tax (see Schedule 45 to FA 2013).

[82] Which can include amendment. See Paragraph 1 (11) (c) "(c)references to an **election being included in a return include** an election being so included as a result of an **amendment** of the return."

Where figures are undetermined a designation can still be made see paragraph 8(5). It is for consideration whether a white box disclosure should be made in such cases. This will essentially depend on the particular circumstances.

(iii.) *Records*

By subparagraph 8 (8):

> **"An individual who makes a designation election must keep a record of each amount designated."**

It is important to ensure that this is done. This will usually be done in practice by the agent. It is for consideration by the agent how long these records should be kept for.

HMRC say the following on this in their Manuals.

> **"RDRM73340 - Temporary repatriation facility: Designating qualifying overseas capital: Designation process: Foreign tax credits**
>
> Paragraph 8(3) and (4) Schedule 10 Finance Act 2025
>
> Where an individual has paid foreign tax on income or capital gains that are also taxable in the UK, they may be able to claim relief for the foreign tax paid (see INTM150000 onwards for further guidance on foreign tax credit relief).
>
> Under the temporary repatriation facility (TRF), the TRF charge is payable on designations of amounts of qualifying overseas capital. These amounts of designated qualifying overseas capital must be net of any foreign tax that has been paid or is payable. As such, foreign tax credit relief is not available against any qualifying overseas capital designated under the TRF.
>
> Where an individual chooses to designate an amount on which foreign tax has already been paid, the TRF rate will only apply to the net amount after foreign tax has been deducted. No further credit can be claimed against the TRF rate of 12% for 2025-26 and 2026-27 or 15% in the 2027-28 tax year.
>
> It will only be possible for an individual to claim a full credit for foreign tax paid overseas if they do not elect to designate the net amount under the TRF and instead remit the funds as an ordinary remittance.
>
> > **Example**
> >
> > Lorenzo is UK resident and a former remittance basis user. He arrived in the UK for the first time on 6 April 2019. On 6 April 2020 he sold his house in Rome. The house had originally cost £50,000 in 2011 but was sold for £350,000, making a gain of £300,000.
> >
> > Lorenzo was charged a withholding tax at 30% on this gain in Italy and paid £90,000 to the Italian tax authorities, leaving £260,000 (£50,000 clean capital and £210,000 net gain) which was paid into a newly opened Italian bank account.

Under the Italy-UK Double Tax Agreement (DTA), as the Italian tax authorities have taxed this gain, a credit can be given in the UK on the Italian tax paid.

Assuming a tax rate of 28% and no other allowances, Lorenzo would have paid tax of £84,000 in the UK on the £300,000 gain if he was taxed on the arising basis. Since he had already paid £90,000 tax in Italy, the tax credit would be restricted to the lower of the UK or Italian tax paid. This means Lorenzo would have been able to claim a foreign tax credit of £84,000 and no additional UK tax would be due.

However, Lorenzo is instead subject to the remittance basis in the 2020-21 tax year, and so does not pay tax on this gain as it arises. He does not make any remittances from this account and by 6 April 2025, the account still contains a balance of £260,000.

Lorenzo decides to remit the £260,000 to the UK in 2025-26. He has three options.

Option 1: He can make no designation and claim a tax credit against the capital gains tax arising on the gross remittance. Assuming a rate of 28% and no other allowances, he would declare a £300,000 gain in his tax return for 2025-26 along with a UK tax liability of £84,000, which is reduced to nil by payment of the Italian tax.

Option 2: He can make a designation under the TRF in the amount of £210,000, because this is the amount of qualifying overseas capital net of foreign tax paid. This would need to be designated in his 2025-26 tax return and he would pay the TRF charge at 12% on this amount, totalling £25,200. He would not be able to claim a further tax credit against this liability because the tax is on a capital amount and not the full gain on remittance (he has effectively claimed the tax credit relief by way of deduction since the TRF charge is calculated on the net amount).

Option 3: He can make a partial designation of some of the gain. The amount designated would be taxed at 12% against which he will not be able to claim an additional tax credit, as per option 2 above. The remaining element of the gain would be grossed up with a proportional tax credit claimed as per option 1. As a result of the mixed fund ordering rules (see RDRM75000 onwards), Lorenzo will be deemed to have remitted the designated qualifying overseas capital before the undesignated net gain."

2.8.6.1.4 Effective Date

06 April 2025

2.8.6.2 Paragraph 9 "Payment of the TRF charge through the income tax system"

2.8.6.2.1 Overview

Paragraph 9 deals with "Payment of the TRF charge through the income tax system".

2.8.6.2.2 Legislation

Paragraph 9 reads as follows.

"Payment of the TRF charge through the income tax system

9(1)An amount of designated qualifying overseas capital is chargeable to the TRF charge for the tax year to which the return in which it is designated relates.

(2)Amounts of TRF charge are to be charged as if they were amounts of income tax.

(3)Section 23 of ITA 2007 (calculation of income tax liability) applies in relation to a person liable to the TRF charge as if paragraph 1(8) were included in the lists of provisions in section 30(1) of that Act (amounts of tax added at Step 7).

(4)For the purposes of the collection and management of the TRF charge, all other enactments applying generally to income tax apply to the TRF charge.

(5)Those enactments include—

(a)those relating to returns of information and the supply of accounts, statements and reports,

(b)those relating to the assessing, collecting and receiving of income tax,

(c)those conferring or regulating a right of appeal, and

(d)those concerning administration, penalties, interest on unpaid tax and priority of tax in cases of insolvency under the law of any part of the United Kingdom.

(6)But section 59A of TMA 1970 (payments on account of income tax) does not apply in relation to amounts of TRF charge.

(7)For the purposes of section 12B of TMA 1970 (as applied as a result of sub-paragraph (4)), the records required to be kept as a result of paragraph 8(8) are to be regarded as records that must be kept for the purposes of enabling an individual to make and deliver a correct and complete return."

2.8.6.2.3 Detail

Paragraph 8 provides that the TRF charge is to be treated as "if they were amounts of income tax." (see paragraph 9 (2)).

The rest of the paragraph is essentially consequential on this.

HMRC say the following in their Manuals.

"RDRM71000 - Temporary repatriation facility: Introduction

The Finance Act 2025 introduced a new temporary repatriation facility (TRF) as part of a wider set of measures removing the concept of domicile as a relevant connecting factor in the tax system.

From 6 April 2025 it is no longer possible to use the remittance basis of taxation. However, former remittance basis users may have amounts of pre-6 April 2025 foreign income and gains which arose during a period in which they were subject to the remittance basis, which are capable of being remitted and taxed in the future.

The TRF is aimed at encouraging former remittance basis users to remit those pre-6 April 2025 foreign income and gains, and a low tax rate will be available for individuals that choose to use the TRF. The TRF is a temporary measure, available for a fixed period of 3 years: the 2025-26, 2026-27 and 2027-28 tax years.

To use the TRF individuals must designate amounts on which they pay the TRF charge. The amount designated can be pre-6 April 2025 foreign income and gains or amounts held overseas where they are uncertain as to the source.

Once designated, amounts are treated as an amount of capital on which the TRF charge is paid. If the amount is subject to foreign tax it is treated as an amount of net capital. No credit for foreign tax paid is available against a TRF charge – see RDRM73330.

Individuals do not have to remit the designated amount during the TRF period in order to benefit from the low tax rate, although they can if they choose to.

In order to be designated, the amount must meet the definition of 'qualifying overseas capital' – this is explained at RDRM72000 onwards. Individuals must meet specific eligibility criteria to be able to use the TRF – see RDRM73200.

The designation process is explained at RDRM73000 onwards, along with guidance on future remittances of designated qualifying overseas capital. Where an individual designates amounts in a mixed fund, the designated qualifying overseas capital will be available for remittance in priority to other income and capital in the fund – RDRM75000 onwards explains this.

Designations are not limited to money held overseas. For example, pre-6 April 2025 foreign income, gains and amounts of uncertain origin that have been used to purchase overseas property could be designated, as could amounts that have been invested in a UK company on which business investment relief (BIR) has been claimed. For details on the scope of designation, see RDRM74000 onwards."

They also say:

"RDRM73400 - Temporary repatriation facility: Designating qualifying overseas capital: TRF charge

Overview

The temporary repatriation facility (TRF) charge is a charge on an amount of designated qualifying overseas capital.

See RDRM72100 onwards for a definition of 'qualifying overseas capital' and RDRM73300 onwards for guidance on the designation process.

The TRF charge is a charge on capital. It is not a tax on income or capital gains. While the mechanism for collection is through HMRC's Income Tax system, this does not affect the character of the charge.

Where a Double Taxation Convention applies to taxes on income and capital gains, but not to taxes on capital, the TRF charge will not be within the scope of the Convention.

As the TRF charge is not a payment of Income Tax or Capital Gains Tax, where a taxpayer has made Gift Aid donations in a tax year, the TRF charge cannot be used to frank Gift Aid claimed by the charity receiving the donation. Donors who have not been charged sufficient tax to cover the Income Tax deducted from their Gift Aid donations are responsible for paying any difference.

Payment of the TRF charge will also not impact an individual's payments on account due for the following tax year.

Otherwise, legislation that applies generally to Income Tax applies to the TRF charge, because amounts of TRF charge are charged in the same way as if they were amounts of Income Tax, which includes:

- completion of tax returns
- record keeping
- rights of appeal
- penalties and interest on unpaid tax

Amount of charge

The amount of the TRF charge is:

12% of the amount of qualifying overseas capital designated in a return for the tax year 2025-26 or 2026-27

15% of the amount of qualifying overseas capital designated in a return for the tax year 2027-28

Payment of charge

If an individual decides to pay the TRF charge using pre-6 April 2025 foreign income or gains from an overseas bank account, they will need to ensure that the amount used to the pay the charge has been designated, otherwise the transfer to the UK to make the payment will be an ordinary remittance, taxed at the usual tax rates.

Former remittance basis users who paid the remittance basis charge (RBC) may be familiar with an exemption at section 809V ITA 2007, which treats money brought to the UK to pay the remittance basis charge as not remitted if direct payment was made to HMRC. There is no exemption in the TRF legislation that would prevent money paid to HMRC to pay the TRF charge being remitted and taxed at the usual tax rates.

Where a former remittance basis user has paid the RBC, this will have no impact on their designation under the TRF. RBCs previously paid cannot be offset against an amount of TRF charge.

Example

Nida is a UK resident and former remittance basis user. She has a property in Australia that she purchased with £50,000 of foreign gains from 2021-22. She plans to sell it in a few years' time and remit the proceeds to the UK. In order to take advantage of the low TRF rate she designates the £50,000 in her 2025-26 tax return.

The amount of the TRF charge due and payable is £6,000 (12% of £50,000). On 31 January 2027 she pays the £6,000 directly to HMRC from an overseas bank account which contains £30,000 of foreign income from 2022-23. The payment of £6,000 would be an ordinary remittance of foreign income taxed at the usual Income Tax rate for 2026-27.

However, Nida decides instead to designate all the foreign income from 2022-23 in her overseas bank account in her 2026-27 tax return, so that she can pay her 2025-26 and 2026-27 TRF charges from it without any Income Tax charges arising when she makes payments to HMRC. When Nida designates the foreign income in 2026-27 a TRF charge of £3,600 (12% of £30,000) will be due. If she pays both TRF charges from her overseas bank account she will have paid a total of £9,600 to HMRC, and the remaining £20,400 can be remitted without a further tax charge. The proceeds from her Australian property that derive from the foreign gains from 2021-22 can also be remitted without a further tax charge. Alternatively, Nida could pay any TRF charge using clean capital."

2.8.6.2.4 Effective Date

06 April 2025

2.8.6.3 Paragraph 10 Overview Individual's gains under section 87(2) or paragraph 8 Schedule 4C

2.8.6.3.1 Overview

Broadly paragraph 10 provides chargeable gains treated as accruing to an individual under section 87(2) or paragraph 8(1) of Schedule 4C , where there is capital payment from a non-UK resident settlement the amount of that payment if it contains designated qualifying overseas capital, is to be reduced by the amount of the payment designated.

2.8.6.3.2 Legislation

Paragraph 10 reads as follows.

"Income tax exemptions and relief

10(1)No liability to income tax arises on the remittance of an amount of designated qualifying overseas capital.

(2) No liability to income tax arises on an amount of income treated as qualifying overseas capital under paragraph 6 if the amount is designated.

(3) But such an amount is to be treated for the purposes of section 97(1) of TCGA 1992 (capital payments not to include amounts chargeable to income tax) as if it were chargeable to income tax.

(4) **No liability to income tax arises on an amount of income treated as qualifying overseas capital under paragraph 7 if the amount is designated.**

(5) Accordingly, the amount—

(a)will be a capital payment for the purposes of sections 86A to 96 of, and Schedule 4C to, TCGA 1992 (see section 97(1) of that Act), and

(b)will, as a result of paragraph 3 or 5 (or both), be qualifying overseas capital.

(6) Any such qualifying overseas capital is to be treated as having been designated by the individual (under that paragraph or those paragraphs), but no liability to the TRF charge is to arise as a result of that deemed designation.

(7) Sub-paragraph (8) applies where—

(a)offshore income gains, within the meaning of the Offshore Funds (Tax) Regulations 2009, are treated as accruing to an individual in a tax year under section 87(2) of TCGA 1992 (as applied by regulation 20 of those regulations) as a result of a capital payment made to an individual, and

(b)an amount of that capital payment is qualifying overseas capital that has been designated by the individual.

(8) The offshore income gains are to be reduced by the amount of that designated qualifying overseas capital.

(9) This paragraph has effect for the tax year 2025-26 and subsequent tax years.

2.8.6.3.3 Detail

Broadly, no IT or CGT is to arise in respect of the designated amounts. Paragraph 10(4) deals with IT. As no IT arises a CGT charge could but that it is treated as having been designated for CGT. Sub-paragraphs 10(1), (2), (5) and (6), provide that any chargeable gains treated as accruing to an individual under section 87(2) or paragraph 8(1) of Schedule 4C TCGA, because of a capital payment from a non-UK resident settlement that contains designated qualifying overseas capital, are to be reduced by the amount of the payment which has been designated.

Sub-paragraphs 10(3), (4), (7) and (8) provide that these gains will not be subject to an additional supplementary charge under section 91 of, or paragraph 13 of Schedule 4C to, TCGA 1992."

This is a complex area on which specialist advice will often be needed.

HMRC say the following on this in their Manuals.

"Exemptions from further Income Tax charges

Paragraphs 10 and 11 Schedule 10 Finance Act 2025

When an amount of designated qualifying overseas capital is remitted on or after 6 April 2025, the amount is exempt from any Income Tax charges on that remittance.

Paragraph 10 also provides Income Tax relief for amounts matched to gains under paragraph 4 (offshore income gains) as these would otherwise be charged to Income Tax.

Paragraph 11 applies where an amount of income is treated as arising to an individual under section 732 ITA 2007 (transfer of assets abroad – benefits charge) that is exempt from a charge to Income Tax. It amends the step calculation at section 733(1) ITA 2007 in respect of these exempt amounts."

2.8.6.3.4 Effective Date

06 April 2025

2.8.7 Part 3: Effect of designation on when amounts remitted etc

2.8.7.1 Paragraph 11 Income tax exemptions: application of transfer of assets abroad rules in future years

2.8.7.1.1 Overview

Paragraph 11 Income tax exemptions: application of transfer of assets abroad rules in future years. Broadly, designated qualifying overseas capital will not be taxed.

Paragraph 11 reads as follows.

"Income tax exemptions: application of transfer of assets abroad rules in future years

11(1)This paragraph applies where an amount of income that is treated as arising to an individual under section 732 of ITA 2007 ("**the deemed income**") is **exempt from income tax by virtue of paragraph 10**.

(2)If the deemed income is qualifying overseas capital by virtue of paragraph 6(1)(c), Chapter 2 of Part 13 of ITA 2007 has effect as though the deemed income had been charged to tax under section 731 of that Act.

(3)Accordingly—

(a)in the application of section 733(1) of ITA 2007 to the individual for subsequent tax years, the amount of the deemed income will be deducted at Step 2 and at paragraph (a) of Step 5, and

(b)in the application of section 733(1) of ITA 2007 to any other individual for subsequent tax years, the amount of the deemed income will be deducted at paragraph (b) of Step 5.

(4)If the deemed income is qualifying overseas capital by virtue of paragraph 7, Chapter 2 of Part 13 of ITA 2007 has effect as though the benefit by reference to which the deemed income was treated as arising had never been provided.

(5) Accordingly, in the application of section 733(1) of ITA 2007 to any individual for subsequent tax years—

(a)that benefit will not be taken into account at Step 1,

(b)no deduction in respect of the deemed income will be made at Step 2 or Step 5, and

(c)the total untaxed benefits will not be reduced in respect of that benefit by virtue of section 734 (previous capital gains charge)."

2.8.7.1.2 Detail

As noted above broadly, designated qualifying overseas capital will not be taxed. The rest of the paragraph sets out the detail of such calculations.
HMRC say in this context as noted above the following.

"Exemptions from further Income Tax charges

Paragraphs 10 and 11 Schedule 10 Finance Act 2025

When an amount of designated qualifying overseas capital is remitted on or after 6 April 2025, the amount is exempt from any Income Tax charges on that remittance.

Paragraph 10 also provides Income Tax relief for amounts matched to gains under paragraph 4 (offshore income gains) as these would otherwise be charged to Income Tax.

Paragraph 11 applies where an amount of income is treated as arising to an individual under section 732 ITA 2007 (transfer of assets abroad – benefits charge) that is exempt from a charge to Income Tax. It amends the step calculation at section 733(1) ITA 2007 in respect of these exempt amounts"

2.8.7.1.3 Effective Date

06 April 2025

2.8.7.2 Paragraph 12 Capital gains tax: main exemption

2.8.7.2.1 Overview

This provides an exemption from CGT but not from the TRF charge.

2.8.7.2.2 Legislation

Paragraph 12 reads as follows.

"Capital gains tax: main exemption

12(1) No gain is treated as accruing under paragraph 1(2) of Schedule 1 to TCGA 1992 on the remittance of an amount of designated qualifying overseas capital.

(2) This paragraph has effect for the tax year 2025-26 and subsequent tax years."

2.8.7.2.3 Detail

This is an exemption from CGT in respect of the remittance of designated qualifying overseas capital which might otherwise arise. This is not an exemption from the TRF charge.

Sub-paragraph 12(2) introduces an additional step A1 before step 1 of section 809Q (3). The additional step A1 requires that "TRF capital" is identified and funds which meet this description are treated as transferred in priority to any other amounts that may be within a mixed fund.

Sub-paragraph 12(3) introduces a new subsection (c) within section 809Q (6). This clarifies that a fund which includes both TRF capital and amounts that are not TRF capital will meet the definition of a being a mixed fund.

Sub-paragraph 12(4) introduces a new subsection 809Q (9). This confirms that the term "TRF Capital" should be understood in sections 809Q and 809R to 809RA of ITA 2007 in the same way it is defined in the present schedule, Schedule 10 to the Finance Act 2025.

Sub-paragraph 12(5) defines "TRF capital" throughout ITA 2007.

HMRC say on this in their Manuals as follows.

> **"... Capital Gains Tax main exemption** [83]
>
> Paragraph 12 Schedule 10 Finance Act 2025
>
> When an amount of designated qualifying overseas capital is remitted on or after 6 April 2025, the amount is exempt from any Capital Gains Tax charges on that remittance..."

2.8.7.2.4 Effective Date

06 April 2025

2.8.7.3 Paragraph 13 – Amendment of section 809R ITA

2.8.7.3.1 Overview

Sub-paragraph 13(1) amends section 809R of ITA 2007.

Sub-paragraph 13(3) introduces a new subsection (4A) within section 809R of ITA 2007.

Sub-paragraph 13(4) amends section 809R (5) of ITA 2007 to ensure that the definition of an offshore transfer is one which neither meets the conditions of section 809Q of ITA 2007 nor section 809RZA of ITA 2007

[83] https://www.gov.uk/hmrc-internal-manuals/residence-domicile-and-remittance-basis/rdrm73600

Sub-paragraph 13(5) amends section 809R (6) of ITA 2007.

Sub-paragraph 13(6) introduces an additional point (c) within section 809R (7) of ITA 2007. So, where a designation is made for some, but not all of the funds, the account being treated as a mixed fund.

Sub-paragraph 13(7) amends section 809R (9) of ITA 2007 to ensure that TRF capital is included within the ordering rules when more than 1 transfer is made to the UK.

2.8.7.3.2 Legislation

Paragraph 13 reads as follows.

"Capital gains tax: reliefs in respect of matched capital payments

13(1) Sub-paragraph (2) applies where—

(a)chargeable gains are treated as accruing to an individual in a tax year under section 87(2) or 89(2) of TCGA 1992 as a result of a capital payment made to an individual by the trustees of a settlement, and

(b)an amount of that capital payment is qualifying overseas capital that has been designated by the individual under paragraph 3.

(2) The gains are to be reduced by the amount of that designated qualifying overseas capital.

(3) Sub-paragraph (4) applies where—

(a)an individual is charged to capital gains tax by virtue of the matching (under section 87A of TCGA 1992) of a capital payment with the section 1(3) amount for the tax year 2024-25 or any earlier tax year,

(b)section 91(2) of TCGA 1992 (increase of tax where capital payment matched to section 1(3) amount for earlier tax year) would (ignoring sub-paragraph (4)) apply in relation to the capital payment mentioned in paragraph (a),

(c)an amount of a capital payment (which may or may not be the payment mentioned in paragraph (a)) is qualifying overseas capital that has been designated by the individual, and

(d)the amount designated is qualifying overseas capital as a result of the fact it would, in accordance with paragraph 3(2), be matched with the section 1(3) amount mentioned in paragraph (a).

(4)Section 91(2) of TCGA 1992 does not apply to capital gains tax payable by the individual in respect of so much of the capital payment mentioned in sub-paragraph (3)(a) as is matched with the amount of the section 1(3) amount as would also, in accordance with paragraph 3(2), be matched with the amount of a capital payment mentioned in sub-paragraph (3)(c).

(5) Sub-paragraph (6) applies where—

(a)chargeable gains are treated as accruing to an individual in a tax year under paragraph 8(1) of Schedule 4C to TCGA 1992 as a result of a capital payment made to an individual by the trustees of a settlement, and (b)an amount of that capital payment is qualifying overseas capital that has been designated by the individual under paragraph 5.

(6) The gains are to be reduced by the amount of that designated qualifying overseas capital.

(7) Sub-paragraph (8) applies where—

(a)an individual is charged to capital gains tax by virtue of the matching (under section 87A of TCGA 1992 as it has effect for the purposes of paragraph 8(3) of Schedule 4C to that Act) of a capital payment with the section 1(3) amount in the Schedule 4C pool for the tax year 2024-25 or any earlier tax year,

(b)paragraph 13(2) of Schedule 4C to that Act (increase of tax where capital payment matched to section 1(3) amount for earlier tax year) would (ignoring sub-paragraph (8)) apply in relation to the capital payment mentioned in paragraph (a),

(c)an amount of a capital payment (which may or may not be the payment mentioned in paragraph (a)) is qualifying overseas capital that has been designated by the individual, and

(d)the amount designated is qualifying overseas capital as a result of the fact it would, in accordance with paragraph 5(2), be matched with the section 1(3) amount mentioned in paragraph (a).

(8)Paragraph 13(2) of Schedule 4C to TCGA 1992 does not apply to capital gains tax payable by the individual in respect of so much of the capital payment mentioned in sub-paragraph (7)(a) as is matched with the amount of the section 1(3) amount in the Schedule 4C pool as would also, in accordance with paragraph 5(2), be matched with the amount of a capital payment mentioned in sub-paragraph (7)(c).

(9) For the purposes of this paragraph—

(a) "section 1(3) amount" has the meaning it has in section 87 of TCGA 1992;

(b) "section 1(3) amount in the Schedule 4C pool" is to be construed in accordance with Schedule 4C to TCGA 1992.

(10) This paragraph has effect for the tax year 2025-26 and subsequent tax years."

2.8.7.3.3 Detail

Sub-paragraph 13(1) amends section 809R of ITA 2007.

Sub-paragraph 13(3) introduces a new subsection (4A) within section 809R of ITA 2007. This subsection (4A) confirms that, when determining the appropriate portion of a mixed fund, TRF capital is to be treated as a "kind of" income or capital. As a result, income that has been designated, gains that have been designated and any other amount that has been designated are all treated as one collective amount known as TRF capital. This amount is separate from the income that has not been designated, the gains that have not been designated and any other amount that has not been designated.

Sub-paragraph 13(4) amends section 809R (5) of ITA 2007 to ensure that the definition of an offshore transfer is one which neither meets the conditions of section 809Q of ITA 2007 nor section 809RZA of ITA 2007. As a result, an offshore transfer will be one which is neither a taxable remittance, meeting the requirements of a condition A transfers under section 809L of ITA 2007, nor a transfer into a TRF capital account which only can receive transfers of TRF capital.

Sub-paragraph 13(5) amends section 809R (6) of ITA 2007 to ensure that transfers from a mixed find are treated as offshore transfers only if they are neither a taxable remittance nor a transfer into a "designated account" which only can receive TRF capital.

Sub-paragraph 13(6) introduces an additional point (c) within section 809R (7) of ITA 2007. The effect of this is that where a designation is made on some, but not all of the funds within an account, this will result in the account being treated as a mixed fund.

Sub-paragraph 13(7) amends section 809R (9) of ITA 2007 to ensure that TRF capital is included within the ordering rules when more than 1 transfer is made to the UK.

HMRC say the following on this in their Manuals. [84]

> **"Reliefs in respect of matched capital payments**
>
> Paragraph 13 Schedule 10 Finance Act 2025
>
> Paragraph 13 prevents a charge to both TRF and to CGT on the same payment.
>
> Where an individual designates an amount of a capital payment as designated qualifying overseas capital because of it being matched to gains under paragraph 3 (section 87 and 89 TCGA 1992 cases) or 5 (Schedule 4C cases), the corresponding chargeable gains deemed to accrue as result of the payment are reduced by the designated amount."

2.8.7.3.4 Effective Date

06 April 2025

2.8.7.4 Paragraph 14 New Sections 809ZA to 809ZD ITA

2.8.7.4.1 Overview

Paragraph 14 introduces 4 new sections 809RZA to 809RZD into ITA 2007. These new sections cover the rules concerning the creation, design and transfers to new designated accounts for holding TRF capital.

[84] https://www.gov.uk/hmrc-internal-manuals/residence-domicile-and-remittance-basis/rdrm73600

2.8.7.4.2 Legislation

Paragraph 14 reads as follows. Temporary disapplication of nominated income ordering rules

> "14 Section 809I of ITA 2007 (remittance basis charge: income and gains treated as remitted) does not apply for a tax year in relation to an individual if—
>
> (a)the tax year is tax year 2025-26, 2026-27 or 2027-28,
>
> (b)the individual
>
> (i)makes a designation of qualifying overseas capital for that tax year, or
>
> (ii)has made such a designation for a previous tax year, and
>
> (c)that section has not applied in relation to that individual for the tax year 2024-25 or an earlier tax year."

2.8.7.4.3 Detail

Paragraph 14 introduces 4 new sections 809RZA to 809RZD into ITA 2007. These new sections cover the rules concerning the creation, design and transfers to new designated accounts for holding TRF capital.

(a.) New subsections 809RZA (1), (2) and (4) set out the conditions necessary for a transfer from a mixed fund to be treated as a transfer of TRF capital into a TRF capital account.

(b.) New subsection 809RZA (3) sets out that where a transfer includes an amount that is not TRF capital this will be treated as a separate non-qualifying transfer.

(c.) New subsections 809RZB(1) to (7) set out the conditions necessary for an account to qualify as a TRF capital account including: that it must be nominated in writing to HMRC, the date of qualification, the balance of the account when it is nominated and the process of withdrawing a nomination.

(d.) New subsections 809RZB (8) confirms the length of time an account can qualify as a TRF capital account.

(e.) New subsection 809RZB (9) confirms the conditions when the account will not qualify as a TRF capital account.

(f.) New subsection 809RZB (10) confirms that the opening balance of a TRF capital account, which cannot be more than £10, will be treated as TRF capital.

(g.) New subsection 809RZB (11) confirms that if interest is payable on TRF capital held in a TRF capital account, any such interest is to be treated as TRF capital.

(h.) New subsection 809RZB (12) confirms that if there is an unremedied breach in a tax year, then the account will cease to qualify for the entire tax year, not just a portion of it.

(i.) New subsection 809RZB (13) confirms that that a breach is to be ignored if it occurs after the account has already ceased to be a TRF capital account in the tax year.

(j.) New subsection 809RZB (14) confirms the definition of an ordinary bank account.

(k.) New subsection 809RZB (15) confirms that "paid into" an account means anything credited.

(l.) New subsections 809RZC (1) and (6) confirm that a breach of the rules takes place when anything other than TRF capital is paid into a TRF capital account.

(m.)New subsections 809RZC (2), (3) and (4) confirm a breach will be remedied if amounts are removed from the account within 30 days of their receipt.

(n.) New subsection 809RZC (5) confirms that where there has been a breach on more than 2 days in any tax year, any subsequent breach cannot be remedied.

(o.) New section 809RZD confirms that where a taxpayer successfully remedies a breach, the transfer of the prohibited sum into and out of the TRF capital account are ignored for the purposes of s809R and s809Q ITA 2007.

(p.) Sub-paragraph 15(2)(a) introduces new rules at section 809RZZA of ITA 2007 which will only apply for the years of the TRF, 2025-26, 2026-27 and 2027-28.

(q.) New subsection 809RZZA (1) confirms that the rules apply for any mixed fund which contains TRF capital.

(r.) New subsection 809RZZA (2) sets out the steps that should be applied to determine the make-up of transfers from a mixed fund containing TRF capital. These steps confirm that transfers of TRF capital "into a TRF capital account" are treated as being paid in priority to any other payments, then remittances to the UK and finally other transfers.

(s.) New subsection 809RZZA (3) confirms that even if the composition of the transfers is impacted by paragraph 2, this does not impact the date on which they are paid.

(t.) New subsection 809RZZA (4) defines that a remittance takes its usual meaning as per condition A in section 809L of ITA 2007.

(u.) New subsection 809RZZA (5) to (6) confirms that "other transfers" are ones which are neither UK remittances nor transfers into a TRF capital account.

(v.) New subsection 809RZZA (7) confirms that TRF capital is a kind of income or gain for apportionment purposes.

2.8.7.4.4 Effective Date

06 April 2025 broadly but see paragraph 21.

2.8.7.5 Paragraph 15 - Confirmation of annualised ordering rules and TRF remedy taken.

2.8.7.5.1 Overview

Paragraph 15(2)(b) confirms that the annualised ordering rules should be reapplied where a remedy is taken in respect of a TRF capital account in the tax years 2025-26, 2026-27 and 2027-28.

2.8.7.5.2 Legislation

Paragraph 15 reads as follows.

"Mixed funds: section 809Q of ITA 2007

15(1) Section 809Q of ITA 2007 is amended as follows.

(2) In subsection (3)—

(a)before Step 1 insert—

"Step A1

Find the amount (if any) of income or capital of the individual for the relevant tax year in the mixed fund immediately before the transfer that is TRF capital.

If the amount of the transfer is equal to, or less than, the amount of TRF capital, treat the transfer as containing only TRF capital.

Otherwise—

(a) treat so much of the transfer as does not exceed the amount of the TRF capital as being comprised of TRF capital, and

(b) apply the following steps to the remainder of the transfer.", and

(b)in Steps 2 to 4, and in the first sentence in Step 5, for "transfer", in each place it occurs, substitute "remainder".

(3) In subsection (6)—

(a)omit the "or" after paragraph (a), and

(b)after paragraph (b) insert ", or

(c)income or capital that is TRF capital and income or capital that is not TRF capital."

(4) After subsection (8) insert—

"(9) For the purposes of this Chapter "TRF capital" means any amount that—

(a)is qualifying overseas capital (within the meaning of Part 1 of Schedule 10 to FA 2025) as a result of paragraph 2 of that Schedule, and

(b)is designated qualifying overseas capital for the purposes of that Part of that Schedule (and see paragraph 8(7) which provides for qualifying overseas capital to be treated as designated qualifying overseas capital from the start of the tax year to which the return in which it is designated relates)."

(5) In section 809Z10 of ITA 2007 (general interpretation), after the definition of "the remittance basis user" insert—

""TRF capital" has the meaning given by section 809Q (9)."

2.8.7.5.3 Detail

This is a specialist area on which appropriate advice should be taken.

HMRC say the following in their Manuals on this.

"RDRM35210 - Remittance Basis: Amounts Remitted: Mixed Funds: Remittances from mixed funds - overview.

Sections 809Q and 809R Income Tax Act 2007

A mixed fund is an overseas fund of money, other property, or both, which contains or consists of more than one type of income, gains or capital, or income, gains or capital from more than one tax year. A simple example would be a single offshore bank account which contains an individual's relevant foreign earnings, interest (relevant foreign income) and some proceeds including a chargeable gain from the disposal of an asset.

From 6 April 2025 a mixed fund may also contain 'TRF capital', if an individual has designated amounts within a mixed fund under the temporary repatriation facility (TRF) - see RDRM75100.

Where Condition A of section 809L ITA 2007 applies (see RDRM33100), the mixed fund rules work to determine if Condition B is also met. They do this by applying ordering rules to the types of income, gains and capital in the fund and (for tax purposes) identifying property brought to the UK out of the fund with the fund's contents in the same order. It can then be determined whether what is brought to the UK satisfies Condition B by virtue of being treated as (for instance) relevant foreign earnings.

The effect of these rules is that foreign income and gains of a taxpayer that are remitted to the UK under section 809L(2) and (3) from a mixed fund are remitted to the UK in a certain order – see RDRM35240 which explains how the ordering rules at section 809Q(3) operate.

There are other rules that determine what is regarded as 'leaving' a mixed fund as a result of an 'offshore transfer', for example, where money is spent outside the UK, or transferring money from a mixed fund to another offshore account – see RDRM35420 which explains how the offshore transfer rules at section 809R operate.

Although the principle behind the rules is relatively straightforward, their application requires detailed knowledge and accurate accounting showing precisely what has entered and left the fund, when and where, with complete details of all transfers where money leaves the mixed fund. This information is required in order to check any amounts remitted from mixed funds.

The mixed fund provisions do not apply to Condition C or Condition D in section 809L (see RDRM33200 and RDRM33400).

The mixed fund provisions also do not apply to foreign income or gains that arose or accrued before 6 April 2008 (see RDRM36000)."

2.8.7.5.4 Effective Date

06 April 2025

2.8.7.6 Paragraph 16 - Amendment of section 809VC (4) ITA confirming no BIR investment post 5 April 2028 and of sections 809VG, 809VN and 809V0 and new section 809VIA introduced

2.8.7.6.1 Overview

Paragraph 16(2) amends section 809VC (4) of ITA 2007 to confirm that Business Investment Relief (BIR) qualifying investments cannot be made after the end of the TRF window, 5 April 2028. It will also not be possible to make a BIR qualifying investment with TRF capital.

2.8.7.6.2 Legislation

Paragraph 16 reads as follows.

Mixed funds: section 809R of ITA 2007

16(1) Section 809R of ITA 2007 is amended as follows.

(2) In subsection (1), for "This section applies" substitute "Subsections (2) to (8) apply".

(3) After subsection (4) insert—

"(4A) For the purposes of subsection (4)—

(a)TRF capital is to be treated as a kind of income or capital, and

(b)TRF capital is not to be regarded as any other kind of income or capital."

(4) In subsection (5) for "section 809Q does not apply" substitute "neither section 809Q nor section 809RZA (2) applies".

(5) In subsection (6)—

(a)in the words before paragraph (a), for "section 809Q as not applying in relation to it, if it" substitute "neither section 809Q nor section 809RZA (2) as applying in relation to it, if they", and

(b)in paragraph (a), for "section 809Q does not apply" substitute "neither section 809Q nor section 809RZA (2) applies".

(6) In subsection (7)—

(a)omit the "or" after paragraph (a), and

(b) after paragraph (b) insert ", or

(c)income or capital that is TRF capital and income or capital that is not TRF capital."

(7) In subsection (9)—

(a)for "step 1" substitute "steps A1 and 1", and

(b)for "step 2" substitute "steps A1 and 2".

2.8.7.6.3 Detail

Paragraph 16(2) amends section 809VC (4) of ITA 2007 to confirm that Business Investment Relief (BIR) qualifying investments cannot be made after the end of the TRF window, 5 April 2028. It will also not be possible to make a BIR qualifying investment with TRF capital.

Paragraph 16(3) amends section 809VG of ITA 2007 to confirm that where there is a remittance following a potentially chargeable event (PCE), the portion of the PCE that is taxable is calculated after deducting any TRF capital within the BIR investment. The portion of the PCE which is treated as TRF capital is treated as remitted in priority to any other kinds of income or capital within the investment. This amount will also not be regarded as remitted again on the occasion of any future PCEs.

Paragraph 16(4) amends section 809VN of ITA 2007 to introduce a new order of disposals when a PCE takes place where there is more than one BIR qualifying investment. The order is TRF capital first followed by any remaining qualifying investments.

Paragraph 16(5) amends section 809VO of ITA 2007 in respect of PCEs affecting qualifying investments made from mixed funds which have subsequently been designated as TRF capital.

This section prioritises the remittance of TRF capital and determines the composition of the remaining funds invested for the purposes of identifying what amounts of undesignated FIG have been remitted or mitigated following a PCE.

Paragraph 16(7) introduces a new section 809VIA of ITA 2007 after 809VI of ITA 2007. This section confirms that an appropriate mitigation step is not required in relation to any element of the proceeds from a PCE that is treated as consisting of TRF capital. If such a step is nevertheless taken in relation to the whole proceeds, the TRF capital will still be treated as remitted with no further tax charge arising.

2.8.7.6.4 Effective Date

06 April 2025

2.8.7.7 Paragraph 17 Mixed funds: TRF capital account

2.8.7.7.1 Overview

Paragraph 17 inserts a new section 809RZA headed "Transfers into TRF capital account" into the ITA.

2.8.7.7.2 Legislation

Paragraph 17 reads as follows.

"Mixed funds: TRF capital account

17After section 809R of ITA 2007 insert—

"809RZA Transfers into TRF capital account

(1) Subsection (2) applies to a transfer made from a mixed fund if—

(a)it is made from a mixed fund that contains TRF capital,

(b)the transfer is to a TRF capital account, and

(c)the amount of the transfer does not exceed the amount of TRF capital in the mixed fund at the time of the transfer.

(2) The transfer is to be treated as a transfer of TRF capital.

(3) Where subsection (2) would apply to a transfer but does not because of paragraph (c) of subsection (1)—

(a)that transfer is to be treated as two separate transfers occurring one immediately after the other, and

(b)the first of those transfers is to be treated as being in the amount of TRF capital in the mixed fund (and accordingly subsection (2) will apply to that deemed transfer but not the second, which may result in the TRF capital account ceasing to be a TRF capital account).

(4) Section 809RZB makes provision about the nomination of an account as a TRF capital account (and see sections 809RZC and 809RZD for the effect of making a transfer that contains amounts that are not TRF capital).

809RZBTRF capital account

(1) An individual may by notice to the Commissioners nominate an account to be a TRF capital account (and more than one nomination may have effect at any time)

(2) The notice must specify the qualifying date for the account.

(3) "The qualifying date" for the account is the first date on which there is paid into the account sums falling within subsection (4) which (in total) are more than £10 at a time when the credit balance of the account was £10 or less.

(4)A sum falls within this subsection if it is TRF capital.

(5) The individual may withdraw the nomination by giving a further notice to the Commissioners, specifying the date with effect from which the nomination is withdrawn.

(6)A notice under subsection (1) or (5) must be in writing and include such information as the Commissioners may reasonably require.

(7)A notice under subsection (1) or (5) must be given no later than—

(a)31 January in the tax year following the tax year in which falls, as the case may be—

(i) the qualifying date for the account, or

(ii)the date with effect from which the nomination is withdrawn, or

(b)such later date as the Commissioners may allow.

(8) If an individual nominates an account under this section, the account is a "TRF capital account" of the individual throughout the period—

(a)beginning with the qualifying date, and

(b)ending with the date before the earliest of the following dates—

(i)the date on which the account is closed or ceases to be an ordinary bank account held by and for the benefit of the individual (alone or jointly with others);

(ii)the date with effect from which the nomination is withdrawn under this section;

(iii)6 April in a tax year in which there is a breach of the TRF deposit rule which is not remedied or cannot be remedied.

(9) The account is not to be a TRF capital account at all if—

(a)at any time on the qualifying date, the account is not an ordinary bank account held by and for the benefit of the individual (alone or jointly with others), or

(b)immediately before the qualifying date, the account has a credit balance of more than £10.

(10) Where the account has a credit balance immediately before the qualifying date (which must be £10 or less), that balance is to be treated as TRF capital for the purposes of this Chapter.

(11) Where interest is payable on TRF capital held in the TRF capital account, any such interest paid into the account is to be treated as TRF capital for the purposes of this Chapter.

(12) The account is not to be a TRF capital account at all if the qualifying date falls in a tax year in which there is a breach of the TRF deposit rule which is not remedied or cannot be remedied.

(13) Subsection (8)(b)(iii) or (12) (as relevant) is to be ignored if the breach occurs on or after a date falling within subsection (8)(b)(i) or (ii).

(14)For the purposes of this section an account is an "ordinary bank account" if it is a cash account in a bank (whether a current or savings account) where sums standing to the credit of the account from time to time represent a debt owed by the bank to the account-holder.

(15) In this section, and in sections 809RZC and 809RZD, a reference to anything "paid into" an account includes anything credited to the account by whatever means.

809RZCBreaches of the TRF deposit rule

(1) There is a breach of the TRF deposit rule if one or more prohibited sums are paid into a TRF capital account on the qualifying date or any day after the qualifying date.

(2)A breach of the TRF deposit rule is remedied if, within 30 days beginning with the day on which the prohibited sums are paid into the account, the required amount is transferred out of the account by way of a single one-off qualifying transfer.

(3)A transfer is "qualifying" if it does not result in the remittance of any amount to the United Kingdom.

(4) "The required amount" is an amount equal to the total of the prohibited sums paid into the TRF capital account on the day of the breach.

(5)If there are 2 days in a tax year on which one or more breaches of the TRF deposit rule occur, subsection (2) does not apply to any breach on any subsequent day in the tax year (and accordingly any breach occurring on any day after the second day in the tax year on which there has been a breach cannot be remedied).

(6)A "prohibited sum" is anything other than a sum that is TRF capital.

809RZDEffect where 30-day deadline is met.

(1) This section applies if the required amount in relation to a breach of the TRF deposit rule was transferred out of the account in accordance with section 809RZC (2).

(2) Sections 809Q and 809R have effect as if—

(a)the intervening transactions had never taken place, and

(b)each prohibited sum represented by the required amount had instead been transferred directly (at the time that sum was paid into the TRF capital account) into the account or other property into which the required amount was transferred by virtue of the single one-off qualifying transfer.

(3) Each of the following is an "intervening transaction"—

(a)each payment into the TRF capital account of a prohibited sum represented by the required amount, and

(b)the single one-off qualifying transfer out of the TRF capital account."

2.8.7.7.3 Detail

This deals with TRF capital accounts.

HMRC say the following in their Manuals about this.

"RDRM75310 - Temporary repatriation facility: Mixed funds: Transfers to a TRF capital account: Transfers to the account

Overview

Section 809RZA Income Tax Act 2007

Ordinarily, where an individual transfers funds from a mixed fund to another offshore account, or spends money from the mixed fund outside the UK without there being a benefit in the UK, this is treated as an 'offshore transfer' – see RDRM35410.

Under the rules for offshore transfers, the transfer from the mixed fund is regarded as consisting of the appropriate proportion of each and every amount of each kind of income and capital as contained in the mixed fund itself, immediately before the offshore transfer.

This means that if an individual designates some of their foreign income and gains within a mixed fund, but there are also undesignated amounts of income and gains and other capital, then an offshore transfer would be regarded as consisting of a proportion of the TRF capital as well as proportions of the other types of income and capital in the mixed fund. It is possible therefore that some TRF capital could be spent offshore and be unavailable for remittance to the UK. See RDRM75100 for definition of 'TRF capital'.

Therefore, to enable individuals to separate out their TRF capital where they have made a partial designation, they are able to transfer their TRF capital from a mixed fund to a special overseas account, known as a TRF capital account. This may help an individual to keep track of where their TRF capital is for remitting amounts to the UK, and to avoid using up TRF capital offshore instead. For details on how to nominate a TRF capital account, see RDRM75320.

An individual is under no obligation to use a TRF capital account; it may not be necessary if they will only make transfers to the UK from the account which contains funds they have designated.

Transfers from the mixed fund

A TRF capital account can only hold TRF capital, so the amount of a transfer from a mixed fund to the TRF capital account cannot exceed the amount of TRF capital in the mixed fund.

Where an individual accidentally makes a transfer of an amount which is higher than the amount of TRF capital in the fund, the transfer is treated as two separate transfers: a deemed transfer of the amount of TRF capital in the fund and a second deemed transfer of non-TRF capital occurring immediately after the first deemed transfer, which is treated as an ordinary offshore transfer – see RDRM35420. The second deemed transfer will breach the TRF deposit rule, which may result in the account ceasing to be a TRF capital account, unless this is remedied within 30 days – see RDRM75340 for further information.

During the TRF period, an annualised basis applies to mixed funds containing TRF capital. This means that during the TRF period, rather than following the transaction-by-transaction basis under the ordinary mixed fund rules, any transfers to TRF capital accounts during the tax year will be deemed to have taken place before any remittances to the UK and any other offshore transfers – see RDRM75500 for an explanation of the annualised basis and examples.

Example

Stefano is UK resident and a former remittance basis user. He came to the UK for the first time on 6 April 2022. On 6 April 2025 he had an overseas bank account which is a mixed fund, comprising:

£200,000 foreign income from 2024-25
£300,000 foreign gains from 2023-24
£100,000 foreign gains from 2022-23

Stefano wants to designate all his foreign income, but he does not intend to remit this immediately to the UK. He is unsure of when he will need these funds but does not want to delay making a designation.

In 2025-26 Stefano designates the £200,000 foreign income and pays the TRF charge of £24,000 (12% of £200,000) on this amount. He does not make any remittances to the UK or any offshore transfers that year. His mixed fund now comprises:

£200,000 TRF capital
£300,000 foreign gains from 2023-24
£100,000 foreign gains from 2022-23

On 31 August 2026 Stefano sets up a TRF capital account and makes a transfer of £300,000 to the account from his mixed fund.

Because the amount of £300,000 exceeds the TRF capital in the mixed fund, the transfer is treated as a deemed transfer of £200,000 TRF capital and a second deemed transfer of £100,000 occurring immediately after. The second deemed transfer is an ordinary offshore transfer, which is comprised of a proportion of what remains in the mixed fund after the first deemed transfer of TRF capital. To prevent the TRF capital account losing its status, Stefano must take action in respect of the second deemed transfer of £100,000 to remedy the accidental breach.

Alternatively, Stefano could keep the £100,000 in the TRF capital account and designate £100,000 of foreign gains in his Self Assessment tax return for 2026-27, as the TRF is still available to him. The amount would therefore be treated as designated on 6 April 2026, so when Stefano made the £300,000 transfer to the TRF capital account it was all TRF capital.

If Stefano does not remedy the breach, then the TRF capital account will lose its status and the £300,000 transfer will be treated as an ordinary offshore transfer between two overseas bank accounts. Therefore, it will contain a proportion of the kinds of income and capital in his offshore account immediately before the transfer – see RDRM35410, subject to the annualised basis applying if there are any other transfers or remittances in 2026-27.

Interest on the account

Where interest is payable on TRF capital held in the TRF capital account, it does not need to be separated out or paid into a different bank account. This is because interest paid into the account is treated as TRF capital for the purposes of the TRF capital account by section 809RZB(11) ITA 2007. This means that the TRF deposit rule is not breached when interest is credited to the account.

Any interest arising on TRF capital in a TRF capital account will be after 6 April 2025 when the remittance basis is no longer available, so it will be taxed on the arising basis in the year the interest arises. Therefore, remitting amounts of interest to the UK along with the TRF capital itself will not result in any further tax charges.

2.8.7.7.4 Effective Date

06 April 2025

2.8.8 Temporary application of annualised basis to mixed funds containing TRF capital.

2.8.8.1 Paragraph 18 Temporary application of annualised basis to mixed funds containing TRF capital

2.8.8.1.1 Overview

Under the temporary repatriation facility (TRF) an annualised basis will apply to any mixed funds which contain TRF capital during a tax year.

2.8.8.1.2 Legislation

Paragraph 18 reads as follows.

"18(1) These following modifications have effect for the tax years 2025-26, 2026-27 and 2027-28.

(2) Chapter A1 of Part 14 of ITA 2007 has effect as if—

(a)after section 809R there were inserted—

"809RZZA Annualised basis for mixed funds containing TRF capital.

(1) This section applies where, at any time in a tax year, a mixed fund contains TRF capital.

(2) If this section applies, the composition of each transfer made from the fund in that tax year at any time is to be determined as follows—

Step 1

Suppose that all transfers made from the mixed fund to a TRF capital account in relation to which section 809RZA (2) applies had been a single transfer made from the fund at the end of the tax year.

Whether that section applies in relation to transfers to a TRF capital account is determined as if all transfers from the mixed fund were made at the end of the tax year but transfers to a TRF capital account were made—

(a) before any other transfer from the mixed fund was made, and

(b) sequentially in the order in which the transfers to a TRF capital account were actually made.

Step 2

Suppose that all the condition A transfers made from the mixed fund in the tax year had been a single transfer made at the end of the tax year immediately after the single transfer mentioned in Step 1.

Step 3

Suppose that all the other transfers made from the account in the tax year had been a single offshore transfer made at the end of the tax year immediately after the single transfer mentioned in Step 2.

Step 4

Applying those suppositions—

(a) find under section 809Q (3) the content of the single transfer mentioned in Step 2, and

(b) find under section 809R (4) the content of the single offshore transfer mentioned in Step 3.

Step 5

Each transfer made from the fund in the tax year, other than a transfer to which section 809RZA (2) is regarded as applying in accordance with Step 1, is treated as containing the specified proportion of each kind of income or capital contained in the relevant deemed transfer.

"The specified proportion" is the amount of the transfer divided by the amount of the relevant deemed transfer.

"The relevant deemed transfer is—

(a)if the transfer is a condition A transfer, the single transfer mentioned in Step 2, and

(b) otherwise, the single offshore transfer mentioned in Step 3.

Step 6

Each transfer made from the fund in the tax year to which section 809RZA(2) is regarded as applying in accordance with Step 1 is to be treated as a transfer to which that section applies (and no other transfer in the tax year is to be regarded as a transfer in relation to which that section applies).

(3) Subsection (2) applies in determining the composition of a transfer for the purposes of sections 809Q and 809R, but it does not otherwise affect the date on which a transfer is considered to occur for the purposes of this Chapter.

(4)A transfer from the fund is a "condition A transfer" if and to the extent that—

(a)condition A in section 809L is met, and

(b)either—

(i)the property or consideration for the service is (wholly or in part), or derives (wholly or in part, and directly or indirectly) from, the transfer, or

(ii)the transfer, or anything deriving (wholly or in part, and directly or indirectly) from the transfer, is used as mentioned in section 809L(3)(c).

(5)A transfer from the fund is an "other transfer" if and to the extent that it is neither a condition A transfer nor a transfer to which section 809RZA (2) is regarded as applying in accordance with Step 1.

(6) Treat a transfer as an "other transfer" if and to the extent that, at the end of the tax year—

(a)it is neither a condition A transfer nor a transfer to which section 809RZA (2) is regarded as applying in accordance with Step 1, and

(b)on the basis of the best estimate that can reasonably be made at that time, it will not become either a condition A transfer or a transfer to which section 809RZA (2) is regarded as applying in accordance with Step 1.

(7) For the purposes of Step 5 in subsection (2)—

(a)TRF capital is to be treated as a kind of income or capital, and

(b)TRF capital is not to be regarded as any other kind of income or capital.", and

(b)in section 809RZD (as inserted by paragraph 17), at the end there were inserted—

"(4) If it is supposed under Steps 1 to 3 of section 809RZZA (2) that single transfers had been made in the intervening period, re-apply those steps in relation to those transfers taking account of subsection (2) and re-apply sections 809Q and 809R accordingly.

(5) "The intervening period" is the period—

(a)beginning with the day on which the breach occurred, and

(b)ending with the day on which the single one-off qualifying transfer was made in accordance with section 809RZC (2).

(6) If more than one qualifying transfer of a sum equal to the required amount was transferred out of the TRF capital account within the 30-day grace period, the first of those transfers is assumed to be the single one-off qualifying transfer.

(7) "The 30-day grace period" is the period of 30 days mentioned in section 809RZC (2)."

2.8.8.1.3 Detail

HMRC say the following on this in their Manuals:

"RDRM75500 - Temporary repatriation facility: Mixed funds: Annualised basis Overview

Paragraph 18 Schedule 10 Finance Act 2025

Under the temporary repatriation facility (TRF) an annualised basis will apply to any mixed funds which contain TRF capital during a tax year – see RDRM75100 for a definition of TRF capital. The application of the annualised basis is limited to the 3 years within the TRF period.

The statutory order of remittances of types of income and capital will be the same as under section 809Q ITA 2007 (see RDRM35220) but instead of identifying the composition of transfers out of the mixed fund on a transaction-by-transaction basis, individuals will be able to total up all their remittances to the UK for a tax year and treat that as a single remittance made at the end of the year in priority to any offshore transfers. This does not apply to offshore transfers to a TRF capital account, which will be treated as having taken place before the deemed single remittance.

The purpose of the annualised basis is to provide for a simplified version of the mixed fund rules during the TRF period, to allow for TRF capital to be transferred to a TRF capital account or remitted to the UK in priority to other funds. The effect is that the composition of a remittance or other transfer may be calculated differently, but the deeming of single transfers at the end of the tax year does not change the date on which the remittance or transfer took place. This is relevant where amounts are transferred between an account using the annualised basis and an account using the transaction-by-transaction basis. The receiving account receives the funds on the date transferred, not at the end of the tax year.

Also, as a designation is treated as having taken place at the start of the tax year for which the designation election has been made, this means that it will be possible for individuals to review any remittances made within a tax year and designate these under the TRF when completing their Self Assessment tax return after the end of that tax year.

Where a bank account which is a mixed fund containing TRF capital closes before the end of a tax year, the remittances and transfers are considered to take place at the end of the tax year for the purpose of ordering the transfers in the account and determining what funds are contained within the transfer. This deemed date does not impact the date on which the amounts are transferred out of the account on or before closure.

Ceasing to apply

The annualised basis will cease to apply during the TRF period if there is no TRF capital in the mixed fund at any time during a tax year. For example, if an amount had been designated in the 2025-26 tax year and then either fully remitted to the UK or transferred to a TRF capital account (see RDRM75310 onwards) in that same tax year so that it is no longer in the fund on 6 April 2026, the annualised basis will not apply to that account in 2026-27 or 2027-28 if no further designations are made. The annualised basis will not cease partway through a tax year if TRF capital is transferred out or start partway through if it was transferred in; it will apply for the entire tax year.

The annualised basis will cease to apply on 6 April 2028 whether or not there is TRF capital in the mixed fund, because it is a temporary basis only applying during the TRF period. The mixed fund ordering rules which provide for TRF capital to take priority where it is remitted to the UK (see RDRM75200) or transferred to a TRF capital account will continue, but they will continue on a transaction-by-transaction basis.

Operating the annualised basis

The legislation provides for a temporary section 809RZZA after the existing mixed fund rules at sections 809Q and 809R ITA 2007. Former remittance basis users who qualified for Overseas Workday Relief prior to 6 April 2025 may note some similarity to how the special mixed fund rules operated.

Section 809RZZA provides a set of steps to be followed where the annualised basis apples to a mixed fund.

At Step 1, suppose that all transfers made from the mixed fund to a TRF capital account, whether this is to the same or different TRF capital accounts, had been a single transfer made from the fund at the end of the tax year.

At Step 2, suppose that all remittances to the UK from the mixed fund had been a single remittance made at the end of the tax year immediately after the single transfer at Step 1.

At Step 3, suppose that all other transfers from the mixed fund had been a single offshore transfer (within the meaning of section 809R) made at the end of the tax year immediately after the single remittance at Step 2.

At Step 4, find the content of the deemed single remittance using the priority ordering rules at section 809Q(3) – see RDRM35240, and find the content of the deemed single offshore transfer using the proportional rules at section 809R(4) – see RDRM35420.

At Step 5, find the content of individual remittances and other transfers by dividing the amount of the transfer by the amount of the single deemed transfer. Any TRF capital that has not been transferred to a TRF capital account is considered to be a kind of income or capital for the purposes of ascertaining what a remittance or transfer comprises.

Step 6 provides that the 'supposed' transfers that form the deemed single transfer at Step 1 are treated as transfers to TRF capital accounts for the purposes of applying the rules at section 809RZA – see RDRM75310.

Where there are multiple transfers between different accounts, individuals will need to take care to ensure which accounts qualify for the annualised approach and which do not, and that transfers into a TRF capital account, remittances and other transfers are treated in the correct order.

Example 1

Francois is UK resident and a former remittance basis user. On 6 April 2025 he has an overseas bank account, which is a mixed fund, comprising:

- £10,000 foreign income from 2023-24
- £25,000 foreign gains from 2023-24
- £20,000 foreign gains from 2020-21
- £20,000 which Francois is not certain of the source
- £60,000 clean capital from an inheritance in 2018-19

On 1 May 2025 Francois gifts £10,000 to his friend Marco, transferring it to Marco's bank account in France.

On 1 June 2025 Francois remits £10,000 to the UK.

On 1 February 2026 Francois spends £30,000 on a car, purchased from a French car dealer, which he keeps at his house in Paris.

On 31 March 2026 Francois remits a further £45,000 to the UK.

Francois decides to take advantage of the TRF to ensure all of his remittances to the UK are taxed at the most efficient rate.

Francois designates all of his foreign income, his entire uncertain amount and his foreign gains from 2023-24 in his 2025-26 tax return, paying the TRF charge on the £55,000. Therefore, the £55,000 is treated as TRF capital from 6 April 2025.

The composition and priority ordering of the mixed fund has now changed to:

- £55,000 TRF capital
- £20,000 foreign gains from 2020-21
- £60,000 clean capital from an inheritance in 2018-19

Because Francois's mixed fund contains TRF capital, the annualised basis will apply to all transfers out of the account from 6 April 2025.

As Francois has not made any transfers to a TRF capital account in 2025-26, to identify the composition of his transfers he will start by deeming that all his remittances comprise a single remittance (Step 2) totalling £55,000, made from the fund at the end of the tax year. Francois will then deem all his other transfers, the gift to Marco and the car purchase, to be a single offshore transfer taking place immediately after the deemed single remittance (Step 3) totalling £40,000.

He will then find the content of the deemed single remittance and single offshore transfer (Step 5). Using the priority ordering rules at s809Q(3), Francois's deemed single remittance of £55,000 will comprise the £55,000 of TRF capital. Using the proportional ordering rules at section 809R(4), his deemed single offshore transfer of £40,000 will comprise £10,000 foreign gains and £30,000 clean capital.

Francois will then find the content of individual remittances and other transfers by dividing the amount of the transfer by the amount of the single deemed transfer. As only TRF capital was remitted, both remittances will comprise TRF capital, but Francois will need to calculate the composition of his other transfers, meaning that:

- the 1 May 2025 gift to Marco of £10,000 will comprise £2,500 foreign gains and £7,500 clean capital
- the 1 February 2026 car purchase of £30,000 will comprise £7,500 foreign gains and £22,500 clean capital

Francois will need to keep records of the composition of the transfers in case he has a future remittance in relation to the gift or the car. His mixed fund on 6 April 2026 comprises:

- £10,000 foreign gains from 2020-21
- £20,000 clean capital from an inheritance in 2018-19

If Francois does not designate any further amounts in the mixed fund, the annualised basis will not apply to any remittances or other transfers from the account in 2026-27 or 2027-28, because there will be no TRF capital in the mixed fund at any time during either tax year.

Example 2

Xavier is UK resident and a former remittance basis user. He became UK resident for the first time on 6 April 2022. On 6 April 2025 he has an overseas bank account A, which is a mixed fund, comprising:

- £600,000 foreign income from 2023-24
- £100,000 foreign gains from 2023-24
- £30,000 foreign gains from 2022-23
- £50,000 pre-arrival clean capital

On 1 August 2025 Xavier pays £10,000 from account A to his Canadian travel agent to book an Alaskan cruise from Vancouver.

On 1 October 2025 Xavier remits £100,000 to the UK. Xavier decides to take advantage of the low TRF rate for this remittance and also anticipates future remittances that he may want to make after the TRF period ends. Because Xavier makes offshore transfers from account A, he wants to ensure his TRF capital doesn't form part of any of these transfers, so he opens a TRF capital account B to keep his unremitted TRF capital in.

On 2 October 2025 Xavier transfers £500,000 to his TRF capital account B.

On 30 October 2025 Xavier transfers a further £30,000 to account B.

On 1 March 2026 Xavier pays £50,000 of his foreign dividend income from 2025-26 into account A.

Xavier designates all of his foreign income and his foreign gains from 2022-23 in his 2025-26 tax return, paying the TRF charge on the £630,000. Therefore, the £630,000 is treated as TRF capital from 6 April 2025. Xavier is also taxable on his foreign dividend income for 2025-26 on the arising basis.

The composition and priority ordering of the mixed fund has now changed to:

- £630,000 TRF capital
- £50,000 taxed foreign dividend income from 2025-26
- £100,000 foreign gains from 2023-24
- £50,000 pre-arrival clean capital

Because Xavier's mixed fund contains TRF capital, the annualised basis will apply to all transfers out of account A from 6 April 2025.

To identify the composition of his transfers, Xavier will start by deeming that all transfers made from the mixed fund to one or more TRF capital accounts had been a single transfer made from the fund at the end of the tax year.

Xavier would then deem all his remittances to comprise a single deemed remittance and all his other transfers to be a single offshore transfer, in that order. Although he only has one remittance and one other transfer in the 2025-26 tax year, the effect of the annualised basis is that the remittance is deemed to have taken place immediately before the other transfer. This is only for identifying the composition of the transfer and does not change the dates the remittance and the other transfer took place.

Therefore, the deemed single transfer of £530,000 to account B comprises £530,000 of TRF capital, the remittance comprises £100,000 of TRF capital, and the other transfer comprises a proportion of what remains in the mixed fund. The payment of £10,000 on 1 August 2025 therefore comprises:

- £2,500 taxed foreign dividend income from 2025-26
- £5,000 foreign gains from 2023-24
- £2,500 pre-arrival clean capital

Example 3

Teuila is UK resident and a former remittance basis user. On 6 April 2025 she has two overseas bank accounts which are both mixed funds. Account A comprises:

- £100,000 foreign income from 2023-24
- £200,000 foreign gains from 2022-23
- £100,000 foreign income from 2021-22
- £80,000 which Teulia is not certain of the source.

  Account B comprises:
- £20,000 foreign income from 2024-25
- £60,000 clean capital from an inheritance in 2020-21

On 1 June 2025 Teuila transfers £100,000 from account A to account B.

On 1 September 2025 Teuila remits £50,000 from account A to the UK. Teuila decides to take advantage of the low TRF rate for this remittance and also anticipates future remittances that she may want to make after the TRF period ends, so she opens a TRF capital account C to keep her unremitted TRF capital in.

On 15 September 2025 Teuila transfers £230,000 from account A to account C.

On 1 December 2025 Teuila spends £45,000 on a statue from account B, purchased from an Australian art dealer, which she keeps at her house in Hawaii.

Teuila designates her foreign income from 2023-24, her entire uncertain amount and half of her foreign gains from 2022-23 in account A in her 2025-26 tax return, paying the TRF charge on the £280,000. Therefore, the £280,000 is treated as TRF capital from 6 April 2025. She makes no designations on any amount in account B.

The composition and priority ordering of account A has now changed to:

- £280,000 TRF capital
- £100,000 foreign gains from 2022-23
- £100,000 foreign income from 2021-22

Because account A contains TRF capital, the annualised basis will apply to all transfers out of account A from 6 April 2025.

Therefore, the deemed single transfer of £230,000 to account C comprises £230,000 of TRF capital, the remittance comprises £50,000 of TRF capital, and the other transfer to account B comprises a proportion of what remains in the mixed fund. Therefore the £100,000 transfer comprises:

- £50,000 foreign gains from 2022-23
- £50,000 foreign income from 2021-22

Although the remittances and transfers were deemed to have taken place at the end of the tax year for the purposes of identifying their composition, they actually took place on 1 June 2025 and 1 September 2025. This means that from 1 June 2025, Teuila's account B comprised:

- £20,000 foreign income from 2024-25
- £50,000 foreign gains from 2022-23
- £50,000 foreign income from 2021-22
- £60,000 clean capital from an inheritance in 2020-21

Therefore, when Teuila purchased the statue on 1 December 2025, which was an offshore transfer from account B, the £45,000 transfer comprised a proportion of all the kinds of income and capital in the fund immediately before the transfer, because account B is operating on a transaction-by-transaction basis:

- £5,000 foreign income from 2024-25
- £12,500 foreign gains from 2022-23

- £12,500 foreign income from 2021-22
- £15,000 clean capital from an inheritance in 2020-21

  The balance of £135,000 remaining in account B therefore comprises:
- £15,000 foreign income from 2024-25
- £37,500 foreign gains from 2022-23
- £37,500 foreign income from 2021-22
- £45,000 clean capital from an inheritance in 2020-21"

2.8.8.1.4 Effective Date

06 April 2025 broadly (but see paragraph 21).

2.8.8.2 Paragraph 19 BIR amendments to ITA

2.8.8.2.1 Overview

Business investment relief (BIR) allows foreign income and gains from years in which an individual was subject to the remittance basis to be invested in a UK company without triggering a remittance and tax charge in certain circumstances. Changes are made to this as set out below.

2.8.8.2.2 Legislation

Paragraph 19 reads as follows.

> **"Business investment relief**
>
> 19(1) ITA 2007 is amended as follows.
>
> (2) In section 809VC (qualifying investments) in subsection (4), after "if" insert "—
>
> (a)the investment is made before 6 April 2028,
>
> (b)none of the money or other property used to make the investment is TRF capital, and (c)".
>
> (3) In section 809VG (income or gains treated as remitted following certain events)—
>
> (a)after subsection (6) insert—
>
> "(6A) Where—
>
> (a)the income or gains mentioned in subsection (1)(a) include amounts designated as TRF capital (in a tax year after the tax year in which the investment is made), and
>
> (b)the portion of the investment affected is less than the whole of the investment,
>
> so much of the affected income or gains as does not exceed the amounts designated is to be treated as being comprised of the TRF capital.
>
> (6B)Where section 809VO (investments made from mixed funds) applies, subsection (8) of that section applies for the purposes of determining the composition of the amount of the affected income or gains that is

not treated as being comprised of TRF capital (referred to as the "relevant affected income and gains" in that subsection) as a result of—

(a)subsection (6A) of this section not applying, or

(b)that subsection only applying to a part of the affected income or gains.",

(b)in subsection (7)—

(i)for "Sections" substitute "Section", and

(ii)for "and 809VO (investments made from mixed funds) make" substitute "makes", and

(c)in subsection (9), after paragraph (a) insert—

"(aa)any part contained in amounts already treated as remitted under section 809VIA (4) following an earlier event,".

(4) In section 809VN (order of disposals etc)—

(a)in subsection (2)(b), for the words from "order" to the end substitute "following order.", and

(b)after subsection (2) insert—

"(2A) The order is—

(a)so much of the qualifying investments as were made using money or other property that is designated as TRF capital (in a tax year after the tax year in which the investment is made) to the extent those qualifying investments were made using that money or other property, and then

(b)in relation to whatever remains, the order in which the qualifying investments were made (that is to say, on a first in, first out basis).", and

(c)in subsection (4), for paragraph (b) substitute—

"(b)assume that a disposal of all or part of that deemed single holding is—

(i)a disposal of so much of the deemed single holding as is from any qualifying investments that were made using money or other property that is designated as TRF capital (in a tax year after the tax year in which the investment is made) to the extent those qualifying investments were made using that money or other property, and

(ii)if any of the deemed single holding remains after the disposal referred to in sub-paragraph (i), a disposal of a holding from qualifying investments until the holdings from all the qualifying investments have been disposed of."

(5) In section 809VO (investments made from mixed funds)—

(a)for subsection (4) substitute—

"(4) The "fixed proportion" is, unless subsection (4B) applies, the proportion of that kind of income or capital contained in the invested property by virtue of subsection (2).

(4A)Subsection (4B) applies, instead of subsection (3), for determining the composition of the holding in connection with the application of subsections (7) and (8) where the holding contains TRF capital (as a result of the designation of income or capital in the holding as TRF capital in the tax year after the tax year in which the relevant event occurred).

(4B) Where this subsection applies, take the following steps to determine the composition of the holding in connection with the application of those subsections—

Step 1

Determine the amounts of each kind of income and capital that the holding was treated as containing by virtue of subsection (3).

Step 2

Reduce the amount of each kind of income and capital by the amount (if any) of that income or capital as is TRF capital.

(4C) Where subsection (4B) applies, the "fixed proportion" is the proportion of that kind of income or capital treated as contained in the invested property by virtue of that subsection (instead of subsection (2))."

(b)in subsection (7), after "proportion" insert "(determined under subsection (4) or (4C) as the case may be)",

(c)in subsection (8)(a)—

(i)before "affected" insert "relevant", and

(ii)before "portion" insert "relevant proportion of the",

(d)in subsection (8)(b), after "(3)" insert "or (4B) (as the case may be)", and

(e)after subsection (8) insert—

"(8A) For the purposes of subsection (8)(a)—

(a)the "relevant affected income or gains" means—

(i)in a case where section 809VG(6A) applies to treat some of the affected income or gains as being comprised of TRF capital, so much of the affected income or gains as is not treated as being comprised of TRF capital, or

(ii)otherwise, all of the affected income or gains, and

(b)the "relevant proportion" of the portion of the investment means—

(i)in a case where section 809VG(6A) applies to treat some of the affected income or gains as being comprised of TRF capital, the proportion of the portion of the investment that is equal to the proportion of the affected income or gains as is not treated as being comprised of TRF capital, or

(ii)otherwise, the whole of the portion of the investment."

(6) In section 809VI (the appropriate mitigation steps), in subsection (3), after "But" insert "—

(a)see also section 809VIA (which makes provision treating the disposal proceeds as reduced where TRF capital is involved), and

(b)".

(7) After that section insert—

"809VIAApplication of appropriate mitigation steps where TRF capital involved.

(1)This section applies in relation to a potentially chargeable event where, if no appropriate mitigation steps were regarded as taken, an amount of TRF capital would (ignoring this section) be treated as remitted to the United Kingdom immediately after the end of the relevant grace period as a result of section 809VG(2).

(2)Where there has been a disposal of all or part of the holding (see section 809VI(1) or (2)(b)), so much of the proceeds of that disposal as are equal to that amount of TRF capital is to be regarded as comprising that TRF capital.

(3) Section 809VI has effect as if references in that section to the disposal proceeds did not include the TRF capital.

(4) Unless section 809VG (2) applies in relation to the potentially chargeable event, the TRF capital is to be treated as remitted to the United Kingdom at the time the potentially chargeable event occurred."

No tax credits for pre-2016-17 dividends etc

Sections 397 to 398 of ITTOIA 2005 (which have been repealed and only have effect in relation to distributions made before tax year 2016-17) do not apply in relation to any amount of designated qualifying overseas capital.

2.8.8.2.3 Detail

HMRC say the following on this.

> **"RDRM74710 - Temporary repatriation facility: Scope of designation: BIR investments: Overview**
>
> Business investment relief (BIR) allows foreign income and gains from years in which an individual was subject to the remittance basis to be invested in a UK company without triggering a remittance and tax charge, provided it has been used to make a 'qualifying investment'. BIR is available for qualifying investments of pre-6 April 2025 foreign income and gains until 5 April 2028.

Once a qualifying investment has been made there are several actions, known as 'potentially chargeable events', which can cause the relief to be lost, unless the foreign income or gains are taken back offshore or used to make another qualifying investment within a specified time; these are known as 'mitigation steps'. Where the relief is lost, the foreign income and gains used to make the investment are treated as remitted to the UK. See RDRM34310 onwards for BIR guidance.

Foreign income or gains that have been used to make qualifying BIR investments are eligible to be designated under the temporary repatriation facility (TRF). They do not have to be taken out of the company to be designated.

Individuals are not required to designate all the foreign income and gains that they have invested in a company or group. They may want to make a partial designation (see RDRM74720) or designate the foreign income or gains within some qualifying investments but not others, where they have multiple investments (see RDRM74730). Where only some of the invested foreign income and gains have been designated, these will be treated as remitted in priority to any undesignated foreign income and gains.

Where the foreign income or gains have been designated and the TRF charge has been paid, no further tax charges will arise if there is a subsequent remittance on the disposal of the investment or a breach of the BIR conditions, that is, where there has been a potentially chargeable event. Also, a mitigation step will not need to be taken – see RDRM74740 for further details.

For the purposes of the BIR rules, amounts of designated qualifying overseas capital to which the rules apply are TRF capital – see RDRM75100 for a definition of 'TRF capital'. "

2.8.8.2.4 Effective Date

6 April 2025

2.8.8.3 Paragraph 21 Commencement

2.8.8.3.1 Overview

The effective date for part 3 of Schedule 10 is 6 April 2025 apart from modifications made by paragraph 14 and paragraph 18).

2.8.8.3.2 Legislation

Paragraph 21 reads as follows:

> "21(1) The amendments made by this Part of this Schedule [i.e. Part 3] have effect for the tax year 2025-26 and subsequent tax years.
> (2) Sub-paragraph (1) does not apply to the modifications made by paragraphs 14 and 18."

2.8.8.3.3 Detail

The effective date for part 3 of Schedule 10 is 6 April 2025 apart from modifications made by paragraph 14 (New Sections 809ZA to 809RZD ITA broadly rules about new designated accounts for holding TRF capital) and paragraph 18 (Modifications for 2025-2026, 2026-27 and 2027-28).

2.8.8.3.4 Effective Date

06 April 2025 see paragraph 21.

2.9 Rebasing of assets for CGT for some former remittance basis users

2.9.1 Section 42 and Schedule 11: Rebasing of assets

2.9.1.1.1 Overview

The government Policy Paper included CGT rebasing under transitional arrangements for current and past remittance basis users. These provisions give effect to it.

Section 42 and Schedule 11 allow former remittance basis users to substitute the value of a personally held foreign asset on 5 April 2017 for their earlier allowable costs for CGT purposes ('rebasing') where certain conditions are met.

It also amends, in consequence of the ending of domicile in the tax system, CGT rebasing rules available to certain former remittance basis users who ceased to be eligible for the remittance basis in 2017.

2.9.1.1.2 The Legislation

The relevant legislation here is section 42 and Schedule 11.

Section 42 is headed "Rebasing of assets".

It reads as follows:

> "Schedule 11 makes provision about the rebasing of assets for individuals who have been subject to the remittance basis."

2.9.1.1.3 Detail

This allows the changes to be made concerning the rebasing of assets for individuals who have been subject to the remittance basis.

2.9.1.1.4 Effective Date

06 April 2025

2.9.1.2 Paragraph 1 Rebasing of assets for individuals who have been subject to the remittance basis.

2.9.1.2.1 Overview

Paragraph 1 Schedule 11 provides for the rebasing of assets for former remittance basis users.

2.9.1.2.2 Legislation

Paragraph 1 reads as follows.

> *"Rebasing of assets for individuals who have been subject to the remittance basis.*
>
> 1(1) This paragraph applies to the disposal of an asset by an individual ("P") where—
>
> (a)the asset was held by P on 5 April 2017,
>
> (b)the disposal is made on or after 6 April 2025,
>
> (c)the asset was not situated in the United Kingdom at any time in the period beginning with 6 March 2024 and ending with 5 April 2025,
>
> (d)P was not domiciled in the United Kingdom at any time in a tax year before tax year 2025-26, and
>
> (e)P has made a claim under section 809B of ITA 2007 (claim for remittance basis) for at least one tax year that is—
>
> (i)one of the tax years from tax year 2017-18 to tax year 2024-25, and
>
> (ii)a tax year for which neither section 809D nor 809E of that Act applied to P (remittance basis applies without claim).
>
> (2) In computing, for the purpose of TCGA 1992, the gain or loss accruing on the disposal, it is to be assumed that P acquired the asset on 5 April 2017 for a consideration equal to its market value on that date.
>
> (3) Sub-paragraph (2) applies notwithstanding section 58(1) of TCGA 1992 (disposals between spouses).
>
> (4) Where under section 127 of TCGA 1992 (including that section as applied by sections 132, 135 and 136 of that Act) an original and a new holding of shares or other securities are treated as the same asset, the condition in sub-paragraph (1)(c) applies to both the original and the new holding.
>
> (5) Section 835BA of ITA 2007 (deemed domicile) applies for the purposes of sub-paragraph (1)(d).
>
> (6) This paragraph and paragraphs 2 and 3 have effect as if they were included in TCGA 1992."

2.9.1.2.3 Detail

Paragraph 1 Schedule 11 provides for the rebasing of assets for former remittance basis users.

a) When does rebasing apply?

Sub-paragraph 1(1) sets out when rebasing applies. It applies to individuals who dispose of an asset on or after 6 April 2025 provided that they have not been UK domiciled at any time before tax year 2025-26 and have made a remittance basis claim for any one of the tax years 2017-18 to 2024-25. The asset being disposed of must have been held by the person on 5 April 2017 and been situated outside the UK throughout the period 6 March 2024 to 5 April 2025.

b) *Rebasing to what date on what basis?*
Sub-paragraph 1(2) provides that the asset is to be rebased to its market value on 5 April 2017.

c) *What about spouses etc?*
Sub-paragraph 1(3) provides that rebasing applies in relation to disposals between spouses and civil partners, notwithstanding that such disposals are normally made for an amount such that neither a gain nor a loss accrues.

d) *What about Share Reorganisations?*
Sub-paragraph 1(4) provides that where, following a reorganisation, an original and a new holding of shares or other securities is treated as the same asset, both the original and new holding must not be situated in the UK from 6 March 2024 to 5 April 2025.

e) *Meaning of UK domiciled*
Sub-paragraph 1(5) provides that a UK domiciled person includes as person who is regarded as domiciled in the UK because of meeting tests at section 835BA of the Income Tax Act 2007.

f) *TCGA Definitions and Concepts.*
Sub-paragraph 1(6) ensures that definitions and other concepts within the Taxation of Chargeable Gains Act 1992 apply to this provision.

2.9.1.2.4 Effective Date

06 April 2025

2.9.1.3 Paragraph 2 Certain assets brought etc to the UK before 6 April 2025 treated as not UK situs.

2.9.1.3.1 Overview

Paragraph 2 treats assets brought to, received or used in the UK prior to 6 April 2025 as not situated in the UK under certain circumstances.

Sub-paragraph 2(2) prescribes that the circumstances are, broadly, where the asset is made available for public access at an approved establishment; is under repair or restoration; is in the UK for the purpose of being sold; or is clothing, footwear, jewellery or a watch for the personal use of the person or their spouse or civil partner, or a minor child.

Sub-paragraph 2(3) prescribes further circumstances in which an asset is to be regarded as not situated in the UK. Broadly, they are where the asset is not regarded as remitted to the UK because it is valued at less than £1,000 or is a temporary import.

Sub-paragraph 2(4) extends subparagraph (2)(d)(i) (clothing, footwear, jewellery or a watch for the personal use of the person's spouse or civil partner) to include such items for the personal use of a someone living with the person as if they were a spouse or civil partner.

Sub-paragraph 2(5) defines "relevant period" for the purpose of the paragraph.

2.9.1.3.2 Legislation

Paragraph 2 reads as follows.

> "Assets becoming situated in the United Kingdom before 6 April 2025
>
> 2(1) This paragraph applies for the purposes of paragraph 1(1)(c) in the case of an asset which, having been situated outside the United Kingdom, becomes situated in the United Kingdom before the end of the relevant period.
>
> (2) The asset is to be regarded as not situated in the United Kingdom at a time in the relevant period when—
>
> (a)it meets the condition in section 809Z(3)(a), (b) or (c) of ITA 2007 (public access),
>
> (b)it meets the condition in section 809Z3(3)(a), (b) or (c) of ITA 2007 (repairs),
>
> (c)the sole or principal purpose of its being situated in the United Kingdom is to sell it or put it up for sale, or
>
> (d)in the case of clothing, footwear, jewellery or a watch, it is for the personal use of—
>
> (i)P or a husband, wife or civil partner of P, or
>
> (ii)a child or grandchild of a person within sub-paragraph (i), if the child or grandchild has not reached the age of 18.
>
> (3) The asset is to be regarded as not situated in the United Kingdom at any time in the relevant period if it is brought to, or received or used in, the United Kingdom in circumstances in which section 809L(2)(a) of ITA 2007 applies but—
>
> (a)by virtue of section 809X(5)(c) of ITA 2007 (notional remitted amount less than £1000) it is treated as not remitted to the United Kingdom, or
>
> (b)by the end of the relevant period it has not failed to meet the temporary importation rule in section 809Z4 of ITA 2007.

(4) Section 809M(3)(a) of ITA 2007 (persons living together) apply for the purposes of sub-paragraph (2)(d)(i).

(5) In this paragraph the "relevant period" means the period beginning with 6 March 2024 and ending with 5 April 2025.

2.9.1.3.3 Detail

1. Sub-paragraph 2(2) prescribes that the circumstances are, broadly, where the asset is made available for public access at an approved establishment; is under repair or restoration; is in the UK for the purpose of being sold; or is clothing, footwear, jewellery or a watch for the personal use of the person or their spouse or civil partner, or a minor child.

2. Sub-paragraph 2(3) prescribes further circumstances in which an asset is to be regarded as not situated in the UK. Broadly, they are where the asset is not regarded as remitted to the UK because it is valued at less than £1,000 or is a temporary import.

3. Sub-paragraph 2(4) extends subparagraph (2)(d)(i) (clothing, footwear, jewellery or a watch for the personal use of the person's spouse or civil partner) to include such items for the personal use of a someone living with the person as if they were a spouse or civil partner.

4. Sub-paragraph 2(5) defines "relevant period" for the purpose of the paragraph.

2.9.1.3.4 Effective Date

06 April 2025

2.9.1.4 Paragraph 3

2.9.1.4.1 Overview

Paragraph 3 allows an election to be made to stop paragraph 1 applying to any disposal made.

Sub-paragraph 3(2) provides that the procedure and time limit for an election is the same as that for making claims under the Taxes Management Act 1970, except that an amount need not be quantified.

Sub-paragraph 3(3) provides that an election is irrevocable.

Sub-paragraph 3(4) provides for the making of any necessary adjustments to give effect to an election.

2.9.1.4.2 Legislation

Paragraph 3 reads as follows.

"Election for paragraph 1 not to apply.

3(1) An individual may make an election for paragraph 1 not to apply to a disposal made by the individual.

(2) Sections 42 and 43 of TMA 1970 (procedure and time limit for claims), except section 42(1A) of that Act, apply in relation to an election under this paragraph as they apply in relation to a claim for relief.

(3) An election under this paragraph is irrevocable.

(4) All such adjustments are to be made, whether by way of discharge or repayment of tax, the making of assessments or otherwise, as are required to give effect to an election under this paragraph."

2.9.1.4.3 Detail

Paragraph 3 allows an election to be made to stop paragraph 1 applying to any disposal made.

Sub-paragraph 3(2) provides that the procedure and time limit for an election is the same as that for making claims under the Taxes Management Act 1970, except that an amount need not be quantified.

Sub-paragraph 3(3) provides that an election is irrevocable.

Sub-paragraph 3(4) provides for the making of any necessary adjustments to give effect to an election.

2.9.1.4.4 Effective Date

06 April 2025

2.9.1.5 Paragraph 4

2.9.1.5.1 Overview

Paragraph 4 amends paragraph 41(4)(b) of Schedule 8 to the Finance (No.2) Act 2017. Schedule 8 introduced 'deemed domicile' rules for income tax and CGT. Paragraph 41 provides that an individual who was a non-UK domiciled remittance basis user prior to 2017-18 and became treated as UK domiciled under the 15 out of 20 rules from 6 April 2017 may rebase foreign situated assets to their value on 5 April 2017.

Rebasing is subject to the person remaining deemed domiciled under the 15 out of 20 rules at all times from tax year 2017-18 until and including the tax year in which the disposal is made. The effect of the amendment introduced by paragraph 4 is that, for disposals in tax year 2024-25 and future years, the person must be deemed domiciled under the 15 out of 20 rules from tax year 2017-18 up to and including 5 April 2025.

2.9.1.5.2 Legislation

Paragraph 4 reads as follows.

"Rebasing under Schedule 8 to F(No.2) A 2017

4(1) In Schedule 8 to F(No.2) A 2017, in paragraph 41(4)(b), for "that in which the disposal was made" substitute "the tax year 2024-25".

(2) The amendment made by this paragraph has effect for the tax year 2025-26 and subsequent tax years.

2.9.1.5.3 Detail

Paragraph 41 provides that an individual who was a non-UK domiciled remittance basis user prior to 2017-18 and became treated as UK domiciled under the 15 out of 20 rules from 6 April 2017 may rebase foreign situated assets to their value on 5 April 2017.

Rebasing is subject to the person remaining deemed domiciled under the 15 out of 20 rules at all times from tax year 2017-18 until and including the tax year in which the disposal is made. The effect of the amendment introduced by paragraph 4 is that, for disposals in tax year 2024-25 and future years, the person must be deemed domiciled under the 15 out of 20 rules from tax year2017-18 up to and including 5 April 2025.

Paragraph 4 amends paragraph 41(4)(b) of Schedule 8 to the Finance (No.2) Act 2017. Schedule 8 introduced 'deemed domicile' rules for income tax and CGT. Paragraph 41 provides that an individual who was a non-UK domiciled remittance basis user prior to 2017-18 and became treated as UK domiciled under the 15 out of 20 rules from 6 April 2017 may rebase foreign situated assets to their value on 5 April 2017.

Rebasing is subject to the person remaining deemed domiciled under the 15 out of 20 rules at all times from tax year 2017-18 until and including the tax year in which the disposal is made. The effect of the amendment introduced by paragraph 4 is that, for disposals in tax year 2024-25 and future years, the person must be deemed domiciled under the 15 out of 20 rules from tax year 2017-18 up to and including 5 April 2025.

2.9.1.5.4 Effective Date

06 April 2025

3 Trusts: connected amendments, transitional provision etc

3.1 Summary

Key Points

- Special provision for trusts – IT CGT
    - Removal of IT and CGT protection for Non-Doms and the Remittance Basis subject to qualifying new residents relief
    - Changes mainly found in section 43 and Parts 1 and 2 Schedule 12
- Further review and changes
- Also changes to the Settlement and Transfer of Assets Provisions
    - section 43 and Schedule 12
- Amendment of particular Acts e.g. ITTOIA is a way change is brought about.

This Chapter offers a detailed legal and technical examination of **Schedule 12 of the Finance Act 2025**, focusing on its impact on **trusts**, especially **settlor-interested offshore trusts**, and the **abolition of domicile-based protections** for UK tax purposes, covering the following core points:

3.1.1 *Overview and Purpose*

- Schedule 12 of FA 2025 enacts sweeping changes for **non-UK trusts**, particularly **settlor-interested trusts.**
- The changes reflect a **shift from domicile-based** to **residence-based taxation** for income tax (IT), capital gains tax (CGT), and inheritance tax (IHT).
- The **remittance basis** is abolished from 6 April 2025, with **new rules** governing trust taxation, including **repeal of protections for "excluded property trusts."**

3.1.2 *Trust Structures Affected*

- Focus is on **"settlor-interested trusts"**, where the settlor or close family has an interest.
- Includes **offshore trusts** that historically benefited from remittance or excluded property protection.
- Existing protections for such trusts are largely **abolished unless within the 4-Year FIG regime**.

3.1.3 *Income Tax Provisions*

- **New Section 643A ITTOIA** taxes trust income where the **settlor is UK resident** and not within the 4-year FIG regime.

- Introduces a **"no longer protected foreign source income"** (NPFSI) category, defined in **new Section 643B**.
- NPFSI includes foreign income previously protected under the remittance basis but now taxable when matched or distributed.
- Sets out a mechanism for **matching income to benefits**, including a **priority ordering** of old vs new income.

3.1.4 *Capital Gains Tax Provisions*

- Amendments made to TCGA **1992 section 86, s87, and s87G**, which apply to gains in offshore trusts.
- Gains now chargeable on UK resident settlors (under section 86) and UK resident beneficiaries (under section 87), even where protections previously applied.
- Provides for **rebasing** in limited cases.
- s87G matching rules modified to reflect **new FIG regime alignment** and transitional gains.

3.1.5 *Anti-Avoidance and Transitional Rules*

- **Transfer of Assets Abroad (ToAA)** and **settlements anti-avoidance** rules retained, with amendments to reflect new scope.
- Detailed rules for **transition from protected to taxable status** for income/gains accumulated before 6 April 2025.
- Special rules apply to **distributions from pre-2025 income/gains** and how these interact with FIG regime eligibility.

3.1.6 *IHT Provisions (Interaction with Schedule 1)*

- **Schedule 1 of FA 2025** introduces the **"long-term residence test"** for IHT.
- **Excluded Property Trusts (EPTs)** lose IHT protection for settlors meeting the long-term residence criteria.
- New provisions impose **UK IHT on trust assets** if the settlor or trust meets the new residence-based threshold.

3.1.7 *Policy Justification and Practical Challenges*

- HMRC's seeming goal to end perceived **unfair advantages** for non-domiciled UK residents.
- Practical difficulties:
    - Tracking **historical income and gains** across old and new regimes.
    - Identifying **"protected" vs "unprotected" income/gains**.
    - Potential for **double taxation** and **complex record-keeping**.
- Detailed **transitional planning and professional advice** is crucial.

3.1.8 *Planning Considerations and Risks*

- Trustees and advisors should:

  - Re-evaluate **distribution strategies**, especially by reference to what was done before April 2025.
  - Consider **acceleration of benefits** before protections lapse.
  - Prepare for enhanced **reporting and matching obligations** under new rules.
- **Update trust deeds** other trust documents and tax documentation.
- Urgent Action Point: early consideration of **jurisdictional issues and possible restructuring.**

3.1.9 Overview

The government Policy Paper published on 29 July 2024 outlined the government's plans to change the taxation of UK resident non-domiciled individuals. [85] These plans included removing from 6 April 2025 the IT and CGT protection for settlor-interested trust structures for non-domiciled and deemed domiciled individuals not within the new relief for qualifying new residents. Changes were also made to IHT and Trusts discussed which are discussed below.

Section 43 and Schedule 12 make special provision about trusts and the introduction of relief for qualifying new residents and the abolition of the remittance basis of taxation.

These provisions also remove certain protections for foreign-source income that have been in the main available since the tax year 2017-18 and make transitional provision in respect of income that arose in past tax years. The FA 2017 had *inter alia* extended the concept of deemed domicile to IT and CGT.

3.2 Further Review

3.2.1 General

We had been told that the government intended to conduct a review of offshore anti-avoidance legislation, including the Transfer of Assets Abroad and Settlements legislation, "to modernise the rules and ensure they are fit for purpose".

3.2.2 Intended purpose of review

The intended purpose of this review, we were told, was:

- to remove ambiguity and uncertainty in the legislation,
- make the rules simpler to apply in practice and
- ensure the anti-avoidance provisions in question are effective.

---

[85] 2024: Non-UK domiciled individuals- Policy Summary - GOV.UK (www.gov.uk)

We were told that "Further details on the review would be provided in due course". It was not anticipated that this review will result in any changes before the start of the 2026/27 tax year."

However, the legislation under consideration makes some changes to the Settlement and Transfer of Assets provisions from 6 April 2025[86] (see Parts 1-3 and para 71 Schedule 12 and section 43(2)). These are considered below.

3.3 The Legislation – section 43

Section 43 is headed "Trusts: connected amendments, transitional provision etc". It reads as follows:

> "(1) Schedule 12 amends legislation relating to the taxation of income and gains arising within trusts and similar structures, and in particular—
>
> (a) contains amendments connected with the introduction of relief for qualifying new residents and the abolition of the remittance basis of taxation (see Chapters 1 and 2), and
>
> (b) removes certain protections for foreign-source income and gains that have been available since the tax year 2017-18 while making transitional provision in respect of income that arose in past tax years.
>
> (2) In that Schedule—
>
> Part 1 amends Chapter 5 of Part 5 of ITTOIA 2005 (settlements: amounts treated as income of settlor or family);[87]
>
> Part 2 amends Chapter 2 of Part 13 of ITA 2007 (transfer of assets)[88]
>
> Part 3 amends Chapter 2 of Part 3 of TCGA 1992 (settlements: chargeable gains)[89] and other provisions of TCGA 1992 relating to trusts and similar structures;
>
> Part 4 contains provision about commencement and transitional provision."

It is convenient to note here that paragraph 70 of Schedule 12 provides that Parts 1 to 3 of the Schedule come into force on 6 April 2025.

3.3.1 *Details of the section*

Subsections (1) and (2) of section 43 introduce Schedule 12, which amends legislation relating to the taxation of income and gains arising within trusts and similar structures as described in Section 43(2) covering ITTOIA, ITA and CGT (see above).

---

[86] See paragraph 71 of Schedule 12

[87] See Chapter 6

[88] See Chapter 6

[89] See Chapter 6

3.3.2 *Details of the Schedule*

3.3.2.1 *Introduction*

The new government said in the Policy Document that it intended to make special provision about trusts and the introduction of relief for qualifying new residents and the abolition of the remittance basis of taxation and to review and modernise "offshore anti-avoidance legislation, including the Transfer of Assets Abroad and Settlements legislation" (see above). Schedule 12 deals with the implementation of this change.

The Schedule is divided into parts as mentioned above. These are:

- Part 1: Settlements (income) (paragraph 1 to 25)
- Part 2: Transfer of assets abroad (paragraph 26 to 50)
- Part 3: Capital Gains Tax (paragraph 51 to 69)
- Part 4: Commencement and Transitional Matters. (paragraph 70)

The full text of the Schedule is not set out here for reasons of length and space but the text of each of the paragraphs in the Schedule is considered in turn below and the relevant paragraph in the Schedule is set out under the subheading "legislation" in the course of that consideration of that paragraph.

3.3.2.2 *Part 1: Settlements (income)*

Part 1 of Schedule 12 amends Chapter 5 of Part 5 ITTOIA (settlements: amounts treated as income of settlor or family). [90]

3.3.2.3 *Paragraph 1*

3.3.2.3.1 **Overview**

Part 1 of Schedule 12 amends the Settlement Provisions (i.e. Chapter 5 Part 5 ITTOIA).

Paragraph 1 gives effect to this set of amendments and is the legal authority for them and the changes made. Paragraph 70 tells us the amendments generally apply from 6 April 2025.

3.3.2.3.2 **Legislation**

Paragraph 1 reads:

> "Chapter 5 of Part 5 of ITTOIA 2005 (settlements: amounts treated as income of settlor or family) is amended in accordance with this Part of this Schedule."

3.3.2.3.3 **Details of the paragraph**

This is the introductory paragraph to Part 1 of Schedule 12. It tells us that the Settlement Provisions are amended in accordance with Part 1 of the Schedule. It is the legal authority for the amendments.

---

[90] See Chapter 6 of *Taxation of Entertainers and Sportspersons* – the Settlement Provisions

3.3.2.3.4 Effective Date

6 April 2025 see paragraph 70.

3.3.2.4 Paragraph 2

3.3.2.4.1 Overview

Paragraph 2 amends section 619 (charge to tax under Chapter 5 Part 5 ITTOIA)[91] in the light of:

(1.) new section 643A (Benefits paid out of protected foreign-source income or transitional trust income) inserted by paragraph 13 of the Schedule; and

(2.) new section 643C (meaning of "available protected income" in section 643A) inserted by paragraph 15 of the Schedule.

The paragraph also reflects the omission (i.e. repeal) of sections 643I to 643M (old onward gift provisions) under paragraph 21 of the Schedule.

Paragraphs 13 and 15 are discussed below.

The position before the change is discussed in Appendix 2 to Chapter 6 headed "Protected Trusts".

3.3.2.4.2 Legislation

i. General:

Paragraph 2 reads:

> "In section 619 (charge to tax under Chapter 5), in subsection (1)—
>
> (a) at the end of paragraph (d), insert ", and";
>
> (b) in paragraph (e), after "protected foreign-source income" insert "or transitional trust income";
>
> (c) omit paragraph (f) and the "and" before it."

Section 619 is headed Charge to tax under Chapter 5. Before amendment it read as follows:

> "(1) Income tax is charged on—
>
> (a) Income which is treated as income of a settlor as a result of section 624 (income where settlor retains an interest),
>
> (b) Income which is treated as income of a settlor as a result of section 629 (income paid to relevant children of settlor),
>
> (c) Capital sums which are treated as income of a settlor as a result of section 633 (capital sums paid to settlor by trustees of settlement), ...
>
> (d) Capital sums which are treated as income of a settlor as a result of section 641 (capital sums paid to settlor by body connected with settlement).

---

[91] See Chapter 6 especially 6.3.1.2 in the *Taxation of Entertainers and Sportspersons* for a discussion of Section 619 before the amendment made by this paragraph.

(e) Benefits whose amount or value is treated as income of the settlor or a close family member as a result of section 643A (benefits provided out of protected foreign-source income), and

(f) Amounts treated as income of the settlor or a close family member by section 643J or 643L (gifts provided out of benefits).

(2) For the purposes of Chapter 2 of Part 2 of ITA 2007 (rates at which income tax is charged) , where income of another person is treated as income of the settlor and is charged to tax under subsection (1)(a) or (b) above, it shall be charged in accordance with whichever provisions of the Income Tax Acts would have been applied in charging it if it had arisen directly to the settlor."

ii. Amended section 619:

As amended section 619 reads as follows:

"619 Charge to tax under Chapter 5

(1) Income tax is charged on—

(a) Income which is treated as income of a settlor as a result of section 624 (income where settlor retains an interest),

(b) Income which is treated as income of a settlor as a result of section 629 (income paid to relevant children of settlor),

(c) Capital sums which are treated as income of a settlor as a result of section 633 (capital sums paid to settlor by trustees of settlement), ...

(d) Capital sums which are treated as income of a settlor as a result of section 641 (capital sums paid to settlor by body connected with settlement), and

(e) benefits whose amount or value is treated as income of the settlor or a close family member as a result of section 643A (benefits provided out of protected foreign-source income or transitional trust income), ...

(f)..............................

(2) For the purposes of Chapter 2 of Part 2 of ITA 2007 (rates at which income tax is charged), where income of another person is treated as income of the settlor and is charged to tax under subsection (1)(a) or (b) above, it shall be charged in accordance with whichever provisions of the Income Tax Acts would have been applied in charging it if it had arisen directly to the settlor."

3.3.2.4.3 Details of the paragraph

This makes necessary amendments following the changes made by paragraphs 13 and 15 of the Schedule particularly for "transitional trust income". Paragraph 13 substitutes a new Section 643A headed "Benefits paid out of protected foreign source income or transitional trust income." This affects what is taxable. It is discussed below.

Paragraph 15 substitutes a new Section 643C headed "Meaning of "Available Protected Income" in Section 643A". This is relevant to the amount of income that is taxable. This is discussed below. Appendix 2 to Chapter 6 in the *Taxation of Entertainers and Sportspersons* discusses *inter alia* Protected Foreign Source Income before the changes.

3.3.2.4.4 Effective Date

6 April 2025 see paragraph 70.

3.3.2.5 Paragraph 3 Person liable - amendment of section 622

3.3.2.5.1 Overview

Paragraph 3 amends section 622 (person liable under the Settlement Provisions) as a consequence of new section 643A (Benefits paid out of protected foreign-source income or transitional trust income) inserted by paragraph 13 of the Schedule and the repeal of sections 643I to 643M (old onward gift provisions) under paragraph 21 of the Schedule.

3.3.2.5.2 Legislation

i. Paragraph 3

Paragraph 3 reads:

> "In section 622 (person liable), for "sections 643A and 643I to 643M" substitute "section 643A (under which a close member of the settlor's family may instead be liable)"."

ii. Amended Section 22

Section 622 is headed "Person liable" and as amended reads as follows.

> "The person liable for any tax charged under this Chapter is the settlor[92], but this is subject to section 643A (under which a close member of the settlor's family may instead be liable)."

3.3.2.5.3 Details of the paragraph

i. Consequential changes

This paragraph makes necessary changes to the wording of section 622 following the introduction of a new section 643A by paragraph 13 and the repeal of sections 643I to 643M (old onward gift provisions) by paragraph 13 is discussed at page 41 below and paragraph 21 of the Schedule. Paragraph 21 is discussed at page 64 below.

ii. Close member of the settlor's family- section 643H

[92] Settlor is defined in section 620(1) ITTOIA as any person by whom the settlement was made. a person is treated as having made a settlement if they have provided funds directly or indirectly for the purposes of this settlement.

The meaning of "**a close member of the settlor's family**" is dealt with by section 643H headed "Meaning of close member of settlor's family in sections 643A to 643EA."

As amended by paragraph 20 this reads as follows.

"(1) For the purposes of sections 643A to 643EA, a person is a close member of the family of the settlor of a settlement at any time if the settlor is living at that time and—

(a) The person is the settlor's spouse or civil partner at that time, or

(b) The person—

(i) is a child of the settlor, or of a person who at that time is the settlor's spouse or civil partner, and

(ii) At that time has not reached the age of 18.

(2) For the purposes of subsection (1), two people living together as if they were a married couple or civil partners are treated as if they were spouses or civil partners of each other."

Example

Clive Partin makes a settlement in favour of his partner Connie Cub and her infant children living with them at the time. Clive is excluded from benefit under the settlement. Clive and Connie have not officially become spouses or civil partners of each other. However, they live together as if they were and Connie sometimes calls herself Mrs Pantin. The children are treated as members of the family. [93]

Connie and her children at the time the settlement is made are close members of the family of the settlor of the settlement i.e. Clive, in these circumstances. Connie and Clive are living together as if they were spouses. The children of Connie are under 18 and she is effectively treated as Clive's spouse by section 643H (2).

3.3.2.5.4 Effective Date

6 April 2025 see paragraph 70.

3.3.2.6 Paragraph 4

3.3.2.6.1 Overview

Paragraph 4 amends section 624 (income where settlor retains an interest) as a consequence of the changes made by paragraph 5 of Schedule 12 discussed immediately following this.

This removes protections inserted by FA 2017 for non-Doms.

---

[93] cf Inheritance (Provision for Family & Dependants) Act 1975 (especially section 1 (1) (d)).

3.3.2.6.2 Legislation

Paragraph 4 reads:

> "In section 624 (income where settlor retains an interest), in subsection (3)—
> (a) after "section 627 (exceptions for certain types of income)," insert "and";
> (b) omit "section 628A (exception for protected foreign-source income)" and the "and" before it."

3.3.2.6.3 Details of the paragraph

This paragraph deals with the necessary consequences of the repeal of sections 628A to 628C (protected foreign-source income and transitional trust income) by paragraph 5 discussed in the next section. These repealed provisions were part of the 2017 changes which gave certain protections for Non-Doms. The repealed sections are set out below in the discussion of paragraph 5.

Section 624 applies where the settlor retains an interest. This phrase has a wide definition.

The meaning of the phrase the settlor retains an interest for these purposes is given by section 625 headed "Settlor's retained interest".

This reads (*inter alia*):

> "(1) A settlor is treated for the purposes of section 624 as having an interest in property if there are any circumstances in which the property or any related property [94]—
> (a) Is payable to the settlor or the settlor's spouse or civil partner,
> (b) Is applicable for the benefit of the settlor or the settlor's spouse or civil partner, or
> (c) Will, or may, become so payable or applicable..."

This is very wide in its ambit. "... any circumstances in which the property or income from or representing it may be paid or applied for the benefit of the settlor or the settlor's spouse or civil partner". Cf the Transfer of Assets case *IRC v Botnar* [1999] STC 205.

This is one of the reasons for the common exclusion of settlor and spouse etc. in a trust deed.

Examples

Lana sets up two offshore trusts.

i. Lana sets up the first trust as a discretionary trust. The class of beneficiaries is any descendant of Moreth who is the mother of Lana. The class would

[94] See subsection (5) In this section "related property", in relation to any property, means income from that property or any other property directly or indirectly representing proceeds of, or of income from, that property or income from it.

thus include Lana. Accordingly, the settlor, Lana, would have retained an interest within the meaning of section 625.

ii. Lana sets up what is sometimes known as "Red Cross Trust". This is a trust with a gift over to Charity such as the Red Cross. There is no named beneficiary but a power for the Trustee to appoint such a beneficiary or class of beneficiaries. Lana is not excluded. Lana is the trustee. She could appoint herself as a beneficiary. Consequently, Lana would have retained an interest within the meaning of section 625.

3.3.2.6.4 Effective Date

6 April 2025 see paragraph 70.

3.3.2.7 Paragraph 5

3.3.2.7.1 Overview

Paragraph 5 omits (i.e. repeals) sections 628A to 628C (protected foreign-source income and transitional trust income) as a consequence of the changes made by repeal of sections 628A-628C paragraph 12 Schedule 12 (discussed below). This is to reflect that from 6 April 2025 the previous definitions and protections for 'protected foreign-source income' and 'transitional trust income' will no longer apply. These are replaced by new section 643ZA ("Protected foreign source income" and "transitional trust income") and new section 643ZB (Protected foreign-source income and transitional trust income not to be taxed elsewhere in Chapter) inserted under paragraph 12 Schedule 12 discussed below.

3.3.2.7.2 Legislation

Paragraph 5 reads:

> "Omit sections 628A to 628C (protected foreign-source income and transitional trust income)."

3.3.2.7.3 Details of the paragraph

i. General

Broadly, section 628B dealt with tainting i.e. adding further assets to the Trust whilst UK domiciled or deemed domiciled which was relevant to Condition F in Section 628A (set out below). Tainting could remove some of the benefit of the protections for certain trusts.

These were domicile related matters and so, no longer appropriate.

This paragraph effectively repeals sections 628A – 628C as they are "omitted". Those sections were introduced by paragraph 22 Schedule 8 Finance (No. 2) Act 2017 (c. 32). This gave special protection to certain income arising under a settlement. By way of oversimplification this was essentially where the Settlor was:

(a) not domiciled in the UK at the time the settlement was created by the settlor (see Condition C in Section 628A set out below);
(b) not domiciled or deemed domiciled in the UK in the year in question (see Condition D in Section 628A set out below).
There were also other conditions.

ii. Text of repealed section 628 – 628C

These sections are set out here for the convenience of the Reader here and read:

"628AException for protected foreign-source income

(1) The rule in section 624(1) does not apply to income which arises under a settlement if it is protected foreign-source income for a tax year.
(2) For this purpose, income arising under a settlement in a tax year is "protected foreign-source income" for the tax year if Conditions A to F are met.
(3) Condition A is that the income would be relevant foreign income if it were income of a UK resident individual.
(4) Condition B is that the income is from property originating from the settlor (see section 645).
(5) Condition C is that when the settlement is created the settlor—
 (a) Is not domiciled in the United Kingdom, and
 (b) If the settlement is created on or after 6 April 2017, is not deemed domiciled in the United Kingdom.
(6) Condition D is that there is no time in the tax year when the settlor is—
 (a) Domiciled in the United Kingdom, or
 (b) Deemed domiciled in the United Kingdom by virtue of Condition A in section 835BA of ITA 2007.
(7) Condition E is that the trustees of the settlement are not UK resident for the tax year.
(8) Condition F is that no property or income is provided directly or indirectly for the purposes of the settlement by the settlor, or by the trustees of any other settlement of which the settlor is a beneficiary or settlor, at a time in the relevant period when the settlor is—
 (a) domiciled in the United Kingdom, or
 (b) Deemed domiciled in the United Kingdom.
(9) In subsection (8) "relevant period" means the period—
 (a) Beginning with the start of 6 April 2017 or, if later, the creation of the settlement, and
 (b) Ending with the end of the tax year.
(10) For the purposes of Condition F, the addition of value to property comprised in the settlement is to be treated as the direct provision of property for the purposes of the settlement.
(11) Section 628B (tainting) contains further provision for the purposes of Condition F.

(12) In this section "deemed domiciled" means regarded for the purposes of section 809(1)(b) of ITA 2007 as domiciled in the United Kingdom as a result of section 835BA of ITA 2007 having effect.

(13) Section 648(3) to (5) (relevant foreign income treated as arising under settlement only if and when remitted) do not apply for the purposes of this section.

628B Section 628A: tainting

The addition of property to a settlement "taints" the settlement if made by the settlor directly or indirectly or by the trustees of another settlement made by the same settlor.

(1) This section applies for the purposes of Condition F in section 628A.

(2) Ignore—

(a)property or income provided under a transaction, other than a loan, where the transaction is entered into on arm's length terms,

(b)property or income provided, otherwise than under a loan, without any intention by the person providing it to confer a gratuitous benefit on any person,

(c) The principal of a loan which is made to the trustees of the settlement on arm's length terms,

(d) The payment of interest to the trustees of the settlement under a loan made by them on arm's length terms,

(e)repayment to the trustees of the settlement of the principal of a loan made by them,

(f)property or income provided in pursuance of a liability incurred by any person before 6 April 2017, and

(g) Where the settlement's expenses relating to taxation and administration for a tax year exceed its income for that year, property or income provided towards meeting that excess if the value of any such property and income is not greater than the amount of—

(i) The excess, or

(ii) If greater, the amount by which such expenses exceed the amount of such expenses which may be paid out of the settlement's income.

(3) Where—

(a) A loan is made to the trustees of the settlement by the settlor or the trustees of a settlement connected with the settlor, and

(b) The loan is on arm's length terms, but

(c) A relevant event occurs,

the principal of the loan is to be regarded as having been provided to the trustees at the time of that event (despite subsection (2)).

(4) In subsection (3) "relevant event" means—

(a) Capitalisation of interest payable under the loan,

(b) Any other failure to pay interest in accordance with the terms of the loan, or

(c)variation of the terms of the loan such that they cease to be arm's length terms.

(5) Subsection (6) applies (subject to subsection (7)) where—

(a) The settlor becomes deemed domiciled in the United Kingdom on or after 6 April 2017,

(b) Before the date on which the settlor becomes deemed domiciled in the United Kingdom ("the deemed domicile date"), a loan has been made to the trustees of the settlement by—

(i) The settlor, or

(ii) The trustees of a settlement connected with the settlor,

(c) The loan is not entered into on arm's length terms, and

(d) Any amount that is outstanding under the loan on the deemed domicile date ("the outstanding amount") is payable or repayable on demand on or after that date.

(6) Where this subsection applies, the outstanding amount is to be regarded as property directly provided on the deemed domicile date by the lender for the purposes of the settlement (despite subsection (2)).

(7) But if the deemed domicile date is 6 April 2017, subsection (6) does not apply if—

(a) The principal of the loan is repaid, and all interest payable under the loan is paid, before 6 April 2018, or

(b) The loan becomes a loan on arm's length terms before 6 April 2018 and—

(i) before that date interest is paid to the lender in respect of the period beginning with 6 April 2017 and ending with 5 April 2018 as if those arm's length terms had been terms of the loan in relation to that period, and

(ii) Interest continues to be payable from 6 April 2018 in accordance with those terms.

(8) For the purposes of this section, a loan is on "arm's length terms"—

(a) In the case of a loan made to the trustees of a settlement, only if interest at the official rate or more is payable at least annually under the loan;

(b) In the case of a loan made by the trustees of a settlement, only if any interest payable under the loan is payable at no more than the official rate.

(9) For the purposes of this section—

a settlement is "connected" with a person if the person is the settlor or a beneficiary of it;

"deemed domiciled" has the same meaning as in section 628A;

"official rate", in relation to interest, means the rate of interest applicable from time to time under section 178 of FA 1989 for the purposes of Chapter 7 of Part 3 of ITEPA 2003.

628C Foreign income arising before, but remitted on or after, 6 April 2017

(1) For the purposes of applying section 809L of ITA 2007 (meaning of remitted to the UK) in relation to transitional trust income, "relevant person" in that section does not include the trustees of the settlement concerned.

(2) "Transitional trust income" means income—

(a) That arises under a settlement in the period beginning with the tax year 2008-09 and ending with the tax year 2016-17 ("the protection period"),

(b) That would be protected foreign-source income for the purposes of section 628A (1) if section 628A (2)—

(i) Had effect for the protection period, and

(ii) So had effect with a reference to conditions A to E (instead of A to F),

(c) That prior to 6 April 2017 has neither been distributed by the trustees of the settlement nor treated under section 624(1) as income of the settlor, and

(d) That would for the tax year in which it arose under the settlement have been treated under section 624(1) as income of the settlor if the settlor had been domiciled in the United Kingdom for that year.

(3) Section 648(3) to (5) (relevant foreign income treated as arising under settlement only if and when remitted), and corresponding earlier enactments, do not apply for the purposes of subsection (2)(a) and (d)."

3.3.2.7.4 Effective Date

6 April 2025 see paragraph 70.

3.3.2.8 Paragraph 6 – Amendment of Section 629 Minor Children Settlements.

3.3.2.8.1 Overview

Paragraph 6 amends section 629 (income paid to relevant children of settlor) following changes made by paragraph 7 of Schedule 12 which removes the exception from the charge under section 629 (the Children provision) for foreign source income for protected income etc.

This is essentially making consequential amendments because of Paragraph 7 which removes the protection for foreign source income from charge under Section 629 given by Section 630A repealed by paragraph 7 which is discussed in the next section.

3.3.2.8.2 Legislation

i. General

Paragraph 6 reads:

"In section 619 (charge to tax under Chapter 5), in subsection (1)—

(a) at the end of paragraph (d), insert ", and";

(b) in paragraph (e), after "protected foreign-source income" insert "or transitional trust income";

(c) omit paragraph (f) and the "and" before it."

ii. Section 619 as amended

Section 619 as amended reads as follows:

"619 Charge to tax under Chapter 5

(1) Income tax is charged on—

(a) Income which is treated as income of a settlor as a result of section 624 (income where settlor retains an interest),

(b) Income which is treated as income of a settlor as a result of section 629 (income paid to relevant children of settlor),

(c) Capital sums which are treated as income of a settlor as a result of section 633 (capital sums paid to settlor by trustees of settlement), ...

(d) Capital sums which are treated as income of a settlor as a result of section 641 (capital sums paid to settlor by body connected with settlement), and]

(e) Benefits whose amount or value is treated as income of the settlor or a close family member as a result of section 643A (benefits provided out of protected foreign-source income or transitional trust income]), ...

(f). . . .

(2) For the purposes of Chapter 2 of Part 2 of ITA 2007 (rates at which income tax is charged)] , where income of another person is treated as income of the settlor and is charged to tax under subsection (1)(a) or (b) above, it shall be charged in accordance with whichever provisions of the Income Tax Acts would have been applied in charging it if it had arisen directly to the settlor."

3.3.2.8.3 Details of the paragraph

This makes a consequential change following on from paragraph 7 which omits (repeals) the exception to section 629 for protected foreign source income. Paragraph 7 is discussed in the next section.

3.3.2.8.4 Effective Date

6 April 2025 see paragraph 70.

3.3.2.9 Paragraph 7

3.3.2.9.1 Overview

Paragraph 7 omits (i.e. repeals) section 630A (exception to section 629 for protected foreign-source income) as a consequence of paragraph 12 of Schedule12 (discussed below). Effectively section 630A is repealed.

3.3.2.9.2 Legislation

i. General

Paragraph 7 reads:

> "Omit section 630A (exception to section 629 for protected foreign-source income)."

ii. Section 630A before repeal

Section 630A ITTOIA read before omission i.e. repeal

> **"630AException for protected foreign-source income**
>
> (1) The rule in section 629(1) does not apply to income which arises under a settlement if it is protected foreign-source income for a tax year.
>
> (2) Sections 628A (2) to (12) and 628B (meaning of "protected foreign-source income") have effect also for this purpose. [see above for the text of sections 628A – C)
>
> (3) Section 648(3) to (5) (relevant foreign income treated as arising under settlement only if and when remitted) do not apply for the purposes of this section."

Section 630A was a 2017 insertion by paragraph 23(2) Schedule 8 F (No 2) A 2017 as part of the 2017 changes. This is swept away by paragraph 7 Schedule 12 FA 2025. This change is in line with the move away from a domicile-based system to a residence-based system.

3.3.2.9.3 Details of the paragraph

Section 630A is effectively repealed by paragraph 7.

Amendment of calculation of available income in section 635.

3.3.2.9.4 Effective Date

6 April 2025 see paragraph 70.

3.3.2.10 Paragraph 8

3.3.2.10.1 Overview

Paragraph 8 amends section 635 (capital sums charge: amount of available income) by removing the references in subsection (2) and subsection (3)(d)(i) to 'unprotected income' and substituting the existing subsection (5) with a new subsection (5) which refers to new section 643ZB (protected foreign source income and transitional trust income not to be taxed elsewhere in Chapter). This reflects that from 6 April 2025 the previous provisions relating to 'protected income' will no longer apply except for the transitional provisions inserted under paragraph 12 Schedule 12 discussed below.

3.3.2.10.2 Legislation

Paragraph 8 reads:

"In section 635 (capital sums charge: amount of available income)—

(a) in subsections (2) and (3)(d)(i), omit "unprotected";

(b) for subsection (5) substitute—

"(5) See also section 643ZB (2) (which provides for certain income not to be counted towards available income for the purposes of this section)."

3.3.2.10.3 Details of the paragraph

This paragraph makes a consequential change following the changes in respect of protected income etc as introduced by the 2017 changes such that the earlier provisions will cease to be applicable from 6 April 2025 subject to the transitional provisions inserted by paragraph 12 Schedule 12. Paragraph 12 inserts new section 643ZA ("protected foreign-source income" and "transitional trust income") and new section 643ZB (protected foreign-source income and transitional trust income not to be taxed elsewhere in Chapter).

This is discussed below.

3.3.2.10.4 Effective Date

6 April 2025 see paragraph 70.

3.3.2.11 Paragraph 9

3.3.2.11.1 Overview

Paragraph 9 changes the calculation of the charge under section 633 by removing the exception for protected income. Section 633 is concerned with the matching of undistributed income with any capital sum (widely defined in section 634 and includes loans) paid directly or indirectly to the settlor. This is consequent upon the move away from domicile-based regime.

Paragraph 9 amends section 636 (capital sums charge: calculation of undistributed income) by removing reference to 'unprotected income' and 'domicile'. This is to reflect that from 6 April 2025 the previous provisions relating to 'protected income' and 'domicile' will cease to apply except for the transitional provisions inserted under paragraph 12 Schedule 12 discussed below.

Section 633 imposes an income tax charge by reference to capital sums paid to the Settlor. [95] The capital sums (widely defined) are matched to undistributed income within the settlement. Paragraph 9 removes an exception to the amount of the charge where protected income (as defined for this purpose) was involved.

3.3.2.11.2 Legislation

Paragraph 9 reads:

> "In section 636 (capital sums charge: calculation of undistributed income)—
> (a) omit "unprotected" in the following places—
> (i) subsection (1);
> (ii) subsection (2) (in both places it occurs);
> (iii) subsection (4);
> (iv) subsection (6);
> (b) in subsection (2)(b), omit "domiciled and"."

Section 636 is relevant to the calculation of the undistributed income. As amended the section reads as follows reads as follows.

> **"636 Calculation of undistributed income**
> (1) For the purposes of section 635, ... income arising under a settlement in any tax year is treated as ... income which has not been distributed so far as it exceeds the total amount of—
> (a) The sums to which subsection (2) applies,
> (b) The expenses to which subsection (4) applies, and
> (c) If the trustees of the settlement are trustees for charitable purposes, the amount to which subsection (6) applies.
> (2) This subsection applies to ... sums paid in the tax year to any persons by the trustees of the settlement that are payments of ... income, or sums treated as representing ... income, and that]—
> (a) Are treated in that year (otherwise than under section 633) as the income of those persons for income tax purposes, or
> (b) Would be treated as mentioned in paragraph (a) if those persons were ... resident] in the United Kingdom and the sums had been paid to them there.
> (3) Subsection (2) is subject to section 637(1).
> (4) This subsection applies to any expenses of the trustees of the settlement paid in the tax year which, in the absence of any express provision of the settlement, would be properly chargeable to ... income.

[95] The Explanatory Notes said the section "...treats as income of the settlor capital sums paid or lent to the settlor by the trustees of the settlement where those payments are matched by undistributed income within the settlement."

(5) Subsection (4)—

(a) Does not apply to expenses so far as they are included in the sums mentioned in subsection (2), and

(b) Is subject to section 637(2) to (7).

(6) This subsection applies to the amount by which—

A > B

where—

A is any ... income arising under the settlement in the tax year in respect of which exemption from tax may be granted under any provision to which subsection (7) applies], and

B is the total amount of any such sums or expenses as are mentioned in subsections (2) and (4) paid in that year which are properly chargeable to the income.

(7) This subsection applies to the following provisions of ITA 2007—

section 521(4) (gifts entitling donor to gift-aid relief),
section 522(5) (gifts of money from companies),
section 523(5) (payments from other charities),
section 524 (profits etc of charitable trades),
section 529 (profits from fund-raising events),
section 530 (profits from lotteries),
section 531 (property income etc),
section 532 (savings and investment income),
section 533 (public revenue dividends),
section 536 (miscellaneous income), and
section 537 (income from estates in administration).

3.3.2.11.3 Details of the paragraph

This paragraph makes necessary changes to reflect that from 6 April 2025 the previous provisions relating to 'protected income' and 'domicile' will cease to apply except for the transitional provisions inserted under paragraph 12 Schedule 12. Paragraph 12 is discussed below.

3.3.2.11.4 Effective Date

6 April 2025 see paragraph 70.

3.3.2.12 Paragraph 10

Consequential changes to Section 637 qualifications to Section 636.

3.3.2.12.1 Overview

Paragraph 10 amends section 637 (qualifications to section 636) by removing reference to 'unprotected income' in subsection (5) and subsection (7A). This is to reflect that from 6 April 2025 the previous provisions relating to 'protected income ceases to apply except for the transitional provisions inserted under paragraph 12 of the Schedule discussed below.

3.3.2.12.2 Legislation

Paragraph 10 reads:

> "In section 637 (qualifications to section 636), in subsections (5) and (7A), omit "unprotected"."

3.3.2.12.3 Details of the paragraph

This paragraph makes amendments to section 637 (qualifications to section 636). It removes the references to 'unprotected income' in subsection (5) and subsection (7A). These references are superfluous as the provisions relating to such protected income cease to apply from 6 April 2025 subject to the transitional provisions introduced by paragraph 12 of Schedule 12 discussed below. These are essentially consequential amendments.

3.3.2.12.4 Effective Date

6 April 2025 see paragraph 70.

3.3.2.13 Paragraph 11 – Change of heading to section 643A

3.3.2.13.1 Overview

Paragraph 11 substitutes the italic heading before section 643A ("Benefits matched with protected foreign-source income") with "Transitional provision about protected foreign-source income and transitional trust income" as a consequence of the enactment paragraph 12 Schedule 12. Paragraph 12 is discussed next.

3.3.2.13.2 Legislation

Paragraph 11 reads:

> "11 For the italic heading before section 643A, substitute—
> "Transitional provision about protected foreign-source income and transitional trust income"."

3.3.2.13.3 Details of the paragraph

This is a helpful change. However, headings in legislation were not generally supposed to affect its interpretation at least in earlier times.[96] It does at least make matters potentially less obscure.

[96] But see now *Regina v. Montila and others (Appellants) (On Appeal from the Court of Appeal (Criminal Division))* [2004] UKHL 50 where it was said "34. The question then is whether headings and side notes, although unamendable, can be considered in construing a provision in an Act of Parliament. Account must, of course, be taken of the fact that these components were included in the Bill not for debate but for ease of reference. This indicates that less weight can be attached to them than to the

3.3.2.13.4 Effective Date

6 April 2025 see paragraph 70.

3.3.2.14 Paragraph 12

3.3.2.14.1 Overview

A number of consequential changes upon paragraph 12 have been noted above.

These include:

Paragraph 5 – Repeal of sections 628A-628C

Paragraph 8 – Amendment of section 635, Calculation of Available Income

Paragraph 10 Consequential changes to Section 637 qualifications to Section 636.

Paragraph 12 inserts:

(a) a new section 643ZA ("protected foreign-source income" and "transitional trust income"); and

(b) a new section 643ZB (protected foreign-source income and transitional trust income not to be taxed elsewhere in Chapter)

into Part 5 ITTOIA

New section 643ZA ("protected foreign-source income" and "transitional trust income") defines what is meant by "protected foreign-source income" and "transitional trust income".

Section 648(3) to (5) (income arising under a settlement) is ignored for the purpose of these definitions.

New section 643ZB (protected foreign-source income and transitional trust income not to be taxed elsewhere in Chapter) ensures that 'protected foreign-source income' and 'transitional trust income' are not subject to tax under section 624(1) (income where settlor retains an interest) or section 629(1) (income paid to relevant children of settlor). This means that 'protected foreign source income' and 'transitional trust income' will not be treated as arising after 5 April 2025 under section 648(3) to (5). Other charges may arise though.

3.3.2.14.2 Legislation

Paragraph 12 reads:

"Before section 643A insert—

"643ZA "Protected foreign-source income" and "transitional trust income"

---

parts of the Act that are open for consideration and debate in Parliament. But it is another matter to be required by a rule of law to disregard them altogether. One cannot ignore the fact that the headings and side notes are included on the face of the Bill throughout its passage through the Legislature. They are there for guidance. They provide the context for an examination of those parts of the Bill that are open for debate. Subject, of course, to the fact that they are unamendable, they ought to be open to consideration as part of the enactment when it reaches the statute book."

(1) In this Chapter—

"protected foreign-source income" means income that—

(a) arose under a settlement in any of the tax years 2017-18 to 2024-25, and

(b) was protected foreign-source income for that tax year within the meaning of section 628A (as that section had effect for that tax year).

"transitional trust income" means income that—

(a) Arose under a settlement in any of the tax years 2008-09 to 2016-17, and

(b) was transitional trust income throughout the tax years 2017-18 to 2024-25 within the meaning of section 628C (as that section had effect for those tax years).

(2) For the purposes of subsection (1) ignore section 648(3) to (5) (foreign income treated as arising under settlement only if and when remitted).

643ZB Protected foreign-source income and transitional trust income not to be taxed elsewhere in Chapter

The rules in sections 624(1) and 629(1) do not apply to protected foreign-source income or transitional trust income (which, by virtue of section 648(3) to (5), may be treated as income arising under the settlement in the tax year 2025-26 or a subsequent tax year).

(3) In the following provisions, "income" does not include protected foreign-source income or transitional trust income—

section 635(2) and (3)(d)(i);

section 636(1), (2) (in the words before paragraph (a)), (4) and (6);

section 637(5) and (7A)."

3.3.2.14.3 Details of the paragraph

Paragraph 12 introduces two new sections into Part 5 ITOIA. These are sections 643ZA and 643ZB.

Section 643ZA deals with PFSI (Protected Foreign Source Income) and TTI (Transitional Trust Income).

Section 643ZA (1) tells us that:

"protected foreign source income" means income that:

(i) Arose under a settlement in any of the years from 2017 to 2024-25. In other words, in the tax years from the 2017 changes coming into force and ending 5 April 2025; and

(ii) was protected income for that year within section 628A.

"Transitional Trust Income" is income that:

(i) arose under a settlement in any of tax years 2008-2009 to 2016-2017;

(ii) was transitional Income throughout 2017-2018 to 2024-2025 within the meaning of old Section 628C (see under heading Paragraph 5 legislation above).

Reference is made in the legislation to section 628A which is repealed by paragraph 5 discussed above.

Section 628A read as follows before repeal:

"628AException for protected foreign-source income

(1) The rule in section 624(1) does not apply to income which arises under a settlement if it is protected foreign-source income for a tax year.

(2) For this purpose, income arising under a settlement in a tax year is "protected foreign-source income" for the tax year if Conditions A to F are met.

(3) Condition A is that the income would be relevant foreign income if it were income of a UK resident individual.

(4) Condition B is that the income is from property originating from the settlor (see section 645).

(5) Condition C is that when the settlement is created the settlor—

(a) Is not domiciled in the United Kingdom, and

(b) If the settlement is created on or after 6 April 2017, is not deemed domiciled in the United Kingdom.

(6) Condition D is that there is no time in the tax year when the settlor is—

(a) Domiciled in the United Kingdom, or

(b) Deemed domiciled in the United Kingdom by virtue of Condition A in section 835BA of ITA 2007.

(7) Condition E is that the trustees of the settlement are not UK resident for the tax year.

(8) Condition F is that no property or income is provided directly or indirectly for the purposes of the settlement by the settlor, or by the trustees of any other settlement of which the settlor is a beneficiary or settlor, at a time in the relevant period when the settlor is—

(a) Domiciled in the United Kingdom, or

(b) Deemed domiciled in the United Kingdom.

(9) In subsection (8) "relevant period" means the period—

(a) Beginning with the start of 6 April 2017 or, if later, the creation of the settlement, and

(b) Ending with the end of the tax year.

(10) For the purposes of Condition F, the addition of value to property comprised in the settlement is to be treated as the direct provision of property for the purposes of the settlement.

(11) Section 628B (tainting) contains further provision for the purposes of Condition F.

(12) In this section "deemed domiciled" means regarded for the purposes of section 809(1)(b) of ITA 2007 as domiciled in the United Kingdom as a result of section 835BA of ITA 2007 having effect.

(13) Section 648(3) to (5) (relevant foreign income treated as arising under settlement only if and when remitted) do not apply for the purposes of this section."

For HMRC's view see TSEM4720 - Settlements Legislation: Rules affecting non-domiciled and deemed domiciled settlors of non-resident trusts from 6 April 2025: Benefits

For details of the rules introduced from 6 April 2018 on the benefit charge see TSEM 4635.

Under the trust protections measures in place up to and including the 5 April 2025, a settlor of a protected settlement was not taxed on the Protected Foreign-Source Income (PFSI) of the structure as it arose, provided it remained offshore, but they were taxed under section 643A ITTOIA 2005 on any benefits that they received, or under section 643J or section 643L ITTOIA 2005 in relation to onwards gifts, to the extent that the benefit or onward gift was matched with the PFSI of the trust.

From 6 April 2025 a charge applies to a settlor or close family member (CFM) under section 643A ITTOIA 2005 to the extent that they: receive a benefit from the settlement, are UK resident, have an untaxed benefits total and there is available protected income (PFSI or TTI).

If there is a choice about individuals as to whom the income is treated as arising, then HMRC can apportion the tax charge on a just and reasonable basis to prevent any potential double taxation.

From 6 April 2025 if a beneficiary receives a benefit from a previously protected settlement which would ordinarily be taxed on that individual under section 643A ITTOIA 2005, but the recipient of the benefit is eligible for and makes a claim to the 4-year FIG regime for the relevant tax year, no tax will be paid by the individual in relation to the benefit. However, that benefit will not be treated as reducing the pool of available relevant income for matching to future benefits paid out of PFSI/TTI, under section 643C ITTOIA 2005.

What is an untaxed benefit?

For each individual you must determine what their untaxed benefits total is. There are 4 steps set out in the legislation at section 643B ITTOIA 2005 to tell you how to do this.

Step 1

Identify each benefit provided by the trustees to that individual at any time when they were UK resident in the current or an earlier tax year. If the individual is a close family member (CFM) then only include the benefits provided to them at a time when they were a CFM.

If a benefit is provided to a CFM at a time when they are not UK resident, but the settlor is UK resident, then the benefit will be included in the settlor's untaxed benefits total for the year.

Step 2

Next identify the amount or value of each benefit for that individual at Step 1 and calculate the total.

Step 3

Then, deduct from the total at Step 2:

1. Any part of it where the individual has already been subject to income tax by a means other than section 643A ITTOIA 2005,
2. Any part that has been subject to income tax by virtue of section 643A, or previously under old section 643J or section 643L ITTOIA 2005 (onward gifts rules from 6 April 2018 – 5 April 2025),
3. Any whole or part benefit that has been taken into account when charging income tax under the Transfer of Assets Abroad (ToAA) legislation (see INTM600000),
4. Any amount required to be deducted by section 643D (2) ITTOIA 2005 (reduction due to previous capital gains tax charge).

Step 4

If the amount at Step 3 of the calculation is greater than nil, then that is the individual's untaxed benefits total for the current tax year.

Meaning of available protected income

To determine the amount of available protected income, there are 5 steps that you need to follow. These are set out at section 643C ITTOIA 2005:

1. Identify any PFSI and TTI that arose at any time under the settlement. This is the total protected income*.
2. Deduct from the total protected income any amount that has been matched under the ToAA legislation in the current or an earlier tax year.
3. Deduct any amount of the total protected income on which the individual or another individual has been subject to income tax in the current or an earlier tax year.

4. Deduct any amount that is treated as income under section 643A ITTOIA 2005 in an earlier tax year.
5. Add back any amount of income that falls within step 4 at a time that the individual or another individual has claimed relief under the 4-year FIG regime for any tax year.

The amount calculated is the total amount of available protected income (API).

*New section 643ZA ITTOIA 2005 defines what is PFSI and confirms that it is only income which arose to the settlement during tax years 2017/18 to 2024/25. New section 643ZA also defines what is TTI and confirms that it is only income which arose to the settlement between tax years 2008/09 to 2016/17.

TSEM4710 - Settlements Legislation: Rules affecting non-domiciled and deemed domiciled settlors of non-resident trusts from 6 April 2025: Removal of Protected Foreign-Source Income (PFSI)

For details of the rules introduced from 6 April 2017 on Protected Foreign-Source Income (PFSI), see TSEM 4610.

From 6 April 2025 the trust protections no longer apply to the settlements legislation and therefore sections 628A through to section 628C and section 630A ITTOIA 2005 have been repealed.

References to PFSI have been removed from various sections, the main ones being sections 624 and 629 ITTOIA 2005.The removal of PFSI means that income arising under the settlement from 6 April 2025 will be treated as income of the UK resident settlor if either of the following charging provisions apply:

- S624 ITTOIA 2005 – income where settlor retains an interest;
- S629 ITTOIA 2005 - income paid to 'relevant' children of settlor

Reference to 'unprotected' income has been removed from sections 635 through to 637 ITTOIA 2005. The removal of the concept of PFSI means that 'protected' income will no longer arise.

New section 643ZB ITTOIA 2005 will ensure PFSI that has arisen between 6 April 2017 and 5 April 2025 and Transitional Trust Income (TTI) that has arisen between 6 April 2008 and 5 April 2017 cannot be taxed under sections 624 or 629. However, if a benefit or onward gift is provided to the settlor or a close family member, there could be a charge under section 643A ITTOIA 2005 to the extent that it can be matched to PFSI/TTI arising before 6 April 2025.

TTI and PFSI-what are they and when do they accrue?

Transitional Trust Income (TTI)	S643ZA ITTOIA 2005	6 April 2008 to 5 April 2017
Protected Foreign-Source Income (PFSI)	S643ZA ITTOIA 2005	6 April 2017 to 5 April 2025

Some questions arising from sections 6432A and 6432B

The new sections 643ZA and 643ZB raise a number of questions including the following.

- What is income for these purposes?
- When was it income that arose under a settlement in any of the tax years 2017-18 to 2024-25?
- When was it was protected foreign-source income for that tax year within the meaning of section 628A (as that section had effect for that tax year)?
- What is income that arose under a settlement in any of the tax years 2008-09 to 2016-17?
- What is income that was transitional trust income throughout the tax years 2017-18 to 2024-25 within the meaning of section 628C (as that section had effect for those tax years)? close up. These will be considered in turn next.

Some answers

1. What is income for these purposes?

The legislation does not specifically define "income" for these purposes. A useful rule of thumb starting point in my view is the proper accounting treatment. Again, in my view a further useful rule of thumb starting point is for what year should it be recognised under the proper accounting treatment.

2. When was it income that arose under a settlement in any of the tax years 2017-18 to 2024-25?

To a large extent this is a question of fact. The relevant information must be obtained and carefully analysed.

3. When was it was protected foreign-source income for that tax year within the meaning of section 628A (as that section had effect for that tax year)?

This is in essence a question of fact. Section 628A in its earlier form is set out above under the subheading "Legislation". The answer to the two preceding questions should help with deciding the position on this in any particular case.

4. What is income that arose under a settlement in any of the tax years 2008-09 to 2016-17?

Again, this is essentially a question of fact. It is broadly the sum of the answers.

5. What is income that was transitional trust income throughout the tax years 2017-18 to 2024-25 within the meaning of section 628C (as that section had effect for those tax years)?

Section 628C is set out above under the subheading Legislation.

The appropriate information must be obtained and analysed in the light of the relevant legislation.

3.3.2.14.4 Effective Date

6 April 2025 see paragraph 70.

3.3.2.15 Paragraph 13 new section 643A substituted

3.3.2.15.1 Overview

Paragraph 13 substitutes a new section for the existing section 643A (deemed income because of benefits for settlor or close family member) with a new section 643A (benefits paid out of protected foreign-source income or transitional trust income).

New section 643A (Benefits paid out of protected foreign-source income or transitional trust income) ensures that income will be treated as arising to a settlor or close member of the settlor's family where benefits are paid out of 'protected foreign-source income' or 'transitional trust income'. The meaning of these phrases is discussed above.

Where the income is treated as arising to more than one individual under section 643A (1), section 643A (3) gives an officer of Revenue and Customs discretion to apply and apportion the tax charge "in a just and reasonable way". This phrase gives a fair degree of leeway and allows reasonable minds to reach different conclusions within the range of reasonable decisions. This can make it hard to advise on.

3.3.2.15.2 Legislation

Paragraph 13 reads:

> 13 For section 643A substitute—
>
> **"643A Benefits paid out of protected foreign-source income or transitional trust income**
>
> (1) If—
>
> (a) an individual to whom this section applies has an untaxed benefits total for a settlement for a tax year (see section 643B),
>
> (b) there is available protected income in relation to the individual, the settlement and the tax year (see section 643C), and
>
> (c) the individual is UK resident for the tax year, an amount equal to so much of the untaxed benefits total as does not exceed the available protected income is treated for income tax purposes as income of the individual for the tax year.
>
> (2) This section applies to—
>
> (a) the settlor, and
>
> (b) anyone who has at any time been a close member of the settlor's family.
>
> (3) If there is a choice about the individuals in whose case income is to be treated as arising under subsection (1), income is to be treated as arising—
>
> (a) to such one or more of them as appears to an officer of Revenue and Customs to be just and reasonable, and

(b) if more than one, in such respective proportions as appear to the officer to be just and reasonable."

3.3.2.15.3 Details of the paragraph

Paragraph 13 substitutes a new section 643 A headed "Benefits paid out of protected foreign-source income or transitional trust income" for the previous one. This is set out above.

When does section 643 A apply?

The new section applies where:

i. An individual to whom the section applies as set out in subsection (2) discussed below under the heading "To whom does the section apply?";
ii. Has an untaxed benefits total for a settlement for a tax year c section 643B
iii. There is available protected income in relation to the individual, the settlement and the tax year; and
iv. The individual is UK resident for the tax year.

Effect of section 643 A applying

Where section 643A applies an amount is treated as income of the individual for income tax purposes for the tax year in question.

The amount so treated is "an amount equal to so much of the untaxed benefits total as does not exceed the available protected income is treated for income tax purposes as income of the individual for the tax year".

3.3.2.15.4 Some questions arising

A number of questions arise in respect of section 643A including the following.

- Who is an individual for these purposes?
- To whom does the section apply?
- What is the Untaxed Benefits total for a settlement for a tax year?
- What is available protected income?
- When does it relate to the individual, the settlement and the tax year?
- When is the individual UK resident for the Tax year in question?

These questions will now be considered in turn.

Who is an individual for these purposes?

The word "Individual" is not defined in the legislation for these purposes.

Accordingly, the usual meaning of the word applies.

Lady Longford's case discussed above treated a trustee who was an individual as not being an individual for supertax purposes in her capacity as a trustee. This is thought to apply more generally.

To whom does the section apply?

This is dealt with by subsection (2) which is set out above.

This tells us the section applies to:

i. The Settlor; and

ii. Anyone who at any time has been a close member of the settlor's family.

This raises the questions as to who is:

i. The Settlor; and

ii. Anyone who at any time has been a close member of the settled family?

The section does not specifically answer these questions itself. However, in the context though the defined terms relevant to the charging provisions must apply.

"Settlor" for these purposes by Section 620(1) means any person by whom the settlement was made. This is extended by subsections (2) and (3) and include any person who has provided funds directly or indirectly for the purpose of the settlement.

Close Family member is dealt with by 643H inserted by para 20 of the schedule and discussed below.

What is the untaxed benefits total?

This is a defined term for these purposes.

This is found in section 643 B. This is amended by paragraph 14 Schedule 12 discussed below.

In essence this is concerned with untaxed benefits.

See the discussion below.

What is the available protected income?

This is again a defined term for these purposes.

The relevant legislation is found in section 643 C.

A new section 643C is substituted by paragraph 15 Schedule 12. This is discussed below. The amount of the available protected income is to be determined by the four steps set out in section 643 C as substituted.

When does it relate to the individual, the settlement and the tax year?

This is very much a fact dependent matter.

Individual is not defined for these purposes, but it is discussed above and is generally thought not to include a trustee even if the trustee is an individual in the capacity of a trustee. (see the supertax case of *Lady Longford -v- IRC* discussed above.

"Settlement" bears the meaning in section 620.

"Tax year" bears its usual meaning of 6 April one year to 5 April following year. [97]

When is the individual UK tax resident for the tax year in question?

This is a matter to be determined using the SRT. This is discussed in Chapter 3 at 3.3 and Appendices 1 and 2.

As noted above "Tax year" bears the usual meaning of 6 April one year to 5 April the following year. [98] HMRC's view on the position.

> TSEM4720 - Settlements Legislation: Rules affecting non-domiciled and deemed domiciled settlors of non-resident trusts from 6 April 2025: Benefits
>
> For details of the rules introduced from 6 April 2018 on the benefit charge see TSEM 4635.
>
> Under the trust protections measures in place up to and including the 5 April 2025, a settlor of a protected settlement was not taxed on the Protected Foreign-Source Income (PFSI) of the structure as it arose, provided it remained offshore, but they were taxed under section 643A ITTOIA 2005 on any benefits that they received, or under section 643J or section 643L ITTOIA 2005 in relation to onwards gifts, to the extent that the benefit or onward gift was matched with the PFSI of the trust.
>
> From 6 April 2025 a charge applies to a settlor or close family member (CFM) under section 643A ITTOIA 2005 to the extent that they: receive a benefit from the settlement, are UK resident, have an untaxed benefits total and there is available protected income (PFSI or TTI).
>
> If there is a choice about individuals as to whom the income is treated as arising, then HMRC can apportion the tax charge on a just and reasonable basis to prevent any potential double taxation.
>
> From 6 April 2025 if a beneficiary receives a benefit from a previously protected settlement which would ordinarily be taxed on that individual under section 643A ITTOIA 2005, but the recipient of the benefit is eligible for and makes a claim to the 4-year FIG regime for the relevant tax year, no tax will be paid by the individual in relation to the benefit. However, that benefit will not be treated as reducing the pool of available relevant income for matching to future benefits paid out of PFSI/TTI, under section 643C ITTOIA 2005.

---

[97] See Section 4 ITA

[98] See section 4 ITA

What is an untaxed benefit?

For each individual you must determine what their untaxed benefits total is. There are 4 steps set out in the legislation at section 643B ITTOIA 2005 to tell you how to do this.

Step 1

Identify each benefit provided by the trustees to that individual at any time when they were UK resident in the current or an earlier tax year. If the individual is a close family member (CFM) then only include the benefits provided to them at a time when they were a CFM.

If a benefit is provided to a CFM at a time when they are not UK resident, but the settlor is UK resident, then the benefit will be included in the settlor's untaxed benefits total for the year.

Step 2

Next identify the amount or value of each benefit for that individual at Step 1 and calculate the total.

Step 3

Then, deduct from the total at Step 2:

1. Any part of it where the individual has already been subject to income tax by a means other than section 643A ITTOIA 2005,
2. Any part that has been subject to income tax by virtue of section 643A, or previously under old section 643J or section 643L ITTOIA 2005 (onward gifts rules from 6 April 2018 – 5 April 2025),
3. Any whole or part benefit that has been taken into account when charging income tax under the Transfer of Assets Abroad (ToAA) legislation (see INTM600000),
4. Any amount required to be deducted by section 643D (2) ITTOIA 2005 (reduction due to previous capital gains tax charge).

Step 4

If the amount at Step 3 of the calculation is greater than nil, then that is the individual's untaxed benefits total for the current tax year.

Meaning of available protected income

To determine the amount of available protected income, there are 5 steps that you need to follow. These are set out at section 643C ITTOIA 2005:

1. Identify any PFSI and TTI that arose at any time under the settlement. This is the total protected income*.

2. Deduct from the total protected income any amount that has been matched under the ToAA legislation in the current or an earlier tax year.
3. Deduct any amount of the total protected income on which the individual or another individual has been subject to income tax in the current or an earlier tax year.
4. Deduct any amount that is treated as income under section 643A ITTOIA 2005 in an earlier tax year.
5. Add back any amount of income that falls within step 4 at a time that the individual or another individual has claimed relief under the 4-year FIG regime for any tax year.

The amount calculated is the total amount of available protected income (API).

*New section 643ZA ITTOIA 2005 defines what is PFSI and confirms that it is only income which arose to the settlement during tax years 2017/18 to 2024/25. New section 643ZA also defines what is TTI and confirms that it is only income which arose to the settlement between tax years 2008/09 to 2016/17.

Close family member

A general useful starting point is https://www.gov.uk/hmrc-internal-manuals/trusts-settlements-and-estates-manual/tsem4700. This is set out below.

The following extracts are helpful as to what HMRC's view is in respect of Close Family Members.

> "TSEM4650 - Settlements Legislation Rules affecting non-domiciled and deemed domiciled settlors of non-resident trusts from 6 April 2017 – 5 April 2025: Meaning of close member of settlor's family
>
> The guidance on this page relates to the period 6 April 2017 - 5 April 2025. From 6 April 2025 the rules around the taxation of non-UK domiciled individuals ended and individuals are taxable based on their residence position only. Detailed guidance on the changes from 6 April 2025 can be found at TSEM4700 onwards.
>
> For the purposes of S643B to S643M a person is a close member of the family of the settlor of a settlement at any time that the settlor is living at the time, and:
>
> - The person is the settlor's spouse or civil partner at that time, or
> - The person is a child of the settlor, or of a person who at that time is the settlor's spouse or civil partner and who has not reached the age of 18.
>
> Two people living together as if they were a married couple or civil partners are treated as if they were spouses or civil partners of each other.

TSEM4745 - Settlements Legislation: Rules affecting non-domiciled and deemed domiciled settlors of non-resident trusts from 6 April 2025: Close family members

For details of the close family member (CFM) rules introduced from 6 April 2018 see TSEM 4650.

From 6 April 2025 the close family member rules remain the same.

A close family member of the settlor's family is a person who at that time is:

- the settlor's spouse or civil partner;
- a child of the settlor, or a child of the settlor's spouse or civil partner, and has not reached age 18 at the time.
- Two people living together as a married couple are treated as spouses/civil partners for this purpose.

As explained in more detail in TSEM4720 (Benefits) a tax charge will arise under section 643A ITTOIA 2005 when a CFM receives a benefit from the trust. If the CFM is UK resident, then the charge will, in most cases, fall to them. There are some exceptions such as them being eligible for the 4-year FIG regime.

If the CFM is not UK resident, then the charge will fall to the settlor.

If there is a choice about who is taxable then HMRC can apportion the charge on a just and reasonable basis.

The onward gift rules (TSEM4755) extend to CFMs in a similar manner."

3.3.2.15.5 Effective Date

6 April 2025 see paragraph 70.

3.3.2.16 Paragraph 14 – Amendment to meaning of "untaxed benefits total in Section 643B"

3.3.2.16.1 Overview

Paragraph 14 amends section 643B (meaning of "untaxed benefits total" in section 643A) to reflect that the move away from a domicile-based regime means domicile will no longer be relevant after 5 April 2025.

3.3.2.16.2 Legislation

Paragraph 14 reads:

"Section 643B (meaning of "untaxed benefits total" in section 643A) is amended as follows.

(2) In subsection (1), for Step 1 substitute—

"Step 1

Identify each benefit provided by the trustees to the individual—

in the current tax year, or an earlier tax year for which the individual was UK resident, and

(b) if the individual is not the settlor, at a time when the individual
was a close member of the settlor's family."

(3) For subsection (2) substitute—

"(2) For the purposes of Step 1 in subsection (1), if—

(a) the trustees provide a benefit to an individual in a given tax year,

(b) the individual is a close member of the settlor's family when the benefit is provided,

(c) the individual is non-UK resident, or is a qualifying new
resident, for the tax year, and

(d) the settlor is UK resident for the tax year,
the benefit is instead treated as provided to the settlor."

This paragraph amends section 643B. As amended it reads:

"643BMeaning of "untaxed benefits total" in section 643A

(1) For the purposes of section 643A, whether an individual has an untaxed benefits total for a settlement for a tax year ("the current year"), and (if so) its amount, are determined as follows—

Step 1 If the individual is the settlor, identify each benefit provided by the trustees to the individual at a time—update this step

(a) when the individual is not relevantly domiciled, and

(b) In a tax year that is the current year or an earlier tax year.

If the individual is not the settlor, identify each benefit provided by the trustees to the individual at a time—

(a) when the individual is a close member of the settlor's family (see section 643H), and

(b) in a tax year that is the current year or an earlier tax year.

Step 2 Identify the amount or value of each benefit identified in the individual's case at Step 1, and calculate the total of those amounts and values. update this step

Step 3 Take the total calculated at Step 2 and deduct from it the following—

(a) any part of it on which the individual is liable to income tax otherwise than under section 643A,

(b) any income treated by section 643A, 643J or 643L as arising, to a person for a tax year earlier than the current year, by reference to any of the benefits identified in the individual's case at Step 1,

(c) where the whole or part of a benefit identified in the individual's case at Step 1 is taken into account in charging income tax under Chapter 2 of Part 13 of ITA 2007, the amount or value of so much of the benefit as is taken into account in doing that, and

(d) any amount required to be deducted by section 643D (2) (gains treated as accruing in a year before the current year).

Step 4 If the result of the calculation at Step 3 is an amount greater than nil, that amount is the individual's untaxed benefits total for the settlement for the current year.

(2) For the purposes of Step 1 in subsection (1), an individual is "relevantly domiciled" at any time if at that time—

(a) The individual is domiciled in the United Kingdom, or

(b) The individual is regarded for the purposes of section 809(1)(b) of ITA 2007 as domiciled in the United Kingdom as a result of section 835BA of ITA 2007 having effect because of Condition A in that section being met.

(3) Sections 742C to 742E of ITA 2007 (value of certain benefits) apply for the purpose of calculating the value of a benefit for the purposes of this section as they apply for the purpose of calculating an income tax charge under Chapter 2 of Part 13 of ITA 2007.

(4) In this section and sections 643C to 643M, a reference to a benefit provided by trustees of a settlement is to—

(a) A benefit treated by subsection (6) as provided by the trustees, or

(b) Any other benefit if it is provided by the trustees directly, or indirectly, out of—

(i)property comprised in the settlement, or

(ii) Income arising under the settlement.

(5) In this section and sections 643C to 643M, a reference to a benefit provided by trustees of a settlement to an individual is to—

(a) A benefit treated by subsection (6) as provided by the trustees to the individual, or

(b) Any other benefit if it is provided by the trustees to the individual directly, or indirectly, out of—

(i)property comprised in the settlement, or

(ii) Income arising under the settlement.

(6) Where—

(a) Income arises under a settlement, and

(b) The income, before being distributed, is the income of a person other than the trustees, a benefit is for the purposes of subsection (4)(a) treated as provided by the trustees and is for the purposes of subsection (5)(a) treated as provided by the trustees to the person.

(7) A benefit treated as provided by subsection (6) is treated—

(a) As consisting of the income mentioned in that subsection, but after any reduction in accordance with Chapter 8 of Part 9 of ITA 2007 for trustees' expenses, and

(b) As provided at the time that income arises.

3.3.2.16.3 Detail

Paragraph 14 amends section 643B as set out above.

Section 643B (1) Step 1 of the calculation to determine an individual's 'untaxed benefits total' is amended to identify each benefit provided by the trustees to the settlor (or close member of the settlor's family if not the settlor) at a time when they were UK resident.

Section 643(B)(2) is amended to ensure that for the purposes of section 643B(1) Step 1, a benefit is treated as being provided to a UK resident settlor where a close member of the settlor's family receives a benefit from the trustees at a time when they are non-UK resident or a 'qualifying new resident' (an individual who qualifies for relief under section 845A of ITTOIA 2005).

Subsection (5) is amended as a consequence of paragraph 17 and paragraph 21 of the Schedule.

3.3.2.16.4 Effective Date

6 April 2025 see Paragraph 70.

3.3.2.17 Paragraph 15

3.3.2.17.1 Overview

Paragraph 15 substitutes the earlier section 643C (Meaning of "available protected income" in section 643A) with a new a section 643C (Meaning of "available protected income" in section 643A) which defines what is meant by "available protected income" in section 643A. This is the total amount of protected foreign-source income and transitional trust income that arose at any time under the settlement (ignoring section 648(3) to (5)), less income matched under the transfer of assets abroad legislation and income that the individual, or another individual has been liable to income tax on or has been treated as income of the individual under section 643A or section 643J or 643L (as they had effect) during the tax year. Any income identified as 'qualifying foreign income' on a "foreign income claim" [99] under the transfer of assets abroad legislation is added back to establish the "available protected income".

3.3.2.17.2 Legislation

Paragraph 15 reads:

> "For section 643C substitute—
>
> "643C Meaning of "available protected income" in section 643A

[99] These two phrases are discussed above

(1) For the purposes of section 643A, take the following steps to determine the amount of available protected income in relation to an individual ("**P**"), a settlement and a tax year ("**the current tax year**")—

Step 1

Identify the total amount of protected foreign-source income and transitional trust income that arose (at any time) under the settlement ("**the total protected income**").

Step 2

Deduct any amount of the total protected income that is matched under the transfer of assets abroad code in the current tax year or an earlier tax year.

Step 3

Deduct any amount of the total protected income on which P or any other individual is liable to income tax in the current tax year or an earlier tax year.

Step 4

Deduct any amount that, in relation to the settlement, is treated under section 643A as P's income in an earlier tax year or as another individual's income in any tax year.

Step 5

Add back the amount of any income falling within Step 4 that is identified as qualifying foreign income on a foreign income claim made by P or any other individual for any tax year.

(2) For the purposes of Step 1 in subsection (1), ignore section 648(3) to (5) (foreign income treated as "arising" under settlement only if and when remitted).

(3) For the purposes of Step 2 in subsection (1), an amount of the total protected income is "matched under the transfer of assets abroad code" if it is matched under section 735A of ITA 2007 with—

(a) benefits provided by the trustees to P or any other individual in the current tax year or in an earlier tax year, and

(b) an amount of income treated as arising to P or any other individual under section 732 of ITA 2007 (or if it would be so matched if section 735A applied for those purposes).

(4) For the purposes of Step 3 in subsection (1), ignore any liability to income tax arising under section 643A above or under section 731of ITA 2007 (transfer of assets abroad: benefits charge).

(5) In Step 4 in subsection (1) and in subsection (4), a reference to section 643A includes, in relation to any of the tax years 2018-19 to 2024-25, section 643J and 643L (**old onward gifting rules**)."

3.3.2.17.3 Details of the paragraph

This Paragraph substitutes a revised section 643 C as set out above.

3.3.2.17.4 Some questions arising

A number of questions arise in respect of the new section 643C.

3.3.2.17.5 Some Relevant Defined Terms

It is important to know the meaning of the terms used in the section. The following terms seem particularly relevant to me.

- the individual in question (subsection (1))
- the tax year in question (subsection (3))
- "P"
- "The current tax year"
- "The total protected income"
- "Transfer of assets abroad code"
- "Qualifying foreign income"
- "Foreign income claim"
- "Settlement"
- "Tax year"
- "Transfer of assets abroad code" matched under the TOA
- Remember subsection (5) on old onward gifting rules

Phrase	Statutory Reference	Comment
"Foreign income claim"	Section 845A	
the individual in question i.e. P	Section 643C (1)	The meaning for FIG purposes
The current tax year	Section 643C (1)	The year in question
the tax year in question	Section 643C (1)	the period in relation to which the amount of available protected income is to be determined.
"P"	Section 643C (1)	the individual in question
"The current tax year"	Section 643C (1)	a tax year in respect of which the determination is required.
"The total protected income"	Step 1 Section 643C	
"Transfer of assets abroad code"	Section 643C (3)	the Section 720 charge
"Qualifying foreign income"	Section 726	Income identified in claim as such which is accepted as such
"Settlement"	Section 620 ITTOIA	Wide definition which includes "arrangements"
"Tax year"	April 6 in one calendar year to April 5 the following calendar year	Section 4 ITA

3.3.2.17.6 Effective Date

6 April 2025 see paragraph 71.

HMRC's view of the new legislation

There is useful information on HMRC's views in the manuals. A useful starting point is **TSEM4700. This reads as follows:**

> TSEM 4700 – Settlements Legislation: Rules affecting non-domiciled and deemed domiciled settlors of non-resident trusts from 6 April 2025: Contents
>
> 1) TSEM4705 **Introduction**
> 2) TSEM4710 **Removal of Protected Foreign-Source Income (PFSI)**
> 3) TSEM4715 **Tainting**
> 4) TSEM4720 **Benefits**
> 5) TSEM4725 **Example – PFSI and the benefits charge**
> 6) TSEM4730 **Example – PFSI, TTI and the benefits charge**
> 7) TSEM4735 **Example -the benefits charge and choice of who is chargeable**
> 8) TSEM4740 **Example – PFSI, the benefits charge and the 4-year FIG regime**
> 9) TSEM4745 **Close family members**
> 10) TSEM4750 **Example – Close family members**
> 11) TSEM4755 **Onward gifts**
> 12) TSEM4760 **Example – Onward gifts**

3.3.2.18 Paragraph 16 Reimbursement of Settlor

3.3.2.18.1 Overview

Paragraph 16 amends section 643E (reimbursement of tax paid by settlor because of section 643A). This is as a consequence of the amendments made by paragraph 14 Schedule 12 discussed above.

Sub-paragraph 16(4) amends section 643E (2) by substituting revised criteria for the right of recovery certificate that the settlor is entitled to require an officer of Revenue and Customs to provide to the Settlor.

3.3.2.18.2 Legislation

Paragraph 16 reads:

> "(1) Section 643E (reimbursement of tax paid by settlor) is amended as follows.
> (2) In the heading, for "section 643A" substitute "643B (2)".
> (3) In subsection (1), for "section 643A (3) or (4)" substitute "section 643B (2) (benefit received by close family member attributed to settlor)".
> (4) In subsection (2), for paragraphs (a) and (b) substitute—
> "(a) the tax year in which income is treated under section 643A as arising to the settlor,
> (b) the amount of income treated as arising, and

(c) the amount of tax paid,".

The updated section 643E reads as follows:

"643EReimbursement of tax paid by settlor because of section 643B (2)]

(1) Where any tax for which the settlor of a settlement is liable as a result of section 643B (2) (benefit received by close family member attributed to settlor) is paid, the settlor is entitled to recover the amount of the tax from the individual concerned.

(2) For the purpose of recovering that amount, the settlor is entitled to require an officer of Revenue and Customs to give the settlor a certificate specifying—

(a) The tax year in which income is treated under section 643A as arising to the settlor,

(b) The amount of income treated as arising, and

(c) The amount of tax paid,

and any such certificate is conclusive evidence of the facts stated in it."

3.3.2.18.3 Details of the paragraph

Various provisions which treat income or gains arising us under a settlement as the Settlor's for tax purposes allow the Settlor a right of reimbursement or of recovery in some circumstances.

This includes section 643E headed "reimbursement of tax paid by settlor"

Paragraph 16 amends section 643 E because of the changes made by paragraph 14. Paragraph 14 is discussed above.

3.3.2.18.4 Effective Date

6 April 2025 see paragraph 70.

3.3.2.19 Paragraph 17 Onward Gifts from non-residents and qualifying new residents

3.3.2.19.1 Overview

It would be possible if provision were not made to prevent it applying by paying or transferring assets to close family to avoid certain charges. Provision in this regard is made by section 643EA.

Paragraph 17 inserts a new section 643EA headed "Onward gifts from non-residents or qualifying new residents".

Where section 643B(2) (close family member's benefits attributed to settlor) does not apply, new section 643EA provides for a benefits charge to arise on a UK resident settlor or a close member of the settlor's family in situations where the trustees provide a benefit to a non-UK resident individual or 'qualifying new resident' (an individual who qualifies for relief under section 845A of ITTOIA

2005 discussed [below]) who then passes it on to the UK resident settlor or a close member of the settlor's family within 3 years of the original benefit being received (or at any time before the original benefit is provided where this was in anticipation of the original benefit being provided).

The benefits charge will apply in the tax year when the onward gift is provided to "close family members".

If there is a series of two or more benefits, then the benefits charge will apply when the final benefit in the series is provided. This puts a great importance on the meaning of "series" in the context. Does it cover a number of payments that just happened to be made or is there more required? Is a deliberate intention to make more than one payment needed? Does the payment need to be made in close proximity of time? What if a payment is missed? Is there an argument to enter into "covenant to pay" as is done on a number of payments out of normal income IHT arrangements. How long could the charge be delayed for? Should the payment to be structured as a conduit? I favour having some documentation for clarity and to help push the timing of the tax charge back if that is what is wanted.

The SOD (inter alia) defines "series" as "A number of things of one kind (immaterial) following one another in temporal succession or in the order of discourse or resourcing". This seems to me to be the likely meaning here.

3.3.2.19.2 Legislation

Paragraph 17 reads:

> "After section 643E insert—
>
> "643EA Onward gifts from non-residents or qualifying new residents
>
> (1) Subsection (2) applies if—
>
> (a) the trustees of a settlement provide a benefit ("**the original benefit**") to an individual ("**the original recipient**"),
>
> (b) the original recipient is **non-UK resident, or is a qualifying new resident,** for the **tax year in which the original benefit is provided**,
>
> (c) Section **643B (2)** (close family member's benefits attributed to settlor) does **not apply to** the **provision of the original benefit to the original recipient**,
>
> (d) at the time when the original benefit is provided—
>
> (i) there are arrangements, or an intention, as regards the (direct or indirect) passing on of the whole or part of the original benefit to another person, and
>
> (ii) it is **reasonable to expect** that, **if** the whole or part of the original benefit is **passed on** to another person in accordance with the arrangements

or intention, that **other person will be UK resident when they receive at least part** of what is passed on to them,

(e) the original recipient provides a benefit ("**the onward gift**") to another person ("**the subsequent recipient**")—

(i) at the time when the original benefit is provided to the original recipient, or at any later time in the **3 years beginning with the day containing that time**, or

(ii) at any time before the original benefit is provided to the original recipient and, it is reasonable to assume, in anticipation of the original benefit's being provided,

(f) the onward gift is of or includes—

(i) the whole or part of the original benefit,

(ii) anything that (wholly or in part, and directly or indirectly) derives from, or represents, the whole or part of the original benefit, or

(iii) any other property, but only if the original benefit is provided with a **view to enabling or facilitating, or otherwise in connection** with, the property's being **provided to the subsequent recipient**, and

(g) the subsequent recipient—

(i) is the settlor, or

(ii) is a close member of the settlor's family at the time when they receive the onward gift or, where the onward gift is provided as mentioned in subsection (1)(e)(ii), at the time given by subsection (4).

(2) So much of the onward gift as falls within subsection (1)(f) is treated for the purposes of section 643B (1) and (2)(a) as a benefit provided by the trustees to the subsequent recipient at the time when the onward gift is provided.

(3) For the purposes of subsection (1)(e), the circumstances in which the original recipient provides a benefit to the subsequent recipient include circumstances where there is a series of two or more benefits starting with a benefit provided by the original recipient and ending with a benefit provided to the subsequent recipient; and in such a case -

(a) the onward gift is treated for the purposes of subsection (1)(e) as provided when the final benefit in the series is provided, and

(b) the reference to the onward gift in subsection (1)(f) is to be read as a reference to each benefit in the series.

(4) Where the onward gift is made as mentioned in subsection (1)(e)(ii), it is treated for the purposes of subsection (2) as made immediately after, and in the tax year in which, the original benefit is provided to the original recipient.

(5) Where the conditions in subsection (1)(e) to (g) are met in any case, it is to be presumed (unless the contrary is shown) that the condition in subsection (1)(d) is also met in that case."

3.3.2.19.3 Details of the paragraph

Paragraph 17 inserts a new section 643 EA into ITTOIA. This is set out above.

There are a number of important words and phrases used which need to be understood to understand how the section works. Some of these are discussed next.

3.3.2.19.4 Definitions, words and phrases

It is important to know the meaning of the terms used in the section. The following terms seem particularly relevant to me.

- "Transfer of assets
- The original benefit
- the original recipient
- Non-UK resident
- Arrangements or intention subsection six
- Reasonable to expect
- The onward gift
- The subsequent recipient
- The day containing that time three year.
- With a view to enabling
- Settlor
- Close member of the settlor's family
- Final benefit
- Tax Year
- Trustees of a settlement
- Series of benefits

The following table may assist the Reader in understanding this:

Phrase	Statutory Reference	Comment
Arrangements or intention	S 643EA (1)(d)(7)	The conditions in subsections 1(e) to (g) are met it is presumed the condition in subsection 1(d) is also met. Section 643 EA subsection (7) provides "arrangements" includes any agreement, understanding, scheme, transaction or series of transactions (whether or not legally enforceable).
Close member of the settlor's family	S 643 H	The meaning of this phrase is discussed at XX The text of the section is set out below.
Final benefit	S 643 A	
Non-UK resident		The usual SRT meaning
Reasonable to expect	S 643EA (1)(d)(ii)	This implies a range of possible answers. A difficult phrase particularly outside its core meaning. Who is to make the judgment? A reasonable person on the Clapham Onmibus? What criteria are to be used?
Series of benefits	S 643EA (3)	
Settlor	section 620 ITTOIA	The person who made or provided funds or assets to the settlement
Tax Year	section 4 ITA	April 6 one year to the following April 6
the day containing that time in three-year period	S 643EA(1)(e)	See discussion above
the onward gift	643EA(1)(c)	
the original benefit	643EA (1)(a)	
the original recipient	643EA (1) (a)	
the subsequent recipient	643EA(1)(e)	
Trustees of a settlement		The usual meaning
With a view to enabling	See Section 643 EA (5) and effect of conditions being fulfilled	Essentially a question of fact but can have wide meaning

The text etc. of section 643H – Close member of the family

Section 643H reads as follows.

> **"643HMeaning of close member of settlor's family in sections 643A to 643EA**
>
> (1) For the purposes of sections 643A to 643EA, a person is a close member of the family of the settlor of a settlement at any time if the settlor is living at that time and—

(a) The person is the settlor's spouse or civil partner at that time, or
(b) The person—
(i) Is a child of the settlor, or of a person who at that time is the settlor's spouse or civil partner, and
(ii) At that time has not reached the age of 18.

(2) For the purposes of subsection (1), two people living together as if they were a married couple or civil partners are treated as if they were spouses or civil partners of each other."

3.3.2.19.5 Effective Date

6 April 2025 see paragraph 70.

3.3.2.20 Paragraph 18 Old remittance rules where straddle of 5/6 April 2025

3.3.2.20.1 Overview

Paragraph 18 amends section 643F (income attributed by section 643A to user of remittance basis) as a consequence of the changes paragraph 13 and paragraph 15 Schedule 12 discussed above. This is to reflect that the previous rules relating to the remittance basis and old sections 643A and 643C will no longer apply after 5 April 2025 but remain effective to the extent that they had effect for the tax year in which the deemed income was treated as arising to the individual where that was before 6 April 2025.

3.3.2.20.2 Legislation

Paragraph 18 reads:

"(1) Section 643F (income attributed by section 643A to user of remittance basis) is amended as follows.
(2) In subsection (1)—
(a) in paragraph (a), for the words from "is treated" to the end substitute "was treated by section 643A as arising to an individual for any of the tax years 2018-19 to 2024-25, and";
(b) in paragraph (b), for "applies" substitute "applied".
(3) In subsection (6)—
(a) in the definition of "protected income", for "forms" substitute "under section 643C formed";
(b) in the definition of "the relevant individual", in paragraphs (a) and (b), for "is treated" substitute "was treated".
(4) At the end insert—
"(7) A reference in this section to section 643A or 643C (or to any provision of that section) is to that section (or provision) as it had effect for the tax year in which the deemed income was treated as arising to the individual."

As amended section 643F reads as follows:

643F Income attributed by section 643A to user of remittance basis

(1) This section applies where—

(a) In the case of a settlement, income ("the deemed income") was treated by section 643A as arising to an individual for any of the tax years 2018-19 to 2024-25, and]

(b) Section 809B, 809D or 809E of ITA 2007 (remittance basis) applied to the individual for that year.

(2) The deemed income is treated as relevant foreign income of the individual.

(3) In the application of section 832 to the deemed income, subsection (2) of that section has effect with the omission of paragraph (b).

(4) For the purposes of Chapter A1 of Part 14 of ITA 2007 (remittance basis) treat a benefit, or any protected income, that relates to any part of the deemed income as deriving from that part of the deemed income.

(5) In subsection (4) "relates" has the meaning given by section 643G.

(6) In this section and section 643G—

"protected income" means the income that under section 643C formed PFSI in the calculation of the settlement's available protected income in the case of the relevant individual for the year, and

"the relevant individual"—

(a) Where the deemed income was treated as income of an individual by section 643A(1)(a) both before and after the application of section 643A (3) and (4), means that individual, and

(b) where the deemed income was treated as income of the settlor by section 643A (3) or (4) after having been treated as income of another individual by section 643A (1), means that other individual.

(7) A reference in this section to section 643A or 643C (or to any provision of that section) is to that section (or provision) as it had effect for the tax year in which the deemed income was treated as arising to the individual."

3.3.2.20.3 Details of the paragraph

Section 643F is amended because of the changes made by paragraphs 13 and 15 (discussed above) which mean the old remittance rules in old sections 643A - 643C will not apply after 5 April 2025 but remain effective for the tax years before 6 April 2025 in which the deemed income was treated as arising.

3.3.2.20.4 Effective Date

6 April 2025 see paragraph 70.

3.3.2.21 Paragraph 19 Benefits and income relating to deemed income

3.3.2.21.1 Overview

Paragraph 19 amends section 643G (section 643F (4): benefits and income "relating" to deemed income) as a consequence of the changes made by paragraph 13 and paragraph 21 of the Schedule 12 discussed elsewhere. This reflects that old section 643A (Deemed income because of benefits for settlor or close family member) and repealed sections 643I to 643M (old onward gift provisions) will no longer apply after 5 April 2025 but remain effective to the extent that they had effect before 6 April 2025.

3.3.2.21.2 Legislation

Paragraph 19 reads:

"(1) Section 643G (section 643F (4): benefits and income "relating" to deemed income) is amended as follows.

(2) In subsection (1)—

(a) in paragraph (a), for "applies" substitute "applied";

(b) after paragraph (a) insert—

(aa) references to section 643A, 643J or 643L (or to a provision of any of those sections) are to that section (or provision) as it had effect for the year,".

(3) In subsection (2)—

(a) in paragraph (b), for "is allowed" substitute "was allowed";

(b) in paragraph (d), for "is", in both places it occurs, substitute "was";

(c) in paragraph (e), for "is", in both places it occurs, substitute "was";

(d) in paragraph (f), for "is treated" substitute "was treated".

3.3.2.21.3 Details of the paragraph

This is essentially a tidying up provision making sure the right cross references and tenses are used.

The past tense is substituted in subsection (1)(a) and subsection (2). This helps with the clarity of what is intended.

3.3.2.21.4 Effective Date

6 April 2025 see Paragraph 70.

3.3.2.22 Paragraph 20 Meaning of close member of settlor's family

3.3.2.22.1 Overview

Paragraph 20 amends section 643H (meaning of close member of settlor's family) as a consequence of the changes made by paragraph 13 and paragraph 17 Schedule 12. These are discussed above.

3.3.2.22.2 Legislation

i. General

Paragraph 20 reads:

"In section 643H (meaning of close member of settlor's family), in the heading and in subsection (1), for "643B to 643M" substitute "643A to 643EA".

ii. Section 643H after amendment reads as follows.

"643HMeaning of close member of settlor's family in sections 643A to 643EA

(1) For the purposes of sections 643A to 643EA, a person is a close member of the family of the settlor of a settlement at any time if the settlor is living at that time and—

(a) The person is the settlor's spouse or civil partner at that time, or

(b) The person—

(i) Is a child of the settlor, or of a person who at that time is the settlor's spouse or civil partner, and

(ii) At that time has not reached the age of 18.

(2) For the purposes of subsection (1), two people living together as if they were a married couple or civil partners are treated as if they were spouses or civil partners of each other.

3.3.2.22.3 Details of the paragraph

This paragraph essentially changes the cross references following the changes made by Paragraph 13 and [17]

3.3.2.22.4 Effective Date

6 April 2025 see paragraph 70.

3.3.2.23 Paragraph 21 Repeal of certain old onward gift provisions

3.3.2.23.1 Overview

Paragraph 21 omits sections 643I to 643M (old onward gift provisions) as a consequence of paragraph 17 of the Schedule. These sections will no longer apply after 5 April 2025 but remain effective to the extent that they had effect before 6 April 2025.

Paragraph 17 is discussed above.

3.3.2.23.2 Legislation

Paragraph 21 reads:

"Omit sections 643I to 643M (old onward gift provisions)."

Section 643I Recipients of onward gifts

Sections 643I to 643M read as follows

(1) Sections 643J to 643L apply if—

(a) In the case of a settlement, an amount—

(i) Is treated by section 643A(1)(a), both before and after the application of section 643A (3) and (4), as income of an individual ("the original beneficiary") for a tax year ("the matching year"), or

(ii) Having been treated by section 643A(1) before the application of section 643A(3) and (4) as income of an individual ("the original beneficiary") for a tax year ("the matching year"), is treated by section 643A(3) or (4) as income of the settlor for the matching year, or

(iii) Is treated by section 643A(1)(b), before the application of section 643A(3) and (4), as income of an individual ("the original beneficiary") for a tax year ("the matching year") but is not treated by section 643A(3), and is not treated by section 643A(4), as income of the settlor for the matching year,

(b) Under section 643G (if it applied also for this purpose) the amount would be matched with a benefit provided in the matching year, or an earlier tax year, to the original beneficiary,

(c) At the time the benefit is provided to the original beneficiary—

(i) There are arrangements, or there is an intention, as regards the (direct or indirect) passing-on of the whole, or part, of the benefit to another person, and

(ii) It is reasonable to expect that, in the event of the whole or part of the benefit being passed on to another person as envisaged by the arrangements or intention, that other person will be UK resident when they receive at least part of what is passed on to them,

(d) The original beneficiary makes, directly or indirectly, a gift ("the onward payment") to a person ("the subsequent recipient")—

(i) At the time the benefit is provided to the original beneficiary, or at any later time in the 3 years beginning with the day containing the start time, or

(ii) At any time before the benefit is provided to the original beneficiary and, it is reasonable to assume, in anticipation of the benefit being provided,

(e) The gift is of or includes—

(i) The whole or part of the benefit,

(ii) Anything that (wholly or in part, and directly or indirectly) derives from, or represents, the whole or part of the benefit, or

(iii) Any other property, but only if the benefit is provided with a view to enabling or facilitating, or otherwise in connection with, the making of the gift of the property to the subsequent recipient,

(f) In a case within paragraph (a)(i), either—

(i) The original beneficiary is non-UK resident for the matching year, or

(ii) Section 809B, 809D or 809E of ITA 2007 (remittance basis) applies to the original beneficiary for the matching year and none of the amount is relevantly remitted in the matching year or in any tax year later than the matching year but not later than the tax year in which the onward payment is made,

(g) In a case within paragraph (a)(ii), section 809B, 809D or 809E of ITA 2007 (remittance basis) applies to the settlor for the matching year and none of the amount is relevantly remitted in the matching year or in any tax year later than the matching year but not later than the tax year in which the onward payment is made, and

(h) The subsequent recipient—

(i) Is the settlor, or

(ii) Is a close member of the settlor's family (see section 643H) at the time the onward payment is made or, where that time is given by subsection (4), at either or both of the time so given and the actual time the onward payment is made.

(2) Where, in a case within subsection (1)(a)(i) and by reference to the amount mentioned in subsection (1)(a), income is treated by section 643J or 643L as arising to a person for a tax year, the original beneficiary is not liable to tax for any later tax year on so much of the amount mentioned in subsection (1)(a) as is equal to that income; and where, in a case within subsection (1)(a)(ii) and by reference to the amount mentioned in subsection (1)(a), income is treated by section 643J as arising to a person for a tax year, the settlor is not liable to tax for any later tax year on so much of the amount mentioned in subsection (1)(a) as is equal to that income.

(3) The amount mentioned in subsection (1)(a) need not be—

(a) The whole amount that in the case of the settlement is treated by section 643A (1), before the application of section 643A (3) and (4), as income of the original beneficiary for the matching year;

(b) The whole amount that would be matched with the benefit mentioned in subsection (1)(b).

(4) Where the onward payment is made as mentioned in subsection (1)(d)(ii), the onward payment is to be treated—

(a) For the purposes of the provisions of this section following subsection (1)(d), and

(b) For the purposes of sections 643J to 643L,

as made immediately after, and in the tax year in which, the benefit is provided to the original beneficiary.

(5) For the purposes of subsection (1)(d)(i)—

(a) If the amount mentioned in subsection (1)(a) is not one that is treated as arising by section 643K, "the start time"—

(i) Is the time the benefit mentioned in subsection (1)(b) is provided to the original beneficiary, or

(ii) Where that benefit is one that section 643M(3) treats as provided, is the time the original benefit in that case (see section 643M(1)(a)) is provided, and

(b) If the amount mentioned in subsection (1)(a) is one that is treated as arising by section 643K in connection with the operation of this section and section 643K on a previous occasion, "the start time" is the time given by this subsection as the start time on that occasion.

(6) Where subsection (1)(d) and (e) are met in any case, it is to be presumed (unless the contrary is shown) that subsection (1)(c) is also met in that case.

(7) In this section (and sections 643J to 643L)—

"arrangements" includes any agreement, understanding, scheme, transaction or series of transactions (whether or not legally enforceable),

"the charging year" means the gift year or, if later, the matching year,

"gift" includes any benefit,

"the gift year" means the tax year in which the onward payment is made (but see subsection (4)),

"make", in relation to a gift that is a benefit, means confer, and

"relevantly remitted" means remitted to the United Kingdom in a tax year for which the original beneficiary is UK resident but, in a case within subsection (1)(a)(ii), means remitted to the United Kingdom in a tax year for which the settlor is UK resident.

(8) Sections 742C to 742E of ITA 2007 (value of certain benefits)—

(a) Apply for the purpose of calculating the value of the onward payment for the purposes of sections 643J to 643L as they apply for the purpose of calculating an income tax charge under Chapter 2 of Part 13 of ITA 2007, and

(b) Apply for that purpose as if their references to a benefit provided were references to a gift made.

(9) Sections 809L to 809Z6 of ITA 2007 (remittance basis: rules about when income is remitted)—

(a) Apply for the purposes of this section and sections 643J to 643L, and

(b) Apply for those purposes in relation to references to remittance of the onward payment as if the onward payment were relevant foreign income of the subsequent recipient.]

643J Cases where income treated as arising to recipient of onward gift

(1) Subsection (3) applies if—

(a) This section applies (see section 643I(1)), and

(b) The subsequent recipient is UK resident for the gift year, and

(c) The subsequent recipient is UK resident for the matching year if that is later than the gift year, and

(d)none of sections 809B, 809D and 809E of ITA 2007 (remittance basis) applies to the subsequent recipient for the charging year.

(2) Subsection (3) also applies if—

(a) This section applies (see section 643I(1)), and

(b) The subsequent recipient is UK resident for the gift year, and

(c) The subsequent recipient is UK resident for the matching year if that is later than the gift year, and

(d) Section 809B, 809D or 809E of ITA 2007 applies to the subsequent recipient for the charging year, and

(e) The whole, or part only, of the onward payment is remitted to the United Kingdom in the charging year.

(3) For income tax purposes, an amount of income—

(a) Equal to the amount or value of so much of the onward payment as is within any of sub-paragraphs (i) to (iii) of section 643I(1)(e), or

(b) Where this subsection applies because of subsection (2) and part only of that much of the onward payment is remitted to the United Kingdom in the charging year, equal to the amount or value of that part,

is treated as income of the subsequent recipient for the charging year, subject to subsection (4).

(4) The amount given by subsection (3) (before adjustment under this subsection) is to be adjusted as follows—

(a) Deduct any part of the amount on which the subsequent recipient is liable to income tax otherwise than under this section, and

(b) If following any adjustment under paragraph (a) the amount exceeds the amount mentioned in section 643I(1)(a), deduct the excess.]

643KCases where deemed income attributed to recipient of onward gift

(1) Subsection (3) applies if this section applies (see section 643I(1)) and—

(a) The subsequent recipient is non-UK resident for the gift year, or

(b) The matching year is later than the gift year and the subsequent recipient is UK resident for the gift year but non-UK resident for the matching year.

(2) Subsection (3) also applies if—

(a) This section applies (see section 643I(1)), and

(b) The subsequent recipient is UK resident for the gift year, and

(c) The subsequent recipient is UK resident for the matching year if that is later than the gift year, and

(d) Section 809B, 809D or 809E of ITA 2007 applies to the subsequent recipient for the charging year, and (e)none, or part only, of the onward payment is remitted to the United Kingdom in the charging year.

(3) Section 643I(1)(a) has effect—

(a) As if the subsequent recipient were an individual to whom, in the case of the settlement, income is treated by section 643A(1)(a), both before and after the application of section 643A(3) and (4), as arising for the charging year, and

(b) As if, subject to subsection (4), the amount of that income—

(i) Were equal to the amount or value of so much of the onward payment as is within any of sub-paragraphs (i) to (iii) of section 643I(1)(e) and is not treated as arising to the settlor as a result of the operation of section 643L, or

(ii) Were, where this subsection applies because of subsection (2) and part only of that much of the onward payment is remitted to the United Kingdom in the charging year, equal to the amount or value of the remainder of that much of the onward payment.

(4) The amount given by subsection (3) (before adjustment under this subsection) is to be adjusted as follows: if that amount exceeds the amount mentioned in section 643I(1)(a) in the case of the original beneficiary, deduct the excess.

(5) Where the amount mentioned in section 643I(1)(a) is treated as arising by this section in connection with the operation of section 643I and this section on a previous occasion, section 643I(1) has effect—

(a) With the omission of its paragraphs (b) and (c),

(b) As if the references in its paragraph (d) to the benefit mentioned in its paragraph (b) were, instead, to what was the onward payment on that previous occasion,

(c) As if the references in its paragraph (d) to when that benefit is provided were, instead, to when that onward payment was made, and

(d) As if the references in its paragraph (e) to that benefit were, instead, to so much of that onward payment as was on that previous occasion within any of sub-paragraphs (i) to (iii) of that paragraph.

643LCases where settlor liable following onward gift

(1) Subsection (3) applies if—

(a) This section applies (see section 643I(1)),

(b) The subsequent recipient is a close member of the settlor's family (see section 643H) when the onward payment is made,

(c) The subsequent recipient is UK resident for the charging year,

(d) Section 809B, 809D or 809E of ITA 2007 applies to the subsequent recipient for the charging year, (e)none, or part only, of the onward payment is remitted to the United Kingdom in the charging year,

(f) There is a time in the charging year when the settlor is UK resident,

(g) There is no time in the charging year when the settlor is domiciled in the United Kingdom, and

(h) There is no time in the charging year when the settlor is regarded for the purposes of section 809B(1)(b) of ITA 2007 as domiciled in the United Kingdom as a result of section 835BA of ITA 2007 having effect because of Condition A in that section being met.

(2) Subsection (3) also applies if—

(a) This section applies (see section 643I(1)),

(b) The subsequent recipient is a close member of the settlor's family when the onward payment is made,

(c) The subsequent recipient is non-UK resident for the charging year,

(d) There is a time in the charging year when the settlor is UK resident,

(e) There is no time in the charging year when the settlor is domiciled in the United Kingdom, and

(f) There is no time in the charging year when the settlor is regarded for the purposes of section 809B(1)(b) of ITA 2007 as domiciled in the United Kingdom as a result of section 835BA of ITA 2007 having effect because of Condition A in that section being met.

(3) For income tax purposes, an amount of income—

(a) Equal to the amount or value of so much of the onward payment as is within any of sub-paragraphs (i) to (iii) of section 643I(1)(e), or

(b) Where this subsection applies because of subsection (1) in a case where part only of that much of the onward payment is remitted to the United Kingdom in the charging year, equal to the amount or value of the remainder of that much of the onward payment,

is treated as arising to the settlor for the charging year, subject to subsection (4).

(4) The amount given by subsection (3) (before adjustment under this subsection) is to be adjusted as follows—

(a) Deduct any part of the amount on which the settlor is liable to income tax otherwise than under this section, and

(b) If following any adjustment under paragraph (a) the amount exceeds the amount mentioned in section 643I(1)(a), deduct the excess.

(5) Where any tax for which the settlor is liable as a result of subsections (3) and (4) is paid, the settlor is entitled to recover the amount of the tax from the subsequent recipient.

(6) For the purpose of recovering that amount, the settlor is entitled to require an officer of Revenue and Customs to give the settlor a certificate specifying—

(a) The amount of the income concerned, and

(b) The amount of tax paid,

and any such certificate is conclusive evidence of the facts stated in it.

643MOnward gift to settlor or close family member by other recipient

(1) Subsection (3) applies if—

(a) The trustees of a settlement provide a benefit ("the original benefit") to an individual ("the original recipient"),

(b) The original recipient is not the settlor,

(c) At the time the original benefit is provided, the original recipient is not a close member of the settlor's family (see section 643H),

(d) The original recipient is not taxed on the original benefit (see subsection (7)),

(e) At the time the original benefit is provided—

(i) There are arrangements, or there is an intention, as regards the (direct or indirect) passing-on of the whole, or part, of the original benefit to another person, and

(ii) It is reasonable to expect that, in the event of the whole or part of the original benefit being passed on to another person as envisaged by the arrangements or intention, that other person will be UK resident when they receive at least part of what is passed on to them,

(f) The original recipient makes, directly or indirectly, a gift ("the onward payment") to a person ("the subsequent recipient")—

(i) At the time the original benefit is provided to the original recipient, or at any later time in the 3 years beginning with the day containing that time, or

(ii) At any time before the original benefit is provided to the original recipient and, it is reasonable to assume, in anticipation of the original benefit being provided,

(g) The gift is of or includes—

(i) The whole or part of the original benefit,

(ii) Anything that (wholly or in part, and directly or indirectly) derives from, or represents, the whole or part of the original benefit, or

(iii) Any other property, but only if the original benefit is provided with a view to enabling or facilitating, or otherwise in connection with, the making of the gift of the property to the subsequent recipient, and

(h) The subsequent recipient—

(i) Is the settlor, or

(ii) Is a close member of the settlor's family at the time the onward payment is made or, where that time is given by subsection (4), at either or both of the time so given and the actual time the onward payment is made.

(2) Where—

(a) There is a series of two or more gifts,

(b) The first gift in the series is made, directly or indirectly, by the original recipient—

(i) At the time the original benefit is provided, or at any later time in the 3 years beginning with the day containing that time, or

(ii) At any time before the original benefit is provided and, it is reasonable to assume, in anticipation of the original benefit being provided,

(c) The recipient of a gift in the series is the person who makes, directly or indirectly, the next gift in the series,

(d) The recipient of the last gift in the series is the settlor or, at the time that last gift is made, is a close member of the settlor's family,

(e) As regards any earlier gift in the series, its recipient—

(i) Is not the settlor, and

(ii) Is not, at the time that earlier gift is made, a close member of the settlor's family, and

(f) The condition in subsection (1)(g) is met in relation to each gift in the series,

the last gift in the series is to be treated for the purposes of subsection (1)(f) as if its maker were the original recipient (and not its actual maker).

(3) So much of the onward payment as is within any of sub-paragraphs (i) to (iii) of subsection (1)(g) is treated for the purposes of Step 1 in section 643B(1) as a benefit provided by the trustees to the subsequent recipient at the time the onward payment is made.

(4) Where the onward payment is made as mentioned in subsection (1)(f)(ii), the onward payment is to be treated, for the purposes of subsections (1)(h) and (3), as made immediately after, and in the tax year in which, the original benefit is provided to the original recipient.

(5) Where subsection (1)(f) to (h) are met in any case, it is to be presumed (unless the contrary is shown) that subsection (1)(e) is also met in that case.

(6) Where the benefit mentioned in section 643I(1)(b) is one that subsection (3) of this section treats as provided, section 643I(1) has effect with the omission of its paragraph (c).

(7) For the purposes of subsection (1)(d), the original recipient is taxed on the original benefit if the original recipient is liable to income tax, or capital

gains tax, by reference to the amount or value of the original benefit; and where the original recipient is so liable by reference to the amount or value of part only of the original benefit, this section applies as if the two parts of the original benefit were separate benefits.

(8) In this section—

"arrangements" includes any agreement, understanding, scheme, transaction or series of transactions (whether or not legally enforceable),

"gift" includes any benefit, and

"make", in relation to a gift that is a benefit, means confer,

and see also section 643B(4) to (7) (interpretation of references to provision of benefits by trustees)"

3.3.2.23.3 Details of the paragraph

This paragraph as noted above omits the old onward gift provisions as a consequence of the changes made by paragraph 17 which inserted the new section 643EA headed "Onward gifts from non-residents or qualifying new residents. The sections do not apply after 5 April 2025 in general but remain effective as they did before 6 April 2025 some/same circumstances [Where there is a straddle of 5/6 April 2025.]

3.3.2.23.4 Effective Date

6 April 2025 see Paragraph 70.

3.3.2.24 Paragraph 22 Amendment of section 643N following paragraph the repeal of 21

3.3.2.24.1 Overview

Paragraph 22 amends section 643N (person liable under section 643J or 643L and remittance basis applies) as a consequence of the repeal of sections 643I to 643M (old onward gift provisions) under paragraph 21 of the Schedule. This reflects that repealed sections 643I to 643M (old onward gift provisions) will no longer apply after 5 April 2025 but remain effective to the extent that they had effect for the tax year in which the income was treated as arising to the individual before 6 April 2025.

3.3.2.24.2 Legislation

Paragraph 22 reads:

"(1) Section 643N (person liable under section 643J or 643L and remittance basis applies) is amended as follows.

(2) In the heading, for "applies" substitute "applied".

(3) In subsection (1)—

(a) in paragraph (a)—

(i) in the words before sub-paragraph (i), for "is treated as arising to an individual for a tax year" substitute "was treated as arising to an individual for the tax year 2024-25 or an earlier tax year";

(ii) in sub-paragraph (i), for "applies" substitute "applied";

(b) in paragraph (b), for "applies" substitute "applied".

(4) In subsection (3), after "onward payment" insert "referred to in section 643I(1)(d)".

(5) At the end insert—

"(5) A reference in this section to section 643I, 643J or 643L (or to a provision of any of those sections) is to that section (or provision) as it had effect for the tax year in which income was treated as arising to the individual."

3.3.2.24.3 Details of the paragraph

This is essentially a tidying up provision consequential on repeals brought about by paragraph 21 Schedule 12. It is concerned with the position pre-6 April 2021 where relevant. It changes the tenses used in the provision to reflect the changes made.

3.3.2.24.4 Effective Date

6 April 2025 see paragraph 70.

3.3.2.25 Paragraph 23 Amendment of section 645 (property or income originating from settlor) consequential on paragraph 5

3.3.2.25.1 Overview

Paragraph 23 amends section 645 (property or income originating from settlor) as a consequence of the changes made by paragraph 5 Schedule 12 (See above). Sub-paragraph 23(3) inserts new subsection (2A) which provides that where the same property is provided by more than one settlor, the property will be attributed and apportioned to each settlor in a just and reasonable way.

3.3.2.25.2 Legislation

i. General

Paragraph 23 reads:

"(1) Section 645 (property or income originating from settlor) is amended as follows.

(2) In subsection (1), for "sections 628A and 644" substitute "section 644".

(3) After subsection (2) insert—

"(2A) If the same property has been provided by more than one settlor for the purposes of the settlement, so much of the property as is attributable to each settlor on a just and reasonable apportionment is treated for the purposes of this section as provided by that settlor."

ii. Text of section 645 as amended

Section 645 as amended reads as follows:

> **"645 Property or income originating from settlor**
>
> (1) References in section 644 to property originating from a settlor are references to—
>
> (a) property which the settlor has provided directly or indirectly for the purposes of the settlement,
>
> (b) property representing property so provided, and
>
> (c) so much of any property which represents both property so provided and other property as, on a just and reasonable apportionment, represents the property so provided.
>
> (2) References in sections 627 and 644 to income originating from a settlor are references to—
>
> (a) income from property originating from the settlor, and
>
> (b) income provided directly or indirectly by the settlor.
>
> (2A) If the same property has been provided by more than one settlor for the purposes of the settlement, so much of the property as is attributable to each settlor on a just and reasonable apportionment is treated for the purposes of this section as provided by that settlor.
>
> (3) In this section references to property or income which a settlor has provided directly or indirectly—
>
> (a) Include references to property or income which has been provided directly or indirectly by another person under reciprocal arrangements with the settlor, but
>
> (b) Do not include references to property or income which the settlor has provided directly or indirectly under reciprocal arrangements with another person.
>
> (4) In this section references to property which represents other property include references to property which represents accumulated income from the other property."

3.3.2.25.3 Details of the paragraph

This paragraph tidies some of the cross references and provides that if there is provision of the same property by more than one settlor the property will be attributed to each settlor in a just and reasonable way.

3.3.2.25.4 Some questions

Paragraph 23 raises some questions including the following:

- What is the same property?
    - This is not an easy question. Where there is joint ownership of property, say a house, each owner has their own rights and obligations.

These can vary depending on whether the holding is as joint tenants or as tenants in common.

Example

If Fru and Mark the parents of Flicka give the family home jointly owned by them to Flicka then the subject matter, namely the house, has moved from parents to daughter.

However, if the parents owned as tenants in common, they each had a separate interest in the house which was a separate property right. On that basis it is not the same property given away.

The question then is should one take a strict legal approach or take a more practical approach and say the parents had given their daughter the house. Subsection (2A) allows a practical approach to be taken on a just and reasonable apportionment basis.

The government say the following:

Joint property ownership: Overview - GOV.UK

"**Joint tenants**

As joint tenants (sometimes called 'beneficial joint tenants'):

- you have equal rights to the whole property
- the property automatically goes to the other owners if you die
- you cannot pass on your ownership of the property in your will

Tenants in common

As tenants in common:

- you can own different shares of the property
- your share of the property does not automatically go to the other owners if you die
- you can pass on your share of the property in your will"

Where there is a joint tenancy, all the co-owners own the whole of the property collectively. It is not correct to mention shares when talking of a joint tenancy. In order to amount to a joint tenancy the four unities must be present:

1. Unity of possession - each party is entitled to occupy the whole of the land and none can exclude the others from any part of it.

2. Unity of interest - each party must hold the same interest in the property

3. Unity of title - each party must acquire their interest through the same transaction

4. Unity of time- interests must have been acquired at the same time

When is there more than one settlor?

This is dealt with by the new subsection (2A). It is to be dealt with on the basis of a just and reasonable apportionment. This always gives scope for discussion.

It is not an exact test and the parameters and metrics are not set out. These are often a "haggle" in practice in my experience.

What is meant by "just and reasonable"?

This is a phrase which allows for much flexibility and in my experience comes down to what deal can be done with HMRC.

3.3.2.25.5 Effective Date

6 April 2025 see paragraph 70

3.3.2.26 Paragraph 24 Amendment to section 646 (adjustment between settlor and trustees etc.)

3.3.2.26.1 Overview

Section 646 ITTOIA provides for recovery of an amount equal to the tax actually paid by a Settlor under section 624 or section 629 from the trustees of the settlement in question on the amount of income arising under the settlement taxed under section 624 (settlor retained interest) or section 629 (minor children). It only covers the tax paid and does not apply to interests and penalties.

Provision is made in the legislation for a settlor to obtain a certificate from HMRC of the amount of tax paid under the relevant provisions.

Paragraph 24 amends section 646 (adjustments between settlor and trustees etc). Sub-paragraph 24(2) amends section 646(2) by substituting revised criteria for the right of recovery certificate that the settlor is entitled to require an officer of Revenue and Customs to provide. Sub paragraph 24(3) amends section 646(6A) by inserting additional criteria for the repayment certificate that an officer of Revenue and Customs may be required to provide.

HMRC updated their Manuals to reflect this.

3.3.2.26.2 Legislation

Paragraph 24 reads:

> "(1) Section 646 (adjustments between settlor and trustees etc) is amended as follows.
>
> (2) In subsection (2), for paragraphs (a) and (b) substitute—
>
> "(a) the tax year in which income was treated as arising to the settlor under section 624 or 629 (as the case may be),
>
> (b) the amount of the income in respect of which the settlor has paid tax, and
>
> (c) the amount of tax paid."
>
> (3) In subsection (6A)—
>
> (a) omit the "and" after paragraph

(b) at the end insert ", and

(c) the tax year in which the income to which the repayment relates was treated as arising to the settlor."

Section 646 ITTOIA as amended reads as follows.

"646 Adjustments between settlor and trustees etc.

(1) A settlor is entitled to recover from—

(a) any trustee, or

(b) any other person to whom the income is payable in connection with the settlement, the amount of any tax paid by the settlor which became chargeable on the settlor under section 624 or 629.

(2) For this purpose, the settlor may require an officer of Revenue and Customs to provide the settlor with a certificate specifying—

(a) The tax year in which income was treated as arising to the settlor under section 624 or 629 (as the case may be),

(b) The amount of the income in respect of which the settlor has paid tax, and

(c) The amount of tax paid.

(3) A certificate provided under subsection (2) is conclusive evidence of the facts stated in it.

(4) Subsection (5) applies if a settlor chargeable to tax under section 624 or 629 obtains a repayment by reason of the payment of the tax by—

(a) Any trustee, or

(b) Any other person to whom the income is payable by virtue of or as a result of the settlement.]

(5) The settlor must pay an amount equal to the repayment to—

(a) The trustee, or

(b) The other person to whom the income is payable by virtue of or as a result of the settlement.

(6) If there are two or more such persons, the amount must be apportioned among them as the case may require.

(6A) For the purpose of subsection (5), the settlor may require an officer of Revenue and Customs to provide the settlor with a certificate specifying—

(a) That the settlor has obtained a repayment as mentioned in subsection (4), ...

(b) The amount of the repayment, and

(c) The tax year in which the income to which the repayment relates was treated as arising to the settlor.

(6B) A certificate provided under subsection (6A) is conclusive evidence of the facts stated in it.

(7) Subject to subsections (6A) and (6B), any question as to—

(a) The amount of a payment under subsection (5), or

(b) An apportionment to be made under subsection (6),

is to be decided by the tribunal and, notwithstanding the provisions of sections 11 and 13 of the Tribunals, Courts and Enforcement Act 2007, the decision of the tribunal is final.

(8) Nothing in sections 624 to 632 is to be read as excluding a charge to tax on the trustees as persons by whom any income is receive."

3.3.2.26.3 Details of the paragraph

This paragraph amends section 646 ITTOIA.

Section 646 allows the Settlor to recover IT actually paid where sections 624 and/or 629 ITTOIA have applied from the trustees of the Settlement.

Provision is also made in respect of tax repayments.

Section 646 ITTOIA also allows the Settlor who pays the tax to recover from the trustees the tax but not any penalties or interest as they may be tax related, but they are not tax.

Example

Lana Peel is a UK resident of Asturian heritage.

She settles a trust under which she is a beneficiary and retains an interest under the trust. [100]She is assessed under section 624 ITTOIA and pays the tax as well as the penalty for late payment of the tax.

The tax paid under section 624 ITTOIA is recoverable by Lana from the trustees, but the penalty is not tax, but a civil penalty paid under the penalty legislation. The certificate will cover the section 624 ITTOIA tax paid but not the penalty.

If part of the tax is later repaid Lana must account to the trustees in respect of the repayment.

Section 646(8) can be a source of controversy.

Section 624(1) tells us "Income which arises under a settlement is treated for income tax purposes as the ***income of the settlor and of the settlor alone***..." where the section applies.

This does not obviously fit with subsection (8).

HMRC say on this at TSEM 4512: [101]

---

[100] See section 625 ITTOIA. HMRC say on this "ITTOIA/S625(1) makes it clear the settlor is treated as having an interest in property if 'that property or any related property is, or will or may become, payable to or applicable for the benefit of the settlor or his spouse or civil partner in any circumstances whatsoever'." https://www.gov.uk/hmrc-internal-manuals/trusts-settlements-and-estates-manual/tsem4200

[101] See https://www.gov.uk/hmrc-internal-manuals/trusts-settlements-and-estates-manual/tsem4512#:~:text=ITTOIA%2FS646(8),on%20the%20income%20as%20recipients.

> "Income arising under a settlement where the settlor retains an interest is treated as that of the settlor and the settlor alone. ITTOIA/S646(8) provides that where the income arises to trustees they are liable to tax on the income as recipients. Tax paid by the trustees in these circumstances is treated as paid on behalf of the settlor and is available to be used against the settlor's own tax liability."

This would seemingly cover income paid under deduction of tax e.g. some royalties and interest payments. It would allow credit for the withholding to the Settlor.

Given the width of the definition of settlement in section 620 ITTOIA income could arise under the settlement which was not paid up to the trustees. On the ordinary meaning of the language the income would not have been received by the trustees but would be within the arrangement settlement.

It would seem then that the better view is that HMRC could not assess the trustees on what they had not received.

Example

Roy Creeve is the settlor of a trust of which he is the life tenant. Accordingly, section 624 could apply. The trust has a holding company below the trust which itself has a number of subsidiaries mainly of an investment nature. Income is paid between the subsidiaries and the holding company. However, no income is paid to the trustees. The trust, the holding company and the subsidiaries would seem to be part of the arrangement to which section 620 applies. However, none of the income in the holding company and subsidiaries has actually been received by the trustees in their bank account or otherwise. On that basis section 646(8) is not applicable as the trustees are not persons by whom any income is received. This seems the better view though there might be an argument on the wide definition of settlement in Section 620. However, section 646(8) does not refer to the settlement but just to trustees. I tend to take the view that trustees are the persons named as such in the Trust Deed.

3.3.2.26.4 Effective Date

6 April 2025 see paragraph 70.

3.3.2.27 *Paragraph 25 Amends section 648 (income arising under a settlement) following replacement of the domicile-based system and repeal of the Remittance Basis*

3.3.2.27.1 Overview

This is essentially a tidying up provision to reflect the change from a domicile-based system to a residence-based system.

Paragraph 25 amends section 648 (income arising under a settlement) by omitting reference to 'domicile' and the 'remittance basis's applying. This is to reflect that from 6 April 2025 the previous provisions relating to 'domicile' and the application of the 'remittance basis" will longer apply as they did before.

3.3.2.27.2 Legislation

Paragraph 25 reads:

> "(1) Section 648 (income arising under a settlement) is amended as follows.
> (2) In subsection (1)(b), omit "domiciled and".
> (3) In subsection (3)—
> (a) for "if, for a tax year, section 809B, 809D or 809E of ITA 2007 (remittance basis) applies", substitute "if, for the tax year 2024-25 or an earlier tax year, section 809B, 809D or 809E of ITA 2007 (remittance basis) applied";
> (b) for "relevant foreign income" substitute "specified foreign income".
> (4) At the end insert—
> "(6) In subsection (3), "specified foreign income" means income that would be relevant foreign income if it were the income of a UK resident individual."

Section 648 ITTOIA is headed "Income arising under a settlement". It reads as follows.

> "(1) References in this Chapter to income arising under a settlement include—
> (a) any income chargeable to income tax by deduction or otherwise, and
> (b) any income which would have been so chargeable if it had been received in the United Kingdom by a person domiciled and resident there.
> (2) But if, in a tax year, the settlor is not UK resident, references in this Chapter to income arising under a settlement do not include income arising under the settlement in that tax year in respect of which the settlor, if actually entitled to it, would not be chargeable to income tax by deduction or otherwise because of not being UK resident.
> (3) And if, for a tax year, section 809B, 809D or 809E of ITA 2007 (remittance basis) applies to the settlor, references in this Chapter to income arising under a settlement include in relation to any relevant foreign income arising under the settlement in that tax year only such of it as is remitted to the United Kingdom (in that tax year or any subsequent tax year) in circumstances such that, if the settlor remitted it, the settlor would be chargeable to income tax.
> (4) See Chapter A1 of Part 14 of ITA 2007 for the meaning of "remitted to the United Kingdom" etc.

(5) Where subsection (3) applies the remitted income is treated for the purposes of this Chapter as arising under the settlement in the tax year in which it is remitted".

After the amendments section 648 reads as follows.

"648 Income arising under a settlement

(1) References in this Chapter to income arising under a settlement include—

(a) Any income chargeable to income tax by deduction or otherwise, and

(b) Any income which would have been so chargeable if it had been received in the United Kingdom by a person ... resident there.

(2) But if, in a tax year, the settlor is not UK resident, references in this Chapter to income arising under a settlement do not include income arising under the settlement in that tax year in respect of which the settlor, if actually entitled to it, would not be chargeable to income tax by deduction or otherwise because of not being UK resident.

(3) And if, for the tax year 2024-25 or an earlier tax year, section 809B, 809D or 809E of ITA 2007 (remittance basis) applied] to the settlor, references in this Chapter to income arising under a settlement include in relation to any specified foreign income arising under the settlement in that tax year only such of it as is remitted to the United Kingdom (in that tax year or any subsequent tax year) in circumstances such that, if the settlor remitted it, the settlor would be chargeable to income tax.

(4) See Chapter A1 of Part 14 of ITA 2007 for the meaning of "remitted to the United Kingdom" etc.

(5) Where subsection (3) applies the remitted income is treated for the purposes of this Chapter as arising under the settlement in the tax year in which it is remitted.

(6) In subsection (3), "specified foreign income" means income that would be relevant foreign income if it were the income of a UK resident individual."

3.3.2.27.3 Details of the paragraph

Section 648 defines income arising under a settlement which is what the Settlor pays tax on where the Settlement Provisions apply.

This used

3.3.2.27.4 Effective Date

6 April 2025 See Paragraph 70.

3.3.2.28 Part 2: Transfer of assets abroad

Part 2 amends Chapter 2 of Part 13 of the Income Tax Act (ITA) 2007 (transfer of assets abroad).

The Transfer of Assets Provisions are discussed in detail in Chapter 6 of the *Taxation of Entertainers and Sportspersons* to which the Reader is referred.

3.3.2.29 Paragraph 26 Amendment of Transfer of Assets Abroad Code in accordance with Part Schedule 12 introduced etc.

3.3.2.29.1 Overview

Paragraph 26 gives effect to the changes made by this Part (i.e. Part 2) of the Schedule 12 depending on the particular circumstances.

3.3.2.29.2 Legislation

Paragraph 26 reads:

> "Chapter 2 of Part 13 of ITA 2007 (transfer of assets abroad) is amended in accordance with this Part of this Schedule."

3.3.2.29.3 Details

This is the authority for the amendments made by Part 2 of the Schedule in this connection.

3.3.2.29.4 Effective date

6 April 2025. See Paragraph 70.

3.3.2.30 Paragraph 27 Amendment of section 718 "Person abroad"

3.3.2.30.1 Overview

Paragraph 27 amends section 718 (meaning of "person abroad" etc) by updating the definition of a person abroad so that a person abroad is any person who is not resident in the UK. Essentially, then any non-resident is a person abroad. This is to reflect that from 6 April 2025 the previous provisions relating to 'domicile' will cease to apply. The reference to domicile is removed.

Subsection 718(3) referring to deemed domicile is also removed.

A qualifying non-resident may have certain exemptions for FIG but is a UK resident and so not a person who is not resident in the UK. Such a person would not be a person abroad with the definition in section 718. However, other avoidance could apply instead of section 720.

3.3.2.30.2 Legislation

Paragraph 27 reads:

> "In section 718 (meaning of "person abroad" etc)—
> (a) in subsection (1), for the words from "means" to the end, substitute "means a person who is resident outside the United Kingdom.";
> (b) omit subsection (3)."

Section 718 as amended reads as follows:

> **718 Meaning of "person abroad" etc**

(1) In this Chapter "person abroad" means a person who is resident outside the United Kingdom.

(2) For the purposes of this Chapter, the following persons are treated as resident outside the United Kingdom—

(a). . . .

(b) The person treated as non-UK resident under section 475(3) (trustees of settlements), and

(c)persons treated as non-UK resident under section 834(4) (personal representatives).

(3)……"

3.3.2.30.3 Details

As noted above.

Paragraph 27 amends section 718 (meaning of "person abroad" etc) by updating the definition of a person abroad so that a person abroad is any person who is not resident in the UK. This is to reflect that from 6 April 2025 the previous provisions relating to 'domicile' will cease to apply.

Subsection 718(3) referring to deemed domicile is also removed.

A qualifying non-resident may have certain exemptions for FIG but is a UK resident and so not a person abroad.

The safer view in my opinion is that a dual resident is a UK resident in many circumstances.

3.3.2.30.4 Effective date

6 April 2025. See Paragraph 70.

3.3.2.31 Paragraph 28 Amendment of power to enjoy income charge following change away from Domicile based system and inappropriateness of section 742 following Brexit

3.3.2.31.1 Overview

Paragraph 28 amends section 720 (charge to tax on income treated as arising under section 721) as a consequence of the changes made by paragraph 32 and paragraph 48 of the Schedule discussed below.

The changes remove reference to section 726 (non-UK domiciled individuals to whom remittance basis applies) dealing with the taxation of remittance basis users and section 742A (post-5 April 2012 transactions: exemption for genuine transactions) which provides an exemption from charge for post 5 April 2012 transactions. Section 742A is being repealed following the UK's withdrawal from the European Union. It's referred, in effect, to compatibility with European Union Freedoms which are no longer relevant since BREXIT.

Paragraph 28 tidies up section 720 to reflect the removal of the Remittance Basis. Paragraph 28 also recognises Brexit and removes the reference to Section 742A paragraph 48 (see below) repeals Section 742A.

3.3.2.31.2 The legislation

Paragraph 28 reads as follows.

> "In section 720 (charge to tax on income treated as arising under section 721)—
> (a) in subsection (4), omit "and section 726 (non-UK domiciled individuals to whom remittance basis applies)";
> (b) in subsection (7), for "742A" substitute "742"."

3.3.2.31.3 Details of the Paragraph

This again is essentially a tidying up provision following the replacement of the Domicile based system.

Paragraph 28 amends section 720 (charge to tax on income treated as arising under section 721) as a consequence of paragraph 32 and paragraph 48 of Schedule 12. These changes remove:

(a) the reference to section 726 (non-UK domiciled individuals to whom remittance basis applies) dealing with the taxation of remittance basis users; and

(b) section 742A (post-5 April 2012 transactions: exemption for genuine transactions) which provides an exemption from charge for post 5 April 2012 transactions.

Section 742A is repealed following the UK's withdrawal from the European Union. This is done by paragraph 48 discussed below.

3.3.2.31.4 Effective date

6 April 2025, See paragraph 70.

3.3.2.32 *Paragraph 29 amendment of section 721 as to amount treated arising to a person abroad following changes to protected foreign source income and replacement of the Domicile based system.*

3.3.2.32.1 Overview

Paragraph 29 is essentially a tidying up provision following the changes to the treatment of protected source income made following the 2017 changes and the replacement of the Domicile based system with a regime based on residence.

3.3.2.32.2 Legislation

Paragraph 29 reads:

> "In section 721 (individuals with power to enjoy income as a result of relevant transactions), for subsections (3B) and (3BA) substitute—

"(3B) The amount of the income treated as arising under subsection (1) is equal to the amount of the income of the person abroad (subject to sections 724 and 725).""

3B and 3BA used to read before substitution. Section 724 is headed "Special rules where benefit provided out of income of person abroad." Section 725 is headed "Reduction in amount charged where controlled foreign company involved."

(3B) The amount of the income treated as arising under subsection (1) is (subject to sections 724 and 725) given by the following rules—

Rule 1 The amount is equal to the amount of the income of the person abroad if the individual—

(a) is domiciled in the United Kingdom at any time in the tax year, or

(b) is at any time in the tax year regarded for the purposes of section 718(1)(b) as domiciled in the United Kingdom as a result of section 835BA having effect because of Condition A in that section being met.

Rule 2 In any other case, the amount is equal to so much of the income of the person abroad as is not protected foreign-source income (see section 721A).

(3BA) In a case in which rule 2 of subsection (3B) applies, so much of the income of the person abroad as is protected foreign-source income for the purposes of that rule counts as "protected income" for the purposes of section 733A(1)(b)(i)

3.3.2.32.3 Details of the paragraph

i. General

Paragraph 29 amends section 721 (individuals with power to enjoy income as a result of relevant transactions) by amending the rules which determine the amount of the income of the person abroad which is treated as arising to an individual. This reflects that from 6 April 2025 'protected foreign-source income' can no longer arise to a person abroad and that the income of the person abroad which is treated as arising to an individual will no longer be calculated by reference to their domicile status.

Paragraph 30 Repeal of sections 721A and 721B meaning of "protected foreign". This omits (i.e. repeals) section 721A and 721 B. This reflects the repeal of the provisions relating to "protected foreign-source income". It is discussed below but is mentioned here for the sake of completeness.

ii. Amended section 721

After amendment section 721 reads as follows:

"721 Individuals with power to enjoy income as a result of relevant transactions

(1) Income is treated as arising to such an individual as is mentioned in section 720(1) or 720A (1) in a tax year for income tax purposes if conditions A to C are met.

(2) Condition A is that the individual has power in the tax year to enjoy income of a person abroad as a result of—

(a) A relevant transfer,

(b)one or more associated operations, or

(c) A relevant transfer and one or more associated operations.

(3) Condition B is that the income of the person abroad would be chargeable to income tax if it were the individual's and received by the individual in the United Kingdom.

(3A) Condition C is that the individual is UK resident for the tax year.

(3B) The amount of the income treated as arising under subsection (1) is equal to the amount of the income of the person abroad (subject to sections 724 and 725).

(3C) Subsection (1) does not apply if—

(a) The individual is liable for income tax charged on the income of the person abroad by virtue of a charge not contained in this Chapter, and

(b) All that income tax has been paid.]

(4) For the purposes of subsection (2), it does not matter whether the income [F7of the person abroad] may be enjoyed immediately or only later.

(5) It does not matter for the purposes of this section—

(a). . . .

(b) Whether the individual is UK resident for the tax year in which the relevant transfer is made (if different from the tax year mentioned in subsection (1)), or

(c) Whether the avoiding of liability to income tax is a purpose for which the transfer is affected.

(6) For the circumstances in which an individual is treated as having the power to enjoy income for the purposes of this section, see section 722."

3.3.2.32.4 Effective date

6 April 2025, See paragraph 70.

3.3.2.33 Paragraph 30

3.3.2.33.1 Overview

Repeal of Sections 721A and 721B

Paragraph 30 repeals of Sections 721A and 721B

The repeal of section 721A and 721B is a consequential amendment reflecting the move to a residence rather than a domicile basis for UK tax.

3.3.2.33.2 Legislation

Paragraph 30 reads:

> "Omit sections 721A and 721B (meaning of "protected foreign-source income" etc)."

3.3.2.33.3 Details of the paragraph

Paragraph 30 omits (i.e. repeals) sections 721A and 721B (meaning of "protected foreign-source income" etc). This is to reflect that the previous provisions relating to 'protected foreign-source income' and 'tainting' cease to apply after 5 April 2025 except for the transitional provisions inserted under paragraph 44 of the Schedule discussed below.

3.3.2.33.4 Effective date

6 April 2025, See paragraph 70.

3.3.2.34 *Paragraph 31 recovery of tax paid by an individual under section 721 from person abroad*

3.3.2.34.1 Overview

This provision introduces a new right of reimbursement for the section 720 charge. It gives the transferor who pays text due under section 721 a right of recovery against the person abroad.

Paragraph 31 makes provision (similar to that in Section 646 ITTOIA) allowing the individual transferor taxed under section 721 to recover tax paid as a result of the application of 721 from the person abroad.

3.3.2.34.2 Legislation

Paragraph 31 reads:

> "After section 725 insert—
>
> **"725A Recovery of tax paid as a result of section 721**
>
> (1) Where any **tax** for which an **individual** is **liable as a result of section 721** is **paid**, the individual is **entitled to recover** the amount of the tax **from the person abroad**.
>
> (2) For the purpose of recovering that amount, the individual is entitled to require an officer of Revenue and Customs to give the individual a certificate specifying—
>
> (a) the tax year in which income is treated under section 721 as arising to the individual,
>
> (b) the amount of income treated as arising, and
>
> (c) the amount of tax paid, and any such certificate is conclusive evidence of the facts stated in it."

3.3.2.34.3 Details of the paragraph

Paragraph 31 inserts new section 725A (Recovery of tax paid as a result of section 721). This provides that from 6 April 2025 a transferor who is liable under section 721 on the income of a person abroad will have the right to recover the tax actually paid by the transferor from that person. The individual must actually pay the tax first.

For the purpose of recovering that amount, the transferor is entitled to require an officer of Revenue and Customs to provide a certificate specifying the criteria listed in new section 725A (2).

This is a similar process to that under Section 646 ITTOIA for tax paid under Section 624 or Section 629 ITTOIA discussed above.

3.3.2.34.4 Effective date

6 April 2025, See paragraph 70.

3.3.2.35 Paragraph 32 amendment of section 726 reflecting change from Domicile system to residence based one.

3.3.2.35.1 Overview

Paragraph 32 amends section 726 which was concerned with the domicile-based remittance basis as a consequence of the withdrawal of the domicile-based Remittance Basis.

3.3.2.35.2 Legislation

i. General

Paragraph 32 reads:

"(1) Section 726 (remittance basis etc) is amended as follows.

(2) For the heading substitute "Qualifying new residents and remittance-basis users: "foreign" deemed income".

(3) For subsection (1) substitute—

"(1) Subsection (2) applies in relation to income treated under section 721 as arising to an individual ("**the deemed income**")—

(a) in the tax year 2024-25 or an earlier tax year if section 809B, 809D or 809E (remittance basis) applied to the individual for that tax year, or

(b) in the tax year 2025-26 or a later tax year if the individual is entitled to claim relief under section 845A of ITTOIA 2005 (qualifying new residents) for that tax year."

(4) After subsection (2) insert—

"(2A) Subsections (3) to (5) apply where the deemed income falls within subsection (1)(a)."

(5) Omit subsections (6) and (7).

(6) At the end insert—

As to income falling within subsection (1)(b), see the table in section 845F of ITTOIA 2005 (under which deemed income that is foreign for the purposes of this section is "qualifying foreign income" and so may be identified in a foreign income claim)."

ii. Amended section 726

After amendment section 726 reads as follows.

Section 726 Qualifying new residents and remittance-basis users: "foreign" deemed income]

(1) Subsection (2) applies in relation to income treated under section 721 as arising to an individual ("**the deemed income**")

(a) In the tax year 2024-25 or an earlier tax year if section 809B, 809D or 809E (remittance basis) applied to the individual for that tax year, or

(b) In the tax year 2025-26 or a later tax year if the individual is entitled to claim relief under section 845A of ITTOIA 2005 (qualifying new residents) for that tax year.

(2) For the purposes of this section the deemed income is "foreign" if (and to [the corresponding extent that) the income mentioned in section 721(2) would be relevant foreign income if it were the individuals.

(2A) Subsections (3) to (5) apply where the deemed income falls within subsection (1)(a).

(3) Treat the foreign deemed income as relevant foreign income of the individual.

(4) For the purposes of Chapter A1 of Part 14 (remittance basis) treat so much of the income within section 721(2) as would be relevant foreign income if it were the individual's as deriving from the foreign deemed income.

(5) In the application of section 832 of ITTOIA 2005 to the foreign deemed income, subsection (2) of that section has effect with the omission of paragraph (b).]

(6) . . . .

(7) . . . .

(8) As to income falling within subsection (1)(b), see the table in section 845H of ITTOIA 2005 (under which deemed income that is foreign for the purposes of this section is "qualifying foreign income" and so may be identified in a foreign income claim).

3.3.2.35.3 Details of the paragraph

Paragraph 32 amends section 726 (remittance basis etc) to remove reference to 'Non-UK domiciled individuals". This is consequential on the move away from a domicile-based system to a residence based one.

The section is amended so that the remittance basis does not apply to income treated as arising to an individual for the years 2025-26 and onwards but will continue to apply to such income as is treated as arising in the year 2024-25 and earlier years. Such earlier income which is remitted to the UK can therefore still be charged. This needs care as it can be a trap for the unwary.

Subsection (1)(b) is amended to apply to 'qualifying new residents' (individuals who qualify for relief under section 845A of ITTOIA 2005) from 6 April 2025, when identifying 'deemed income' which would be assessable under section 720. Subsections 726(6) and 726(7) are removed and subsection 726(8) is added to include what is meant by "qualifying foreign income" for the purposes of amended subsection (1)(b).

3.3.2.35.4 Effective date

06 April 2025 See Paragraph 70.

3.3.2.36 Paragraph 33 Amendment of Section 727 to reflect the repeal of the Remittance Basis.

3.3.2.36.1 Overview

Paragraph 33 amends section 727 to reflect the changes made by paragraph 48 which repeals section 742A (discussed below).

3.3.2.36.2 Legislation

i. General

Paragraph 33 reads:

"In section 727 (charge to tax on income treated as arising under section 728)"—

(a) omit subsection (3A);

(b) in subsection (5), for "742A" substitute "742"."

ii. Text of section 727 after amendment

Section 727 ITA after amendment reads as follows.

"727Charge to tax on income treated as arising under section 728

(1) The charge under this section applies for the purpose of preventing the avoiding of liability to income tax by individuals who are... UK resident by means of relevant transfers.

(2) Income tax is charged on income treated as arising to such an individual under section 728 (individuals receiving capital sums as a result of relevant transactions).

(3) Tax is charged under this section on the amount of income treated as arising in the tax year.

(3A) . . . .

(4) The person liable for any tax charged under this section is the individual to whom the income is treated as arising.

(5) For exemptions from the charge under this section, see sections 736 to [F3742] (exemptions where no tax avoidance purpose or genuine commercial transaction [F4, etc]).

(6) For rules about the availability of deductions and reliefs where income is charged under this section, see section 746 (deductions and reliefs where individual charged under section 720 or this section)."

3.3.2.36.3 Details of the paragraph

Paragraph 33 amends section 727 (charge to tax on income treated as arising under section 728) as a consequence of paragraph 48 of the Schedule which repeals Section 742A linked to European Freedoms. The changes remove reference to section 730 (non-UK domiciled individuals to whom the remittance basis applies) dealing with the taxation of remittance basis users and section 742A (post-5 April 2012 transactions: exemption for genuine transactions) which provides an exemption from charge for post 5 April 2012 transactions.

Section 742A is repealed following the UK's withdrawal from the European Union. [102]

Sections 727, 730 and 742A are discussed in Chapter 6 of *Taxation of Entertainers and Sportspersons*.

3.3.2.37 Paragraph 34 amendment of Section 728 (Capital Sums Charge) so charge on amount of income of person abroad.

3.3.2.37.1 Overview

Paragraph amends section 728 (the capital sum charge) so the charge is on the amount of the income arising to the person abroad. The definition of person abroad has been amended (see above).

3.3.2.37.2 Legislation

i. General

Paragraph 34 reads:

"In section 728 (individuals receiving capital sums as a result of relevant transactions), for subsections (1A) and (1B) substitute—

"(1A) The amount of the income treated as arising under subsection (1) is equal to the amount of the income of the person abroad (subject to subsection (2)).""

ii. Text of amended section 728

Section 728 after the amendment reads as follows.

"728 Individuals receiving capital sums as a result of relevant transactions

[102] Brexit took place at 23:00 GMT on 31 January 2020.

(1) Income is treated as arising to such an individual as is referred to in section 727(1) [or 727A (1) in a tax year for income tax purposes if—

(a) Income has become the income of a person abroad as a result of—

(i) A relevant transfer,

(ii)one or more associated operations, or

(iii) A relevant transfer and one or more associated operations, F2...

(b) The capital receipt conditions are met in respect of the individual in the tax year (see section 729), and

(c) The individual is UK resident for the tax year].

(1A) The amount of the income treated as arising under subsection (1) is equal to the amount of the income of the person abroad (subject to subsection (2)).

(2) Section 725 (reduction in amount charged where controlled foreign company involved) applies for determining the amount of income treated as arising under subsection (1) as if—

(a) In subsection (1) of that section—

(i) The reference to section 721 were a reference to this section, and

(ii) The reference to section 721(2) were a reference to subsection (1)(a) of this section, and

(b) Subsections (2A) and (2B) of that section were omitted.

(2A) Subsection (1) does not apply if—

(a) The individual is liable for income tax charged on the income of the person abroad by virtue of a charge not contained in this Chapter, and

(b) All that income tax has been paid.

(3) It does not matter for the purposes of this section—

(a). . . .

(b) Whether the individual is UK resident for the tax year in which the relevant transfer abroad is made (if different from the tax year mentioned in subsection (1)), or

(c) Whether the avoiding of liability to income tax is a purpose for which that transfer is affected."

3.3.2.37.3 Details of the paragraph

Paragraph 34 amends section 728 (individuals receiving capital sums as a result of relevant transactions) by substituting for subsections (1A) and (1B) a new subsection (1A). This amends the rules that determine the amount of the income of the person abroad that is to be treated as arising to an individual to reflect that from 6 April 2025 'protected foreign-source income' can no longer arise to a person abroad and the income of the person abroad will no longer be calculated by reference to the individual's domicile status.

3.3.2.37.4 Effective Date

06 April 2025 see paragraph 70.

3.3.2.38 Paragraph 35 Repeal of Section 729A on Protected Foreign Source Income.

3.3.2.38.1 Overview

Paragraph 35 repeals Section 729 A which dealt with the meaning of "protected foreign source income". It is no longer relevant generally in the new residence-based regime.

3.3.2.38.2 Legislation

Paragraph 35 reads:

> "Omit section 729A (meaning of "protected foreign-source income")."

3.3.2.38.3 Details of the paragraph

Paragraph 35 omits (i.e. repeals) Section 729A (meaning of "protected foreign-source income") as a result of paragraph 44 of the Schedule (Transitional Provisions about Protected Foreign-Source Income and Transitionally Protected Income) discussed below.

3.3.2.38.4 Effective Date

06 April 2025. See paragraph 70.

3.3.2.39 Paragraph 36 Recovery of tax paid by transferor as a result of section 728 from person abroad.

3.3.2.39.1 Overview

This introduces a right of recovery from the person abroad by the transferor similar to that for section 721 introduced by paragraph 31 discussed above.

Paragraph 36 inserts the new section 729B which entitles the transferor to recover the tax actually paid by the transferor by reference to section 728 (Capital Sum) from the person abroad. This is similar to Section 646ITTOIA and the provision in respect of Section 721 introduced by paragraph 31 (see above), the new Section 725A.

3.3.2.39.2 Legislation

Paragraph 36 reads:

> "36 Before section 730 insert—
>
> **"729B Recovery of tax paid as a result of section 728**
>
> (1) Where any tax for which an individual is liable as a result of section 728 is paid, the individual is entitled to recover the amount of the tax from the person abroad.

(2) For the purpose of recovering that amount, the individual is entitled to require an officer of Revenue and Customs to give the individual a certificate specifying—

(a) the tax year in which income is treated under section 728 as arising to the individual,

(b) the amount of income treated as arising, and

(c) the amount of tax paid,

and any such certificate is conclusive evidence of the facts stated in it."

3.3.2.39.3 Details of the paragraph

This Paragraph 36 inserts new section 729B (Recovery of tax paid as a result of section 728). This provides that from 6 April 2025 a transferor who is assessable under section 728 on the income of a person abroad will have the right to recover the tax paid from that person for the purpose of recovering that amount, the transferor is entitled to require an officer of Revenue and Customs to provide a certificate specifying the criteria listed in new section 729B(2).

3.3.2.39.4 Effective Date

06 April 2025 see paragraph 70.

3.3.2.40 Paragraph 37 amendment of section 730 following removal of domicile-based system.

3.3.2.40.1 Overview

Paragraph 37 amends section 730 in light of the change from the domicile-based regime to a residence-based regime.

3.3.2.40.2 Legislation

i. General

Paragraph 37 reads:

"(1) Section 730 (remittance basis etc) is amended as follows.

(2) For the heading substitute "Qualifying new residents and remittance-basis users: "foreign" deemed income".

(3) For subsection (1) substitute—

"(1) Subsection (2) applies in relation to income treated under section 728 as arising to an individual ("the deemed income")—

(a) in the tax year 2024-25 or an earlier tax year if section 809B, 809D or 809E (remittance basis) applied to the individual for that tax year, or

(b) in the tax year 2025-26 or a later tax year if the individual is entitled to claim relief under section 845A of ITTOIA 2005 (qualifying new residents) for that tax year."

(4) After subsection (2) insert—

"(2A) Subsections (3) to (5) apply where the deemed income falls within subsection (1)(a)."

(5) Omit subsections (6) and (7).

(6) At the end insert—

"(8) As to income falling within subsection (1)(b), see the table in section 845F of ITTOIA 2005 (under which deemed income that is foreign for the purposes of this section is "qualifying foreign income" and so may be identified in a foreign income claim)."

ii. Amended section 730

The amended section 730 reads as follows:

730 Qualifying new residents and remittance-basis users: "foreign" deemed income]

(1) Subsection (2) applies in relation to income treated under section 728 as arising to an individual ("the deemed income")—

(a) In the tax year 2024-25 or an earlier tax year if section 809B, 809D or 809E (remittance basis) applied to the individual for that tax year, or

(b) In the tax year 2025-26 or a later tax year if the individual is entitled to claim relief under section 845A of ITTOIA 2005 (qualifying new residents) for that tax year.]

(2) For the purposes of this section the deemed income is "foreign" if (and to the corresponding extent] that) the income mentioned in section 728(1)(a) would be relevant foreign income if it were the individual's.

(2A) Subsections (3) to (5) apply where the deemed income falls within subsection (1)(a).]

(3) Treat the foreign deemed income as relevant foreign income of the individual.

(4) For the purposes of Chapter A1 of Part 14 (remittance basis) treat so much of the income within section 728(1)(a) as would be relevant foreign income if it were the individual's as deriving from the foreign deemed income.

(5) In the application of section 832 of ITTOIA 2005 to the foreign deemed income, subsection (2) of that section has effect with the omission of paragraph (b).

(6). . . .

(7). . . .

(8) As to income falling within subsection (1)(b), see the table in section 845H of ITTOIA 2005 (under which deemed income that is foreign for the purposes of this section is "qualifying foreign income" and so may be identified in a foreign income claim).

3.3.2.40.3 Details of the paragraph

Paragraph 37 amends section 730 (remittance basis etc) to remove reference to 'Non-UK domiciled individuals'. This section is amended so that the remittance basis does not apply to income treated as arising to an individual for the years 2025-26 onwards but will continue to apply to such income that is treated as arising in the in the year 2024-25 and earlier years. This reflects the time of the charge to a residence-based system and preserves the position before the change so far as relevant.

Subsection (1)(b) is amended to apply to 'qualifying new residents' (individuals who qualify for relief under section 845A of ITTOIA 2005) from 6 April 2025 when identifying 'deemed income' which would be assessable under section 727.

Subsections (6) and (7) are removed and a new subsection 730(8) is added to include what is meant by "qualifying foreign income" for the purposes of amended subsection (1)(b).

3.3.2.40.4 Effective date

6 April 2025 (see paragraph 70.)

3.3.2.41 Paragraph 38 Update of benefits charge (the Non Transferor Charge) to apply on a residence basis etc.

3.3.2.41.1 Overview

Paragraph 38 changes the Benefits charge in section 730 so it applies to non-transferors on a residence basis. This is essentially a tidying up operation following the change to a residence-based system.

3.3.2.41.2 Legislation

Paragraph 38 reads:

"(1) Section 731 (charge to tax on income treated as arising under section 732) is amended as follows.

(2) In subsection (1), for "individuals receiving a benefit" substitute "non-transferors receiving a benefit".

(3) Omit subsections (1A) to (1C) and (2A).

(4) In subsection (3), omit ", but this is subject to section 733A".

(5) In subsection (4), for "742A" substitute "742"."

3.3.2.41.3 Details of the paragraph

Paragraph 38 amends section 731 (charge to tax on income treated as arising under section 732. This is the Non-Transferor charge on those receiving benefits. From 6 April 2025 the benefits charge will apply to non-transferors rather than individuals. The charge is now residence based. See paragraph 39 discussed next.

It also removes reference to section 742A in subsection (4) as this section has been repealed by paragraph 48 discussed below. This included reference to EU freedoms.

3.3.2.42 Paragraph 39 Deemed income where benefit received by UK resident non-transferor

3.3.2.42.1 Overview

Paragraph 39 amends section 732 so it applies on a residence rather than a domiciled basis.

3.3.2.42.2 Legislation

i. General

Paragraph 39 reads:

"(1) Section 732 (deemed income where benefit received) is amended as follows.

(2) In the heading, for "Individuals" substitute "non-transferors".

(3) In subsection (1)—

(a) in paragraph (b), for "receives a benefit in a tax year" substitute

"who is UK resident for a tax year receives a benefit in that tax year";

(b) for paragraph (d) substitute—

"(d) the individual is not liable to income tax under

(4) Omit subsection (4)."

ii. Amended section 732

Section 732 as amended reads as follows:

732 Non-transferors receiving a benefit as a result of relevant transactions

(1) This **section applies** if—

(a) A **relevant transfer** occurs,

(b) An **individual who is UK resident** for a tax year **receives a benefit** that tax year,

(c) The **benefit is provided out of assets which are available for the purpose** as a result of—

(i) The transfer, or

(ii)one or more associated operations,

d) The individual is not liable to income tax under section 720 or 727 by reference to the transfer and would not be so liable if the effect of sections 726 and 730 were ignored, and

(e) The individual is not liable to income tax, under any provision that is none of section 731 of this Act and sections 643A, 643J and 643L of ITTOIA 2005, on the amount or value of the benefit ....

(2) Income is treated as arising to the individual for income tax purposes for any tax year for which section 733 provides that income arises.

(3) Also see that section for the amount of income treated as arising for any such tax year.

(4) . . . ."

3.3.2.42.3 Details of the paragraph

Paragraph 39 amends section 732 (deemed income where benefit received). This restricts the benefits charge to non-transferors unless the transitional provisions about 'protected foreign source income' and 'transitionally protected income' apply. Subsection (1)(d) is amended to remove reference to individuals who are relevantly domiciled.

3.3.2.42.4 Effective Date

06 April 2025 – see paragraph 70.

3.3.2.43 Paragraph 40 amendment of section 730 total untaxed benefits calculation.

3.3.2.43.1 Overview

Paragraph 40 amends "the total untaxed benefits" calculation in Section 733.

3.3.2.43.2 Legislation

i. General

Paragraph 40 reads:

"(1) Section 733 (income charged under section 731) is amended as follows.

(2) In subsection (1), in Step 2, omit the words from "except that" to "for an earlier tax year".

(3) After subsection (2) insert—

"(2A) For the purposes of subsection (1), the amount deducted at Step 2 does not include the amount of any income on which tax was not charged under section 731 by virtue of—

(a) section 735AD (2) (transferor not taxable under benefits charge except where benefit matched to protected foreign-source income etc), or

(b) section 731(1A) (equivalent provision for tax years 2024-25 and earlier)."

ii. Amended section 733

The amended Section 733 reads as follows:

"733Income charged under section 731

(1) To find the **amount** (if any) **of the income treated as arising under section 732(2)** for any tax year in respect of benefits provided as mentioned in section 732(1)(c) take the following steps.

Step 1

Identify the amount or value of such benefits received by the individual in the tax year and in any earlier tax years in which section 732 has applied.

The sum of those amounts and values is **"the total benefits"**.

Step 2

Deduct from the total benefits the total amount of income treated as arising to the individual under section 732(2) for earlier tax years as a result of the relevant transfer or associated operations.

The result is **"the total untaxed benefits" ....**

Step 3

Identify the amount of any income which—

(a) Arises in the tax year to a person abroad, and

(b) As a result of the relevant transfer or associated operations can be used directly or indirectly for providing a benefit for the individual.

That amount is **"the relevant income of the tax year"** in relation to the individual and the tax year.

Step 4

Add together the relevant income of the tax year and the relevant income of earlier tax years in relation to the individual (identified as mentioned in Step 3).

The sum of those amounts is **"total relevant income"**.

Step 5

Deduct from total relevant income—

(a) The amount deducted at Step 2, and

(b) Any other amount which may not be taken into account because of section 743(1) and (2) (no duplication of charges).

The result is "**the available relevant income"**.

Step 6

Compare the total untaxed benefits and the available relevant income.

The amount of the income treated as arising under section 732(2) for any tax year is the total untaxed benefits unless the available relevant income is lower. If the available relevant income is lower, it is the amount of income treated as so arising.

(2) Subsection (1) is subject to section 734 (reduction in amount charged: previous capital gains tax charge).

(2A) For the purposes of subsection (1), the amount deducted at Step 2 does not include the amount of any income on which tax was not charged under section 731 by virtue of—

(a) Section 735AD (2) (transferor not taxable under benefits charge except where benefit matched to protected foreign-source income etc), or

(b) Section 731(1A) (equivalent provision for tax years 2024-25 and earlier).

(2B) For the purposes of subsection (1), if in a tax year—

(a) Income is treated as arising to an individual under section 732(2), and

(b) The income is identified as qualifying foreign income on a foreign income claim, the income is treated for later tax years as not having been charged to income tax under section 731.

(2C) It follows from subsection (2B) that—

(a) In the application of subsection (1) to the individual for subsequent tax years, the amount of the income will be deducted at Step 2 and at paragraph (a) of Step 5, but

(b) in the application of subsection (1) to any other individual for subsequent tax years, the amount of the income will not be deducted at paragraph (b) of Step 5.

(2D) See paragraph 11 of Schedule 10 to FA 2025 (temporary repatriation facility) for special provision about income that is treated as arising under section 732 but that is exempt from income tax under that Schedule.]

(3) See also section 740(5) to (7) (which makes provision about relevant income and benefits where relevant transactions include both transactions before 5 December 2005 and transactions after 4 December 2005 and exemptions under this Chapter cease to apply).

3.3.2.43.3 Details of the paragraph

Paragraph 40 amends 'the total untaxed benefits' calculation in section 733 (income charged under section 731) for the purposes of calculating the income treated as arising to an individual under section 732.

3.3.2.43.4 Effective Date

06 April 2025 see paragraph 70.

3.3.2.44 Paragraph 41 Repeals of Section 733A to 733E and 734A on protected foreign source income

3.3.2.44.1 Overview

Paragraph 41 repeals some of the old provisions about protected foreign source income as no longer being appropriate or needed.

3.3.2.44.2 Legislation

Paragraph 41 reads:

> "Omit sections 733A to 733E and 734A (old provision about protected foreign-source income)."

3.3.2.44.3 Details of the paragraph

Paragraph 41 omits sections 733A to 733E and section 734A (old provision about protected foreign-source income) as a consequence of paragraph 44 of the Schedule.

3.3.2.44.4 Effective Date

06 April 2025 see paragraph 70.

3.3.2.45 Paragraph 42 Amendment of Section 735. Remittance Basis etc.

3.3.2.45.1 Overview

Paragraph 42 amends section 735 to deal with the ending of the domicile-based system and to ensure the Remittance Basis does not apply to "deemed income" treated as arising after 5 April 2025 but continues to apply to earlier years. Provision is also made in respect of qualifying new residents.

3.3.2.45.2 Legislation

i. General

Paragraph 42 reads:

> "(1) Section 735 (remittance basis etc) is amended as follows.
>
> (2) For the heading substitute "Qualifying new residents and remittance-basis users: "foreign" deemed income".
>
> (3) For subsection (1) substitute—
>
> "(1) Subsection (2) applies in relation to income treated under section 732 as arising to an individual ("the deemed income")—
>
> (a) in the tax year 2024-25 or an earlier tax year if section 809B, 809D or 809E (remittance basis) applied to the individual for that tax year, or
>
> (b) in the tax year 2025-26 or a later tax year if the individual is entitled to claim relief under section 845A of ITTOIA 2005 (qualifying new residents) for that tax year."
>
> (4) After subsection (2) insert—
>
> "(2A) Subsections (3) to (5) apply where the deemed income falls within subsection (1)(a)."
>
> (5) At the end insert—
>
> "(6) As to income falling within subsection (1)(b), see the table in section 845F of ITTOIA 2005 (under which deemed income that is foreign for the purposes of this section is "qualifying foreign income" and so may be identified in a foreign income claim)."

ii. Amended section 735

Section 735 as amended reads as follows:

> **735 Qualifying new residents and remittance-basis users: "foreign" deemed income]**
>
> (1) Subsection (2) applies in relation to income treated under section 732 as arising to an individual ("the deemed income")—

(a) In the tax year 2024-25 or an earlier tax year if section 809B, 809D or 809E (remittance basis) applied to the individual for that tax year, or

(b) In the tax year 2025-26 or a later tax year if the individual is entitled to claim relief under section 845A of ITTOIA 2005 (qualifying new residents) for that tax year.

(2) For the purposes of this section the deemed income is "foreign" if (and to the extent that) the relevant income to which it relates would be relevant foreign income if it were the individuals.

(2A) Subsections (3) to (5) apply where the deemed income falls within subsection (1)(a).

(3) Treat the foreign deemed income as relevant foreign income of the individual.

(4) For the purposes of Chapter A1 of Part 14 (remittance basis) treat relevant income, or a benefit, that relates to any part of the foreign deemed income as deriving from that part of the foreign deemed income.

(5) In the application of section 832 of ITTOIA 2005 to the foreign deemed income, subsection (2) of that section has effect with the omission of paragraph (b).

(6) As to income falling within subsection (1)(b), see the table in section 845H of ITTOIA 2005 (under which deemed income that is foreign for the purposes of this section is "qualifying foreign income" and so may be identified in a foreign income claim)".

3.3.2.45.3 Details of the paragraph

Paragraph 42 amends section 735 (remittance basis etc) to remove reference to 'Non-UK domiciled individuals' and ensure that the remittance basis does not apply to benefits provided to an individual for the tax years 2025-26 onwards, but that it continues to apply to benefits provided for the year 2024-25 and earlier. Subsection (1)(b) is amended to apply to 'qualifying new residents' (individuals who qualify for relief under section 845A of ITTOIA 2005) from 6 April 2025 when identifying 'deemed income' which would be assessable under section 731 (Charge to tax on income treated as arising under section 732).

This is essentially a necessary tidying up provision.

3.3.2.45.4 Effective Date

06 April 2025 See paragraph 70.

3.3.2.46 Paragraph 43 Amendment of section 735 Matching Rules consequential on paragraph 44 and new sections 735AA to 735AB

3.3.2.46.1 Overview

Paragraph 43 amends the matching rules in section 735A because of the new sections 735A to 735AG. It also provides for a deduction from benefits where there are overlapping charges.

3.3.2.46.2 Legislation

Paragraph 43 reads:

"(1) Section 735A (matching rules) is amended as follows.

(2) In subsection (1), for paragraph (b) substitute—

"(b) deduct from those benefits any benefit so far as—

(i) chargeable gains (or offshore income gains) are 1treated as mentioned in section 734(1)(d) as accruing by reference to the benefit,

(ii) income is treated as mentioned in section 735AG(1)(b) as arising by reference to the benefit under section 643A, 643J or 643L of ITTOIA 2005 (settlements: benefits charge), or

(iii) income is treated as arising by reference to the benefit under section 732(2) and that income is identified in a foreign income claim,".

(3) in subsection (6), for "the individual, or as a result of section 733A another person" substitute "a person"."

3.3.2.46.3 Details of the paragraph

Paragraph 43 amends section 735A (matching rules) as a consequence of paragraph 44 of Schedule 12. This paragraph is discussed in the next section. Paragraph 44 is concerned with transitional provision concerning PSI and TPI. New subsection (1)(b) provides for a deduction from benefits in cases where there are chargeable gains, there is an overlapping settlements charge, or income is identified in a foreign income claim.

This is essentially a factual matter.

3.3.2.46.4 Effective Date

06 April 2025 see paragraph 70.

3.3.2.47 Paragraph 44 Transitional Provisions about Protected Foreign-Source Income and Transitionally Protected Income

3.3.2.47.1 Overview

Paragraph 44 inserts new sections 735AA to 735AG under the italic heading Transitional provision about protected foreign-source income and transitionally protected income. This is discussed in more detail below.

"Protected foreign source income" is a defined term. See section 735AB.

"Transitionally protected income" is a defined term. See section 735AB.

Section 735AB is set out below.

3.3.2.47.2 Legislation

Paragraph 44 reads:

"After section 735A insert—

"Transitional provision about protected foreign-source income and transitionally protected income 735AA Settlements to which following sections apply

(1) Sections 735AB to 735C apply if—

(a) a relevant transfer occurred before 6 April 2025,

(b) the person abroad was—

(i) the trustees of a settlement, or

(ii) a company in which the trustees of a settlement were participators or indirect participators, and

(c) protected foreign-source income or transitionally protected income arose in relation to the transfer.

(2) In sections 735AB to 735C—

44 After section 735A insert—

"Transitional provision about protected foreign-source income and transitionally protected income

735AA Settlements to which following sections apply

(1) Sections 735AB to 735C apply if—

(a) a relevant transfer occurred before 6 April 2025,

(b) the person abroad was—

(i) the trustees of a settlement, or

(ii) a company in which the trustees of a settlement were participators or indirect participators, and

(c) protected foreign-source income or transitionally protected income arose in relation to the transfer.

(2) For any tax year after one in which such income is so treated, the amount of income treated as arising to the individual under section 732(2) in respect of benefits provided as mentioned in section 732(1)(c) as a result of the transfer or operations in question is calculated as follows.

(3) The amount is calculated under section 733(1) as if the total untaxed benefits were reduced by the amount of that income.

(4) The reference in subsection (1)(b) to income treated as arising under section 643A of ITTOIA 2005 includes, in relation to any of the tax years 2018-19 to 2024-25, a reference to income treated as arising under section 643J or 643L of ITTOIA 2005 (settlements code: old onward gift

provisions). (5) In this section "the total untaxed benefits" has the same meaning as in section 733(1) (see Step 2)."

"the relevant transfer" means the transfer referred to in subsection (1)(a);

"the settlement" means the settlement referred to in subsection (1)(b)(i) or (ii) (as the case may be);

"the settlor" means the settlor of that settlement.

(3) For the purposes of subsection (1)(b)(ii), the trustees of a settlement are "indirect participators" in a company if they are participators in the first in a chain of two or more companies where the last company in the chain is the person abroad and where each company in the chain (except the last) is a participator in the next company in the chain.

735AB "Protected foreign-source income" and "transitionally protected income"

(1) For the purposes of sections 735AA to 735AF—

"protected foreign-source income", in relation to the relevant transfer, means income of the person abroad that by reference to the transfer—

(a) would have been treated as arising to the settlor under section 721 in any of the tax years 2017-18 to 2024-25 had it not been protected foreign-source income within the meaning of section 721A (as that section had effect for that tax year), or

(b) would have been treated as arising to the settlor under section 728 in any of the tax years 2017-18 to 2024-25 had it not been protected foreign-source income within the meaning of section 729A (as that section had effect for that tax year);

"transitionally protected income", in relation to the relevant transfer, means income of the person abroad that by reference to the transfer—

(a) was treated as arising to the settlor under section 721 or 728 in a tax year earlier than the tax year 2017-18,

(b) was not remitted to the United Kingdom in a tax year earlier than the tax year 2017-18, and

(c) was transitionally protected income within the meaning of section 726(7) or 730(7) throughout the tax years 2017-18 to 2024-25 (as that section had effect for those tax years).

In subsection (1), in paragraph (b) of the definition of "transitionally protected income", "remitted to the United Kingdom" is to be read in accordance with Chapter A1 of Part 14 (read with section 726 or 730 as the case may be).

735AC Transitionally protected income not to be taxed on remittance

Section 832 of ITTOIA 2005 (relevant foreign income charged on remittance basis) does not apply to transitionally protected income.

735AD Settlor liable for benefits charge despite being transferor

(1) For the purposes of section 732 (benefits charge: deemed income), subsection (1)(d) of that section (benefits charge confined to individuals not liable under section 720 or 727) is to be disregarded where the individual who receives the benefit is the settlor.

But any income treated as arising to the settlor under section 732(2) is not taxed under section 731 unless the income would, assuming that section 735A applied for this purpose by reference to the settlor, be matched under that section with an amount of relevant income that is protected foreign-source income or transitionally protected income in relation to the relevant transfer.

735AE Settlor liable in place of close family member

(1) If—

(a) a benefit is provided to an individual in a given tax year out of assets which are available for the purpose as a result of—

(i) the relevant transfer, or

(ii) one or more associated operations,

(b) the individual is a close member of the settlor's family at the time when the benefit is provided,

(c) the individual is non-UK resident, or is a qualifying new resident, for the tax year in which the benefit is provided, and

(d) the settlor is UK resident for that tax year,

the benefit is instead treated for the purposes of section 732 and section 735AD (1) as provided to the settlor.

(2) For the purposes of this section, a person is a "close member of the settlor's family" at any time if the settlor is living at that time and—

(a) the person is the settlor's spouse or civil partner at that time, or

(b) the person—

(i) is a child of the settlor, or of a person who at that time is the settlor's spouse or civil partner, and

(ii) at that time has not reached the age of 18.

(3) For the purposes of subsection (2), two people living together as if they were a married couple or civil partners are treated as if they were spouses or civil partners of each other.

(4) Where any tax for which the settlor is liable as a result of this section is paid, the settlor is entitled to recover the amount of the tax from
the individual concerned.

(5) For the purpose of recovering that amount, the settlor is entitled to require an officer of Revenue and Customs to provide the settlor with a certificate specifying—

(a) the tax year in which income was treated as arising to the settlor,

(b) the amount of income treated as arising, and

(c) the amount of tax paid, and any such certificate is conclusive evidence of the facts stated in it.

735AF Onward gifts from non-residents or qualifying new residents

(1) Subsection (2) applies if—

(a) a benefit ("the original benefit") is provided to an individual ("the original recipient") out of assets which are available for the purpose as a result of—

(i) the relevant transfer, or

(ii) one or more associated operations,

(b) the original recipient is non-UK resident, or is a qualifying new resident, for the tax year in which they receive the original benefit,

(c) section 735AE (1) (close family member's benefits attributed to settlor) does not apply to the provision of the original benefit to the original recipient,

(d) at the time when the original benefit is provided—

(i) there are arrangements, or there is an intention, as regards the (direct or indirect) passing on of the whole or part of the original benefit to another person, and

(ii) it is reasonable to expect that, if the whole or part of the original benefit is passed on to another person in accordance with the arrangements or intention, that other person will be UK resident when they receive at least part of what is passed on to them,

(e) the original recipient provides a benefit ("the onward gift") to another person ("the subsequent recipient")—

(i) at the time when the original benefit is received by the original recipient, or at any later time in the 3years beginning with the day containing that time, or

(ii) at any time before the original benefit is received by the original recipient and, it is reasonable to assume, in anticipation of the original benefit's being provided, and

(f) the onward gift is of or includes—

(i) the whole or part of the original benefit,

(ii) anything that (wholly or in part, and directly or indirectly) derives from, or represents, the whole or part of the original benefit, or

(iii) any other property, but only if the original benefit is provided with a view to enabling or facilitating, or otherwise in connection with, the property's being provided to the subsequent recipient.

(2) For the purposes of sections 732, 735AD(1) and 735AE(1), so much of the onward gift as falls within subsection (1)(f) is (so far as would not otherwise be the case) treated as a benefit provided to the subsequent recipient out

of assets which are available for the purpose as a result of an associated operation in relation to the relevant transfer.

(3) For the purposes of subsection (1)(e), the circumstances in which the original recipient provides a benefit to the subsequent recipient include circumstances where there is a series of two or more benefits starting with a benefit provided by the original recipient and ending with a benefit provided to the subsequent recipient; and in such a case—

(a) the onward gift is treated for the purposes of subsection (1)(e) as provided when the final benefit in the series is provided, and

(b) the reference to the onward gift in subsection (1)(f) is to be read as a reference to each benefit in the series.

(4) Where the conditions in subsection (1)(e) and (f) are met, it is to be presumed, unless the contrary is shown, that the condition in subsection (1)(d) is also met.

(5) In subsection (1)(d), "arrangements" includes any agreement, understanding, scheme, transaction or series of transactions (whether or not legally enforceable).

735AG Deduction allowed for previous settlements charge

(1) This section applies if—

(a) benefits provided as mentioned in section 732(1)(c) are received in a tax year, and

(b) income is treated under section 643A of ITTOIA 2005 as arising to a person in that or a subsequent tax year by reference (direct or indirect) to the whole or part of any benefits so provided.

(2) For any tax year after one in which such income is so treated, the amount of income treated as arising to the individual under section 732(2) in respect of benefits provided as mentioned in section 732(1)(c) as a result of the transfer or operations in question is calculated as follows.

(3) The amount is calculated under section 733(1) as if the total untaxed benefits were reduced by the amount of that income.

(4) The reference in subsection (1)(b) to income treated as arising under section 643A of ITTOIA 2005 includes, in relation to any of the tax years 2018-19 to 2024-25, a reference to income treated as arising under section 643J or 643L of ITTOIA 2005 (settlements code: old onward gift provisions).

(5) In this section "the total untaxed benefits" has the same meaning as in section 733(1) (see Step 2)."

3.3.2.47.3 Details of the paragraph

General

Paragraph 44 inserts new sections 735AA to 735AG under the italic heading Transitional provision about protected foreign-source income and transitionally protected income.

(1) When do the transitional provisions apply?

New section 735AA (Settlements to which following sections apply) sets out the conditions for when the transitional provisions apply to a settlement or an underlying company.

New section 735AB ("Protected foreign-source income" and "transitionally protected income") defines "Protected foreign-source income" and "transitionally protected income" for the purposes of new sections 735AA to 735AF.

(2) Transitionally protected income not to be on remittance.

New section 735AC (Transitionally protected income not to be taxed on remittance) ensures that 'transitionally protected income' will not be subject to an income tax charge when remitted to the UK.

(3) Settlor also? Transferor can be liable. Benefits charge.

New section 735AD (Settlor liable for benefits charge despite being transferor) disregards section 732(1)(d) (benefits charge confined to individuals not liable under section 720 or 727) where the settlor receives the benefit. New subsection 735AD (2) ensures that income treated as arising to the settlor under section 732(2) is not taxed under section 731 unless the income would be matched to 'protected foreign-source income' or 'transitionally protected income' if section 735A (matching rules) applied.

(4) Settlor may be liable instead of close family member.

New section 735AE (Settlor liable in place of close family member) provides for a benefits charge to arise on a UK resident settlor when a close member of the settlor's family receives a benefit as a result of a relevant transfer and/or one or more associated operations at a time when they are non-UK resident, or a 'qualifying new resident' (an individual who qualifies for relief under section 845A of ITTOIA 2005) In these circumstances the benefit is treated for the purposes of section 732 as provided to the UK resident settlor. New subsection 735AE (4) gives the settlor the right to recover the tax paid from the close member of the settlor's family.

(5) Onward gifts from Non-Residents or qualifying non-residents

New section 735AF (Onward gifts from non-residents or qualifying new residents) provides for the benefits charge to arise where a benefit is provided to an individual out of assets available as a result of a relevant transfer and/or associated operations where the original recipient is non-UK resident or is a 'qualifying new resident' (an individual who qualifies for relief under section

845A of ITTOIA 2005) in the tax year in which they receive the benefit. If, at the time when the original benefit was provided there was an arrangement in place for the whole or part of it to be passed to another person who is UK resident and the onward gift is made within three years of the original benefit being received, the onward gift is treated as a benefit provided to the subsequent recipient. If the original recipient provides a benefit ("the onward gift") to another person ("the subsequent recipient") before the original benefit is provided to the original recipient and, it is reasonable to assume this was in anticipation of the original benefit's being provided, the benefits charge will apply in the tax year when the benefit is provided to the original recipient rather than when the onward gift is made.

(6) Deduction for earlier settlement charge

New section 735AG (Deduction allowed for previous settlements charge) allows a deduction from amounts charged under section 732(1) if the benefit has been treated as income under section 643A of ITTOIA 2005.

3.3.2.47.4 Effective Date

06 April 2025 see paragraph 70.

Paragraph 45 Liability where historically the remittance basis applied

3.3.2.47.5 Overview

Paragraph 45 amends section 735B to cover situations where income is treated as arising to a beneficiary during the tax years 2017-18 to 2024-25 on which the settlor is liable who was a remittance basis user, so that this income continues to be treated as relevant foreign income of the settlor. A charge can therefore still arise by reference to such unremitted income.

It is intended to deal with historic liability under section 733A where the remittance basis applied as the new heading suggests.

3.3.2.47.6 Legislation

Paragraph 45 reads:

"(1) Section 735B (settlor charge: remittance-basis users) is amended as follows.

(2) For the heading substitute "Historical liability under section 733A where remittance basis applied".

(3) For subsection (1) substitute—

"(1) This section applies in relation to income if—

(a) the income was treated under section 732 as arising to an individual ("the beneficiary") for any of the tax years 2017-18 to 2024-25,

(b) the settlor was under section 733A (2) or (3) (as it had effect for that tax year) liable for tax on the income, and

(c) section 809B, 809D or 809E (remittance basis) applied to the settlor for that year.""

3.3.2.47.7 Details of the paragraph

Paragraph 45 amends section 735B (settlor charge: remittance-basis users) as a consequence of paragraph 41 and paragraph 44 Schedule 12 (discussed below). This section is amended to deal with situations where income is treated as arising to a beneficiary during the tax years 2017-18 to 2024-25 on which the settlor is liable and was a remittance basis user, such that this income continues to be treated as relevant foreign income of the settlor. The new heading is intended to make this clearer.

3.3.2.47.8 Effective Date

06 April 2025 see paragraph 70.

3.3.2.48 Paragraph 46 amended section 735C now headed "Historical operation of section 733C or 733E where remittance basis applied"

3.3.2.48.1 Overview

Paragraph 46 amends section 735C as a result of changes made by paragraphs 41 and 44 discussed above.

3.3.2.48.2 Legislation

i. General

Paragraph 46 reads:

"(1) Section 735C (old onward gifts provisions: remittance-basis users) is amended as follows.

(2) For the heading substitute "Historical operation of section 733C or 733E where remittance basis applied".

(3) In subsection (1)—

(a) in paragraph (a)—

(i) for the words before sub-paragraph (i) substitute "the income was treated as arising to an individual for any of the tax years 2018-19 to 2024-25";

(ii) in sub-paragraph (i), for "applies" substitute "applied";

(b) in paragraph (b), for "applies" substitute "applied".

(4) After subsection (4) insert—

"(5) A reference in subsection (1) to section 733C or 733E (or to any provision of either section) is to that section (or provision) as it had effect for the tax year for which income was treated as arising to the individual."

ii. Amended section 735C

The amended section 735C reads as follows:

> **735 Qualifying new residents and remittance-basis users: "foreign" deemed income**
>
> (1) Subsection (2) applies in relation to income treated under section 732 as arising to an individual ("the deemed income")—
>
> (a) In the tax year 2024-25 or an earlier tax year if section 809B, 809D or 809E (remittance basis) applied to the individual for that tax year, or
>
> (b) In the tax year 2025-26 or a later tax year if the individual is entitled to claim relief under section 845A of ITTOIA 2005 (qualifying new residents) for that tax year.
>
> (2) For the purposes of this section the deemed income is "foreign" if (and to the extent that) the relevant income to which it relates would be relevant foreign income if it were the individual's.
>
> (2A) Subsections (3) to (5) apply where the deemed income falls within subsection (1)(a).
>
> (3) Treat the foreign deemed income as relevant foreign income of the individual.
>
> (4) For the purposes of Chapter A1 of Part 14 (remittance basis) treat relevant income, or a benefit, that relates to any part of the foreign deemed income as deriving from that part of the foreign deemed income.
>
> (5) In the application of section 832 of ITTOIA 2005 to the foreign deemed income, subsection (2) of that section has effect with the omission of paragraph (b).
>
> (6) As to income falling within subsection (1)(b), see the table in section 845H of ITTOIA 2005 (under which deemed income that is foreign for the purposes of this section is "qualifying foreign income" and so may be identified in a foreign income claim)."

3.3.2.48.3 Details of the paragraph

Paragraph 46 amends section 735C (old onward gifts provisions: remittance-basis users) as a consequence of paragraph 41 (repeal of old provision of Protected Foreign Source Income) and paragraph 44 (Insertion of Transitional Provision) Schedule 12. This section is amended to deal with situations where income is treated as arising to an individual for any of the tax years 2018-19 to 2024-25 as a result of section 733C to 733E and the remittance basis applied to the individual in the year. This income continues to be treated as relevant foreign income of the individual.

3.3.2.48.4 Effective Date

06 April 2025 see paragraph 70.

3.3.2.49 *Paragraph 47 Removal of cross reference to repealed section 742A as no longer appropriate post BREXIT*

3.3.2.49.1 Overview

Paragraph 47 is essentially a tidying up provision removing the reference to a section that has been repealed (section 742A) and substituting a reference to section 742 headed "Partial exemption where later associated operations fail conditions", in section 736 which deals with exemptions.

3.3.2.49.2 Legislation

Paragraph 47 reads:

"In section 736 (exemptions: introduction)—

(a) in subsection (1), for "742A" substitute "742";

(b) omit subsection (2A)."

3.3.2.49.3 Details of the paragraph

Paragraph 47 amends section 736 (exemptions: introduction) as a consequence of paragraph 48 of the Schedule. This amendment removes the reference to section 742A as this has been repealed. (see paragraph 48 discussed next). This is essentially a tidying up exercise.

Section 742A was referred to in section 736 but has been repealed by paragraph 48 of the Schedule discussed below.

Section 742A was headed "Post-5 April 2012 transactions: exemption for genuine transactions".

This was inserted by paragraph 7 Schedule 10Finance Act 2013 (c. 29). The Explanatory Notes said of this provision one of the necessary conditions for the relief was met "… where, if the transaction in question were to be considered to be a genuine one (when viewed objectively, having regard to the circumstances under which it was effected and any other relevant circumstances), and gave rise to a transfer of assets charge, that liability would *constitute an unjustified and disproportionate restriction on a relevant EU treaty freedom.*" [Emphasis supplied]. Post BREXIT this was inappropriate.

Paragraph 47 also omits (i.e. repeals) section 736 (2A). Before repeal this read: "(2A) The exemption given by section 742A applies only in the case of a relevant transaction effected on or after 6 April 2012."

This was inserted by FA 2013 as part of the UK's plan to stop the reference to the CJEU started in February 2010 see Chapter 6 of *Taxation of Entertainers and Sportspersons.*

3.3.2.49.4 Effective Date

6 April 2025 see paragraph 70.

3.3.2.50 Paragraph 48 Repeal of section 742A

3.3.2.50.1 Overview

Paragraph 48 repeals section 742A ITA. Its link to European Union Law was no longer appropriate post BREXIT. See also paragraph 47 above which is also concerned with reference to section 442A.

3.3.2.50.2 Legislation

Paragraph 48 reads:

> "Omit section 742A (post-5 April 2012 transactions: exemption for genuine transactions)."

3.3.2.50.3 Details of the paragraph

Paragraph 48 omits section 742A (post-5 April 2012 transactions: exemption for genuine transactions). This means that from 6 April 2025, individuals will no longer be able to claim an exemption from the section 720 charges on the basis that their EU treaty freedoms have been infringed as discussed in respect of paragraph 47.

3.3.2.50.4 Effective Date

06 April 2025 see paragraph 70.

3.3.2.51 Paragraph 49 Change "to be taken into account in charging IT" where TRF election so no section 731 charge

3.3.2.51.1 Overview

Paragraph 49 amends section 744 headed meaning of "taking income into account in charging income tax" for section 743. It covers the position where income is not taxed under section 731 because an election is made under the 'temporary repatriation facility'.

3.3.2.51.2 Legislation

Paragraph 49 reads:

> "In section 744 (meaning of "taking income into account in charging income tax" for section 743), at the end insert—
>
> "(5) Where an amount would have been charged to income tax under section 731 but for an election under Schedule 10 to FA 2025 (temporary repatriation facility), subsection (4) applies as if the amount had been charged to income tax under that section."
>
> In section 747 (amounts corresponding to accrued income profits and related interest), in subsection (1)(b) and subsection (4)(b), omit "or domiciled".

Section 744(4) reads as follows.

> (4) In the case of tax charged under section 731 (charge to tax on income treated as arising to non-transferors where benefit received as a result of relevant transfers), they are references to the amount of relevant income taken into account under section 733 (income charged under section 731) in calculating the amount to be charged in respect of the benefit for the tax year in question.

3.3.2.51.3 Details of the paragraph

Paragraph 48 amends section 744 (meaning of "taking income into account in charging income tax" for section 743) by inserting new subsection 744(5).

New subsection (5) ensures that where income is not taxed under section 731 because an election is made under the 'temporary repatriation facility', subsection (4) will apply as if that income had been charged to income tax."

The effect of this is essentially to treat the amount in respect of which TRF has been claimed as if it was an amount on which tax had been paid.

3.3.2.51.4 Effective Date

06 April 2025 see paragraph 70.

3.3.2.52 Paragraph 49 Removal of reference to domicile in section 747

3.3.2.52.1 Overview

Paragraph 49 removes domicile references in section 747 dealing with amounts corresponding to accrued income, profits and related interest. This is essentially a tidying up exercise.

3.3.2.52.2 Legislation

Paragraph 49 reads:

> "In section 747 (amounts corresponding to accrued income profits and related interest), in subsection (1)(b) and subsection (4)(b), omit "or domiciled"."

3.3.2.52.3 Details of the paragraph

Paragraph 49 amends section 747 (Amounts corresponding to accrued income profits and related interest) by removing reference to 'domicile'. This is to reflect that the previous provisions relating to 'domicile' ceased to apply from 6 April 2025.

This is essentially a tidying up provision.

3.3.2.52.4 Effective Date

06 April 2025 see paragraph 70.

3.3.2.53 Paragraph 50 Amendment of Tribunal's jurisdiction on appeal

3.3.2.53.1 Overview

Paragraph 50 amends section 751 (tribunal's jurisdiction on appeals) as a consequence of paragraph 48 of the Schedule. This removes reference to section 742A as this section has been repealed following BREXIT by paragraph 48 (see above).

3.3.2.53.2 Legislation

Paragraph 50 reads:

"In section 751 (tribunal's jurisdiction on appeals), omit paragraph (da)."

Section 751 headed "The tribunal's jurisdiction on appeals" before the amendment read:

"On any appeal that is notified to the tribunal, the jurisdiction of the tribunal includes jurisdiction to affirm or replace any decision taken by an officer of Revenue and Customs in exercise of the officer's functions under—

(za) Section 720A (4) or 727A (4) (whether individual treated as involved in closely-held companies),

(a) Section 737 (exemption: all relevant transactions post-4 December 2005 transactions),

(b) Section 738 (meaning of "commercial transaction"),

(c) Section 739 (exemption: all relevant transactions pre-5 December 2005 transactions),

(d) Section 742 (partial exemption where later associated operations fail conditions),

(da) Section 742A (post-5 April 2012 transactions: exemption for genuine transactions), [This is the Provision removed]

(e) Section 743(2) (no duplication of charges: choice of persons in relation to whom income is taken into account)."

The words highlighted above are the words omitted.

3.3.2.53.3 Details of the paragraph

The Tribunal's jurisdiction therefore no longer covers the section 742A position. Presumably, this is because section 742A has been repealed.

3.3.2.53.4 Effective Date

06 April 2025 see paragraph 70.

3.3.2.54 Part 3: Settlements (chargeable gains)

Part 3 deals with the position of settlements and chargeable gains under the new disposition.

3.3.2.55 Paragraph 51 Part 3 amends Chapter 2 Part 3 TCGA

3.3.2.55.1 Overview

Part 3 amends Chapter 2 of Part 3 TCGA 1992 (settlements: chargeable gains) and other provisions of TCGA relating to settlements.

3.3.2.55.2 Legislation

Paragraph 51 reads:

> "TCGA 1992 is amended in accordance with this Part of this Schedule."

3.3.2.55.3 Details of Paragraph

This gives effect authority to the amendments made to TCGA by Part 3 Schedule 12.

3.3.2.55.4 Effective Date

6 April 2025 see paragraph 70.

3.3.2.56 Paragraph 52 territorial scope after insertion of section 87HA

3.3.2.56.1 Overview

Paragraph 52 amends section 1A of TCGA 1992 (territorial scope) as a consequence of paragraph 63 and new section 87HA (capital payments routed via non-residents or qualifying new residents) inserted by paragraph 63 Schedule 12. See below.

3.3.2.56.2 Legislation

Paragraph 52 reads:

> "In section 1A (territorial scope), in subsection (2)(e), omit "87K, 87L". "

3.3.2.56.3 Details of Paragraph

This paragraph makes consequential amendments following changes made by paragraph 63 which inserts the new section 87 HA discussed at p131 below.

[87K and L set out at p121]

3.3.2.56.4 Effective Date

6 April 2025 see paragraph 70.

3.3.2.57 Paragraph 53 Use of Personal losses

3.3.2.57.1 Overview

Paragraph 53 omits section 1E (4) TCGA (losses deductible only when within scope of tax etc). This charge will allow personal losses to be used against gains treated as accruing to an individual under section 87 (gains attributed to beneficiaries of non-UK resident settlements), new section 87HA (capital payments routed via non-residents or qualifying new residents) and section 89(2) (migrant settlements).

3.3.2.57.2 Legislation

i. General

Paragraph 53 reads:

"In section 1E (losses deductible only when within scope of tax etc), omit subsection (4)."

ii. Section 1E TCGA before repeal

Section 1E TCGA before repeal read:

"1E Losses deductible only when within scope of tax etc

(1) A loss is not an allowable loss if it accrues in a tax year at a time when, had a gain accrued instead, the gain would not have been chargeable to capital gains tax under this Act for the tax year (and see also sections 16(2) and 16A).

(2) In addition, the only allowable losses that qualify for deduction from chargeable gains under section 1A (3) (non-UK residents) are those accruing to the person on disposals of assets within that subsection.

(3) An allowable loss counts for the purposes of subsection (2) even if it accrues in a tax year in which the person was UK resident.

(4) No allowable losses may be deducted from chargeable gains treated as accruing to an individual as a result of section 87, 87K, 87L or 89(2) (read, where appropriate, with section 1M).

(5) If—

(a) Amounts (or elements of amounts) treated as accruing to an individual as a result of section 86 relate to different settlements, and

(b) The deduction of allowable losses does not reduce the amounts or elements to nil,

the deduction applicable to each amount is the proportion that the amount concerned bears to the total of the amounts.

(6) The deduction of allowable losses also has effect subject to Schedule 1 (UK resident individuals not domiciled in UK).

(7) For the only case in which an allowable loss accruing in a tax year may be carried back to an earlier tax year, see section 62 (death)

The section after amendment reads as follows

"87B Section 87: remittance basis

(1) This section applies if—

(a) chargeable gains are treated under section 87, 87K or 87L as accruing to an individual in a tax year, and

(b) Section 809B, 809D or 809E of ITA 2007 (remittance basis) applies to the individual for that year, ...

(c). . . .

[2) The chargeable gains are chargeable gains accruing on the disposal of an asset situated outside the United Kingdom.

(3) For the purposes of Chapter A1 of Part 14 of ITA 2007 (remittance basis) treat relevant property or benefits as deriving from the chargeable gains.

(4) For the purposes of subsection (3) property or a benefit is "relevant" if the capital payment, or onward payment (see section 87I(1)(c)),] by reason of which the chargeable gains are treated as accruing consists of—

(a) The payment or transfer of the property or its becoming property to which section 60 applies, or

(b) The conferring of the benefit"

3.3.2.57.3 Details of Paragraph

Previously, Section 1E TCGA permitted an individual's losses for the current year to be used against gains arising under Section 87. This is no longer the case

3.3.2.57.4 Effective Date

The effective date is 6 April 2025 see paragraph 70.

3.3.2.58 Paragraph 54 Consequential amendments to section 62 (Death: General Provisions)

3.3.2.58.1 Overview

Paragraph 55 amends section 62 (death: general provisions) as a consequence of paragraph 63 and new section 87HA (Capital payments routed via non-residents or qualifying new residents) discussed below.

3.3.2.58.2 Legislation

i. General

Paragraph 54 reads:

"In section 62 (death: general provisions), in subsection (2A) (a), omit ", 87K,"

ii. Section 87K

Section 87K dealt with attribution and recipients of onward gifts. It read:

"87K Attribution of gains or payments to recipient of onward gift

(1) Where this section applies (see section 87I), G is—

(a) The amount or value of so much of the onward payment as is within any of sub-paragraphs (i) to (iii) of section 87I(1)(d), or

(b) If lower, the amount of the original payment.

(For the meaning of R and U, see section 87J.)

(2) If R is greater than nil, sections 87 and 87A have effect for the gift year and later tax years—

(a) As if a capital payment was received from the trustees by the subsequent recipient—

(i) As a beneficiary of the settlement (whether or not the subsequent recipient is otherwise a beneficiary of the settlement), and

(ii) At the time the subsequent recipient received the onward payment,

(b) As if that capital payment consisted of—

(i)R, if G is greater than R, or

(ii) So much of R as is equal to G, if G is not greater than R, and

(c) As if so, much of the original payment as is equal to that capital payment was not received by the otherwise-liable person.

(3) If G is greater than R, and if U is greater than nil—

(a) Chargeable gains are treated as accruing to the subsequent recipient in the gift year (but see section 87L (3) and (4)),

(b) The amount of those gains is—

(i) U, if (G – R) is greater than U, or

(ii) So much of U as is equal to (G – R), if (G – R) is not greater than U, and

(c) The chargeable gains treated by section 87 as accruing to the otherwise-liable person by reason of the original payment are treated as from the end of the gift year as reduced by that amount, with that reduction being made from so much of those gains as has not by then been remitted to the United Kingdom in a tax year in which the otherwise-liable person is resident in the United Kingdom.

(4) If this section applies by reference to the original payment also in relation to a gift received from the original beneficiary in a tax year earlier than the gift year, this section applies in relation to the onward payment as if—

(a) The amount given by section 87J for R were reduced by the amount of any capital payment given by subsection (2) in relation to that earlier year, and

(b) The amount given by section 87J for U were reduced by the amount of any gains given by subsection (3) in relation to that earlier year."

3.3.2.58.3 Details of Paragraph

Reference to section 87K is removed from section 62 TCGA.

3.3.2.58.4 Effective Date

6 April 2025 see paragraph 70.

3.3.2.59 Paragraph 55 Amendment of section 86 to reflect move away from domicile-based system

3.3.2.59.1 Overview

Paragraph 55 amends section 86 TCGA. This is the section which provides for the net trust gains of a settlement to be attributed to settlor with an interest in a non-resident or dual resident settlement in some circumstances. T

Paragraphs 55 (2), (3) and (5) amend section 86 (attribution of gains to settlors with interest in non-resident or dual resident settlements) and insert a new subsection 86(6) as a consequence of the ending of the domicile basis in the tax system and new Schedule D1.

Sub-paragraph 55 (4) omits subsection 86(4)(b). The effect is that from 6 April 2025 gains attributed under section 86 cease to be treated as the highest part of the individual's chargeable gains.

3.3.2.59.2 Legislation

Paragraph 55 reads:

> "(1) Section 86 (attribution of gains to settlors with interest in non-resident or dual resident settlements) is amended as follows.
>
> (2) In subsection (1)(c), omit "is domiciled in the United Kingdom at some
>
> (4) In subsection (4), omit paragraph (b) and the "and" before it.
>
> "(6) See also paragraph 3 of Schedule D1 (foreign gain claims: foreign gains and losses of the trustees ignored for the purposes of subsection (1)(e))."

3.3.2.59.3 Details of Paragraph

This is essentially a tidying up provision essentially only removing references to domicile-based matters following the change to a residence-based regime.

3.3.2.59.4 Effective Date

The effective date is 6 April 2025 see paragraph 70.

3.3.2.60 Paragraph 56 amendment of section 86A for temporary non-residents following section 87HA insertion

3.3.2.60.1 Overview

Paragraph 56 amends section 86A (attribution of gains to settlor where temporarily non-resident) as a consequence of paragraph 63 and new section 87HA discussed below.

3.3.2.60.2 Legislation

Paragraph 56 reads:

> "In section 86A (attribution of gains to settlor where temporarily non-resident), in subsection (1)(b), omit ", 87K, 87L".

The text of sections 87K and 87L is set out [above].

A person is temporarily non-resident if having been UK resident (for 4 out of the 7 tax years before) then became non-UK resident and returns to UK residence after a period of 5 years or less of non-residence. It should be noted that this requires more than 5 years of non-residence so care needed with timing.

Care is needed with year of departure and return because only five years of non-residence is not sufficient usually this means non-residence for a full six tax years. Gains can be charged on return.

3.3.2.60.3 Details of Paragraph

This is essentially a tidying up provision. Sections 87K and 87L (old onward gifting provisions) are repealed by paragraph 63 of Schedule 12 as discussed below.

The Reader is referred to HMRC's Residence and FIG regime Manual see:

https://www.gov.uk/hmrc-internal-manuals/residence-and-fig-regime-manual

3.3.2.60.4 Effective Date

The effective date is 6 April 2025 see paragraph 70.

3.3.2.61 Paragraph 57 new subsection 87(8) consequential on Schedule D1

3.3.2.61.1 Overview

Paragraph 58 inserts new subsection 87(8) into section 87 (non-UK resident settlements: attribution of gains to beneficiaries) as a consequence of new Schedule D1.

3.3.2.61.2 Legislation

Paragraph 57 reads:

> "In section 87 (non-UK resident settlements: attribution of gains to beneficiaries), at the end insert—
>
> "(8) See also paragraph 4 of Schedule D1 (foreign gain claims: capital payments ignored for the purposes of this section and Schedule 4C)."

3.3.2.61.3 Details of Paragraph

This inserts a cross reference in section 87 to paragraph 4 of Schedule D1. This reminds the reader that certain payments are ignored for the purposes of section 87 and paragraph 4 Schedule DI, the text of which is set out below.

Paragraph 4 Schedule DI is set out again here for the convenience of the Reader. It reads as follows.

> **Relief in respect of deemed gains under sections 87 and 89(2) and Schedule 4C**
>
> 4(1) This **paragraph applies** if—
>
> (a) A settlement is for a tax year—
>
> (i)one to which **section 87 or 89(2) applies** (attribution of gains to beneficiaries of settlements), or

(ii) A **relevant settlement** in relation to a **Schedule 4C** pool, within the meaning of paragraph 8A of Schedule 4C (transfers of value: attribution of gains etc),

(b) A beneficiary of the settlement receives a capital payment from the trustees in that tax year, and

(c) The **individual** identifies the **capital payment in a foreign gain claim** for that tax year.

(2) The **capital payment is to be disregarded** (in that tax year and in later tax years) for the purposes of sections 87, 87A and 89(2) and paragraph 8 of Schedule 4C.

(3) The following apply for the purposes of this paragraph as they apply for the purposes of section 87—

(a) Section 87G (which provides for capital payments made to a close member of the settlor's family to be treated in certain cases as received by the settlor);

(b) Section 97 (which makes provision about the construction of "capital payment", "settlement", "trustees" and "beneficiary").

3.3.2.61.4 Effective Date

The effective date is 6 April 2025 see paragraph 70.

3.3.2.62 Paragraph 58 amendment of section 87B following repeal of domicile-based Remittance Basis

3.3.2.62.1 Overview

Paragraph 58(1) to (4) amends section 87B (section 87: remittance basis) because of the end of the remittance-based system and the domicile basis.

Section 87B provided that gains treated as accruing in a tax year to a remittance basis user on receipt of a capital payment from a non-UK resident settlement were treated as chargeable gains accruing on the disposal of an asset situated outside the UK. This ceased to apply for gains treated as accruing in tax year 2025-26 or later. Accordingly, such gains are potentially UK taxable.

Paragraph 58 (5) inserts new subsection 87B (5) as a consequence of paragraph 63 and new section 87HA (the new provision headed "Onward gifts from non-resident or qualifying new resident" (as to which see below)) to ensure that subsection 87B(1)(a) continues to operate by reference to how it applied for the tax year in which the chargeable gains were treated as accruing to the individual.

3.3.2.62.2 Legislation

i. General

Paragraph 58 reads:

"(1) Section 87B (section 87: remittance basis) is amended as follows.

(2) In subsection (1)—

(a) in paragraph (a)—

(i) for "are treated" substitute "were treated";

(ii) for "a tax year" substitute "the tax year 2024-25 or an earlier tax year";

(b) in paragraph (b), for "applies" substitute "applied".

(3) In subsection (2), for "chargeable gains accruing" substitute "treated as having accrued".

(4) In subsection (4), for "are treated as accruing consists of" substitute "were treated as accruing consisted of".

(5) At the end insert—

"(5) The references in this section to sections 87I(1)(c), 87K and 87L (which were repealed by Part 3 of Schedule 12 to the Finance Act 2025) are to those provisions as they had effect for the tax year in which the chargeable gains were treated as accruing to the individual."

ii. Section 87B as amended

Section 87B as amended reads as follows:

"87B Section 87: remittance basis

(1) This section applies if—

(a) Chargeable gains are treated under section 87[87K or 87L] as accruing to an individual in a tax year, and

(b) Section 809B, 809D or 809E [of ITA 2007] (remittance basis) applies to the individual for that year, ...

(c). . . .

(2) The chargeable gains are chargeable gains accruing on the disposal of an asset situated outside the United Kingdom.

(3) For the purposes of Chapter A1 of Part 14 of ITA 2007 (remittance basis) treat relevant property or benefits as deriving from the chargeable gains.

(4) For the purposes of subsection (3) property or a benefit is "relevant" if the capital payment, or onward payment (see section 87I(1)(c)),] by reason of which the chargeable gains are treated as accruing consists of—

(a) The payment or transfer of the property or its becoming property to which section 60 applies, or

(b) The conferring of the benefit

(5) The references in this section to sections 87I(1)(c), 87K and 87L (which were repealed by Part 3 of Schedule 12 to the Finance Act 2025) are to those provisions as they had effect for the tax year in which the chargeable gains were treated as accruing to the individual.

3.3.2.62.3 Details of Paragraph

Sub-paragraphs 58(1) to (4) amend section 87B (section 87: remittance basis) as a consequence of the ending of the remittance basis of taxation following the move away from a domicile-based system.

Section 87B provides that gains treated as accruing in a tax year to a remittance basis user on receipt of a capital payment from a non-UK resident settlement are treated as chargeable gains accruing on the disposal of an asset situated outside the UK. This ceases to apply for gains treated as accruing in tax year 2025-26 or later.

Sub-paragraph 59(5) inserts new subsection 87B(5) as a consequence of paragraph 63 and new section 87HA (capital payments routed via non-residents or qualifying new residents) to ensure that subsection 87B(1)(a) continues to operate by reference to how it applied for the tax year in which the chargeable gains were treated as accruing to the individual.

3.3.2.62.4 Effective Date

The effective date is 6 April 2025 see paragraph 70.

3.3.2.63 *Paragraph 60 Amendment of section 87D following substitution of section 87HA*

3.3.2.63.1 Overview

Paragraph 60 omits (i.e. repeals) subsection 87D (1) (sections 87 and 87A: capital payments to non-residents disregarded) as a consequence of paragraph 63 and new section 87HA.

3.3.2.63.2 Legislation

Paragraph 60 reads:

> **(1) Section 87D** (sections 87 and 87A: capital payments to non-residents disregarded) is amended as follows.
> (2) In subsection (1), omit paragraph (b) and the "and" before it."
> Sections 87 and 87A TCGA read before amendment as follows.
> **"87Non-UK resident settlements: attribution of gains to beneficiaries**
> (1) This section applies to a settlement for a tax year ("the relevant tax year") if [there is no time in that year when the trustees are resident in the United Kingdom].
> (2) Chargeable gains are treated as accruing in the relevant tax year to a beneficiary of the settlement who has received a capital payment from the trustees in the relevant tax year or any earlier tax year if all or part of the capital payment is matched (under section 87A as it applies for the relevant tax

year) with [the section 1(3) amount] for the relevant tax year or any earlier tax year.

(2A) If the relevant tax year is a split year as respects the beneficiary, the gains are treated as accruing in the UK part of that year.

(3) The amount of chargeable gains treated as accruing is equal to—

(a) The amount of the capital payment, or

(b) If only part of the capital payment is matched, the amount of that part.

(4) The section 1(3) amount] for a settlement for a tax year for which this section applies to the settlement is—

(a) The amount upon which the trustees of the settlement would be chargeable to tax under section 1(3)] for that year if they were resident ... in the United Kingdom in that year, or

(b) If section 86 applies to the settlement for that year, the amount mentioned in paragraph (a) minus the total amount of chargeable gains treated under that section as accruing in that year.

(5) The section 1(3) amount] for a settlement for a tax year for which this section does not apply to the settlement is nil.

(5A) Where (apart from this subsection) the amount mentioned in subsection (4)(a) would include a chargeable gain or allowable loss to which section 1A(3)(b) or (c) applies (disposals by non-UK residents within the charge to capital gains tax), so much of the gain or loss as would be so included is to be disregarded for the purposes of determining the section 1(3) amount.]

(5B) Where (apart from this subsection) the amount mentioned in subsection (4)(a) would include an amount of chargeable gains treated as accruing under section 103KA(2) or (3) (carried interest gains), the amount of the gains is to be disregarded for the purposes of determining the section 1(3) amount.

(6) For the purposes of this section a settlement arising under a will or intestacy is treated as made by the testator or intestate at the time of death.

(7) . . . .

87ASection 87: matching

(1) This section supplements section 87.

(2) The following steps are to be taken for the purposes of matching capital payments with section 1(3) amounts.

Step 1

Find the section 1(3) amount] for the relevant tax year.

Step 2

Find the total amount of capital payments received by the beneficiaries from the trustees in the relevant tax year.

Step 3

The section 1(3) amount] for the relevant tax year is matched with—

(a) If the total amount of capital payments received in the relevant tax year does not exceed the section 1(3) amount] for the relevant tax year, each capital payment so received, and

(b) otherwise, the relevant proportion of each of those capital payments.

"The relevant proportion" is the section 1(3) amount] for the relevant tax year divided by the total amount of capital payments received in the relevant tax year.

Step 4

If paragraph (a) of Step 3 applies—

(a) reduce he section 1(3) amount] for the relevant tax year by the total amount of capital payments referred to there, and

(b) reduce the amount of those capital payments to nil.

If paragraph (b) of that Step applies—

(a) reduce the section 1(3) amount] for the relevant tax year to nil, and

(b) reduce the amount of each of the capital payments referred to there by the relevant proportion of that capital payment.

Step 5

Start again at Step 1 (unless subsection (3) applies).

If the section 1(3) amount] for the relevant tax year (as reduced under Step 4) is not nil, read references to capital payments received in the relevant tax year as references to capital payments received in the latest tax year which—

(a) is before the last tax year for which Steps 1 to 4 have been undertaken, and

(b) is a tax year in which capital payments (the amounts of which have not been reduced to nil) were received by beneficiaries.

If the section 1(3) amount] for the relevant tax year (as so reduced) is nil, read references to [the section 1(3) amount] for the relevant tax year as the section 1(3) amount] for the latest tax year—

(a) which is before the last tax year for which Steps 1 to 4 have been undertaken, and

(b) for which the section 1(3) amount] is not nil.

(3) This subsection applies if—

(a) All of the capital payments received by beneficiaries from the trustees in the relevant tax year or any earlier tax year have been reduced to nil, or

(b) The section 1(3) amounts] for the relevant tax year and all earlier tax years have been reduced to nil.

(4) The effect of any reduction under Step 4 of subsection (2) is to be taken into account in any subsequent application of this section."

3.3.2.63.3 Details of Paragraph

Paragraph 60 omits subsection 87D (1) (sections 87 and 87A: capital payments to non-residents disregard) as a consequence of paragraph 63 and new section 87HA (capital payments routed via non-residents or qualifying new residents).

Paragraphs 60 (1) to (3) amend section 87G (settlor liable if capital payment received by close family member) and inserts new subsection 87G(2A), because of paragraph 63 which inserts the new section 87HA (capital payments routed via non-residents or qualifying new residents). It provides that section 87G does not apply where for the tax year in which the original recipient received the capital payment both the settlor is a qualifying new resident, and the original recipient is UK resident.

Sub-paragraph 60(4) inserts new subsection 87G(4)(c). This amends the content of a certificate that an officer of Revenue and Customs may be required to give a person seeking recovery from the original recipient of the amount tax payable under sections 87 and 87A.

3.3.2.63.4 Effective Date

The effective date is 6 April 2025 see paragraph 70.

3.3.2.64 *Paragraph 61 Amendment of section 87 H following substitution of section 87 HA*

3.3.2.64.1 Overview

Paragraph 61 amends section 87H (meaning of 'close member of settlor's family) as a consequence of paragraph 63 and new section 87HA (capital payments routed via non-residents or qualifying new residents) which are discussed in the next section.

3.3.2.64.2 Legislation

Paragraph 61 reads:

> "In section 87H (meaning of "close member of the settlor's family"), in subsection (1), for "87D, 87G and 87L" substitute "87D and 87G".

3.3.2.64.3 Details of Paragraph

This is essentially a tidying up provision. Section 87L is replaced by section 87HA substituted by paragraph 63 for sections 87I to 87M (set out in the next section). This is discussed in the next section.

3.3.2.64.4 Effective Date

6 April 2025 see paragraph 70.

3.3.2.65 Paragraph 62 Substitution of new section 87HA for old section 87I to 87M

3.3.2.65.1 Overview

Paragraph 62 substitutes a new section 87HA (capital payments routed via non-residents or qualifying new residents) for sections 87I to 87M (onward gifting provisions). Broadly, this provides that where a non-resident settlement makes a capital payment to a UK resident via a non-resident person or a qualifying new resident, then the payment is treated for the purpose of sections 87, 87A, 87D (2) and 87G (2) as if it were made directly to the UK resident at the time when the onward gift is made. This means the payment is not tax free as it generally would be if there were no "onward gifting" and the "true" recipient were non-UK resident or a qualifying new resident.

3.3.2.65.2 Legislation

Paragraph 62 reads:

> "For sections 87I to 87M (old onward gifting provisions) substitute—
>
> "**87HA Onward gifts from non-residents or qualifying new residents**
>
> (1) Subsection (2) applies if—
>
> (a) a person **("the original recipient")** receives a capital payment **("the original benefit")** from the trustees of a settlement,
>
> (b) the original recipient is not resident in the United Kingdom, or is a qualifying new resident, for the tax year in which they receive the original benefit,
>
> (c) section 87G (2) (close family member's benefits attributed to settlor) does not apply to the provision of the original benefit to the original recipient,
>
> (d) at the time when the person receives the original benefit—
>
> (i) there are arrangements, or an intention, as regards the (direct or indirect) passing on of the whole or part of the original benefit to another person, and
>
> (ii) it is reasonable to expect that, if the whole or part of the original benefit is passed on to another person in accordance with the arrangements or intention, that other person will be resident in the United Kingdom when they receive at least part of what is passed on to them,
>
> (e) the original recipient provides a benefit **("the onward gift")** to a person **("the subsequent recipient")**—
>
> (i) at the time when the original benefit is provided to the original recipient or at any later time in the 3 years beginning with the day containing that time, or
>
> (ii) at any time before the original benefit is made to the original recipient and, it is reasonable to assume, in anticipation of the original benefit's being made,

(f) the onward gift is of or includes—
(i) the whole or part of the original benefit
(ii) anything that (wholly or in part, and directly or indirectly) derives from, or represents, the whole or part of the original benefit, or
(iii) any other property, but only if the original benefit is provided with a view to enabling or facilitating, or otherwise in connection with, the providing of the onward gift to the subsequent recipient, and
(g) the subsequent recipient is resident in the United Kingdom for the tax year in which they receive the onward gift.

(2) So much of the onward gift as falls within subsection (1)(f) is treated for the purposes of sections 87, 87A, 87D (2) and 87G (2) as a capital payment received from the trustees by the subsequent recipient at the time when the onward gift is provided.

(3) Where subsection (2) applies, the subsequent recipient is treated as having received the capital payment as a beneficiary of the settlement (whether or not they are otherwise a beneficiary of it).

(4) For the purposes of subsection (1)(e), the circumstances in which the original recipient provides a benefit to the subsequent recipient include circumstances where there is a series of two or more benefits starting with a benefit provided by the original recipient and ending with a benefit provided to the subsequent recipient; and in such a case—
(a) the onward gift is treated for the purposes of subsection (1)(e) as provided when the final benefit in the series is provided, and
(b) the reference to the onward gift in subsection (1)(f) is to be read as a reference to each benefit in the series.

(5) Where the onward gift is made as mentioned in subsection (1)(e)(ii), the onward gift is treated for the purposes of subsection (2) as made in the tax year in which the original benefit is made to the original recipient.

(6) Where the conditions in subsection (1)(e) to (g) are met, it is to be presumed (unless the contrary is shown) that the condition in subsection (1)(d) is also met.

(7) In this section, "arrangements" includes any agreement, understanding, scheme, transaction or series of transactions (whether or not legally enforceable).""

3.3.2.65.3 Details of Paragraph

This paragraph substitutes sections 87I to 87M (onward gifting provisions) with new section 87HA (capital payments routed via non-residents or qualifying new residents). Broadly, this provides that where a non-resident settlement makes a capital payment to a UK resident via a non-resident person or a qualifying new resident, then the payment is treated for the purpose of sections 87, 87A, 87D (2) and 87G (2) as if it were made directly to the UK resident at the time when the onward gift is made. This means this can be a UK tax charge which would not necessarily be the case if the payment were to a non UK resident or a qualifying new resident.

3.3.2.65.4 Effective Date

The effective date is 6 April 2025 see paragraph 70.

3.3.2.66 Paragraph 63 Removing cross references to repealed sections 87K and 87L in section 91

3.3.2.66.1 Overview

Paragraph 63 amends section 91 (increase in tax payable under section 87 or 89(2)) as a consequence of paragraph 63 and the new section 87HA.

3.3.2.66.2 Legislation

Paragraph 63 reads:

> "In section 91 (increase in tax payable under section 87 or 89(2)), in subsection (1)(a), omit ", 87K, 87L"."

3.3.2.66.3 Details of Paragraph

Sections 87K and 87L are repealed by the substitution of section 87HA (capital payments routed via non-residents or qualifying new residents) by paragraph 63. This is essentially a tidying up provision admitting references to repealed sections.

Sections 87K and 87L are set out at p146.

3.3.2.66.4 Effective Date

The effective date is 6 April 2025 see paragraph 70.

3.3.2.67 Paragraph 64 Amendment of section 97 dealing with relationship to the Settlement and Transfer of Assets Abroad provisions

3.3.2.67.1 Overview

Paragraph 65 amends subsections 97(1)(a)(ii) and 97(3) (supplementary provisions) in consequence of Parts 1 and 2 of Schedule 12 and the modifications made as discussed above. This accords with the general principle that payments chargeable to income tax should not also be liable to CGT.

The amendment to subsection 97(1) makes clear that, for the purposes of sections 86 to 96 of, and Schedule 4C to, TCGA 1992, a 'capital payment' does not include a payment chargeable to income tax under either Chapter 5 of Part 5 of ITTOIA 2005 (settlements) or Chapter 2 of Part 13 of ITA 2007 (transfer of assets abroad).

The amendment to subsection 97(3) confirms that although the benefit (or part of it) is treated under those provisions as an individual's income for a tax year after that in which it is received, this does not prevent it being treated as a capital payment for the purposes of sections 86 to 96 of, and Schedule 4C, to TCGA 1992 in relation to any earlier tax year. Care accordingly needed with capital payments.

3.3.2.67.2 Legislation

Paragraph 64 reads:

> ""In section 97 (supplementary provisions)—
>
> (a) in subsection (1)(a)(ii), for the words from "any of sections 643A" to the end of the sub-paragraph, substitute "Chapter 5 of Part 5 of ITTOIA 2005 (settlements) or Chapter 2 of Part 13 of ITA 2007 transfer of assets abroad)";
>
> (b) in subsection (3), for the words from "section 643A" to "ITA 2007", substitute "Chapter 5 of Part 5 of ITTOIA 2005 (settlements) or Chapter 2 of Part 13 of ITA 2007 (transfer of assets abroad)".

3.3.2.67.3 Details of Paragraph

This paragraph clarifies that "capital payment" for attribution of gains etc. provisions in TCGA does not include a payment chargeable to IT under the Settlement provisions or the Transfer of Assets provisions.

3.3.2.67.4 Effective Date

The effective date is 6 April 2025 see paragraph 70.

3.3.2.68 Paragraph 65 Amendment of section 279A TCGA following subsection of new section 87 HA

3.3.2.68.1 Overview

Paragraph 65 amends section 279A (deferred unascertainable consideration: election for treatment of loss) as a consequence of paragraph 63 and new section 87HA discussed at p131 above.

Paragraph 63 and new section 87HA are discussed at p131.

3.3.2.68.2 Legislation

Paragraph 65 reads:

> "In section 279A (deferred unascertainable consideration: election for treatment of loss), in subsection (7)(b), omit ", 87K, 87L".

3.3.2.68.3 Details of Paragraph

This is essentially a tidying up provision. Sections 87K and 87 L are repealed by the substitution of section 87 HA by paragraph 63 discussed at p131 above.

The text of sections 87K and 87 L are set out at p146.

3.3.2.68.4 Effective Date

The effective date is 6 April 2025 see paragraph 70.

3.3.2.69 *Paragraph 66 Amendment of section 279C following substitution of new section 87 HA*

3.3.2.69.1 Overview

Paragraph 66 amends section 279C (effect of election under section 279A) as a consequence of paragraph 63 and new section 87HA (capital payments routed via non-residents or qualifying new residents).

3.3.2.69.2 Legislation

Paragraph 66 reads:

> "In section 279C (effect of election under section 279A), in subsection (6)(c), omit ", 87K, 87L"."

3.3.2.69.3 Details of Paragraph

This omits references to section 87K and 8A in section 279C.

3.3.2.70 *Paragraph 67– Amendment of paragraph 3 Schedule 1 TCGA*

3.3.2.70.1 Overview

Paragraph 67 omits paragraph 3(5)(b) of Schedule 1 to TCGA 1992 (UK resident individuals not domiciled in UK) as a result of paragraph 54 which is concerned with personal losses. It is discussed above.

3.3.2.70.2 Legislation

Paragraph 67 reads:

> "In Schedule 1 (UK resident individuals not domiciled in UK), in paragraph 3(5), omit paragraph (b) and the "and" before it."
>
> Paragraph 3 read before amendment and repeal as follows.
>
> "3(1) This paragraph applies in the case of an individual for a tax year if—
>
> (a) The remittance basis applies to the individual for the tax year, and
>
> (b) An election under section 16ZA has effect for the tax year.
>
> (2) Allowable losses accruing to the individual must be matched to chargeable gains accruing to the individual in accordance with paragraph 4.
>
> (3) If allowable losses are matched to chargeable gains accruing on disposals of foreign assets—
>
> (a) Which actually accrue in the tax year, but
>
> (b) Which are, as a result of paragraph 1, treated as not accruing in the tax year, the amount of those gains is reduced by the matched amount (and the allowable losses are reduced accordingly).

(4) So far as allowable losses are matched to other chargeable gains, they are deducted from chargeable gains accruing to the individual in the tax year.

(5) This is subject to—

(a)paragraph 2 (no use of allowable losses against foreign gains remitted in later year), and

(b) Section 1E (4) (prohibition of deduction of losses from gains treated as accruing under section 87, 87K, 87L or 89(2))."

Paragraph 67 amends paragraph 3 Schedule 1 TCGA by omitting paragraph 3(5)(6). The wording of paragraph 3 is set out above.

3.3.2.70.3 Effective Date

The effective date is 6 April 2025 see paragraph 70.

3.3.2.71 Paragraph 68 Certain attributions to beneficiaries amended

3.3.2.71.1 Overview

Paragraph 68 amends paragraphs 1A (1) and 8(6) of Schedule 4C (transfers of value: attribution of gains to beneficiaries) as a consequence of paragraph 63 and new section 87HA (capital payments routed via non-residents or qualifying new residents).

3.3.2.71.2 Legislation

Paragraph 68 reads:

"Schedule 4C (transfers of value: attribution of gains to beneficiaries) is amended as follows.

In paragraph 8(6), after "87G (2)," insert "87HA (2),". "

3.3.2.71.3 Details of Paragraph

This, even by my standards, is a specialised area on which appropriate advice should be sought if it seems likely to apply.

3.3.2.71.4 Effective Date

The effective date is 6 April 2025 see paragraph 70.

3.3.2.72 Paragraph 69 Amendments to Schedule 5 TCGA to reflect move away from Domicile basis

3.3.2.72.1 Overview

Paragraph 69 amends Schedule 5 TCGA to reflect the change away from a domicile basis. Schedule 5 supplements section 86 TCGA which broadly attributes trust gains of Settlor interested offshore trusts to the settlor.

3.3.2.72.2 Legislation

Paragraph 69 reads:

"(1) Schedule 5 (attribution of gains to settlors with interest in non-resident or dual resident settlement) is amended as follows.

(2) In paragraph 1 (construction of section 86(1)(e): losses etc), after sub-paragraph (6) insert—

"(6A) In construing section 86(1)(e) as regards a particular year of assessment, if—(a) section 86 did not apply to the settlement in a year of assessment ending before 6 April 2025 ("the earlier year"), but (b) that section would have applied to the settlement in the earlier year if the condition in section 86(1)(e) (settlor domiciled in the United Kingdom) had been met in the earlier year, deductions shall be made in respect of losses accruing in the earlier year, but only so far as those losses have not been taken into account for the purposes of section 87 in determining the section 1(3) amount for the settlement for the earlier year."

(3) Omit paragraphs 5A and 5B (protections for deemed domiciles etc).

(4) After paragraph 5 insert—

"Old section 87 rebasing elections to apply in relation to section 86

5C (1) This paragraph applies if—

(a) the trustees of the settlement made (at any time) an election under paragraph 126(1) of Schedule 7 to the Finance Act 2008 (remittance basis: capital gains rebasing), and

(b) an amount of chargeable gains would (apart from this paragraph) be treated as accruing to the settlor under section 86(4) in a tax year ("the relevant tax year").

(2) The settlor is not charged to capital gains tax on so much of the chargeable gains as exceeds the relevant proportion of those gains.

(3) For that purpose, "the relevant proportion" is—

A

B

where—

A is the amount that would be treated under section 86(4) as accruing to the settlor in the relevant tax year if immediately before 6 April 2008 every relevant asset had been sold by the trustees and immediately re-acquired by them at its market value at that time, and

B is the amount mentioned in sub-paragraph (1)(c).

(4) In sub-paragraph (3), "relevant asset" means an asset—

(a) that was disposed of in the relevant tax year, and

(b) that was comprised in the settlement from the beginning of 6 April 2008 until its disposal."

(5) In paragraph 6 (right of recovery), in sub-paragraph (3)—

(a) omit the "and" after paragraph (a);

(b) after paragraph (b) insert ", and

(c) the tax year in which gains were treated as accruing under section 86(4),".

3.3.2.72.3 Details of Paragraph

Sub-paragraph 69 (2) inserts new sub-paragraph 1(6A) into Schedule 5 (attribution of gains to settlors with interest in non-resident or dual resident settlement) as a consequence of sub-paragraph 56(2) discussed above. The effect is to enable unused allowable losses that have accrued for the purposes of attributing gains in non-resident settlements to beneficiaries to be usable for the purposes of attributing gains to settlors.

3.3.2.72.3.1 Deemed Domicile Repeals.

Sub-paragraph 69 (3) omits paragraphs 5A and 5B of Schedule 5, which protected deemed domiciles from rules that attribute to settlors' gains accruing to non-resident or dual resident settlements.

3.3.2.72.3.2 New paragraph 5C inserted.

Sub-paragraph 69 (4) inserts new paragraph 5C into Schedule 5 in consequence of the ending of domicile in the tax system and paragraph 55 (amendments to section 86 of TCGA 1992). As a result of those amendments, gains accruing to non-resident settlements with a UK resident non-UK domicile settlor that has an interest in the settlement will become attributable to the settlor under section 86 (attribution to settlors) rather than section 87 (attribution to beneficiaries).

New paragraph 5C transfers the effect of transitional rules introduced in 2008 on the then amendment of the application of section 87. Under those rules, trustees may elect to make a one-off rebasing of their assets to 5 April 2008 for CGT purposes. Subparagraph 70(4) transfers the effect of such an election through to the computation of gains that become attributable to UK resident settlors under section 86.

3.3.2.72.3.3 Content of HMRC certificate.

Sub-paragraph 69 (5) inserts new sub-paragraph 6(3)(c) into Schedule 5. This amends the content of a certificate that an officer of Revenue and Customs may be required to give a person seeking recovery from the trustees of a settlement of the amount of tax payable under section 86.

3.3.2.72.4 Effective Date

6 April 2025 see paragraph 70.

3.3.2.73 Part 4: Commencement and transitional provision

Part 4 contains provisions about commencement and transitional provision. Broadly, the provisions come into force on 6 April 2023.

3.3.2.74 Paragraph 70 Parts 1-3 come into force 6 April 2025

3.3.2.74.1 Overview

Paragraph 70 provides that Parts 1 to 3 of the Schedule come into force on 6 April 2025.

3.3.2.74.2 Legislation

Paragraph 70 reads:

> "70(1) The amendments made by paragraphs 1 to 53, 55 to 64 and 67 to 69 have effect for the tax year 2025-26 and subsequent tax years.
>
> (2) The amendment made by paragraph 54 to section 62 of TCGA 1992 (death: general provisions) has effect in relation to deaths occurring on or after 6 April 2025
>
> (3) The amendments made by paragraphs 65 and 66 to sections 279A and 279C of TCGA 1992 (deferred unascertainable consideration: election for treatment of loss) have effect in relation to disposals made on or after 6 April 2025 of rights to which section 279A of that Act applies."

3.3.2.74.3 Details of Paragraph

This is the general provision under which Parts 1 to 3 of Schedule 12 come into force on 6 April 2025.

Parts 1-3 deal with the following.

Part 1 amends Chapter 5 of Part 5 of ITTOIA 2005 (settlements: amounts treated as income of settlor or family); [103]

Part 2 amends Chapter 2 of Part 13 of ITA 2007 (transfer of assets) [104]

Part 3 amends Chapter 2 of Part 3 of TCGA 1992 (settlements: chargeable gains) [105] and other provisions of TCGA 1992 relating to trusts and similar structures;

3.3.2.74.4 Effective Date

The effective date is 6 April 2025 see paragraph 70.

3.3.2.75 Paragraph 71 Section 743EA and straddle over 6 April 2025

3.3.2.75.1 Overview

Paragraph 71 provides that new section 643EA of ITTOIA 2005, as inserted by paragraph 17 of Schedule 12, applies where the original benefit was made by the settlement before 6 April 2025 and the onward gift is made on or after 6 April 2025; and makes consequential provision for such cases. In other words,

---

[103] See Chapter 6 of *Taxation of Entertainers and Sportspersons*

[104] Ibid

[105] Ibid

it deals with the situation where the original benefit and the onward gift straddle 6 April 2025.

3.3.2.75.2 Legislation

Paragraph 71 reads:

> ""**Onward gifts: settlements (income)**
>
> 71 Section 643EA of ITTOIA 2005 (onward gifts from non-residents or qualifying new residents), as inserted by paragraph 17 of this Schedule,
>
> (1) applies where the onward gift is provided on or after 6 April 2025, even if the original benefit was provided before that date.
>
> (2) Where the original benefit was provided before 6 April 2025, that section applies as if for subsection (1)(b) there were substituted—
>
> "(b) either—(i) the original recipient is non-UK resident for the tax year in which the original benefit is provided, or (ii) section 809B, 809D or 809E of ITA 2007 (remittance basis) applies to the original recipient for that tax year,".
>
> (3) In this paragraph, "the original benefit" and "the onward gift" have the same meanings as in section 643EA of ITTOIA 2005; and in a case within section 643EA (3) "the onward gift" means the final benefit in the series."

Paragraph 17 which inserts section 643EA ITTOIA is discussed above.

3.3.2.75.3 Details of Paragraph

Again, this deals with the position where the original benefit and the onward gift straddle 6 April 2025.

3.3.2.75.4 Effective Date

The effective date is 6 April 2025 see paragraph 70.

3.3.2.76 Paragraph 72 Continued application of section 643M ITTOIA to earlier events despite repeal

3.3.2.76.1 Overview

Paragraph 72 provides that despite the repeal of section 643M ITTOIA, by paragraph 21 Schedule 12 (discussed above), this section continues to have effect so far as is relevant to the continued application of section 643B by reference to past events.

3.3.2.76.2 **Legislation**

Paragraph 72 reads:

> "Despite the repeal of section 643M of ITTOIA 2005 by paragraph 21 of this Schedule, that section continues to have effect so far as—
>
> (a) it provided before its repeal for a benefit of a particular amount to be treated for the purposes of section 643B of that Act as having been provided to a particular person at a particular time, and (b) the receipt

of the benefit by the person is relevant to the application of section 643B of that Act in the tax year 2025-26 or a later tax year."

3.3.2.76.3 Details of Paragraph

In broad terms section 643 ITTOIA continues to have effect where relevant to past events.

3.3.2.76.4 Effective Date

The effective date is 6 April 2025 see paragraph 70.

3.3.2.77 Paragraph 73 straddle over 6 April 2025 and section 745F ITA

3.3.2.77.1 Overview

Paragraph 73 provides that new section 735AF ITA 2007, as inserted by paragraph 44 Schedule 12, applies where the original benefit was made by the settlement before 6 April 2025 and the onward gift is made on or after 6 April 2025; and makes consequential provision for such cases.

3.3.2.77.2 Legislation

Paragraph 73 reads:

"Onward gifts: transfer of assets abroad

73 Section 735AF of ITA 2007 (onward gifts from non-residents or qualifying new residents), as inserted by paragraph 44 of this Schedule, applies where the onward gift is provided on or after 6 April 2025, even if the original benefit was provided before that date.

(2) Where the original benefit was provided before 6 April 2025, that section applies as if for subsection (1)(b) there were substituted—(b) either— the original recipient is non-UK resident for the tax year in which the original benefit is provided, or (ii) section 809B, 809D or 809E of ITA 2007 (remittance basis) applies to the original recipient for that tax year,".

In this paragraph, "the original benefit" and "the onward gift" have the same meanings as in section 735AF of ITA 2007; and in a case within section 735AF (3) "the onward gift" means the final benefit in the series."

Section 735AF is headed "Onward gifts from non-residents or qualifying new residents". It reads as follows.

(1) Subsection (2) applies if—

(a) A benefit ("the original benefit") is provided to an individual ("the original recipient") out of assets which are available for the purpose as a result of—

(i) The relevant transfer, or

(ii)one or more associated operations,

(b) The original recipient is non-UK resident, or is a qualifying new resident, for the tax year in which they receive the original benefit,

(c) Section 735AE (1) (close family member's benefits attributed to settlor) does not apply to the provision of the original benefit to the original recipient,

(d) At the time when the original benefit is provided—

(i) There are arrangements, or there is an intention, as regards the (direct or indirect) passing on of the whole or part of the original benefit to another person, and

(ii) It is reasonable to expect that, if the whole or part of the original benefit is passed on to another person in accordance with the arrangements or intention, that other person will be UK resident when they receive at least part of what is passed on to them,

(e) The original recipient provides a benefit ("the onward gift") to another person ("the subsequent recipient")—

(i) At the time when the original benefit is received by the original recipient, or at any later time in the 3 years beginning with the day containing that time, or

(ii) At any time before the original benefit is received by the original recipient and, it is reasonable to assume, in anticipation of the original benefit's being provided, and

(f) The onward gift is of or includes—

(i) The whole or part of the original benefit,

(ii) Anything that (wholly or in part, and directly or indirectly) derives from, or represents, the whole or part of the original benefit, or

(iii) Any other property, but only if the original benefit is provided with a view to enabling or facilitating, or otherwise in connection with, the property's being provided to the subsequent recipient.

(2) For the purposes of sections 732, 735AD(1) and 735AE(1), so much of the onward gift as falls within subsection (1)(f) is (so far as would not otherwise be the case) treated as a benefit provided to the subsequent recipient out of assets which are available for the purpose as a result of an associated operation in relation to the relevant transfer.

(3) For the purposes of subsection (1)(e), the circumstances in which the original recipient provides a benefit to the subsequent recipient include circumstances where there is a series of two or more benefits starting with a benefit provided by the original recipient and ending with a benefit provided to the subsequent recipient; and in such a case—

(a) The onward gift is treated for the purposes of subsection (1)(e) as provided when the final benefit in the series is provided, and

(b) The reference to the onward gift in subsection (1)(f) is to be read as a reference to each benefit in the series.

(4) Where the conditions in subsection (1)(e) and (f) are met, it is to be presumed, unless the contrary is shown, that the condition in subsection (1)(d) is also met.

(5) In subsection (1)(d), "arrangements" includes any agreement, understanding, scheme, transaction or series of transactions (whether or not legally enforceable).

3.3.2.77.3 Details of Paragraph

This is also in essence a straddle provision.

3.3.2.77.4 Effective Date

The effective date is 6 April 2025 see paragraph 70.

3.3.2.78 Paragraph 74 Straddle over 5 April 2025 of capital payment and onward gift and Section 87HA

3.3.2.78.1 Overview

Paragraph 74 provides that new section 87HA of TCGA 1992, as inserted by paragraph 63 Schedule 12, applies where the capital payment was made by the settlement before 6 April 2025 and the onward gift is made on or after 6 April 2025; and makes consequential provision for such cases.

3.3.2.78.2 Legislation

Paragraph 74 reads:

"Onward gifts: settlements (chargeable gains)

(1) Section 87HA of TCGA 1992 (benefits routed via non-residents or qualifying new residents), as inserted by paragraph 63 of this Schedule, applies where the onward gift is provided on or after 6 April 2025, even if the original benefit was provided before that date.

(2) Where the original benefit was provided before 6 April 2025, that section applies as if for subsection (1)(b) there were substituted—

"(b) either—

(i) the original recipient is non-UK resident for the tax year in which they receive the original benefit, or (ii) section 809B, 809D or 809E of ITA 2007 (remittance basis) applies to the original recipient for that tax year,".

(3) In this paragraph, "the original benefit" and "the onward gift" have the same meanings as in section 87HA of TCGA 1992; and in a case within section 87HA (4) "the onward gift" means the final benefit in the series."

Section 87HA is discussed above.

The text of section 87HA is set out above.

87A Section 87: matching

(1) This section supplements section 87.

(2) The following steps are to be taken for the purposes of matching capital payments with section 1(3) amounts.

Step 1

Find the section 1(3) amount for the relevant tax year.

Step 2

Find the total amount of capital payments received by the beneficiaries from the trustees in the relevant tax year.

Step 3

The section 1(3) amount for the relevant tax year is matched with—

(a) if the total amount of capital payments received in the relevant tax year does not exceed the section 1(3) amount for the relevant tax year, each capital payment so received, and

(b) otherwise, the relevant proportion of each of those capital payments.

"The relevant proportion" is the section 1(3) amount for the relevant tax year divided by the total amount of capital payments received in the relevant tax year.

Step 4

If paragraph (a) of Step 3 applies—

(a) reduce the section 1(3) amount for the relevant tax year by the total amount of capital payments referred to there, and

(b) reduce the amount of those capital payments to nil.

If paragraph (b) of that Step applies—

(a) reduce the section 1(3) amount for the relevant tax year to nil, and

(b) reduce the amount of each of the capital payments referred to there by the relevant proportion of that capital payment.

Step 5

Start again at Step 1 (unless subsection (3) applies).

If the section 1(3) amount for the relevant tax year (as reduced under Step 4) is not nil, read references to capital payments received in the relevant tax year as references to capital payments received in the latest tax year which—

(a) is before the last tax year for which Steps 1 to 4 have been undertaken, and

(b) is a tax year in which capital payments (the amounts of which have not been reduced to nil) were received by beneficiaries.

If the section 1(3) amount for the relevant tax year (as so reduced) is nil, read references to the section 1(3) amount for the relevant tax year as the section 1(3) amount for the latest tax year—

(a) which is before the last tax year for which Steps 1 to 4 have been undertaken, and

(b) or which the section 1(3) amount is not nil.

(3) This subsection applies if—

(a) all of the capital payments received by beneficiaries from the trustees in the relevant tax year or any earlier tax year have been reduced to nil, or

(b) the section 1(3) amounts for the relevant tax year and all earlier tax years have been reduced to nil.

(4) The effect of any reduction under Step 4 of subsection (2) is to be taken into account in any subsequent application of this section.]]

Section 1(3) TCGA reads

"(3) Capital gains tax is charged on the total amount of chargeable gains accruing to a person in a tax year after deducting—

(a) Any allowable losses accruing to the person in the tax year, and

(b) So far as not previously deducted under this subsection, any allowable losses accruing to the person in any previous tax year."

In simplistic terms the section 1(3) amount is the amount on which CGT is chargeable for the tax year in question.

3.3.2.78.3 Details of Paragraph

This is also in essence a straddle provision.

3.3.2.78.4 Effective Date

The effective date is 6 April 2025 see paragraph 70.

3.3.2.79 Paragraph 75 Continued application of sections 87K and 87L despite repeal where relevant after 6 April 2025

3.3.2.79.1 Overview

Paragraph 76 provides that despite the repeal of sections 87K and 87L of TCGA 1992, by paragraph 63 Schedule 12 (discussed above), those sections continue to have effect so far as is relevant to the continued application of sections 87 and 87A by reference to past events.

3.3.2.79.2 Legislation

Paragraph 76 reads:

"Despite the repeal of sections 87K and 87L of TCGA 1992 (old onward gifting rules) by paragraph 63 of this Schedule, each of those sections continues to have effect so far as—

(a) before its repeal, it provided for section 87 and 87A of that Act to have effect as if a capital payment of a particular amount had been received at a particular time by a particular person, and

(b) the receipt of the capital payment by that person is relevant to the application of sections 87 and 87A in the tax year 2025-26 or a later tax year."

Sections 87K and 87L read as follows before their repeal.

87K Attribution of gains or payments to recipient of onward gift

(1) Where this section applies (see section 87I), G is—

(a) The amount or value of so much of the onward payment as is within any of sub-paragraphs (i) to (iii) of section 87I(1)(d), or

(b) If lower, the amount of the original payment.

(For the meaning of R and U, see section 87J.)

(2) If R is greater than nil, sections 87 and 87A have effect for the gift year and later tax years—

(a) As if a capital payment was received from the trustees by the subsequent recipient—

(i) As a beneficiary of the settlement (whether or not the subsequent recipient is otherwise a beneficiary of the settlement), and

(ii) At the time the subsequent recipient received the onward payment,

(b) As if that capital payment consisted of—

(i)R, if G is greater than R, or

(ii) So much of R as is equal to G, if G is not greater than R, and

(c) As if so, much of the original payment as is equal to that capital payment was not received by the otherwise-liable person.

(3) If G is greater than R, and if U is greater than nil—

(a) Chargeable gains are treated as accruing to the subsequent recipient in the gift year (but see section 87L (3) and (4)),

(b) The amount of those gains is—

(i) U, if (G – R) is greater than U, or

(ii) So much of U as is equal to (G – R), if (G – R) is not greater than U, and

(c) The chargeable gains treated by section 87 as accruing to the otherwise-liable person by reason of the original payment are treated as from the end of the gift year as reduced by that amount, with that reduction being made from so much of those gains as has not by then been remitted to the United Kingdom in a tax year in which the otherwise-liable person is resident in the United Kingdom.

(4) If this section applies by reference to the original payment also in relation to a gift received from the original beneficiary in a tax year earlier than the gift year, this section applies in relation to the onward payment as if—

(a) The amount given by section 87J for R were reduced by the amount of any capital payment given by subsection (2) in relation to that earlier year, and

(b) The amount given by section 87J for U were reduced by the amount of any gains given by subsection (3) in relation to that earlier year.

87L Cases where settlor liable following onward gift

(1) Subsection (2) applies where—

(a) Ignoring this section and section 87M, a person is treated by section 87K (2) as receiving a capital payment from the trustees of a settlement at a time ("the time of receipt") in a tax year,

(b) The settlor is resident in the United Kingdom at any time in that year, and

(c) The person mentioned in paragraph (a) is a close member of the settlor's family (see section 87H) at the time of receipt.

(2) Sections 87 and 87A have effect for that year, and later tax years, as if the capital payment—

(a) Was received from the trustees by the settlor—

(i) As a beneficiary of the settlement (whether or not the settlor is otherwise a beneficiary of the settlement), and

(ii) At the time of receipt, and

(b) Was not received by the person mentioned in subsection (1)(a).

(3) Subsection (4) applies where—

(a) In the case of a settlement, chargeable gains are (ignoring this section and section 87M) treated by section 87K (3) as accruing to a person in a tax year ("the subsequent recipient"),

(b) The settlor is resident in the United Kingdom at any time in that year, and

(c) The subsequent recipient is a close member of the settlor's family when the subsequent recipient receives the onward payment (see section 87I(1)(c)) by reference to which the chargeable gains are treated as accruing.

(4) Section 87K(3)(a) has effect as if its reference to the subsequent recipient a reference to the settlor were, and references (however expressed) to chargeable gains treated as accruing by this section are to chargeable gains treated by section 87K(3)(a) as accruing to the settlor as a result of the operation of this subsection.

(5) Where, in the case of a settlement, any tax is chargeable on the settlor as a result of this section and is paid, the settlor is entitled to recover the full amount of the tax from the person mentioned in subsection (1)(a) or (3)(a), as the case may be.

(6) For the purpose of recovering that amount, the settlor is entitled to require an officer of Revenue and Customs to give the settlor a certificate specifying—

(a) The amount of tax paid, and

(b) The amount of the gains on which the tax is paid,

and any such certificate is conclusive evidence of the facts stated in it.

3.3.2.79.3 Details of Paragraph

This provision deals with the position where despite their repeal sections 87K and 87L continue to have application to past events.

3.3.2.79.4 Effective Date

6 April 2025 see paragraph 70.

4 Inheritance Tax

Key Points IHT and FA 2025

- Residence replaces domicile as basis for IHT charge
    - Fundamental changes
    - Started 6 April 2025
- Policy paper important as to policy and so for interpretation
- Deemed domicile abolished
- Long Term UK resident ("LTR") an important concept in connecting facts of post 5. April 2025
- 10-Year tail after ceasing to be UK resident
- Double Death Conventions ("DDC") e.g. with US may be relevant on death IHT charge but complex. US DDC may help with inter vivos gifts and trusts
- Excluded property trusts and other protections abolished for LTRS with some transitional provisions
- Significant effect for many long term residents
- Careful review needed
- Sections 44-46 FA 2025 deal with this. Schedule 13 important
- How HMRC will apply this in practice not entirely clear

4.1 Summary

The shift to a **residence-based IHT regime** under FA 2025 represents a **seismic policy shift**, particularly for:

- **UK-resident non-doms**
- **Settlor-interested trusts**
- **High-net-worth individuals (HNWIs)** with international ties such as some ESPs

It significantly increases compliance complexity and **IHT risk exposure**, especially during the **10-year tail period**. Meticulous tracking of residence history, professional planning, and timely restructuring as well as full recording of all relevant information are now essential.

This chapter provides an analysis of the **Inheritance Tax (IHT) reforms** introduced under the **Finance Act 2025**, particularly the shift from a **domicile-based** to a **residence-based** IHT regime. It focuses on practical implications, transitional provisions, and the risks for individuals—especially non-domiciled UK residents and those with offshore trusts. The following core matters are considered in this section of the Supplement:

1. Core Legislative Change

- From **6 April 2025**, IHT exposure is based on **residence**, not **domicile.**
- The new rule introduces the concept of a **"long-term resident" ("LTR")**:
    - A person is an LTR if **UK-resident for at least 10 out of the past 19 tax years.**
    - This LTR status brings **worldwide assets** within the scope of UK IHT.

2. The 10-Year "Tail" Rule

- IHT exposure continues for up to **10 years after ceasing UK residence**.
- Even after leaving the UK, **former LTRs remain taxable** on worldwide assets unless the full 10-year period has passed.

3. Impact on Excluded Property Trusts (EPTs)

- The previous exemption from IHT for **EPTs** (based on non-UK domicile) **no longer applies** to LTRs.
- **Trusts become liable to UK IHT** on relevant property if the settlor is, or becomes, an LTR.
- **Historic EPT protections do not continue** unless very specific transitional reliefs apply. Such arrangements need careful review.

4. Transitional and Carve-Out Provisions

- Transitional rules exist but are limited:
    - **Trusts settled before 6 April 2025** may get limited protection if the settlor is not an LTR on that date.
    - **Chargeable events (e.g. death, 10-year charges)** occurring after 5 April 2025 are governed by the new regime.
- **Carve-outs for pre-2025 trust gains or remittances** exist but require precise tracking and documentation and careful consideration.

5. Interaction with Double Taxation Conventions (DTCs)

- **DTCs on estate/inheritance taxes** (e.g. UK–US DDC) may **override UK IHT rules**, depending on facts and treaty interpretation.
- This could still provide **protection for certain US citizens** and others with DTC-covered domicile/residence claims.
- The UK-USC DDC has wider coverage than the other UK DDC's (see Some Thoughts at the end of this supplement).

6. Planning and Practical Issues

- **Identifying LTR status** is now central to IHT planning. Historical UK residence data over at least **12 years** must be maintained.

- **Life insurance** is recommended as a hedge against IHT exposure, particularly during the 10-year tail.
- **Changing residence now is not an immediate IHT escape**—only the passage of time reduces exposure.

7. HMRC Guidance and Future Review

- There is a lack of full HMRC guidance and an **absence of a comprehensive impact assessment**.
- The government seemingly intends to consult further on the **design of the residence-based IHT regime**, but changes are already Law.

4.1.1 General

This part of the Supplement is concerned with the changes made to IHT by FA 2025.

The "headline" in respect of IHT in this context is the change from a Domicile based system to a Residence based regime. This is a "fundamental" change to the basis on which IHT is charged and to its original design.

The basis for IHT from 6 April 2025 is long term UK residence rather than "domicile". This has similarities to Deemed Domicile under the Old Regime which was a residence-based extension to the general concept of domicile for IHT purposes where there was a significant period of residence. This extension had been included since the introduction of CTT (now called IHT). However, the New Regime is self-contained and must be considered on its own.

The change to a residence-based regime will have a significant effect on the ESPs who came to the UK who were domiciled outside the UK and were accepting of IHT on UK situs assets but not on worldwide assets on death with a 10-year tail.

The UK/US death taxes treaty [106] may help in some cases but careful advice is needed. [107] This is discussed below. There seemed to be an increase in inquiries about this from such individuals after the Autumn Budget October 2024 and publication of the legislation in my experience although many individuals were concerned before the election. A significant number have left the UK in my experience as the ten-year tail on Worldwide assets for IHT was the last straw.

---

[106] There are Double Death Duty Treaties or Double Death Conventions ("DCC"). Some of these are discussed in the Further Thoughts section below.

[107] The changes to APR and BPR have caused concern as well. Insurance solutions can sometimes assist depending on age and fitness of the individuals.

4.1.2 *Policy Paper or Policy Summary*

The 29 July 2024 Policy Paper outlining the then new government's plans to change the taxation of non-UK domiciled individuals [108] included the intention to replace the domicile-based IHT system with a new residence-based system from 6 April 2025. This is what happened.

The 30 October 2024 Budget confirmed that this was to be the case. This legislation in FA 2025 under discussion here is part of its implementation.

From its start as Capital Transfer Tax (and after it was renamed Inheritance Tax), IHT used Domicile as the connecting factor for charge. UK Domiciliaries were charged on their worldwide assets. There were special provisions for individuals domiciled outside the UK. The provisions in the FA 2025 concerning this are considered in this section.

4.1.3 *Deemed Domicile*

Domicile was given an extended meaning for IHT to include "deemed domicile" [109] from its introduction as CTT [110] as noted above. This was residence based and intended to bring longer term UK residents with an offshore domicile into the charge to IHT. It was often referred to as "deemed domicile" as noted above.

An individual was treated as domiciled in the UK for IHT purposes if they had been resident in the UK for 17 out of the preceding 20 years till 2017. This was often referred to as "deemed domicile". This was acceptable to many HNWIs as by careful planning, particularly by using EPTs set up before becoming deemed domicile the impact could be reduced to acceptable levels for many.

Deemed domicile was extended to IT and CGT by F(No.2) A 2017. It had not applied to IT and CGT before then. It did afterwards.

The period became 15 years out of the 20 years preceding the year in question rather than 17 out the preceding 20 years. This is discussed below.

There was thus a period of long-term residence by reference to a twenty-year period for IHT for charging purposes treated as meeting the Domicile requirement. This was achieved by the deemed domicile concept. [111]

It is this regime, in particular, that FA 2025 replaces with the new residence – based system from 6 April 2025.

---

[108] 2024: Non-UK domiciled individuals- Policy Summary - GOV.UK (www.gov.uk)

[109] See section 267 IHTA Persons treated as domiciled in United Kingdom

[110] Name changed to IHT from Capital Transfer Tax by section 100 FA 1986.

[111] Section 267 IHTA. For changes over time see https://www.legislation.gov.uk/ukpga/1984/51/section/267

4.1.4 *Tail for IHT after leaving the UK*

The domicile-based legislation before FA 2025 meant there could be a "tail"[112] after an individual left the UK of up to four years before potential liability to IHT was generally lost after leaving the UK.

This tail was effectively extended to a period of ten years by FA 2025. This is complicated matter which is discussed below.

The extension to 10 years has been "the straw that broke the camel's back" for many formerly UK resident non-doms. The prospect of a 40%[113] charge on the value of their worldwide assets was too much for them as from their perspective they regarded this as double taxation.[114] Accordingly, a significant number of them have ceased to be UK resident to start the clock running as soon as possible in my experience. Some have taken out term assurance against the risk of dying within the period of the tail applicable to them.

Many such UHNWI ESPS have houses in a number of places around the World which makes it much easier from them to achieve non-residence in the UK than it is for others who would need to sell their house and find a new job buy a new home and make arrangements for their children's education etc. Many such ESPs have a degree of flexibility as to what they do when. They can, for example, choose which tournaments they play in or if retired not work and so not have difficulties with the Deeming Rule in some circumstances where work is done in the UK which can mean any presence in the UK rather than just at Midnight is the test for day counting. For many such ESP's it is a question of changing their routine and spending less time in the UK which is much less onerous than for many other people who do not have the infrastructure in place. These only seem to be increasing at present.

4.1.5 *Excluded Property etc.*

Excluded Property is property excluded from a person's estate for IHT purposes and so not charged to IHT. This used to be by reference to the situs of the property and the Domicile of the individual in question which could include the settlor of a trust.

---

[112] Broadly, the period after the individual left the UK during which an IHT charge could arise.

[113] Current rate of IHT on death at the time of writing.

[114] This was not always accurate as the wealth was often inherited so double taxation was not necessarily the case. The perspective though was what mattered. I am aware of at 21 UHNWIs (lowest worth more than US$ 7bn who left the UK as a result. This is 27.27% of the 77 individuals the Warwick Report would leave the UK as a result on which the Government seemingly relied notwithstanding representations from the professional bodies and others.

This special treatment of offshore situs property continues but is now modified to a residence basis rather than a domicile based one. This is discussed below.

Section 44 headed "Excluded property: domicile test replaced with long-term residence test" is the main provision that replaces the existing domicile-based rules for IHT with revised tests by reference to a person's residence by making amendments to IHTA. This is discussed below.

These amendments took effect from 6 April 2025.

Sections 45–46 FA 2025 follow on from the section 44 changes making more detailed provision in respect of the move away from Domicile.

Section 45 makes corresponding changes for settled property to those in section 44 (see below).

Section 46 makes "Consequential, connected and transitional provision" in relation to this (see below).

These sections are each in turn below after considering what was said in committee.

Finance Bill Committee

James Murray, the Exchequer Secretary to the Treasury said the following on IHT in the Finance Bill Committee.

"Clauses [now sections] 44 to 46 and Schedule 13 make changes to replace the current domicile-based system of inheritance tax with the new residence-based system. Currently, an individual's domicile status determines whether their non-UK assets are in scope of inheritance tax. The non-domiciled individual's personal non-UK assets are not in scope until they become deemed domiciled. However, if such assets are placed into a trust they will remain out of scope in perpetuity, even if an individual later settles in the UK.

The changes made by clause 44 will mean that from April this year [2025], an individual will be in scope for inheritance tax on their personal, non-UK assets if they have been resident in the UK for at least 10 out of the least 20 tax years. An individual will then remain in scope for between three and 10 years after leaving the UK, depending on how long they were resident in the UK.

The changes made by clause 45 will mean that, subject to transitional points, any non-UK assets that an individual places in a trust will be liable for inheritance tax charges when the settlor is a long-term resident. This will also apply to such assets treated as owned by a beneficiary who is a long-term UK resident. Although non-UK assets in existing protected trusts will be in the 10-yearly inheritance tax charging regime when the settlor is a long-term resident, it is important to note that those non-UK assets in existing protected trusts will be kept out of the settlor's or beneficiary's death estate. Any new assets put into trust will be fully in scope for trust charges or charges on a death whenever the settlor is a long-term UK resident. This matches the current treatment of people with UK domicile.

Clause [now section] 46 and Schedule 13 make changes to the remaining inheritance tax areas to depend on a person's long-term UK residence instead of their domicile, and to provide for commencement. For example, a surviving spouse or civil partner can elect to be treated as a long-term UK resident instead of electing to be treated as a UK domicile. This will have effect for 10 years.

Four minor amendments, 62 to 65, have been made to Schedule 13 to insert a missing word, to correct cross-references to the new definition of excluded property in a settlement, and to ensure that all fiscal domicile definitions are removed unless they are needed for a double taxation convention to work. The Government are committed to making the tax system fairer, so that everyone who is a long-term resident in the UK pays their taxes here. The new regime therefore ensures that individuals, in the future, will not be able to keep their assets out of scope of inheritance tax indefinitely. At the same time, our approach ensures that non-UK assets in existing protected trusts will be kept out of the settlor's or beneficiary's death estate. I therefore commend clauses 44 to 46 and schedule 13, alongside Government amendments 62 to 65, to the Committee."

4.2 Some Relevant Legislation

4.2.1 General

This section of the Supplement sets out the text of the legislation in sections 44 to 46 FA 2025. This legislation is what makes the relevant changes which are in point here. This is mainly achieved by amending the IHTA as noted above. Each of the sections in the legislation will then be discussed in more detail below.

4.2.2 Section 44 - "Excluded property: domicile test replaced with long-term residence test"

Section 44 is headed "Excluded property: domicile test replaced with long-term residence test". It reads as follows:

"(1) IHTA 1984 is amended as follows.
(2) In section 6 (excluded property), in subsections (1) and (1A), for "domiciled outside the United Kingdom" substitute "who is not a long-term UK resident".
(3) After section 6 insert—
"6A "Long-term UK resident": individuals
(1) For the purposes of this Act, an individual is a "**long-term UK resident**" at all times in a tax year if they were **UK resident for at least 10 of the previous 20 tax years**.
(2) But an individual is not a long-term UK resident at any time in a tax year ("**the current tax year**") if they were non-UK resident—

(a) for **any 10 consecutive tax years during the 19 tax years before** the **current** tax year, or

(b) for at least the required number of consecutive tax years ending with the tax year before the current tax year.

(3) To determine "**the required number**" for the purposes of subsection (2)(b), take the 20 tax years ending with the last tax year for which the individual was UK resident and find the number of those tax years for which the individual was UK resident ("**the number of resident years**").

The required number is the number in the second column of the following table corresponding to the number of resident years.

Number of resident years	Required number
13 or less	3
14	4
15	5
16	6
17	7
18	8
19	9
20	10

(4) In this section, "UK resident" means resident in the United Kingdom and "non-UK resident" means not resident in the United Kingdom.

(5) For the purposes of this section, a question as to whether the individual was UK resident for the tax year 2012-13 or an earlier tax year is to be determined as it would have been determined for income tax purposes for that tax year (and as to later tax years see Schedule 45 to the Finance Act 2013 (statutory residence test)).

(6) See also—

(a) section 6B (which modifies this section in its application to young persons);

(b) sections 267ZC to 267ZE (under which a person may be treated as a long-term UK resident as the result of an election)."

6B "Long-term UK resident": young persons

In the application of section 6A(1) for the purpose of determining whether a young person is a long-term UK resident at any time in a tax year ("the current tax year"), that subsection has effect as if—

(a) for "20" there were substituted the number of whole tax years for which the person was alive before the current tax year, and

(b) for "10" there were substituted half the number mentioned in paragraph (a) (rounded up, if not a whole number, to the next whole number).

(2) In subsection (1), "young person" means an individual who was under the age of 20 immediately before the current tax year.

(3) For the purposes of this Act, an individual is not a long-term UK resident at any time in a tax year if they were under the age of 1 (or were not yet born) immediately before the tax year.

6C "Long-term UK resident": bodies corporate

For the purposes of this Act, a body corporate is a "long-term UK resident" at all times in a tax year if the body—

(a) is incorporated in the United Kingdom, or

(b) was (if in existence before the beginning of the tax year) within the charge to corporation tax on income at any time during the previous tax year by virtue of section 5(1) of the Corporation Tax Act 2009 (UK resident companies)."

This section comes into force on 6 April 2025".

4.2.2.1 *Some questions raised by section 44*

Section 44 raises a number of questions including the following:

- What is excluded property? Why does it matter? This is discussed below.
- Who is "Long-term UK resident"? This is discussed below.
- Do the rules differ for individuals, trusts and bodies corporate? This is discussed below.
- Are there special rules for young persons? This is discussed below.
- What about trusts? This is discussed below.

These questions are discussed below after some comments about trusts.

4.2.3 *Trusts*

4.2.3.1 *General*

The question about trusts is quickly answered so is dealt with first. There are special rules for trusts found in Section 45 which is headed "Corresponding change for settled property".

Section 45 is set out next and discussed below under the heading "Settled Property".

Subsection (4) of section 45 provides for commencement.

It reads "This section [i.e. section 45] comes into force on 6 April 2025." Accordingly, the relevant provisions apply after 5 April 2025.

4.2.4 *Section 45 Settled Property "Corresponding change for settled property"*

Section 45 is headed "Corresponding change for settled property". It provides:

"(1) IHTA 1984 is amended as follows.

(2) In section 48 (excluded property)—

(a) in the heading, at the end insert ": reversionary interests and Treasury securities";

(b) omit subsections (3) to (3F).[115]

(3) After section 48 insert—

"48ZA **Excluded property**: property situated outside the UK etc

(1) If **property comprised in a settlement**—

(a) is **situated outside the United Kingdom**, or

(b) is a holding in an authorised unit trust or a share in an open-ended investment company,

this section applies to the property and section 6(1) and (1A) (general excluded property rule) does not.

(2) **If** the **settlor is alive**, the **property is excluded** property at any time **when the settlor is not a long-term UK resident**.

---

[115](3)Where property comprised in a settlement is situated outside the United Kingdom—

(a)the property (but not a reversionary interest in the property) is excluded property unless the settlor was domiciled in the United Kingdom at the time the property became comprised in the settlement (but see also subsection (3F)), and

(b)section 6(1) above applies to a reversionary interest in the property but does not otherwise apply in relation to the property ;

but this subsection is subject to subsections (3B) to (3E) below and to Schedule A1.

(3A)Where property comprised in a settlement is a holding in an authorised unit trust or a share in an open-ended investment company—

(a)the property (but not a reversionary interest in the property) is excluded property unless the settlor was domiciled in the United Kingdom at the time the property became comprised in the settlement (but see also subsection (3F)), and

(b)section 6(1A) above applies to a reversionary interest in the property but does not otherwise apply in relation to the property ;

but this subsection is subject to subsections (3B) and (3E) below and to Schedule A1.

(3B)Property is not excluded property by virtue of subsection (3) or (3A) above if—

(a)a person is, or has been, beneficially entitled to an interest in possession in the property at any time,

(b)the person is, or was, at that time an individual domiciled in the United Kingdom, and

(c)the entitlement arose directly or indirectly as a result of a disposition made on or after 5th December 2005 for a consideration in money or money's worth.

(3C)For the purposes of subsection (3B) above—

(a)it is immaterial whether the consideration was given by the person or by anyone else, and

(b)the cases in which an entitlement arose indirectly as a result of a disposition include any case where the entitlement arose under a will or the law relating to intestacy.

(3D)Where paragraphs (a) to (d) of section 74A(1) are satisfied, subsection (3)(a) above does not apply at the time they are first satisfied or any later time to make the relevant settled property (within the meaning of section 74A) excluded property.

(3E)In a case where the settlor of property comprised in a settlement is not domiciled in the United Kingdom at the time the property became comprised in the settlement (but see also subsection (3F)), the property is not excluded property by virtue of subsection (3) or (3A) above at any time in a tax year if the settlor was a formerly domiciled resident for that tax year.

(3F)If—

(a)an amount is payable in respect of property ("the existing property") comprised in a settlement, and

(b)the amount represents an accumulation of income which (once accumulated) becomes comprised in the settlement,

subsections (3)(a), (3A)(a) and (3E) have effect, in the case of the amount, as if any reference to the time it became comprised in the settlement were to the time the existing property became comprised in the settlement.

(3) If the settlor **died on or after 6 April** 2025, the property is **excluded property** if the **settlor** was **not a long-term UK resident immediately before they died**.
(4) If the settlor **died before 6 April 2025**, the property is **excluded property** if the **settlor** was **not domiciled in the United Kingdom when the property became comprised in the settlement**.
(5) Subsections (2) and (3) do not apply at any time to property to which section 49(1) [116] (certain interests in possession) applies if, at that time, the person beneficially entitled to the interest is a long-term UK resident.
(6) Subsections (2) to (4) do not apply to property if—

(a) an individual has been beneficially entitled to an interest in possession in the property—

(i) at any time on or after 6 April 2025 while a long-term UK resident, or
(ii) at any time before that date while domiciled in the United Kingdom, and

(b) the entitlement arose directly or indirectly as a result of a disposition made on or after 5 December 2005 for a consideration in money or money's worth.

(7) For the purposes of subsection (6)—

(a) it is immaterial whether the consideration was given by the individual or by anyone else, and
(b) the cases in which an entitlement arose indirectly as a result of a disposition include any case where the entitlement arose under a will or the law relating to intestacy.

(8) Where the conditions in paragraphs (a) to (d) of section 74A (1) (arrangements involving acquisition of interest in settled property etc) are satisfied, none of subsections (2) to (4) applies at the time when the conditions are first satisfied or at any later time to make the relevant settled property (within the meaning of section 74A) excluded property.
(9) If—

(a) an amount is payable in respect of property ("the existing property") comprised in a settlement, and
(b) the amount represents an accumulation of income which (once accumulated) becomes comprised in the settlement, subsection (4) has effect in the case of the amount as if the reference to the time when it became comprised in the settlement were to the time when the existing property became comprised in the settlement.

(10) Subsections (2) to (4) are subject to Schedule A1 (overseas property with value attributable to UK residential property).

---

116 Treat life tenant as beneficially entitled to the underlying property in which the I.P. exists subject to exceptions including if entitled after 2 March 2006 see sections 49(1) and 49(1A)

(11) The reference in subsection (1) to property comprised in a settlement does not include a reversionary interest in the property (and accordingly this section does not apply to such an interest and section 6(1) does)."
(4) This section comes into force on 6 April 2025. "

4.2.4.1 *Examples relevant to section 45 amending section 48 IHTA.*

The position after these changes come into force will depend on the long-term UK resident status of the relevant person as discussed below.

An example may be of some assistance in understanding this complex provision.

Example

Desi Tern is an Asturian citizen and domiciliary who lives in the UK.
Desi sets up a settlement which holds UK registered shares, some UK land and some Asturian shares and some Asturian land in the trust fund.
The UK land and shares are UK situs assets and so *ex hypothesi* cannot constitute Excluded Property as they are not situated outside the UK. This is the case both before and after the change.
The Asturian land and shares could be excluded property. This depends on Desi's long term UK resident status.

i. Desi comes to the UK for the first time in a year one having never been to the UK before and until his arrival had never been UK resident. He dies in year which is after 5 April 2025 and [six] tax years after the year in which Desi been the UK resident.
Desi is not a long-term UK resident as he has only been UK resident for [6/7] years.
Accordingly, section 48 ZA (2) provides that at times when Desi was alive the Asturian land and shares are excluded property as he was not a long-term UK resident.
By section 48 ZA (3) The same property is excluded property in respect to the charge on death as Desi was not a long-term UK resident immediately before death.

ii. If Desi had died before 6 April 2025 and was domiciled in Astoria immediately before his death the Asturian land and shares would be Excluded Property see section 48 ZA (4)

iii. If Desi died having been in the UK for 11 years in one continuous stretch before the year of death Desi Desi would be UK long term resident as he met the criteria to be a long-term UK resident. Accordingly, IHT would be chargeable, without more as Desi is long term UK resident.

iv. If Desi's child Tone was the life tenant of the settlement and Tone was a long-term UK resident, then the Astorian shares and lands would not be excluded property.

4.2.5 *Section 46 - "Consequential, connected and transitional provision*

Section 46 is headed "Consequential, connected and transitional provision". It reads:

> "In Schedule 13—
>
> Part 1 contains amendments to IHTA 1984 and related legislation that are consequential on, connected with or incidental to the new excluded property tests introduced by sections 44 and 45;
>
> Part 2 contains provision about commencement and transitional provision".

Section 45 and Schedule 13 are discussed below.

For reasons of space the full text of Schedule 13 is not included here. Relevant extracts are included in the discussion of the Schedule below.

4.3 Replacement of Domicile Test by Long-Term Residence Test - section 44 FA 2025

4.3.1 *Introductory*

This part of the Supplement discusses "the long-term residence test" introduced by section 44.

As noted above section 44 replaces the existing domicile-based rules for IHT with revised tests relating to an individual's residence as foreshadowed in the Policy Summary. It does so by making amendments to IHTA1984.

The amendments took effect from 6 April 2025.[117]

It was intended to replace Domicile (both actual and deemed) as the connecting factor for charging IHT. The new connecting factor is "Long term UK resident".

4.3.1.1 *"Long-Term UK Resident"*

The important new concepts introduced by FA 2025 include that of "Long-term UK resident". This is broadly that the person was resident for at least 10 of the twenty tax years before the year in question. They are therefore 21 years that need consideration. Collecting such information from clients for such a period is likely to be an interesting logistical issue. This is an important matter as the onus of proof will be on the taxpayer to show they are not a long-term UK resident if HMRC makes a determination that they are.

The new section 6A IHTA deals with LTR for individuals.

[117] See subsection (4) provides for commencement. It reads "(4) This section comes into force on 6 April 2025."

The new section 6C IHTA deals with LTR for bodies corporate.

There are special rules in the new section 6B IHTA for young persons.

These are each discussed below

4.3.1.2 The Text of the Section

For the convenience of the Reader the text of the section is repeated here. Section 44 is headed "Excluded property: domicile test replaced with long-term residence test". It reads as follows:

"(1) IHTA 1984 is amended as follows.
(2) In section 6 (excluded property), in subsections (1) and (1A), for "domiciled outside the United Kingdom" substitute "who is not a long-term UK resident".
(3) After section 6 insert—
"6A "Long-term UK resident": individuals
(1) For the purposes of this Act, an individual is a **"long-term UK resident"** at all times in a tax year if they were **UK resident for at least 10 of the previous 20 tax years**.
(2) But an **individual is not a long-term UK resident** at any time in a tax year (**"the current tax year") if they were non-UK resident—**

> (a) for **any 10 consecutive tax years during the 19 tax years before the current tax year, or**
> (b) for at least **the required number of consecutive tax years ending** with the tax year **before the current tax year**.

(3) To determine **"the required number**" for the purposes of subsection (2)(b), take the 20 tax years ending with the last tax year for which the individual was UK resident and find the number of those tax years for which the individual was UK resident ("the number of resident years").
The required number is the number in the second column of the following table corresponding to the number of resident years.

Number of resident years	**Required number**
13 or less	3
14	4
15	5
16	6
17	7
18	8
19	9
20	10

(4) In this section, "UK resident" means resident in the United Kingdom and "non-UK resident" means not resident in the United Kingdom.

(5) For the purposes of this section, a question as to whether the individual was UK resident for the tax year 2012-13 or an earlier tax year is to be determined as it would have been determined for income tax purposes for that tax year (and as to later tax years see Schedule 45 to the Finance Act 2013 (statutory residence test)).

(6) See also—

(a) section 6B (which modifies this section in its application to young persons);

(b) sections 267ZC to 267ZE (under which a person may be treated as a long-term UK resident as the result of an election).

For the convenience of the Reader sections 6B and 6C are set out again here.

6B "Long-term UK resident": young persons

In the application of section 6A (1) for the purpose of determining whether a young person is a long-term UK resident at any time in a tax year ("**the current tax year**"), that subsection has effect as if—

(a) for "20" there were substituted the number of whole tax years for which the person was alive before the current tax year, and

(b) for "10" there were substituted half the number mentioned in paragraph (a) (rounded up, if not a whole number, to the next whole number).

(2) In subsection (1), "young person" means an individual who was under the age of 20 immediately before the current tax year.

(3) For the purposes of this Act, an individual is not a long-term UK resident at any time in a tax year if they were under the age of 1 (or were not yet born) immediately before the tax year.

6C "Long-term UK resident": bodies corporate

For the purposes of this Act, a body corporate is a "long-term UK resident" at all times in a tax year if the body—

(a) is incorporated in the United Kingdom, or

(b) was (if in existence before the beginning of the tax year) within the charge to corporation tax on income at any time during the previous tax year by virtue of section 5(1) [118] of the Corporation Tax Act 2009 (UK resident companies)."

This section comes into force on 6 April 2025".

---

[118] Section 5 is headed "Territorial scope of charge".

(1)A UK resident company is chargeable to corporation tax on income on all its profits wherever arising (but see Chapter 3A for an exemption from charge in respect of profits of foreign permanent establishments).

(2)A non-UK resident company is within the charge to corporation tax on income] only if—

(a)it carries on a trade of dealing in or developing UK land (see section 5B), ...

(b)it carries on a trade in the United Kingdom (other than a trade of dealing in or developing UK land) through a permanent establishment in the United Kingdom,

(c)it carries on a UK property business, or

(d)it has other UK property income....

4.3.2 *Approach taken here*

The approach taken here in discussing this matter is to follow the structure of the sections.

Accordingly, Long Term Residence for individuals is considered first.

The meaning of Long-Term Residence for Young Persons is then considered followed by that for bodies corporate.

Before that Excluded Property is considered as it is matter much affected by the change.

It should be noted that although section 6(1) talks of resident for at least 10 of the previous 20 tax years section 6(2) talks of consecutive years.

4.4 Long Term Residence and Excluded Property

4.4.1 *Retention of concept of Excluded Property*

4.4.1.1 *General*

The concept of Excluded Property is retained for IHT but in a modified form that is not Domicile based, but residence related. In other words, certain non-UK situs property is not within the charge to IHT (i.e. is excluded from charge) where a non-UK long term resident is involved and certain other conditions are met. Under the revised legislation this is no longer to depend on the domicile of the person in question but on their long-term residence status.

Excluded Property relates to non-UK situs property held by an individual who meets certain criteria. It does not apply to UK situs property. Such property is excluded from a person's estate on death. [119] Hence, the label Excluded Property is used. Excluded property is defined in section 6 IHTA. It is discussed below.

---

[119] See section 5 IHTA headed "Meaning of estate". It reads as follows.

"(1)For the purposes of this Act a person's estate is the aggregate of all the property to which he is beneficially entitled, except that—

(a)the estate of a person—

(i)does not include an interest in possession in settled property to which section 71A or 71D below applies, and

(ii)does not include an interest in possession that falls within subsection (1A) below unless it falls within subsection (1B) below, and

(b)***the estate of a person immediately before his death does not include excluded property*** or a foreign-owned work of art which is situated in the United Kingdom for one or more of the purposes of public display, cleaning and restoration (and for no other purpose). [Emphasis supplied]

(b)the estate of a person immediately before his death does not include excluded property or a foreign-owned work of art which is situated in the United Kingdom for one or more of the purposes of public display, cleaning and restoration (and for no other purpose).]

(1A)An interest in possession falls within this subsection if—

(a)it is an interest in possession in settled property,

(b)the settled property is not property to which section 71A or 71D below applies,

In the past this was domicile based. This is now to be long term UK residence based.

4.4.1.2 Mechanics of change from Domicile to Long Term Residence

The situs of UK property is not dealt with in the IHTA but is generally decided by case law, statute and occasionally double taxation treaties, agreements or conventions. The situs of an asset is important for Inheritance Tax because

- Being located outside the UK may cause the asset to be excluded property (IHTM27211)
- The location of an asset determines whether or not the value of the asset receives relief under a Double Taxation Convention (DTC) (IHTM27161).

IHTA84/S158 tells us to look first at the DTC that applies to see if it contains any situs rules. If the convention does not contain situs rules we must follow the general law ruling on the assets in question.

DTCs drafted before 1975 usually contain detailed rules about situs. Those drafted after 1975 usually do not." [120]

Section 44 (2) provides that the definitions of excluded property in sections 6(1) and 6(1A) IHTA 1984 from 6 April 2025 are to use the concept of an individual's long-term UK residence rather than their domicile.

(c)the person is beneficially entitled to the interest in possession,

(d)the person became beneficially entitled to the interest in possession on or after 22nd March 2006, and

(e)the interest in possession is—

(i)not an immediate post-death interest,

(ii)not a disabled person's interest, and

(iii)not a transitional serial interest.

(1B)An interest in possession falls within this subsection if the person—

(a)was domiciled in the United Kingdom on becoming beneficially entitled to it, and

(b)became beneficially entitled to it by virtue of a disposition which was prevented from being a transfer of value by section 10 below.

(2)A person who has a general power which enables him, or would if he were sui juris enable him, to dispose of any property other than settled property, or to charge money on any property other than settled property, shall be treated as beneficially entitled to the property or money; and for this purpose "general power" means a power or authority enabling the person by whom it is exercisable to appoint or dispose of property as he thinks fit.

(3)In determining the value of a person's estate at any time his liabilities at that time shall be taken into account, except as otherwise provided by this Act.

(4)The liabilities to be taken into account in determining the value of a transferor's estate immediately after a transfer of value include his liability for inheritance tax on the value transferred but not his liability (if any) for any other tax or duty resulting from the transfer.

(5)Except in the case of a liability imposed by law, a liability incurred by a transferor shall be taken into account only to the extent that it was incurred for a consideration in money or money's worth."

[120] see https://www.gov.uk/hmrc-internal-manuals/inheritance-tax-manual/ihtm27071

Section 44 (3) inserts new sections 6A, 6B and 6C into IHTA 1984 (set out above). These deal with the meaning of long-term UK resident for individuals, young persons and bodies corporate respectively.

The new section 6A (1) defines an individual as a 'long-term UK resident' for a tax year when they have been resident for at least 10 out of the previous 20 tax years. However, this is subject to the exceptions in new subsections 6A (2) and (3). This is discussed below.

The 20-year period is likely to cause taxpayers and their advisers some practical issues. Few if any taxpayers will have records available for such a period. The onus of proof will be on the taxpayer to show it is not the case that they have been UK resident for at least 10 out of the previous 20 years. If HMRC make a determination on the basis that the taxpayer was UK resident that determination stands unless the taxpayer can prove on the balance of probabilities this was not the case. This requires suitable admissible evidence to do so.

Further the rules have changed on this over the last 20 years. The SRT was introduced by FA 2013. Before then IR 20 was used. This is discussed below and some extracts from IR 20 are set out in the Annexe.

4.4.1.3 *Some Relevant Legislation etc. Excluded Property*

"Excluded property" is a defined term in the IHTA.

Section 6 IHTA is headed "Excluded property".

4.4.1.4 *Pre Change Version*

Before the current changes section 6 read as follows:

> "Property situated outside the United Kingdom is excluded property if the person beneficially entitled to it is an individual domiciled outside the United Kingdom.
>
> (1A) A holding in an authorised unit trust and a share in an open-ended investment company is excluded property if the person beneficially entitled to it is an individual domiciled outside the United Kingdom.
>
> (1B) A relevant decoration or award is excluded property if it has never been the subject of a disposition for a consideration in money or money's worth.
>
> (1BA) In subsection (1B) "relevant decoration or award" means a decoration or other similar award—
>
> (a)that is designed to be worn to denote membership of—
>
> (i)an Order that is, or has been, specified in the Order of Wear published in the London Gazette ("the Order of Wear"), or
>
> (ii)an Order of a country or territory outside the United Kingdom,
>
> (b)that is, or has been, specified in the Order of Wear,
>
> (c)that was awarded for valour or gallant conduct,

(d)that was awarded for, or in connection with, a person being, or having been, a member of, or employed or engaged in connection with, the armed forces of any country or territory,

(e)that was awarded for, or in connection with, a person being, or having been, an emergency responder within the meaning of section 153A (death of emergency service personnel etc), or

(f)that was awarded by the Crown or a country or territory outside the United Kingdom for, or in connection with, public service or achievement in public life.

(1C) In subsection (1B) the reference to a disposition of the decoration or other award includes—

(a)a reference to a disposition of part of it, and

(b)a reference to a disposition of an interest in it (or in part of it).

(2)Where securities have been issued by the Treasury subject to a condition authorised by section 22 of the Finance (No. 2) Act 1931 (or section 47 of the Finance (No. 2) Act 1915) for exemption from taxation so long as the securities are in the beneficial ownership of persons [of a description specified in the condition], the securities are excluded property if they are in the beneficial ownership of such a person.

(3) Where the person beneficially entitled to the rights conferred by any of the following, namely—

(a)war savings certificates;

(b)national savings certificates (including Ulster savings certificates);

(c)premium savings bonds;

(d)deposits with the National Savings Bank or with a trustee savings bank;

(e)a certified SAYE savings arrangement within the meaning of section 703(1) of the Income Tax (Trading and Other Income) Act 2005; is domiciled in the Channel Islands or the Isle of Man, the rights are excluded property.

(4) Property to which this subsection applies by virtue of section 155(1) or (5A) below is excluded property.

(5) This section is subject to Schedule A1 (non-excluded overseas property)." [121]

4.4.1.5 Post Change Version

After the changes made by section 44 it reads as follows: (1) "Property situated outside the United Kingdom is excluded property if the person beneficially entitled to it is an individual [domiciled outside the United Kingdom].

(1A) A holding in an authorised unit trust and a share in an open-ended investment company is excluded property if the person beneficially entitled to it is an individual ~~domiciled outside the United Kingdom.~~

[121] This includes Overseas property with value attributable to UK residential property such as shares in an overseas company owning UK residential property and certain associated loans.

(1B) A relevant decoration or award is excluded property if it has never been the subject of a disposition for a consideration in money or money's worth.

(1BA) In subsection (1B) "relevant decoration or award" means a decoration or other similar award—

(a)that is designed to be worn to denote membership of—

(i)an Order that is, or has been, specified in the Order of Wear published in the London Gazette ("the Order of Wear"), or

(ii)an Order of a country or territory outside the United Kingdom,

(b)that is, or has been, specified in the Order of Wear,

(c)that was awarded for valour or gallant conduct,

(d)that was awarded for, or in connection with, a person being, or having been, a member of, or employed or engaged in connection with, the armed forces of any country or territory,

(e)that was awarded for, or in connection with, a person being, or having been, an emergency responder within the meaning of section 153A (death of emergency service personnel etc), or

(f)that was awarded by the Crown or a country or territory outside the United Kingdom for, or in connection with, public service or achievement in public life.

(1C) In subsection (1B) the reference to a disposition of the decoration or other award includes—

(a)a reference to a disposition of part of it, and

(b)a reference to a disposition of an interest in it (or in part of it).

(2) Property situated outside the United Kingdom is excluded property if the person beneficially entitled to it is an individual ~~domiciled outside the United Kingdom~~ who is not a long-term UK resident.

(1A) A holding in an authorised unit trust and a share in an open-ended investment company is excluded property if the person beneficially entitled to it is an individual ~~domiciled outside the United Kingdom~~ who is not a long-term UK resident~~.~~

(1B) A relevant decoration or award is excluded property if it has never been the subject of a disposition for a consideration in money or money's worth.

(1BA) In subsection (1B) "relevant decoration or award" means a decoration or other similar award—

(a)that is designed to be worn to denote membership of—

(i)an Order that is, or has been, specified in the Order of Wear published in the London Gazette ("the Order of Wear"), or

(ii)an Order of a country or territory outside the United Kingdom,

(b)that is, or has been, specified in the Order of Wear,

(c)that was awarded for valour or gallant conduct,

(d)that was awarded for, or in connection with, a person being, or having been, a member of, or employed or engaged in connection with, the armed forces of any country or territory, (e)that was awarded for, or in connection with, a person being, or having been, an emergency responder within the meaning of section 153A (death of emergency service personnel etc), or

(f)that was awarded by the Crown or a country or territory outside the United Kingdom for, or in connection with, public service or achievement in public life.

(1C) In subsection (1B) the reference to a disposition of the decoration or other award includes—

(a)a reference to a disposition of part of it, and

(b)a reference to a disposition of an interest in it (or in part of it).

(2)Where securities have been issued by the Treasury subject to a condition authorised by section 22 of the Finance (No. 2) Act 1931 (or section 47 of the Finance (No. 2) Act 1915) for exemption from taxation so long as the securities are in the beneficial ownership of persons [of a description specified in the condition], the securities are excluded property if they are in the beneficial ownership of such a person.

(3) Where the person beneficially entitled to the rights conferred by any of the following, namely—

(a)war savings certificates;

(b)national savings certificates (including Ulster savings certificates);

(c)premium savings bonds;

(d)deposits with the National Savings Bank or with a trustee savings bank;

(e)a certified SAYE savings arrangement within the meaning of section 703(1) of the Income Tax (Trading and Other Income) Act 2005;

is domiciled in the Channel Islands or the Isle of Man, the rights are excluded property.

(4) Property to which this subsection applies by virtue of section 155(1) or (5A) below is excluded property.

(5) This section is subject to Schedule A1 (non-excluded overseas property)." [122]

4.4.2 *ESPs Medals Treasury securities Premium Bonds etc.*

Whilst an ESP is not generally going to have won a "relevant decoration or award" certainly in the past some individuals have won an Olympic Medal and the VC. [123]

A number of athletes have served in the armed forces in recent times so it can be worthwhile checking on such service.

---

122 This includes Overseas property with value attributable to UK residential property such as shares in an overseas company owning UK residential property and certain associated loans.

123 See e.g. https://www.forcesnews.com/services/tri-service/how-british-army-officer-won-olympic-gold-and-vc

4.4.2.1 *Long term UK resident*

The meaning of this phrase is dealt with by the legislation itself. The relevant legislation is Sections 6A to 6C inserted by section 44(3) (see above).

6A "Long-term UK resident": individuals

The meaning of this term is dealt with by section 6A "Long-term UK resident": individuals.

This Section reads as follows:

"(1) For the purposes of this Act, an individual is a "long-term UK resident" at all times in a tax year if they were UK resident for at least 10 of the previous 20 tax years.[Emphasis supplied]

(2) But an individual is not a long-term UK resident at any time in a tax year ("the current tax year") if they were non-UK resident—

(a) for any 10 consecutive tax years during the 19 [124] tax years before the current tax year, or

(b) for at least the required number of consecutive tax years ending with the tax year before the current tax year.

(3) To determine "the required number" for the purposes of subsection (2)(b), take the 20 tax years ending with the last tax year for which the individual was UK resident and find the number of those tax years for which the individual was UK resident ("the number of resident years").

The required number is the number in the second column of the following table corresponding to the number of resident years.

Number of resident years	Required number
13 or less	3
14	4
15	5
16	6
17	7
18	8
19	9
20	10

(4) In this section, "UK resident" means resident in the United Kingdom and "non-UK resident" means not resident in the United Kingdom.

(5) For the purposes of this section, a question as to whether the individual was UK resident for the tax year 2012-13 or an earlier tax year is to be determined as it would have been determined for income tax purposes for that

[124] It is interesting to note difference from periods for qualifying new residents and other related matter

tax year (and as to later tax years see Schedule 45 to the Finance Act 2013 (statutory residence test)).

(6) See also—

(a) section 6B (which modifies this section in its application to young persons);

(b) sections 267ZC to 267ZE (under which a person may be treated as a long-term UK resident as the result of an election)."

4.4.2.2 *Overview*

The starting point on the meaning of "long-term UK resident" is found in new section 6A (1) IHTA which deals with individuals. This reads as follows:

> "For the purposes of this Act, **an individual** is a **"long-term UK resident"** at all times **in a tax year if they were UK resident for at least 10 of the previous 20 tax years.**"

This is subject to the new section 6A (2) which in broad terms provides that an individual will **not be a long-term UK resident if they were not resident in the UK** for

(a) **any 10 consecutive tax years during the 19 years before the current year**; or

(b) for a number of **consecutive tax years** (often referred to as "**the tail period**") **preceding the current year** as set out in subsection 6A(3).

New subsection 6A (3) sets out how the tail period is calculated. This reads:

> "(3) To determine "**the required number**" for the purposes of subsection (2)(b), **take the 20 tax years ending with the last tax year for which the individual was UK resident** and **find the number of those tax years for which the individual was UK resident** ("**the number of resident years**").

Broadly, the tail is tapered depending on how many years exceeding 10 years the individual had been resident in the UK, at the time the individual was last resident in the UK. This is subject to a minimum of 3 years.

For example, if an individual had at that time i.e. when the individual was last resident in the UK that individual had been UK resident for 10 or 12 years out of the last 20 they will have the minimum 3 year tail, if they were resident for 17 years they will have a 7 year tail.

The Examples above and below will help to understand this.

4.4.3 Definitional Issues and section 6A

4.4.3.1 *Introductory*

Section 6A raises a number of definitional issues including the following:

- Who is an "individual" for these purposes?
- What is a tax year?
- How is residence to be determined?
- What is "the required number"?

- What is "the number of resident years"?
- Are there any special rules? If so, what are they?
- What about "young persons"?
- What about sections 267ZC to 267ZE?

These questions will be considered in turn next.

4.4.3.2 Who is an individual for these purposes?

An individual is essentially a human being in their individual capacity. In *Lady Longford v IRC* [1928] UKHL J0322-2 it was held for Surtax purposes that a human being who was a trustee was not an individual for those purposes despite being a human being as they were acting in a different capacity or as it is sometimes put "wearing a different hat".

"Individual" for these purposes does not include a juridical or legal person such as a company.

An individual can be referred to as a natural person in contrast to a juristic person. It is the natural person which is the meaning used in the legislation in my opinion.

The position as regards:

i. Trustees

ii. Companies

is discussed below. Section 6A only deals with individuals.

4.4.3.3 What is a tax year? Definitions of "tax year" and "long-term UK resident" in IHTA

4.4.3.3.1 "Tax year"

"Tax year" essentially has the same meaning for these purposes as for IT.

FA 2025 makes specific provision about this and amends section 272 IHTA.

Section 272 is amended by paragraph 24(8) Schedule 13 FA 2025. This reads

> "(4) Also in subsection (1), at the appropriate places insert—
>
> ""tax year" means a year beginning with 6 April and ending with the following 5 April;";
>
> ""the tax year 2025-26" means the tax year beginning with 6 April 2025 (and any corresponding expression in which two years are similarly mentioned is to be read in the same way) ..."

This is essentially the same meaning as for IT. [125]

---

[125] See section 4 ITA headed "Income tax an annual tax". This provides:

4.4.3.3.2 "long-term UK resident"

Paragraph 24 also inserts the following into section 272 IHTA "long-term UK resident" has the meaning given by sections 6A to 6C … These sections are discussed below.

Examples relevant to section 6A

These are general examples intended to help understand section 6A. [126]

i. Tommy Atkins is 34 years of age has lived in the UK all his life and dies in the UK. He has a domicile of origin in Ireland.

   Tommy was resident in the UK for at least 10 years as he has lived in the UK for most of his life. It is accepted by HMRC that on the facts he has not lost his domicile of origin in Ireland, and he is not deemed domiciled in the UK. On that basis subject to the deemed domicile rules Tommy could have claimed the remittance basis in earlier times because of his Domicile of Origin outside the UK.

   Under the new rules it is likely that Tommy would meet the test in section 6A of being a long-term resident. He was UK resident for at least 10 of the previous 20 tax years and so would be a "long-term UK resident". He would seem unlikely to meet any of the escape conditions not to be a "long-term UK resident". The IHT consequences as a long-term UK resident would therefore flow.

ii. Ian Blucip is an adult aged 40 of Dystopian heritage where he was born. Ian has a domicile of origin in Dystopia which he retains. He came to the UK 11 years before the current tax year and has been UK resident for all those 11 years without any break as well as for the current year. Ian would meet the test in section 6A (1) to be a "long-term UK resident that he was UK resident for at least 10 of the previous 20 tax years. He does not meet any of the escape conditions.

   Ian is therefore a long-term UK resident as he was UK resident for at least ten of the twenty years before the current year (see section 6A (1) IHTA).

   The IHT consequences as a long-term UK resident therefore flow. The way in which residence falls can have a significant effect.

"(1) Income tax is charged for a year only if an Act so provides.
(2) A year for which income tax is charged is called a "tax year".
(3) A tax year begins on 6 April and ends on the following 5 April.
(4) "The tax year 2007-08" means the tax year beginning on 6 April 2007 (and any corresponding expression in which two years are similarly mentioned is to be read in the same way).
(5) Every assessment to income tax must be made for a tax year.
(6) Subsection (5) is subject to Chapter 15 of Part 15 (by virtue of which an assessment may relate to a return period)."

[126] Any missing information shall be deemed to help give the answer in the example.

iii. Des Rerorer is of Utopian heritage and has a domicile of origin in Utopia. He is 43years of age. He has been in the UK off and on for a number of years.

He was UK resident for five years and then went back to Utopia for 16 consecutive years. He came back to the UK and was resident in the UK in the current year and the year before. Accordingly, Des was not UK long term resident as he was not UK resident for more than 10 years in the previous 19 years before the current tax year. He was resident in Utopia for 16 consecutive years in the previous 19 years (see section 6A(2). He does not meet the required number (3) either as in both UK presences they are 2 years and not 3 consecutive years.

If Des had spent 8 years rather than 11 years in Utopia and so longer in the UK, he would be a UK long term resident as he was UK resident for 12 consecutive years in the preceding 20 years.

Des has been UK resident for 11 out of the 22 years before the current year but only 9 years out of the previous 20 years. This is because only 3 of the 5 years of earlier UK residence count.

Accordingly, if Des spent 10 years in the UK out of the preceding 20 years in the Year 5 to 15 as a continuous period of 10 years before the current year when he was UK resident, he would be long-term UK resident.

Year	Residence	Comment
Childhood etc	Utopia	[till 18]
Later till 20		
Five years [3]	UK resident	20-25
11 years [8]	Utopia	[25-36]
Six years before [9] The current year	UK	[36-42]
Current Year	UK	[43]

Des is not a long term UK resident see section 6A (2) (a) IHTA

However, if Des's sister Katrina Ljus spent years:

1 and 2 in the UK

3 to 8 [5] years in Utopia

9 to 11 [2] in the UK

13 to 15 [2] in Utopia

in more year there would be no continuous block of 10 years so she would not be long term UK resident under limb 1 despite spending longer overall in the UK than her brother.

4.4.3.4 *How is residence to be determined?*

The legislation gives some guidance on the answer to this question. It provides in section 6A (4) and (5) that:

> "(4) In this section, "UK resident" means resident in the United Kingdom and "non-UK resident" means not resident in the United Kingdom.
>
> (5) For the purposes of this section, a question as to whether the individual was UK resident for the tax year 2012-13 or an earlier tax year is to be determined as it would have been determined for income tax purposes for that tax year (and as to later tax years see Schedule 45 to the Finance Act 2013 (statutory residence test))."

Before FA 2013 introduced the SRT there was no general statutory definition of residence for UK tax purposes. HMRC produced their own administrative code published in an Inland Revenue pamphlet generally known as IR 20. Some extracts from IR 20 are set out in the Annexe to this section of the Supplement. [127]

4.4.3.5 *What is the required number?*

Introduction

This phrase appears in section 6A(2) which reads:

> "But an individual is not a long-term UK resident at any time in a tax year ("the current tax year") if they were non-UK resident—
>
> (a) for any 10 consecutive tax years during the 19 tax years before the current tax year, or
>
> (b) for at least the required number of consecutive tax years ending with the tax year before the current tax year.

It should be noted that there are two limbs to section 6A(2). Fulfilment of either of these alternative limbs is sufficient for that individual not to be a long-term UK resident.

Only the second limb refers the required number.

Both limbs require "consecutive years". By way of reminder the COD tells us that consecutive means "a. following continuously; proceeding in logical sequence ..."

The two limbs are as follows. The individual is not long-term UK resident if:

i. not UK resident for any 10 **consecutive tax** years in the 19 tax years **before** the current tax year; and

[127] 20 years from 2025 goes back to 2005 so the Revenue Amendment Code in IR20 is therefore relevant to the determination of residence for such years. Extracts from IR 20 are included in the Annexe.

ii. not UK resident for at least the required number of **consecutive tax** years ending with the current tax year.

The two limbs will now each be considered in turn.

It should be noted first that the two limbs have different tests:

i. Limb a.

This limb is concerned with UK tax residence for **any 10 consecutive years out of the 19** tax years **before the current tax year**. So, if the individual was UK resident consecutively for 11 of the proceeding 19 tax years, they would be long term UK resident.

ii. Limb b.

This limb is concerned with residence for the **required number of consecutive tax years before the current year**. This limb is concerned with the consecutive years before the current year.

Each limit refers to "consecutive" tax years. The COD gives the meaning of this as "the following continuously proceeding as a logical sequence". It is the "continuously preceding" meaning have the draft person had in mind.

4.4.3.5.1 Relevant Legislation on "the required number"

The relevant legislation is mainly found in section 6A (3).

This reads as follows:

> "(3) To determine "the required number" for the purposes of subsection (2)(b), take the 20 tax years ending with the last tax year for which the individual was UK resident and find the number of those tax years for which the individual was UK resident ("the number of resident years").

The number of resident years is therefore the number of years in the 20 years including the last year when the individual was UK resident.

The required number is the number in the second column of the following table corresponding to the **number of resident years.**

Number of resident years	Required number
13 or less	3
14	4
15	5
16	6
17	7
18	8
19	9

20	10

Example

Tern side left the UK two years ago. These are called years 1 and 2. The last tax year for which she was UK resident was year 3.

4.4.3.6 *What is "the number of resident years"?*

The number of resident years is a defined term for these purposes.

Section 6A (3) provides:

> (3) To determine "the required number" for the purposes of subsection (2)(b), take the 20 tax years ending with the last tax year for which the individual was UK resident and find the number of those tax years for which the individual was UK resident (**"the number of resident years"**).

The **required number** is the number in the second column of the following table corresponding to the **number of resident years. The required number is a number of consecutive years resident in the UK.**

Number of resident years	Required number
13 or less	3
14	4
15	5
16	6
17	7
18	8
19	9
20	10

Examples

i. Bryony has been UK resident for 12 years out of the previous 20 years ending with the last year in which she was UK resident. The last year in which Bryony was UK resident is the current year. Bryony has been UK resident for twelve of those previous years. Accordingly, the number of her resident years is 12. This is 13 or less so the table tells us that the required number i.e. the number in the second column of the Table is 3 consecutive tax years of non-UK residents see section 6A (2)(b) and (3).

Consecutive years of non-residence

If Bryony was resident for two years consecutively at times but not for three years consecutively in that period, then section 6 A (2)(b) and 6A (3) would not be fulfilled even if there were other years of non-consecutive residence. However, if there were three consecutive tax years of UK residence in that period, she would be a long-term UK resident.

ii. Robert was UK resident for 10 years or so the required number of consecutive tax year is 3. The issue will then depend on how Robert's presence in the UK breakdown. If Robert's residence is as follows:

- 10-9 UK
- 8-7 non-UK
- 6-4 UK
- 3-2 non-UK
- 1 UK

Robert would not be long term UK resident as there is no period of 3 years of UK residence.

If Robert is residence as follows:

- 10-8 non-UK
- 7-5 UK
- 4-2 non-UK

The required number is a number of consecutive years resident in the UK. Robert would be UK long term resident as this is a period of 3 years consecutive in the UK i.e. 7-5 that he was the UK resident, in years 7, 6 and 5 three consecutive years in the UK resident.

iii. Wayne has been in the UK for more than 20 years ending in the last year of his residence in the UK. The questions then are:

1. Was Wayne resident for any consecutive 10 years in the 19 years before the current tax year i.e. the year in question? and
2. Was Wayne UK resident for at least the required number of consecutive tax years? The required number here will be 10 years as he is potentially UK resident for 20 years or more.

Are there any special rules? If so, what are they?

There are special rules that apply here. These include provision about:

- Young people
- Bodies corporate

4.4.3.6.1 What about young persons?

Introduction

Special provision is made about young persons by section 6B inserted by FA 2025. This is necessary as a young person ex hypothesi will not have a twenty-year history if they have not attained the age of 20 years.

Overview

New section 6B modifies the section 6A 'long-term UK resident' tests for individuals aged under 20 years in the **previous** tax year, where they are too young (i.e. less than 20 years) for the main tests otherwise to work. [128]

As noted above section 6A (1) provides that:

> "For the purposes of this Act, an individual is a "long-term UK resident" at all times in a tax year if they were UK resident for at least 10 of the previous 20 tax years."

The Table etc. in section 6A is essentially by reference to 20 years as the person has not been alive that long.

If a person has not been alive for 20 years then how is the test to be applied?

It does not then work as one cannot go back 20 years.

Section 6B (set out below) provides a solution where the individual has not been alive for 20 years.

Instead of 20 years the number of years the individual was alive before the current tax year is to be used in determining whether "a young person" is a long-term resident.

This approach deals with the problem of the treatment of the years before birth which otherwise arises.

The 10-year period of UK residence is modified to half the number substituted for the 20-year period. This is equivalent to the ratio of 10 to 20 in section 6A (i.e. 1:2).

Example

Nigel is 14 years old in the current year and so under 20 years in the previous tax year. His heritage is from Sodor where he has a Domicile of Origin. His family came to the UK when he was 10.

Nigel was alive therefore for 13 years before the current year. [129] Half of 13 is six and a half which is rounded up to seven (see Section 6B (1) (6) set out below).

Nigel has been in the UK since he was 10. Accordingly, Nigel has been UK resident for 4 years. This is the number of [years of tax years] ending with the last tax year for which Nigel was UK resident (see section 6A (3) set out above). The number of tax resident years is 4 which is less than 7 which is the number of consecutive years substituted for 10 in section 6A as a result of section 6B.

---

[128] See the Explanatory Notes to the Bill

[129] parts of a year have been ignored for the purposes of this example.

4.4.3.6.2 Relevant Legislation

Section 6B is headed ""Long-term UK resident": young persons". It provides:

> "(1) In the application of section 6A (1) [set out above] for the purpose of determining whether a young person is a long-term UK resident at any time in a tax year ("**the current tax year**"), that subsection has effect as if—
>
> (a) for "20" there were substituted the **number of whole tax years** for which the person was **alive before the current tax year**, and
>
> (b) for "10" there were substituted half the number mentioned in paragraph (a) (rounded up, if not a whole number, to the next whole number).
>
> (2) In subsection (1), "young person" means an individual who was under the age of 20 immediately before the current tax year.
>
> (3) For the purposes of this Act, an individual is not a long-term UK resident at any time in a tax year if they were under the age of 1 (or were not yet born) immediately before the tax year."

Some Questions arising from section 6B

Section 6B raises a number of questions including the following.

- Who is a "young person" for these purposes?
- What is meant by "the current tax year"?
- What is meant by the number of whole tax years for which the person was alive before the current tax year? Why does it matter?
- What is meant by "half the number mentioned in paragraph (a) (rounded up, if not a whole number, to the next whole number)"? Why does it matter?
- What about an individual who has not reached the age of 1?
- What about sections 267ZC to 267ZE?
- This will now be considered in turn.

4.4.3.6.3 Who is a young person for these purposes?

The legislation deals with the meaning of "young person" for these purposes in Section 6B.

Section 6B (2) provides:

> "(2) In subsection (1), "**young person**" means an **individual** who was **under the age of 20 immediately before the current tax year**."
>
> The meaning of individual is discussed above. When a person attains a particular age is discussed below.
>
> The phrase "was under the age of 20 immediately before the current tax year". attained the age of 20 on 6th April XX.
>
> **Example**
>
> *i.* Tom Sewel is in his 13th year during the current tax year. Accordingly, he was 12 immediately before the current tax year and so under the age of

20. The legislation talks in terms of whole tax years. Tom therefore falls within section 6 B (2).

ii. Tom Lewes attain the age of 20 in the current tax year on 1 May. The current tax year started on 6 April. The previous tax year ended on 5 April. So, in these circumstances Tom "was under the age of 20 immediately before the current tax year".
Tom therefore falls within section 6B (2)

iii. Tom Slewe attains the age of 21 in the current year on 1 May. The current year started on 6 April. So, in these circumstances it is not the case that Tom "was under the age of 20 immediately before the current tax year".

Tom therefore does not fall within section 6B (2).

iv. Stem Lowe attains the age of 21 in the current tax year on 1 May. The current tax year started on 6 April. The previous tax year ended on 5 April. Tom was not under the age of 20 immediately before the current tax year so section 6B does not apply.

v. Stem was born on 1 January in the previous tax year which ended on 5 April. He was thus some 3 months or so old then. Accordingly, he had not attained the age of 1 then. This means Tom is "an individual [who] is not a long-term UK resident at any time in a tax year [the current year] if they were under the age of 1 (or were not yet born) immediately before the tax year" i.e. on 5 April.
It is important to check which year is the current tax year and the other resident dates.
Current Tax Year

The meaning of the current tax year is discussed above. It is essentially the year in question.

When does an individual attain a particular age.

This matter is the subject of general legislation for English Law. [130]

This is the vital matter for these purposes.

In my view this is a matter to be determined for these purposes in accordance with UK Law.

Section 9 Family Law Reform Act 1969 is headed "Time at which a person attains a particular age". It reads as follows:
"(1) The time at which a person attains a particular age expressed in years shall be the commencement of the relevant anniversary of the date of his birth.

[130] More accurately England and Wales see section 28 of the Act. The position in Scotland and Northern Ireland should be carefully checked where relevant. See example Section 6 Age of Legal Capacity Act (Scotland) 1991. This seems to give the same outcome as for English Law but appropriate advice should be taken.

(2) This section applies only where the relevant anniversary falls on a date after that on which this section comes into force, and, in relation to any enactment, deed, will or other instrument, has effect subject to any provision therein."

The FLRA and section 9 in particular came into force on 1 January 1970. [131]

Examples

i. Nat Fint was born on 1 June Year 0 [132] at 22.59. The anniversary of Nat's birth is therefore on 1 June at the commencement of that day which is when he attained the relevant age by reason of section 9 FLRA.

ii. What if Nat had died at 22:58 on 1 June in Year 10. Nat would not have reached the time he was actually born at and so arguably had not attained the age of 10. However, by section 9 FLRA the age expressed in years is attained at the commencement of the relevant anniversary of his birth. On these facts he would have attained the age of 10. If Natt had died on 30th, May he would not have attained the age of 10 as he did not reach the commencement of the relevant anniversary of his date of birth.

iii. An even more extreme example would be of Nat had died before the actual time of his birth on the first anniversary of his birth. He had then not survived a full year since birth, but Nat had survived beyond the commencement of the day which was the day of the anniversary of Nat's birth. He was therefore one year old at the date of his birth. This is the effect of Section [6(B)(3)] Section 9 in part 1 of the Act.

4.4.3.6.4 What is meant by the current tax year?

By section 6B (1) "In the application of section 6A (1) for the purpose of determining whether a young person is a long-term UK resident at any time in a tax year (**"the current tax year"**), ..."

In effect, the current tax year is the year in question, the year for which it is sought to determine whether the young person is long term resident.

Example

Nespor Young was born on 5 April year 0. The question arises as to whether Nespor was UK long term resident in Year 10. The current tax year will be 10 years in those circumstances as that is the year in question.

4.4.3.6.5 What is meant by the number of whole tax years for which the person was alive before the current tax year? Why does it matter?

Section 6B (1) provides in determining a young person's long term residence status in the current tax year "the number of whole tax years for which the

---

[131] see The Family Law Reform Act 1969 (Commencement Number 1) [Order 1969]

[132] This is taken to be after the coming into force of the Family Law Reform Act 1969

young person was alive before the current tax year is substituted for 20 in section 6A (1).

Accordingly, it is necessary to determine the number of whole tax years for which the person was alive before the current tax year.

It is to be noted that for section 6B (1)(a) there is no rounding up as there is in section 6B (1) (b). This is discussed next.

Example

Leo T Whax was born on 1 March in year 1. The question arises as to the whole number of years Leo was alive before the current year which is year 10. The year before was year 9 so Leo will have been alive for 9 whole tax years before year 10.

4.4.3.6.6 What is meant by "half the number mentioned in paragraph (a) (rounded up, if not a whole number, to the next whole number)"? Why does it matter?

The comparison for this determination of long-term *residence* needs a number. If the number of years substituted for 20 years was 9 then, half would be 4.5. This is not a whole number so by section 6B (1)(6) it is to be rounded up to the next whole number. Accordingly, 4.5 years would become five years.

It matters because it determines what the required number is.

4.4.3.6.7 What about an individual who has not reached the age of 1?

By section 6B (3) "For the purposes of this Act, an individual is not a long-term UK resident at any time in a tax year if they were under the age of 1 (or were not yet born) immediately before the tax year."

Section 9 FLRA as to the time an individual attains an age can also be relevant here. It is discussed above.

4.4.3.6.8 **Companies and Long -term residence – section 6C**

Sections 6A and 6B deal with individuals.

They do not deal with bodies corporate such as limited companies or LLCs.

Bodies corporate are dealt with by section 6C headed ""Long-term UK resident": bodies corporate"

Section 6C provides a long-term UK resident test for corporate bodies, such as limited companies which will be relevant, for example, in establishing whether settled property in a settlement made by a corporate body is excluded property under the new rules discussed above. It is not relevant to the main excluded property tests in section 6(1) and 6(1A) which only apply to individuals. This section reads as follows:

"6C "Long-term UK resident": bodies corporate
For the purposes of this Act, a body corporate is a "long-term UK resident" at all times in a tax year if the body—
(a) is incorporated in the United Kingdom, or
(b) was (if in existence before the beginning of the tax year) within the charge to corporation tax on income at any time during the previous tax year by virtue of section 5(1) of the Corporation Tax Act 2009 (UK resident companies)."

Section 5(1) CTA09
This reads as follows.
"5Territorial scope of charge
(1) A UK resident company is chargeable to corporation tax on income] on all its profits wherever arising (but see Chapter 3A for an exemption from charge in respect of profits of foreign permanent establishments) ..."

4.4.3.7 *Some Questions arising*

It might be arguable that this could extend the period of non-UK residence on a literal interpretation. However, it would be likely to provide a GAAR Opinion that such an approach was abusive. It would seem a forlorn hope [133] but is mentioned for the sake of completeness.

4.4.3.7.1 General

Section 6C raises a number of questions including the following:

i. What is a body corporate for these purposes?
ii. What is a body incorporated in the UK?
iii. What is a body within the charge to corporation tax on income at any time during the previous tax year by virtue of section 5(1) CTA 2009?

These questions will be considered in turn next.

4.4.3.7.2 What is a body corporate for these purposes?

Bodies corporates are corporations. They are to be contrasted with a natural person.

According to the Oxford Concise Dictionary of Law "A body corporate or company is an entity that is a legal personality i.e. it is capable of enjoying and being subject to legal rights and duties"

Thus, a limited liability company is a body corporate. An English general partnership would not be as it does not have a separate legal personality.

[133] From the Dutch "verloon hoop" a lost heap. "Hoop" was also used to refer to a contingent of troops. Essentially, it is a suicide attack by troops with no realistic chance of success.

4.4.3.7.3 What is a body incorporated in the UK?

A body incorporated in the UK is one whose existence, separate legal personality and rights and duties are governed by the law of one of the constituent jurisdictions of the United Kingdom or of the UK itself. [134]

The use of the word "incorporated" implies a separate legal personality. [135] On that basis a General Partnership under English law would not be covered as it does not have a separate legal personality. This is in contrast to a Scottish general partnership that is a matter of General Scots Law does have a separate legal personality.

4.4.3.7.4 What is a body within the charge to corporation tax on income at any time during the previous tax year by virtue of section 5(1) CTA 2009?

Section 5 CTA 2009 provides (inter alia):

> "(1) A **UK resident company is chargeable to corporation tax on all its profits wherever** arising (but see Chapter 3A for an exemption from charge in respect of profits of foreign permanent establishments).
> (2)**A non-UK resident company is within the charge to corporation tax on income** only if—
> (a)it carries on **a trade of dealing in or developing UK land** (see section 5B), ...
> (b)it carries on a **trade in the United Kingdom** (other than a trade of dealing in or developing UK land) through a permanent establishment in the United Kingdom,
> (c)it carries on a **UK property business**, or
> (d)it has **other UK property income**."

4.4.4 *Company for CTA purposes*

CTA 2010 provides a definition for CT purposes in section 1121 headed "Company".

> "(1) In the Corporation Tax Acts "company" means any body corporate or unincorporated association, but does not include a partnership, a co-ownership scheme (as defined by section 235A of the Financial Services and Markets Act 2000), a local authority or a local authority association.
>
> (2) Subsection (1) needs to be read with section 617 (under which the trustees of an authorised unit trust are treated for certain purposes as a UK resident company). This reads as follows:
>
> The Schedule to IA 1978 deals with the meaning of "the Corporation Tax Acts".

It provides:

[134] This may be important depending on when the company was incorporated. Cf *Salamon v Salamon Ltd* [1897] AC 22

[135] cf *Salamon v Salamon Ltd* [1897] AC

> ""The Corporation Tax Acts" means the enactments relating to the taxation of the income and chargeable gains of companies and of company distributions (including provisions relating to income tax)."

This includes CTA 2009.

Accordingly, "Company" for these purposes would generally bear the meaning in section 1121 CTA 2010 set out above.

A company incorporated in the UK is automatically UK resident (see section 14 CTA).[136]

A company incorporated outside the UK is resident where its centre of management and control is located.

4.5 Position concerning settled property following move away from Domicile

4.5.1 *Section 45: Corresponding change for settled property*

4.5.1.1 *Overview*

Section 44 considered above only deals with persons. It does not deal with relationships which is what some consider trusts or settlements to be. Trusts and settlements are dealt with for this purpose by section 45.

Section 45 introduces revised tests for IHT in respect of settled property by reference to the settlor's residence rather than their domicile as was the case before these changes.

The legislation does so by amending the IHTA.

The amendments to the IHTA have effect from 6 April 2025 (see section 45(4)).

4.5.1.2 *The Legislation*

Section 45 is headed **"Corresponding change for settled property".** It reads as follows:

> "(1) IHTA 1984 is amended as follows.
> (2) In section 48 (excluded property)—
>> (a) in the heading, at the end insert ": reversionary interests and Treasury securities";
>> (b) omit subsections (3) to (3F).
>
> (3) After section 48 insert—

---

[136] Section is headed "**14 Companies incorporated in the United Kingdom." It reads as follows.**

(1)A company which is incorporated in the United Kingdom is UK resident for the purposes of the Corporation Tax Acts.

(2)Accordingly, even if a different place of residence is given by a rule of law, the company is not resident in that place for the purposes of the Corporation Tax Acts.

"48ZA Excluded property: property situated outside the UK etc

(1) **If property comprised in a settlement—**

(a) **is situated outside the United Kingdom**, or

(b) is a **holding in an authorised unit trust** or a share in an open-ended investment company,

this section applies to the property and **section 6(1) and (1A)** (general excluded property rule) **does not**.

(2) If the **settlor is alive**, the property is **excluded property** at any time **when the settlor is not a long-term UK resident**.

(3) If the **settlor died on or after 6 April 2025**, the property is **excluded property if the settlor was not a long-term UK resident immediately before they died.**

(4) If the **settlor died before 6 April 2025**, the property is **excluded property if** the settlor was **not domiciled in the United Kingdom when the property became comprised in the settlement**.

(5) Subsections (2) and (3) do not apply at any time to property to which section 49(1) (certain interests in possession) applies if, at that time, the person beneficially entitled to the interest is a long-term UK resident.

(6) Subsections **(2) to (4) do not apply** to property if—

(a) an individual has been beneficially **entitled to an interest in possession** in the property—

(i) at any time **on or after 6 April 2025 while a long-term UK resident**, or

(ii) at **any time before** that date while **domiciled in the United Kingdom**, and

(b) the **entitlement arose** directly or indirectly as a result of a **disposition made on or after 5 December 2005 for a consideration in money or money's worth.**

(7) For the purposes of subsection (6)—

(a) it is immaterial whether the consideration was given by the individual or by anyone else, and

(b) the cases in which an entitlement arose indirectly as a result of a disposition include any case where the entitlement arose under a will or the law relating to intestacy.

(8) Where the conditions in paragraphs (a) to (d) of section 74A (1) (arrangements involving acquisition of interest in settled property etc) are satisfied, none of subsections (2) to (4) applies at the time when the conditions are first satisfied or at any later time to make the relevant settled property (within the meaning of section 74A) excluded property.

(9) If—

(a) an amount is payable in respect of property ("the existing property") comprised in a settlement, and

(b) the amount represents an accumulation of income which (once accumulated) becomes comprised in the settlement, subsection (4) has effect in the case of the amount as if the reference to the time when it became comprised in the settlement were to the time when the existing property became comprised in the settlement.

(10) Subsections (2) to (4) are subject to Schedule A1 (overseas property with value attributable to UK residential property).

(11) The reference in subsection (1) to property comprised in a settlement does not include a reversionary interest in the property (and accordingly this section does not apply to such an interest and section 6(1) does)."

(4) This section comes into force on 6 April 2025. "

4.5.1.3 Details of Section 45

Section 45 (1) tells us that the IHTA is amended as set out in the section.

Section 45 (2) amends section 48 of the IHTA 1984 to remove subsections 48(3) to (3F) and to clarify that section 48 now determines the excluded property status of reversionary interests and Treasury securities. [The heading is revised.]

Section 45 (3) inserts section 48ZA to IHTA 1984.

4.5.2 *Section 48ZA – a quick look*

This section provides that section 48ZA applies to property held in a settlement. This is property which is:

- non-UK situs property, or
- an interest in a holding in an authorised unit trust or
- a share in an open-ended investment company, and
- not a reversionary interest.

Such property is excluded property (and so not subject to IHT charges).

Section 48ZA (2) provides the excluded property status of the settled property will not be fixed at the time the property is added to the settlement. Instead, property comprised in a settlement will only be excluded property at times when the settlor is not long-term UK resident.

When a settlor is long-term UK resident, any property they have settled (even when not long term UK resident) will be subject to IHT. This is an important matter to note.

Section 48ZA (3) provides that where the settlor of a trust dies on or after 6 April 2025, the excluded property status of the settled property will depend on the settlor's long-term residence status at their death not on their domicile then or at any time before.

If the settlor was not a long-term UK resident, then any non-UK settled property can be excluded property if the relevant conditions (discussed below) are met.

This is decided not on domicile but on the individuals long term Resident status as at death.

If the settlor was long-term UK resident at death, then all the settled property will be within the charge to IHT for the duration of the trust.

Examples

Ace was UK resident in the year of her death and was UK long term resident under Section 6A (2) (a) as Ace was the UK resident for more than 10 years (19) consecutively during the 19 years before the current tax year (i.e. the year of duty).

Ace was born with a Domicile of the origin in Asturia which she never lost as she as HMRC accepted Act had lived continuously in the UK of 15 years out of the previous 9 years before the "current year" i.e. the year of death she had set up a settlor interested trust in a year some time before she was long-term UK resident [Domiciled.]

4.5.2.1 Death before 6 April 2025

Section 48ZA (4) provides that where the settlor died before 6 April 2025, the excluded property tests previously applicable at the settlor's death will continue. This means that broadly the status of the property will depend on the settlor's domicile at the time the property became comprised in the settlement.

A qualifying interest in possession is essentially one where the holder of the interest is entitled to the income as it arises. [137]

4.5.2.2 QIIP (Qualifying Interest in Possession)

Section 45 (5) introduces an additional test for qualifying interest in possession (QIIP) settlements so that where the settlor is alive or dies on or after 6 April 2025, the property comprised in the settlement is only excluded property if both the settlor and the beneficiary with the QIIP are not long-term UK resident.

Example

Nikki is domiciled in Isle of Mann but has been resident continuously in the UK for the last 20 years. She set up 11 years before she became UK resident and while she was domiciled out of the UK a settlement. Nikki is UK resident on 6 April 2025 and thought?? she is a Settlor and the lifetime (beneficiary).

4.5.2.3 Purchased interests

There is a provision to stop a purchased interest in possession being treated as Excluded Property. This stopped an IHT avoidance arrangement which was also blocked by changes made by FA 2010.

[137] See *IRC v Pearson*

Section 48ZA (6) and (7) disapply the settlor long-term UK residence tests for excluded property if at any time an individual with a 'purchased' interest in possession was long-term UK resident on or after 6 April 2025 or had a UK domicile before that date.

Section 48ZA (8) provides that where the anti-avoidance provision in section 74A IHTA 1984 relating to 'purchased' interests in a settlement applies to settled property, that property will not be excluded property under subsections (2) to (4) of new section 48ZA above.

Example

Bridget a UK domiciliary bought an interest under a settlement settled by an Isle of Man Incorporated Company at market value and received an option in respect of the reversionary interest under the settlement which was the only other interest in possession under the settlement. Before section 74 A - C were inserted into IHTA by FA 2010 the settlor of the trust was a non-UK domiciliary as it was accompanying incorporated outside the UK.

Accordingly, so far as the asset in the trust fund were non-UK situs assets. They were excluded assets as Bridget was the UK domiciliary who purchased an interest in possession. No exchanged property treatment is available. This would also be the case when she became long term UK resident.

Accumulated income and settlor death before 6 April 2025

Section 48ZA (9) provides that where the settlor has died before 6 April 2025 and the settled property includes accumulated income, this will be treated as becoming comprised in the settlement at the same time as the property from which it was derived.

Section 48ZA (10) confirms that the inserted excluded property definition for settlements is subject to Schedule A1 IHTA 1984 (overseas property with value attributable to UK residential property).

Section 48ZA (11) confirms that the reference in subsection (1) to property comprised in a settlement does not include a reversionary interest in the property.

4.5.2.4 Some Questions on section 48ZA

Section 48ZA raises a number of questions including the following.

i. What is excluded property and its effect?

ii. Who is the settlor?

iii. When is the settlor a long-term UK resident Immediately before they died?

iv. When does property become comprised in a settlement? Why does it matter?

v. What interest in possession does section 48ZA (5) apply to? Why does it matter?

vi. What is the effect of section 48ZA (6) and (7) on purchased interests?

vii. What is the effect of section 48ZA (8)? Why does it matter?

viii. What about accumulated income in a settlement if the settle dies before 6 April 2025? Later death?

ix. What about overseas property with significant value attributable to UK residential property?

4.5.2.4.1 What is excluded property and its effect?

Dealing firstly with the effect of there being excluded property it is that excluded property is excluded from the charge to IHT.

The first thing to note about excluded property is that it is non UK site as property. Property that is UK situs property cannot be excluded property. For property comprised in the settlement section 47ZA applies and not section 6(1) and (1A).

Post 5 April 2025 non UK situs property comprised in a settlement is excluded property:

- If the settlor is alive when the settlor is not a long term UK resident (see section 482A(2);
- If the settlor died after 5 April 2025 if the settlor was not a long term UK resident immediately before they died;
- If the settlor died before 6 April 2025 and the settlor was not domiciled in the UK when the property became comprised in the settlement.

There are exclusions for certain IPs falling within section 49 if the person became beneficially entitled where the person is a long-term UK resident see section 48ZA (5) Interests in possession acquired for money or money's worth see section 48ZA (6).

4.5.2.4.2 Who is the settlor?

The settlor is essentially the economic settlor i.e. the person who provided the assets in the Trust Fund. It also includes anyone else making the settlement e.g. by signing the trust deed (see section 44 IHTA). Where there is more than one settlor interesting questions of attribution can arise.

4.5.2.4.3 When is a settlor a UK long term resident immediately before they died?

This is essentially a question of fact. The facts need to be considered against the tests set out above.

4.5.2.4.4 Interests in Possession falling in section 48ZA (5)

This refers to section 49(1) IHTA. This reads as follows:

"(1)A person beneficially entitled to an interest in possession in settled property shall be treated for the purposes of this Act as beneficially entitled to the property in which the interest subsists."

4.5.2.4.5 What is the effect of section 48ZA (6) and (7) on purchased interests?

The effect where these subsections apply is that there is no excluded property treatment.

4.5.2.4.6 What is the effect of section 48ZA (8)?

This provision stops excluded property treatment where there is a purchased interest under a settlement falling within section 74 IHTA. This is essentially an anti-avoidance provision concerned with purchased interests under a pre-funded trust.

4.5.2.4.7 Accumulated income in a settlement where the Settlor dies before 6 April 2025

The accumulated income is treated as being comprised in the settlement at the same time as the property from which the income is derived (see section 48ZA(a).)

4.5.2.4.8 Overseas property with significant value attribute UK residential property

The use of an offshore company to hold UK residential property is ignored and treated as transparent. The relative value is not treated as excluded property (see section 482A (10)).

4.5.2.5 Effective Date

Subsection 45(4) provides for commencement. Section 45 comes into force on 6 April 2025.

4.5.3 Section 46 and Schedule 13: Consequential, connected and transitional provision

4.5.3.1 Overview

Section 46 and Schedule 13 set out additional changes to the IHTA consequential on or connected to the changes which replace the domicile-based inheritance tax (IHT) system with a new residence-based system.

Schedule 13 is in two parts.

Part 1 of the Schedule sets out the amendments. These are essentially consequential and transitional amendments following the other changes to IHT made by FA2025.

Part 2 contains the commencement and transitional provisions.

4.5.3.2 Legislation

Section 46 is headed "Consequential, connected and transitional provision".

It reads as follows:

> "In Schedule 13—
>
> Part 1 contains amendments to IHTA 1984 and related legislation that are consequential on, connected with or incidental to the new excluded property tests introduced by sections 44 and 45;
>
> Part 2 contains provision about commencement and transitional provision."

Schedule 13 is not set out here, but the relevant paragraphs are set out in the discussion of each paragraph below.

4.5.3.3 Details of Schedule 13

4.5.3.3.1 Overview

As noted above Schedule 13 is divided into two parts. These are headed as follows.

Part 1: Amendments to IHTA 1984 and related legislation (paragraphs 1 – 43)

Part 2: Commencement and transitional provision (paragraphs 44 – 50)

References to paragraph numbers in what follows are to paragraphs of Schedule 13 unless the context otherwise requires.

4.5.3.4 Part 1: Amendments to IHTA 1984 and related legislation

4.5.3.4.1 General

Paragraph 1 helpfully provides "IHTA 1984 is amended as follows".[138] This confirms the heading to the Part and authorises the amendments. This paragraph accordingly is not discussed further.

Paragraph 2 New section 5 (1B)

4.5.3.4.2 Overview

This paragraph introduces a new subsection 5 (1B) into IHTA. The test for whether an interest in possession falls within section 5(1B) is now to be by reference to long term residence rather domicile. It is aimed at an avoidance technique where a person was UK domiciled. It now applies to UK long term residents.

Paragraph 2 inserts a substitute subsection 5(1B) into IHTA 1984. This is a new subsection 5 (1B). It provides that whether an interest in possession falls within

[138] It is interesting to contrast the descriptive nature of section 46.

section 5(1B) is to be determined by reference to whether the person is a long-term UK resident rather than as before whether they were UK domiciled.

4.5.3.4.3 Legislation

The paragraph reads as follows:

> "In section 5 (meaning of estate), for subsection (1B) substitute—
>
> "(1B) An interest in possession falls within this subsection if—
>
> (a) the person became beneficially entitled to it on or after 15 December 2009 by virtue of a disposition that was prevented from being a transfer of value by section 10 (no gratuitous benefit), and
>
> (b) the person—
>
> (i) has been a long-term UK resident at any time on or after 6 April 2025 while beneficially entitled to it, or
>
> (ii) became beneficially entitled to it at a time before 6 April 2025 while domiciled in the United Kingdom."

4.5.3.4.4 Detail

Section 53 FA 2010 provides broadly that if an IiP is a purchased interest it is treated as part of the purchase's estate.

Section 53 inserted the then new subsection (1B) into section 5 so that a further category of IIP was included in a person's estate. These were interests:

1. To which a UK domiciled individual was entitled;
2. acquired in an arm's length transaction within section 10 IHTA.

This is amended to replace domicile with long term UK residence.

Example

Erin Tres acquired an interest in possession from a non-connected 3rd party for a commercially negotiated price with both parties being fully advised including by professional valuers and others. It does not involve any gratuitous benefit within section 1 IHTA

Erin was born with a Domicile of Origin in the UK and had lived all his life in the UK. Accordingly, both before and after the change the purchased interest would not be Excluded Property.

4.5.3.4.5 Effective date

The effective date is 6 April 2025. See paragraph 45.

4.5.3.5 Paragraph 3 Repeal of section 6(3) IHTA - Exclusion of certain savings products owned by CI or IoM domiciled persons

4.5.3.5.1 Overview

Paragraph 3 repeals subsection 6(3) [139] so that certain savings products are no longer excluded

property when beneficially owned by a person domiciled in the Channel Islands or the Isle of Man.

4.5.3.5.2 Legislation

Paragraph 3 of Schedule 13 reads:

> "In section 6 (excluded property), omit subsection (3)."
>
> Section 6(3) used to read:
>
> "(3) Where the person beneficially entitled to the rights conferred by any of the following, namely—
>
> (a)war savings certificates;
>
> (b)national savings certificates (including Ulster savings certificates);
>
> (c)premium savings bonds;
>
> (d)deposits with the National Savings Bank or with a trustee savings bank;
>
> (e)a certified SAYE savings arrangement] within the meaning of [F6section 703(1) of the Income Tax (Trading and Other Income) Act 200];
>
> is domiciled in the Channel Islands or the Isle of Man, the rights are excluded property."
>
> Not many ESPs were Manx domiciled in my experience. There are some who were IoM resident. [140] More were Channel Island resident in my experience. [141]However, each case must be considered as per circumstances and facts.

4.5.3.5.3 Effective date

The effective date is 6 April 2025. See paragraph 45.

---

[139] Section 6 is headed "Excluded property". Subsection (3) read:
"(3)Where the person beneficially entitled to the rights conferred by any of the following, namely—
(a)war savings certificates;
(b)national savings certificates (including Ulster savings certificates);
(c)premium savings bonds;
(d)deposits with the National Savings Bank or with a trustee savings bank;
(e)a certified SAYE savings arrangement within the meaning of section 703(1) of the Income Tax (Trading and Other Income) Act 2005;
is domiciled in the Channel Islands or the Isle of Man, the rights are excluded property."

[140] E.g. Nigel Mansell who was IoM resident during most of his F1 career see https://en.wikipedia.org/wiki/Nigel_Mansel He now lives in the Channel Islands.

[141] See preceding footnote

4.5.3.6 *Consequential amendments following general definition of tax year in section 272 IHTA - Paragraphs 4,5,7 and 13*

4.5.3.6.1 Overview

Paragraphs 4, 5, 7 and 13

Paragraphs 4, 5 and 7 and 13 provide for consequential amendments to subsections 8D (9), 13A (3), 28 A(3) and 75A (4) omitting the definition of "tax year" which is now to be defined generally in section 272 IHTA see paragraph 28 of the Schedule discussed below. This is essentially a tidying up provision.

4.5.3.6.2 Legislation

Paragraph 4 reads as follows.

> "4 In section 8D (9), omit the definitions of "tax year" and "the tax year 2017-18"."

There is now a general definition of "tax year" inserted into section 272 IHTA by paragraph 28 (5) Schedule 13. Accordingly, a specific provision is no longer needed.

Paragraph 5 reads as follows.

> "5 In section 13A (3), omit the definition of "tax year"."

There is now a general definition of "tax year" inserted into section 272 IHTA by paragraph 28 (5) Schedule 13. Accordingly, a specific provision is no longer needed.

Paragraph 7 reads as follows.

> "7 In section 28A, omit subsection (3)."

This used to read "(3) In this section "tax year" means a year beginning on 6 April and ending on the following 5 April."

There is now a general definition of "tax year" inserted into section 272 IHTA by paragraph 28 (5) Schedule 13. Accordingly, a specific provision is no longer needed.

Paragraph 13 reads as follows.

> "In section 75A, omit subsection (4)."

This used to read "(4) In this section "tax year" means a year beginning on 6 April and ending on the following 5 April."

There is now a general definition of "tax year" inserted into section 272 IHTA by paragraph 28 (5) Schedule 13. Accordingly, a specific provision is no longer needed.

4.5.3.6.3 Detail

There is now to be one general definition of "tax year" in the IHTA.

There was no longer any need for a specific provision in each individual piece of the legislation

4.5.3.6.4 Effective Date

The effective date is 6 April 2025. See paragraph 45.

4.5.3.7 Paragraph 6 Consequential change to subsection 18(2) one spouse long-term UK resident other not

4.5.3.7.1 Overview

Paragraph 6 makes a consequential change to subsection 18(2) capping the amount of exemption available when the transferor is a long-term UK resident, but their spouse or civil partner is not. It is also relevant to note that there are additional changes in respect of any spouse exemption election see paragraphs 24 to 27 below. This is essentially moving over from mismatched domiciles to mismatched long term residence.

4.5.3.7.2 Legislation

Paragraph 6 reads:

> "In section 18 (transfers between spouses or civil partners), in subsection (2), for "domiciled in the United Kingdom" substitute "a long-term UK resident,".

4.5.3.7.3 Detail

This reflects the move away from domicile to long term resident status as the basis for IHT. It deals with the situation where the two partners have a difference in status.

Section 18 is the provision which makes transfers between spouses transfers with the same domicile status outside the charge to IHT. As noted above the change made by this paragraph is a reflection of the change away from domicile.

4.5.3.7.4 Effective Date

The effective date is 6 April 2025. See paragraph 45.

4.5.3.8 Paragraph 7

This is considered above with paragraphs 4,5 and 13. It is a consequential from the introduction of a general definition of tax year inserted into section 272 IHTA by paragraph 28(5) of Schedule 13.

4.5.3.9 *Paragraph 8 Long term residence rather than domicile for exemption from charge on termination of an interest in possession and transitional provision*

4.5.3.9.1 Overview

Paragraph 8 amends the test at subsection 53(4)[142] by reference to whether a person is a long-term UK resident instead of whether they are UK domiciled.

Paragraph 8 also introduces a new transitional provision at new subsection 53(4A) so that there is no charge under section 52 on termination of an interest in possession in relation to excluded property which was comprised in a settlement immediately before 30 October 2024 provided it subsequently remains excluded property (under the pre-6 April 2025 rules).

4.5.3.9.2 Legislation

Paragraph 8 reads as follows:

> "(1) Section 53 (exceptions from charge under section 52) is amended as follows.
>
> (2) In subsection (4), for "domiciled in the United Kingdom" substitute "a long-term UK resident".
>
> (3) After subsection (4) insert—
>
> "(4A) Tax shall not be chargeable under section 52 above if—
>
> > (a) the settled property became comprised in the settlement before 30 October 2024,
> >
> > (b) immediately before 30 October 2024, the settled property 5 was excluded property by virtue of section 48(3) or (3A) (as
> >
> > it had effect at that time),
> >
> > (c) the person whose interest comes to an end became beneficially entitled to the interest before 30 October 2024, and
> >
> > (d) at all times on and after 30 October 2024 and before the time when the person's interest in possession in it comes to an end, the settled property—
> >
> > > (i) was situated outside the United Kingdom and was not property to which paragraph 2 or 3 of Schedule A1 applied (overseas property with value attributable to UK residential property), or

[142] Section 53 is headed "Exceptions from charge under section 52. (4)Tax shall not be chargeable under section 52 above if on the occasion when the interest comes to an end—
(a)the settlor's spouse or civil partner, or
(b)where the settlor has died less than two years earlier, the settlor's widow or widower or surviving civil partner, becomes beneficially entitled to the settled property and is domiciled in the United Kingdom." **Now applies** where a person is a long-term UK resident instead of whether they are UK domiciled."
Section 52 is headed "Charge on termination of interest in possession".

(ii) was a holding in an authorised unit trust or a share in an open-ended investment company."

4.5.3.9.3 Detail

This is essentially moving from a domicile basis to a residence basis for an exemption from charge under section 52.

4.5.3.9.4 Effective Date

The effective date is 06 April 2025. See paragraph 45.

4.5.3.10 Paragraph 9 Amendment of the tests in subsections 54(2) and 54(2B) (e

4.5.3.10.1 Overview

Paragraph 9 amends the tests at subsections 54(2) and 54(2B) (e) by reference to whether a person is a long-term UK resident instead of whether they are UK domiciled. An additional transitional provision is introduced at new subsections 54(2C) and (2D) so that there is no charge on death in relation to excluded property which was comprised in a settlement immediately before 30 October 2024 provided it subsequently remains excluded property (under the pre-6 April 2025 rules). Section 54 deals with certain matters left out of account in valuing the estate of a deceased.

4.5.3.10.2 Legislation

Paragraph 9 provides:

"(1) Section 54 (exceptions from charge on death) is amended as follows.
(2) In subsections (2) and (2B)(e), for "domiciled in the United Kingdom" substitute "a long-term UK resident".
(3) After subsection (2B) insert—
"(2C) Where—
- (a) a person who is entitled to an interest in possession in settled property dies,
- (b) the settled property became comprised in the settlement before 30 October 2024,
- (c) immediately before 30 October 2024, the settled property was excluded property by virtue of section 48(3) or (3A) (as it had effect at that time),
- (d) the person became beneficially entitled to the interest before 30 October 2024, and
- (e) at all times on and after 30 October 2024 and before the person's death, the settled property-
  - (i) was situated outside the United Kingdom and was not property to which paragraph 2 or 3 of Schedule A1 applied (overseas property with value attributable to UK residential property), or
  - (ii) was a holding in an authorised unit trust or a share 40 in an open-ended investment company,

the value of the settled property shall be left out of account in determining for the purposes of this Act the value of the person's estate immediately before their death. (2D)

Section 54 provides that certain matters are left out of account in valuing the deceased estate on death. This includes where the settled spouse or civil partner becomes entitled and is UK domiciled.

Where a person became beneficially entitled to an interest in possession in settled property on or after 22 March 2006, subsection (2C) applies in relation to the interest only if it is-

(a) an immediate post-death interest [IPDI],

(b) a disabled person's interest [DPI], or

(c) a transitional serial interest [TSI], or

(d) falls within section 5(1B) (certain interests acquired with no gratuitous benefit)."

4.5.3.10.3 Detail

This is essentially a tidying up operation following the move to residence from domicile as a basis. There is also a transitional provision as noted above.

4.5.3.10.4 Effective date

6 April 2025. See paragraph 45.

4.5.3.11 Paragraph 10 Amendment of subsection 64(1B) and insertion of new subsection 64(1BZA)

4.5.3.11.1 Overview

Paragraph 10 removes the tests at subsection 64(1B) for whether a settlement's income is relevant property at a ten-year anniversary by reference to the settlor's domicile, or whether they were a formerly domiciled resident. It then inserts new subsection 64(1BZA).

New subsection 64(1BZA) provides the new rule that income is relevant property where the settlor is long-term UK resident. It further provides conditions when the settlor has died either before or on or after 6 April 2025.

4.5.3.11.2 Legislation

Paragraph 10 reads as follows:

"(1) Section 64 (charge at ten-year anniversary) is amended as follows.

(2) In subsection (1B), for the words from the beginning to "ten-year anniversary falls" substitute "Where the settlor of property comprised in a settlement meets the condition in subsection (1BZA)".

(3) After that subsection insert—

"(1BZA) The condition is that the settlor—

(a) is alive and is not a long-term UK resident immediately before the ten-year anniversary,

(b) died on or after 6 April 2025 and was not a long-term UK resident immediately before their death, or

(c) died before 6 April 2025 and was not domiciled in the United Kingdom when the property became comprised in the settlement."

(4) In subsection (1BA), for "subsection (1B)" substitute "subsection (1BZA)(c)"

4.5.3.11.3 Detail

Section 64 deals with the 10-year anniversary charge. This is done by amending and inserting subsection 64 (1B2A). This requires the settlor not be a long-term resident immediately before the relevant 10-year anniversary or the death to be out with the charge.

As amended section 64 IHTA reads as follows.

"64 Charge at 10 year anniversary

(1) Where immediately before a ten-year anniversary all or any part of the property comprised in a settlement is relevant property, tax shall be charged at the rate applicable under sections 66 and 67 below on the value of the property or part at that time.

(1A) For the purposes of subsection (1) above, property held by the trustees of a settlement immediately before a ten-year anniversary is to be regarded as relevant property comprised in the settlement at that time if—

(a)it is income of the settlement,

(b)the income arose before the start of the five years ending immediately before the ten-year anniversary,

c)the income arose (directly or indirectly) from property comprised in the settlement that, when the income arose, was relevant property, and

(d)when the income arose, no person was beneficially entitled to an interest in possession in the property from which the income arose.

(1B) Where the settlor of property comprised in a settlement meets the condition in subsection (1BZA)], income of the settlement that arose (directly or indirectly) from the property] is not to be regarded as relevant property comprised in the settlement as a result of subsection (1A) above so far as the income—

(a)is situated outside the United Kingdom, or

(b)is represented by a holding in an authorised unit trust or a share in an open-ended investment company.

(1BZA) The condition is that the settlor—

(a)is alive and is not a long-term UK resident immediately before the ten-year anniversary,

(b)died on or after 6 April 2025 and was not a long-term UK resident immediately before their death, or

(c)died before 6 April 2025 and was not domiciled in the United Kingdom when the property became comprised in the settlement.]

(1BA) If—

(a)an amount is payable in respect of property ("the existing property") comprised in a settlement, and

(b)the amount represents an accumulation of income which (once accumulated) becomes comprised in the settlement,

subsection (1BZA) (c)] has effect, in the case of the amount, as if any reference to the time it became comprised in the settlement were to the time the existing property became comprised in the settlement.

(1C) Income of the settlement is not to be regarded as relevant property comprised in the settlement as a result of subsection (1A) above so far as the income—

(a)is represented by securities issued by the Treasury subject to a condition of the kind mentioned in subsection (2) of section 6 above, and

(b)it is shown that all known persons for whose benefit the settled property or income from it has been or might be applied, or who are or might become beneficially entitled to an interest in possession in it, are persons of a description specified in the condition in question.

(2) For the purposes of subsection (1) above, a foreign-owned work of art which is situated in the United Kingdom for one or more of the purposes of public display, cleaning and restoration (and for no other purpose) is not to be regarded as relevant property."

4.5.3.11.4 Effective Date

The effective date is 6 April 2025. See paragraph 45.

4.5.3.12 Paragraph 11 Amendment of section 65 and insertion of new section 48ZA

4.5.3.12.1 Overview

Paragraph 11 amends section 65 (the Exit Charge) in consequence of the changes to section 48 and provides for the insertion of new section 48ZA. The new definition of excluded property which depends on the settlor's long-term UK residence will apply with regard to charges on exits from relevant property settlements.

4.5.3.12.2 Legislation

Paragraph 11 reads:

"(1) Section 65 (exit charges etc) is amended as follows.

(2) In subsection (7), for "section 48(3)(a) above" substitute "section 48ZA".

(3) In subsection (7A), for the words from "becomes excluded property" to the end, substitute "is invested in a holding in an authorised unit trust or a share in an open-ended investment company and thereby becomes excluded property by virtue of section 48ZA".

(4) Omit subsection (7B).

(5) In subsection (7C), for "section 48(3)(a) above" substitute "section 48ZA".

(6) In subsection (8), for the words from the beginning to "subsection (8A))", substitute "If the condition in subsection (8ZA) is met in relation to property comprised in a settlement".

(7) After subsection (8) insert—

"(8ZA) The condition is that the settlor—

(a) is alive and is not a long-term UK resident,

(b) died on or after 6 April 2025 and was not a long-term UK resident immediately before they died, or

(c) died before 6 April 2025 and was not domiciled in the United Kingdom when the property became comprised in the settlement."

(8) In subsection (8A), for "subsection (8)" substitute "subsection (8ZA) (c)".

Section 65 IHTA as amended reads as follows.

"65 Charge at other times.

(1) There shall be a charge to tax under this section—

(a) where the property comprised in a settlement or any part of that property ceases to be relevant property (whether because it ceases to be comprised in the settlement or otherwise); and

(b) in a case in which paragraph (a) above does not apply, where the trustees of the settlement make a disposition as a result of which the value of relevant property comprised in the settlement is less than it would be but for the disposition.

(2) The amount on which tax is charged under this section shall be—

(a) the amount by which the value of relevant property comprised in the settlement is less immediately after the event in question that it would be but for the event, or

(b) where the tax payable is paid out of relevant property comprised in the settlement immediately after the event, the amount which, after deducting the tax, is equal to the amount on which tax would be charged by virtue of paragraph (a) above.

(3) The rate at which tax is charged under this section shall be the rate applicable under section 68 or 69 below.

(4) Subsection (1) above does not apply if the event in question occurs in a quarter beginning with the day on which the settlement commenced or with a ten-year anniversary.

(5) Tax shall not be charged under this section in respect of—

(a)a payment of costs or expenses (so far as they are fairly attributable to relevant property), or

(b)a payment which is (or will be) income of any person for any of the purposes of income tax or would for any of those purposes be income of a person not resident in the United Kingdom if he were so resident, or in respect of a liability to make such a payment.

(6) Tax shall not be charged under this section by virtue of subsection (1)(b) above if the disposition is such that, were the trustees beneficially entitled

to the settled property, section 10 or section 16 above would prevent the disposition from being a transfer of value.

(7) Tax shall not be charged under this section by reason only that property comprised in a settlement ceases to be situated in the United Kingdom and thereby becomes excluded property by virtue of section 48ZA.

(7A) Tax shall not be charged under this section by reason only that property comprised in a settlement is invested in a holding in an authorised unit trust or a share in an open-ended investment company and thereby becomes excluded property by virtue of section 48ZA].

(7B) . . . .

(7C) Tax shall not be charged under this section by reason only that property comprised in a settlement ceases to any extent to be property to which paragraph 2 or 3 of Schedule A1 applies and thereby becomes excluded property by virtue of section 48ZA.

(7D) Tax shall not be charged under this section where property comprised in a settlement or any part of that property—

(a)is, by virtue of paragraph 5(2)(a) of Schedule A1, not excluded property for the two-year period referred to in that paragraph, but

(b)becomes excluded property at the end of that period.

(8) If the condition in subsection (8ZA) is met in relation to property comprised in a settlement], tax shall not be charged under this section by reason only that the property is invested in securities issued by the Treasury subject to a condition of the kind mentioned in section 6(2) above and thereby becomes excluded property by virtue of section 48(4)(b) above.

(8ZA) The condition is that the settlor—

(a)is alive and is not a long-term UK resident,

(b)died on or after 6 April 2025 and was not a long-term UK resident immediately before they died, or

(c)died before 6 April 2025 and was not domiciled in the United Kingdom when the property became comprised in the settlement.

(8A) If—

(a)an amount is payable in respect of property ("the existing property") comprised in a settlement, and

(b)the amount represents an accumulation of income which (once accumulated) becomes comprised in the settlement,

subsection (8ZA) (c)] has effect, in the case of the amount, as if any reference to the time it became comprised in the settlement were to the time the existing property became comprised in the settlement.]

(9) For the purposes of this section trustees shall be treated as making a disposition if they omit to exercise a right (unless it is shown that the omission was not deliberate) and the disposition shall be treated as made at the time or latest time when they could have exercised the right.

4.5.3.12.3 Detail

Paragraph 11 amends section 65 in consequence of the changes to section 48 and insertion of new section 48ZA.

The new definition of excluded property which depends on the settlor's long-term UK residence will apply with regard to charges on exits from relevant property settlements.

Section 65 IHTA is amended so that the condition in new section 64(8ZA)[143] applies (discussed below).

This is that the settlor:

a. Is alive and not a long-term UK resident;

b. Died after 5 April 2025; or

c. Died before 6 April 2025 and was not UK domiciled when the property became comprised in the settlement.

4.5.3.12.4 Effective Date

The effective date is 6 April 2025. See paragraph 45.

4.5.3.13 Paragraph 12 Amendment of section 74A

4.5.3.13.1 Overview

Paragraph 12 amends section 74A, which contains anti- avoidance provisions relating to 'purchased' interests in settled property, so that the tests for section 74A's application depend on a person's long-term UK residence for periods after 6 April 2025.

4.5.3.13.2 Legislation

Paragraph 12 provides:

> "Section 74A (arrangements involving acquisition of interest in settled property etc) is amended as follows.
> (1) In subsection (1)—
> (a) in paragraph (b)(i), omit "domiciled in the United Kingdom";
> (b) after paragraph (b) insert—
> "(ba) the individual—

[143] (8ZA) The condition is that the settlor—
(a)is alive and is not a long-term UK resident,
(b)died on or after 6 April 2025 and was not a long-term UK resident immediately before they died, or
(c)died before 6 April 2025 and was not domiciled in the United Kingdom when the property became comprised in the settlement.]

(i) is a long-term UK resident at any time on or after 6 April 2025 during the course of the arrangements, or

(ii) acquired the interest, or became able to acquire it, at a time before 6 April 2025 while

domiciled in the United Kingdom.".

(3) For subsection (2) substitute—

"(2) Condition A is that the relevant settled property is excluded property at any time during the course of the arrangement are in trust under and offshore settlement established by a non-UK domiciled settlor with the non-UK situs asset in it such that it was an excluded property trust. This stops similar arrangements being and after the move away from domicile. Ignore for this purpose—

(a) section 48ZA (8) (as it has effect on and after 6 April 2025);

(b) section 48(3D) (as it had effect before 6 April 2025).""

4.5.3.13.3 Detail

This is the amendment of an anti-avoidance provision to reflect the move away from a domicile-based system to a long-term residence are Sections 74AC is inserted to deal with a particular type of avoidance arrangement. This involved a UK domiciled individual buying interests under prefunded trusts.

4.5.3.13.4 Effective Date

The effective date is 6 April 2025. See paragraph 45.

4.5.3.14 Paragraph 13 Amendment of section 75A (4) etc

4.5.3.14.1 Overview

Paragraph 13 amends section 75A by omitting subsection (4).

4.5.3.14.2 Legislation

Paragraph 13 provides:

"In section 75A, omit subsection (4)."

Section 75A (4) used to read:

"(4)Where, by virtue of this section, a liability is not taken into account in determining the value of a person's estate immediately before death, the liability is also not to be taken into account in determining the extent to which the estate of any spouse or civil partner of the person is increased for the purposes of section 18."

18 Transfers between spouses or civil partners.

(1) A transfer of value is an exempt transfer to the extent that the value transferred is attributable to property which becomes comprised in the estate of the transferor's spouse [F2or civil partner] or, so far as the value transferred is not so attributable, to the extent that that estate is increased.

(2) If, immediately before the transfer, the transferor but not the transferor's spouse [F3or civil partner] is domiciled in the United Kingdom the value in respect of which the transfer is exempt (calculated as a value on which no tax is chargeable) shall not exceed [F4the exemption limit at the time of the transfer,] less any amount previously taken into account for the purposes of the exemption conferred by this section.

(2A) For the purposes of subsection (2), the exemption limit is the amount shown in the second column of the first row of the Table in Schedule 1 (upper limit of portion of value charged at rate of nil per cent).]

(3) Subsection (1) above shall not apply in relation to property if the testamentary or other disposition by which it is given—

(a)takes effect on the termination after the transfer of value of any interest or period, or

(b)depends on a condition which is not satisfied within twelve months after the transfer; but paragraph (a) above shall not have effect by reason only that the property is given to a spouse [F6or civil partner] only if he survives the other spouse [F6or civil partner] for a specified period.

(4) For the purposes of this section, property is given to a person if it becomes his property or is held on trust for him.

4.5.3.14.3 Effective Date

The effective date is 6 April 2025. See paragraph 45.

4.5.3.15 Paragraph 14 Amendment of section 80 – initial interest of a settlor or spouse etc.

4.5.3.15.1 Overview

This is aimed at arrangements transferring assets into a life interest trust for one's spouse and carrying a spouse relief under the rules at the time. This amendment is making sure an anti-avoidance provisions essentially continues to work.

Paragraph 14 makes an amendment to section 80.

This provides that, where that section deems settled property in which the settlor, or their spouse or civil partner, has an initial qualifying interest in possession it is to be treated as becoming comprised in the settlement at a later date, this will apply for the purposes of the excluded property rules in section 48 and section 48ZA.

4.5.3.15.2 Legislation

Paragraph 14 reads:

> "In section 80 (initial interest of settlor or spouse), in subsection (1), after "for the purposes of this Chapter" insert "(including sections 48 and 48ZA (excluded property) as they apply for the purposes of this Chapter)".

Section 80 before amendment read as follows:

> "80 Initial interest of settlor or spouse or civil partner.
>
> (1)Where a settlor or his spouse or civil partner is beneficially entitled to a qualifying interest in possession in property immediately after it becomes comprised in the settlement, the property shall for the purposes of this Chapter be treated as not having become comprised in the settlement on that occasion; but when the property or any part of it becomes held on trusts under which neither of those persons is beneficially entitled to a qualifying interest in possession, the property or part shall for those purposes be treated as becoming comprised in a separate settlement made by that one of them who ceased (or last ceased) to be beneficially entitled to a qualifying interest in possession in it.
>
> (2) References in subsection (1) above to the spouse or civil partner of a settlor include references to the widow or widower or surviving civil partner of a settlor.
>
> (3) This section shall not apply if the occasion first referred to in subsection (1) above occurred before 27th March 1974.
>
> (4) Where the occasion first referred to in subsection (1) above occurs on or after 22nd March 2006, this section applies—
>
> (a)as though for "a qualifying interest in possession" in each place where that appears in subsection (1) above there were substituted a postponing interest, and
>
> (b)as though, for the purposes of that subsection, each of the following were a "postponing interest"—
>
> (i)an immediate post-death interest;
>
> (ii)a disabled person's interest."

4.5.3.15.3 Detail

Paragraph 14 amends section 80 IHTA. This provides that, where that section deems settled property in which the settlor, or their spouse or civil partner, has an initial qualifying interest in possession to be treated as becoming comprised in the settlement at a later date, this will apply for the purposes of the excluded property rules in section 48 and section 48ZA.

Section 80 IHTA is concerned with avoidance using an initial qualifying interest so that the amount transferred in was low etc.

HMRC say the following on this.

> "IHTM42231 - The settlement: initial qualifying interest in possession of settlor or spouse
> A special rule applies where the settlor or their spouse (or civil partner) had an immediate and qualifying interest in possession (QIIP) in the settled property and a later time the QIIP ends, and property becomes relevant property

The rule (IHTA/S80) is that when none of the persons above have a QIIP then for the purposes of relevant property charges

- any continuing settlement is a separate settlement that is deemed to commence at that later time and
- the settlor is the last of those persons to have a QIIP.

This rule may therefore alter the calculation of the rate of tax on future proportionate and anniversary charges.

That is because

- the historic value in the deemed settlement will be at the value at the later date
- the deemed settlor may have a different cumulative total at the later date and
- the deemed settlor may have a different domicile, and this may affect the availability of excluded property (see below)
- if the deemed settlement commences on a death, then settlements made by the deceased's may be related settlements or be treated as same-day additions.

However, the date of the anniversary charge is not affected. It is still determined by the 10-year cycle based on the first settlement.

Impact of the rule on excluded property

If the deemed settlor is not domiciled or is not treated as domiciled in the UK at the later date the settled property may be excluded property.

However, when the rule applies then an additional domicile test must first be satisfied and guidance on this point is at IHTM42603.

Impact of Finance Act 2020

Although the wording of the legislation has been altered to accommodate other changes the rules above have not changed."

4.5.3.15.4 Effective Date

The effective date is 6 April 2025. See paragraph 45.

4.5.3.16 *Paragraph 15 Amendment of section 81 (property moving between settlements)*

4.5.3.16.1 Overview

Paragraph 15 makes two amendments to section 81. These are:

1. Sub-paragraph 15(a) provides that where section 81 deems property transferred from one settlement to another it is to be treated as remaining in the first settlement, this will apply for the purposes of the excluded property rules in section 48 and section 48ZA as updated.
2. The sub-paragraph 15(b) amendment clarifies the existing effect of section 81 by confirming that although property is deemed to remain in the first settlement it is nevertheless treated as held on the trusts of the

second settlement for certain IHT purposes. It is understood that arrangements had been set up in the past to take advantage of the duality. There was apparently some uncertainty as to how they worked.

4.5.3.16.2 Legislation

Paragraph 15 reads as follows:

"In section 81 (property moving between settlements), in subsection (1)—

(a) after "for the purposes of this Chapter" insert "(including sections 48 and 48ZA (excluded property) as they apply for the purposes of this Chapter)";

(b) at the end insert "(but held on the trusts of the second)"."

Before the amendments section 81 headed "Property moving between settlements" read as in plain text – amendments in Italics: [add]

"(1)Where property which ceases to be comprised in one settlement becomes comprised in another then, unless in the meantime any person becomes beneficially entitled to the property (and not merely to an interest in possession in the property), it shall for the purposes of this Chapter "(including sections 48 and 48ZA (excluded property) as they apply for the purposes of this Chapter) be treated as remaining comprised in the first settlement .

(2)Subsection (1) above shall not apply where the property ceased to be comprised in the first settlement before 10th December 1981; but where property ceased to be comprised in one settlement before 10th December 1981 and after 26th March 1974 and, by the same disposition, became comprised in another settlement, it shall for the purposes of this Chapter be treated as remaining comprised in the first settlement (but held on the trusts of the second).

(3) Subsection (1) above shall not apply where a reversionary interest in the property expectant on the termination of a qualifying interest in possession subsisting under the first settlement was settled on the trusts of the other settlement before 10th December 1981."

4.5.3.16.3 Detail

Section 81 is concerned with property moving between settlements and treatment of such property for IHT.

The principle is to treat the property involved for IHT purposes as remaining in the first trust for IHT purposes. The amendment recognises that for general law purposes the property is held on the trusts of the settlement to which the property Is transferred.

HMRC said the following on the position before amendment in the IHT Manual.

"IHTM42603 - Foreign element: additional test of domicile

Where an overseas domicile is claimed and IHTA84/S80 or S81 is in point, and it is claimed that property is excluded under IHTA84/S48 you must apply a double test of domicile

The statutory rules are set out in IHTA84/S82A1B, S82 and S82A, and you may need to test the domicile of more than one person or the domicile of the same person on different dates.

A: When IHTA84/S80 applies

When IHTA/s80 applies then the Act provides for a deemed settlor and a deemed trust with a deemed commencement date (IHTM42231)

If the settlor of the deemed trust is domiciled in the UK (or deemed to be domiciled in the UK) at the deemed commencement date, then the foreign assets in the trust cannot be excluded property in the first place.

However, if that settlor is not domiciled in the UK at the deemed commencement date, then the foreign assets in the deemed trust can only be excluded property if an additional test is met.

The additional test is that the settlor of the original trust must be domiciled outside the UK when the assets became comprised in the original trust.

In summary, excluded property can only be available if both the original settlor and the deemed settlor were non-domiciled.

These rules were not altered by Finance Act 2020.

> **Example**
>
> In 2001 Mr and Mrs A were not domiciled in the UK and neither were born in the UK. Mr A created a trust that provided for an interest in possession for himself for life and then to his surviving spouse following which the trusts were discretionary for the wider family.
>
> Mr A died in 2012 and Mrs A died in 2019 by which time she had become deemed UK domiciled. On both deaths the assets were outside the UK and excluded property.
>
> However, following Mrs A's death IHTA/S80 applies, and a deemed settlement arises. The assets in the trust can no longer be excluded property and will be subject to a ten-year anniversary (TYA) charge in 2021."
>
> On the other hand, if Mrs A had continued to be domiciled outside the UK then the foreign assets will continue to be excluded property because the original settlor (Mr A) was non-domiciled when the assets became comprised in the original trust.

B: When IHTA84/S81 applies

When IHTA/S81 applies then assets in a trust ('T1') that become comprised in another trust ('T2') are deemed to remain in T1 for the purpose of calculating Inheritance Tax (IHT) trust charges (IHTM42229) But when that happens the availability of excluded property status may be denied.

If the settlor of T1 was domiciled in the UK (or deemed to be domiciled in the UK) when the assets become comprised in T1 then the foreign assets in the trust cannot be excluded property in the first place.

However, if the settlor of T1 was not domiciled in the UK when the assets originally became comprised in T1 then the transferred assets (which are deemed to remain in T1) can only continue to have excluded property status if an additional domicile test is met.

The additional domicile test depends upon the time when IHTA/s81 applies, i.e. the assets in T1 become comprised in T2.

1. IHTA/S81 transfers prior to 22 July 2020

The additional test is that the settlor of T2 must also have been non-domiciled at the time the assets in T2 originally became comprised in T2 (IHTA/S82).

Put simply, excluded property status can only be available for the transferred assets if the settlors of both T1 and T2 were historically non-domiciled.

1. IHTA/S81 transfers on or after 22 July 2020 (Finance Act 2020)

The deeming effect of IHTA/S81 remains but the additional domicile test is different and is set out in the new IHTA/S82A.

The new legislation no longer depends on the domicile of the settlor of recipient trust (T2). Instead, the additional domicile test focuses on the domicile of the settlor of T1 or the domicile of the person that caused the assets to become comprised in another trust.

- The trustees use their trust powers to transfer assets from T1 to T2

In this case the transferred assets can only continue to have excluded property status if the settlor of T1 is not domiciled in the UK at the time the assets are transferred to T2.

If further transfers are then made from T2 to T3 or from T2 back to T1 then these are labelled as 'qualifying transfers' and the settlor of T1 must continue to be non-domiciled on each of these occasions. But if at the time of a qualifying transfer the settlor of T1 is UK domiciled then the transferred assets can no longer have excluded property status.

If the settlor of T1 is no longer living at the time of a qualifying transfer (and the death is not a qualifying transfer) then the additional domicile test is treated as satisfied.

- The assets are transferred to T2 because of an assignment or the exercise of a general power of appointment

In this case the transferred assets can only continue to have excluded property status if at the time of an assignment or the exercise of the power (which must occur on or after 22 July 2020) the assignor or the power holder is not domiciled or deemed domiciled in the UK.

Note that the assets may not become comprised in T2 immediately when the assignment is made or the power is exercised. If the qualifying transfer occurs at a later time, then the assignor or power holder must not be a formerly domiciled resident at the time the assets do move to T2 (as well as being non-domiciled at the time of the assignment or exercise).

Consult with Technical advisors at an early stage if the facts are not clearly covered by the guidance above including situations where there are transfers after 22 July 2020 that may be affected by earlier trust-to-trust transfers or where the analysis may depend on the effect of the judgment in *Barclays Wealth v HMRC* (2017) EWCA Civ 1512.

4.5.3.16.4 Effective Date

The effective date is 6 April 2025. See paragraph 45.

4.5.3.17 Paragraph 16 New section 81B substituted

4.5.3.17.1 Overview

Paragraph 16 substitutes a new section 81B. It adds to Section 80 discussed above.

New section 81B relates to property to which section 80 applies and provides that, where property would otherwise be excluded property under the tests in section 48ZA it will only be excluded property if the settlor or their spouse or civil partner with the initial interest also meets those conditions.

4.5.3.17.2 Legislation

Paragraph 16 provides:

> "For section 81B substitute—
>
> "81B Excluded property: property to which section 80 applies
>
> (1) This section applies where—
>
> > (a) property is treated under section 80(1) as becoming comprised in a settlement, and
> >
> > (b) the property would, apart from this section, be excluded property by virtue of meeting the condition in any of 17 Omit sections 82 and 82A (excluded property: property to which section 80 applies."

Before the change section 81B read:

> "81BExcluded property: property to which section 80 applies
>
> (1) This section applies to property to which section 80 (initial interest of settlor etc) applies.
>
> (2) If the property would apart from this section be excluded property by virtue of section 48(3)(a) or (3A)(a), the property is at any time in a tax year to be regarded as excluded property for the purposes of this Chapter, except sections 78 and 79, only if Conditions A and B are met.
>
> (3) Section 65(8) has effect in relation to the property only if Condition A is met (in addition to any condition mentioned in that provision).
>
> (4) Condition A is that the actual settlor was not domiciled in the United Kingdom at the time of the occasion first referred to in section 80(1).
>
> (5) Condition B is that the actual settlor is not a formerly domiciled resident for the tax year.

(6) In this section "the actual settlor" means the person who is the settlor of the property in relation to the settlement first mentioned in section 80(1).

(7) Where the occasion first referred to in section 80(1) occurred before the day on which the Finance Act 2020 was passed, this section has effect as if, in subsection (2), "or (3A) (a)" were omitted."

4.5.3.17.3 Detail

Paragraph 16 substitutes a new section 81B as set out above.

4.5.3.17.4 Effective Date

The effective date is 6 April 2025. See paragraph 45.

4.5.3.18 Paragraph 17 Repeal of sections 82 and 82A

4.5.3.18.1 Overview

Paragraph 17 repeals sections 82 and 82A which related to the excluded property status of settled property in cases where there were transfers between settlements to which section 81 applied. (See also the discussion of paragraphs 15 and 16 above).

Where such transfers have taken place, the excluded property status of the property will now be determined in accordance with the tests in subsections 48(3) and 48(ZA) which depend on the long- term residence status of the settlor of the first settlement rather than domicile.

4.5.3.18.2 Legislation

Paragraph 17 reads:

"Omit sections 82 and 82A (excluded property: property to which section 81 applies). "

Sections 82 and 82A used to read before amendment as follows.

"82Excluded property : property to which section 81 applies (old cases)]

(1)In a case where, apart from this section, property to which section ... 81 applies would be excluded property by virtue of section 48(3)(a) above, that property shall not be taken to be excluded property at any time ("the relevant time") for the purposes of this Chapter (except sections 78 and 79) unless Conditions A and B are satisfied.

(2) Section 65(8) above shall not have effect in relation to property to which section ... 81 applies unless Condition A below is satisfied (in addition to the condition in section 65(8) that the settlor was not domiciled in the United Kingdom when the property became comprised in the settlement).

(3) Condition A referred to in subsections (1) and (2) above is—

(a). . . . .

(b)in the case of property to which subsection (1) or (2) of section 81 above applies, that the person who is the settlor in relation to the second of the settlements mentioned in the subsection concerned,

was not domiciled in the United Kingdom when that settlement was made.

(4) Condition B referred to in subsection (1) above is—

(a). . . .

(b)in the case of property to which subsection (1) or (2) of section 81 above applies, that the person who is the settlor in relation to the first or second of the settlements mentioned in that subsection,

was not a formerly domiciled resident for the tax year in which the relevant time falls.

(5) This section does not apply in relation to a case to which section 82A applies".

Section 82A reads as follows.

"**82AExcluded property: property to which section 81 applies (new cases)**

(1) This section—

(a)applies where, at any time on or after the day on which the Finance Act 2020 is passed, property ceases to be comprised in a settlement ("the first settlement") but is treated as a result of section 81 as remaining comprised in that settlement for the purposes of this Chapter, and

(b)applies whether or not at any subsequent time the property is comprised in the first settlement without regard to that section.

(2)If the property would apart from this section be excluded property by virtue of section 48(3)(a) or (3A)(a), the property is to be regarded as excluded property for the purposes of this Chapter, except sections 78 and 79, at any time only if the non-domicile condition is met in relation to each qualifying transfer occurring on or before that time.

(3)Section 65(8) has effect in relation to the property at any time only if (in addition to the condition mentioned there) the non-domicile condition is met in relation to each qualifying transfer occurring on or before that time; but, for the purposes of this subsection, the non-domicile condition has effect with the omission of subsection (6)(a)(ii).

(4) For the purposes of this section each of the following is a "qualifying transfer"—

(a)the occasion on which section 81 applies to the property; and

(b)any subsequent occasion on which the property would, if the effect of section 81 were ignored, become comprised in a settlement to which this Chapter applies (including the first settlement).

(5) But a qualifying transfer does not occur as a result of—

(a)an assignment by a beneficiary of an interest in a settlement, or

(b)an exercise of a general power of appointment,

unless the time of the assignment or exercise of the power falls on or after the day on which the Finance Act 2020 is passed.

(6) For the purposes of this section "the non-domicile condition" is—

(a)in a case where a qualifying transfer occurs as a result of an assignment by a beneficiary of an interest in a settlement or an exercise of a general power of appointment, that the beneficiary or the person exercising the power—

(i)was not domiciled in the United Kingdom at the time of the assignment or exercise of the power, and

(ii)is not a formerly domiciled resident for the tax year in which the time mentioned in subsection (2) falls;

(b)in a case in which section 81 applies which is not within paragraph (a), that the person who was the settlor of the property in relation to the first settlement was not domiciled in the United Kingdom immediately before the time when the property ceased to be comprised in the first settlement;

(c)in any other case, that the person who was the settlor of the property in relation to the first settlement was not domiciled in the United Kingdom immediately before the time of the subsequent occasion.

(7) If—

(a)the settlor mentioned in subsection (6)(b) or (c) has died before the time mentioned there, and

(b)the death does not give rise to a qualifying transfer, the non-domicile condition is treated as met.

(8) In this section any reference to a qualifying transfer occurring as a result of—

(a)an assignment by a beneficiary of an interest in a settlement, or

(b)an exercise of a general power of appointment,

includes the transfer occurring partly as a result of the assignment or exercise of the power.

(9) In this section any reference to an assignment includes an assignation."

4.5.3.18.3 Detail

Paragraph 17 repeals sections 82 and 82A which related to the excluded property status of settled property in cases where there were transfers between settlements to which section 81 applied. Where such transfers have taken place, the excluded property status of the property will now be determined in accordance with the tests in subsections 48(3) and 48(ZA) which depend on the long-term residence status of the settlor of the first settlement.

4.5.3.18.4 Effective Date

The effective date is 6 April 2025. See paragraph 45.

4.5.3.19 *Paragraphs 18 and 19 Consequential amendments to relating to transactions of close companies*

4.5.3.19.1 Overview

Paragraphs 18 and 19 provide for consequential amendments to the provisions relating to transactions of close companies (sections 94 and 136 IHTA), to replace domicile references with long-term UK residence ones. This is consequential on the move from a domicile-based regime to a long term residence basis.

4.5.3.19.2 Legislation

Paragraphs 18 and 19 read as follows:

> "18 In section 94 (close companies: charge on participators), in subsection (2)(b),for "domiciled outside the United Kingdom" substitute "not a long-term UK resident".
>
> 19 In section 136 (transfers within three years before death: transactions of close companies), in subsection (3), for "domiciled in the United Kingdom" substitute "a long-term UK resident"."

4.5.3.19.3 Detail

The amount of a transfer of value made by a close company can be apportioned to individual participators in the company. There is currently an exemption for Non-Doms in some circumstances.

See section 94 (2)(b) which reads "if any amount which would otherwise be apportioned to an individual who is domiciled outside the United Kingdom is attributable to the value of any property outside the United Kingdom, that amount shall not be apportioned."

This is now to be on residence basis so long-term UK resident is substituted for domiciled in the UK.

Section 136 has a similar exception, and a similar change is made.

HMRC say the following about this in their IHT Manuals on sections 136 IHTA.

> **IHTM14645 - Lifetime transfers: specific lifetime reliefs: shares and securities: transactions of close companies**
>
> IHTA/S136 applies where the transferred asset consists of shares in a close company (IHTM14851) and between the date of transfer and the date of death or sale there was a 'relevant transaction', that is
>
> - transfer of value by the company, or
> - an alteration in the company's unquoted share or loan capital or in the rights attaching the unquoted shares or debentures of the company
>
> but the transaction is one which does not give rise to an adjustment for capital receipts (IHTM14642), payment of calls (IHTM14643) or changes in shareholdings (IHTM14644).

This section of the Act operates by increasing the market value of the transferred asset at the date of death or sale by the difference between

- the market value at the time of the transfer, and
- what that value would have been if the 'relevant transaction' had occurred before rather than after the transfer.

The basic relief under IHTA/S136(2) assumes that the 'relevant transaction' would have had the effect of reducing the value of the transferred asset. Exceptionally, the 'relevant transaction' might have had the effect of increasing the value of that asset at the time of the transfer. In those circumstances IHTA/S136(4) means that you should reduce the market value at the date of death or sale to what it would have been if the 'relevant transaction' had not occurred.

IHTA/S136(3) provides for the IHTA/S136(2) increase to be adjusted if the 'relevant transaction' is a transfer of value by the company which increases the estate of the transferor or spouse/civil partner (IHTM11032) of the transferor.

Similar provisions are made for transfers of interests in land by IHTA/S137. Examples showing how these provisions apply are included at IHTM14662 and IHTM14663.

HMRC say the following on section 94 in their manuals.

IHTM16241 - Close companies and settled property: introduction

In the case of absolute lifetime transfers where a transfer of value is made by a close company IHTA84/S94 provides that a claim to Inheritance Tax (IHT) shall arise as if each individual [identified as a 'participator'] to whom an amount [of the transfer] is apportioned under this section had made a transfer of value. (See the lifetime transfer/close company guidance from IHTM14851)

So the rules relating to transfers by close companies 'look through' the company to its members to produce personal claims to IHT on absolute lifetime transfers of value by those individuals. Where the identified participator is another close company, we simply look through that, and so on.

If trustees of settled property are among the participators in the close company, the same system is followed, with some modifications in IHTA84/S99 to cater for the fact that a trustee, as such, should not be treated as an individual making a lifetime transfer.

Generally, the taxable results produced by IHTA84/Part IV are the same for transfers by the company, or alterations of capital in the company, but IHTA84/S100 specifically deals with alterations of capital where a trustee is the participator.

Where the individual became entitled to the interest in possession on or after 22 March 2006, S100 applies only if the interest in possession is

- an immediate post-death interest,
- a disabled person's interest, or
- a transitional serial interest (IHTM16061), IHTA84/S100(1A).

Practice

Shares and Assets Valuation (SAV) decides all questions on what is a close company, who is a participator, value, apportionment etc. You should consult Shares Valuation at an early stage in all cases.

Where the amount apportioned to the trustee is less than 5% of the value transferred no claim to IHT is raised upon it, and it is left out of account for all cumulation purposes.

Liability for IHT falls primarily on the company but if it does not pay it is generally the joint and several responsibility of the beneficiaries and participators, save that trustees who have less than the above 5% apportioned to them cannot be made liable.

Consideration

If consideration is given for the transfer or alteration then the amount of the consideration will be allowed under IHTA84/S52 (2) where the trusts are interest in possession.

BR and AR

Business relief or agricultural relief may be due on property chargeable under the 'close company' provisions. But in many cases the subject of the transfer will not satisfy the statutory conditions for

- relevant business property (IHTM25141) and
- agricultural property (IHTM24030).

You must therefore analyse the subject matter of the transfer carefully, because of the high probability that in such transactions the transfer is of cash or of company assets which, taken by themselves, will not qualify for either relief.

4.5.3.19.4 Effective Date

The effective date is 6 April 2025. See paragraph 45

4.5.3.20 Paragraph 20 Consequential amendment to section 155 (visiting forces etc)

4.5.3.20.1 Overview

Paragraph 20 makes a consequential amendment to section 155 (visiting forces etc) to remove the reference to domicile. Not many entertainers are members of the Armed Forces [144] more sports persons are because of the enhanced opportunities.

4.5.3.20.2 Legislat*ion*

Paragraph 20 reads:

> "In section 155 (visiting forces etc), in subsections (2) and (5B), omit "or domicile"."

[144] Elvis Presley famously was in the US Army. He served from 1958-1960 fulfilling his draft obligation. He made G.I. Blues after his discharge.

4.5.3.20.3 Detail

This is a consequential amendment arising from the move away from a domicile-based system for IHT.

4.5.3.20.4 Effective Date

The effective date is 6 April 2025. See paragraph 45.

4.5.3.21 Paragraph 21 Replacement of domicile-based conditions in section 157 concerning foreign currency accounts on death

4.5.3.21.1 Overview

Paragraph 21 replaces the conditions in section 157 relating to domicile for determining when foreign currency accounts are left out of account on a death. It substitutes conditions relating to residence and long-term UK residence in relation to property held by individuals. In the case of settled property new tests apply which relate to the trustees' residence and the long-term UK resident status of the settlor.

4.5.3.21.2 Legislation

> Paragraph 21 provides: "(1) Section 157 (non-residents' bank accounts) is amended as follows.
>
> "(2)In subsection (2)—
>
> > (a)omit "is not domiciled and not resident in the United Kingdom";
> >
> > (b)at the end insert "is neither resident in the United Kingdom nor a long-term UK resident".
>
> (3) In subsection (3), for the words from "if the settlor" to the end, substitute "if—
>
> > (a)the trustees are resident in the United Kingdom immediately before the beneficiary's death,
> >
> > (b)the settlor is alive and is a long-term UK resident immediately before the beneficiary's death,
> >
> > (c)the settlor died on or after 6 April 2025 and was not a long-term UK resident immediately before they died, or
> >
> > (d)the settlor died before 6 April 2025 and was not domiciled in the United Kingdom when the property became comprised in the settlement."

4.5.3.21.3 Detail

In essence, section 157 IHTA excluded certain foreign currency accounts from the estate on death by reference to domicile. Broadly, this is now to be judged by residence and long-term residence status

HMRC said the following in their Manuals on this Topic.

> "IHTM04380 - Value left out of account: foreign currency bank accounts

> IHTA84/S157 excludes from the charge on death only the balance on a 'qualifying foreign currency account' of a depositor who was neither domiciled (IHTM13000) in the UK for Inheritance Tax purposes nor resident (or ordinarily resident if the death was before 6 April 2013) here for Income Tax purposes at the time of their death. There is a corresponding exclusion for the balance on such an account held by trustees on the death of a beneficiary domiciled and resident outside the UK who had a qualifying interest in possession (IHTM16062) in it provided the settlor was not domiciled in the UK when the settlement was made and the trustees had no ties with the UK at the time of the beneficiary's death.
>
> Under FA96/SCH37/PARA12 a qualifying account is defined as 'a foreign currency account with a bank or the Post Office'. A foreign currency account is one that is denominated in a currency other than Sterling and under ICTA88/S840A a 'bank' means
>
> - the Bank of England
> - an institution authorised under the Banking Act 1987
> - a relevant European institution
> - any international organisation designated as a Bank by Treasury Order.
>
> Where the conditions are met, the balance on the account, whether in credit or in debit should be left out of account. You should refer any case of difficulty, especially if you are seeking to disallow a debit balance, to Technical."

Following the amendments made by paragraph 21. This is now a residence and a long-term residence basis.

4.5.3.21.4 Effective Date

The effective date is 6 April 2025. See paragraph 44.

4.5.3.22 Paragraph 22 Amendment of section 218 (non-resident trustees)

4.5.3.22.1 Overview

Paragraph 22 amends section 218 to provide that where a professional person is concerned with the making of a settlement and has reason to believe that the settlor is a long-term UK resident, they must make a return to HM Revenue and Customs within 3 months. Fortunately for the author there is an exception for barristers in the legislation.

4.5.3.22.2 Legislation

Paragraph 22 reads as follows:

> "In section 218 (non-resident trustees), in subsection (1) (a), [145] for "domiciled in the United Kingdom" substitute "a long-term UK resident"."

---

[145] **218Non-resident trustees.**

(1)Where any person, in the course of a trade or profession carried on by him, *other than the*

4.5.3.22.3 Detail

This is a consequential change as a result of the move away from a domicile-based system of IHT.

It is important that advisers ensure that their procedures are updated to take account of this. Rather than domicile this should now be geared to long term residence status. Failure to comply with this requirement lead to penalties.

4.5.3.22.4 Effective Date

The effective date is 6 April 2025. See paragraph 45.

4.5.3.23 Paragraph 23 Repeal of deemed domicile provision

4.5.3.23.1 Overview

> Paragraph 23 repeals section 267 which defined when a person was deemed to be UK domiciled for IHT purposes. (See the saving provision in Part 2 of this Schedule).

4.5.3.23.2 Legislation

Paragraph 23 reads as follows:

> "Omit section 267 (persons treated as domiciled in United Kingdom)."

4.5.3.23.3 Detail

As is well known IHT used be based on domicile as a connecting factor for UK purposes. This covered actual domicile under general common law principles but was extended by statute by reference to the residence of the individual in question often referred to as "deemed domicile" which is discussed above.

This is no longer relevant following the introduction of the long-term residence-based system. Accordingly, the provision dealing with this section 267 IHTA is repealed. It is effectively a consequential amendment.

4.5.3.23.4 Effective Date

The effective date is 6 April 2025. See paragraph 45.

---

profession of a barrister, has been concerned with the making of a settlement and knows or has reason to believe—

(a)that the settlor was domiciled in the United Kingdom, and

(b)that the trustees of the settlement are not or will not be resident in the United Kingdom,

he shall, within three months of the making of the settlement, make a return to the Board stating the names and addresses of the settlor and of the trustees of the settlement.

4.5.3.24 Paragraph 24 Amendment of section 267ZA before repeal

4.5.3.24.1 Overview

Paragraph 24 amends section 267ZA so that the conditions for an election for a spouse or civil partner to be treated as UK domiciled refer to times before 6 April 2025. This amendment has effect before repeal by paragraph 26.

4.5.3.24.2 Legislation

Paragraph 24 provides:

> "Section 267ZA (election to be treated as domiciled in the United Kingdom) (as it has effect before its repeal by paragraph 26) is amended as follows.
>
> *(1)* Section 267ZA (election to be treated as domiciled in the United Kingdom) (as it has effect before its repeal by paragraph 26) is amended as follows.
>
> *(2)* In subsections (3) and (4), for "on or after 6 April 2013 and" substitute "before 6 April 2025 but".
>
> *(3)* (3) Omit subsection (5).
>
> *(4)* (4) In subsection (8)—
>
> (a) for "is or was domiciled" substitute "was domiciled";
>
> (b) after "section 267" insert "(deemed domicile)".

4.5.3.24.3 Detail

This is a consequential amendment following the change to a residence basis for IHT.

Section 267ZA allowed certain elections as to domicile to be made. This is clearly not something that should apply after 5 April 2025. However, provision has to be made in respect of the position before 6 April 2025. This paragraph deals with that.

Section 267ZA is repealed by paragraph 26 discussed below.

The repeal of the section takes place after the amendment by paragraph 24 has been made.

4.5.3.24.4 Effective Date

The effective date is 6 April 2025. See paragraph 45.

4.5.3.25 Paragraph 25 Amendment of section 267ZB

4.5.3.25.1 Overview

Paragraph 25 amends section 267ZB so that the date specified in a notice on which a domicile election is treated as having taken effect is before 6 April 2025. This amendment has effect before repeal by paragraph 26.

4.5.3.25.2 Legislation

Paragraph 25 reads:

> "In section 267ZB (section 267ZA: further provision about election) (as it has effect before its repeal by paragraph 26), in subsection (4)(a), for "6 April 2013 or a later date" substitute "5 April 2025 or an earlier date"."

4.5.3.25.3 Detail

This is a consequential amendment following on from paragraphs 24 and 26. It effectively treats a domicile election where applicable as having taken place before the 6 April 2025 when the change to the long-term residence system starts.

Section 267ZB is repealed by paragraph 26.

4.5.3.25.4 Effective Date

The effective date is 6 April 2025.

4.5.3.26 Paragraph 26 Repeal of sections 267ZA and 267ZB from 6 April 2032

4.5.3.26.1 Overview

Paragraph 26 then repeals sections 267ZA and 267ZB, but with effect from 6 April 2032 (see the commencement provision in Part 2 of this Schedule).

4.5.3.26.2 Legislation

Paragraph 26 reads as follows:

> "Omit sections 267ZA and 267ZB (election to be treated as domiciled in the United Kingdom)"

4.5.3.26.3 Detail

This paragraph repeals sections 267ZA and 267ZB (domicile elections) with effect from 6 April 2032 (see below). see paragraph 27 below for their replacements.

4.5.3.26.4 Effective Date

The effective date is not but **6 April 2032** (see paragraph 45 in Part 2 of the Schedule below)

4.5.3.27 Paragraph 27 new sections 267ZC and 267ZD

4.5.3.27.1 Overview

Paragraph 27 introduces new sections 267ZC and 267ZD.

Broadly, these provide for an election by a person's spouse or civil partner to be treated as long-term UK resident for IHT purposes, to have effect for 10 successive tax years from the date of the election.

The paragraph also introduces new section 267ZE. This applies where an election has been made by a spouse or civil partner to be treated as UK domiciled, which has effect immediately before 6 April 2025. It applies to cases where the election was made before 6 April 2025 as well as those made after. This section:

- provides that the spouse or civil partner will be treated as a long-term UK resident at all
- times on or after 6 April 2025 if that would not otherwise be the case,
- sets a lapse period for elections made before 30 October 2024 if the elector has not been resident in the UK for 4 successive tax years from the date of the election, or
- sets a lapse period for elections made after 30 October 2024 if they have not been resident in the UK for 10 successive tax years from the date of election.

4.5.3.27.2 Legislation

Paragraph 27 reads as follows:

"Before section 267A insert -

"**267ZC Election to be treated as a long-term UK resident**

(1) A person ("P") who would not otherwise be a long-term UK resident is treated as one for the purposes of this Act at any time when an election under this section has effect

(2) An election under this section may be made -

(a) if condition A or B is met, by P;

(b) if condition B is met, by P's personal representatives.

(3) Condition A is that, at any time within the period of 7 years ending with the date on which the election is made, P had a spouse or civil partner who was a long-term UK resident.

(4) Condition B is that a person ("the deceased") dies and, at any time within the period of 7 years ending with the date of their death, the deceased was -

(a) a long-term UK resident, and

(b) the spouse or civil partner of P.

267ZD Further provision about elections under section 267ZC

(1) An election under section 267ZC—

(a) must be made by notice in writing to HMRC, and

(b) has effect from such date as is, in accordance with subsection(2), specified in the notice.

(2) The date specified in a notice under subsection (1)(a) ("the specified date") must—

(a) be after 5 April 2025,

(b) be within the period of 7 years ending with—

(i) in the case of a lifetime election, the date on which the election is made;

(ii) in the case of a death election, the date of the

deceased's death, and

(c) meet the condition in subsection (3).

(3) The condition is that—

(a) in the case of a lifetime election—

(i) the person making the election was, on the specified date, married to or in a civil partnership with the spouse or civil partner, and

(ii) the spouse or civil partner was, on the specified date, a long-term UK resident;

(b) in the case of a death election—

(i) the person who is, by virtue of the election, to be treated as a long-term UK resident was, on the specified date, married to or in a civil partnership with the deceased, and

(ii) the deceased was, on the specified date, a long-term UK resident.

(4) A death election may only be made within—

(a) the period of 2 years beginning with the date of the deceased's death, or

(b) such longer period as an officer of Revenue and Customs may in the particular case allow.

(5) Subsection (6) applies if—

(a) an election is made under section 267ZC,

(b) a disposition is made, or another event occurs, during the period beginning with the date on which the election first has effect and ending with the date on which the election is made, and

(c) the effect of the election is that the disposition or event gives rise to a transfer of value.

(6) This Act applies with the following modifications in relation to the transfer of value—

(a) subsections (1) and (6)(c) of section 216 (delivery of accounts)

have effect as if the period specified in subsection (6)(c) of that section were the period of 12 months from the end of the month in which the election is made, and

(b) sections 226 (payment: general rules) and 233 (interest on unpaid tax) have effect as if the transfer were made at the time when the election is made.

(7) An election under section 267ZC cannot be revoked.

(8) If a person who made a lifetime election is, for a period of 10 successive tax years beginning after the date on which the election is made, not resident in the United Kingdom, the election ceases to have effect at the end of that period.

(9) For the purposes of this section—

"death election" means an election made under section 267ZC in circumstances where Condition B in subsection (4) of that section is met;

"lifetime election" means any other election made under section 267ZC.

267ZE Subject of domicile election treated as a long-term UK resident

(1) This section applies where an election under section 267ZA has effect in relation to a person immediately before 6 April 2025 (whether the election was made before or after that date).

(2) The person is treated for the purposes of this Act (so far as would not otherwise be the case)—

(a) as being a long-term UK resident, and

(b) as having been one at all times on and after 6 April 2025.

(3) But if the person is not resident in the United Kingdom for a relevant lapse period beginning at any time after the election is made, subsection (2) ceases to apply to them at the end of that period.

(4) In subsection (3) "relevant lapse period" means—

(a) if the election was made before 30 October 2024, a period of 4 successive tax years;

(b) if the election was made on or after that date, a period of 10 successive tax years."

4.5.3.27.3 Detail

This is essentially a consequential amendment.

4.5.3.27.4 Effective Date

The effective date is 6 April 2025.

4.5.3.28 *Paragraph 28 Consequential amendments to section 272 (general interpretation)*

4.5.3.28.1 Overview

Paragraph 28 contains consequential amendments to section 272 (general interpretation). It amends the definition of "foreign- owned" to substitute conditions relating to long- term UK residence. It also inserts new definitions of "long-term UK resident", "tax-years" and "the tax year 2025-26".

4.5.3.28.2 Legislation

Paragraph 28 reads as follows:

"(1) Section 272 (general interpretation) is amended as follows.
(2) The existing text becomes subsection (1).
(3) In subsection (1), in the definition of "foreign-owned"—
(a) in paragraph (a), for "domiciled outside the United Kingdom" substitute "not a long-term UK resident";

(b) for paragraph (b) substitute—
"(b) if the property is comprised in a settlement, in the case of which the settlor—

(i) is alive and is at that time not a long-term UK resident,

(ii) died on or after 6 April 2025 and was not a long-term UK resident immediately before they died, or

(iii) died before 6 April 2025 and was domiciled outside the United Kingdom when the property became comprised in the settlement, and section 48ZA(9) (accumulation of income) applies for the purposes of this paragraph as it applies for the purposes of section 48ZA (4)."

(4) Also in subsection (1), at the appropriate places insert— 15
""long-term UK resident" has the meaning given by sections 6A to 6C;";
""tax year" means a year beginning with 6 April and ending with the following 5 April;";
""the tax year 2025-26" means the tax year beginning with 6 April 2025 (and any corresponding expression in which two years are similarly mentioned is to be read in the same way);".
(5) After subsection (1) insert—
"(2) A reference in this Act to a settlor's being alive or dying is to be read, in relation to a settlor who is a body corporate, as a reference (respectively) to the body's being in existence or ceasing to exist.""

4.5.3.28.3 Detail

It is provided that a reference to a settlor's being alive or dying is to be read in relation to a corporate settlor as a reference to the body being in existence or ceasing to exist. Insofar as this change affects the interpretation of subsection 201(1)(d) which relates to the settlor's liability to IHT on settled property where the trustees are non-resident, this clarifies the existing law.

***4.5.3.28.4* Effective Date**

The effective date is 6 April 2025.

4.5.3.29 Paragraph 29 Amendment of Schedule A1

***4.5.3.29.1* Overview**

This paragraph amends Schedule A 1.

4.5.3.29.2 Legislation

Paragraph 29 reads as follows.

29(1) Schedule A1 (non-excluded overseas property) is amended as follows.

(2) In paragraph 1, for "48(3)(a)" substitute "48ZA".

(3) In paragraph 5(2)(a), for "or 48(3)(a), (3A) or substitute "section 48(4) or section 48ZA".

Detail

This amends Schedule A 1 as noted above.

4.5.3.29.3 Effective Date

The effective date is 6 April 2025.

4.5.3.30 *Paragraph 30 Consequential amendment to Schedule 4 (Maintenance funds for historic buildings etc)*

4.5.3.30.1 **Overview**

Paragraph 30 makes a consequential amendment to Schedule 4 (Maintenance funds for historic buildings etc) to replace the reference to domicile with a reference to long-term UK residence.

4.5.3.30.2 Legislation

Paragraph 30 reads as follows.

> "30 In Schedule 4 (maintenance funds for historic buildings etc), in paragraph 10(8), for "domiciled in the United Kingdom" substitute "a long-term UK resident"."

4.5.3.30.3 Detail

This is a consequential amendment following the move away from a domicile-based system for IHT to a long-term residence-based system.

4.5.3.30.4 Effective Date

The effective date is 6 April 2025.

4.5.3.31 *Paragraph 31 Amendment of section 102 FA 1986 rules for gifts with reservation of benefit*

4.5.3.31.1 Overview

Paragraph 31 amends section 102 FA 1986 rules for gifts with reservation of benefit.

4.5.3.31.2 Legislation

Paragraph 31 provides:

> "(1) Section 102 of FA 1986 (gifts with reservation) is amended as follows. 30
> (2) In subsection (1), for "(5) and (6)" substitute "(5), (6) and (7A)".
> (3) After subsection (7) insert—
> "(7A) This section does not apply if—
> the disposal of property by way of gift took place before 30 October 2024,
> (b) the property became settled property by virtue of the gift,
> (c) immediately before 30 October 2024, the property was excluded property for the purposes of the 1984 Act by virtue of section 48(3) or (3A) (as it had effect at that time), and

(d) at all times on and after 30 October 2024 and before the relevant time, the property—

(i) was situated outside the United Kingdom and was not property to which paragraph 2 or 3 of Schedule A1 to the 1984 Act applied (overseas property with value attributable to UK residential property), or

(ii) was a holding in an authorised unit trust or a share in an open-ended investment company (within the meaning, in either case, of the 1984 Act).

(7B) In subsection (7A), "the relevant time" means—

(a) if the property ceases to meet the condition in subsection (2) at any time before the donor's death, that time;

(b) otherwise, the time of the donor's death.""

4.5.3.31.3 Detail

Paragraph 31 amends section 102 FA 1986 rules for gifts with reservation of benefit and provides that section 102 FA 1986 does not apply to property settled before 30 October 2024 if it was excluded property by virtue of subsections 48(3) or (3A) immediately before that date, and provided it subsequently remains excluded property (under the pre-6 April 2025 rules)

4.5.3.31.4 Effective Date

The effective date is 6 April 2025.

4.5.3.32 Paragraph 32-35 Schedule 15 to FA 2004 (pre-owned assets charge)

4.5.3.32.1 Overview

Paragraphs 32 to 35 provide make amendments to Schedule 15 of the Finance Act 2004 (pre-owned assets charge) in consequence to the changes effected by paragraph 30 to the rules to Gifts with Reservation.

4.5.3.32.2 Legislation

The legislation reads as follows:

32 Schedule 15 to FA 2004 (pre-owned assets charge) is amended as follows.

33 In paragraph 11 (exemptions from charge), in sub-paragraph (5), after paragraph (b) insert—

"(ba) would fall to be so treated but for section 102(7A) of the 1986 Act (cases where property was excluded property under the old inheritance tax regime),".

34 In the italic heading before paragraph 12, for "resident or domiciled outside the United Kingdom" substitute "non-UK resident or not a long-term UK resident".

35 (1) Paragraph 12 is amended as follows.

(2) In sub-paragraph (2), for "domiciled outside the United Kingdom" substitute "not a long-term UK resident".

(3) Omit sub-paragraph (3).

(4) For sub-paragraph (4) substitute—

"(4) In this paragraph, "long-term UK resident" has the same meaning as in IHTA 1984."

4.5.3.32.3 **Detail**

Paragraphs 32 to 35 provide make amendments to Schedule 15 of the Finance Act 2004 (pre-owned assets charge) in consequence to the changes effected by paragraph 30 to the rules to Gifts with Reservation.

These amendments substitute references to domicile with references to long-term UK residence and ensure that property which is not subject to the gift with reservation rules will not be subject to the pre-owned assets charge where there was excluded property under the old rules.

4.5.3.32.4 **Effective Date**

The effective date is 6 April 2025.

4.5.3.33 *Paragraph 36 Section 41 of the Constitutional Reform and Governance Act 2010 (tax status of MPs and members of the House of Lords)*

4.5.3.33.1 Overview

This deals with the tax status of MPs and certain Lords.

Not many MPs and Lords are currently ESPs so this is not expected to apply to many likely clients. However, it is possible that a sportsperson from the Commonwealth might be appointed to the House of Lords or to one of the Bishoprics whose incumbent sits in the House of Lords. If so they would need to consider the tax position carefully. Hence the inclusion of this information.

The Explanatory Notes from 2010 tell us that:

"Section 41: Tax status of MPs and members of the House of Lords

Section 41 provides that MPs and most members of the House of Lords are to be deemed resident, ordinarily resident and domiciled in the UK ("ROD") for the purposes of income tax, capital gains tax and inheritance tax. This means that they will be liable to pay these taxes in the UK on their worldwide income, gains, and assets regardless of their actual status in the UK, and that they will be unable to access the remittance basis of taxation.

The section provides that MPs and peers are deemed ROD for the whole of each tax year in which they are a member of either House (including those tax years in which they are a member for only part of the year). This means that they will be deemed ROD from the start of the tax year in which they become a member of that House and to the end of the tax year in which they cease to be a member. Subsection (7) provides that the section applies from the start of the tax year 2010-2011, but under subsection (8)(a) it will only apply in that tax year to MPs who are members of the new Parliament meeting in 2010. Subsection (9) defines a tax year for the purposes of inheritance tax as running from 6 April to 5 April (the phrase is already defined in other legislation for the other taxes).

Section 41 applies to a person who has been elected as an MP after they have taken the oath of allegiance at the start of a new Parliament (as they are required to do under the Parliamentary Oaths Act 1866). For the purposes of the section, an MP ceases to be a member when the Parliament to which they were elected has been dissolved or their seat is otherwise vacated (by resignation, death or disqualification).

For the purposes of section 41, a member of the House of Lords is someone who is entitled to receive a writ of summons. Subsection (6)(a) specifically disapplies the provision for members of the judiciary who are disqualified from sitting and voting in the House under section 137 of the Constitutional Reform Act 2005. If such an individual were to leave the House on assuming judicial office during the course of a tax year, or return to the House after retiring during the course of a tax year, they will be deemed ROD for the whole of the tax year in question. Subsection (6)(b) disapplies the provision for the Lords Spiritual.

Subsection (10) provides that any temporary suspension or disqualification from entitlement to receive a writ imposed in the circumstances set out in paragraphs (a) or (b) are discounted when determining whether a person is entitled to receive a writ of summons (and is therefore a member of the House of Lords for the purposes of the section). While a peer is subject to such temporary suspension or disqualification, the deeming provision would still apply to them."

Paragraph 35 removes subsections 41(2) and (3) of the Constitutional Reform and Governance Act 2010 so that existing references to domicile are removed. It adds a new subsection 41(2) to provide that members of the House of Commons or the House of Lords are for income tax, capital gains tax and IHT purposes treated as UK resident, and for IHT purposes long-term UK resident, for any year during which they are a member.

Constitutional Reform and Governance Act 2010

4.5.3.33.2 Legislation

Paragraph 36 reads as follows:

"In section 41 of the Constitutional Reform and Governance Act 2010 (tax status of MPs and members of the House of Lords), for subsections (2) and (3) substitute—

"(2) The person is to be treated—

a. as resident in the United Kingdom for the whole of that tax year for the purposes of income tax, capital gains tax and inheritance tax, and

b. as a long-term UK resident at all times in that tax year for the purposes of inheritance tax."

4.5.3.33.3 Detail

The tax adviser should be aware of this legislation in case it could apply but any actual case will require careful consideration by reference to the particular circumstances involved.

4.5.3.33.4 Effective Date

The effective date is 6 April 2025.

4.5.3.34 *Paragraph 37-43 Consequential amendments to the Inheritance Tax (Delivery of Accounts) (Excepted Estates) Regulations 2004 (S.I. 2004/2543)*

***4.5.3.34.1* Overview**

Paragraphs 37 to 43 provide for consequential amendments to the Inheritance Tax (Delivery of Accounts) (Excepted Estates) Regulations 2004 (S.I. 2004/2543) to substitute reference to domicile with references to long- term residence.

Inheritance Tax (Delivery of Accounts) (Excepted Estates) Regulations 2004 (S.I. 2004/2543)

It is important that advisers ensure that their procedures are updated to take account of this. Rather than domicile this should now be geared to long term residence status.

***4.5.3.34.2* Legislation**

The paragraphs in question read as follows.

"37 The Inheritance Tax (Delivery of Accounts) (Excepted Estates) Regulations 2004 are amended in accordance with paragraphs 37 to 42.

38 In regulation 2 (interpretation)—

(a) the existing text becomes paragraph (1);

(b) after that paragraph insert—

"(2) A reference in these Regulations to a person's being domiciled in the United Kingdom includes a reference to the person's being treated as so domiciled for the purposes of the 1984 Act."

39 (1) Regulation 4 (excepted estates) is amended as follows.

(2) In paragraphs (2)(a) and (3)(a), for ", domiciled in the United Kingdom" substitute "and was a long-term UK resident immediately before their death".

(3) For paragraph (5)(b) substitute—

"(b) that person—

(i) was not a long-term UK resident at any time on or after 6 April 2025, and

(ii) was not domiciled in the United Kingdom at any time before that date;"

40 In regulation 5 (spouse, civil partner and charity transfers), in paragraph (2), for the words from "was not domiciled" to the end substitute "—

(a)was, at any time in the period beginning with 6 April 2025 and ending with the time of the transfer, not a long-term UK resident,

(b) was, at any time before 6 April 2025, not domiciled in the United Kingdom."

41 In regulation 5A (IHT threshold), in paragraph (4)(a), for "died domiciled in the United Kingdom" substitute "was a long-term UK resident immediately before their death".

42 In regulation 6 (production of information), in the heading, for "domiciled in the United Kingdom" substitute "a long-term UK resident".

43 (1) Regulation 6A (production of information) is amended as follows.

In the heading, for "deceased domiciled outside the United Kingdom" substitute "cases within regulation 4(5)".

(3) In paragraph (2)(g), for "domicile" substitute "place of tax residence".

4.5.3.34.3 Detail

These are essentially consequential changes flowing from the change to a long-term residence basis for IHT as a replacement for a domiciled based system.

4.5.3.34.4 Effective Date

The effective date is 6 April 2025.

4.5.3.35 Paragraph 44 Inheritance Tax (Delivery of Accounts) (Excepted Settlements) Regulations 2008 (S.I. 2008/606)

4.5.3.35.1 Overview

Paragraph 44 provides for consequential amendments to the Inheritance Tax (Delivery of Accounts) (Excepted Settlements) Regulations 2008 (S.I. 2008/606) with similar effect.

It is important that advisers ensure that their procedures are updated to take account of this. Rather than domicile this should now be geared to long term residence status.

4.5.3.35.2 Legislation

Paragraph 44 provides:

"(1) In the Inheritance Tax (Delivery of Accounts) (Excepted Settlements) Regulations 2008, regulation 4 (excepted settlement) is amended as follows.

(2) In paragraph (3)(a), for "is domiciled in the United Kingdom" substitute "meets the condition in paragraph (3A)".

(3) After paragraph (3) insert—

"(3A) The condition in this paragraph is—

(a) in relation to times on or after 6 April 2025, that the settlor is a long-term UK resident;
(b) in relation to times before that date, that the settlor is domiciled in the United Kingdom (or treated as such for the purposes of the 1984 Act)."

4.5.3.35.3 Detail

These are essentially consequential changes flowing from the change to a long-term residence basis for IHT as a replacement for a domiciled based system.

4.5.3.35.4 Effective Date

The effective date is 6 April 2025. See paragraph 45.

4.5.3.36 Part 2: Commencement and transitional provision

Part 2 deals with commencement and transitional provision in respect of the Part 1 of the schedule. These broadly are effects on 6 April 2025. This is an exception for paragraph 26 which comes into force essentially on 6 April 2032.

Paragraph 45 contains commencement provisions. The amendments in part 1 of the Schedule come into force on 6 April 2025 with the exception of paragraph 26 which comes into force on **6 April 2032**.

4.5.3.37 Paragraph 45

4.5.3.37.1 Overview

Paragraph 45 contains commencement provisions. The amendments in part 1 of the Schedule come into force on 6 April 2025 with the exception of paragraph 26

Paragraph 26, which repeals subsections 267ZA and 267ZB (domicile elections) comes into force on 6 April 2032, at which time those provisions will have no further purpose.

4.5.3.37.2 Legislation

45(1) Part 1 of this Schedule, other than paragraph 26, comes into force on 6 April 2025.
(2) Paragraph 26 (repeal of sections 267ZA and 267ZB) comes into force on 6 April 2032.
(3) The amendments made by paragraph 12 to section 74A of IHTA 1984 (arrangements involving acquisition of interest in settled property etc) have effect where the relevant time (as defined in section 74C(5) of that Act) is on or after 6 April 2025 (even if the arrangements were entered into before that date).
(4) The amendment made by paragraph 19 to section 136 of IHTA 1984 (transactions of close companies) has effect in relation to relevant transactions (within the meaning of that section) on or after 6 April 2025.

(5) The amendments made by paragraphs 37 to 43 to the Inheritance Tax (Delivery of Accounts) (Excepted Estates) Regulations 2004 (S.I. 2004/2543) have effect in relation to deaths occurring on or after 6 April 2025.

(6) The amendments made by paragraph 44 to the Inheritance Tax (Delivery of Accounts) (Excepted Settlements) Regulations 2008 (S.I. 2008/606) have effect in relation to chargeable events (within the meaning of regulation 2 of those Regulations) occurring on or after 6 April 2025.

4.5.3.37.3 **Detail**

As noted above this deals with commencement of the amendments made by Part 1 of the Schedule. Essentially, they came into effect on 6 April 2025 except for paragraph 26 which comes into force on 6 April 2032.

4.5.3.37.4 **Effective Date**

6 April 2025 see paragraph 45

4.5.3.38 Paragraph 46 Long term residence for certain pre-30 October 2024 leavers

4.5.3.38.1 Overview

Paragraph 45 contains transitional rules for certain individuals who have left the UK. There are certain conditions for this treatment to apply discussed below. This is an important provision for certain leavers.

4.5.3.38.2 **Legislation**

Paragraph 46 reads as follows

"46 (1) An individual who would otherwise be a long-term UK resident at any time in a given tax year ("the relevant tax year") is treated for the purposes of IHTA 1984 as not being a long-term UK resident at that time if the individual—

(a) was not domiciled in the United Kingdom on 30 October 2024,

(b)has been resident in the United Kingdom for no tax year in the period beginning with the tax year 2025-26 and ending with the relevant tax year, and

(c)either—

(i)was resident in the United Kingdom for none of the 3 tax years immediately preceding the relevant tax year, or

(ii)was resident in the United Kingdom for fewer than 15 of the 20 tax years immediately preceding the relevant tax year.

(2)For the purposes of sub-paragraph (1)(a), in determining where an individual was domiciled on 30 October 2024, ignore section 267 (deemed domicile) and sections 267ZA and 267ZB (domicile elections) of IHTA 1984."

4.5.3.38.3 Details

Paragraph 46 contains transitional rules for certain individuals who have left the UK. An individual who is not UK domiciled on 30 October 2024 and who is not UK resident for the tax year 2025-26 or any later year will not be treated as long-term UK resident under the new test in section 6A. Instead they will continue to be outside the scope of IHT in relation to their non-UK assets provided they do not meet the existing deemed domicile test in subsection 267(1)(b) which required them to have 15 years UK residence.

4.5.3.38.4 **Effective Date**

6 April 2025. See paragraph 44

4.5.3.39 Paragraph 47

4.5.3.39.1 Overview

Paragraph 47 deals withe position after its amendment of section 81 IHTA by paragraph 15 (see above) where property comprised in the settlement ceased to be so comprised in the first settlement before 6 April 2025.

4.5.3.39.2 **Legislation**

Paragraph 47 reads as follows.

> 47 The amendment of section 81(1) of IHTA 1984 by paragraph 15(b) of this Schedule (trusts on which property moving between settlements is held) is to be disregarded in construing section 81(1) in a case where the property in question ceased to be comprised in the first settlement before 6 April 2025.

4.5.3.39.3 **Detail**

Paragraph 47 (see also paragraph 15) provides that the additional wording to section 81 ("(but held on the trusts of the second)") is to be disregarded in relation to property that ceased to be comprised in the first settlement before 6 April 2025.

4.5.3.39.4 Effective date

6 April 2025. See paragraph 44.

4.5.3.40 Paragraph 48 Savings

4.5.3.40.1 Overview

Paragraph 48 provides savings where consideration is given to a person's domicile status for periods before 6 April 2025 and the application of DDCs.

4.5.3.40.2 **Legislation**

Paragraph 48 reads as follows

48 The repeal of section 267 of IHTA 1984 (persons treated as domiciled in United Kingdom) by paragraph 23 is to be disregarded—

(1)

(a)in determining for the purposes of that Act any question as to where a person was domiciled at any time before 6 April 2025, and

(b) in determining any question as to where a person is treated as domiciled for the purposes of that Act at any time on or after that date, so far as that question is relevant to the application of any double taxation arrangements.

(2) In sub-paragraph (1)(b), "double taxation arrangements" means arrangements having effect under section 158 of IHTA 1984]

4.5.3.40.3 Details

Sub-paragraph 48(1) saves repealed section 267 when considering a person's domicile before 6 April 2025 and also in determining questions relating to a person's domicile for the purposes of the IHTA when considering the application of double taxation arrangements at any time after that date. This provides for the continued application of existing double tax conventions having effect under section 158 with reference to an individual's fiscal domicile for IHT purposes.

4.5.3.40.4 Effective Date

6 April 2025 – See paragraph 44.

45(1) Part 1 of this Schedule, other than paragraph 26, comes into force on 6 April 2025.

(2) Paragraph 26 (repeal of sections 267ZA and 267ZB) comes into force on 6 April 2032.

(3) The amendments made by paragraph 12 to section 74A of IHTA 1984 (arrangements involving acquisition of interest in settled property etc) have effect where the relevant time (as defined in section 74C(5) of that Act) is on or after 6 April 2025 (even if the arrangements were entered into before that date).

(4) The amendment made by paragraph 19 to section 136 of IHTA 1984 (transactions of close companies) has effect in relation to relevant transactions (within the meaning of that section) on or after 6 April 2025.

(5) The amendments made by paragraphs 36 to 42 to the Inheritance Tax (Delivery of Accounts) (Excepted Estates) Regulations 2004 (S.I. 2004/2543) have effect in relation to deaths occurring on or after 6 April 2025.

(6) The amendments made by paragraph 43 to the Inheritance Tax (Delivery of Accounts) (Excepted Settlements) Regulations 2008 (S.I. 2008/606) have effect in relation to chargeable events (within the meaning of regulation 2 of those Regulations) occurring on or after 6 April 2025.

Certain pre-commencement emigrants treated as not being long-term UK residents

46 (1) An individual who would otherwise be a long-term UK resident at any time in a given tax year ("the relevant tax year") is treated for the purposes of IHTA 1984 as not being a long-term UK resident at that time if the individual—

(a) was not domiciled in the United Kingdom on 30 October 2024,

(b) (b) has not been resident in the United Kingdom for any tax year in the period beginning with the tax year 2025-26 and ending with the relevant tax year, and

(c) either—

(i) was not resident in the United Kingdom for any of the 3 tax years immediately preceding the relevant tax year, or

(ii) was not resident in the United Kingdom for more than 14 15of the 20 tax years immediately preceding the relevant tax year.

(2) For the purposes of sub-paragraph (1)(a), in determining where an individual was domiciled on 30 October 2024, ignore section 267 (deemed domicile) and sections 267ZA and 267ZB (domicile elections) of IHTA 1984.

Property moving between settlements

47 The amendment of section 81(1) of IHTA 1984 by paragraph 15(b) of this Schedule (trusts on which property moving between settlements is held) is to be disregarded in construing section 81(1) in a case where the property in question ceased to be comprised in the first settlement before 6 April 2025.

Settlor's death etc: application to bodies corporate

48 The insertion of section 272(2) of IHTA 1984 by paragraph 28(5) of this Schedule (meaning of references to dying or being alive in the case of corporate settlors) is to be disregarded in construing section 201(1)(d) of IHTA 1984 in relation to property that became comprised in the settlement before 6 April 2025.

Appendix 1: ANNEXE

Some pertinent matters.

1. *Residence before the SRT*

General

1. Before 2013 when the Finance Act 2013 introduced the statutory residence test ("**SRT**"), there was no general statutory provision for the determination of an individual's tax residence. Accordingly, case law and practice had to be relied on. There was some specific provision e.g. section 334 ICTA 1988 [146] but in the main the position was determined by case law and practice. This was not always clear and fair.

2. The Inland Revenue produced an Administrative Code said to be based on the case law which was often determinative in many cases. This was published as a revenue pamphlet numbered IR 20 with the title "Residents' and Non-Residents' Liability to Tax in the UK". It has since been withdrawn. As IR20 may be relevant in determining residence over a twenty-year period (e.g. for long term residence) which can stretch back before 2013, extracts from IR20 are set out below.

3. Prior to the enactment of FA 1993, the importance of the distinction between taxpayers who had available accommodation [147] in the United Kingdom and those who did not was emphasised in IR 20. The Revenue view seemed to be that prima facie a person who was present in the United Kingdom at any time in a year of assessment when that person had accommodation available in the UK was UK resident. [148]The intention of the 1993 according to the Chief Secretary to the Treasury was to remove the available accommodation rule. [149]

4. There was also another concept that was used which was effectively abolished by Finance Act 2013 for tax. This was ordinary residence. The distinction between this and "residence" was not always clear.

---

[146] UK citizen abroad for a temporary purpose see *Reed v Clark* [1985]

[147] The Inland Revenue said at paragraph 4.2 of IR 20 ""available accommodation" has never been defined in the Taxes Act. Whether accommodation in the United Kingdom was treated as available for your use depended on all the circumstances." They continued at 4.3 "for accommodation to be treated as available you have to be able actually to use it as and when you wished. You did not have to own or rent a house, apartment or other accommodation for it to be available for your use. For example, of property owned or rented by your husband or wife would usually be treated as available for your use…."

[148] Shipwright and Price *UK Taxation And Intellectual Property* 2nd edition 1996 Sweet & Maxwell Page 30ff ISBN 0 421 475 609

[149] Inland Revenue Press Release 16 March 1993 [1993] STI 468

Ordinary Residence

There was also another concept that was used for tax purposes before it was abolished by Finance Act 2013. This was ordinary residence. The distinction between this and resonant simplicity was not always clear. Ordinary residence was relevant to section 334 ICTA (UK citizen abroad for a temporary purpose).

This term was used in tax legislation till FA 2013 in effect "retired" it. It was a defined term. It is used in other parts of the Law which also suffer from the lack of a definition.

The Home Office [150] say this about Ordinary Residence:

> "The term ordinary residence is not defined in the immigration or nationality acts and has not been defined in any Act of Parliament [including for tax purposes]. The leading case in this area is R v Barnet LBC ex parte Shah [1983] 1 All ER 226. The House of Lords found that the concept of ordinary residence implied:
>
> - ordinary residence is established if there is a regular habitual mode of life in a particular place for the time being, whether of short or long duration, the continuity of which has persisted apart from temporary or occasional absences, residence must be both:
>   - voluntary
>   - adopted for a settled purpose
> - a person can be ordinarily resident in more than one country at the same time, distinguishing it from domicile
> - ordinary residence is proven more by objective evidence than evidence of an individual's state of mind at a point in time".

This seems a helpful outline for the earlier tax position as well as for nationality purposes. This may be for a different purpose, but the comments appear relevant.

Significant Change - FA 1991

1. FA 1991 introduced significant changes to CGT and Offshore Trusts.
2. Section 80 FA 1981 modified the position for 1981-82 and following tax years. It applied where the trustees were not resident or ordinarily resident in the UK in the relevant tax year.
3. This was repealed by TCGA Schedule 12 and essentially became sections 86 and 87 TCGA which are still around today. This also dealt with some of the difficulties following the case of *Leedale v Lewis* [1982] STC 835

---

[150] https://assets.publishing.service.gov.uk/government/uploads/system/uploads/attachment_data/file/655489/Nationality-policy-assessing-ordinary-residence-v2.0EXT.pdf

4. Section 89 FA 1991 dealt with settlements where the Settlor has an interest in the settlement. This was afforced by Schedule 16. This is essentially section 86 today.
5. Section 90 FA 1991 dealt with beneficiaries. Beneficiaries were charged on a matching basis where the beneficiary had received a capital payment to trust gains which had not already been taxed on the Settlor. This was dealt with in Schedule 17. This is essentially section 87 TCGA today.

2. *Residence of the Trustees of the Settlement*

Brief Summary of the Rules

1. There have been various changes to the rules determining the residence of trusts for Income Tax and Capital Gains Tax over time. In particular, before amendment of the relevant provisions by Finance Act 2006, the rules for determining trustee residence for Income Tax and Capital Gains Tax purposes were different. The position in respect of Income Tax was also impacted by the introduction of section 110 Finance Act 1989.
   The rules can be broadly summarised as follows:
   a. Prior to 2007/08, a settlement with non-resident trustees would be regarded as resident for Capital Gains Tax if a majority of the trustees were UK resident and the administration of the trust was carried on in the UK,
   b. Up to and including 1988/89, a non-UK settlement would only be regarded as UK resident for Income Tax purposes if all of the trustees were UK resident (see Dawson v IRC [1989] STC 473).
   c. Between1989/90and 2006/07, a settlement with non-UK resident trustees was regarded as UK resident for Income Tax purposes where the settlor was resident or ordinarily resident at the time the settlement was created.
   d. From 2007/08 onwards, for both Income Tax and Capital Gains Tax purposes, where trustees included a mix of UK and non-UK trustees, the trust is regarded as UK resident where the settlor of the trust was UK resident or UK domiciled at the time the settlement was created (sections476 ITA 2007 and s69(2B) TCGA1992).

Appendix 2: Inland Revenue Pamphlet IR 20 Extracts

1. *Part I: Meaning of residence, ordinary residence and domicile*

Residence and ordinary residence

1.1 The terms "**residence**" and "**ordinary residence**" are not defined in the Taxes Acts. The guidelines to their meaning in this Chapter and in Chapters 2 (residence status of those leaving the United Kingdom) and 3 (those coming to the United Kingdom) are largely based on rulings of the Courts. This booklet sets out the main factors that are taken into account, but a final decision on your residence status can only be made on the facts in your particular case.

Residence

1.2 To be regarded as **resident** in the United Kingdom you must normally be physically present in the country at some time in the tax year. You will always be resident if you are here for **183** days or more in the year. **There are no exceptions to this**. A count is made of the total number of days you spend in the United Kingdom – it does not matter if you come and go several times during the year or if you are here for one stay of 183 days or more. The days of arrival in and departure from the United Kingdom are normally ignored in counting the days spent in the United Kingdom. If you are here for less than 183 days, you may still be treated as resident for the year under other tests (see Chapter 3, and in particular paragraph 3.3).

Ordinary Residence

1.3 If you are resident in the United Kingdom year after year, you are treated as ordinarily resident here. You may be resident but not ordinarily resident in the United Kingdom for a tax year, if, for example, you normally live outside the United Kingdom but are in this country for 183 days or more in the year. Or you may be ordinarily resident but not resident for a tax year if for example, you usually live in the United Kingdom but have gone abroad for a long holiday and do not set foot in the United Kingdom during that year.

Residence in both the United Kingdom and another country

1.4 It is possible to be resident (or ordinary resident) in both the United Kingdom and some other country (or countries) at the same time. If you are resident (or ordinarily resident) in another country, this does **not** mean that you cannot **also** be resident (or ordinarily resident) in the United Kingdom. Where, however, you are resident both in the United Kingdom and a country with which the United Kingdom has a **double taxation agreement**, there may be special provisions in the agreement for treating you as a resident of only one of the countries for the purposes of the agreement (see paragraph 10.2).

Leaving, or coming to, the United Kingdom part way through a tax year

1.5 You are either resident or not resident in the United Kingdom for the **whole** of a tax year. But, by concession, the tax year is **split**, so that you can be treated as resident in the United Kingdom for part of a year, where

- you have been not ordinarily resident in the United Kingdom and you come to live here permanently or to stay for at least three years. You are treated as resident from the date of your arrival: or
- you come to the United Kingdom to take up employment which is expected to last for at least two years. You are treated as resident from the date of your arrival; or
- you leave the United Kingdom to live abroad permanently and on your departure you are not ordinarily resident in the United Kingdom. You are treated as resident up to and including the date of your departure; or
- you leave the United Kingdom to take up full-time employment abroad and meet certain conditions (see paragraphs 2.2-2.3). You are treated as resident up to and including the date of your departure (and from the date when you return to the United Kingdom).

Where a tax year is split this way, your tax liabilities which are affected by residence status are calculated on the basis of the period you are treated as resident here (see also paragraph 6.4).

Married people

1.6 If you are married, your residence status depends on your own circumstances and need not be the same as that of your spouse. Suppose, for example, your husband or wife leaves the United Kingdom for full-time employment abroad and you accompany or later join your spouse. If you yourself return to this country to resume living here without having been away for a full tax year, you are regarded as remaining resident and ordinarily resident here, even if your spouse is treated as not resident and not ordinarily resident. (In the case of married women, see paragraphs 5.6-5.7 for information on domicile, and paragraphs 8.5-8.6 on entitlement to tax allowances and reliefs).

2. *Leaving the United Kingdom*

Short absences

2.1 You are resident and ordinarily resident in the United Kingdom if you usually live in this country and only go abroad for short periods – for example, holiday or on business trips.

Working abroad

2.2 If you leave the United Kingdom to work full-time abroad under a contract of employment, you are treated as not resident and not ordinarily resident if you meet **all** the following conditions

- your absence from the United Kingdom and your employment abroad both last for at least a whole tax year
- during your absence any visits you make to the United Kingdom
  - total less than 183 days in any tax year, and
  - average less than 91 days a tax year (the average is taken over the period of absence up to a maximum of four years; any days spent in the United Kingdom because of exceptional circumstances beyond your control, for example the illness of yourself or a member of your immediate family, are not normally counted for this purpose)
- for tax years before 1993-94, where there was accommodation in the United Kingdom available for your use, either all duties of your employment were performed abroad, or any duties you performed in the United Kingdom were incidental to your duties abroad (see paragraphs 6.7-6.8 for the meaning of "incidental" Chapter 4 on the meaning of "available accommodation").

2.3 If you meet all of the above conditions, you are treated as not resident and not ordinarily resident in the United Kingdom from the day after you leave the United Kingdom to the day before you return to the United Kingdom at the end of your employment abroad and as resident and ordinarily resident from that date.

If you do not meet all these conditions, you remain resident and ordinarily resident unless paragraphs 2.7-2.8 apply to you. Special rules apply in the case of Crown employees and employees of the European Community (see paragraph 2.11).

Accompanying spouse

2.4 If you are the husband or wife of someone who leaves the United Kingdom within the terms of paragraph 2.2 and you accompany or later join your spouse abroad, you may also by concession be treated as not resident and not ordinarily resident from the day after your departure to the day before your return, even if you are not yourself in full-time employment abroad. This applies where:

- you are abroad for a complete tax year, and
- during your absence any visits you make to the United Kingdom
  - total less than 183 days in the tax year
  - average less than 91 days a tax year (the average is taken over the period of absence up to a maximum of four years; any days spent in the United

Kingdom because of exceptional circumstances beyond your control, for example the illness of yourself or a member of your immediate family, are not normally counted for this purpose).

Where the tax years of your departure or return are split in this way, your tax liabilities which are affected by residence status are calculated on the basis of the period you are treated as resident in the United Kingdom.

2.5 For tax years before 1993-94, a further condition applied. If you had accommodation in the United Kingdom available for your use, you were resident for any tax year – or part of a tax year, in the case of the years of your departure or return – during which you made a visit to this country. The split year treatment applied where you made no visits to the United Kingdom between the date of your departure and the following 5 April, or, for the year of return, between 6 April and the date of return. You were treated as not ordinarily resident from the day after leaving the United Kingdom to the day before returning, provided that

- your absence was for three years or more, and
- visits here averaged less than 91 days a tax year.

If you absence was expected to be for three years or more but was cut short because your spouse's employment abroad was terminated unexpectedly, you might still be treated as not ordinarily resident for the period of your absence, provided that this shorter absence included a whole tax year and any visits to the United Kingdom averaged less than 91 days a tax year.

Leaving the United Kingdom permanently

2.6 If you go abroad permanently, you will be treated as remaining resident and ordinarily resident if your visits to the United Kingdom average 91 days or more a year.

For tax years before 1993-94, if you went abroad permanently but had accommodation in the United Kingdom available for your use, you were treated as resident for any tax year during which you visited the United Kingdom (see Chapter 4 for details of when accommodation was regarded as available). The length of the visit did not matter. If you came to the United Kingdom in most tax years, you remained ordinarily resident.

2.7 If you claim that you are no longer resident and ordinarily resident, you will normally be asked to give some evidence that you have left the United Kingdom permanently – for example, that you have taken steps to acquire accommodation abroad to live in as a permanent home, and if you continue to own property in the United Kingdom, the reason is consistent with your stated aim of permanent residence abroad. If you can provide this, you may be treated as **provisionally** not resident and not ordinarily resident from the day after the date of your departure. Normally this provisional ruling is confirmed after you have lived abroad for a whole tax year, as long as your visits to the United Kingdom since leaving have averaged less than 91 days a tax year.

2.8 If you do not have this evidence, a decision is postponed for up to three years. The decision will be based on what has actually happened since you left the United Kingdom. Until then you are **provisionally** treated as remaining resident in the United Kingdom. You continue to receive tax allowances and reliefs (see paragraph 8.1). Your tax bill may be adjusted when the final decision has been made.

Tax treatment after leaving the United Kingdom

2.9 For details of the tax treatment of your earnings from employment after you have ceased to be resident in the United Kingdom, see Chapter 6 and in particular paragraphs 6.1-6.3 and the table following paragraph 6.13. For similar details in the case of any unearned income you may have (for example, interest from United Kingdom investments) see Chapter 7 and in particular paragraph 7.3. [Not included in this print.]

2.10A number of special provisions applying to those who leave the United Kingdom are dealt with as follows

Earnings of those who leave the United Kingdom part way through the year	paragraph 6.4
United Kingdom Government securities, interest arising in year of departure from United Kingdom	paragraph 7.5
Investment income of those leaving the United Kingdom	paragraph 7.11-7.13
tax allowance	paragraph 8.7
capital gains	paragraph 9.3

Special classes of employees

2.11 Special rules apply to some employees working abroad. If you fall into one of the classes shown below, write to the Inland Revenue office shown – the addresses appear in paragraph 8 if the Introduction. Please give your National Insurance number and details of your employment abroad. The Revenue will advise you of your tax position.

Class	Write to Inland Revenue
Crown employees e.g. civil servants, diplomats, members of the armed forces, etc.)	Public Departments (Technical Unit) Foreign Section
European Community (EC) employees	Claims Branch (International)

Employees working in oil and gas exploration and extraction industries (where the employer is not resident in the United Kingdom)	Foreign Group, HMIT Centre 1
Merchant Navy seafarers	Marine Section, HMIT Cardiff 6

3. *Coming to the United Kingdom*

Coming to the United Kingdom permanently or indefinitely

3.1 You are treated as resident and ordinarily resident from the date you arrive if your home has been abroad and you come to the United Kingdom

- to live her permanently, or
- intending to stay here for three years or more.

Visitors to the United Kingdom

3.2 If you come to the United Kingdom other than to live here permanently as in paragraph 3.1, the guidelines in the rest of this Chapter will govern your residence and ordinary residence position in the United Kingdom.

The Chapter deals in turn with three main groups coming to this country

- short term visitors – where you visit the United Kingdom for only limited periods in one or more tax years
- those coming for employment
- longer term visitors – where you come to the United Kingdom to stay indefinitely or for an extended period, perhaps stretching over several tax years.

You may fall within one or more of these categories, depending on your precise circumstances.

4. *Short term* visitors

Residence

4.1 You will be treated as **resident** for a tax year if

- you are in the United Kingdom for 183 days or more in the tax year (see paragraph 1.2), or
- you visit the United Kingdom regularly and after four tax years your visits during those years average 91 days or more a tax year. You are treated as resident from the fifth year. However
  - any days spent in the United Kingdom for exceptional circumstances beyond your control, for example the illness of yourself or a member of your immediate family, are not counted for this purpose
  - you are treated as resident from 6 April of the first year if it is clear when you first come to the United Kingdom that you **intend** making such visits
- you are treated as resident from 6 April of the tax year in which you **decide** that you will make such visits, where this decision is made before the start of the fifth tax year.

For example,

- you come to the United Kingdom with no definite intentions but your visits during the tax years 1993-94 to 1996-97 average at least 91 days a tax year; you are resident from 6 April 1997
- you first come to the United Kingdom during 1993-94 intending that between then and 5 April 1997 your visits will average at least 91 days a tax year; you are resident from 6 April 1993
- you first come to the United Kingdom during 1993-94 with no definite intentions and you spend, say, 60 days here, you come again during 1994-1995 and decide you will come regularly in future years and your visits will average at least 91 days a tax year; you are resident from 6 April 1994.

For tax years before 1993-94; you are treated as resident if you had accommodation in the United Kingdom available for your use and you visited the United Kingdom, no matter how short the visit (see Chapter 4 on "available accommodation"; paragraphs 4.4-4.5 describe circumstances where accommodation was ignored).

Ordinary Residence

4.2 You will be treated as ordinary resident if you come to the United Kingdom regularly and

- your visits average 91 days or more a tax year; any days spent in the United Kingdom for exceptional circumstances beyond your control, for example the illness of yourself or a member of your immediate family, are not normally counted for this purpose, or
- for tax years before 1993-94, you had accommodation in the United Kingdom available for your use.

4.3 The date from which you are treated as ordinarily resident depends on your intentions. You will be ordinarily resident

- from 6 April of the tax year of your first arrival, if it is clear when you first come here that you **intend** visiting the United Kingdom regularly for at least four tax years
- from 6 April of the fifth tax year after you have visited the United Kingdom over four years, if you originally came with no definite plans about the number of years you will visit
- from 6 April of the tax year in which you **decide** you will be visiting the United Kingdom regularly, if that decision is made before the start of the fifth year.

For example,

- you first come to the United Kingdom during 1993-94, you intend visiting regularly until at least 5 April 1997 and your visits will average at least 91 days a tax year. You are ordinarily resident from 6 April 1993

- you come to the United Kingdom with no definite intentions but you visit regularly during the tax years 1993-94 to 1996-97 and your visits average at least 91 days a tax year. You are ordinarily resident from 6 April 1997
- you first come to the United Kingdom during 1993-94 with no definite intentions; you come again in 1994-95 and 1995-96 and during 1995-96 you decide you will come regularly in future years, and your visits will average at least 91 days a tax year. You are ordinarily resident from 6 April 1995.

Those coming for employment

4.4 You are treated as resident in the United Kingdom from the day you arrive to the day you depart (see paragraph 1.5) if you come to the United Kingdom to work for at least **two years**. If you come to work for less than two years or do not know how long you will be here, you will **only** be treated as resident for the tax year if

- you spend 183 days or more in the United Kingdom in the tax year, or
- for tax years before 1993-94, you had accommodation in the United Kingdom available for your use (see Chapter 4).

For your ordinary residence status see paragraphs 3.8-3.11

Longer term visitors

4.5 For your residence status see paragraph 3.3.

4.6 You will be ordinary resident in the United Kingdom from the date you arrive, whether to work here or not, if it is clear that you intend to stay for at least three years.

If you come to the United Kingdom as a student for an extended period of study or education, see paragraph 3.13.

4.7 You will be treated as ordinarily resident from the beginning of the tax year after the third anniversary of your arrival if you come to, and remain, in the United Kingdom but you

- do not originally intend to stay for at least three years, and
- do not buy accommodation or acquire it on a lease of three years or more.

For example, if you arrive in the United Kingdom on 21 November 1993 and you are still in the United Kingdom on 6 April 1997, you are ordinarily resident from 6 April 1997.

4.8 If, after you have come to the United Kingdom, you decide to stay for at least three years from the date of your original arrival, you will be treated as ordinarily resident from

- the day you arrive if your decision is made in the year of arrival, or
- the beginning of the tax year in which you make your decision when this is after the year of arrival.

For example, you arrive in the United Kingdom on 4 January 1994 and decide to stay permanently on 16 May 1994. You are ordinarily resident from 6 April 1994

4.9 if you come to and remain in the United Kingdom, you will be treated as ordinarily resident

- from the day you arrive, if
- you already own accommodation here
- you buy accommodation during the tax year of arrival
  or
- you have or acquire accommodation on a lease of three years or more during the tax year of arrival
- from 6 April of the tax year in which such accommodation becomes available, when this occurs after the year of arrival.

4.10 If you are treated as ordinarily resident **solely** because you have accommodation here (paragraph 3.11) and you dispose of the accommodation and leave the United Kingdom within three years of your arrival, you may be treated as not ordinarily resident for the duration of your stay if this is to your advantage.

4.11 If you are a **student** who comes to the United Kingdom for a period of study or education and you will be here for less than **four years**, you will be treated as not ordinarily resident, providing

- you do not own or buy accommodation here, or acquire it on a lease of three years or more, and
- on leaving the United Kingdom you will not be returning regularly for visits which average 91 days or more a tax year.

Tax treatment after arrival in the United Kingdom

4.12 For details of the tax treatment of your entire earnings from employments both in the United Kingdom and abroad after you have become resident in the United Kingdom, see Chapter 6 and in particular paragraphs 6.1-6.3, 6.9-6.11 an the table following paragraph 6.13. For details of the treatment of any investment income you may have, see Chapter 7 and in particular paragraph 7.2

4.13 A number of special provisions applying to those coming to the United Kingdom are dealt with as follows:

Earnings of those who come to the United Kingdom part way through a tax year	paragraph 6.4
lump sums from overseas pension schemes and provident funds	paragraph 6.12

United Kingdom Government securities: interest arising in year of arrival in United Kingdom	paragraph 7.5
investment income of those coming to the United Kingdom part way through a tax year	paragraphs 7.14-7.16
tax allowances	paragraph 8.7
capital gains	paragraph 9.3

Available accommodation

4.14 Before 6 April 1993 one of the considerations in deciding your residence status was whether you had "available accommodation" in the United Kingdom. Due to a change in the law in 1993 this Chapter is only relevant for tax years before 1993-1994.

4.15 "Available accommodation" has never been defined in the Taxes Acts. Whether accommodation in the United Kingdom was treated as available for your use depended on all the circumstances.

4.16 For accommodation to be treated as available you had to be able actually to use it as and when you wished. You did not have to own or rent a house, apartment or other accommodation for it to be available for your use. For example, a property owned or rented by your husband or wife would usually be treated as available for your use. Accommodation provided by your employer might be regarded as available in certain circumstances.

4.17 In some cases accommodation which you owned might be treated as not available for your use, for example if it was

- let out on a lease, under the terms of which you had no right to stay in the property
- left empty of furniture, so that it was not in a state to be lived in
- only available for your use during part of the year when you were not in the United Kingdom
- owned purely as an investment, and not used or usable by you when you were in the United Kingdom
- too far away from the place visited to be reasonably used, where your only stay in the United Kingdom in a tax year was a brief business trip.

Accommodation rented for your use might also be ignored if it was:

- rented furnished for less than two years
- rented unfurnished for less than one year

4.18 Accommodation that was available for your use might be ignored if you were working full-time

- in a business or profession carried on wholly abroad. (The accommodation was **not** ignored where your business or profession had a branch or a place of business in the United Kingdom in the tax year, even if you yourself did no work in the United Kingdom)

- in an employment abroad and
  - all your duties were performed abroad, or
  - any duties you performed in the United Kingdom were merely incidental to your overseas duties (see paragraphs 6.7-6.8).

5. Domicile

5.1 Domicile is a general law concept. It is not possible to list all the factors that affect your domicile but some of the main points are explained in this Chapter.

5.2 Broadly speaking you are domiciled in the country where you have your permanent home. Domicile is distinct from nationality or residence. You can only have one domicile at any given time.

Domicile of origin

5.3 You normally acquire a **domicile of origin** from your father when you are born. It need not be the country in which you are born. For example, if you are born in France while your father is working there, but his permanent home is in the United Kingdom, you domicile of origin is in the United Kingdom.

Domicile of dependency

5.4 Until you have the legal capacity to change it – see paragraph 5.5 – your domicile will follow that of the person on whom you are legally dependent. If the domicile of that person changes, you automatically acquire the same domicile (a **domicile of dependency**) in place of your domicile of origin.

Domicile of choice

5.5 You have the legal capacity to acquire a new domicile (a **domicile of choice**) when you reach age 16. To do so, you must broadly leave your current country of domicile and settle in another country. You need to provide strong evidence that you intend to live there permanently or indefinitely. Living in another country for a long time, although an important factor, is not enough in itself to prove you have acquired a new domicile.

Married women

5.6 Before 1974, when you married you automatically acquired your husband's domicile. After marriage this domicile would change at the same time as your husband's domicile changed. If your marriage ended, you kept your husband's domicile until such time as you legally acquire a new domicile.

5.7 From 1 January 1974 your domicile is no longer necessarily the same as your husband's domicile. It is decided by the same factors as for any other individual who is able to have an independent domicile. If, however, you were married before 1974 and had acquired your husband's domicile (see paragraph

5.6) you **retain** this after 1 January 1974 until such time as you legally acquire a new domicile.

Tax treatment of those not domiciled in the United Kingdom

5.8 Those who are resident in the United Kingdom but not domiciled here receive special tax treatment in respect of income and gains arising outside the United Kingdom. For details see paragraphs 6.11 (income tax) and 9.5 (capital gains tax). The Inland Revenue will consider the question

Appendix 3: Some Relevant Definitions

Word or Phrase	Statute	Comment etc.
Adjusted Net Income s58 ITA and 845G		section 845G (1) Subsection (2) applies for the purpose of determining the adjusted net income under section 58 of ITA 2007 of an individual for a tax year for which the individual has made a foreign income claim.
"BIR"		Business Investment Relief See https://www.gov.uk/guidance/business-investment-relief
Consequential Claim		
"the current tax year"	S 6A (2) IHTA	(2)But an individual is not a long-term UK resident at any time in a tax year ("the current tax year") if they were non-UK resident— (a)for any 10 consecutive tax years during the 19 tax years before the current tax year, or (b)for at least the required number of consecutive tax years ending with the tax year before the current tax year.
CTT		Capital Transfer Tax renamed IHT in 1986 see section 100 FA 1986 "1)On and after the passing of this Act, the tax charged under the Capital Transfer Tax Act 1984 (in this Part of this Act referred to as "the 1984 Act") shall be known as inheritance tax ..." 25th July 1986 date Act passed
"Disqualified Income"	S 845 I	Includes Performance Income see below
Disqualified Individual s 845B (4)		(4) An individual is disqualified for a tax year if the individual would, for the purposes of section 41 of the Constitutional Reform and Governance Act 2010, be regarded as— (a)a member of the House of Commons for any part of that tax year, or (b)a member of the House of Lords for any part of that tax year.
"the existing property"	S 48(9) ZA IHTA	(9) If— (a)an amount is payable in respect of property ("the existing property") comprised in a settlement, and

		(b)the amount represents an accumulation of income which (once accumulated) becomes comprised in the settlement, subsection (4) has effect in the case of the amount as if the reference to the time when it became comprised in the settlement were to the time when the existing property became comprised in the settlement.
"FIG"		Foreign Income and Gains
"Foreign Income Claim"	S 845 A	(1)An individual may make a claim for relief for a tax year under this section (a "foreign income claim") if the individual is a qualifying new resident for that year (see section 845B).
Individual	Not defined	
"ITA"		Income Tax Act 2007
"ITEPA"		Income Tax (Earnings and Pensions) Act 2003
"ITTOIA"		Income Tax (Trading and Other Income Act) 2005
"Long-term UK resident"	S 6A IHTA	Individual resident in the UK for at least 10 of the previous 20 years
The New Regime		The meaning in the Introduction as the new residence-based regime replacing the Domicile based regime for IT, CGT and IHT.
"Non-Doms"		individuals domiciled outside the UK colloquially
"Non-UK resident"	S 6A (4) IHTA	Inserted by FA 2025
"the number of resident Years"	S 6A (3) IHTA	Inserted by FA 2025
The Old Regime		The previous domiciled based regime
"OWR"	S41 - X	Overseas Workday Relief
"Performance Income"	S 845 H	Income directly or indirectly from the performance of entertainment or sport which is Disqualified Income under section 845 G and so does not fall within Chapter 1 Part 2 FA 2025
"the Policy Paper" or "Policy Summary"	Not a statutory matter	The government on 29 July 2024 published a policy paper (2024: Non-UK domiciled individuals- Policy Summary - GOV.UK) outlining the

		planned changes to the taxation of non-UK domiciled individuals. (www.gov.uk) This included replacing the remittance basis of tax with a residence-based regime, providing 100% relief on foreign income and gains for new arrivals to the UK in their first four years of tax residence, provided they have not been UK tax resident in any of the 10 consecutive years prior to their arrival
"QAHC"		Qualifying Asset Holding Company
"Qualifying employment income"	S 41 N ITEPA	means— (a) qualifying general earnings, (b) qualifying third party income, and (c) qualifying securities income.
"Qualifying foreign third-party income"		41N (5) Section 41U defines what it means— (a) for third party income to be "qualifying third party income", and (b)for qualifying third party Income to be "qualifying foreign third party income"
"qualifying general earnings"	S41N(4) and S41J	(4) Section 41T defines what it means— (a)for general earnings to be "qualifying general earnings", and (b)for qualifying general earnings to be "qualifying foreign general earnings".
"Qualifying New Resident"		(1) For the purposes of this Chapter, an individual is a qualifying new resident for a tax year if— (a)the individual is UK resident for that tax year, (b)the individual is not disqualified for that tax year, and (c)for each of the 10 tax years before that tax year, the individual was not UK resident. (2) An individual is also a qualifying new resident for a tax year if— (a)the individual is UK resident for that tax year, (b)the individual is not disqualified for that tax year, and

		(c)that tax year is one of the next three tax years after a qualifying tax year in relation to the individual.
"qualifying securities income"	S41N(6) and S41V	Section 41 N(6) Section 41V defines what it means— (a)for securities income to be "qualifying securities income", and (b)for qualifying securities income to be "qualifying foreign securities income".
"Qualifying Year" s41M(i)	S845B (3)	(3)A tax year is a qualifying tax year in relation to an individual if— (a)the individual was a qualifying new resident for that tax year as a result of subsection (1), (b)the individual would have been a qualifying new resident for that tax year as a result of that subsection, but was not only as a result of the individual being disqualified for that tax year, or (c)the tax year— (i)is the tax year 2022-23, 2023-24 or 2024-25, and (ii)is a tax year to which paragraph (a) or (b) would have applied in relation to the individual had this section had effect for that tax year.
Relevant Business	S845C (3)	(3)In this section "relevant business" means— (a)a trade, profession or vocation, or (b)a property business.
"the required number"	S 6A (3) IHTA	See the Table in the section 6
"return"		Section 8 TMA
the Settlement Provisions	Chapter 5 Part 5 ITTOIA	Discussed in Chapter 6 of *Taxation of Entertainers and Sportspersons* and FA 2025 recent changes in section on Trusts
Tax Year		the period starting on 6 April one calendar year and ending 5 April in the following calendar year
"TCGA"		Taxation of Chargeable Gains Act 1992
Transitionally protected income		

"TRF"		Temporary Repatriation Facility
"UK resident"	Section 6A (4) IHTA	(4) In this section, "UK resident" means resident in the United Kingdom and "non-UK resident" means not resident in the United Kingdom.
"young person"	S 6B (2) IHTA	**means an individual who was under the age of 20 immediately before the current tax year.**

5 Relief for New Residents for Foreign Gains

5.1 Summary

This section of the Supplement provides a legal and technical commentary on the **new Capital Gains Tax (CGT) relief** introduced under **Section 39 and Schedule D1 of the Finance Act 2025**. This new relief is part of the UK's broader move from a **domicile-based to residence-based tax system**. This section deals with the new CGT relief.

This relief offers **significant tax advantages** to **internationally mobile individuals** relocating to the UK, especially those with foreign investments or interests in offshore trusts. However, it comes with **strict documentation**, **timing**, and **reporting requirements**, and must be **actively claimed** to be effective.

The following matters are considered:

5.1.1 *Purpose of the Reform*

- The relief is designed to **replace the remittance basis** for new arrivals to the UK.
- It provides **100% CGT exemption on foreign gains** for **individuals** who are **qualifying new resident** during broadly their **first four years of UK tax residence**, if they were **non-resident in the UK for the 10 years prior to their arrival in the UK**.

5.1.2 *Who Qualifies?*

- A **"qualifying new resident"** is defined in the new legislation as an individual who must:
    - **Not** have been **UK tax resident in any of the previous 10 tax years**, and
    - Be **within** their **first four tax years** of UK residence after arriving.

5.1.3 *How the Relief Works*

- **Foreign gains** (on non-UK assets) are **excluded** from CGT where a proper **foreign gain claim** has been made in the self-assessment tax return.
- The Relief applies to:
    - **Individual's own foreign gains** (Paragraph 2),
    - **Attributed gains** from **non-resident trusts** where the individual is the **settlor** (Paragraph 3),
    - **Attributed gains** where the individual is a **beneficiary** receiving capital payments from non-resident trusts (Paragraph 4).

5.1.4 *Key Provisions in the Legislation*

- **Schedule D1** inserted into the **Taxation of Chargeable Gains Act 1992 (TCGA)** matters providing:
  - Definitions for **"qualifying foreign asset,"** **"qualifying foreign gain,"** and **"foreign gain claim."**
  - Claim must be made **within 12 months** from 31 January after the end of the relevant tax year.
  - Foreign gains must be **clearly identified** in the return.

5.1.5 *Consequences of Making a Claim*

- If a foreign gain claim is made:
  - **No CGT annual exemption** is available for that claim year.
  - **Qualifying foreign losses** are **not deductible**.
  - Some **income tax allowances** are restricted.

5.1.6 *Effective Date*

- The relief and related legislative changes came into effect **from 6 April 2025** for the **2025–26 tax year** and subsequent tax years.

5.1.7 *Case studies in the text below*

- Case studies like **Carla Petfiele-Fingis** and **David Lineuil** illustrate how foreign gains are excluded under the new regime.
- Example of **Devina Ludiani** explores how trust gains attributed to a settlor are relieved.

5.1.8 *Interaction with Trusts*

- Reliefs extend to **offshore trusts** through:
  - **Section 86** (settlor-interested trusts),
  - **Section 87** (beneficiary charges),
  - **Schedule 4C** (capital payments attribution),

These gains are **excluded from attribution** if a valid claim is made and the relevant conditions are met.

5.2 Introduction

This part of the Supplement deals with the CGT changes introduced by Chapter 1 of Part 2 FA 2025 following the change to a residence-based system for CGT following the removal of the Remittance Basis and the domicile-based basis for UK tax.

A new CGT relief for new residents on foreign gains is introduced as foreshadowed in the Policy Paper.

This is dealt with by section 39 and Schedule D1. The Schedule is introduced into the TCGA by section 39 FA 2025. The relief is similar to that for qualifying new residents for IT discussed above.

5.3 Finance Bill Committee

5.3.1 General

There was no debate in the Committee on what became section 39 of the Act and Schedule DI TCGA.

Hansard just records "Clause 39 ordered to stand part of the Bill."

5.3.2 Section 39: Claim for relief on foreign gains

5.3.2.1 Overview

Section 39 introduces a new CGT relief for new residents on foreign gains and makes consequential amendments.

The new relief applies for tax year 2025-2026 and subsequent years. The government policy paper published on 29 July 2024 included replacing the remittance basis of tax with a residence-based regime, providing 100% relief on foreign income and gains for new arrivals to the UK in up to their first four years of tax residence, provided they have not been UK tax resident in any of the **10 consecutive years prior to their arrival.** The taxpayer will have the onus of proof to show this.

The legislation in question here seeks to implement this in respect of foreign gains.

The relief is given by deducting an amount equal to the sum of those gains qualifying for relief from the total amount of chargeable gains accruing to the individual. The amount of the gains deducted accordingly is not then subject to CGT.

> **Example**
>
> Carla Petfiele-Fingis is a qualifying new resident. In her first year of UK residence, she has net gains of £3m. Of these gains £2m qualify for relief so only £1m is taxable (£3m - £2m). Thus, the qualifying gains (£2m) are not charged to CGT, and the relief is effectively given.

Subsection (1) of section 39 provides that the section amends the Taxation of Chargeable Gains Tax Act 1992 (generally referred to as the TCGA in this Supplement).

Schedule D1 inserted.

Subsection (2) of section 39 inserts new Schedule D1 to TCGA 1992.

The new Schedule provides relief for new residents on foreign gains that qualify. It is discussed in the next section below headed "Details of new Schedule D1".

5.3.2.2 *Effective Date*

The effective date for this legislation is 06 April 2025. See section 39 (11) which reads "The amendments made by this section have effect for the tax year 2025-26 and subsequent tax years." The tax year 2025-2026 started in April 2025.

5.3.2.3 *Legislation*

Section 39 is headed "Claim for relief on foreign gains".

It provides:

> "(1) TCGA 1992 is amended as follows.
>
> (2) Before Schedule 1 insert—
>
> "Schedule D1 Section 1a (2) (Za) Relief for New Residents on Foreign Gains"
>
> [*Note to Reader The text of the Schedule is set out below.*]
>
> (3) In section 1A (territorial scope), in subsection (2), before paragraph (a) insert—
>
>> "(za)Schedule D1 (relief for new residents on foreign gains),".
>>
>> (4) In section 1E (losses deductible only when within scope of tax), in subsection (6), for "Schedule 1 (UK resident individuals not domiciled in the UK)" substitute "paragraph 5 of Schedule D1 (relief for new residents on foreign gains)."
>
> (5) In section 1K (annual exempt amount), in subsection (6)—
>
>> (a)the words from "section" to the end become paragraph (a) of that subsection, and
>>
>> (b)after that paragraph insert ", or
>>
>> (b)the individual makes a foreign gain claim, a foreign income claim or a foreign employment election for that tax year."
>
> (6) In section 16 (computation of losses), at the end insert—
>
>> "(4) A **qualifying foreign loss** accruing to an individual in a tax year is not an allowable loss if a foreign gain claim, a foreign income claim or a foreign employment election has effect in relation to the individual for that tax year.

(5) In subsection (4), "qualifying foreign loss" has the same meaning as in Schedule D1 (see paragraph 6 of that Schedule)."

(7) In section 288 (interpretation), in subsection (1) at the appropriate places insert—

""**foreign employment election**" means a claim under section 41M of ITEPA 2003;";

""**foreign gain claim**" means a claim under paragraph 1 of Schedule D1;";

""**foreign income claim**" means a claim under section 845A of ITTOIA 2005;";

""**qualifying new resident**" has the meaning given by section 845B of ITTOIA 2005 (which sets out the circumstances in which an individual will be a qualifying new resident following a period of 10 years of non-residence);".

(8) In Schedule 1A, in paragraph 1, after "2B(4)(b)" insert "or paragraph 6 of Schedule D1".

(9) In Schedule 1C (annual exempt amount in cases involving settled property), in paragraph 1(4), for the words from "who" to the end substitute "to whom subsection (6) of that section does not apply."

(10) In Schedule 2 to FA 2022 (qualifying asset holding companies), in paragraph 46—

(a)in the heading (as amended by section 37(3)(a)), after "income" insert "or gain", and

(b)in sub-paragraph (6A) (as inserted by section 37(3)(c)), after "claim)" insert "and paragraph (c) of the definition of "qualifying foreign gain" in paragraph 6 of Schedule D1 to TCGA 1992 (foreign gain claims)".

(11) The amendments made by this section have effect for the tax year 2025-26 and subsequent tax years. "

5.3.3 *Details of section 39*

Section 39 inserts Schedule D1 into the TCGA before Schedule 1. This Schedule is headed "Relief for New Residents on Foreign Gains."

5.3.3.1 Consequentials

Schedule 9 and Consequential Amendments:

5.3.3.1.1 General

As a result of the insertion of updated and cross-checked new Schedule D1 a number of consequential amendments are needed. These are made in particular by paragraph 2 Schedule 9 to the 2025 Act.

5.3.3.1.2 Subsection (3) Amendments of Section 1A (2)

Subsection (3) of 39 amends subsection 1A (2) of TCGA 1992, which refers to charging provisions that apply to UK residents, as a consequence of new Schedule D1.

5.3.3.1.3 Subsection (4) amendment of Section 1E (6)

Subsection (4) amends subsection 1E (6), which refers to provisions affecting the deduction of allowable losses, as a consequence of new Schedule D1.

5.3.3.1.4 Subsection (5) Amendments of Section 1 (K) 6.

Subsection (5) amends subsection 1K(6) to deny an individual entitlement to the CGT annual exempt amount for a tax year where for that year they make a foreign gain claim (under new Schedule D1), a foreign income claim (under new section 845A to Income Tax (Trading and Other Income) Act (ITTOIA) 2005, as inserted by section 37) or a foreign employment election (under new section 41M to Income Tax (Earnings and Pensions) Act (ITEPA) 2003, as inserted by section 38 FA 2025.

5.3.3.1.5 Subsection (6) new Section 16 (4) and (5).

Subsection (6) inserts new subsections 16(4) and (5) into section 16 TCGA to provide that a qualifying foreign loss accruing to an individual in a tax year (as defined in new Schedule D1) is not an allowable loss if for that year they make a foreign gain claim (under new Schedule D1), a foreign income claim (under new section 845A to ITTOIA 2005) or a foreign employment election (under new section 41M to ITEPA 2003).

5.3.3.1.6 Subsection (7) inserts various definitions into section 288.

Subsection (7) inserts various definitions into Section 288 TCGA the general definition section, including that for qualifying new resident.

5.3.3.1.7 Subsection (8)

Subsection (8) amends paragraph 1 (introduction) of Schedule 1A (assets deriving 75% of value from UK land etc) as a consequence of new Schedule D1.

5.3.3.1.8 Subsection (9)

Subsection (9) amends paragraph 1(4) (introduction) of Schedule 1C (annual exempt amount in cases involving settled property) as a consequence of subsection (5).

5.3.3.1.9 Subsection (10)

Subsection (10) amends subparagraph 46(6A) of Schedule 2 to the Finance Act 2022 (qualifying asset holding companies) to confirm that subparagraphs 46(4) to (6) of that Schedule also apply for the purposes of 'a qualifying Asset Holding

Company gain' found in the definition of 'qualifying foreign gain' in paragraph 6 of new Schedule D1.

5.3.3.1.10 Subsection (11) Commencement

Subsection (11) provides for commencement. This is effectively 6 April2025.

5.4 Details of new schedule D1

5.4.1 General

Schedule D1 sets out further detail in respect of the relief for foreign capital gains introduced by Section 39 as discussed above.

Paragraph 1 Schedule D1 provides that an individual who is a qualifying new resident [(defined for the purposes of TCGA 1992 at subsection 39(7))] may make a claim for the reliefs found in paragraphs 2, 3 and 4 of the Schedule so far as relevant here.

Section 39 (7) reads as follows.

> "(7) In section 288 (interpretation), in subsection (1) at the appropriate places insert—
>
> ""**foreign employment election**" means a claim under section 41M of ITEPA 2003;";
>
> ""**foreign gain claim**" means a claim under paragraph 1 of Schedule D1;";
>
> ""**foreign income claim**" means a claim under section 845A of ITTOIA 2005;";
>
> ""**qualifying new resident**" has the meaning given by section 845B of ITTOIA 2005 (which sets out the circumstances in which an individual will be a qualifying new resident following a period of 10 years of non-residence);" This is discussed earlier in this Supplement.

5.4.2 Reliefs

There are three particular reliefs. These cover gains of an individual and the gains of offshore settlements attributed to the Settlor or a beneficiary on receipt of a capital payment.

The reliefs are as in the following Table.

Provision in Schedule	Description
Paragraph 2	Relief for Individual's gains
Paragraph 3	Relief for section 86 gains attributed to the Settlor
Paragraph 4	Relief for section 87 gains attributed to a Beneficiary on receipt of a capital payment.

5.4.3 *Section 1A (2) (za)*

5.4.3.1 *Legislation*

The Schedule is headed "Schedule D1 - Relief for new residents on foreign gains".

It reads as follows:

1. Claim for relief for qualifying new residents.

1(1) An individual may make a claim for relief for a tax year under this paragraph (a "foreign gain claim") if the individual is a qualifying new resident for that tax year.

(2) Paragraphs 2, 3 and 4 set out the reliefs that may be obtained by making a foreign gain claim.

(3)A foreign gain claim must be made in a return.

(4)A foreign gain claim in relation to a tax year must be made before the end of the period of 12 months beginning with 31 January after the end of that tax year.

(5)A foreign gain claim may not be made as a consequential claim (within the meaning of section 43C(5) of the Management Act) if the circumstances which give rise to the consequential claim result from a loss of tax brought about carelessly or deliberately by the individual or a person acting on the individual's behalf.

(6) For the purposes of this paragraph—

(a) "return" means a return under section 8 of the Management Act (personal return),

(b)references to a claim being included in a return include a claim being so included as a result of an amendment of the return, and

(c)subsections (5) to (7) of section 118 of the Management Act (loss of tax brought about carelessly or deliberately) apply as they apply for the purposes of that Act.

2. Relief for qualifying foreign gains

2(1) Where an individual makes a foreign gain claim for a tax year, the individual is entitled to relief for each qualifying foreign gain accruing to the individual in that year that is identified in the claim.

(2) The relief is given by deducting an amount equal to the sum of those gains from the total amount of chargeable gains accruing to the individual.

3. Relief in respect of deemed gains under section 86.

3(1) This paragraph applies if—

(a)an amount of chargeable gains would (but for this paragraph) be treated as accruing to an individual in a tax year under section 86(4) (attribution of gains to settlors of non-resident settlements),

(b)a qualifying foreign gain accrued in that tax year to the trustees of the settlement concerned (or would have done on the assumption in section 86(3)), and (c)the individual identifies the gain mentioned in paragraph (b) in a foreign gain claim for that tax year.

(2) For the purposes of section 86(1)(e) as it applies to the individual, the following are to be disregarded (in that tax year and in later tax years)—

(a)the gain mentioned in sub-paragraph (1)(b);

(b)any qualifying foreign loss that accrued to the trustees in that tax year (or that would have so accrued on the assumption in section 86(3)).

4. Relief in respect of deemed gains under sections 87 and 89(2) and Schedule 4C.

4(1) This paragraph applies if—

(a)a settlement is for a tax year—

(i)one to which section 87 or 89(2) applies (attribution of gains to beneficiaries of settlements), or

(ii)a relevant settlement in relation to a Schedule 4C pool, within the meaning of paragraph 8A of Schedule 4C (transfers of value: attribution of gains etc),

(b)a beneficiary of the settlement receives a capital payment from the trustees in that tax year, and

(c)the individual identifies the capital payment in a foreign gain claim for that tax year.

(2) The capital payment is to be disregarded (in that tax year and in later tax years) for the purposes of sections 87, 87A and 89(2) and paragraph 8 of Schedule 4C.

(3) The following apply for the purposes of this paragraph as they apply for the purposes of section 87—

(a)section 87G (which provides for capital payments made to a close member of the settlor's family to be treated in certain cases as received by the settlor).

(b)section 97 (which makes provision about the construction of "capital payment", "settlement", "trustees" and "beneficiary").

5. Other effects of claim

5 For other effects of making a foreign gain claim, see—

(a)section 1K(6)(b) (annual exempt amount), which provides that where a foreign gain claim has effect in relation to an individual for a tax year, the individual has no entitlement to an annual exempt amount for that year,

(b)section 16(4) (computation of losses), which provides that where a foreign gain claim has effect in relation to an individual for a tax year, qualifying foreign losses accruing to the individual in that year are not allowable losses, and

(c)sections 845C to 845E of ITTOIA 2005, which set out some income tax consequences of making a foreign gain claim.

6. Interpretation of Schedule

6 In this Schedule—

"**Qualifying foreign asset**" means an asset that—

(a)is situated outside the United Kingdom, and

(b)does not derive at least 75% of its value from UK land (see Schedule 1A).

"**Qualifying foreign gain**" means—

(a)a chargeable gain accruing on the disposal of a qualifying foreign asset,

(b)a chargeable gain treated as accruing as a result of section 3 (gains of non-UK resident close companies attributed to UK residents) where the gain accruing to the non-UK resident close company to which the deemed gain relates accrued on the disposal of a qualifying foreign asset, or

(c)a qualifying QAHC gain, but a chargeable gain falling within paragraph (a) or (b) is not a qualifying foreign gain if it is a gain to which paragraph 1(2) of Schedule 1 applies (pre-2025-26 gains subject to the remittance basis);

"**Qualifying foreign loss**" means a loss accruing on the disposal of an asset that is a qualifying foreign asset;

"**Qualifying QAHC gain**" means the foreign proportion (see paragraph 46(4) to (6) of Schedule 2 to FA 2022) of a chargeable gain accruing on the disposal of shares in a QAHC (within the meaning of that Schedule) other than a chargeable gain to which paragraph 46(3) of that Schedule applies."

(3) In section 1A (territorial scope), in subsection (2), before paragraph (a) insert—

"(za)Schedule D1 (relief for new residents on foreign gains),".

(4) In section 1E (losses deductible only when within scope of tax), in subsection (6), for "Schedule 1 (UK resident individuals not domiciled in the UK)" substitute "paragraph 5 of Schedule D1 (relief for new residents on foreign gains)."

(5) In section 1K (annual exempt amount), in subsection (6)—

(a)the words from "section" to the end become paragraph (a) of that subsection, and

(b)after that paragraph insert ", or

(b)the individual makes a foreign gain claim, a foreign income claim or a foreign employment election for that tax year."

(6) In section 16 (computation of losses), at the end insert—

"(4)A qualifying foreign loss accruing to an individual in a tax year is not an allowable loss if a foreign gain claim, a foreign income claims or a foreign employment election has effect in relation to the individual for that tax year.

(5) In subsection (4), "qualifying foreign loss" has the same meaning as in Schedule D1 (see paragraph 6 of that Schedule)."

(7) In section 288 (interpretation), in subsection (1) at the appropriate places insert—

""**foreign employment election**" means a claim under section 41M of ITEPA 2003;";

""**foreign gain claim**" means a claim under paragraph 1 of Schedule D1;";

""**foreign income claim**" means a claim under section 845A of ITTOIA 2005;";

""**qualifying new resident**" has the meaning given by section 845B of ITTOIA 2005 (which sets out the circumstances in which an individual will be a qualifying new resident following a period of 10 years of non-residence);".

(8) In Schedule 1A, in paragraph 1, after "2B(4)(b)" insert "or paragraph 6 of Schedule D1".

(9) In Schedule 1C (annual exempt amount in cases involving settled property), in paragraph 1(4), for the words from "who" to the end substitute "to whom subsection (6) of that section does not apply."

(10) In Schedule 2 to FA 2022 (qualifying asset holding companies), in paragraph 46—

(a)in the heading (as amended by section 37(3)(a)), after "income" insert "or gain", and

(b)in sub-paragraph (6A) (as inserted by section 37(3)(c)), after "claim)" insert "and paragraph (c) of the definition of "qualifying foreign gain" in paragraph 6 of Schedule D1 to TCGA 1992 (foreign gain claims)".

(11) The **amendments made by this section** have **effect for** the **tax year 2025-26** and **subsequent** tax **years**.

Discussion of the legislation

5.4.3.2 *Claim for relief for qualifying new residents Paragraph 1*

5.4.3.2.1 Overview

An individual may make a claim for relief from CGT in accordance with the Schedule for a tax year (a "**foreign gain claim**") if the individual is a "qualifying new resident" for that tax year.

5.4.3.2.2 Legislation

i. General

Paragraph 1 It reads as follows:

"1 (1) An individual may make a claim for relief for a tax year under this paragraph (a "**foreign gain claim**") if the individual is a **qualifying new resident [discussed earlier in this Supplement]** for that tax year.

(2) I Paragraphs 2, 3 and 4 [of Schedule D1] set out the reliefs that may be obtained by making a foreign gain claim.

(3) A foreign gain **claim must be made in a return**.

(4) A foreign gain claim in relation to a tax year **must be made before the end of the period of 12 months beginning with 31 January after the end of that tax year**.

(5) A foreign gain claim **may not be made as a consequential claim** (within the meaning of section 43C(5) of the Management Act) **if** the circumstances which give rise to the **consequential claim result from a loss of tax brought about carelessly or deliberately** by the individual or a person acting on the individual's behalf.

(6) For the purposes of this paragraph—

(a) "**return**" means a return under section 8 of the Management Act (personal return),

(b) references to a claim being **included in a return include** a claim being so included as a result of **an amendment of the return**, and

(c) **subsections (5) to (7) of section 118 of the Management Act (loss of tax brought about carelessly or deliberately add relevant parts of Section 8 and 118 TMA) apply** as they apply for the purposes of that Act."

ii *Section 8 TMA*

Section 8 TMA is referred to in Paragraph 1

So far as relevant section 8 TMA headed "Personal return" reads as follows.

"(1)For the purpose of establishing the amounts in which a person is chargeable to income tax and capital gains tax for a year of assessment, and the amount payable by him by way of income tax for that year, he may be required by a notice given to him by an officer of the Board—

(a) to make and deliver to the officer a return containing such information as may reasonably be required in pursuance of the notice, and

(b) to deliver with the return such accounts, statements and documents, relating to information contained in the return, as may reasonably be so required.

(1A) . . . .

(1AA) For the purposes of subsection (1) above—

(a)the amounts in which a person is chargeable to income tax and capital gains tax are net amounts, that is to say, amounts which take into account any relief or allowance a claim for which is included in the return; and

(b)the amount payable by a person by way of income tax is the difference between the amount in which he is chargeable to income tax and the aggregate amount of any income tax deducted at source ...

(1H) The Commissioners—

(a)shall prescribe what constitutes an electronic return, and

(b)may make different provision for different cases or circumstances.]

(1I) Where a person is required to make and deliver a return under this section, the person may be required by an officer of His Majesty's Revenue and Customs to include in the return any information that is specified or described in regulations made by the Commissioners (whether or not the information is relevant for the purpose mentioned in subsection (1)).

(1J) The Commissioners may only specify or describe information in regulations under subsection (1I) if the Commissioners consider that the information is relevant for the purpose of the collection and management of any of the taxes listed in section 1.

(1K) A person who fails to comply with a requirement imposed on them by virtue of subsection (1I) is liable to a penalty of £60.

(1L) Regulations under subsection (1I) may make different provision for different purposes.]

(2) Every return under this section shall include a declaration by the person making the return to the effect than the return is to the best of his knowledge correct and complete."

So far as relevant section 118 TMA headed "Personal return" reads as follows.

"(5) For the purposes of this Act a loss of tax or a situation is brought about carelessly by a person if the person fails to take reasonable care to avoid bringing about that loss or situation.

(6) Where—

(a)information is provided to Her Majesty's Revenue and Customs,

(b)the person who provided the information, or the person on whose behalf the information was provided, discovers some time later that the information was inaccurate, and

(c)that person fails to take reasonable steps to inform Her Majesty's Revenue and Customs,

any loss of tax or situation brought about by the inaccuracy shall be treated for the purposes of this Act as having been brought about carelessly by that person.

(7) In this Act references to a loss of tax or a situation brought about deliberately by a person include a loss of tax or a situation that arises as a result of a deliberate inaccuracy in a document given to Her Majesty's Revenue and Customs by or on behalf of that person."

5.4.3.2.3 Detail

This paragraph only applies to individuals. This is essentially an individual as opposed to a juristic or legal person such as a company. This is discussed at a number of points in this section.

This paragraph raises a number of questions including the following.

(1.) Who is an individual for these purposes

(2.) What is a foreign gain claim?

(3.) When is an individual a "qualifying new resident" for that tax year

(4.) What is meant by the claim must be made in a return?

(5.) Within what time a claim for relief must be made

(6.) What is a consequent claim?

These questions will be considered in turn next. [X refers to equivalent IT discussion.

5.4.3.2.4 Who is an individual for these purposes?

An individual for these purposes is a human being as opposed to a legal or juristic person. It is usually considered to be an individual in their capacity as themselves not some other capacity such as an individual trustee (see *Lady Longford v IRC* [1928] UKHL J0322-2).

5.4.3.2.5 What is a foreign gain claim?

A foreign gain claim is a defined term for these purposes.

Paragraph 1 Schedule D 1 TCGA is headed "Claim for relief for qualifying new residents".

So far as relevant here it provides as follows.

> "1(1) An individual may make a claim for relief for a tax year under this paragraph (a "**foreign gain claim**") if the individual is a qualifying new resident for that tax year..."

5.4.3.2.6 When is an individual a "qualifying new resident" for that tax year?

"Qualifying new resident" is also a defined term here. Section 39(7) provides that section 288 TCGA is to have the following inserted.

"qualifying new resident" has the meaning given by section 845B of ITTOIA 2005." This section sets out the circumstances in which an individual will be a qualifying new resident following a period of 10 years of non-residence.

This is discussed in the section on FIG.

5.4.3.2.7 What is meant by the claim must be made in a return?

This is discussed above.

5.4.3.2.8 Within what time must a claim for relief be made?

This is dealt with by paragraph 1(4). So far as relevant this reads as follows.

"(4) A foreign gain claim in relation to a tax year **must be made before the end of the period of 12 months beginning with 31 January after the end of that tax year**."

5.4.3.2.9 What is a consequent claim?

This is discussed below.

5.4.3.2.10 Effective Date

The effective date is 06 April 2025

See paragraph 6 (11)

5.4.3.3 Relief for qualifying foreign gains paragraph 2 - Individual's gains

5.4.3.3.1 Overview

Paragraph 2 of Schedule D1 provides for relief on qualifying foreign gains (defined at paragraph 6 discussed below) accruing to the individual which are identified in the foreign gain claim. The relief is given by deducting the specified gains from the individual's total chargeable gains for the tax year.

Example

David Lineuil from Asturia is a qualifying new resident in his first year of UK residence. He makes a gain on the disposal of shares in an Austurian company which trades in upmarket goods and has no assets or presence in the UK. He also makes gains in that year on the disposal of UK situs assets totalling 100. David makes a foreign gains claim in the relevant tax return in respect of the year of arrival which clearly identifies the 200 gain as a qualifying foreign gain.

The net gains (the section 1(2) gains) for the year are 300 ignoring any foreign gains claim. There is a foreign gains claim for the tax year in question which identifies qualifying gains liable to CGT are reduced to 200 (300 less 100). It is assumed all the conditions for relief are met,

The individual must be a qualifying new resident for the relief to apply. This is a defined term at section 39(7) discussed above.

This, so far as relevant here, reads as follows.

> ""qualifying new resident" has the meaning given by section 845B of ITTOIA 2005 (which sets out the circumstances in which an individual will be a qualifying new resident following a period of 10 years of non-residence)"

The subsection is discussed above.

5.4.3.3.2 Legislation

Paragraph 2 reads as follows.

> "*Relief for qualifying foreign gains*
>
> 2(1) Where an individual makes a foreign gain claim for a tax year, the individual is entitled to relief for each qualifying foreign gain accruing to the individual in that year that is identified in the claim.
>
> (2) The relief is given by deducting an amount equal to the sum of those gains from the total amount of chargeable gains accruing to the individual."

5.4.3.3.3 Details

Paragraph 2 raises a number of questions including the following.

(1.) Who is an individual for these purposes?

(2.) What is meant by "makes a foreign gain claim"?

(3.) What is meant by for a tax year and in that year?

(4.) What is meant by relief for each qualifying foreign gain?

(5.) What is meant by is identified in the claim?

(6.) What is meant by relief is given by deducting an amount equal to the sum of those gains from the total chargeable gains?

5.4.3.3.4 "Individual"

This is not a defined term in the legislation for these purposes. Accordingly, it bears its ordinary meaning. This is usually an individual human as opposed to a legal or juristic person.

5.4.3.3.5 "Makes a foreign gain claim"

A foreign gain claim is defined in paragraph 1 discussed above. A claim must be made in a return. The relief is to be given by reference to the qualifying foreign gains identified in the claim. Also, the discussion under heading (Identified Foreign Claims) below. It is important to make clear exactly what is being claimed and what the qualifying foreign gains are and what their amount is.

5.4.3.3.6 "For a tax year"

Tax year bears it usual meaning of 6 April one year to the following 5 April. The individual must make a foreign gains claim for that year for there to be relief in respect of that year.

5.4.3.3.7 "Relief for each qualifying foreign gain"

The relief is to be given by reference to the qualifying foreign gains in the claim. See also the discussion under the heading "that is identified in the claim" below.

5.4.3.3.8 Accruing to the individual in that year

Devina comes to the UK for the first time ever in the year in question. She is a qualifying new resident. She disposes of assets resulting in £1m to Devina. Under Section 867C6A she makes a foreign gain. In my view, it will usually be best to provide full details, so it is as clear as possible what gains the claim is made in respect of and for which year. Hopefully the propriety software tax return will allow this to be done easily.

The phrase "that year" refers back to "where an individual makes a foreign gain claim for a tax year ..." Accordingly, it is the year in respect of which the claim is made and the foreign gain identified in the claim that matter. The year is a "Tax Year"

That is identified in the claim.

The claim which identifies the foreign gain in question are the gains on which she receives the relief.

This refers back to the phrase earlier in paragraph 1(i) "each qualifying foreign [accruing] to the individual in that year [i.e. the year of claim] identified in the claim". It is important to get this right as otherwise the claim may be denied.

The details of the gains in respect of which the claim(s) is made must be set out clearly and each of the qualifying foreign gains identified. It must be clear what is claimed. More detail rather than less should be supplied in my view.

5.4.3.3.9 Effective Date

The effective date is 06 April 2025. See paragraph 6(11).

5.4.3.4 Relief in respect of deemed gains under section 86(3) - gains attributed to the Settlor

5.4.3.4.1 Overview

Paragraph 3 of Schedule D1 provides for relief where the qualifying new resident is the settlor of a non-UK resident trust and the trust's gains are attributed to the qualifying new resident as the Settlor of the trust. This is the charge under section 86 TCGA.

Relief is limited to the qualifying foreign gains identified in the claim.

The same comment made in respect of a claim under paragraph 2 also apply here. It is important that the claim clearly identifies the gains in question and in respect of which tax year and their amounts.

Relief is given by disregarding the identified amount in computing the amount of trustees' gains attributable to the individual for the tax year and future years.

Example

Devina Ludiani is an UK resident individual. She is a qualifying new resident. She is the settlor of the Games Trust having provided all the capital of the trust fund. The trustee of this trust is resident in Kintesta and nowhere else. Kintesta is a jurisdiction which levies no tax. There is power in the Trust Deed to name Devina as a beneficiary. Accordingly, she has an interest in the trust for the purposes of section 86 and Schedule 5 TCGA. The trustees make a gain of £1m in the tax year in question on qualifying foreign assets which is attributed to Davina as the settlor of the trust under section 86. It is a qualifying foreign gain. Davina duly claims relief under paragraph 3 in her tax return for the relevant year and clearly identifies and specifies the qualifying foreign gain.

5.4.3.4.2 Legislation

Paragraph 3 reads as follows.

"(1) This paragraph applies if:

(a) an amount of chargeable gains would (but for this paragraph) be treated as accruing to an individual in a tax year under section 86(4) (attribution of gains to settlors of non-resident settlements),

(b) a qualifying foreign gain accrued in that tax year to the trustees of the settlement concerned (or would have done on the assumption in section 86(3)), and

(c) the individual identifies the gain mentioned in paragraph (b) in a foreign gain claim for that tax year.

(2) For the purposes of section 86(1)(e) as it applies to the individual, the following are to be disregarded (in that tax year and in later tax years)—

(a) the gain mentioned in sub-paragraph (1)(b);

(b) any qualifying foreign loss that accrued to the trustees in# that tax year (or that would have so accrued on the assumption in section 86(3))."

Section 86 TCGA is discussed below.

5.4.3.4.3 Details

The paragraph applies to an individual who is the settlor of an offshore trust. The meaning of individual has been discussed above.

This paragraph raises a number of issues some of which are discussed in the following paragraphs.

The questions include the following:

These will each be considered in turn next.

1. *What is an amount of chargeable gains that would (but for the relief) be treated as accruing to an individual in a tax year under section 86(4).*

   Section 86(4) provides as follows.

   "(4) Where this section applies—

   (a) chargeable gains of an amount equal to that referred to in subsection (1)(e) above shall be treated as accruing to the settlor in the year or if, as respects the settlor, the year is a split year, in the UK part of that year."

   Section 86 (1) (e) reads as follows:

   "(1) This section applies where the following conditions are fulfilled as regards a settlement in a particular year of assessment—

   ...

   (e)by virtue of disposals of any of the settled property originating from the settlor, there is an amount on which the trustees would be chargeable to tax for the year under section 1(3) if the assumption as to residence specified in subsection (3) below were made; ..."

2. *What is a qualifying foreign gain accrued in that tax year to the trustees of the settlement?*

3. Qualifying foreign gain is a defined term for these purposes. It is defined in paragraph 6 of the Schedule. It reads as follows

4. *What is meant by would have done on the assumption in section 86(3)?*

   The assumptions set out in the Section 86(3) are as follows:

   "(3)Where subsection (2)(a) above applies, the assumption as to residence is that the trustees are resident ... in the United Kingdom throughout the year;

and where subsection (2)(b) above applies, the assumption as to residence is that the double taxation relief arrangements do not apply."

5. *What is meant by the individual identifies the gain mentioned in paragraph (b) in a foreign gain claim for that tax year?*
   The individual is the settlor in question (see discussion in this section).
6. *What is meant by for section 86(1)(e) as it applies to the individual?*
   The following are to be disregarded (in that tax year and in later tax years)—
   (a) the gain mentioned in sub-paragraph (1)(b);
   (b) any qualifying foreign loss that accrued to the trustees in that tax year (or that would have so accrued on the assumption in section 86(3)).
   Section 86 (3) is set out above.
7. *What is the effect of paragraph 3 applying?*
   Where paragraph 3 applies to an individual settlor who identifies a qualifying gain in a foreign gain claim who is a qualifying new resident can get the relief for foreign gains where the conditions are fulfilled.

5.4.3.4.4 Effective Date

The effective date is 06 April 2025. See paragraph 6(11).

5.4.3.5 Relief in respect of deemed gains under section 87 and Schedule 4C – Paragraph 4

5.4.3.5.1 Overview

In so far as a beneficiary receives a capital payment resulting in a charge under Section 87TCGA relief may be available to a qualifying new resident.

This paragraph is concerned in particular with CGT and the beneficiary charge under section 87 TCGA. Paragraph 4 of Schedule D1 provides for relief where the qualifying new resident is a beneficiary of a non-resident trust and the trust's gains are attributed to them on receipt of a capital payment.

Relief is limited to the capital payment amount identified in the claim. It is given by disregarding the identified capital payments in computing the amount attributed to the individual for the tax year and future years (and the trustees' pool of attributable gains is not reduced).

In broad terms, Section 87 TCGA applies to gains accruing to trustees which have not been charged on the Settlor under section 86 where a capital payment is made to a beneficiary out of the Trust. The capital payment can be matched with trust gains up to the amount of the capital payments and the recipient beneficiary charged to CGT in so far as the beneficiary is within the charge to CGT. This is done on a rolling basis.

5.4.3.5.2 Legislation

4 (1) This paragraph applies if—

(a) A settlement is for a tax year—

(i) One to which section 87 applies (attribution of gains to beneficiaries of non-resident settlements), or

(ii) A relevant settlement in relation to a Schedule 4C pool, within the meaning of paragraph 8A of Schedule 4C (transfers of value: attribution of gains etc),

(b) A beneficiary of the settlement receives a capital payment

from the trustees in that tax year, and

(c) The individual identifies the capital payment in a foreign gain claim for that tax year.

(2) The capital payment is to be disregarded (in that tax year and in 5 later tax years) for the purposes of sections 87 and 87A and paragraph 8 of Schedule 4C.

(3) The following apply for the purposes of this paragraph as they apply for the purposes of section 87—

What is the settlement for these purposes?

This is an important question to consider. This include the word "arrangement" the definition and is wider than the Lord Wilberforce approach that applies for Section 86.

Two miscellaneous points to note:

(a) section 87G (which provides for capital payments made to a close member of the settlor's family to be treated in certain cases as received by the settlor);

(b) section 97 (which makes provision about the construction of "capital payment", "settlement", "trustees" and "beneficiary").

5.4.3.5.3 Details

This paragraph raises a number of questions including the following:

(1.) What is the settlement for these purposes?

The definition of Settlement in section 620 ITTOIA applies for these purposes (see Section 9 (7)[151] TGCA).

[151] (7) In sections 86A to 96 and Schedule 4C and in ... this section—
"settlement" has the meaning given by section 620 of ITTOIA 2005, and
"settled property" and references (however expressed) to property comprised in a settlement

(2.) *When does section 87 apply to a settlement?*

(3.) *What is the relevant settlement in relation to a Schedule 4 C pool?*

This is a specialist area on which appropriate advice must be taken.

(4.) *How does the individual identify the capital payment in a foreign gain claim for that year?*

The individual must make absolutely clear in the return what it is that is the gain in respect of which relief is sought and for what tax year. There should be no fear of being longwinded about this if it is needed in order to be clear.

(5.) What is the effect of paragraph 4 (1) applying?

This is dealt with by paragraph 4(2) which reads as follows.

"(2) The capital payment is to be disregarded (in that tax year and in 5 later tax years) for the purposes of sections 87 and 87A and paragraph 8 of Schedule 4C."

5.4.3.5.4 Effective Date

The effective date is 06 April 2025. See paragraph 6(ii).

5.4.3.6 Other effects of claim - Paragraph 5

5.4.3.6.1 Overview

Paragraph 5 of new Schedule D1 signposts that making a claim for a tax year results in (a) the CGT annual exempt amount not being available for that year

(b) qualifying foreign losses not being allowable losses; and

(c) certain income tax allowances and losses being unavailable.

These are discussed below.

5.4.3.6.2 Legislation

Paragraph reads as follows:

"For other effects of making a foreign gain claim, see—

(a) section 1K(6)(b) (annual exempt amount), which provides that where a foreign gain claim has effect in relation to an individual for a tax year, the individual has no entitlement to an annual exempt amount for that year,

(b) section 16(4) (computation of losses), which provides that where a foreign gain claim has effect in relation to an individual for a tax year, qualifying foreign losses accruing to the individual in that year are not allowable losses, and

---

shall be construed accordingly.

(c) sections 845C and 845D of ITTOIA 2005, which set out some income tax consequences of making a foreign gain claim."

5.4.3.6.3 Details

Claim needed and made within time

The Claim must be made in a tax return no later than 12 months after 31 January following the end of the tax year.

Example

Liam Cant is a qualifying new resident. Liam makes a foreign gains claim. The effect of this is:

(a). Liam loses the CGT Annual Exempt Amount (£3,000 at the time of writing [152])

(b). Liam has made £50,000 of qualifying foreign losses in the tax year in question. These losses will not be allowable losses for CGT.

(c). There are also IT consequences as discussed above.

5.4.3.6.4 Effective Date

The effective date is 06 April 2025. See paragraph 6(11).

5.4.3.7 Interpretation of the Schedule Paragraph 6

5.4.3.7.1 Overview

Paragraph 6 of new Schedule D1 defines various terms for the purposes of new Schedule D1.

5.4.3.7.2 Legislation

Paragraph 6 is headed "**Interpretation of Schedule**". It reads as follows:

"6 In this Schedule—

"**qualifying foreign asset**" means an asset that—

(a) is situated outside the United Kingdom, and

(b) does not derive at least 75% of its value from UK land (see Schedule 1A);

"qualifying foreign gain" means—

'(a)a chargeable gain accruing on the disposal of a qualifying foreign asset,

(b) a chargeable gain treated as accruing as a result of section 3 (gains of non-UK resident close companies attributed to UK residents) where the gain accruing to the non-UK resident close company to which the deemed gain relates accrued on the disposal of a qualifying foreign asset, or

152 It has been higher in the past see https://www.gov.uk/guidance/capital-gains-tax-rates-and-allowances

(c) a qualifying QAHC gain, but a chargeable gain falling within paragraph (a) or (b) is not a qualifying foreign gain if it is a gain to which paragraph 1(2) of Schedule 1 applies (pre-2025-26 gains subject to the remittance basis);

"qualifying foreign loss" means a loss accruing on the disposal of an asset that is a qualifying foreign asset;

"qualifying QAHC gain" means the foreign proportion (see paragraph 46(4) to (6) of Schedule 2 to FA 2022) of a chargeable gain accruing on the disposal of shares in a QAHC (within the meaning of that Schedule) other than a chargeable gain to which paragraph 46(3) of that Schedule applies."

(3) In section 1A (territorial scope), in subsection (2), before paragraph (a) insert—

"(za) Schedule D1 (relief for new residents on foreign gains),".

(4) In section 1E (losses deductible only when within scope of tax), in subsection (6), for "Schedule 1 (UK resident individuals not domiciled in the UK)" substitute "paragraph 5 of Schedule D1 (relief for new residents on foreign gains)."

(5) In section 1K (annual exempt amount), in subsection (6)—

(a) the words from "section" to the end become paragraph (a) of that subsection, and

(b) after that paragraph insert ", or

(b) the individual makes a foreign gain claim, a foreign income claim or a foreign employment election for that tax year."

(6) In section 16 (computation of losses), at the end insert—

"(4) A qualifying foreign loss accruing to an individual in a tax year is not an allowable loss if a foreign gain claim, a foreign income claim or a foreign employment election has effect in relation to the individual for that tax year.

(5) In subsection (4), "qualifying foreign loss" has the same meaning as

in Schedule D1 (see paragraph 6 of that Schedule)."

(7) In section 288 (interpretation), in subsection (1) at the appropriate places insert—

""*foreign employment election*" means a claim under section 41M of ITEPA 2003;";

""*foreign gain claim*" means a claim under paragraph 1 of Schedule D1;";

""*foreign income claim*" means a claim under section 845A of ITTOIA 2005;";

""*qualifying new resident*" has the meaning given by section 845B of ITTOIA 2005 (which sets out the circumstances in which an individual will be a qualifying new resident following a period of 10 years of non-residence);".

(8) In Schedule 1A, in paragraph 1, after "2B(4)(b)" insert "or paragraph 6 of Schedule D1".

(9) In Schedule 1C (annual exempt amount in cases involving settled property), in paragraph 1(4), for the words from "who" to the end substitute "to whom subsection (6) of that section does not apply."

(10) In Schedule 2 to FA 2022 (qualifying asset holding companies), in paragraph 46—

(a) in the heading (as amended by section 37(3)(a)), after "income" insert "or gain", and

(b) in sub-paragraph (6A) (as inserted by section 37(3)(c)), after "claim)" insert "and paragraph (c) of the definition of "qualifying foreign gain" in paragraph 6 of Schedule D1 to TCGA 1992 (foreign gain claims)".

(11) The amendments made by this section have effect for the tax year 2025-26 and subsequent tax years."

5.4.3.7.3 Details

This is the Interpretation Paragraph for the Schedule. The Details are set out above.

5.4.3.7.4 Effective date

The effective date is 06 April 2025. See Paragraph 6 (11).

Appendix 4: Table of some relevant definitions

Word or Phrase	Meaning	Statutory Reference	Inserted by erred to etc.	Comment
assumption in section 86(3))	(3) Where subsection (2)(a) above applies, the assumption as to residence is that the trustees are resident ... in the United Kingdom throughout the year; and where subsection (2)(b) above applies, the assumption as to residence is that the double taxation relief arrangements do not apply.	Section 86 TCGA	Paragraph 3 Schedule D1	(2) The condition as to residence is that— (a)there is no time in the year when the trustees are resident in the United Kingdom, or (b)there is such a time but, whenever the trustees are resident in the United Kingdom during the year, they fall to be regarded for the purposes of any double taxation relief arrangements as resident in a territory outside the United Kingdom.
Consequential claim				For a discussion of this see above
"foreign employment election"	a claim under section 41M of ITEPA 2003	Section 41M ITEPA Section 288 TCGA	Section 39(7)	
"foreign gain claim"	a claim under paragraph 1 of Schedule D1	paragraph 1 of Schedule D1 Section 288 TCGA	Section 39(7)	
""foreign income claim"	a claim under section 845A of ITTOIA 2005	Section 845A ITTOIA Section 288 TCGA	Section 39(7)	
individual	Not defined			*Lady Longford* Surtax case

Loss of tax brought about carelessly or deliberately	Term imported from TMA	Paragraph 1(6)(c) Schedule D1		Section 118 TMA (5) For the purposes of this Act a loss of tax or a situation is brought about carelessly by a person if the person fails to take reasonable care to avoid bringing about that loss or situation. (6) Where— (a)information is provided to Her Majesty's Revenue and Customs, (b)the person who provided the information, or the person on whose behalf the information was provided, discovers some time later that the information was inaccurate, and (c)that person fails to take reasonable steps to inform Her Majesty's Revenue and Customs, any loss of tax or situation brought about by the inaccuracy shall be treated for the purposes of this Act as having been brought about carelessly by that person. (7) In this Act references to a loss of tax or a situation brought about deliberately by a person include a loss of tax or a situation that arises as a result of a

				deliberate inaccuracy in a document given to Her Majesty's Revenue and Customs by or on behalf of that person.
Period of 12 months beginning with 31 January after the end of that tax year				
"**Qualifying foreign asset**"	an asset that— (a)is situated outside the United Kingdom, and (b)does not derive at least 75% of its value from UK land (see Schedule 1A). or (c) a qualifying QAHC gain, but a chargeable gain falling within paragraph (a) or (b) is not a qualifying foreign gain if it is a gain to which paragraph 1(2) of Schedule 1 applies (pre-2025-26 gains subject to the remittance basis);		Paragraph 6	

"Qualifying foreign gain"	'(a)a chargeable gain accruing on the disposal of a qualifying foreign asset, (b) a chargeable gain treated as accruing as a result of section 3 (gains of non-UK resident close companies attributed to UK residents) where the gain accruing to the non-UK resident close company to which the deemed gain relates accrued on the disposal of a qualifying foreign asset, or (c) a qualifying QAHC gain, but a chargeable gain falling within paragraph (a) or (b) is not a qualifying foreign gain if it is a gain to which paragraph 1(2) of Schedule 1 applies (pre-2025-26 gains subject to the remittance basis);		Paragraph 6	
"Qualifying foreign loss"	a loss accruing on the disposal of an asset that is a qualifying foreign asset;	Section 39(4) and (5) cross referencing paragraph 6 Schedule D1		See also section 16 TCGA qualifying foreign asset see above and paragraph 6
"qualifying new resident"	the meaning given by section 845B of ITTOIA	section 845B ITTOIA	Section 39(7)	
"Qualifying QAHC gain" means	the foreign proportion (see paragraph 46(4) to (6) of Schedule 2 to FA 2022) of a	paragraph 6 Schedule D1		See paragraph 46 Schedule 2 FA 2022

	chargeable gain accruing on the disposal of shares in a QAHC (within the meaning of that Schedule) other than a chargeable gain to which paragraph 46(3) of that Schedule applies."			
Return	A return under section 8 TMA	Paragraph 1(6)(a) Schedule D1 TCGA		On amendment of return see 1(6)(6) Schedule D1 TCGA
"for that tax year."				
Tax year	The period from 6 April one calendar year to 5 April the following year	Section 4 ITA		

6 Some first thoughts, and possibilities

6.1 Summary

6.1.1 Introduction and Context

This section of the Supplement discusses some of the implications and potential planning strategies related to the UK's new residence-based system for Income Tax, Capital Gains Tax), and Inheritance Tax. It focuses particularly on changes for "non-doms" noting client concerns, government objectives, and various approaches to managing tax liabilities in light of the significant FA 2025 changes. It is intended to spark discussion, and nothing must be implemented without having first obtained full, reliable, reputable detailed advice and acting in accordance with it.

6.1.2 Client Objectives and Government Intentions

Clients generally want to preserve their prior tax benefits at minimal cost and risk. For some, such as US citizens, this may be partially achievable through the UK-US Double Death Convention (DDC) and Foreign Tax Credits (FTCs), but outcomes depend heavily on the particular circumstances. Client and Government intentions do not always align.

6.1.3 Residence Status and Tax Implications

There is a distinction between individuals who have never been UK resident and those who have been. Non-residents are generally taxed only on UK-source income, akin to the previous regime. For new residents, especially those qualifying for FIG specific tax benefits may apply, though performance income generally remains excluded from reliefs for ESPs.

6.1.4 Planning Strategies and Approaches

Several bespoke and complex planning approaches are outlined but only for discussion purposes. These include the following:

1. Leaving the UK Completely

This option, often considered by ultra-high-net-worth individuals (UHNWIs), involves ceasing UK residency and relocating, but is not an immediate or straightforward solution due to the 10-year IHT tail and because of practical constraints such as family and work commitments. Proper timing, compliance, and careful selection of a new principal residence are crucial. Popular destinations include Dubai, Italy, Ireland, Portugal, Singapore, Spain, and Switzerland.

2. Ceasing UK Residency Without Severing Ties

This is a less drastic approach, this involves spending fewer than 16 days in the UK to meet the First Automatic Overseas Resident Test under the Statutory Residence Test (SRT), with strict record-keeping and avoidance of UK work to circumvent the "Deeming Rule." This strategy may benefit from applicable DDCs, especially for US citizens, to reduce IHT exposure on worldwide assets. It effectively allows 30 days but only 15 nights in the UK.

3. Use of Portfolio Bonds and Insurance Wrappers

Portfolio bonds, based on the *Willoughby* case analysis, can provide a contractual right to payments disconnected from direct asset ownership, potentially reducing tax liabilities. However, Personal Portfolio Bond (PPB) legislation imposes anti-avoidance charges, making this area technically complex and requiring specialist advice.

Insurance can also be used for funding, such as term life assurance to cover IHT risks during the 10-year tail period. This has proved popular with some ESPs.

4. Restructuring Arrangements

This involves reorganizing assets, including image rights and endorsement arrangements, in the light of the abolition of the remittance basis and the exclusion of performance income from qualifying income reliefs. Tax planning must be comprehensive, with full documentation and valuations, and may include investments with tax advantages. Care is needed to avoid triggering unintended tax charges.

5. Starting the Clock Again and Fragmentation of Ownership

Transferring assets to reduce value of the individual in question's estate, using potentially exempt transfers (PETs), and fragmenting ownership can lower IHT exposure. Using this for another to start the clock running again can be of use. Fixing the value of shares and issuing growth shares with low initial value may facilitate gifting above the nil-rate band. Detailed planning and valuations are essential, with careful attention to the Disclosure of Tax Avoidance Schemes (DOTAS) rules.

6. Accepting IHT on UK Assets but Protecting Non-UK Assets

Some clients may choose to accept IHT on UK situs assets while structuring to protect rest of world assets, aiming to replicate pre-2025 positions. This requires early planning before becoming a long-term UK resident and consideration of asset situs and exclusions such as certain gilts.

6.1.5 Double Taxation Conventions (DDCs)

There is a fuller analysis of DDCs, focusing on the UK-US, UK-Italy, and UK-India treaties. These conventions aim to prevent double taxation on estates. The UK-US DDC is notable for covering inter vivos transfers and generation-skipping trusts, offering planning opportunities for US citizens.

6.1.5.1 Key Provisions of the UK-US DDC

- Defines domicile, nationality, and residence to allocate taxing rights.
- Provides exceptions for immovable property and business property of permanent establishments.
- Contains mutual agreement procedures for resolving disputes.
- Includes anti-discrimination clauses and information exchange provisions.
- Can be terminated with six months' notice, emphasizing legislative risk.

6.1.5.2 UK-Italy and UK-India DDCs

These older treaties focus on estate duties (predecessors to IHT) and primarily cover death duties, excluding inter vivos gifts and trusts. They establish situs rules for various asset classes, domicile determination rules, and credit mechanisms to alleviate double taxation. Both treaties can be terminated and require careful interpretation due to their age and the evolution of UK tax law.

6.1.6 Legal and Compliance Considerations

The document stresses the importance of full transparency, comprehensive record-keeping, and commercial justification for tax planning strategies. It highlights HMRC's scrutiny, especially of offshore elements and complex arrangements, and the necessity of specialist advice across relevant jurisdictions. Legislative risk and changes in tax law or treaties must be factored into planning.

6.1.7 Client Information Gathering

An Appendix provides an initial questionnaire for advisors to collect essential client information, including residence history, nationality, family circumstances, assets, health, and existing structures. This helps tailored and effective planning aligned to client objectives and risk profiles.

This is intended as a guide to the navigation of the complexities of UK residence-based taxation and international double taxation relief. It emphasises the importance of bespoke planning, risk management, and compliance in the new landscape introduced by 2025.

6.2 Introduction

Key Points Purpose

- The purpose of this section is to set out some points for discussion as an aid to helping clients achieve what they want including:
    - Keep what it is they had that they wish to so far as possible (important limitation)
    - Issue of lack trust in "Perfidious Albion" affects many clients. Even if IHT changes – the question is are the government to be trusted to stick to them? What protection can be built in?
- In UK already
    - What nationality?
    - If US Citizen may be advantageous because of DTA and DDC.
    - If not, why stay? Deliberate provocative question intended to help in securing real intentions.
- Position if they keep coming to UK? FIG for four years but not for Performance Income so not good for ESPs.
    - What wanted?
    - Some questions and approaches set out below

6.2.1 *General*

The preceding paragraphs have set out some of the technicalities of the new residence-based system in the UK for IT, CGT and IHT. The question then is what is the effect and how can that be ameliorated, if possible and wanted?

6.2.2 *Clients' Wants*

The next area to consider is what can now be done to preserve the earlier tax position, if anything, for the benefit of the client is as risk free a way as possible. This is a frequent request in my recent experience. The people I come across liked what they had before and would like to "keep" it, if possible, at limited cost and risk. Clients always have high (impossible?) requirements.

For some clients, such as US citizens, this may be possible at least to some extent[153] (see the discussion of the UK US DDC below). As ever, it all depends on the facts which the advisor must investigate thoroughly.

What does come across to me in discussions, as at the time of writing, is the intense anger at and lack of trust in the UK government that is now prevalent. The discussion of a UK Wealth Tax at the time of writing this, adds to the lack

[153] Compliance is also important here. For U.S. citizens coming to the UK full advice is needed so, for example, full tax credits for UK tax are available in the US and all the requisite IRS forms have been filed.

of trust. The prospect of an exit charge has led to requests for escape plans to be in place. However, this assumes at least some notice will be given.[154]

6.2.3 *Government wants and "Non-Dom" Perception*

One thing is clear and that is that the UK wishes to collect more tax from UK resident "non-doms", as they used to be called colloquially. My experience is that the increases in IT and CGT are much less resented than the "unwarranted" 10-year IHT hike as the ten-year tail etc. is perceived.[155] This is what seems to be what has driven many "non doms" from the UK and is likely to continue to do so. The ending of the efficacy of Excluded Properly Trusts and the ten-year tail as a result of the change to long term UK residence has been the proverbial "straw that broke the camel's back". It was not part of the Spring 2024 announcement but was part of the 2024 Autumn Budget.[156]

This change has also made the UK a less attractive place for an ESP to base themselves in the view of many ESPs, in my recent experience. This is not just for tax purposes but a perceived change in the attitude of the indigenous population and as to the provision of service. This is hard to test but the perception does seem to be there strongly at least anecdotally. It does not show signs in my experience of abating short term.

There seems to be no single approach that fits all that can be used. Much depends on the individual's particular circumstances and wants. This is an area which needs very bespoke and comprehensive planning often with very specialist advice.

6.2.4 *Different Positions*

6.2.4.1 *General*

Much depends in this context on the residence status of the ESP in question and how long they have been in the UK, if they have been in the UK. This is often a

[154] This is not necessarily the case. There is a conspiracy theory that a government could pass emergency legislation during a country wide power cut that stops the internet so that no money movement was possible. The emergency legislation could include the return of Exchange Control so that movement afterwards would be a criminal offence unless prior approval and permission had been obtained.

[155] It is also perceived as double taxation. This may not be an accurate reflection of what has been done but the perception is certainly hard to shake. One interlocutor even described it as a "betrayal" after having lived here.

[156] As noted elsewhere a further impact assessment was not done to reflect the change. This seems unfortunate to say the least given what has happened. It has sought to rely on what was done for the Spring budget and the 2017 changes. This is like comparing apples and oranges and is an inappropriate approach to policy which should be based on sound data.

useful general starting point in discussion with the ESP particularly what their UK connections are and which matter to them and which less so. This is not a pure tax point but a practical one. Their offshore connections are also relevant and should be investigated.

6.2.4.2 UK present or not?

The position differs for (a) those in the UK from that of (b) those not in the UK.

If the ESP has never been UK resident, then many of the potential issues are easier as the ESP is not generally within the charge to UK tax on a residence basis and so taxable generally only on a source basis. That is not really different from the position under the Old Regime. If they are not resident in the UK broadly the issues under discussion here, do not arise. By going somewhere other than the UK as not becoming UK resident many of the perceived difficulties do not arise and, on balance, there is a smaller overall tax bill. My recent experience is that many individuals perceive places other than the UK as more welcoming and more to their taste particularly if they have less "harsh" regimes as one client described the UK as having.

6.2.5 *New Arrivals – Qualifying New Residents and Performance Income*

The general position of those in the UK differs for those who have not been resident in the UK for:

- 4 years; and / or
- 10 out of the preceding 20 years who may be UK long term residents;

for whom there may be IT and CGT benefits for up to four years[157].

This is the FIG regime for qualifying new residents which is discussed earlier in the Supplement

6.2.6 *Portfolio Bonds etc. (See also "Insurance" below)*

A suggestion I am being asked about more recently is the use of Portfolio Bonds intended to provide a disconnect between the ESP and say the "Image Right" payments. This based on the House of Lords analysis in the *Willoughby* case discussed below. This can be useful in the UK. However, the offshore position must also be considered as if there is a higher offshore tax charge saving UK tax may not be of much use.

In some jurisdictions such bonds can also be helpful. For example, if there is no stockholding in the relevant insurance corporation, there is no PFIC (Passive

---

[157] The UK has been used as a "stepping stone" jurisdiction where there is say a big capital gain on a disposal in the current jurisdiction which coming to the UK for less than four years may alleviate.

Foreign Investment Company (PFICs) Regulations defining when an insurance company is caught).[158] The offshore tax position should always be carefully checked and appropriate advice taken.

6.2.6.1 Leaving the UK

This requires careful planning and full and proper compliance. Timing for best advantage must be considered including the tax position where it is intended to be principally resident. See https://www.gov.uk/tax-right-retire-abroad-return-to-uk

6.2.6.2 Coming to the UK

Again, those coming to the UK need careful planning and arrangement. https://www.gov.uk/tax-come-to-uk.

Availability of FTCs also needs to be investigated. For example, a US citizen is liable to US tax on a worldwide basis subject to certain exceptions. If there are FTCs available for this in the UK or vice versa, this may reduce the tax loss for such persons as may the UK US DDC for IHT.

6.2.6.3 Insurance

Bonds – A rave from the grave.

As noted above these are becoming quite the thing. However, they have some issues. See the discussion below:

6.2.6.4 Clear knowledge of facts essential

As ever it is important to know the facts. An Initial Questionnaire to use with clients is set out as Appendix 1 at the end of this section to assist with the acquisition of some of the initial relevant information. It is not exhaustive and intended merely as a starting point from which many other questions will certainly arise.

6.2.6.5 Some Danish questions to recognise or not to recognise?

An interesting development at the time of writing is the Danish proposal to protect facial characteristics.[159] Depending on how this develops it might provide an interesting alternative to "Image Rights". This needs to be kept under review and it will be particularly interesting to see how the EU reacts to this. It may also provide an escape from the restriction of FIG relief for "performance income". Payment for the use of facial characteristics would not seem to arise from

---

[158] https://www.irs.gov/instructions/i8621#en_US_202201_publink100010010

[159] See e.g. https://www.theguardian.com/technology/2025/jun/27/deepfakes-denmark-copyright-law-artificial-intelligence

the performance of entertainment or sporting activity in quite the same way and to the same degree as endorsement and similar income.

6.3 Some approaches

Key Points – Some Approaches

- Some possibilities are considered here for discussion purposes
- Must be measured and considered responses if they are to stand any chance of being effective and successful
- Careful thought must be given to the likelihood of successful challenge along with where on the risk profile is the Client in question. In many cases specialist advice will be necessary as this is a technically challenging area and one HMRC are likely to focus on given the potential amounts involved.
- Possibilities include:
  1. Leaving the UK completely
  2. Ceasing to be UK resident
  3. Putting in "firebreaks"
  4. Restructuring arrangements including image rights and endorsement arrangements
  5. Using insurance for funding and or as a wrapper
  6. Starting the clock again
  7. Checking nationality etc. and possible applicability of any relevant DDC
  8. Fragmenting and splitting ownership
  9. Fixing the value and giving away the value above that
  10. Accepting IHT on UK assets but seeking to protect rest of world assets

i. General Comments

The approaches to dealing with the significant changes brought about by the FA 2025 must be measured and considered if they are to stand any chance of being effective and successful. Facial recognition arguably, at least, does not result directly or indirectly[160] from performance of sport or entertainment on usual principles of statutory construction. Careful thought must be given to the likelihood of successful challenge along with where on the risk profile is the Client in question. In many cases specialist advice will be necessary as this is a technically challenging area and one HMRC are likely to focus on.

The client must also be made aware that the law may change again in the future so it is not a "perpetual solution". There is what is sometimes called "legislative risk". Accordingly, the position must be kept under review. "Legislative risk" is nothing new particularly where estate planning is concerned which can be a

[160] cf the use of "derive" in the 1987 Regulations.

long-term matter compared to transactional planning which is often more "one off" in nature.

ii. Some possibilities to consider

A number of matters to consider occur to me including the following. These derive from matters that have gone across my desk recently and questions I have been asked:

1. Leaving the UK completely
2. Ceasing to be UK residents
3. Putting in "firebreaks"
4. Restructuring arrangements including image rights and endorsement arrangements
5. Using insurance for funding and or as a wrapper
6. Starting the clock again
7. Checking nationality etc and possible applicability of any relevant DDC
8. Fragmenting and splitting ownership
9. Fixing the value and giving away the value above that
10. Accepting IHT on UK assets but seeking to protect rest of world assets.

These will now each be commented on in turn at a high level. They are put forward as ideas for discussion and treated as such. Nothing should be done without taking full appropriate advice covering all relevant jurisdictions and acting on that advice. These reasons and their commercial justifications should be recorded in suitable documents which should be retained for future reference.

6.3.1 *Leaving the UK completely*

Key Points – Leaving UK completely

- Not as easy not just buying an airline ticket to somewhere
- NB Two Important Matters
    - Not an immediate solution e.g. 10 year tail for IHT
    - Is it practicable and acceptable to others?
- Easier with UHINWI's as in practice much of the infrastructure needed is already there e.g. 13 Houses around the world
- Go for automatic overseas tests? Certainty vs restriction consideration
- Care with Deeming Rule if work done in the UK
- Go where? Ensure necessary permissions etc. obtained
- Ensure meet compliance requirements

6.3.1.1 General

"I am off completely" has been the "knee jerk reaction" of many affected by the changes, witness the 10,000 plus millionaires said to have left the UK recently. [161] However, it is not always as simple, as clients sometimes like to think, as buying a plane ticket. It is something that needs careful thought and planning.

Two immediate points need to be made. These are:

a. It does not provide an immediate solution e.g. 10 year tail for IHT; and
b. It is not always practicable and or acceptable to others.

Point a. reflects the fact that there is generally a 10-year tail before UK IHT ceases to apply to a long-term UK resident who ceases to be UK resident. This must not be forgotten and possible mitigation considered.

Point b. reflects the fact that an individual may have other relationships and obligations as well as performances and appearances that impose restrictions on what is possible. This may include family members and others. [162] Work obligations such as directors' meetings and the like can also impact.

This approach is often easier to deal with for UHINWI ESPs with houses etc. around the World and a routine and structure set up as to where they are when. Such persons already have much of the necessary infrastructure in place to make such a change. Further, they do not need e.g. to sell a property to acquire another as they already have a number of suitable properties usually chosen because they are liked rather than a quick acquisition under pressure. They can

[161] https://www.imidaily.com/europe/uk-lost-10800-millionaires-in-2024-as-non-dom-changes-spark-record-exodus/

[162] Some more significant than others.

also provide a base in the short term from which to find a more suitable property if that is what is wanted so reducing hassle and stress as e.g. the interim property does not need to be sought first which can help with timing. Where relevant they have also dealt with the education of children etc. It is often only a matter of changing routine to exclude the UK from the itinerary or if (2) Ceasing to be UK resident discussed next is used to spend less than 16 midnights in the UK.[163] There seem to be some useful apps coming onto the market to assist with this seemingly linked to GPS to show where the individual is when. These can be useful where the HINWI is not into careful recording of information. It is important not to work in the UK because of the "Deeming Rule" discussed below.

It is important for the advisor to discover the pressure points on relationships etc. It should be part of the information gathering exercise the advisor undertakes. This should also include making sure that other more individual concerns that the individual may not wish to share with other family members because of the hurt and difficulty it could engender are covered. A sensitive approach may be needed.

Such matters are important knowledge for a trusted or advisor to have. It is also important for the adviser to be aware of the conflicts this may bring and how to deal with them.

6.3.1.2 *Where to go?*

It is one thing to decide to leave the UK, but it is also necessary practically to decide where one is going to which is to be the principal tax residence. This is important in practice as it is much easier to show HMRC UK residence has been lost if the replacement can be shown. Whilst technically this is not necessarily the case practically it seems to be. Care is also needed with where "the Home" is as the SRT treats a person with a home in the UK as resident where the second UK Automatic Residence test is met.

Ideally, the majority of the tax year should be spent in the new country of tax residence. The UK family home should generally be sold and available accommodation avoided. Presentationally, different hotels, Airbnb's and the like are much more helpful than reserving and retaining a suite at a "swanky" London

---

[163] This is in order to fall within the first automatic overseas resident's test. Some may regard this as overly cautious, but it can still give up to 30 days in The UK assuming there is no Home in the UK. If the conditions in the first automatic overseas residence test are met, then under the legislation the individual would automatically be overseas resident and so has a strong statutory basis for their status. Some clients find this comforting

Hotel where clothes etc. are kept. It may be less convenient but it is usually worth it because of the potential tax saving. Popular destinations seem to include[164] the following:

- Dubai
- Italy
- Ireland
- Portugal
- Singapore
- Spain
- Switzerland

There is a Jurisdiction Table in Appendix 3 (at the end of this section) which seeks to provide some relevant information on places I have seen used.

The table includes information as to whether or not there is a DDS. It also includes some URLs for further information including the ICAEW resources. Each case needs detailed individual consideration. The visa and rights of residence position needs detailed consideration. Being thrown out of a country does not help the tax planning. Many accounting firms provide useful country guides to which the Reader is referred as appropriate. I have also found BDO's article entitled "FIG Regime: How does the UK's tax regime for new residents compared globally" a useful source of information.[165]

6.3.2 Ceasing to be UK resident

Key Points Ceasing to be UK resident

- Not perpetual solution – 10 year IHT Tail
- Heed what others want
- Keep good records
    - Apps to help
- DDCs? Any applicable? What covered?
- US Citizens
    - DDCs?
    - Not Green Card – consider change of UK status
- HMRC views

6.3.2.1 General

This is a less drastic and more technical approach than leaving the UK completely but there are many overlapping issues.

---

[164] This is not exhaustive

[165] Other advisers' publications are available

Ceasing to be UK resident without severing ties completely with the UK may be a more acceptable approach to some clients. It is sometimes an approach that may fit in better with their social lives and so sweeten the pill. Approaches (1) and (2) should both be discussed with the client in my view and the pros and cons carefully considered. Although an understandable reaction sweeping away all ties with the UK may not be realistic or sensible. This is certainly likely to be so the case if done on a "forced sale" basis.

The ceasing residence approach does not solve the ten-year tail immediately but may help in the longer term. Term insurance may ease the issue in appropriate cases. However, in some circumstances with restructuring assets are held personally and a suitable location for principal residence found it may well assist here. It is essential that proper clear records are kept showing limited presence in the UK. The "apps" mentioned above may help with this.

For example, becoming a resident of one of the jurisdictions with which the UK has a double death tax convention ("**DDC**") may assist with the tax on death position as broadly in those circumstances it is only UK assets that are generally taxable. It may also be possible to restructure what assets are held and where situate. This may help with succession planning and reducing the value of the taxable estate for IHT purposes.

DDC are discussed in more detail below. They also raise the important question of Domicile and the relevance of deemed domicile. This needs careful research and advice in any particular case. The position in the other jurisdictions more generally must not be forgotten and appropriate advice sought.

Accordingly, if an appropriate convention applies and the assets are held personally and are non-UK situs assets then the position on death may be ameliorated. This is tended to be the main concern in my experience of non-dom clients. Some conventions go wider, and cover *inter vivos* transactions and certain trusts e.g. the UK US DDC.

6.3.2.2 Automatic Overseas Resident Tests

The SRT can be a helpful matter here. It can give legislative certainty to an acceptable extent in many of the circumstances under consideration in this context.

If the taxpayer who was UK resident in one or more of the three preceding tax years before the year in question the first overseas test can be met if the taxpayer spends less than 16 days in the UK in the year in question.[166] If so, then the individual comes fully within the First Automatic Overseas Resident Test. This can allow the First Automatic Overseas Test to be met.

This statutory test is found in paragraph 12 Schedule 45 FA 203 and reads as follows.

> "12 The first automatic overseas test is that—
> (a) **P** [i.e. the person in question] was **resident in the UK** for **one or more** of **the 3 tax years preceding year X** [i.e. the year in question],
> (b) the number of days in year X that P spends in the UK is less than 16, and
> (c) P does not die in year X."

There are special rules for the year of death.[167]

6.3.2.3 Spends less than 16 days in UK in year in question

This usually means a maximum of 15 midnights in the UK as it is the end of the day that is taken[168] which HMRC treat midnight UK time in most cases. However, this can mean more than 15 days physically in the UK if the individual leaves the UK before midnight on the second day. The effect of this usually means a maximum of 30 days in the UK which fits the schedule of many HINWI non-doms in my experience. If less certainty is required, then a longer period may be possible, but this depends on the precise circumstances. In my experience a number of ESPs have found the first Automatic overseas Test attractive. Depending on when they left the UK it may also assist with long term UK resi-

[166] See paragraph 12 Schedule 45 FA 2013
"The first automatic overseas test is that—
(a) P [the individual in question] was resident in the UK for one or more of the 3 tax years preceding year X [the year in question],
(b) the number of days in year X that P spends in the UK is ***less than 16***, and
(c) P does not die in year X."
This is on the basis that the individual had been UK resident which is often the case. If not resident in the preceding three years the 45 (less than 46) days then the Second Automatic Offshore residence test may apply. See paragraph 13 which provides:
"The second automatic overseas test is that—
(a) P was resident in the UK for none of the 3 tax years preceding year X, and
(b) the number of days that P spends in the UK in year X is less than 46."
Complications can arise in year 4 though if care is not taken.

[167] For HMRC's views on this see https://www.gov.uk/hmrc-internal-manuals/residence-and-fig-regime-manual/rfig20900

[168] Paragraph 23(1) FA 2013:
"If P is not present in the UK at the end of a day, that day does not count as a day spent by P in the UK. ..."

dence. For example, paragraph 46 Schedule 13 provides that "Certain pre-commencement emigrants treated as not being long-term UK residents"[169] (see below for further discussion).

This approach in practice means no work being done in the UK as this may bring the "Deeming Rule"[170] into play. This rule, where applicable, means one is looking not at midnights but any day of physical presence in the UK whether or not including midnight.

I have seen the acquisition of "bolt holes" in the Channel Islands, the Isle of Man and France as protection against this. This may also include special provision for transport from the UK to such bolt holes so as not to spend more than 15 nights in the UK. Many clients consider this a sensible cost to preserve the tax benefits.

For many HINWIs this approach may only mean a readjustment to their usual routine where they have houses in many jurisdictions around the World. Many such persons will not be open to "working" in the UK which also helps with the deeming rule. They often do not need to although this depends on the particular circumstances.

---

[169] Section 46(1)An individual who would otherwise be a long-term UK resident at any time in a given tax year ("the relevant tax year") is treated for the purposes of IHTA 1984 as not being a long-term UK resident at that time if the individual—

(a) was not domiciled in the United Kingdom on 30 October 2024,

(b) has been resident in the United Kingdom for no tax year in the period beginning with the tax year 2025-26 and ending with the relevant tax year, and

(c) either—

 (i) was resident in the United Kingdom for none of the 3 tax years immediately preceding the relevant tax year, or

 (ii) was resident in the United Kingdom for fewer than 15 of the 20 tax years immediately preceding the relevant tax year.

[170] Paragraph 23(1) FA 2013

"... (3)The deeming rule applies if—

 (a) P has at least 3 UK ties for a tax year,

 (b) the number of days in that tax year when P is present in the UK at some point in the day but not at the end of the day ("qualifying days") is more than 30, and

 (c) P was resident in the UK for at least one of the 3 tax years preceding that tax year.

(4) The deeming rule is that, once the number of qualifying days in the tax year reaches 30 (counting forward from the start of the tax year), each subsequent qualifying day in the tax year is to be treated as a day spent by P in the UK.

(5) The deeming rule does not apply for the purposes of sub-paragraph (3)(a) (so, in deciding for those purposes whether P has a 90-day tie, qualifying days in excess of 30 are not to be treated as days spent by P in the UK)."

Example

Steen Gixtith has been UK resident for the last two tax years before the present tax year. He spends the following time in the UK.

Arrive	*Depart at*	*Total*
Second Monday in April	12 noon following Thursday	3 nights (Monday, Tuesday, Wednesday)
Friday in July	following Wednesday	5 nights (Friday, Saturday, Sunday, Monday, Tuesday)
December 23	Noon December 30	7 nights (23,24,25,26,27,28,29)
Overall Total		**15** (3+5+7)

Total 15 nights (3+5+7) which (*ex hypothesi*) is less than 16 nights and so the First Automatic Non-resident Test would be met.

If Steen had left on 31 December that would be 16 nights. The First Automatic Non-resident Test would not then be met.[171]

Day visits (i.e. leave before Midnight) or meeting in say Paris could help keep the count down.

Again, this is a matter that needs careful planning and record keeping.

This assumes no work in the UK so deeming rule issue.

This is a matter that is very much dependent on individual circumstances and wishes. It requires careful and prospective planning.

If the person was not UK resident for any of the preceding three tax years, then the number of days potentially in the UK goes up. The relevant test refers to "fewer than 46 days in the UK in the tax year". This means 45 or fewer days (midnight subject to the deeming rule) in the UK. It is important to check the previous residence position and to be certain it is correct if more than 15 days might be spent in the UK in the year. Full and proper record keeping in a verifiable and advisable / accessible / admissible form is essential.

6.3.2.4 *What is there in the UK by way of chargeable assets?*

It is important for the advisor to know what there actually is in the UK by way of chargeable assets. This is a simple sounding question but not one that clients can always answer easily. Not all clients keep full, admissible up to date records in my experience. However, the information is essential. The onus of proof will be on the taxpayer. This can be vital in any discussion/dispute with the Fisc.

This information includes what assets are there in the UK. It also includes relationships. What family ties are there in the UK? What other similar ties and relationships are there?

[171] Hence the acquisition of non-UK bolt holes and special transport arrangements.

These can be relevant for the purposes of the SRT and need careful consideration along with all the other circumstances.

Practical issues such as grandmothers and grandchildren must be considered[172] particularly the effect on the amount of time in the UK. Also, family homes and UK based businesses can be important in this context. They can raise difficult issues as to what to do with them. In purely tax terms it will usually be best to get rid of them, but this can raise non-financial concerns which are important to some but sometimes not as much to others.

That said it may be possible to structure things for the individual(s) in question only to be in the UK for less than 16 days a tax year, so the first automatic overseas residence test is met as is considered under the heading "Automatic Overseas Residence Tests" above. This is not necessarily as restrictive as it sounds.

Detailed information is needed when considering this as is an understanding of the personal relationships and circumstances that the persons involved. Underlying the important matters though remain the two points made at the start of [this section] namely the time needed to escape the tail and the practicalities in doing so.

6.3.2.5 US Citizens etc

The position of those who are US citizens or Green Card[173] holders may be different. The US double death convention ("DDC") is discussed in more detail below which may be of help in some circumstances. Generally, it only applies to US Citizens. Accordingly, the individual's status must be carefully checked and considered.

The DDC can also impact the IHT charge on *inter vivos* transfers and death and in respect of some trusts. They may help some lifetime planning by Redistributing assets within the wanted group.

The US charge to tax on income and gains by reference to nationality and the like must not be forgotten. This may mean FTC's are available. The UK US DTA on income and gains may assist here and should be considered as well as the UK US DDC on death duties etc.

---

[172] This is not intentionally sexist but reflects how this has manifested itself in practice as far as I am concerned.

[173] Green card holders are not technically US Citizens and so problems can arise. The card is evidence of a right to reside permanently in the USA. See https://www.uscis.gov/green-card

This approach can be used in a seemingly successful way if a carefully considered and an appropriate plan is put in place. This will often require specialist advice including offshore advice.

The UK US DDC is considered in more detail below.

As noted above ceasing to be UK resident without severing ties completely with the UK may be a more acceptable approach to some clients than quitting the UK completely. However, the residence position under the SRT rules must be kept under careful review.

6.3.2.6 *HMRC's views – IHT DTR etc.*

The following extracts from the IHT publications may help to understand HMRC's views on this and some of the mechanics. They cover treaty relief and unilateral relief. They are included for the Reader's convenience.[174]

6.3.3 *Double taxation conventions*

According to HMRC "Double taxation conventions are treaties (agreements) which help prevent you being taxed in the UK and another country. This can happen if a person was domiciled or deemed domiciled (fiscally domiciled) in another country when they die.

You might be able to reclaim the tax through a double taxation convention, if the other country charges Inheritance Tax on the same property or gift the UK is taxing.

The UK has a number of bilateral double tax conventions for taxes on estates, gifts and inheritances."

6.3.3.1 *How double taxation conventions work*

For the purpose of the agreement, they allow:

- the country in which the transferor is (or in the case of a death, was) domiciled or deemed domiciled to tax all property wherever it is
- the other country to tax only specified types of property, such as immovable property, in its territory

From 6 April 2025, a person is treated as having deemed UK domicile if they are a long-term UK resident (section 48ZA of the Inheritance Tax Act 1984, as amended by the Finance Act 2025). This is discussed later.

---

[174] https://www.gov.uk/guidance/inheritance-tax-double-taxationrelief#:~:text=The%20following%20double

If you still suffer double taxation, there are rules for deciding which country gives credit for the other's tax.

6.3.3.2 Countries the UK has double taxation conventions with

The following double taxation conventions apply to Inheritance Tax.

Country	Date of entry into force
Republic of Ireland	2 October 1978
South Africa	6 May 1979
USA	11 November 1979
Netherlands (amended)	16 June 1980 3 June 1996
Sweden (amended)	19 June 1981 14 July 1989
Switzerland	7 March 1995

Treaties with France, Italy, India and Pakistan were in place before 1975 during the Estate Duty era and have different rules to eliminate double taxation. They do not include provision for deemed domicile.

6.3.4 If there is no double taxation convention

If a transfer is liable to Inheritance Tax and also to a similar tax imposed by another country with which the UK does not have an agreement, you may be able to get relief under Unilateral Relief provisions.

HMRC say the following in the IHT Manual.

> **IHTM27160 - Foreign property: Double Taxation Conventions: What is Double Taxation Relief?**
>
> For more information on the effect of long-term UK residence in respect of Double Taxation Conventions, please refer to IHTM47070.
>
> Inheritance Tax Double Taxation Conventions
>
> https://www.gov.uk/guidance/inheritance-tax-double-taxation-relief
>
> The Double Taxation Relief (Taxes On Estates of Deceased Persons and On Gifts) (United States of America) Order 1979
>
> Statutory Instrument 1979 No. 1454
>
> https://www.legislation.gov.uk/uksi/1979/1454/made

HMRC say this on the change to a long-term residence test.

> **"IHTM47070 - Long-term UK residence test: Introduction to Double Taxation Conventions**
>
> From 6 April 2025 a person's UK Inheritance Tax position will depend on whether they are a long-term UK resident (IHTM47000).

A double taxation convention between the UK and a foreign country may apply if a person is in scope for UK Inheritance Tax or its equivalent in the convention country.[175] The UK currently has 10 double taxation conventions in place which have been negotiated between the fiscal authority in each country. (IHTM27161).

A double taxation convention seeks to eliminate double taxation by assigning taxing rights to one country or the other and, on occasions where both countries retain their right to tax the same assets, it determines which country will allow and apply a credit.

Where primary taxing rights cannot be established, a tiebreaker set out within the convention will be applied.

Each convention varies in its approach to eliminating double taxation and some only apply in respect of duty or taxes imposed on death whilst others also apply for charges imposed on other occasions i.e. lifetime transfers.

From 6 April 2025, where a double tax convention operates by reference to whether the UK treats a person as UK domiciled for Inheritance Tax purposes (deemed domicile), a person will be treated as UK domiciled if they are a long-term UK resident.

Deemed domicile is relevant to some of the double tax conventions (IHTM47071) but not others (IHTM47072).

However, where a person is treated as domiciled or long-term resident in the UK for the purposes of Inheritance Tax because they have made a spousal domicile election (IHTM13040) or a long-term UK residence election (IHTM47031) this will be disregarded in applying any of the existing double tax conventions. (IHTA84/267ZF(3) and (4))

IHTM47071–Long-term UK residence test: Post 1975 Double Taxation Conventions

If a person is a long-term UK resident they will be deemed to be domiciled in the UK under the terms of these conventions."

6.3.4.1 Republic of Ireland

Taxes covered are UK Inheritance Tax and Republic of Ireland capital acquisition tax and gift tax.

A person will be regarded as domiciled in either contracting state if they are domiciled under general law or treated as so under their respective laws.

Each state retains the right to tax assets under their own law and where this results in both states taxing the same property, the situs and credit provisions within the convention will determine which state has subsidiary taxing rights.

[175] The DDCs are discussed further below where it will be seen that it can be a complicated matter.

6.3.4.2 *South Africa*

Taxes covered are UK Inheritance Tax and estate duty and donations tax in South Africa.

A person will be regarded as domiciled in either contracting state if they are domiciled under general law or treated as so under their respective laws.

Taxing rights can vary depending on residence in either state for income tax purposes and whether the person was a national of South Africa or a national of the UK.

6.3.4.3 *USA*

Taxes covered are UK Inheritance Tax and federal estate duty or gift tax in the United States, including generation skipping transfers.

A person will be regarded as domiciled in the UK if they are domiciled under general law or treated as so under UK law.

A person will be regarded as domiciled in the US if they were a resident or a national of the US at any time during the preceding three years.

Taxing rights can vary depending on residence in either state for income tax purposes and whether the person was a national of the United States of America or a national of the UK.

6.3.4.4 *Netherlands*

Taxes covered are UK Inheritance Tax and succession duty, gift tax and transfer duty in the Netherlands.

A person will be regarded as domiciled in the UK if they are domiciled under general law or treated as so under UK law.

A person will be regarded as domiciled in the Netherlands if they are a resident of the Netherlands. Currently, Dutch nationals are regarded as resident in the Netherlands for 10 years after their departure.

6.3.4.5 *Sweden*

Taxes covered are UK Inheritance Tax and Swedish inheritance tax and gift tax.

A person will be regarded as domiciled in either contracting state if they are domiciled under general law or treated as so under their respective laws.

Inheritance tax and gift tax was abolished in Sweden on 31 December 2004.

6.3.4.6 *Switzerland*

Taxes covered are UK Inheritance Tax and cantonal and communal taxes on estates and inheritances in Switzerland. It does not apply to settlements in Switzerland where there is no interest in possession.

A person will be regarded as domiciled in the UK if they are domiciled under general law or treated as so under UK law.

A person will be regarded as domiciled in Switzerland if they are domiciled or resident of Switzerland under Swiss law or are a Swiss national and their succession must be governed under Swiss Civil Law.

Taxing rights in either state can be restricted in cases of temporary residence by reason of employment provided the person has retained the domicile of the state in which they are a national.

The UK DDC for US Italy and India are considered further below to which the reader is referred.

6.4 Putting in "firebreaks" - one other prophylactic to consider is the use of "firebreaks"

Key Points – firebreaks

- Bonds
    - Useful technical stuff but practical problems
    - NB PPB
- Lord Nolan in *Willoughby*
- PPB Issues
- Can be bespoke
- Detailed bespoke advice needed

6.4.1 *Introductory*

This approach essentially is looking to create a structure where the taxpayer is sufficiently distanced as a matter of law (and substance) from the underlying assets to mean that IHT does not arise on the death of that individual. This is not always easy to achieve because of the associated operations, close family member and similar legislation and the *Ramsay / Arrowtown* approach on finding facts realistically and applying the statute purposively. It requires care and concentration and a good team.

The idea is to keep the benefit within the desired group but in such a way that it has a low value and or the underlying assets are not the taxpayers in so far as possible so as to reduce the amount of IHT on death. It may be possible to fund any residual IHT on the main person by life assurance. Appropriate quotes should be obtained.

The most often raised approach to this that I have encountered so far has been the proposed use of portfolio bonds.

These are essentially "insurance wrappers" which give a right to a payment of a sum on the occurrence of a contingency such as the death of the life in being by reference to specified assets in the insurance company's general fund.

6.4.2 *Willoughby v IRC*

This approach relies on the analysis of Lord Nolan in Willoughby v IRC [1997] 70 TC 57 as to what a bond holder actually has which is essentially a contractual right against the Insurance Company to be paid a sum of money on the occurrence of a contingency but no rights in the underlying assets by reference to which the sum assured is to be calculated.

Lord Nolan said the *Willoughby* Case that:

> "My Lords, there is a basic fallacy in this argument. It lies in the proposition that the "underlying reality" is that the holder of the bond continues to manage and benefit from "his own portfolio of investments."
>
> As my noble and learned friend Lord Hoffmann pointed out in the course of argument, so far from the underlying investments being owned by the bond holder, he has no legal or equitable interest in them whatever. As Clause 12 of the Policy makes clear the allocation of investment units to the bond for which the policy provides is purely notional. Units are referred to solely for the purpose of computing benefits under the policy. The reality in truth is that the bond holder has a contractual right to the benefits promised by the policy, no more and no less. It is therefore quite wrong to describe the bond holder as having, in the words of the appellants' printed case "in substance all the advantages of direct personal ownership without the tax disadvantages." The significance of this misdescription would become all too apparent if--perish the thought--Royal Life were to become insolvent and unable to meet its obligations to the bond holders.
>
> This fallacy goes to the heart of the Commissioners' case. For the attack which they have launched against Professor and Mrs. Willoughby and other Royal Life bond holders is limited as I have said to those who hold personal portfolio bonds, that is to say bonds under which the bond holder has effective control of the investment policy, the Commissioners accepting that the remaining offshore bonds issued by Royal Life do not involve the avoidance of tax.
>
> Like the Special Commissioner and the Court of Appeal, I am unable to follow the reasoning of the Commissioners. The personal portfolio bond holder may fare better or worse in terms of benefits by reason of his control over investment policy than does his fellow bond holder with the standard type of bond,

but the difference between them seems to me to have nothing to do with tax or with tax avoidance. I can see no reason why Parliament should have intended to distinguish between them in fiscal terms.

It follows that, in agreement with the Court of Appeal, I would affirm the clear and carefully reasoned decision of the Special Commissioner upholding the respondents' claim for exemption under section 741(*a*). It is therefore unnecessary to decide whether the Special Commissioner was equally entitled to hold that the respondents had established their claim to the protection conferred by section 741(*b*) on "bona fide commercial transactions . . . not designed for the purpose of avoiding liability to taxation." At first sight the point seems a straightforward one, but the precise scope of the phrase "bona fide commercial" as it occurs in the related context of section 703(1) of the Act, which also deals with tax avoidance, has given rise to dispute in a number of cases of which *Commissioners of Inland Revenue v. Goodwin* [1976] 1 W.L.R. 191, a decision of your Lordships' House is an example. In the instant case your Lordships did not think it necessary to call upon counsel for the respondents, and in company with the Court of Appeal I think it better to defer consideration of section 741(*b*) until a case arises in which it is crucial to the decision.[176]"

6.4.3 *Revenue Response – PPB legislation*

The Revenue's response as the good losers that they are was to change the law and introduce a charge on PPBs.

HMRC make the following comments on this:

"**IPTM7705 - Personal portfolio bonds (PPB): introduction**

In law, it is the insurer, not the policyholder, that owns the property that determines the benefits under a life policy. Where the policyholder has the ability to select the property that determines the policy benefits, the policyholder retains nearly all the advantages of direct personal ownership of that property. Without the PPB legislation, because the property is held in the 'envelope' of a life insurance policy, the policyholder would not have to pay income tax on dividend and interest income arising from the investments nor capital gains tax on disposals when the investments underlying the policy are altered. Tax on any gains on the policy would be deferred until the policy comes to an end.

PPB legislation

The PPB legislation is an anti-avoidance measure which imposes a yearly charge to tax on life insurance and capital redemption policies, and life annuity contracts in some circumstances, where the policyholder is able to select the property that determines the benefits payable on those policies/contracts.

Where the chargeable person is an individual, the relevant legislation is contained in ITTOIA05/S515 to S526.

[176] See: https://publications.parliament.uk/pa/ld199798/ldjudgmt/jd970710/willough.htm

> Where the chargeable person is a company, the loan relationship rules apply from the start of the first accounting period of the company to begin on or after 1 April 2008 - IPTM3900 onwards.
>
> The rules as they apply to companies before 1 April 2008 are contained in The Personal Portfolio Bonds (Tax) Regulations 1999, or 'PPB Regulations' (SI 1999/1029).
>
> **PPB Guidance**
>
> Although the guidance in IPTM7710 onwards mainly refers to 'policies' and 'policyholders' it should be read as applying not only to life insurance policies, but also to life annuity contracts and capital redemption policies, which are also within the scope of the PPB legislation.
>
> HMRC staff may contact BAI Financial Services Team (Insurance) if they have a query on PPBs which is not covered in the guidance."

This is a complicated area on which specialist bespoke advice would be needed. Nothing should be done without such advice that can be relied on.

One of the major problems is getting existing assets into the structure without creating a PPB.

Various drafting stratagems seem to be in vogue.

6.5 Restructuring arrangements including image rights and endorsement arrangements

Key Points

- Complex area much dependent on what done in the past
- Bespoke specialist advice often needed
- Advisor needs to full details of what was done, document bible, valuations then and now etc. as a starting point
- Often issue removal of remittance basis and its effect for UK based ESPs
- FIG problem of performance income (see sections 843I and J)
- What do with taxed income?
- FOTRA Arrangements
- Cease to be UK based?
    - Sometimes simplest and most certain approach
    - Other jurisdiction tax needs to be considered
    - Others' wants

i. General

This is a complex and bespoke area where specialist advice will often be necessary as it can involve matters such as the use of Bonds and moving assets[177] so

[177] What these are is not always clear. This is especially so with Personality Rights and in the UK as

the old adage "If it moves tax it" is in play. The advisor will need full details of the assets in question and of all that has been done and current valuations and costs of acquisition etcetera as a first step.

Full documentation including earlier advice will be needed including details of returns and correspondence with the relevant revenues. Details of advisers and providers in the relevant jurisdictions will also be needed.

The old saying "If you're going to Dublin I wouldn't start from here"[178] has a clear resonance in the kind of circumstances under consideration here. Often the fundamental protection behind the arrangements namely the Remittance Basis has been removed. The Advisor should remember the old adage "if it moves tax it" in this context as moving things around can give rise to tax charges if care is not taken.

In the past arrangements and structures for non-doms from a UK perspective often split matters into UK assets and income and rest of the world assets and income. This was often done to take advantage of the remittance basis in the UK. As the remittance basis has been abolished this is often now irrelevant other than say for a short time for new residents. For new residents it will often be better to start from scratch. The fact that performance income is not qualifying income (see sections 843I and J) whether or not remitted to the UK will need different solutions such as payment for something that does not result directly or indirectly from the performance of the sport or entertainment hence the interest in such matters as the Danish approach to Facial Characteristics.

One of the questions to consider is what to do with the taxed income. This walks us into investment advice which is beyond my pay grade. However, it may be that there are some tax advantage investments that could be used. I believe that some gilts and T-bonds[179] have tax breaks that financial planners can take advantage of. This can produce good returns which may be tax free I believe. I also believe in the past some of these have also had advantages on death. It is something on which specific advice must be taken from an authorised entity.

FOTRA (Free of Tax to Residents Abroad) gilts can be excluded property for non-UK residents.[180]

---

the House of Lords has told us that they do not exist in the UK despite being dealt with in the UK virtually every day (e.g. the Premier League Player's Contract).

[178] Cf https://briscoelab.org/2016/07/09/i-wouldnt-start-from-here/

[179] Treasury Bonds such as gilts

[180] See section 6(2) IHTA which reads:

"(2)Where securities have been issued by the Treasury subject to a condition authorised by section 22 of

6.6 Using insurance for funding and or as a wrapper

Key Points – Using insurance

- Funding arrangement
    - E.g. protection during 10 Year run off if death occurs within the period
    - Costs
    - Similar to PET planning
- Insurance as a wrapper
    - What trying to achieve?
    - How?
    - What are the obstacles ?

i. General

It is not unusual to take out term life assurance where, for example, a PET has been made to deal with the risk of IHT becoming payable in the seven years till the gift ceases to be a PET.

In theory, a similar approach could be considered for the 10-year tail. Cost will be an important factor. However, this will depend to a large extent on the age and health of the taxpayer. These are crucial matters in determining the level of premium involved. The adviser needs knowledge of the client's medical history and consent to medical examination. In my view, this should generally be dealt with sooner rather than later.

It may also be that the premiums are cheaper than the tax even on a discounted basis. Proper calculations are needed. However, it is a matter on which proper valuations and comparative calculations are needed. The issue of legislative change must also be considered. What is the likelihood of IHT being abolished or going back to an 80% rate.

These are essentially matters for the client to decide upon.

This requires bespoke advice, and it is important that several and quotations are obtained valuations (so an average can be used where appropriate).

It is also important to ensure that there is a genuine commercial reason for what is being done. Saving tax is not such a reason in this case as far as HMRC are

the Finance (No. 2) Act 1931 (or section 47 of the Finance (No. 2) Act 1915) for exemption from taxation so long as the securities are in the beneficial ownership of persons of a description specified in the condition, the securities are excluded property if they are in the beneficial ownership of such a person."
See https://www.gov.uk/hmrc-internal-manuals/international-manual/intm368010 They can also have IT and CGT advantages which I am told can provide good net returns. Proper Financial Services advice must be taken on this.

concerned. There also needs to be admissible evidence of this. Such evidence should be retained and in a readily accessible form.

ii. Special Insurance Providers

I am aware of a number of insurance approaches that are being developed. These can be technically complex and require careful analysis in the light of the particular circumstances of the client in question It is too early to reach conclusions, in my view, on some of these arrangements until the full practicalities. These need careful review. Some are considerably better than others that I have explored. However, this does not mean that the adviser should ignore them or not keep themselves apprised at what is out there in the Market. They can be useful matters in appropriate cases.

6.7 Starting the clock again

Key Points – Starting the clock again

- How long till UK long term residence?
- How long abroad to stop it?
- Rearrange assets so value of client's estate reduced?
- PETS
- DDC

6.7.1 General

If a person is about to become a long-term UK resident it is worth considering whether the clock can be restarted by appropriate transfers At least as to part of the Estate.

Much will depend on the particular circumstances the individuals and entities involved.

However, if arrangements can be made to reduce the amount in the individual's estate this can reduce the tax charge. If there are individuals or entities that are not long-term UK residents, gifts to them may not always attract UK tax. Much will depend on the particular circumstances and risk profile of the client.

A gift to an individual may be a PET and so not liable to immediate IHT. Relief for *inter vivos* may be available to a US citizenship under the UK US DDC.

However, IT and CGT and the position in relevant foreign jurisdictions must also be considered.

6.7.2 Associated operations etc.

a. General

There are number of anti-avoidance matter to be particularly aware of here.

These are:

- Associated Operations; and
- Same Settlement
- Section IHTA is headed "Associated operations."

It provides as follows.

"(1) In this Act "associated operations" means, subject to subsection (2) below, **any two or more operations of any kind**, being—

(a) operations which **affect the same property**, or one of which affects some property and the other or others of which affect property which represents, whether **directly or indirectly**, that **property, or income arising from that property**, or any property representing accumulations of any such income, or

(b) **any two operations of which one is effected with reference to the other**, or with a **view to enabling the other to be effected or facilitating its being effected**, and **any further operation** having a like relation to any of those two, and so on.

whether those operations are effected by the **same person or different persons**, and **whether or not they are simultaneous**; and **"operation" includes an omission**.

(2) The granting of **a lease for full consideration in money** or money's worth shall **not** be taken to be **associated with any operation effected more than three years after the grant**, and no operation effected on or after 27th March 1974 shall be taken to be associated with an operation effected before that date.

(3) Where a transfer of value is made by associated operations carried out at **different times** it shall be **treated as made at the time of the last of them**; but where any one or more of the earlier operations also constitute a transfer of value made by the same transferor, the value transferred by the earlier operations shall be treated as reducing the value transferred by all the operations taken together, except to the extent that the transfer constituted by the earlier operations but not that made by all the operations taken together is exempt under section 18 above."

The words "enabling", "facilitate" and "with a view to" and "with reference to" in the section give a wide meaning to the provision can have a wide impact. It is not obvious what is not connected particularly if a "but for" test is used.

For HMRC's views on definition etc. see IHTM14826–Lifetime transfers: associated operations: definition of terms.[181]

---

[181] See https://www.gov.uk/hmrc-internal-manuals/inheritance-tax-manual/ihtm14822#:~:text=The%20definition%20of%20associated%20operations,taken%20at%20th

6.7.3 *HMRC View*

6.7.3.1 *Objective view first as to what involved*[182]

HMRC seem to think an objective view should be taken first. This is at least a practical approach and avoids inquiry into a person's subjective intention at that stage. This identifies the property and operations involved which I consider a helpful starting point.

They say:

> **"IHTM14823 - Lifetime transfers: associated operations: the objective test**
>
> When considering if the associated operations provisions apply to a series of operations (IHTM14826) you should firstly apply the objective test set out in IHTA84/S268(1)(a). To be relevant associated operations for the objective test, the two or more operations must be
>
> - operations which affect the same property, or
> - operations, one of which affects some property and the other(s) affects
>   - property which represents the first property, or
>   - income arising from that property, or property which represents accumulated income from the property.
>
> If the operations do not qualify under the objective test, consider the subjective test. (IHTM14824)
>
> i. then apply the subjective approach for "effected with reference to, enabling of facilitating" the other
>
> IHTM14824 - Lifetime transfers: associated operations: the subjective test
>
> If you have considered the objective test (IHTM14823) and determined that it does not apply, you must then consider the subjective test set out in IHTA84/S268(1)(b). To be relevant associated operations for the subjective test, there must be two or more operations (IHTM14826), of which
>
> - one is effected with reference to the other, or
> - one is effected with a view to enabling the other to be effected, or
> - one facilitates the effecting of the other.
>
> If one of the operations is similarly linked to a further operation, all the operations are associated.
>
> If none of the above conditions are met and the objective test (IHTM14823) has also not been met, then the operations are not associated operations."

This at least gives an approach that the taxpayer can use that as far as the tests are concerned are similar to those outlined by HMRC. They may not give the

---

e%20same%20time

[182] Similar to the *Arrowtown* approach of finding the facts realistically to which to apply the statute purposively

same outcome though as there is a mixture of objective and subjective and a view to be taken as to the linkage in the arrangements.

6.7.3.2 Gift

The relevant section of the IHTA on PET is set out here for the convenience of the reader. This is section 3A which reads as follows.

> **"3A Potentially exempt transfers.**
>
> (1) Any reference in this Act to a potentially exempt transfer is a reference to a transfer of value—
>
> (a) which is made by an individual on or after 18th March 1986 but before 22nd March 2006; and
>
> (b) which, apart from this section, would be a chargeable transfer (or to the extent to which, apart from this section, it would be such a transfer); and
>
> (c)to the extent that it constitutes either a gift to another individual or a gift into an accumulation and maintenance trust or a disabled trust;
>
> . . . . .
>
> (1A) Any reference in this Act to a potentially exempt transfer is also a reference to a transfer of value—
>
> (a) which is made by an individual **on or after 22nd March 2006**,
>
> (b) which, apart from this section, would be a chargeable transfer (or to the extent to which, apart from this section, it would be such a transfer), and
>
> (c) to the extent that it constitutes—
>
> (i)a **gift** to another individual,
>
> (ii)a gift into a disabled trust, or
>
> (iii)a gift into a bereaved minor's trust on the coming to an end of an immediate post-death interest.
>
> (1B) Subsections (1) and (1A) above have effect subject to any provision of this Act which provides that a disposition (or transfer of value) of a particular description is not a potentially exempt transfer.
>
> (2) Subject to subsection (6) below, a transfer of value falls within subsection (1)(c) or (1A)(c)(i)] above, as a gift to another individual,—
>
> (a) to the extent that the value transferred is attributable to property which, by virtue of the transfer, becomes comprised in the estate of that other individual, . . . , or
>
> (b) so far as that value is not attributable to property which becomes comprised in the estate of another person, to the extent that, by virtue of the transfer, the estate of that other individual is increased,
>
> . . .
>
> (3) Subject to subsection (6) below, a transfer of value falls within subsection (1)(c) above, as a gift into an accumulation and maintenance trust or a disabled trust, to the extent that the value transferred is attributable to

property which, by virtue of the transfer, becomes settled property to which section 71 or 89 of this Act applies.

(3A) Subject to subsection (6) below, a transfer of value falls within subsection (1A)(c)(ii) above to the extent that the value transferred is attributable to property which, by virtue of the transfer, becomes settled property to which section 89 below applies.

(3B) A transfer of value falls within subsection (1A)(c)(iii) above to the extent that the value transferred is attributable to settled property (whenever settled) that becomes property to which section 71A below applies in the following circumstances—

(a) under the settlement, a person **("L")** is beneficially entitled to an interest in possession in the settled property,

(b) the interest in possession is an immediate post-death interest,

(c) on or after 22nd March 2006, but during L's life, the interest in possession comes to an end,

(d) L is beneficially entitled to the interest in possession immediately before it comes to an end, and

(e) on the interest in possession coming to an end, the property—
(i)continues to be held on the trusts of the settlement, and
(ii)becomes property to which section 71A below applies.

(4) A potentially exempt transfer which is made seven years or more before the death of the transferor is an exempt transfer and any other potentially exempt transfer is a chargeable transfer.

(5) During the period beginning on the date of a potentially exempt transfer and ending immediately before—
(a)the seventh anniversary of that date, or
(b)if it is earlier, the death of the transferor,
it shall be assumed for the purposes of this Act that the transfer will prove to be an exempt transfer.

(6) Where, under any provision of this Act . . . tax is in any circumstances to be charged as if a transfer of value had been made, that transfer shall be taken to be a transfer which is not a potentially exempt transfer.

(6A) The reference in subsection (6) above to any provision of this Act does not include section 52 below except where the transfer of value treated as made by that section is one treated as made on the coming to an end of an interest which falls within section 5(1B) below.

(7) In the application of this section to an event on the happening of which tax is chargeable under section 52 below, the reference in subsection (1)(a) or (1A)(a) above to the individual by whom the transfer of value is made is a reference to the person who, by virtue of section 3(4) above, is treated as the transferor.

6.7.3.3 *Same settlement for IHT*

Section 81 can treat assets moved between settlements as remaining in the old settlement and being part of the new if care not taken.

Before considering this section 80 should be considered as this can provide a trap for the unwary on the basis of what has gone across my desk over the years. Section 80 reads as follows.

> **"80 Initial interest of settlor or spouse or civil partner[183].**
>
> (1) Where a settlor or his spouse or civil partner is beneficially entitled to a qualifying interest in possession in property immediately after it becomes comprised in the settlement, the property shall for the purposes of this Chapter (including sections 48 and 48ZA (excluded property) as they apply for the purposes of this Chapter) be treated as not having become comprised in the settlement on that occasion; but when the property or any part of it becomes held on trusts under which neither of those persons is beneficially entitled to a qualifying interest in possession, the property or part shall for those purposes be treated as becoming comprised in a separate settlement made by that one of them who ceased (or last ceased) to be beneficially entitled to a qualifying interest in possession in it.
>
> (2) References in subsection (1) above to the spouse or civil partner of a settlor include references to the widow or widower or surviving civil partner of a settlor.
>
> (3) This section shall not apply if the occasion first referred to in subsection (1) above occurred before 27th March 1974.
>
> (4) Where the occasion first referred to in subsection (1) above occurs on or after 22nd March 2006, this section applies—
>
> (a) as though for " a qualifying interest in possession" in each place where that appears in subsection (1) above there were substituted a postponing interest, and
>
> (b) as though, for the purposes of that subsection, each of the following were a "postponing interest"—
>
> (i)an immediate post-death interest;
>
> (ii)a disabled person's interest.

The other section mentioned above is section 81. It reads as follows.

> **"81 Property moving between settlements.**

[183] https://www.legislation.gov.uk/ukpga/1984/51/section/80

(1) Where property which ceases to be comprised in one settlement becomes comprised in another then, unless in the meantime any person becomes beneficially entitled to the property (and not merely to an interest in possession in the property), it shall for the purposes of this Chapter (including sections 48 and 48ZA (excluded property) as they apply for the purposes of this Chapter) be treated as remaining comprised in the first settlement (but held on the trusts of the second).

(2) Subsection (1) above shall not apply where the property ceased to be comprised in the first settlement before 10th December 1981; but where property ceased to be comprised in one settlement before 10th December 1981 and after 26th March 1974 and, by the same disposition, became comprised in another settlement, it shall for the purposes of this Chapter be treated as remaining comprised in the first settlement.

(3) Subsection (1) above shall not apply where a reversionary interest in the property expectant on the termination of a qualifying interest in possession subsisting under the first settlement was settled on the trusts of the other settlement before 10th December 1981."

Care is needed where property is moved between settlements. In appropriate circumstances moving assets out of trust may give greater flexibility. It can be worth investigating this. If a US national is involved, then it should be remembered that US UK DDC covers some *inter vivos* transactions. This may allow more flexibility in the particular circumstances.

The UK US DDC is discussed below.

6.8 Checking nationality etc and applicability of DDC

Key Points – Check nationality and applicability of DDC

- Checking this may help with planning e.g. whether a DDC may apply
- For HMRC's view on Domicile after the introduction of the long-term residence system see IHTM 47001 ff set out in the text below
- It seems reasonably safe to rely on this given that the logic may not be obvious to all. Practically, this is HMRC's view which is always subject to legislative risk

It is sensible to check the nationality (including multiple nationalities) of and heritage including domicile and residence history of the client in question. This can be important in considering the applicability of any relevant double death convention, any DDC.

Care will also be needed with CGT charges if no section 260 relief is available on change. Sometimes a PET may be involved if a gift between individuals and depending on the type of asset some CGT relief might be available e.g. gift of business assets.[184]

A list of DDCS in force can be found at:
https://www.gov.uk/guidance/inheritance-tax-double-taxation-relief
The DDC are usually based on Domicile. This raises questions now this has been replaced with long term residence for IHT purposes. HMRC's view on when domicile remains relevant following the introduction of the long-term residence test is found in IHTM 47001 set out below.

6.8.1 *Certain pre-commencement emigrants treated as not being long-term UK residents*

Broadly non-resident non-doms who left the UK before 30 October 2024 (Budget Day) and have not returned are not treated as long term UK residents[185]. This should always be investigated.

The legislation prevents certain individuals being treated as long term UK residents if:

- (i) they were not UK domiciled on 30th October 2024;
- (ii) not UK resident after 5th April 2025
- (iii) not UK resident:
    - a) for any of the years before the year in question; or
    - b) in the UK for more than 15 years of the 20 years before the tax year in question.

The legislation is found in paragraph 46 Schedule 13 FA 2025. It reads as follows.

> "46(1) An individual who would otherwise be a long-term UK resident at any time in a given tax year ("the relevant tax year") is treated for the purposes of IHTA 1984 as not being a long-term UK resident at that time if the individual—
>
> (a) was not domiciled in the United Kingdom on 30 October 2024,
>
> (b) has been resident in the United Kingdom for no tax year in the period beginning with the tax year 2025-26 and ending with the relevant tax year, and
>
> (c) either—

---

[184] See https://www.gov.uk/gift-holdover-relief see section 165 TCGA and the restriction in section 166 on the relief for gifts to non-residents.

[185] Bonus for having left early

(i) was resident in the United Kingdom for none of the 3 tax years immediately preceding the relevant tax year, or

(ii) was resident in the United Kingdom for fewer than 15 of the 20 tax years immediately preceding the relevant tax year.

(2) For the purposes of sub-paragraph (1)(a), in determining where an individual was domiciled on 30 October 2024, ignore section 267 (deemed domicile) and sections 267ZA and 267ZB (domicile elections) of IHTA 1984."

It is also worth noting paragraph 49 in this connection. It reads as follows

"49(1) The repeal of section 267 of IHTA 1984 (persons treated as domiciled in United Kingdom) by paragraph 23 is to be disregarded in determining for the purposes of that Act any question as to where a person was domiciled at any time before 6 April 2025.

(2) In construing section 267 of IHTA 1984, so far as saved by sub-paragraph (1), the repeal of the definition of "formerly domiciled resident" by paragraph 28(3)(b) is also to be disregarded."

6.8.2 *HMRC views*

Some extracts from the IHT manual illustrate this.

IHTM47001 - Long-term UK residence test: Introduction and when domicile will remain relevant

From 6 April 2025, Inheritance Tax moved from being based on domicile (IHTM13000)

to being based on long-term UK residence (IHTM47000). An individual is a long-term UK resident if they have been resident in the UK for at least 10 out of the last 20 tax years immediately preceding the tax year in which the chargeable event (including death) arises. Where an individual is a long-term UK resident and becomes non-UK resident, they will remain in scope for inheritance tax for a minimum of 3 years and a maximum of 10 years depending on the amount of time they resided in the UK (IHTM47202)

Domicile will remain relevant:

- for deaths and lifetime transfers of value prior to 6 April 2025;
- *where the common law concept of domicile arises such as within designated Double Taxation Conventions* (IHTM27161), and;
- for property comprised in a settlement, domicile will remain relevant:
- for charges which arise before 6 April 2025,
- where the settlor died before 6 April 2025, or
- where transitional provision for gifts with reservation of benefit or qualifying interest in possession charges apply.
- If these circumstances apply, please refer to Chapter 13:
  Domicile (IHTM13000)

The following summarises when chargeability of foreign property depends on long-term UK residence or domicile.

Foreign unsettled property (IHTM04260)

- For deaths and lifetime transfers of value on or after 6 April 2025, foreign property will be chargeable if the deceased was a long-term UK resident immediately before their death or the transfer.
- For deaths and lifetime transfers of value before 6 April 2025, foreign property will be chargeable if the deceased was domiciled in the UK immediately before their death or the transfer.

Foreign settled property (IHTM04271)

- Where a settlement has a living settlor, charges on foreign settled property which arise on or after 6 April 2025 will depend upon whether the settlor is a long-term UK resident at the time of the charge.
- Where a settlor died on or after 6 April 2025, charges on foreign settled property which arise on or after 6 April 2025 will depend upon whether the settlor was a long-term UK resident immediately before their death.
- Where a settlor died before 6 April 2025, charges on foreign settled property which arise on or after 6 April 2025 will depend upon the domicile of the settlor at the time the property became comprised in the settlement.
- For qualifying interest in possession trusts there is an additional test from 6 April 2025. Property comprised in the settlement is only excluded property if both the settlor and interest in possession beneficiary are not long-term UK resident at the time of the chargeable event.
- Charges on foreign settled property which arise before 6 April 2025 will depend upon the domicile of the settlor at the time the asset became comprised in the settlement.
- There will be occasions where some foreign property may still be chargeable even if the individual (or settlor) is not a long-term UK resident or, when still relevant, non-domiciled. This will include, for example, cases where the value of value attributable to UK the foreign property includes residential property (IHTM43011) whether comprised in a settlement or not.

Transitional provisions

- Where excluded property was comprised in a settlement on or before 30 October 2024, it will not be subject to charge under the gift with reservation provisions, on death, where the property remains settled property and is situated outside the UK at the time of the chargeable event (See further guidance at IHTM47060).
- Where excluded property is comprised in a qualifying interest in possession settlement before 30 October 2024, it will not be subject to certain charges under the interest in possession regime where the property is situated

outside the UK at the time of the chargeable event (See further guidance at IHTM47051).

- In both cases, whether the foreign property comprised in the settlement at 30 October 2024 was excluded property will depend on the domicile (IHTM13000) of the settlor at the time the property became comprised in the settlement.

Double taxation conventions

Domicile may remain relevant where there is an existing double taxation convention in operation between the UK and the relevant foreign country and its terms use the concept of common law domicile

(see IHTM47070 and IHTM27161).

DDCs

The terms of any relevant DDC must be carefully considered in the light of the particular circumstances of the individual matter in point. Often DCC apply to individuals and not to trusts. If property is in a trust, it may be worth considering whether or not it would be worthwhile appointing property out of the trust to the individual to take advantage of the DDC. Appropriate valuations and calculations will obviously need to be done.

The risk of change such as the termination of the DDC and other legislative change will also be an important consideration.

This is a matter that ultimately is one for the client to decide as there is no right or wrong answer till after the taxable event has occurred.

Summaries of DDCs relating to the US, Italy and India are set out below.

6.9 Fragmenting and splitting ownership

Key Points – Fragmenting and splitting ownership

- Old planning but new context
- Reduce the value of estate on death
- Detailed planning needed
- Care with GWR
- Reliefs?
- PETs
- Business Assets

This can be a way of reducing the value of the individual's estate and so the charge on the death of the main person with the valuable assets. For example, the individual could make gifts of the shares as business assets up to the new limit. Sometimes gifts to individuals will qualify as PET's (see Section 3A IHT set out above).

It can also fit into succession planning. Much will depend on what the value of the assets is and how they are held.

Care with GWR's is needed. The value of GWR's can be included in the Donor's estate on death. This would defeat the purpose of the rearrangement.

6.10 Fixing the value and giving away the value above that

Key Points - Fixing the value and giving away the value above

- Relates to fragmentation etc. as discussed above.
- Useful where shares are involved because of their flexibility
- DOTAS Financial hallmark
- If fix value of old shares new shares likely to have low value and so low charge to tax
- Full valuation advice essential
- Record commercial justification

This is related to the previous item. It is essentially a variation on it. It is particularly useful for companies with a share capital. Shares can have almost infinitely variable rights and so infinitely variable values. Growth in value shares can be useful here. DOTAS must be borne in mind as shares are included in the Financial Products Hallmark which can apply.

Example

Val Heuhig is a UK residence of Ruritanian heritage. Val is not yet a UK long term resident. Valves assets are held in a Ruritanian incorporated resident company, Vafan Ltd. It has 100 ordinary shares in issue all held by Val. A share for share reorganisation takes place to fix the value of the ordinary shares to their current value by providing that the holder thereof is entitled to an amount equal to the current net asset value At the time of change and to dividends of no more than an amount equal to the average amount of dividends per year for the last three years before the change followed by a right issue of say 1P shares Or equivalent which are potentially entitled to the rest of the distributable profits and income then there should be no value shift for IHT or CGT.

Appropriate valuations would of course be necessary. I always recommend more than one valuation for safety's sake. These new shares, i.e. growth and value shares, are likely to have a low value Roundabout par when his seat and can be given away at that time with no real concern as to UK IHT or CGT of any significance. The value of the ordinary shares retained is likely to be unnamed fixed amount. This can help planning say using term assurance by having a value as to which IHT is like used to be charged. This at least reduces one of the variables.

Diagrams

1. Reconstruction

0. Starting Point

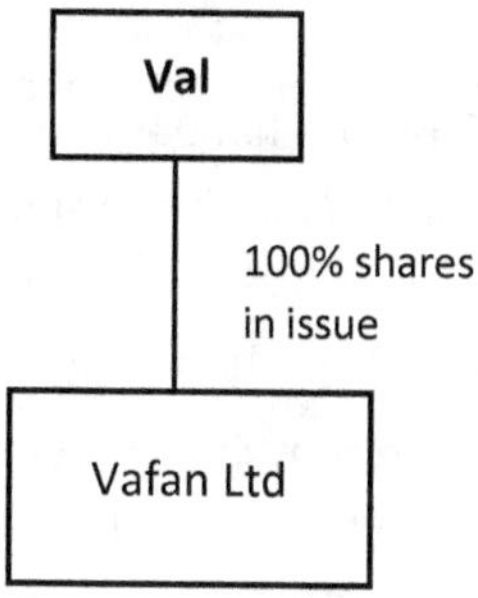

1. Reconstruction

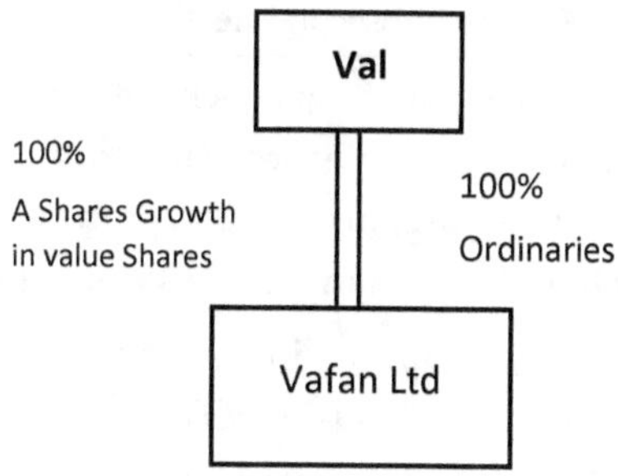

2. Gift of A shares

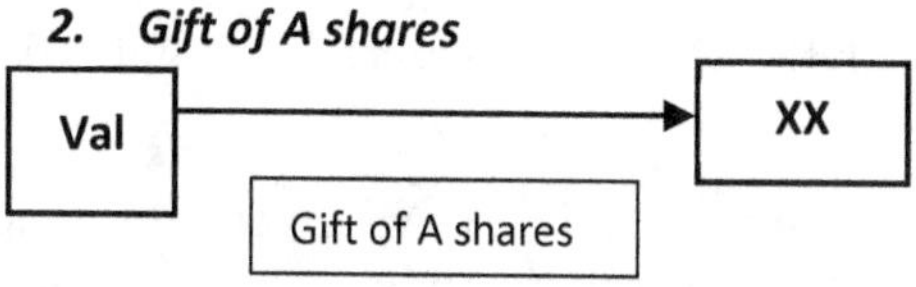

- Value of estate before and after gift?
- Within annual exemption?
- Within Nil rate band?

Another approach might be to form a new company with different ownership and to do a name swap. New business can then be put through the new company. Care is needed with flight districts etc.

The old companies unlikely to be an asset with a diminishing value.

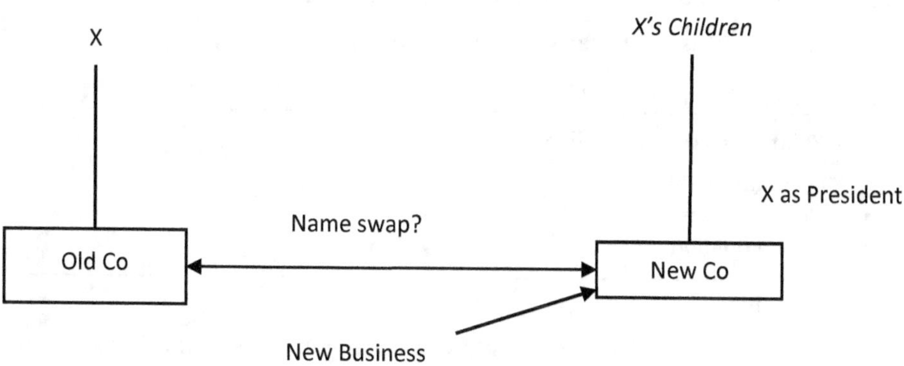

6.10.1 *Accepting IHT on UK assets but seeking to protect rest of world assets.*

Key Points

- Back to position before changes?
- UK situs assets almost invariably attract IHT
- Leave to spouse but second death tax exposure?

This is essentially trying to get back to the position before the changes came into force. This is something that some non-doms accepted in the past and might yet do again if they are prepared to accept the legislative risk. It was IHT on worldwide assets that drove many UHINWI's out of the UK in my experience.

UK situs assets will almost invariably attract IHT. There may be some exceptions such as certain gilts (see FOTRA mentioned below) but favourite houses in Mayfair it is wished to keep for sentimental reasons will not fall within the exceptions. It may be possible to defer the charge by leaving the property to the individual's spouse or civil partner with the same long term resident status. But consider UK ties.

However, a charge is likely to arise on the second death. Arrangements aimed at preventing this have essentially been stopped by legislation see e.g. Section 110 Finance Act 2010.

This approach will require early planning generally before the taxpayer has become UK long-term resident as worldwide assets will become liable to IHT thereafter giving away assets with a non UK situs which may fall to be treated as excluded property may be a cost effective way of dealing with matters as no UKIHT should arise on the gift if it is treated as excluded property and or if it is treated as a PET.

Again, much will depend on the precise circumstances.

For a Table of situs of property (see Appendix 2).

6.10.2 *Need to warn clients*

Key Points - need to warn clients

- Legislative risk
- No guarantees
- Second opinion

6.10.2.1 General

It is important that clients enter into any arrangements on the basis of full knowledge and transparency and with their eyes wide open. No guarantees of success. Issue of legislative change.

Anything done that results in less tax being paid than HMRC thinks should be paid is likely to spark their interests especially if there is an offshore element. This is particularly the case at a time when the government they answer to is seemingly short of cash.

Clients often think that tax is a yes or no, black or white matter. This may be the case with PAYE where the table gives you the answer but something like the matters under consideration here involves judgement and interpretation. This means there is scope for reasonable minds to disagree with the range of possible reasonable views.

Consideration must be given to matters such as DOTAS particularly where shares are involved as the Financial Instruments hallmark may apply. It applies to shares with rights only there for tax reasons. This is an important consideration.

The *Ramsay / Arrowtown* adage to find the facts realistically and apply the statute purposively must also be carefully considered.

It is important that the matter can be justified commercially. I always recommend keeping a memorandum setting this out with the Bible. The contemporaneous record why something is being done and the commercial reasons justifying it being done should be prepared and retained with the Bible of documents relating to what was done. It is very useful to have such a document if inquiries arise a number of years down the Pike when those originally involved have moved on. Commercial justification is not a certain "get out of gaol" card but can help. HMRC unlike a number of clients do not regard saving tax as a commercial justification.

It may be sensible for the advisor to seek a second opinion on complex matters such as these where dealing with potentially feisty clients and partly as a sanity check and partly as an insurance for the client when it comes to penalties etc. There are a number of persons out there who offer such a service. "I would say this wouldn't I" but the Tax Bar has much to recommend it for this purpose. An opinion for the client and the client's advisor's benefits can prove very useful particularly as regards penalties and their mitigation. It is also something that can properly fall to the client's account.

It is important to be realistic when considering these matters and to remember that in a tax case the onus of proof is on the taxpayer. This makes for a different dynamic from the usual commercial case. It is also vital to consider the position outside the UK where this is relevant. Generally, appropriate offshore advice should always be sought as the adviser may not be qualified in the relevant jurisdictions.

6.10.3 *Estate Duty or IHT relief on domicile basis? What allows relief under DDCs?*

Key Points – Estate duty or IHT

- Domicile based system replaced but DDCs on domicile so how work given change to residence-based system?
- Section 158 IHTA
- DDC How wide is its particular coverage? Does the particular DDC just apply on death? What about *inter vivos* transfers and death?

6.10.3.1 *General*

The DDCs in force were entered into before the change to long term UK residence for the basis for IHT. They were not aimed at IHT on the basis of long-term UK residency. They were aimed at Estate Duty in some cases. Estate Duty was abolished by FA 1975 (see particularly section 49 of that Act).

Estate Duty was the predecessor in the UK to what is now known as IHT. Some of the Conventions were made when Estate Duty was in force and reflect this.

The relief given by some of the treaties or conventions read literally is from Estate Duty not IHT. Some of the more modern treaties etc refer to IHT which is what we have today.

This raises the question what gives authority for these Treaties and Conventions to apply to give relief from IHT when they refer to Estate Duty. They also refer to Domicile which raises the question of its current relevance and what about long term residence?

The answer is found in the legislation.

6.10.3.2 *Some legislation*

The authority for double tax conventions relating to Estate Duty and IHT is found in large part in section 158 IHTA. This is headed "Double taxation conventions". It reads as follows.

> "(1) If Her **Majesty by Order in Council declares—**
>
> (a)that arrangements specified in the Order have been **made with the government** of any **territory outside the United Kingdom** with a view to **affording relief from double taxation in relation to inheritance tax** payable under the laws of the United Kingdom **and any tax imposed under the laws of that territory** which is of a **similar** character or is chargeable on **or by reference to death or gifts inter vivos**, and

(b) that it is **expedient that those arrangements should have effect**;
the arrangements shall, notwithstanding anything in this Act, **have effect so far as they provide for relief from inheritance tax**, or for determining the place where any property is to be treated as situated for the purposes of the tax.

(1ZA) For the purposes of this section, arrangements made with a view to affording relief from double taxation include any arrangements which modify the effect of arrangements so made.

(1ZB) Arrangements to which effect is given under this section may include provision conferring (with or without other functions) functions relating to the determination of matters arising under the arrangements on a public authority in the United Kingdom or in a territory outside the United Kingdom.

(1A) . . . .

(2) Any arrangements to which effect is given under this section may include provision for relief in cases occurring before the making of the arrangements and provisions as to property which is not itself subject to double taxation.

(3) Any Order in Council under this section which revokes an earlier Order may contain such transitional provisions as appear to Her Majesty to be necessary or expedient.

(4) An Order under this section shall not be submitted to Her Majesty in Council unless a draft of it has been laid before, and approved by resolution of, the House of Commons.

(5) Where any arrangements have effect by virtue of this section, no obligation as to secrecy shall prevent the Board or an authorised officer of the Board from disclosing to any authorised officer of the government with which the arrangements are made such information as is required to be disclosed under the arrangements.

(6) Where **arrangements with** the **government** of any territory **outside the United Kingdom** are specified **under any Order in Council** which—

(a)was made, or has effect as made, under ***section 54 of the Finance (No.2) Act 1945*** [Emphasis supplied] or section 2 of the Finance Act (Northern Ireland) 1946, and

(b)**had effect immediately before the passing of this Act,**

the Order shall notwithstanding the repeal of that section by the Finance Act 1975, **remain in force** and **have effect as if** any provision made by those **arrangements in relation to estate duty extended to inheritance tax chargeable by virtue of section 4 above** [headed Transfers on Death]; but the Order may be amended or revoked by an Order in Council made under this section."

As the UK is a "dualist" jurisdiction International Treaties need to be given effect in municipal or domestic law to have effect in UK law (see e.g. *Cheney v Conn* [1968] 1 All ER 779[186]).

The mechanics for doing this are an Order in Council.

That deals with the issue of future IHT Conventions and how effect was given to existing IHT conventions.

The UK US DDC (discussed below) was made under paragraph 7 of Schedule 7 to the Finance Act 1975. This was repealed by Capital Transfer Tax Act 1984 (see sections 274, 277 and Schedules, 7 and 9). Paragraph 7 became section 158 IHTA.

The CTT Act 1984 became the IHTA (see section 100 (1) (a) FA 1986 which provided that "the 1984 Act may be cited as the Inheritance Tax Act 1984".

That does not deal with the issue of the Estate Duty Treaties and Conventions.

The Italy and India Estate Duty Convention Orders were made under section 56(2) [*sic*] F (No. 2) A 1945 as were the others but 56 Supplementary to 54].

In such circumstances section 158(6) IHTA applies. This provides:

> "(6) Where arrangements with the government of any territory outside the United Kingdom are specified under any Order in Council which—
>
> (a) was made, or has effect as made, under section **54** of the Finance (No.2) Act 1945 or section 2 of the Finance Act (Northern Ireland) 1946, and
>
> (b) had effect immediately before the passing of this Act,
>
> the Order shall notwithstanding the repeal of that section by the Finance Act 1975, remain in force and have effect as if any provision made by those arrangements in relation to estate duty extended to inheritance tax chargeable by virtue of section 4 above [headed "Transfers on Death"]; but the Order may be amended or revoked by an Order in Council made under this section."

The arrangements leading to the Convention were made under section 54 but the Order in Council was authorised by section 56 – hence the different references as different matters referred to.

The Conventions had effect immediately before the passing of the 1984 Act and

> "... so remain in force and have effect as if any provision made by those arrangements in relation to estate duty extended to inheritance tax..."

[186] Spending on nuclear weapons funded by UK tax but convention against nuclear weapons sought to be a ground to justify paying less income tax. As the Treaty had not been given effect in the municipal i.e. UK Law it meant the collection of tax was legal.

HMRC's manual reads as follows. This is mainly found in IHTM 47001ff. This refers to life transfers. It should be noted that section 158(6) IHTA (set out above) refers to Section 4 IHTA headed "Transfers on Death". The relationship between the section and the manual is not pellucid in my view.

> "**IHTM47001 - Long-term UK residence test: Introduction and when domicile will remain relevant**
>
> From 6 April 2025, Inheritance Tax moved from being based on domicile (IHTM13000) to being based on long-term UK residence (IHTM47000). An individual is a long-term UK resident if they have been resident in the UK for at least 10 out of the last 20 tax years immediately preceding the tax year in which the chargeable event (including death) arises. Where an individual is a long-term UK resident and becomes non-UK resident, they will remain in scope for inheritance tax for a minimum of 3 years and a maximum of 10 years depending on the amount of time they resided in the UK (IHTM47202)
>
> Domicile will remain relevant:
>
> - for deaths and lifetime transfers of value prior to 6 April 2025;
> - **where the common law concept of domicile arises such as within designated Double Taxation Conventions** (IHTM27161), and;
> - for property comprised in a settlement, domicile will remain relevant:
>   - for charges which arise before 6 April 2025,
>   - where the settlor died before 6 April 2025, or
>   - where transitional provision for gifts with reservation of benefit or qualifying interest in possession charges apply.
>
> If these circumstances apply, please refer to Chapter 13: Domicile (IHTM13000)
>
> The following summarises when chargeability of foreign property depends on long-term UK residence or domicile.
>
> **Foreign unsettled property** (IHTM04260)
>
> - For deaths and lifetime transfers of value **on or after 6 April** 2025, **foreign property will be chargeable** if the deceased was a **long-term UK resident** immediately before their death or the transfer.
> - For deaths and lifetime transfers of value before 6 April 2025, foreign property will be chargeable if the deceased was domiciled in the UK immediately before their death or the transfer.
>
> **Foreign settled property** (IHTM04271)
>
> - Where a settlement has a living settlor, charges on foreign settled property which arise **on or after 6 April 2025** will **depend upon whether the settlor is a long-term UK resident** at the time of the charge.
> - Where a settlor died on or after 6 April 2025, charges on foreign settled property which arise on or after 6 April 2025 will depend upon whether the settlor was a long-term UK resident immediately before their death.

- Where a settlor died before 6 April 2025, charges on foreign settled property which arise on or after 6 April 2025 will depend upon the domicile of the settlor at the time the property became comprised in the settlement.
- For qualifying interest in possession trusts there is an additional test from 6 April 2025. Property comprised in the settlement is only excluded property if both **the settlor and interest in possession beneficiary are not long-term UK resident at the time of the chargeable event.**
- Charges on foreign settled property which arise before 6 April 2025 will depend upon the domicile of the settlor at the time the asset became comprised in the settlement.

There will be occasions where some foreign property may still be chargeable even if the individual (or settlor) is not a long-term UK resident or, when still relevant, non-domiciled. This will include, for example, cases where the value of the foreign property includes value attributable to UK residential property (IHTM43011) whether comprised in a settlement or not.

Transitional provisions

- Where excluded property was comprised in a settlement on or before 30 October 2024, it will not be subject to charge under the gift with reservation provisions, on death, where the property remains settled property and is situated outside the UK at the time of the chargeable event (See further guidance at IHTM47060).
- Where excluded property is comprised in a qualifying interest in possession settlement before 30 October 2024, it will not be subject to certain charges under the interest in possession regime where the property is situated outside the UK at the time of the chargeable event (See further guidance at IHTM47051).
- In both cases, whether the foreign property comprised in the settlement at 30 October 2024 was excluded property will depend on the domicile (IHTM13000) of the settlor at the time the property became comprised in the settlement.

Double taxation conventions

Domicile may remain relevant where there is an existing double taxation convention in operation between the UK and the relevant foreign country and its **terms use the concept of common law domicile** (see IHTM47070 and IHTM27161)."

6.10.4 *Some further legislation- Double taxation conventions operating by reference to deemed domicile*

Special provision is made for "Double taxation conventions operating by reference to deemed domicile".

This is done by section 267ZF IHTA inserted by Finance Act 2025, s 46, Sch 13, Pt 1, paras 1, 27.

The section reads as follows.

> "**Double taxation conventions operating by reference to deemed domicile**
>
> (1) This section applies to a case in which the application of any arrangements having effect under section 158 (double taxation conventions) depends (to any extent) on whether a person is treated as domiciled in the United Kingdom for the purposes of inheritance tax.
>
> (2) The person is treated as domiciled in the United Kingdom for the purposes of inheritance tax if they are a long-term UK resident.
>
> (3)Sections 276ZC to 267ZE (persons treated as long-term resident by virtue of election) are to be disregarded in applying this section in relation to any arrangements that are specified in an Order in Council made under section 158 of IHTA 1984 before 17 July 2013 (other than by way of amendment by an Order made on or after that date).
>
> (4) Nothing in this section affects the interpretation of any such arrangements as are mentioned in section 158(6) (certain pre-1975 arrangements)."

6.11 Double Death Conventions ("DDC")

Key Points Sample DDCs

- US UK DDC
- Italy UK DDC
- India UK DDC

The UK has a number of DDC with foreign countries. See page 14 above under heading "HMRC's view IHT DTR etc".

This section looks at three sample DDCs.

These are the following.

- US UK DDC
- Italy UK DDC
- India UK DDC

These are broadly representative of the types of DDCs encountered.

6.11.1 US UK DDC

6.11.1.1 Overview

The UK US DDC is one of the more modern DDCs. See page 14 for HMRC short summary.

It caters not only IHT on death but also on *inter vivos* transfer.[187]

Special provision is made about trusts see Article 5 below. It is likely to offer some exciting possibilities for some ESPS and other HINWIs. This will be specific bespoke planning which will often require specialist advice across a number of jurisdictions.

The UK US DDC is given effect in UK law by The Double Taxation Relief (Taxes on Estates of Deceased Persons and on Gifts) (United States of America) Order 1979 SI 1979 No 1454.[188]

6.11.1.2 Explanatory Note to SI

The Explanatory Note to the SI reads as follows.

> "The Double Taxation Convention with the United States of America which forms the Schedule to this Order applies to death duties and gift taxes. The taxes covered by the Convention are the United Kingdom capital transfer tax and the United States estate and gift taxes. The Convention will also apply to any tax of a substantially similar character which may be imposed by either country.
>
> Under the Convention, the country in which the transferor was domiciled or of which he was a national can tax property wherever it is situated. The other country may tax specified categories of property, namely immovable property situated in its territory and business property of a permanent establishment or a fixed base in its territory. Where the transferor was domiciled in neither country both countries may tax except where the transferor was a national of the other, in which case the country of nationality normally has the sole right to tax except in respect of the specified categories of property. There are special rules for trusts.
>
> Where both countries impose tax, the Convention provides rules for determining which country is to give credit for the other's tax. In general, the country in which the transferor was not domiciled is required to give credit. But the country in which the transferor was domiciled is required to give credit for the other country's tax on the specified categories of property.
>
> Rules are provided for determining a person's domicile for the purposes of the Convention and a definition of nationality is also provided.
>
> There are provisions for dealing with cases in which tax, though chargeable, is not paid.
>
> There are provisions which extend the reliefs available in both countries for transfers by an individual to his or her spouse.

[187] NB section 158(6) IHTA seemingly is a limitation to death charges. It seems HMRC accept that it may go wider.

[188] https://www.legislation.gov.uk/uksi/1979/1454/made

> There are provisions for safeguarding nationals of one country from discriminatory taxation in the other country, and for the exchange of information and consultation between the taxation authorities of the two countries.
>
> The Convention applies to any person who is within the scope of a tax covered by the Convention.
>
> The Convention takes effect immediately on entry into force, thirty days after the exchange of instruments of ratification."

The instruments of ratification were exchanged on 11 October 1979 (see end of S.I.)

6.11.1.3 Article 1 Scope

This DDC applies to any person within the scope of a tax to which the Convention applies see Article I.

The Taxes Covered are dealt with by Article 2 discussed next.

6.11.1.4 Article 2 Taxes Covered

This Convention applies to what used to be called Capital Transfer Tax ("**CTT**") and is now called IHT (see Article 2 (1)(b)).

CTT was renamed IHT by FA 1986.[189]

The Convention also applies to any identical or substantially similar taxes(see Article 2(2)).

6.11.1.5 Article 3 Definitions

6.11.1.5.1 *General*

This is essentially a boilerplate Article. However, it contains important definitions for the purposes of the DDC.

It is important to study though as the definitions are vital in construing and interpreting the DDC. The definitions are essentially in Article 3(1)

6.11.1.5.2 *USA, UK, enterprise*

(i) the term "United States" means the United States of America, but does not include Puerto Rico, the Virgin Islands, Guam or any other United States possession or territory;

(ii) the term "United Kingdom" means Great Britain and Northern Ireland;

(iii) the term "enterprise" means an industrial or commercial undertaking;

---

[189] Section100 headed "Capital transfer tax to be known as inheritance tax". It is the same tax but with a different name.

Puerto Rico is not included for DDC purposes nor are the Virgin Islands, Guam and some other territories. The relevant details should always be carefully checked.

6.11.1.5.3 *"Tax" in DDC*

The definition of tax in article 3(1)(f) should also be noted. It reads as follows.

> "(f)the term "tax" means :
>
> (i) the Federal gift tax or the Federal estate tax, including the tax on generation-skipping transfers, imposed in the United States, or
>
> (ii) the capital transfer tax imposed in the United Kingdom, or
>
> (iii) any other tax imposed by a Contracting State to which this Convention applies by virtue of the provisions of paragraph (2) of Article 2,
>
> as the context requires; ..."

6.11.1.5.4 *National*

"National" is another defined term in Article 3(1)(e) to be aware of as it appears in Articles 4 (Fiscal Residence) and 5 (Taxing Rights) as well as 10 (Non-discrimination). The definition is as follows.

> "(e) the term "nationals" means :
>
> in relation to the United States, United States citizens, and
>
> (ii) in relation to the United Kingdom, any citizen of the United Kingdom and Colonies, or any British subject not possessing that citizenship or the citizenship of any other Commonwealth country or territory, provided in either case he had the right of abode in the United Kingdom at the time of the death or transfer."

6.11.1.5.5 *Contracting State*

There is also a definition of "Contracting State". This reads as follows.

> "(g) the term "Contracting State" means the United Kingdom or the United States as the context requires."

The terms jurisdiction, state, country are used in this section in a similar way.

6.11.1.5.6 *Undefined terms*

Provision is made for terms not defined in the Convention. This is found in Artice 3(2). This reads as follows.

> "As regards the application of the Convention by a Contracting State, any term not otherwise defined shall, unless the context otherwise requires and subject to the provisions of Article 11 (Mutual Agreement Procedure), have the meaning which it has under the laws of that Contracting State relating to the taxes which are the subject of the Convention."

6.11.1.6 Article 4 Fiscal Residence

6.11.1.6.1 ***General***

Article 4 of the DDC deals with fiscal residence for the purposes of the Convention. This is particularly relevant to the question as to which Country has the taxing rights (discussed under the heading "Article 5" below). Article 4 relates only to individuals.

Article 4 is essentially concerned with individuals and their domicile. It is not concerned with long term residence. It does not refer to that concept as such. This is unsurprising as it only became relevant after 05 April 2025.

Article 4 does not deal with Trusts which are dealt with to some extent by Article 5.

6.11.1.6.2 ***Individual's Domicile***

By Article 4(1) an ***individual*** was domiciled:

1) *in the United States:*
   - if he [*sic*] was a resident[13] (domiciliary) thereof (i.e. USA); or
   - if he was:
     i. a "national thereof" (i.e. USA); and
     ii. had been a resident (domiciliary) thereof (i.e. USA) at any time during the preceding three years; and
2) *in the United Kingdom:*
   - if he was domiciled in the United Kingdom in accordance with the law of the United Kingdom; or
   - is treated as so domiciled for the purposes of a tax which is the subject of this Convention.

The second part of this provision covers deemed domicile as it was called under section 267 IHTA[190] under the Old Regime. Section 267[191] was repealed by paragraph 23 Schedule 13 FA 2025 from 06 April 2025. There appears to be no substitution of long-term residence for these purposes.

---

[190] As a starting point see https://www.irs.gov/individuals/international-taxpayers/determining-an-individuals-tax-residency-status

[191] Section 267 was headed "Persons treated as domiciled in United Kingdom". It read as follows:

"(1)A person not domiciled in the United Kingdom at any time (in this section referred to as " the relevant time ") shall be treated for the purposes of this Act as domiciled in the United Kingdom (and not elsewhere) at the relevant time if—

(a)he was domiciled in the United Kingdom within the three years immediately preceding the relevant time, or

(b)he was resident in the United Kingdom in not less than seventeen [15 after F(No2)A 2017] of the

6.11.1.6.3 Schedule 13 FA 2025

There are two provisions particularly to note here. These are paragraphs 46 and 49 of Schedule 13 to the 2025 Act.

6.11.1.7 Dual Domicile

6.11.1.7.1 *General*

Articles 4(2) to 4(4) deal with the position where an individual was at any time domiciled in both states under Article 4(1).

6.11.1.7.2 *Deemed UK domiciled where UK national-Article 4(2)*

Article 4(2) applies to deem a person for the purposes of the Convention to be domiciled in the UK at the time in question if that individual was:

a) treated as domiciled in both states (i.e. the UK and the US) under paragraph 4 (1);
b) a national of the United Kingdom but not of the United States, and
c) not resident in the United States for Federal income tax purposes in seven or more of the ten taxable years ending with the year in which that time falls,

he shall be deemed to be domiciled in the United Kingdom at that time.

On "resident in the United States for Federal income tax" see https://www.irs.gov/individuals/international-taxpayers/us-residents.

6.11.1.7.3 *Deemed US domiciled where US national-Article 4(3)*

Article 4(3) applies to deem a person to be domiciled in the US at the time in question if that individual is:

- treated as domiciled in both states (i.e. the UK and the US) under paragraph 4 (1);
- a US but not a national of the UK
- not resident in the United Kingdom in seven or more of the ten income tax years of assessment ending with the year in which that time falls,

For the purposes of paragraph (3), the question of whether a person was so resident ((i.e. in the UK) is determined as for income tax purposes. However, this to be done without regard to any dwelling-house available to him in the United Kingdom for his use. Availability of accommodation was a factor for residence till repealed by FA1996.

---

twenty years of assessment ending with the year of assessment in which the relevant time falls."

Example

Tusic Ziten dies in the UK. The issue here is Tusic's DDC domicile at death.

He was born in US so is a US citizen[192] and so a US National but not a UK national. Tusic was in UK for many years before his death when he was resident in Utopia so could be within Article 4(1) but Scuti does meet Article 4(2)(ii) as he was not US resident in the last three years of his life.

6.11.1.7.4 *General Rule (Article 4(4)) where Article 4(2) and (3) not deal with dual domicile*

Article 4(4) says in its opening words:

> "Where by reason of the provisions of paragraph (1) an individual was domiciled in both Contracting States, then, subject to the provisions of paragraphs (2) and (3), his status shall be determined as follows:..."

Accordingly, where:

1. an individual was domiciled in both the UK and the US under Article 4(1);
2. Article 4(2) and (3) do not determine the matter by Nat Well trying Nationality and residence;

The further rules in 4(4) apply using the following tests.

6.11.1.7.4.1 Test 1 Permanent Home

> (a)the individual shall be deemed to be domiciled in the Contracting State in which he had a permanent home available to him. If the individual had a permanent home in both Countries or neither the next test applies.

The question of an available permanent home is essentially one of fact. It is not a defined term in the DDC. Often the position will be relatively clear from the facts. However, difficulties can arise at the margins.

This is not a defined term for the purposes of the Convention nor for general UK law.

HMRC say the following in their Manuals[193].

> **"Permanent home.**
>
> An individual is a resident of the State in which they have a permanent home available to them (though not necessarily owned by them)..."

HMRC tells that a "permanent home" for the purposes of Double Taxation Conventions (DTCs) refers to a dwelling that an individual has arranged and retained for their permanent use. This means the individual must have the dwelling available to them at all times continuously, rather than occasionally or for

---

[192] See 14 amendment

[193] See INTM154020 - Double taxation agreements: residence: Dual residents

short-term stays such as travel for pleasure, business, or education. The concept of permanence excludes situations where the dwelling is rented out to unrelated parties, as the individual would no longer have possession or the ability to stay there during that period (see generally *McCabe v Revenue and Customs Commissioners.*)

6.11.1.7.4.2 Test 2 Centre of Vital Interests

If the individual had a permanent home available to him in both Contracting States, or in neither Contracting State, the individual shall be deemed to be domiciled in the Contracting State with which his personal and economic relations were closest (centre of vital interests). If the location of the individual's centre of vital interests cannot be determined the next test is to be applied which is habitual abode.

This again is essentially a question of fact. The only guidance is the phrase "... state with which his personal and economic interests were closest. What is not included in personal interests is an interesting question.

6.11.1.7.4.3 Test 3 Habitual abode

(i) *General*

If the Contracting State in which the individual's centre of vital interests was located cannot be determined, the individual shall be deemed to be domiciled in the Contracting State in which he had an habitual abode.

(ii) *Meaning of habitual abode*

This is not a defined term for these purposes and there is not much guidance that is easily discoverable. It is essentially a matter of fact and degree.

If the individual had an habitual abode in both Contracting States or in neither of them, the next test is to be applied which is nationality.

6.11.1.7.4.4 Test 4 Nationality

If the individual had an habitual abode in both Contracting States or in neither of them, he shall be deemed to be domiciled in the Contracting State of which he was a National.

National is a defined term for the purposes of this DDC. Article 3(1)(e) provides:

> "(e)the term "nationals" means:
>
> i. in relation to the United States, United States citizens, and
>
> ii. in relation to the United Kingdom, any citizen of the United Kingdom and Colonies, or any British subject not possessing that citizenship or the citizenship of any other Commonwealth country or territory,

> provided in either case he had the right of abode in the United Kingdom at the time of the death or transfer."

If the individual was a national of both Countries or neither the next test applies which is mutual agreement.

6.11.1.7.4.5 Test 5 Mutual Agreement

If the individual was a national of both Contracting States or of neither of them, the competent authorities of the Contracting States shall settle the question by mutual agreement.

Example

Raw Ward is a UK citizen and a British subject. He does not fall within tests 1-4 on the facts as HMRC agree. Essentially, the two jurisdictions negotiate who has the taxing right. This is more of a public law matter although it has private law consequences. Raw May be allowed to make written representation but would not be a party to the negotiations between the two states. This can prove frustrating especially to the more combative ESP's and their families. See Article 11 on the mutual agreement process discussed below.

6.11.1.7.5 *Resident of a US possession who became a US Citizen by reason of this neither domiciled in or national of US*

(i) *General*

There is an exclusion from Treaty benefits for an individual who became a US citizen via a connection with a US possession.

Article 4(5) tells us that an individual who was a resident (domiciliary) of a possession of the United States and who became a citizen of the United States solely by reason of his:

a) being a citizen of such possession, or
b) birth or residence within such possession,

shall be considered as neither domiciled in nor a national of the United States for the purposes of this Convention.

6.11.1.7.6 "Possession of the US"

A useful starting point on the meaning of "Possession of the US" I find is U.S. Code: Title 15 — COMMERCE AND TRADE

15 U.S. Code[194] § 1171 - Definitions

So far as relevant this reads as follows.

---

[194] https://www.senate.gov/legislative/HowTo/how_to_us_code.htm The *U.S. Code* is prepared by the Office of Law Revision Counsel, U.S. House of Representatives, and published by the Government Printing Office. The *Code* is published every six years.

(b) The term "**State**" includes the District of Columbia, Puerto Rico, the Virgin Islands, and Guam.

(c) The term "possession of the United States" means any **possession of the United States** which is not named in paragraph 1 (b) of this section."

It should be noted that Article 3(1) of the Convention provides

(a) the term "United States" means the United States of America, but does not include Puerto Rico, the Virgin Islands, Guam or any other United States possession or territory;

How a client became a US citizen should therefore be a question for the advisor to ask a US citizen client. It is included in the initial questionnaire in Appendix 1.

6.11.1.8 Article 5 Taxing Rights

6.11.1.8.1 *Introductory*

The fiscal domicile of an individual (considered above under the heading Article 4) matters because it is a vital matter in determining taxing rights under Article 5, the article in question here. Article 11 deals with the mutual Agreement process. It is discussed below.

Article 5 essentially sets out which state has the taxing rights.

6.11.1.8.2 *General Principle Article 5 (1)*

Article 5(1) sets at the general principle for the purposes of the Convention and Taxing Rights which is that if the decedent or transferor was domiciled in one of the states at the time of death or transfer property shall not be taxable in the other state. This is subject to the provisions of Articles 6 and 7. Accordingly, property will therefore be taxable in the state of the individual's fiscal domicile provided that the property is not land situate in the other jurisdiction or business property of a permanent establishment.

Example

Dom was domiciled in the US under the DCC, at the time of his death. Subject to the exceptions considered below, the assets and property are generally taxable in the US (the state of Dom's fiscal domicile i.e. US) and not in the UK (the other state).

Provision is made where the individual was a national of the other state.

Article 5 (1) (b) provides "(b) Sub-paragraph (a) shall not apply if at the time of the death or transfer the decedent or transferor was a national of that other State and does not fall within the provisions of Article 4 or 5."

6.11.1.9 *Articles 6 and 7 Immovable Property Business Property of a Permanent Establishment exception to the General Principle*

These two Articles (i.e. articles 6 and 7) set out special rules for taxing rights about Land and the Business Property of a Permanent Establishment. Land is situated where it is and the permanent establishment business property is linked more to the place where the pe business is carried on.

Accordingly, such assets are to be taxed in the Country in which they are situate.

Articles 6 and 7 are discussed in more detail below.

6.11.1.9.1 *Domiciled in neither UK or US but National of one Article 5(2)*

Article 5 (2) tells us that "Subject to the provisions of the said Articles 6 and 7, if at the time of the death or transfer the decedent or transferor was domiciled in neither Contracting State and was a national of one Contracting State (but not of both), property which is taxable in the Contracting State of which he was a national shall not be taxable in the other Contracting State".

Consequently, if the individual was not domiciled in either state at the relevant time of transfer or death but was a national of one of the states but not both, property in the state of which the individual was a national shall not be taxable in the other state by virtue of Article 5. However, this is subject to Articles 6 and 7 discuss below.

Example

Mio Delic was a national of the US but not the UK and was not domiciled for DCC purposes in either the UK or the USA when she died owning a house in Mayfair, interests in Delaware LLCs and shares in Canadian companies and a significant portfolio of investments. The UK would only have taxing rights over the house in Mayfair as between the US and the UK the taxing rights would go with nationality i.e. to the US as Mio is a US citizen.

6.11.1.9.2 *US and Trusts and Settlements Article 5(3)*

6.11.1.9.2.1 1. General

Paragraph 5(3) reads "Paragraphs (1) and (2) shall not apply in the United States to property held in a generation-skipping trust or trust equivalent on the occasion of a generation-skipping transfer; but, subject to the provisions of the said Articles 6 and 7, tax shall not be imposed in the United States on such property if at the time when the transfer was made the deemed transferor was domiciled in the United Kingdom and was not a national of the United States."

Consequently, there is no charge to US tax on property held in a generation-skipping trust or trust equivalent on a generation-skipping transfer if at the time when the transfer was made the deemed transferor was domiciled in the United Kingdom and was not a national of the United States." This does not apply to a US national though. There could be a charge to US tax on the creation of such a trust subject to any exemptions. This is an area on which specialist advice is essential before anything is done. However, there can be reasonably generous exemption limits. This should be checked in every case.

2. *GSST*

Investopedia[195] tells us the following about GSST.

> **"What Is the Generation-Skipping Transfer Tax (GSTT)?**
>
> The generation-skipping transfer tax is a federal tax on a gift or inheritance that prevents the donor from avoiding estate taxes by skipping children in favor of grandchildren. With the generation-skipping transfer tax, grandchildren receive the same amount as if the inheritance were coming from their parents.
>
> Before the generation-skipping transfer tax was introduced in 1976, wealthy individuals were legally able to gift money and bequeath property to their grandchildren, without paying federal estate taxes the way they would if the bequest had been made to their children. The legislation effectively closed the loophole where inheritances could skip a generation to avoid double estate taxation..."
>
> **Example**
>
> Henrieta Chrin is a British subject and proud of it. She is not a US national.
>
> Henrieta sets up a trust for her grandchildren Dandi and Chreleng for which her daughter their mother and her partner are excluded. There is a generation skipped here
>
> GSST is not generally an issue for US tax because Henrieta was domiciled in the UK and not a US national. However, UK tax may be chargeable. There should not be double taxation.

It may be that the facts fit the situation when such a trust was set up. This should be checked.

If the settlor had renounced US citizenship before the trust was setup and they were domiciled in the UK the relief might be available. However, it would be important to ensure that no adverse US tax consequences arose such as being classified as a "covered expatriate" and owing exit taxes.

Some detailed calculations would be needed as well as full advice for all jurisdictions.

I am aware of some US citizens who had already left the USA, but when they thought someone, they disapproved of who might be elected President decided

[195] https://www.investopedia.com/terms/g/generation-skipping-transfer-ta I x.asp

that they no longer wished to be US citizens. It may be that they could benefit from the DDC if the other circumstances were right. It would at least appear to prevent a double charge.

It is worthy of investigation.

6.11.1.9.3 *UK and property comprised in a settlement Article 5(4)*

(i) General

Paragraph 5(4) provides:

> "Paragraphs (1) and (2) shall not apply in the United Kingdom to property comprised in a settlement; but, subject to the provisions of the said Articles 6 and 7, tax shall not be imposed in the United Kingdom on such property if at the time ***when the settlement was made*** the **settlor** was ***domiciled in the United States*** and was not a national of the United Kingdom."

(ii) When is property comprised in a settlement?

Paragraph (4) applies to "property comprised in a settlement". It is therefore important to know what this means. In broad terms, this is the property comprising the trust fund of the Settlement in question. (cf. Section 64 IHTA).

Property falling within Articles 6 and 7 (Immovables and Permanent Establishment property – see c. above) is not covered by paragraph 5(4).

Paragraph (4) provides *inter alia* that paragraphs 5(1) and 5(2) do not apply to property comprised in a settlement.

(iii) Paragraph 5(1)

Paragraph 5(1) sets out the general rule that "if the decedent or transferor was domiciled in one of the states at the time of death or transfer property shall not be taxable in the other state" see b. above.

> **Example**
>
> Tone Aste a US national domiciled in the US and the DDC gives a valuable painting to Donna. This is an *inter vivos* transfer which could attract IHT in the UK. A painting does not attract Article 6 or 7. Accordingly it is only taxable in the US if instead of a painting the gift was of a house in Mayfair and so Real Property Article 6 would apply and so may be taxed in the UK.

However, it seems likely FTCs could be available in the US.

(iv) Paragraph 5(2)

Paragraph 5(2) tells us that if the individual was not domiciled in either state at the relevant time of transfer or death but was a national of one of the states but not both, property in the state of which the individual was a national shall not be taxable in the other state by virtue of Article 5. (see above).

It is not immediately obvious to me how these paragraphs could have applied to a discretionary trust. There would seemingly not be an individual treated as entitled to the assets in the trust fund with a relevant domicile or nationality.

However, where there was an Interest in Possession trust before the 2006 changes the assets in the trust fund were treated as property to which the beneficial holder of the interest in possession was beneficially entitled so far as it was property in which the interest in possession subsisted (see section 49 IHTA as originally enacted).

Such treatment can sometimes still apply to an Interests in Possession to which the person became beneficially entitled before 22 March 2006 other than by way of purchase etc. or to an IPDI etc.

In such circumstances paragraphs 5(1) and (2) would not apply where the conditions in paragraph 5(4) were fulfilled.

The position is then that "... subject to the provisions of the said Articles 6 and 7, tax shall not be imposed in the United Kingdom on such property if at the time when the settlement was made the settlor was domiciled in the United States and was not a national of the United Kingdom."

The phrase *"such property"* refers grammatically to "property comprised in a settlement" (see Article 5(4) set out above.

Tax (i.e. IHT) is not imposed on "such property" if two conditions were satisfied "at the time when the settlement was made", broadly when constituted. These conditions are the settlor:

- was domiciled in the United States; and
- was not a national of the United Kingdom.

In other words, there is no UK charge to IHT if when the settlement was made the settlor was domiciled in the US and was not a UK national.

It does not seem on the wording that an offshore trust is required. However, it might give an advantage subject to the US position. It is worth considering whether the trust should be in a suitable US state. Careful appropriate US advice would be essential though.

6.11.1.9.4 *Transfer in*

DDC Article 5(1) sets out the general rule that:

> "If transferor was domiciled in one of the states at the time of ... transfer property shall not be taxable in the other state."

The reference to "property" presumably is to the property transferred.

If the transferor was not domiciled in the UK on the transfer into settlement there should not be a charge to UK IHT because of Article 5(1). However, this paragraph is subject to the rest of the Article.

Paragraph 5(2) applies "… if the individual was not domiciled in either state at the relevant time of transfer or death…" then nationality comes into play. However, if the transferor is domiciled in the US, then this condition cannot apply.

6.11.1.9.4.1 Settlement

Paragraph 5(3) provides "Paragraphs (1) and (2) shall not apply in the United States to property held in a generation-skipping trust or trust equivalent on the occasion of a generation-skipping transfer; but, subject to the provisions of the said Articles 6 and 7, tax shall not be imposed in the United States on such property if at the time when the transfer was made the deemed transferor was domiciled in the United Kingdom and was not a national of the United States."

6.11.1.9.4.2 "Settlement" etc.

Settlement is not a defined term for DDC purposes here. It is a defined term in the IHTA (see sections 272 and 43 IHTA).

Section 43(2) IHTA reads as follows.

> "(2) "Settlement" means any disposition or dispositions of property, whether effected by instrument, by parol or by operation of law, or partly in one way and partly in another, whereby the property is for the time being—
> (a) held in trust for persons in succession or for any person subject to a contingency, or
> (b) held by trustees on trust to accumulate the whole or part of any income of the property or with power to make payments out of that income at the discretion of the trustees or some other person, with or without power to accumulate surplus income, or
> (c) charged or burdened (otherwise than for full consideration in money or money's worth paid for his own use or benefit to the person making the disposition) with the payment of any annuity or other periodical payment payable for a life or any other limited or terminable period,
>
> or would be so held or charged or burdened if the disposition or dispositions were regulated by the law of any part of the United Kingdom; or whereby, under the law of any other country, the administration of the property is for the time being governed by provisions equivalent in effect to those which would apply if the property were so held, charged or burdened."

6.11.1.9.4.3 Settlor

This is dealt with by section 44 IHTA which reads as follows.

> "44 Settlor.

"(1)In this Act "settlor", in relation to a settlement, includes any person by whom the settlement was made directly or indirectly, and in particular (but without prejudice to the generality of the preceding words) includes any person who has provided funds directly or indirectly for the purpose of or in connection with the settlement or has made with any other person a reciprocal arrangement for that other person to make the settlement.

(2) Where more than one person is a settlor in relation to a settlement and the circumstances so require, this Part of this Act (except section 48(4) to (6)) shall have effect in relation to it as if the settled property were comprised in separate settlements."

6.11.1.9.5 *"Non-Payment"*

This is dealt with by Article 5(5). This reads as follows.

(5) If by reason of the preceding paragraphs of this Article any property would be taxable only in one Contracting State and tax, though chargeable is not paid (otherwise than as a result of a specific exemption, deduction, exclusion, credit or allowance) in that State, tax may be imposed by reference to that property in the other Contracting State notwithstanding those paragraphs.

(6) If at the time of the death or transfer the decedent or transferor was domiciled in neither Contracting State and each State would regard any property as situated in its territory and in consequence tax would be imposed in both States, the competent authorities of the Contracting States shall determine the situs of the property by mutual agreement.

6.11.1.9.6 *Article 6 Immovable Property (Real Property)*

Article 6 deals with immovables Real Property. It reads as follows.

"**Immovable Property (Real Property)**

ARTICLE 6.— (1) Immovable property (real property) may be taxed in the Contracting State in which such property is situated.

(2) The term "immovable property" shall be defined in accordance with the law of the Contracting State in which the property in question is situated, provided always that debts secured by mortgage or otherwise shall not be regarded as immovable property. The term shall in any case include property accessory to immovable property, livestock and equipment used in agriculture and forestry, rights to which the provisions of general law respecting landed property apply, usufruct of immovable property and rights to variable or fixed payments as consideration for the working of, or the right to work, mineral deposits, sources and other natural resources; ships, boats, and aircraft shall not be regarded as immovable property.

(3) The provisions of paragraphs (1) and (2) shall also apply to immovable property of an enterprise and to immovable property used for the performance of independent personal services."

Real property i.e. immovable property may be taxed in the states in which the immovable property in question is situate. This seems sensible and should usually be obvious.

Example

May Fare, is a US citizen domiciled for DDC purposes in the US. She owns a large house in Kensington London and stocks or shares in a Delaware corporation. As a matter of English Law the house would be English Real Property, and the Delaware shares would not be. The house but not the shares or stocks would fall in the UK purview for IHT (see Article 6.1).

The phrase "Immovable property" is to be interpreted in accordance with the law in which the property in question is situate.[196] However, this is not to include debt secured by a mortgage or otherwise.

6.11.1.9.7 ***Ships etc.***

Ships, boats and aircraft are not to be regarded as immovable property. However, their situs is likely to be where they are registered. So Sam's luxury superyacht registered in say the Isle of Man would not be UK situs. However, it is not real property for English law purposes.

Immovable property does include matters properly accessory to the immovable property including livestock and equipment used in agriculture and forestry and rights under the general law of that state respecting landed property e.g. which may include easements, restricted covenants, rights of light and potentially contractual licences.

Usufructs[197] of land and mineral rights etc are covered.[198]

6.11.1.10 Article 7 Business Property of a Permanent Establishment and Assets Pertaining to a Fixed Base Used for the Performance of Independent Services

Article 7 deals with the business property of a permanent establishment and assets forming part of the business property of a permanent establishment. This Article reads as follows.

"ARTICLE 7.—

---

[196] This in theory could be complicated and involve issues of Renvoi and Double Renvoi. In most cases it is likely to be obvious.

[197] See *Shipwright and Harris on Usufructs* see Lexology and Addington Chambers Website www.addingtonchambers.com

[198] Usufructs exist in Louisiana see Louisiana Civil Code Title III Personal Servitudes Chapter 2—Usufruct. This flows from the Louisiana Purchase in April 1803 which brought with it certain aspects of the draft Napoleonic Code which became law in France in 1804. Louisiana is the only state in the USA with a civil law base system. Usufructs are a matter of Roman Law in origin and are widely used in Europe.

(1) Except for assets referred to in Article 6 (Immovable Property (Real Property)) assets forming part of the business property of a permanent establishment of an enterprise may be taxed in the Contracting State in which the permanent establishment is situated.

(2) (a) For the purposes of this Convention, the term "permanent establishment" means a fixed place of business through which the business of an enterprise is wholly or partly carried on.

(b)The term "permanent establishment" includes especially:

(i) a branch;

(ii) an office;

(iii) a factory;

(iv) a workshop; and

(v) a mine, an oil or gas well, a quarry, or any other place of extraction of natural resources.

(c) A building site or construction or installation project constitutes a permanent establishment only if it lasts for more than twelve months.

(d) Notwithstanding the preceding provisions of this paragraph, the term "permanent establishment" shall be deemed not to include:

(i) the use of facilities solely for the purpose of storage, display, or delivery of goods or merchandise belonging to the enterprise;

(ii) the maintenance of a stock of goods or merchandise belonging to the enterprise solely for the purpose of storage, display or delivery;

(iii) the maintenance of a stock of goods or merchandise belonging to the enterprise solely for the purpose of processing by another enterprise;

(iv) the maintenance of fixed place of business solely for the purpose of purchasing goods or merchandise, or of collecting information, for the enterprise;

(v) the maintenance of a fixed place of business solely for the purpose of carrying on, for the enterprise, any other activity of a preparatory or auxiliary character; or

(vi) the maintenance of a fixed place of business solely for any combination of activities mentioned in paragraphs (i)—(v) of this sub-paragraph.

(e) Notwithstanding the provisions of sub-paragraphs (a) and (b) where a person—other than an agent of an independent status to whom sub-paragraph (f) applies—is acting on behalf of an enterprise and has, and habitually exercises, in a Contracting State an authority to conclude contracts in the name of the enterprise, that enterprise shall be deemed to have a permanent establishment in that State in respect of any activities which that person undertakes for the enterprise, unless the activities of such person are limited to those mentioned in sub-paragraph (d) which, if exercised through a fixed place of business, would not make this fixed place of business a permanent establishment under the provisions of that sub-paragraph.

(f) An enterprise shall not be deemed to have a permanent establishment in a Contracting State merely because it carries on business in that State through a broker, general commission agent or any other agent of an independent status, provided that such persons are acting in the ordinary course of their business.

(g) The fact that a company which is a resident of a Contracting State controls or is controlled by a company which is a resident of the other Contracting State or which carries on business in that other State (whether through a permanent establishment or otherwise) shall not of itself constitute either company a permanent establishment of the other.

(3) Except for assets described in Article 6 (Immovable Property (Real Property)), assets pertaining to a fixed base used for the performance of independent personal services may be taxed in the Contracting State in which the fixed base is situated."

6.11.1.10.1 Relationship to Article 6 (Immovable property) for DDC purposes.

Article 7 provides that such business property and assets may be taxed in the state in which the permanent establishment is situated (see Article 7(1)).

This is subject to Article 6 (Immovable Property (Real Property)) discussed above. This is presumably to give only one exception. I find a useful starting point is to look at the accounts relating to the permanent establishment. If the asset is listed there it is likely to be a business asset. Difficulties can arise though where there is an effect a "flat above the shop". is the flat a business asset given that it is for residential occupation?

6.11.1.10.2 What is business property?

Permanent establishment broadly follows the general approach in the MTC.

It is the property that is used in this business that this is aimed at. It is essentially a matter of fact and proof.

6.11.1.11 Article 8 Deductions, Exemptions Etc

Special rules are provided for deductions, exemptions etc in Article 8 for DDC purposes.

The Article reads as follows.

"ARTICLE 8.—

(1) In determining the amount on which tax is to be computed, permitted deductions shall be allowed in accordance with the law in force in the Contracting State in which tax is imposed.

(2) Property which passes to the spouse from a decedent or transferor who was domiciled in or a national of the United Kingdom and which may be taxed in the United States shall qualify for a marital deduction there to the extent that a marital deduction would have been allowable if the decedent or transferor had been domiciled in the United States and if the gross estate of the decedent had been limited to property which may be taxed in the United States or the transfers of the transferor had been limited to transfers of property which may be so taxed.

(3) Property which passes to the spouse from a decedent or transferor who was domiciled in or a national of the United States and which may be taxed in the United Kingdom shall, where

- (a) the transferor's spouse was not domiciled in the United Kingdom but the transfer would have been wholly exempt had the spouse been so domiciled, and
- (b) a greater exemption for transfers between spouses would not have been given under the law of the United Kingdom apart from this Convention,

be exempt from tax in the United Kingdom to the extent of 50 per cent of the value transferred, calculated as a value on which no tax is payable and after taking account of all exemptions except those for transfers between spouses.

(4)

- (a) Property which on the death of a decedent domiciled in the United Kingdom became comprised in a settlement shall, if the personal representatives and the trustees of every settlement in which the decedent had an interest in possession immediately before death so elect and subject to sub-paragraph (b), be exempt from tax in the United Kingdom to the extent of 50 per cent of the value transferred (calculated as in paragraph (3)) on the death of the decedent if:
  - (i) under the settlement, the spouse of the decedent was entitled to an immediate interest in possession,
  - (ii) the spouse was domiciled in or a national of the United States,
  - (iii) the transfer would have been wholly exempt had the spouse been domiciled in the United Kingdom, and
  - (iv) a greater exemption for transfers between spouses would not have been given under the law of the United Kingdom apart from this Convention.
- (b) Where the spouse of the decedent becomes absolutely and indefeasibly entitled to any of the settled property at any time after the decedent's death, the election shall, as regards that property, be deemed never to have been made and tax shall be payable as if on the death such property had been given to the spouse absolutely and indefeasibly.

(5) Where property may be taxed in the United States on the death of a United Kingdom national who was neither domiciled in nor a national of the United

States and a claim is made under this paragraph, the tax imposed in the United States shall be limited to the amount of tax which would have been imposed had the decedent become domiciled in the United States immediately before his death, on the property which would in that event have been taxable. "

Essentially, in computing the amount taxed in the jurisdiction the taxable amount for that jurisdiction is to be computed in accordance with the law of "that jurisdiction".

6.11.1.12 Article 9 Credits

Special rules are provided for credits in Article 9 for DDC purposes.

The Article reads as follows.

"ARTICLE 9.—

(1) Where under this Convention the United States may impose tax with respect to any property other than property which the United States is entitled to tax in accordance with Article 6 (Immovable Property (Real Property)) or 7 (Business Property of a Permanent Establishment and Assets Pertaining to a Fixed Base Used for the Performance of Independent Personal Services) (that is, where the decedent or transferor was domiciled in or a national of the United States), then, except in cases to which paragraph (3) applies, double taxation shall be avoided in the following manner:

  (a) Where the United Kingdom imposes tax with respect to property in accordance with the said Article 6 or 7, the United States shall credit against the tax calculated according to its law with respect to that property an amount equal to the tax paid in the United Kingdom with respect to that property.

  (b) Where the United Kingdom imposes tax with respect to property not referred to in sub-paragraph (a) and the decedent or transferor was a national of the United States and was domiciled in the United Kingdom at the time of the death or transfer, the United States shall credit against tax calculated according to its law with respect to that property an amount equal to the tax paid in the United Kingdom with respect to that property.

(2) Where under this Convention the United Kingdom may impose tax with respect to any property other than property which the United Kingdom is entitled to tax in accordance with the said Article 6 or 7 (that is, where the decedent or transferor was domiciled in or a national of the United Kingdom), then, except in the cases to which paragraph (3) applies, double taxation shall be avoided in the following manner:

  (a) Where the United States imposes tax with respect to property in accordance with the said Article 6 or 7, the United Kingdom shall credit against the tax calculated according to its law with respect to that property an amount equal to the tax paid in the United States with respect to that property.

(b) Where the United States imposes tax with respect to property not referred to in sub-paragraph (a) and the decedent or transferor was a national of the United Kingdom and was domiciled in the United States at the time of the death or transfer, the United Kingdom shall credit against the tax calculated according to its law with respect to that property an amount equal to the tax paid in the United States with respect to that property.

(3) Where both Contracting States impose tax on the same event with respect to property which under the law of the United States would be regarded as property held in a trust or trust equivalent and under the law of the United Kingdom would be regarded as property comprised in a settlement, double taxation shall be avoided in the following manner:

(a) Where a Contracting State imposes tax with respect to property in accordance with the said Article 6 or 7, the other Contracting State shall credit against the tax calculated according to its law with respect to that property an amount equal to the tax paid in the first-mentioned Contracting State with respect to that property.

(b) Where the United States imposes tax with respect to property which is not taxable in accordance with the said Article 6 or 7 then

(i) where the event giving rise to a liability to tax was a generation-skipping transfer and the deemed transferor was domiciled in the United States at the time of that event,

(ii) where the event giving rise to a liability to tax was the exercise or lapse of a power of appointment and the holder of the power was domiciled in the United States at the time of that event, or

(iii) where (i) or (ii) does not apply and the settlor or grantor was domiciled in the United States at the time when the tax is imposed,

the United Kingdom shall credit against the tax calculated according to its law with respect to that property an amount equal to the tax paid in the United States with respect to that property.

(c) Where the United States imposes tax with respect to property which is not taxable in accordance with the said Article 6 or 7 and sub-paragraph (b) does not apply, the United States shall credit against the tax calculated according to its law with respect to that property an amount equal to the tax paid in the United Kingdom with respect to that property.

(4) The credits allowed by a Contracting State according to the provisions of paragraphs (1), (2) and (3) shall not take into account amounts of such taxes not levied by reason of a credit otherwise allowed by the other Contracting State. No credit shall be finally allowed under those paragraphs until the

tax (reduced by any credit allowable with respect thereto) for which the credit is allowable has been paid. Any credit allowed under those paragraphs shall not, however, exceed the part of the tax paid in a Contracting State (as computed before the credit is given but reduced by any credit for other tax) which is attributable to the property with respect to which the credit is given.

(5) Any claim for a credit or for a refund of tax founded on the provisions of the present Convention shall be made within six years from the date of the event giving rise to a liability to tax or, where later, within one year from the last date on which tax for which credit is given is due. The competent authority may, in appropriate circumstances, extend this time limit where the final determination of the taxes which are the subject of the claim for credit is delayed."

6.11.1.13 Article 10 Non-Discrimination

This is provided for by Article 10 and is based on Nationality as in the equivalent DTA. This reads as follows.

"ARTICLE 10.—

(1)

(a) Subject to the provisions of sub-paragraph (b), nationals of a Contracting State shall not be subjected in the other State to any taxation or any requirement connected therewith which is other or more burdensome than the taxation and connected requirements to which nationals of that other State in the same circumstances are or may be subjected.

(b)Sub-paragraph (a) shall not prevent the United States from taxing a national of the United Kingdom, who is not domiciled in the United States, as a non-resident alien under its law, subject to the provisions of paragraph (5) of Article 8 (Deductions, Exemptions Etc).

(2) The taxation on a permanent establishment which an enterprise of a Contracting State has in the other Contracting State shall not be less favourably levied in that other State than the taxation levied on enterprises of that other State carrying on the same activities.

(3) Nothing contained in this Article shall be construed as obliging either Contracting State to grant to individuals not domiciled in that Contracting State any personal allowances, reliefs and reductions for taxation purposes which are granted to individuals so domiciled.

(4) Enterprises of a Contracting State, the capital of which is wholly or partly owned or controlled, directly or indirectly, by one or more residents of the other Contracting State, shall not be subject in the first-mentioned Contracting State to any taxation or any requirement connected therewith

which is other or more burdensome than the taxation and connected requirements to which other similar enterprises of the first-mentioned State are or may be subjected.

(5) The provisions of this Article shall apply to taxes which are the subject of this Convention."

The definitions of tax, national in permanent establishment in the DDC should be noted (see particularly Articles 3, 7 and any defined terms in the local law if not defined in the DDC).

6.11.1.14 Article 11 Mutual Agreement Procedure

Provision as to mutual agreement procedure is made in Article 11. This reads as follows.

ARTICLE 11.—

(1) Where a person considers that the actions of one or both of the Contracting States result or will result in taxation not in accordance with the provisions of this Convention, he may, irrespective of the remedies provided by the domestic laws of those States, present his case to the competent authority of either Contracting State.

(2) The competent authority shall endeavour, if the objection appears to it to be justified and if it is not itself able to arrive at an appropriate solution, to resolve the case by mutual agreement with the competent authority of the other Contracting State, with a view to the avoidance of taxation not in accordance with the Convention. Where an agreement has been reached, a refund as appropriate shall be made to give effect to the agreement.

(3) The competent authorities of the Contracting States shall endeavour to resolve by mutual agreement any difficulties or doubts arising as to the interpretation or application of the Convention. In particular the competent authorities of the Contracting States may reach agreement on the meaning of the terms not otherwise defined in this Convention.

(4) The competent authorities of the Contracting States may communicate with each other directly for the purpose of reaching an agreement as contemplated by this Convention.

This allows the taxpayer to present their case to the Competent authority of either jurisdiction. By Article 3(d) Competent authority in the US means the Secretary of the Treasury and in the UK the Commissioner of the Inland Revenue (now HMRC.)

6.11.1.15 Article 12 Exchange of Information

Article 12 provides an older form of Exchange of Information provision. It has been overtaken by more recent treaty provisions, bilateral and multilateral e.g. the MLAAT. The Article provides as follows.

> **"ARTICLE 12.** The competent authorities of the Contracting States shall exchange such information (being information available under the respective taxation laws of the Contracting States) as is necessary for the carrying out of the provisions of this Convention or for the prevention of fraud or the administration of statutory provisions against legal avoidance in relation to the taxes which are the subject of this Convention. Any information so exchanged shall be treated as secret and shall not be disclosed to any persons other than persons (including a court or administrative body) concerned with the assessment, enforcement, collection, or prosecution in respect of the taxes which are the subject of the Convention. No information shall be exchanged which would disclose any trade, business, industrial or professional secret or any trade process."

6.11.1.16 Article 13 Effect on Diplomatic and Consular Officials and Domestic Law

This is dealt with by Article 13.

6.11.1.17 Article 14 Entry into Force

This is dealt with by Article 14.

The Convention tells us it was "Done in duplicate at London this 19th day of October 1978."

It also says in the SI that "Instruments of ratification were exchanged on 11 October 1979."

6.11.1.18 Article 15 Termination

As mentioned above the client must be made aware that the DDC can be terminated by six months' prior notice. There is thus no "perpetual solution" .

Article 15 deals with termination. It reads as follows.

> **"ARTICLE 15.—**
>
> (1) This Convention shall remain in force until terminated by one of the Contracting States. Either Contracting State may terminate this Convention, at any time after five years from the date on which the Convention enters into force provided that at least six months' prior notice has been given through the diplomatic channel. In such event the Convention shall cease to have effect at the end of the period specified in the notice, but shall continue to apply in respect of the estate of any individual dying before the end of that period and in respect of any event (other than death) occurring before the end of that period and giving rise to liability to tax under the laws of either Contracting State.
>
> (2) The termination of the present Convention shall not have the effect of reviving any treaty or arrangement abrogated by the present Convention or by treaties previously concluded between the Contracting States.

6.11.2 Italy UK DDC

6.11.2.1 General

The Italian Convention dates from an earlier time than the UK US DDC.

It dates from February 1966 as far as signing goes.

It was brought into force for UK tax purposes by the Double Taxation Relief (Estate Duty)(Italy) Order 1968 SI 1968 No. 304.

This was at a time before the introduction of what came to be known as IHT. Estate duty was still in force then.

The convention is concerned with "... the avoidance of double taxation on the estates of deceased persons..." It does not cover *inter vivos* gifts and transfers nor does it deal with trusts. It is a domicile based document.

6.11.2.2 Explanatory Note to the SI

The Explanatory Note to the SI reads as follows.

> "The Convention with Italy which is scheduled to this Order provides (in Article IV) a code of rules for determining the situs of categories of property which may be subject to duty on the death of a person dying domiciled in either country and (in Article VI) a supplementary system of credits. The code does not apply where the effect would be to bring within either country's charge property which, apart from the code, would be outside the charge of the country in question (paragraph (3) of Article III).
>
> In some cases the situs code will itself eliminate double taxation: example, on the death of a person domiciled in the United Kingdom, shares in a company incorporated in the United Kingdom will not be liable to duty in Italy even though the share certificates were physically located Italy at the date of the deceased's death. But where, notwithstanding the application of the situs code, property is chargeable with duty by both countries, Article VI provides for a credit to be given by the country in which the property is not situated for duty paid in the other country. in Rules are provided in paragraph (2) of Article II to establish the domicile of a deceased person for the purposes of this Convention when he would otherwise be deemed to be domiciled in both countries. Article VIII provides for the exchange of information between the taxation authorities of the two countries. The Convention, which extends also to the Estate Duty (separate from that in Great Britain) which is imposed in Northern Ireland (Article will apply in connection with deaths occurring after the date of exchange of instruments of ratification."

6.11.2.3 Article I Taxes Covered

By Article I (1) the duties covered by this DDC are:

a) in the UK estate duty and

b) Italy succession duty and estate duty.

However, all is not lost for IHT as far as this DDC is concerned.

Article 1(2) provides that this DDC shall apply to any other duties of a substantially similar character to estate duty et cetera imposed after the signature of the Convention.

IHT then called CTT was imposed by FA and so after 15th February 1966, the date the convention was signed (see the execution part of the convention).

Also, section 158(6) IHTA would extend the coverage to IHT as discussed above

6.11.2.4 Article II Definitions etc.

6.11.2.4.1 General

Most of this Article is boilerplate. However, it is important that it is properly considered as it is integral to the interpretation and understanding of the DDC.

Article II (1) (e) tells us that in this DDC "duty" means the two estate duties referred to in Article I (see above). In other words, it means the estate duty imposed in Great Britain or the succession duty and estate duty imposed in Italy, as the context requires.

Because of the extension to IHT by section 158 IHTA this DDC can apply to IHT on death.

6.11.2.4.2 Determination of place of domicile

This is dealt with by Article II (2).

For the purposes of the convention whether a person was domiciled in one of the countries in question is to be determined in accordance with the law in force in that territory. Presumably this is as at the date of death.

It is to be noted that there is no general definition of domicile for these purposes in the DDC.

The paragraph sets out the rules to determine the place of domicile of an individual. It would seem that one is to use the law in force in the territory in question at the time of death in determining this.

6.11.2.4.3 Rule 1 Domicile to be determined in accordance with the law of jurisdiction seeking duty

The question whether the deceased was domiciled at death in any part of the territory of either Great Britain or Italy is to be determined in accordance with the law of the territory seeking to enforce duty in force presumably at the time of death.

6.11.2.4.4 Rule 2 Dual Domicile

If the deceased as a result of Rule 1 is deemed to be domiciled in each of the territories, then the deceased should be deemed to be domiciled in the territory in which

1) The deceased had a permanent home available at the time of death;
2) If the Deceased had a permanent home available to them in each of Great Britain and Italy or no permanent home available in either jurisdiction in the jurisdiction in which the deceased had his centre vital interests i.e. where his personal economic relations were closest;
3) If the deceased centre of vital interest cannot be determined or they have no permanent home in either jurisdiction the jurisdiction in which the deceased has an habitual abode;
4) If the deceased had an habitual abode in both jurisdictions or neither in the country of the deceased nationality;
5) If the deceased was a national of both Great Britain and Italy or neither than in the country decided on by mutual agreement between Great Britain and Italy.

(i) Some Questions

Article II[2]raises a number of questions including the following.

1) What is a "Permanent home" for DDC purposes?
2) What is the meaning of Centre of Vital Interests other than as where his personal and economic interest were closest - how test?
3) Who is a "National" for DDC purposes?
   National is not a defined term in the DDC and so article 2(3) applies
4) What is meant by "Mutual agreement" for DDC purposes?
   This is a negotiation between the contracting states. The taxpayer may be allowed to make representations.

(ii) Some Answers

(1) What is a permanent home for DDC purposes?

This is not a defined term for the purposes of the Convention nor for general UK law.

HMRC say the following in their Manuals.[199]

[199] See INTM154020 - Double taxation agreements: residence: Dual residents

> **"Permanent home.**
>
> An individual is a resident of the State in which they have a permanent home available to them (though not necessarily owned by them)..."

HMRC tells that a "permanent home" for the purposes of Double Taxation Conventions (DTCs) refers to a dwelling that an individual has arranged and retained for their permanent use. This means the individual must have the dwelling available to them at all times continuously, rather than occasionally or for short-term stays such as travel for pleasure, business, or education. The concept of permanence excludes situations where the dwelling is rented out to unrelated parties, as the individual would no longer have possession or the ability to stay there during that period (see generally *McCabe v Revenue and Customs Commissioners*.)

(2) What is meant by Centre of Vital Interests?

This is not a defined term in the Convention. The DDC does say it is where his personal and economic interests are closest. The DDC does not provide a test. HMRC say the following in their Manuals:[200]

> **"Centre of vital interests.**
>
> An individual is a resident of the State to which their 'personal and economic relations' (a wide expression intended to cover the full range of social, domestic, financial, political and cultural links and relationships) are closer ..."

It is essentially a matter of fact and degree.

They also say the term "centre of vital interests" (COVI) is used in the context of determining an individual's residence status under double tax treaties. It refers to the state with which an individual has the closest personal and economic ties. A temporary relocation to another state for a specific purpose is unlikely to shift the COVI (see *Oppenheimer v Revenue and Customs Commissioners*).

(3) National

This is not a defined term in the DDC and so bears its usual meaning.

National is not a defined term in the DDC and so article 2(3) applies.

(4) Mutual Agreement

This is not a defined term in the DDC and so bears it's usually meaning.

[200] See INTM154020 - Double taxation agreements: residence: Dual residents

6.11.2.4.5 *Undefined terms* – Article 2(3)

Any term not otherwise defined in the DDC is to have the meaning under the law of the jurisdiction relating to that duty.

It seems therefore that domicile for these purposes means domicile in the UK sense for UK purposes. There is no general definition in the DDC of Domicile for these purposes so it is an undefined term. Accordingly, it is to have the meaning in the law of that jurisdiction i.e. the UK.

6.11.2.5 Article III Situs of property – general

6.11.2.5.1 General

Article III (1) tells us that the situs of property for the purposes of this DDC is to be determined in accordance with Article IV (discussed next) where the individual was domiciled in one of the relevant territories at the time of their death. This is an important matter in allocating taxing rights between the contracting parties and how the tax arises.

6.11.2.5.2 Applies even if exemption in the other jurisdiction

Article III (2) tells us that Article IV only applies if otherwise duty would be imposed:

1) Under the law of each jurisdiction; or
2) Under the law of one of the jurisdictions and but for some specific exemption would also be imposed under the law of the other jurisdiction; and
3) Would not lead to duty that would not otherwise arise

Paragraph (1) does not apply if its application results in duty being imposed in a jurisdiction where it would not otherwise be imposed.

This is not always an easy provision to understand and apply given that the purpose of the DDC is to allocate taxing rights. A pragmatic sensible approach is suggested.

6.11.2.6 Article IV Situs of assets - specifics

6.11.2.6.1 General

This Article sets out the specific rules to determine the situs of assets for the purposes of the DDC. This can be important in allocating taxing rights and how the tax arises.

6.11.2.6.2 Land

Land is located for the purposes of this DDC where the land is situate see Article IV (1). This may sound circular but is likely to be obvious in practice. The assets covered by this Article are sometimes referred to as "immovables".

Rights or interest other than security interests which constitutes immovables are located where the land to which they relate is located. A right of way or restrictive covenant related to an English freehold is situate in England for the purposes of the DDC. A mortgage is likely to be treated as a debt and situate where the debtor was resident at the time of death.

Whether the rights or interests constitute immovables is to be determined in accordance with the law of the place where the land to which they relate its located.

> **Example**
>
> Ian Tail, a Brit, owns a Palazzo between Bologna and Milan with its own vineyards and associated servitudes. It was brought with help of a mortgage charged on the property.
>
> The Land is in Italy and is treated located in Italy as are the associated servitudes. The charge to support the mortgage is not treated as situate in Italy as land under the Article.

6.11.2.6.3 Tangible movable property

1) *General*

Subject to the rest of the Article such rights or interests other than security interests are situated for DDC purposes at the place where they were located at the time of death.

2) *Goods in transit*

Such property which is in transit (*in transitu*) ought to be treated for the purposes of the DDC as located at the place of the destination of the transit.

3) *Banknotes, legal tender where issued etc*

These are to be treated as tangible movable property for these purposes. A promissory note or bill of exchange which is negotiable would be located where it was at the time of death notwithstanding Article IV (3) considered next.

4) *Debts etc*

These are generally located at the place where the debtor was residing at the time of death.

This applies to both secured and unsecured debts.

Example

Rod Bet is an Asturian national resident in the UK who owes $1m to Roc Tedic, a financier resident in Dystopia, when he dies.

The debt is a UK situs debt as Rod was UK resident when he died.

5) *Bank accounts*

These are deemed to be situate at the branch where the account was kept. Life was simpler when the DDC was assigned as e.g. there was no internet banking

6) *Securities et cetera*

Securities issued by government, local governments or public authorities are located if:

i. In bearer form where located at the time of death; and
ii. In registered or inscribed form at the place of registration or inscription.

7) *Shares, debentures et cetera of a company*

These are located where the company was incorporated.

See Levy v Abercoris Slate (1887) 36 Ch D 215 Chitty J on meaning of debenture

8) *Partnership interest etc*

This is located where the business was carried on. If the business was carried on in more than one place, then an appropriate apportionment is to be made between the branches. An appropriate proportion of the interest is treated as situate at each of those places and duty applied accordingly.

9) *Goodwill*

Business or professional asset this is situate where the business etc is carried on.

If the business is carried on at more than one place an appropriate apportionment is to be made. An appropriate proportion is treated with situated each of those places and duty is applied accordingly.

10) *Ships and aircraft and shares in them*

These are treated as located at the place of registration of the ship or aircraft.

11) *Patents, trademarks and designs*

These are located where they were registered. However, and yes you could arise with unregistered trademark in the UK.

12) *Copyright, copyright licences and licences of patents, trademarks or designs*

These are located where the rights are rising from them were exercisable.

13) *Rights of action etc*

Where these are rights or causes of action *ex delicto* which survive for the benefit of the deceased's estate they are situate where the right or cause of action arose.

14) *Other property*

Any other properties situate in the jurisdiction where the deceased was domiciled at the time of their death.

Summary Table

[*follows treaty order not alphabetic*]

Asset	Location
Land	Where the land is located Article IV (1). Sometimes called immovables. Rights etc other than security interests which are immovables located where the relative land is located. Whether the rights etc. are immovables determined in by the law of place where the land is
Tangible movable property	Where located at the time of death
Goods in transit	Such property in transit (*in transitu*) located at the destination of the transit.
Banknotes, legal tender where issued etc	Treated as tangible movable property for these purposes.
Debts etc	located at the place where the debtor was residing at the time of death. Applies to both secured and unsecured debts.
Bank accounts	Situate at the branch where the account was kept.
Securities et cetera	Securities received by government, local governments or public authority are located if: In bearer form where located at the time of death; and In registered or inscribed form at the place of registration or inscription.
Shares, debentures et cetera of a company	These are located where the company was incorporated. *Levy v Abercoris Slate* (1887) 36 Ch D 215 Chitty J on meaning of debenture.
Partnership interest etc	This is located where the business was carried on. If the business was carried on in more than one place then an appropriate apportionment is to be made. An appropriate proportion of the interest is treated as situate at each of those places and duty applied accordingly.
Goodwill	Business or professional asset this is Scituate where the business etc is carried on. If the business is carried on more than one place in appropriate apportionment is to be made. An appropriate proportion is treated with situated each of those places and duty is applied accordingly.
Ships and aircraft and shares in them	located at the place of registration of the ship or aircraft.

Patents, trademarks and designs	Where registered.
Copyright, copyright licences and licences of patents, trademarks or designs	located where the rights arising from them were exercisable.
Rights of action etc	Where these arise *ex delicto* and survive for the deceased's estate where the right or cause of action arose
Other property	Any other property is situate in the jurisdiction where the deceased was domiciled at the time of their death.

6.11.2.7 Article V Deductions

The deductions permitted by the law in force of the country in which the duty is imposed is to be used in computing the amounts of duty (see Article V(1)).

Where duty is imposed on a deceased's estate by the jurisdiction in which the deceased was not domiciled at the time of their death but was Domiciled in the other jurisdiction no account is to be taken of property situate outside the "former territory" i.e. "the territory at the time of … death [the deceased] was not domiciled in that territory" in determining the amount or rate of duty this is subject to the proviso that this does not apply to duty an asset passing under a settlement governed by its law. It may be arguable this helps with the 10-year tail.

6.11.2.8 Article VI Credit

Where duty is imposed by one jurisdiction on property situate in the other jurisdiction credit shall be allowed by "the former party" i.e. the jurisdiction in which the property is not situate for the duty imposed in the jurisdiction where the asset is situate attributable to the property in question Article VI (1).

Example

If Jon Riscuti, an Italian citizen, who is resident and domiciled in Italy dies owning a house in Mayfair which attracts IHT in the UK then Italy (the jurisdiction in which the house is not situate) is to give credit for the UK IHT for Italian purposes. This assumes there is a charge to Italian tax on the house under Italian law.

6.11.2.9 Article VII Time limit for credit or refund

There is a time limit of five years from the death or if a later event causes duty to be payable 5 years from that later event.

6.11.2.10 *Article VIII Exchange of information*

This is an old-fashioned limited provision compared some of the more recent agreements which can lead to automatic exchange of information e.g. the MLAAT. However, this provision should be noted.

6.11.2.11 *Article IX Extension by UK*

The UK is responsible for the external and international relations of certain countries such as the Crown Dependencies and the British Overseas Territories.

This Article allows the DDC to be extended to such countries.

It is similar to Article 30 of the MLAAT which the UK has extended to the Isle of Man, the Channel Islands and the BVI. It is understood no such extension has been made for this DDC.

6.11.2.12 *Article X Application to Northern Ireland*

There was a different estate duty regime in Northern Ireland when this DDC was negotiated. This is no longer the case. It is understood that HMRC treat this DDC as covering Northern Ireland.

6.11.2.13 *Article XI and XII Ratification entry into force and termination*

It is important that clients know that this DDC can be terminated so it can form part of their risk assessment.

6.11.3 *India UK DDC*

6.11.3.1 *General*

The Indian DDC dates from 1956. Things have changed in the 69 or so years since then to the time of writing.

It was signed on 3 April 1956. It was bought into force for UK tax purposes by the Double Taxation Relief (Estate Duty) (India) Order 1956 SI 1956 No. 998.

This was all at a time before the introduction of what came to be known as IHT.[201] Estate Duty was still in force in the UK. The convention is concerned with the "… Avoidance of double taxation on the estates of deceased persons…"

It does not cover *inter vivos* gifts and transfers nor does it deal with trusts.

---

[201] CTT was announced in his Budget speech by Denis Healey on 26 March 1974. This announcement was given effect by Part III FA 1975. This was consolidated as the Capital Transfer Act 1984. The tax was renamed IHT by section 100 FA 1986.

6.11.3.2 *Explanatory Note to the SI*

A useful overview of the DDC is found in the Explanatory Note to the SI which reads as follows.

> "Article V of the double estate duty Agreement with India which is scheduled to this Order provides a code of rules for determining the situs of the categories of property which may pass on the death of a person who dies domiciled in either country. The code of rules does not apply where the effect of applying it would be to bring within either country's charge to duty property which, apart from the code, would be outside the charge of the country in question (Paragraph (2) of Article IV). The estate duty chargeable in India to which a British company may become liable in certain circumstances on the death of a shareholder is not affected by the Agreement (Paragraph (2) of Article III).
>
> For cases in which duty is charged by both countries, Article VI provides a system of "credits". Where property has a situs in one country and not in the other, the country of situs will retain its duty and the other country will allow a "credit" (Paragraph (1)); otherwise, both countries will allow "credits", the sum of which will eliminate the smaller of the two duties (Paragraph (2)).
>
> Provision is made for the exchange of information between the taxation authorities of the two countries.
>
> The Agreement applies to the estate duty (separate from the British estate duty) which is imposed in Northern Ireland.
>
> The Agreement is effective as regards the estates of persons who die on or after the date when it comes into force. But provision is made for the Agreement to be applied to the estate of any person who dies before the date on which the Agreement comes into force and after 15th October 1953, if the accountable person so elects."

6.11.3.3 *Article I Taxes Covered*

By Article 1 the duties covered by the DDC are:

a. In India estate duty under the Estate Duty Act 1953;[202] and
b. In the UK the estate duty imposed in Great Britain.

These are referred to in this DDC as "duty" (see Article II (1)(e)).

There is no extension to any other duty of a substantially similar nature as there is in the Italian DDC in Article I (2).

---

[202] Indian estate duty was abolished in 1985 see https://www.business-standard.com/politics/decoded-the-history-and-political-relevance-of-inheritance-tax-in-india-124042500736_1.html for an interesting discussion of it. It is understood that India has no estate duty at present. There has been talk of introducing Inheritance Tax in India but as yet this has not been done on a general basis.

However, the arrangements were authorised under section 54 and given effect through an SRO within section 56 F(No 2) A 1945. Accordingly, as discussed above the DDC is extended to cover IHT on death by section 158(6) IHTA.

Section 158 IHTA discussed above effectively continues the DDC for IHT purposes. HMRC

6.11.3.4 Article II Definitions

6.11.3.4.1 General

Most of this Article is boilerplate. It is important that it is properly considered as the definitions are integral to the interpretation and understanding of the DDC.

6.11.3.4.2 Meaning of "Duty"

Article II (1) (e) tells us that in this DDC "duty" means the two estate duties referred to in Article I (see above). In other words, it means the estate duty imposed in Great Britain[25] or the estate duty imposed in India, as the context requires.

Because of the extension to IHT by section 158 IHTA duty here includes IHT.

6.11.3.4.3 Determination of place of domicile

This is dealt with by Article II (2).

For the purposes of the convention whether a person was domiciled in one of the countries in question shall be determined in accordance with the law in force in that territory at the time in question. Presumably this is as at the date of death.

It is to be noted that there is no general definition of domicile for these purposes.

The paragraph sets out the rules to determine the place of domicile. It would seem that one is to use the law in force in the territory in question at the time of death in determining this.

6.11.3.4.4 Rule 1

The question whether the deceased was domiciled at death in any part of the territory of either Great Britain or India is to be determined in accordance with the law of the territory seeking to enforce duty in force presumably at the time of death.

6.11.3.4.5 Rule 2 Dual Domicile

If the deceased as a result of Rule 1 is deemed to be domiciled in each of the territories then the deceased should be deemed to be domiciled in the territory in which:

1) The deceased had a permanent home available at the time of death;
2) If the Deceased had a permanent home available to them in each of Great Britain and Italy or no permanent home available in either jurisdiction in the jurisdiction in which the deceased had his centre vital interests IE where his personal economic relations were closest;
3) If the deceased centre of vital interest cannot be determined all they have no permanent home in either jurisdiction the jurisdiction in which the deceased has an habitual abode;
4) If the deceased had an habitual abode in both jurisdictions or neither in the country of the deceased nationality;
5) If the deceased was a national of both Great Britain and Italy or neither than in the country decided on by mutual agreement between Great Britain and Italy.

It should be noted that the following words or phrases are amongst those not defined in the DDC.

Some questions

Some questions arise as to what is meant by the following.

1) Permanent home
2) Central vital interests other than as where his personal and economic interest were closest dash how test?
3) National
4) Mutual agreement

Some answers

(1) What is a permanent home for DDC purposes?

This is not a defined term for the purposes of the Convention nor for general UK law.

HMRC say the following in their Manuals.[203]

> **"Permanent home.**
>
> An individual is a resident of the State in which they have a permanent home available to them (though not necessarily owned by them)..."

(2) What is meant by Centre of Vital Interests?

[203] See INTM154020 - Double taxation agreements: residence: Dual residents

This is not a defined term in the Convention. The DDC does say it is where his personal and economic interests are closest. The DDC does not provide a test. HMRC say the following in their Manuals:[204]

> **"Centre of vital interests.**
>
> An individual is a resident of the State to which their 'personal and economic relations' (a wide expression intended to cover the full range of social, domestic, financial, political and cultural links and relationships) are closer ..."

It is essentially a matter of fact and degree.

(3) National

This is not a defined term in the DDC and so bears its usual meaning.

National is not a defined term in the DDC and so article 2(3) applies.

(4) Mutual Agreement

This is not a defined term in the DDC and so it bears its usual meaning.

These are discussed elsewhere in this part of the Supplement.

6.11.3.4.6 Undefined terms

Any term not otherwise defined in the DDC Is to have the meaning under the law of the jurisdiction relating to that duty.

It seems therefore that domicile for these purposes means domicile in the UK sense. There is no general definition of domicile for these purposes, so it is an undefined term. Accordingly, it, is to have the meaning in the law of that jurisdiction i.e. the UK or where appropriate India.

6.11.3.5 Article III Restrictions

This Article restricts the application of the DDC to some extent. Article III(3) tells us that 2 on the death of a person who was not domiciled at the time of his death in any part of Great Britain but was domiciled in some part of India.

> **ARTICLE III.—**
>
> (1) Subject to paragraph (2) of this Article, duty shall not be imposed in India on the death of a person who was not domiciled at the time of his death in any part of India but was domiciled in some part of Great Britain on any property situate outside India:
>
> Provided that nothing in this paragraph shall prevent the imposition of duty in India on—

[204] See INTM154020 - Double taxation agreements: residence: Dual residents

(a)any settled property of which the deceased was life tenant where the settler was domiciled in India at the time the settlement took effect; or

(b)property that passes under a disposition or devolution regulated by the law of some part of India.

(2) Nothing in the present Agreement shall affect any provision of the law of India imposing duty on shares in or debentures of a company incorporated outside India which carries on business in India and which has been treated for the purposes of the Indian Income-tax Act, 1922 (XI of 1922), as resident in India for two out of the three completed assessments immediately preceding the death; nor shall anything in the present Agreement be considered to confer a right to a credit against duty so imposed for any duty imposed in Great Britain on any such shares or debentures.

(3) Duty shall not be imposed in Great Britain on the death of a person who was not domiciled at the time of his death in any part of Great Britain but was domiciled in some part of India on any property situate outside Great Britain:

Provided that nothing in this paragraph shall prevent the imposition of duty in Great Britain on any property which passes under a disposition or devolution regulated by the law of some part of Great Britain.

6.11.3.6 *Article IV Situs of Property - General*

Where an individual was domiciled at the time of their death in one of the relevant jurisdictions the situs of the property passing on death for the purposes of the imposition of duty and of credit is to be determined exclusively in accordance with the rules set out in Article V.

This is subject to the provisor who these rules do not apply where the effect if they were applied would be to bring within either country's charge to duty property which would otherwise be outside that country's charged duty [See Article IV (2)]

6.11.3.7 *Article V Situs of Property - Specifics*

Article IV makes provision about the situs of assets for the purposes of the DDC. This is summarised in the following table.

Summary Table

Asset	Location
Land	Where the land is located Article IV (1). Sometimes called immovables. Rights etc other than security interests which are immovables located where the relative land is located. Whether the rights etc. are immovables determined in by the law of place where the land is.
Tangible movable property	Where located at time of death.
Goods in transit	Such property in transit (in transitu) located at the destination of the transit.
Banknotes, legal tender where issued etc	Treated as tangible movable property for these purposes.
Debts etc	located at the place where the debtor was residing at the time of death. Applies to both secured and unsecured debts.
Bank accounts	Situate at the branch where the account was kept.
Securities et cetera	Securities received by government, local governments or public authority are located if: In bearer form where located at the time of death; and In registered or inscribed form at the place of registration or inscription.
Shares, debentures et cetera of a company	These are located where the company was incorporated. Levy v Abercoris Slate (1887) 36 Ch D 215 Chitty J on meaning of debenture
Partnership interest etc	This is located where the business was carried on. If the business was carried on in more than one place then an appropriate apportionment is to be made. An appropriate proportion of the interest is treated as situate at each of those places and duty applied accordingly.
Goodwill	Business or professional asset this is Scituate where the business etc is carried on. If the business is carried on more than one place in appropriate apportionment is to be made. An appropriate proportion is treated with situated each of those places and duty is applied accordingly.
Ships and aircraft and shares in them	located at the place of registration of the ship or aircraft.
Patents, trademarks and designs	Where registered.
Copyright, copyright licences and licences of patents, trademarks or designs	located where the rights arising from them were exercisable.

Rights of action etc	Where these arise ex delicto and survive for the deceased's estate where the right or cause of action arose
Other property	Any other property is situate in the jurisdiction where the deceased was domiciled at the time of their death.

6.11.3.8 Article VI Credit

Where duty is imposed by one jurisdiction on property situate in the other jurisdiction credit shall be allowed by "the former party" i.e. the jurisdiction in which the property is not situate for the duty imposed in the jurisdiction where the asset is situate attributable to the property in question Article VI (1)

Example

If a house was owned in Mayfair which attracted duty in India then India as the state in which the property is not would need to give credit against its own duty. At present it is understood that there would be no duty in India as estate duty was abolished in 1985.

6.11.3.9 Article VII Time limit for credit or refund – 6 years

There is a time limit of five years from the death or if a later event causes duty to be payable 5/6 years from that later event.

By article VII no payment of interest is due in respect of the refund or credit.

6.11.3.10 Article VIII Exchange of information

This is an old-fashioned limited provision compared some of the more recent agreements which can lead to automatic exchange of information e.g. The MLAAT. However this provision should be noted.

6.11.3.11 Article IX Extension by UK

The UK is responsible for the external and international relations of certain countries such as the crime dependencies and the British overseas territories.

This Article allows the DDC to be extended to such countries.

Is similar to Article 30 of the MLAAT which the UK has extended to the Isle of Man, the Channel Islands and the BVI. It is understood no such extension has been made for this DDC.

6.11.3.12 Article X Northern Ireland

There was a different estate duty regime in Northern Ireland when this DDC was negotiated. This is no longer the case.

6.11.3.13 Article XI Coming into force

The DDC came into force in 1956.

It remains in force at the time of writing.

6.11.3.14 Article X II Termination

It is important that clients know that this DDC can be terminated so it can form part of their risk assessment and planning.

6.12 Conclusion

What is set out above is solely for the purposes of discussion and to stimulate thought. No action should be taken in respect of anything set out above without obtaining appropriate advice.

This is likely to be a developing area and new techniques etc. are likely to emerge. We will seek to contribute to this.

Appendix 5: Some questions for clients?

Full name	
Current Correspondence address	
Activities (if any). Any work in the UK. Details	
Self-employed or employed?	
Where currently resident?	
What time if any spent in the UK in the last 21 years?	
Are there any consecutive periods of UK residence?	
Nationality, Green Card etc.?	
Additional Nationalities? Residence permits, Cartes de Séjour etc.?	
Citizenship? If US national how became US citizen Did residence etc. in a US possession lead to this?	
What family is there?	
Details e.g. name, address, status, age, schooling, disabilities, special circumstances, wishes?	
What residential property is available where?	
Where does the Client consider home?	
What residential property in the UK?	
Where was the client domiciled (deemed or actual) on 30th October 2024?	
Details of time spent in such properties over the last [20] years?	
Health?	
Insurable?	
Life expectancy factors?	
What structures and arrangements if any are in place e.g. image right structures, family branding? Full details and documentation needed.	
Is there or will there be income from performances? Will it be "performance Income"? (income that results directly or indirectly from performance of entertainment or sport)	
What else might be relevant in the particular circumstances?	

Appendix 6: Table of Situs of Assets

IHT

IHTM27071 - Foreign property: locality of assets (situs): introduction starting point as no general statutory provision

CGT

Section 275 TCGA starting point

Type of Asset	General Rule	CGT	IHT	Comment
ADRS	Where enforceable	No specific provision so where enforceable	No specific provision so where enforceable IHTM25193 - Other holdings of unquoted shares: American Depositary Receipts	American Depositary Receipts
Aircraft	See below			See also the Cape Town Convention , https://www.icao.int/cape-town-convention-and-protocol
Bank Accounts		Foreign currency accounts (debts receivable) held by UK residents who are domiciled within the UK are regarded as UK-situs assets, even if the account is actually maintained offshore section 275(1)(c))TCGA https://www.gov.uk/hmrc-internal-manuals/residence-domicile-and-remittance-basis/rdrm33570	IHTM27093 - Foreign property: debts: bank accounts A bank account is a debt, and under general law is situated at the branch of the bank where the account is kept: *R v Lovitt* [1912] AC 212. This general law rule may be modified for Inheritance Tax (IHT) purposes by a Double Taxation Convention.	Bank Account does not give a right in the money actually handed over or in it but a right to payment of an equivalent sum i.e. a debt liability Sometimes special provisions
Bearer Warrants	Broadly, treated in same way as bearer shares			Much will depend on the documentation
Beneficial Interests				

Type of Asset	General Rule	CGT	IHT	Comment
In Underlying Property				e.g. Nomineeship
Personal Rights Against The Legal Holder of the Property				e.g. Trust
Branch Registers				
Business Assets				
Canadian etc Companies				Special rules in some cases
Causes of Action				
Chattels	Generally, in the jurisdiction the chattel is in at any particular time subject to exceptions see e.g. *New York Life Insurance Co v Public Trustee* [1924] 2 Ch. 101, 109 (CA), *Alloway v Phillips* [1980] 1 W.L.R. 888 (CA)	TCGA 1992, s. 275 (b)	Household and personal goods (chattels) are situated where they happen to be at the relevant time. So UK situs chattels are usually chargeable to Inheritance Tax. IHTM27075 IHTM27075 - Foreign property: locality of assets (situs): household and personal goods Household and personal goods (chattels) are situated where they happen to be at the relevant time. So UK situs chattels are usually chargeable to Inheritance Tax.	Artwork brought into the UK for sale might have a different treatment, if it was ordinarily outside the UK. Specialist advice should be sought. Chattels, i.e. tangible moveable property (including rights and interests therein, other than by way of security)

Type of Asset	General Rule	CGT	IHT	Comment
			But, under IHTA84/S5(1)(b) and IHTA84/S64(2), if a work of art normally kept outside the UK would become liable to IHT because it happened to be in the UK at the relevant date, the liability will be waived if it was brought here solely for public exhibition, cleaning or restoration. Any case where this provision is invoked, or the taxpayer or agent says it may apply, must be referred to Heritage.	
Choses in Action	Generally, situate in jurisdiction where they are properly recoverable or enforceable Alloway v Phillips [1980] 1WLR 888. *New York Life Insurance Company v Public Trustee* [1924] 2Ch 101 .			Called Things in Action in section 136 LPA New third category
Company that has no Share Capital				Broadly treat corporators' rights as if shareholders' rights
Contractual Funds				FCP Continental structure Fonds commun de placement (FCPs) translates to "investment funds" or

Type of Asset	General Rule	CGT	IHT	Comment
				"mutual funds", and are open-ended collective investment funds. The legal structure is neither a trust or a company and are more like an open ended partnership. similar to common contractual funds in Ireland, tax transparent funds in the UK and *fondsen voor gemene rekening* in the Netherlands. They are typically issued in the French-speaking countries of Europe
Copyright, Design Right, Franchises and Corresponding Rights,				
Corporate Debtors				
Corresponding Rights				
Cyrptoassets	Since cryptoassets are digital and do not have a physical location, their situs is complex and depends on specific tax rules to determine location for tax purposes			Fetchi Property of the Third Kind Situs where holder domiciled?
Debts		FA 2025 para 9 Schedule 19, removed the situs of assets of foreign currency bank accounts		

Type of Asset	General Rule	CGT	IHT	Comment
		held by non-domiciled individual. A debt, secured or unsecured, is situated in the United Kingdom if and only if the creditor is resident in the United Kingdom. (TCGA 1992, s275 (c)) This does not include Municipal or government shares or debentures. UK if creditor is UK resident; otherwise, where the debtor is resident. This reverses the common law rule that treats a debt as situated where the debtor is resident		
Debt which Is owed by a Bank				
Municipal Debt				Municipal or government shares or Debentures country of issuer country of issuer
Simple Debts				
Secured Debts	See the discussion of Debts			
Crown Debt	See the discussion of Debts			

Type of Asset	General Rule	CGT	IHT	Comment
Deeply Discounted Securities	See the discussion of Debts			
Depositary Receipts	See ADRs above			See ADR and GDR
GDRS	See ADRs above			Global Depositary Receipts
Goodwill of a business	Generally, in the jurisdiction where the premises are to which the goodwill is attached e.g. *Muller & Co's Margarine Limited* [1901] AC 217	The situation of good-will as a trade, business or professional asset is at the place where the trade, business or profession is carried on. (TCGA 1992, s275 (g))		
Government Securities	Much depends under what authority and where issued	TCGA 1992, s275		Power to issue on special terms Municipal or government shares or debentures country of issuer
	See chattels			
Immobilised Securities	Terms of issue important		IHTM27077 - Foreign property: locality of assets (situs): Eurobonds HMRC regard the situs of securities dealt with through computerised clearing systems (for example, Euroclear;	Securities such as Eurobonds listed on Euroclear

Type of Asset	General Rule	CGT	IHT	Comment
			CEDEL) as determined by the terms of issue of the particular security.	
Immovable Property	Essentially where the land is. This a realistic practical approach		Immovable property is situated where it is actually located. IHTM27074	Sometimes called Real Property and usually includes associated rights
Intangible Property	Often where enforceable	If asset A is subject to UK law (see section 275B(2)) at the time it is created, it shall be taken for the purposes of this Act to be situated in the United Kingdom at all times. TCGA 1992, s275A (3)		
Certain Intangible Assets	Some special rules	See sections 275A and B TCGA		Special CGT Rules
International Conventions	Terms of Convention can be important			Goes to enforceability because of jurisdiction allocation Interesting issue as the interface of public and private rights cf the Mutual Agreement Article in DTAs
Judgment Debt		A judgment debt is situated where the judgment is recorded. TCGA 1992, s275 (k)		
Immovables	Where the land is. Realistic \and practical solution		See above	Essentially land – Civilian Law term
Inscribed And Registered Securities	Usually where the relevant register is			Starting point where register is This category covers registered

Type of Asset	General Rule	CGT	IHT	Comment
	subject to any special rules in relative legislation etc.			shares or debentures in non-UK incorporated companies. Per CG 12440, registration will normally be in the country where the company was incorporated. If registered on more than one register, they are located where the principal register is located.
Interests under a Trust	Broadly where enforceable			Personal rights against trustee for single beneficiary but the class of beneficiaries as a whole seemingly as a whole group has the equitable interest under the so-called Rule in *Saunders v Vautier*
Land and Interests In Land	Generally, in the jurisdiction where the land is physically located.	Land and Building including rights therein, other than by way of security. TCGA 1992, s. 275 (a)	Immovable property is situated where it is actually located. Land is usually classed as immovable property, so it is generally governed by the law of the country in which it is situated. IHTM27074 IHTM27074 - Foreign property: locality of assets (situs): land and interests in land Immovable property is situated where it is actually located. But, different legal systems may take opposing	Broadly, where the land is and in whose jurisdiction, it lies. Land and buildings (including rights and interests therein, other than by way of security). This will include leasehold interests and tenancies, but is not applicable to a debt that is secured over land.

Type of Asset	General Rule	CGT	IHT	Comment
			views as to whether some types of interest in land or relating to land are movable or immovable property. 'These differences are resolved (under Private International Law, and also by specific provision in Double Taxation Conventions where these apply) by the adoption of the view taken by the law of the country in which the land itself is situated': *Johnstone v Baker* (1817), 4 Madd 474; *Macdonald v Macdonald* [1932) SLT (HL) 381. Land is usually classed as immovable property, so it is generally governed by the law of the country in which it is situated. This issue may be important when deciding whether spouse or civil partner exemption (IHTM11032) applies to the property. You should resolve any questions about ownership (for example, where joint property is involved) before considering the valuation.	
Licences Or Other Rights	Broadly where enforceable			

Type of Asset	General Rule	CGT	IHT	Comment
Money From A Life Policy	Much depends on the analysis of the policy cf the *Willoughby* case			
Multiple Registers	Which is the register in question. What is the position under the relative law as to the relationship between the registers			
Mutual Funds	Complex depends on close analysis of the arrangements			
OEICS	Complex depends on close analysis of the arrangements			Open Ended Investment Company shares are essentially shares in a company and follow those rules generally
Other Financial Products	No general rule			Careful analysis of what involved needed
Partnership Interests	In practice often where the rights can be enforced			In English Law partner has no interest in the underlying assets so partnership interest effectively property right itself
Patents, Trade Marks, Registered Designs *copyright, design right, franchises and corresponding rights.*	Generally, secured in the jurisdiction which governs that particular rights existence i.e. the right that it is sought to enforce. See e.g. *IRC v Muller & Co's Margarine Ltd* [1901] A.C. 217; *RJ Reuter Co Ltd v Mulhens* [1954] Ch. 50, 95–96 (CA). 134 *Coin*	TCGA 1992, s. 275 (h) and (j) There is a distinction between two groups of rights. Patents, trademarks, registered designs and corresponding rights are situated where they are registered, and if registered in more than one register, where each register is situated. But		Essentially IP rights are to stop another doing certain things in a given territory without the owner's consent. e.g. right to enforce copyright in France although UK copyright allows this [illegible word here] French right being enforced.

Type of Asset	General Rule	CGT	IHT	Comment
	Controls Ltd v Suzo International (UK) Ltd [1999] Ch. 33.	licences or other rights in respect of any such rights are situated in the United Kingdom if they or any right derived from them are exercisable in the United Kingdom. Moreover, copyright, design right, franchises and corresponding rights, and licences or other rights in respect of any such rights, are situated in the United Kingdom if they or any right derived from them are exercisable in the United Kingdom		
Renounceable Letters Of Allotment	In practice where the issuer is registered	Letters of allotment should be treated as located in the country where the company issuing the letters is registered. CG12400		[In *Young v Phillips* [1984] BTC 311, non-domiciled taxpayers passed the value of their interests in UK companies into renounceable letters of allotment. They took the letters of allotment to Jersey and renounced them in favour of Jersey companies. They appealed against capital gains tax assessments, on the grounds that the letters of allotment were situated wherever they were at any time, and that the taxpayers had dis-

Type of Asset	General Rule	CGT	IHT	Comment
				posed of assets situated outside the UK. It was held that the letters of allotment were enforceable in the UK and were thus situated there at the time of disposal. The taxpayers' appeal thus failed.
Rights of action in contract or tort	Broadly situate in jurisdiction where the action may be brought but some associated issues			
Securities issued by International Organisations	Some special rules	S265 TCGA 1992. Once such an organisation has been designated any securities issued by it are deemed for the purposes of Capital Gains Tax to be located outside the UK. The list of organisations that have been designated under this provision is as follows. • International Bank for Reconstruction and Development • Asian Development Bank • African Development Bank • The European Economic Community • The European Investment Bank • The European Bank for		

Type of Asset	General Rule	CGT	IHT	Comment
		Reconstruction and Development • The European Coal and Steel Community • The European Atomic Energy Community		
Shares	Usually where registered if registered shares			This category covers registered shares or debentures in non-UK incorporated companies. Per CG 12440, registration will normally be in the country where the company was incorporated. If registered on more than one register, they are located where the principal register is located.
Shares Or Debentures	Usually where registered if registered shares Unregistered debentures often in practice where can be enforced			Municipal or government shares or debentures country of issuer
Ships	See Ships or aircraft			IHTM27073 - Foreign property: locality of assets (situs): ships 'A ship on the high seas is deemed to be situated at its port of registry but when it comes within territorial waters this artificial situs is displaced by the actual situs': Trustees Executors &

Type of Asset	General Rule	CGT	IHT	Comment
				Agency Co Ltd v IRC [1973) Ch 254. So, on the date of a transfer of value the value of a ship is chargeable to Inheritance Tax in the UK if it is within UK territorial waters
Ship Or Aircraft and any interest or right over the ship or aircraft.		A ship or aircraft is situated in the United Kingdom if and only if the owner is then resident in the United Kingdom, and an interest or right in or over a ship or aircraft is situated in the United Kingdom if and only if the person entitled to the interest or right is resident in the United Kingdom. TCGA 1992, s. 275 (f)	'A ship on the, high seas is deemed to be situated at its port of registry but when it comes within territorial waters this artificial situs is displaced by the actual situs': *Trustees Executors & Agency Co Ltd v IRC* [1973) Ch 254. So, on the date of a transfer of value the value of a ship is chargeable to Inheritance Tax in the UK if it is within UK territorial waters.	This is contrary to the general rules of international law (per CG12430) and also has the effect that, for a remittance basis user, a ship or aircraft is UK situs property unless held via an non-resident company
Specialties			IHTM27079 - Foreign property: specialty debts: bonds and debentures under seal A specialty debt is: • a debt made by deed, or • a deed which records or creates obligations, or • a debt incurred by way of statute, or • a certain type of debt that is given the nature	Speciality Debts are mainly governed by caselaw with statutory modifications for some purposes HMRC practice

Type of Asset	General Rule	CGT	IHT	Comment
			of a specialty debt by statute The debt may be secured or unsecured. At present the law by which the situs of such debts is determined is largely set out in a number of Privy Council decisions from 1891 onwards. HMRC has revised its previous approach to the Inheritance Tax (IHT) treatment of such debts, which was that where the debt is situated depends on where the relevant document is to be found. HMRC will take the following approach, which will apply regardless of when the specialty debt was created. Secured specialty debts Where the debt is solely secured on land or other tangible property situated in the UK the situs of the debt will also be in the UK. HMRC considers the situs of the debt follows the genuine interest of the creditor in the secured property, not merely the personal obligation of the debtor to repay (which may be situated elsewhere, for	

Type of Asset	General Rule	CGT	IHT	Comment
			example where the debtor is resident). Any claim that a debt secured on UK assets is not UK situs property must be sent to Technical. Unsecured specialty debts Where the debt is not secured the view of the Courts is that the situs of the debt is usually where the relevant deed or instrument evidencing the debt is found. HMRC will generally adopt this approach to unsecured specialty debts. However, it is possible to exploit this approach artificially by, for example, removing the document from the UK to avoid an IHT charge. Where the creditor and debtor are both resident in the UK but the deed evidencing the debt has been removed from the UK, it may be possible for HMRC to argue that the debt is nevertheless situated in the UK for the purposes of the IHT charge. For this reason all cases in which a specialty debt is claimed to be situated outside the UK should be	

Type of Asset	General Rule	CGT	IHT	Comment
			referred to Technical. Finance (No 2) Act 2017 From 6 April 2017, in cases where the loan monies have been used by the debtor to acquire UK residential property, then you should also consider the guidance at IHTM04313. In such a case the debt may not be excluded property for IHT purposes even if it is regarded as having a situs outside the UK. IHTM27080 - Foreign property: specialty debts: Treasury Bills, British Savings Bonds, National Savings Income Bonds Treasury Bills and British Savings Bonds are treated as specialty debts and situs will follow the normal principles for unsecured specialty debts (IHTM27079). National Savings Income Bonds are securities registered on the National Savings Stock Register and are situated in the UK.	
Tangible Property				General Rule

Type of Asset	General Rule	CGT	IHT	Comment
Trade Marks etc.	Essentially a right to stop others doing certain things in a given territory without the owner's permission. Generally, situate in the jurisdiction governs the IP's existence. [WIPO Treaties]	? - See above. Are we not looking at the same trademarks?		
Transfers Endorsed In Blank	Often relate to the governing law but not always enforceable so careful analysis needed			Check legality
Unadministered Estates	Depends on the relevant governing law. Can be complex where assets in a number of jurisdictions	IHTM27072 - Foreign property: locality of assets (situs): unadministered estates In general, a person who takes an absolute interest in the residue of an estate is entitled, not to the assets of the testator, but to a right of action, enforceable against the executors. This is the case under English law and many other legal systems. This means the executors must administer the estate and transfer the clear residue, or a share of it to the beneficiary. The same rule applies in the case of intestacy. This is a similar rule to the *jus crediti* (IHTM25091) to which a beneficiary is entitled in Scotland.		In UK right to have estate administered properly not give right in underlying assets as a matter of general law

Type of Asset	General Rule	CGT	IHT	Comment
		But, for Inheritance Tax, the deceased is treated as having a direct interest (in the whole or a share) in the net assets of the residuary estate (IHTM22031). For this reason you must consider the situs of each of the underlying assets separately. For example, the excluded property provisions in IHTA84/S6 (2) may apply to qualifying securities included in an unadministered estate (IHTM04260) and as a result they may not be chargeable to Inheritance Tax.		
Unit Trusts	Depends on analysis of structure. Is there an interest in the underlying assets?			Depends on form set up. Is there a right to a share of the underlying assets? Note that, for the purposes of TCGA 1992, a unit in a unit trust scheme is treated in the same way as a share in a company (TCGA 1992, s. 99).
Works of Art	Some special Rules			Copyright and physical matter ownership can be split cf *Re Dickens*

Appendix 7: Jurisdiction Table

Jurisdiction	UK DDC	Local Taxes	Comment
Dubai	X	The UAE does not levy income tax on individuals. However, it levies 5 per cent value added Tax on the purchase of goods and services, levied at each stage of the supply chain and ultimately borne by the end consumer. The UAE also levies excise tax on specific goods that are harmful to health, and corporate tax on the net income or profit of corporations and other entities from their business. https://u.ae/en/information-and-services/finance-and-investment/taxation#:~:text=The%20UAE%20does%20not%20levy,borne%20by%20the%20end%20consumer.	A useful starting point is https://u.ae/en/information-and-services/finance-and-investment/taxation https://u.ae › finance-and-investment › taxation
France	✓ 1963 No. 1319 [205]	French Tax can be complicated. https://www.service-public.fr/particuliers/vosdroits/comment-faire-si can help practically https://www.icaew.com/technical/by-country/europe/france/tax-in-france can be a useful tool	A useful starting point is https://www.revenue.ie/en/life-events-and-personal-circumstances/moving-to-or-from-ireland/moving-or-returning-to-ireland/the-tax-system-in-ireland.aspx https://www.service-public.fr/particuliers/recherche?keyword=impots
India	✓ 1956 No. 998 [206]	Central and state taxes must be taken into account https://www.eoiparis.gov.in/content/A-Key-Pillar-of-Nation-Building.pdf https://www.icaew.com/technical/by-country/south-asia/india/tax-in-india can be a useful tool	A useful starting point is https://www.revenue.ie/en/life-events-and-personal-circumstances/moving-to-or-from-ireland/moving-or-returning-to-ireland/the-tax-system-in-ireland.aspx https://www.incometax.gov.in/iec/foportal/
Ireland	✓ S.I. No. 279/197	https://taxinstitute.ie/ can provide useful information as can the Irish Revenue https://www.revenue.ie	A useful starting point is https://www.revenue.ie › moving-or-returning-to-ireland

[205] The Double Taxation Relief (Estate Duty) (France) Order 1963
[206] The Double Taxation Relief (Estate Duty) (India) Order 1956

	8 [207] and 1978 No 1107	https://www.icaew.com/technical/by-country/europe/ireland/tax-in-ireland can be a useful tool	
Italy	✓ 1968 No. 304 [208]	https://www.icaew.com/technical/by-country/europe/italy/tax-in-italy can be a useful tool	A useful starting point is https://www.revenue.ie/en/life-events-and-personal-circumstances/moving-to-or-from-ireland/moving-or-returning-to-ireland/the-tax-system-in-ireland.aspx https://www.agenziaentrate.gov.it/portale/agenzia/amministrazione-trasparente/servizi-erogati/carta-servizi/servizi-per-gli-stranieri/services-for-foreign-citizens
Netherlands	✓ SI 1996 No. 730 [209]	https://www.icaew.com/technical/by-country/europe/netherlands/tax-in-netherlands is a useful tool	A useful starting point is https://www.revenue.ie/en/life-events-and-personal-circumstances/moving-to-or-from-ireland/moving-or-returning-to-ireland/the-tax-system-in-ireland.aspx https://www.government.nl/topics/themes/taxes-benefits-and-allowances
Pakistan	✓ 1957 No. 1522 [210]	https://www.icaew.com/technical/by-country/south-asia/pakistan/tax-in-pakistan can be a useful tool	A useful starting point is https://www.revenue.ie/en/life-events-and-personal-circumstances/moving-to-or-from-ireland/moving-or-returning-to-ireland/the-tax-system-in-ireland.aspx https://fbr.gov.pk/
Portugal		https://www.icaew.com/technical/by-country/europe/portugal/tax-in-portugal is a useful tool	A useful starting point is https://www.revenue.ie/en/life-events-and-personal-circumstances/mov-

[207] Double Taxation Relief (Taxes on Estates of Deceased Persons and Inheritances and on Gifts) (United Kingdom [Ireland]) Order, 1978

[208] The Double Taxation Relief (Estate Duty) (Italy) Order 1968

[209] The Double Taxation Relief (Taxes on Estates of Deceased Persons and Inheritances and on Gifts) (Netherlands) Order 1996

[210] The Double Taxation Relief (Estate Duty) (Pakistan) Order, 1957

			ing-to-or-from-ireland/moving-or-returning-to-ireland/the-tax-system-in-ireland.aspx Only Portuguese assets?
Singapore		https://www.icaew.com/technical/by-country/south-east-asia/singapore/tax-in-singapore is a useful tool	A useful starting point is https://www.revenue.ie/en/life-events-and-personal-circumstances/moving-to-or-from-ireland/moving-or-returning-to-ireland/the-tax-system-in-ireland.aspx A useful starting point is https://www.revenue.ie/en/life-events-and-personal-circumstances/moving-to-or-from-ireland/moving-or-returning-to-ireland/the-tax-system-in-ireland.aspx Estate Duty abolished 2008
South Africa	✓ 1979 No. 576 [211]	https://www.icaew.com/technical/by-country/africa/south-africa/tax-in-south-africa is a useful tool	A useful starting point is https://www.revenue.ie/en/life-events-and-personal-circumstances/moving-to-or-from-ireland/moving-or-returning-to-ireland/the-tax-system-in-ireland.aspx Similar to US UK DDC
Spain		https://www.icaew.com/technical/by-country/europe/spain/tax-in-spain is a useful tool	A useful starting point is https://sede.agenciatributaria.gob.es/Sede/en_gb/inicio.html See also https://www.gov.uk/world/tax-benefits-pensions-and-working-abroad-spain Unilateral relief can be of assistance
Sweden	✓ 1981 No. 840 [212]	See https://skatteverket.se/servicelankar/otherlanguages/inenglish.4.12815e4f14a62bc048f4edc.html	A useful starting point is https://sweden.se/life/society/taxes-in-sweden

[211] The Double Taxation Relief (Taxes on Estates of Deceased Persons and on Gifts) (Republic of South Africa) Order 1979

[212] The Double Taxation Relief (Taxes on Estates of Deceased Persons and Inheritances and On Gifts) (Sweden) Order 1981

		https://www.icaew.com/technical/by-country/europe/sweden/tax-in-sweden is a useful tool	
Switzerland	✓ 1994 No. 3214 [213]	https://www.gov.uk/guidance/living-in-switzerland can be of assistance in navigating this complex position https://www.icaew.com/technical/by-country/europe/switzerland/tax-in-switzerland can be a useful tool	A useful starting point for federal tax is https://www.estv.admin.ch/estv/en/home.html Cantonal tax must be checked as it can vary considerably. There are 26 cantons. The municipal position must also be considered https://www.revenue.ie/en/life-events-and-personal-circumstances/moving-to-or-from-ireland/moving-or-returning-to-ireland/the-tax-system-in-ireland.aspx UK treaty, exempts from inheritance tax in Switzerland immovable property located outside Switzerland.
USA	✓ 1979 No. 1454 [214]	Federal and state taxes must be considered and in some cases city taxes https://www.icaew.com/technical/by-country/north-america/us/tax-in-us can be a useful tool	A useful starting point is https://www.revenue.ie/en/life-events-and-personal-circumstances/moving-to-or-from-ireland/moving-or-returning-to-ireland/the-tax-system-in-ireland.aspx https://www.irs.gov/ Always check the state and other local tax positions e.g. NY up to 16% https://www.tax.ny.gov/pit/estate/etidx.htm [215]

[213] The Double Taxation Relief (Taxes on Estates of Deceased Persons and Inheritances) (Switzerland) Order 1994

[214] The Double Taxation Relief (Taxes on Estates of Deceased Persons and On Gifts) (United States of America) Order 1979

[215] 12 States and DC impose such taxes see https://taxfoundation.org/data/all/state/estate-inheritance-taxes/

www.ingramcontent.com/pod-product-compliance
Lightning Source LLC
LaVergne TN
LVHW052208200926
848481LV00001B/53